D1269146

Poe's Helen Remembers

Poe's Helen Remembers

Edited by John Carl Miller

University Press of Virginia

Charlottesville

Publication of this volume was assisted by a grant from the Old Dominion University Research Foundation, Inc.

THE UNIVERSITY PRESS OF VIRGINIA
Copyright © 1979 by the Rector and Visitors
of the University of Virginia

First published 1979

Frontispiece: Sarah Helen Whitman in 1838, age thirty-five. From a painting by C. Giovanni Thompson. (Photograph courtesy Providence, R.I., Athenaeum Library.)

Library of Congress Cataloging in Publication Data

Whitman, Sarah Helen Power, 1803–1878.
    Poe's Helen remembers.

    "Correspondence that passed between John Ingram and Sarah Helen Whitman from late 1873 through mid-1878."
    Includes index.
    1. Poe, Edgar Allan, 1809–1849—Biography—Sources. 2. Whitman, Sarah Helen Power, 1803–1878—Correspondence. 3. Ingram, John Henry, 1842—1916. 4. Authors, American—19th century—Biography. I. Ingram, John Henry, 1842–1916, joint author. II. Miller, John Carl. III. Title.
    PS2630.5.W5   1979   818'.3'09 [B]   79–742 ISBN 0–8139–0771–3

Printed in the United States of America

To those mentors and friends,
professors in the University of Virginia
and giants in the earth,
James Southall Wilson,
Armistead Churchill Gordon, Jr.,
John Cook Wyllie, and
Francis Lewis Berkeley, Jr.

ALMANZOR. Stand off; I have not leisure yet to die.
Dryden, *The Conquest of Granada*

Contents

1875

1876

Illustrations

Preface

When John Henry Ingram of London reached Mrs. Sarah Helen Whitman, Poe's former fiancée, in Providence, Rhode Island, with a written plea for her help in his efforts to write a truthful and redemptive biography of Edgar Allan Poe, her swift reply that she would gladly write out her memories of Poe for his use made him realize at once that he had found his "Providence." Her responses proved that of all the correspondents he had reached in America and all the others he was to reach, she was the most reliable and intelligent source of firsthand biographical memories and materials about Edgar Poe that he was ever to find.

This volume offers students, teachers, scholars, and future biographers, as well as that large public which is always interested in new and reliable information about Poe, the voluminous and largely unknown and unpublished correspondence that passed between John Ingram and Sarah Helen Whitman from late 1873 through mid-1878. The texts of that correspondence are established and here presented in their entirety for the first time. They contain discussions of almost every poem and tale as well as many of the critical articles Poe wrote, and they offer new information about him that Ingram did not take full advantage of, even though he received it first; no subsequent biographer has ever fully explored and used this rich store. This correspondence dramatically presents the changing relationships between Ingram and Mrs. Whitman, it offers much unknown information about other British and American writers of the period, in addition to that about Poe, and finally and perhaps most importantly, it reveals the long and sometimes painful gestation of the first reliable biography of Edgar Allan Poe. John Ingram was an impassioned biographer. Mrs. Whitman was a superbly gifted person, a poet and an acute critic who had a deep and clear insight into Edgar Poe's human personality and habits as well as into his accomplishments as a writer. It took this particular combination of persons to build Poe's biography as we now have it.

This volume has no precedent in Poe literature, for here, together with searching questions and well-founded factual answers, are presented for the first time since their publication more than one hundred years ago a number of important magazine and newspaper articles about Poe, several of which exist in a single copy only, while others are in collections not readily accessible. In these articles readers can see for themselves how quickly Ingram rushed into print with the new information about Poe that he was receiving almost daily from Mrs. Whitman, information that became and has remained permanent elements in Poe biography.

After Ingram's two-volume biography of Poe appeared in 1880, he thought he was through with his job, that he reigned alone as the sole arbiter of everything concerning Edgar Poe; in short, Ingram was convinced that his was the definitive biography. That he was mistaken is a matter of record, for the controversies he sparked by his publications and the interest he aroused, particularly in America, in Edgar Poe were forces that compelled him to go on with his researches until his death in 1916, as a concluding volume will show. In it I expect to reproduce documented evidence of his attempts to defend his untenable position as the only authority about things concerning the life and writings of Edgar Allan Poe.

JOHN C. MILLER

Old Dominion University

Acknowledgments

The holographs of John Ingram's seventy-one letters and three post-cards addressed to Mrs. Whitman are in the Sarah Helen Whitman Papers in the Brown University Library. I am grateful to Librarians Stuart C. Sherman and John H. Stanley for permission to work in these papers and to publish these important and almost unknown letters and to the members of their staffs, especially Mmes. Russo and Trescott, for their never-failing efficient and courteous help. I especially appreciate Brown University Library's permission to reproduce in this volume a copy of the painting of Mrs. Whitman, executed by John Nelson Arnold, which now hangs in their Caleb Fiske Harris Room.

The holographs of Mrs. Whitman's ninety-four replies to John Ingram's letters are in the Manuscript Department of the University of Virginia Library. I am grateful to that library's Curators of Manuscripts, Mr. Edmund Berkeley, Jr., Miss Anne Freudenberg, and their helpful staffs for permission to reproduce Mrs. Whitman's letters here, along with two letters addressed to John Ingram by Rose Peckham, a young artist friend of Mrs. Whitman's. I owe and offer my appreciation too for the swift and deft responses to my many requests for help to Messrs. Michael Plunkett and Gregory Johnson of the Manuscript Department, as well as Mmes. Ann M. Jenkins, Lucille Richards, and Pauline Page, of the library's Communication Service, for their many courtesies shown me in supplying requested reproductions of materials.

I offer my appreciation to Mrs. Sylvia Moubayad, Librarian of the Providence Athenaeum, and to her staff, in particular Mrs. Muriel Borts and Miss Cynthia Saccoccia, for their gracious reception and their courteously furnishing from their valuable holdings copies of materials I needed. I am especially grateful for their permission to reproduce here as frontispiece a copy of the beautiful painting of Sarah Helen Whitman, executed by C. Giovanni Thompson, which now hangs in the Art Room of their library.

Reference librarians Mrs. Eileen Donahue of the Library of Congress and Mr. Roger Leachman of the University of Virginia Library and his staff, especially Mr. Ray English, gave unstintingly to me both their time and expert knowledge in helping solve many problems that developed in my researches in their libraries. To both I offer my sincere gratitude.

My appreciation is offered also to Jeffrey Johnson, graduate student in English at Old Dominion University, to Lori and Bill York, Dan Decker, Richard Klepal, and Anthony Brezovski, all of whom were my students, for their valuable help in preparing the manuscript for the press.

Several letters herein written by Ingram and Mrs. Whitman were first printed in my article "Poe's Biographers Brawl," which appeared in *American History Illustrated*, November 1976, and are here reprinted by the gracious permission of that magazine's managing editor, Mrs. Christine Ritter, as well as some material first printed in that article, here reprinted in my Introduction.

In their letters John Ingram and Mrs. Whitman often discuss other correspondence. When these letters are important to Poe biography, I have reproduced them. For permission to print letters written by Maria Poe Clemm and Marie Louise Shew Houghton, I am grateful to Mrs. Saundra Taylor, Curator of Manuscripts in the Josiah K. Lilly Library, Indiana University, Bloomington, and to Messrs. Stuart C. Sherman and John H. Stanley, Brown University librarians.

Old Dominion University's Research and Publications Foundation, headed by Mr. Ernest Maygarden, has my deep appreciation for awarding two summer grants in which I was able to continue research for this volume and for agreeing to sponsor its publication. The Research Committees of the Department of English and the School of Arts and Letters of Old Dominion University have provided funds and personal encouragement that literally made this volume possible.

Finally, I offer my thanks to Provost Charles O. Burgess, Deans Vernon Peele and Heinz K. Meier, and to my various departmental chairmen, Professors James B. Reece, Karl F. Knight, Donald Hammond, and David L. Shores, for reducing my teaching load and making it possible for me to have a semester's leave on a professorial research assignment that permitted me to work in the University of Virginia Library in the spring of 1976.

Editorial Method

All textual materials are numbered and interleaved, magazine and newspaper articles usually by date of publication, letters and postcards strictly by the dates on which they were written. For the correspondence, the names of the writer and the recipient are then given (and the notation "Postcard" where it is applicable). Item numbers of the Whitman letters are those of the Ingram Poe Collection, which is described in my book *John Henry Ingram's Poe Collection at the University of Virginia* (Charlottesville: University of Virginia Press, 1960). Mrs. Whitman addressed all of her letters from Providence, Rhode Island, and her address is given only once; after his first letter, Ingram's address is given only when it is not that of his previous letter.

I have made every effort to reproduce the materials as their authors wrote them. Establishing the texts of John Ingram's letters presented many problems. He wrote with a stub pen on both sides of very thin pages, and the black ink frequently bled through, obscuring the obverses. Over the years many of the pages have crumbled at their edges, making it difficult if not impossible to read exactly what he wrote. In some cases I have supplied educated guesses at what I thought he intended to write, but these are always enclosed in square brackets. Mrs. Whitman's letters offered their particular difficulties too. She was wildly inconsistent in using or omitting the ordinary, expected marks of punctuation, but she was consistent in misspelling several words: *received, weird, separate*, and *enemies*. She often opened a quotation with its mark but forgot to close it, and she occasionally used double quotation marks within double marks or misplaced them. These obvious errors I have silently corrected, in addition to other changes detailed below that I felt clarity required.

In both sides of the correspondence I have silently corrected and regularized the spelling of all proper names. When either writer used an opening initial or wrote only the initials of a person and I thought there was any chance of misunderstanding, I have supplied the missing letters in brackets. Superscripts are written out but abbreviations are retained

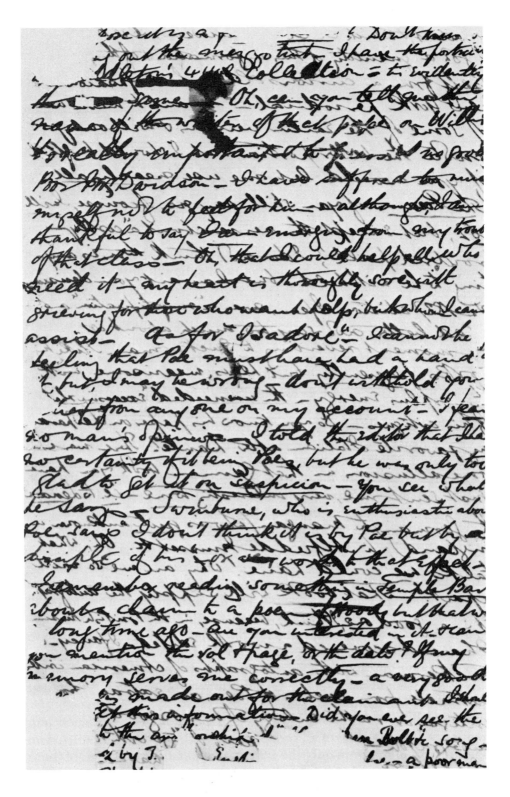

Page 6 of Ingram's letter of Apr. 2, 1874. (Courtesy Brown University Library.)

and periods supplied. Full titles of magazines and newspapers and of published and therefore known works are corrected and regularized, but the writers' short titles are retained when it is clear what magazine or book they refer to. Variant spellings (American versus British) have not been regularized, and individual variations have been retained, as in Mrs. Whitman's shifting back and forth in using *i*'s and *e*'s to begin *enclose, entrust,* or *enquiry*. Ingram's spelling of *Lotos* and Mrs. Whitman's variant *Lotus* are preserved in the case of William Fearing Gill's book *Lotos Leaves.*

I have lightly regularized punctuation within sentences and silently supplied missing terminal marks and opening capital letters. Both writers vacillated between underlining and quoting (or not marking) titles of works; I have regularized these. Also, as he himself admitted, Ingram underscored for emphasis far too much. I have retained (as italics) only the emphases that seemed reasonable and (when it was possible to determine) that were not added by Mrs. Whitman or Ingram as they read and reread the letters.

Capitalization has been modernized and correct dates supplied whenever possible. Inadvertent repetitions, such as "Had I been wealthy, long ere this I'd have properly have investigated the whole subject," are silently corrected.

All editorial interpolations are enclosed in square brackets; authorial insertions in quotations are enclosed in ornamental brackets. Ellipsis points have been modernized. Long quotations in the letters are printed as extracts.

Neither writer paid much attention to paragraphing, Ingram especially feeling that the large amounts he paid for transatlantic postage justified using all possible space available. Occasionally, when the subjects discussed obviously switched and the new one was carried on for some length, I have arbitrarily broken the discourse into paragraphs, but I did not do so with many of the brief reportings of details.

I have reproduced surviving enclosures in the letters that have direct bearings on matters concerning Poe, Mrs. Whitman, or Ingram. When these enclosures were holograph letters, I have printed them as written, without regularization; the same procedure is employed in letters reproduced in the notes. Nonpertinent enclosures are listed and described in my 1960 book.

The magazine and newspaper articles are reprinted verbatim except for the modernization of ellipses and the numbering of footnotes. Typographical errors in these articles are silently corrected.

Introduction

Ingram's "Providence" Comes to His Aid

When John Ingram addressed his first letter to Mrs. Whitman asking for her help in writing Poe's biography, he had just passed his thirty-first birthday on November 16, 1873. He was not completely unknown as a writer in England, for he had published and suppressed in 1863, after the manner of Poe's supposed suppression of *Tamerlane*, a small volume of verses called *Poems by Dalton Stone*, again imitating Poe's use of a pseudonym in his first volume. He had gone on to compile, sift all previous publications on the subject, and finally produce in 1869 a large volume on the history and symbolism of flowers. In addition, he had lectured in London on American literature, had learned to write and speak at least four languages other than his native English, and in 1868 had been awarded a commission in the British Civil Service, with a job in the General Post Office, which he held for the next thirty-five years and by means of which he supported his mother and two sisters. His father's death several years before had forced him to withdraw from the City of London College.

As a boy John Ingram found and read repeatedly Edgar Poe's poems and tales and became a fanatical admirer of the American writer. When he later read Rufus Griswold's 1850 biography of Poe, in which Griswold said that Poe was an immoral and dishonest man who, as a writer, was insanely jealous of any of his fellow authors, Ingram *instinctively* disbelieved Griswold's many unsavory allegations. He found his life's work by resolving to learn everything he possibly could about Poe and to write a truthful and definitive biography that would prove Griswold to have been a liar. Mrs. Whitman's replies to his letters made him joyously aware that he had found a literary gold mine of the primary source materials he so badly needed and hoped for in writing his long-planned biography.

Ingram had begun reading and gathering materials about Poe perhaps as early as the late 1860s, but since the British Museum Library's holdings of American magazines and newspapers were limited, he had been especially pleased to find a copy of *Edgar Poe and His Critics*, Mrs. Whitman's small, beautifully written defense of Poe. He quickly prepared and published in the London *Mirror* for January 26, 1874, a thin article which he called "New Facts about Edgar Allan Poe," of which no known copy survives. After he received Mrs. Whitman's first letter, he had more, much more, to offer his readers, and he promptly published a second article in the same weekly, which appeared on February 21, 1874, called "More New Facts about Edgar Allan Poe." Of this only a single known copy survives in the Ingram Poe Collection in the University of Virginia Library. It is reproduced in the text that follows.

When Mrs. Whitman replied to Ingram's first letter, she was within six days of her seventy-first birthday and she was wearily familiar with requests from would-be biographers of Poe who had written or come to her for help. But there was something different about this letter from England; the strong handwriting and choice of words showed her that the writer obviously worshiped Poe and hated Griswold and that he was determined to clear Poe's name of some, if not all, of the untruths Griswold had published about the dead poet. Ingram had not neglected to inform her that he had already published two books, that he was a recognized member of the British literati as well as being a Fellow of the Royal Historical Society. It could have been any or all of these things that impressed her, for she did answer his letter very quickly. After first warning him that he would find his job difficult, if not impossible, she proceeded to write many more pages in which Ingram easily recognized her acute intellect, her sense of humor, and her factual and intimate knowledge of Edgar Poe's personality and writings. This letter became the beginning of the building of truthful and reliable Poe biography.

Sarah Helen Power was born in Providence, Rhode Island, on January 19, 1803, exactly six years to the day before Edgar Poe was born in Boston. Her father, Nicholas Power, disappeared at sea sometime after 1813, when her sister, Susan Anna, was born, and the two girls grew up with their mother; their father's return, after nineteen years of silence, apparently surprised them all. Sarah Helen married John Winslow Whitman on July 10, 1828, and moved with him to Boston, where he had started his law practice. After his death, five years and fifteen days later, she promptly returned to Providence to resume her life with her mother and her mentally affected sister, whose eccentricities even then governed the household, and Sarah Helen, apparently with much satisfaction, returned to her former activities—writing and receiving letters from the more important and well-known American literati, taking occasional trips to the mountains and the beaches; she joined a tour for a trip to Europe in 1857. She wrote better than average verses, and these were published in book form by George Whitney in Providence in 1853, at his request.

Edgar Poe had appeared at her door in September 1848, armed with a letter of introduction written in New York City by Maria J. McIntosh. He had immediately declared his love for Sarah Helen, asking her to marry him at once. Of course she temporized, flattered as she was by both his person and his undeniable abilities as a writer. Her mother and her sister, as well as her neighbor, William J. Pabodie, made strong objections to the proposed marriage, as, apparently, did many of her friends. But Mrs. Whitman did consent to a conditional engagement, after several stormy scenes with Poe and she had extracted from him a sacred promise that he would never drink again. This engagement was broken in December of that same year, and not without Poe's connivance.

When Poe died in Baltimore the next October, Mrs. Whitman must have realized that she had lost her best chance for literary and personal immortality by refusing to become the second Mrs. Edgar Allan Poe, for she was too good a critic of her own verses and his not to recognize that his writings would rank him among the very first of American authors.

Lurid stories had been told and retold as well as published about the breaking of her engagement to Poe, and these she had tried to correct by personal letters and sometime quiet but firm vocal denials. It was not until Rufus Wilmot Griswold died in 1857 that she began writing her defense of Poe, for Griswold had both a powerful personality and strong hatred for Poe, and he was so well known as an editor and author that he had access to almost every important magazine published in America—and Mrs. Whitman was afraid of him. When she did write her *Edgar Poe and His Critics*, published in 1860, she did not attempt to controvert every lie Griswold had written about Poe, but she did say that he had lied, and she attempted to give interested readers another and different view of Poe's personality and writings.

After the Civil War, when writers literally besieged her, she graciously tried to help everyone who asked, for she was extremely anxious that an able and truthful biographer retell the story of Poe's life, and especially the circumstances surrounding her broken engagement to him. One by one they came: Thomas Cottrell Clarke, who had once offered to finance Poe's dreamed-of-magazine, the *Stylus*; an anonymous writer using the initials S.E.R., who burned to write a redemptive biography but who unfortunately went insane before the work was even started; James Wood Davidson, of South Carolina, an early defender of Poe's reputation and one of the first attackers of Griswold's veracity; William Gowans, who had actually boarded for a time with the Poe family in New York City; Richard Henry Stoddard, a New York writer who did not ask for her help and who not very politely snubbed her written efforts to correct two of the more glaring errors he had written about Poe; and William Fearing Gill of Boston and New York, an impulsive but ardent admirer of Poe with whom she talked at length and whom she allowed to use some of her firsthand materials about Poe, actions she was later to regret deeply.

When none of these writers produced anything that came close to fitting her wishes, she began to despair that an impassioned and able biographer would ever appear to straighten out the record for all time. She still had an enormous amount of primary source materials for Poe biography, but her mother was dead and she alone was responsible for her insane sister, whose behavior grew harder to handle as the years passed, and she too was growing old.

It was at this point that John Ingram's first letter reached her, changing her whole outlook about the possibilities of her association and engagement to Poe being told with both dignity and tact, and she promptly began a correspondence with him. It began somewhat formally but quickly became friendly and then affectionate, even though they never met face to face. Her reply changed Ingram's career and life, too, and together they gave to us the longest, most reliable account we have of Poe's life and writings.

Poe's Helen Remembers

England

12 Wolsey Road,
Mildmay Park, London, N.

20 Dec. 1873—

Dear Mrs. Whitman,

I am sending this in the forlorn hope that it may reach your hands safely and induce you to kindly aid me in my efforts to clear the memory of my favorite author, Edgar Poe, from the cruel slanders of the late D. Griswold. For many years past I have been collecting material for a new life of the poet, but here in England, I work under great difficulties, the only American works of reference which I can see being those in the British Museum. Nearly all the newspapers which I require (that is, which are mentioned in Griswold's Memoir) are absent from the above library, and of the few there, such as The Tribune &c., I have not yet succeeded in doing much with in consequence of not having any certain dates or data to go by, & hitherto, my literary & official duties have prevented me going through even that one paper consecutively. A little while ago I was delighted to see your work, "Edgar Poe and his Critics" in the Museum, as it strengthened & confirmed me in my desire to do my best in vindication of Poe. I at once sent to Trübner for the book but was told that it had long been out of print— Allibone, in his Dictionary, I think, says you have written several things in defence of our mutual favorite. If so, they are not in our Museum. I have just written a prelude to my more lengthy defence of Poe, for one of our monthlies, and as soon as it appears you shall have a copy or will

Page 1 of Ingram's first letter to Mrs. Whitman, Dec. 20, 1873. (Courtesy Brown University Library.)

1. *John H. Ingram to Sarah Helen Whitman*

England
12 Wolsey Road
Mildway Park, London, N.

Dear Mrs. Whitman,   20 Dec. 1873

I am sending this in the forlorn hope that it may reach your hands safely and induce you to kindly aid me in my efforts to clear the memory of my favorite author, Edgar Poe, from the cruel slanders of the late Dr. Griswold. For many years past I have been collecting material for a new life of the poet, but here, in England, I work under great difficulties, the only American works of reference which I can see being those in the British Museum. Nearly all the newspapers which I require (that is, which are mentioned in Griswold's "Memoir") are absent from the above library, and of the few there, such as the *Tribune* &c., I have not yet succeeded in doing much with in consequence of not having any certain dates or *data* to go by, &, hitherto, my literary & official duties have prevented me going through even one paper consecutively. A little while ago I was delighted to see your work *Edgar Poe and His Critics* in the Museum, as it strengthened & confirmed me in my desire to do my best in vindication of Poe.[1] I at once sent to Trübners for the book but was told that it had long been out of print. Allibone, in his *Dictionary, I think,* says you have written several things in defense of our mutual favorite: if so, they are not in our Museum.[2] I have just written a prelude to my more lengthy defense of Poe, for one of our monthlies, and as soon as it appears you shall have a copy & will then see what use I have made of my slender materials. Over leaf I will give you references to such papers as I cannot obtain, and which, for reasons stated, might prove useful in the vindication. If you can I feel assured you will aid me by pointing out their value for the purpose desired, and by letting me know how, & for how much, they may be procured & I will gladly remit the needful. I have written to an English acquaintance to find out your address if possible & he *may* call on you—'Tis a Mr. T. Clarke. By the way, a Mr. T. C. Clarke (of Baltimore), stated to be a friend of Edgar Poe's, was said by the papers to be about to write a new life of the poet: can you say the result?[3] Do you know of anything of Poe's besides the writings contained in the four (4) vols. published under Griswold's supervision by Redfield & by Widdle[ton], New York?[4] I have just written to a "Rosalie Poe," Hick's Landing, Virginia, said by the papers to be Poe's sister & only surviving relative. I don't know whether the address was sufficient to find her. Amongst the chief things I hope for Poe's life is the *correct* dates of his birth, departure to & return from England, entering University at Charlottesville, publication of 1st edition of poems &c. Did this first collection contain anything not republished? *Any* particulars of his journey in Europe: did Poe ever reach Greece, visit Italy &c.? Date of his entry & departure from West Point? Can it be disproved that he was expelled therefrom? Can it be *disproved* that he deserted from the army? Can you point to a single anecdote of Griswold's which has been publicly refuted, or even denied in print? *One only would be a help* to my special pleading. Some I have disproved and have made others look very improbable, but your book is the only publication I have yet seen which declares Griswold's statements incorrect. What are those letters of John Neal & George Graham which Griswold alludes to? Can any copy of them be obtained? Bought or borrowed? In which papers, can you say, did they appear, and about what dates? I have seen Powell's "Memoir" in *Poets of America*, & the letter of Willis, but not a single fact, *specially* pointed out to be denied: can you furnish any or one?[5] New York *Tribune*, or *Saturday Evening Post*? The libel on Poe by Dr. Dunn English is said to have appeared in the New York *Mirror* on 23 June 1846.[6] Files of the papers are in British Museum, but *that particular number* is missing! Poe is said to have prepared a sketch of his own life for Brooks's *Museum* (of Baltimore?[7]). Do you know if it ever appeared? Griswold says the family of "S. D. Lewis" were good friends of Poe's—do you know anything of *them*? Do you know any particulars of poor Poe's death? Did you see the poem in New York *Tribune*, 13 Nov. [18]49, in response to Griswold's remark, "The poet hath no friends"? Have you seen a poem by "C. Gardette" called "The Fire Fiend"? Mrs. Macready published it in the London *Star* as by Poe, & stated that Mrs. Clemm gave it to her as Poe's: that is strange! I pronounced it a forgery at once, but it is sometimes reprinted here as Poe's, but I shall stop that, I trust, for the future.[8] Papers, which I cannot get in London, appeared on Poe in the following, according to Allibone. Do they contain anything of use to me?—

   Democratic Review (J. Savage), XXVIII, pp. 66, 162
   Boston *Living Age*, XXV, p. 77
   New York *Electric* [*Eclectic*] *Magazine*, XV, p. 262
   Wallace's *Literary Criticisms*—

Many others are mentioned, but I have either seen them or can do so.

   In *E. Poe & His Critics* you alluded to Poe's portrait, and the engraving therefrom as being bad: cannot a photo be taken? I would willingly subscribe for a dozen copies. In same book you mention that many of the anecdotes retailed by Griswold were disproved in New York *Tribune*, and one more recently in the *Home Journal*: can you furnish me dates of the former publication, which I can see, & particulars of the latter, which I cannot? Pardon my long, rambling scrawl & forgive my intrusion, for the sake of the object. I have thrown my requests into a disconnected form, I fear, just as they have occurred to me. I might have asked more, probably, but shall be only too glad if you can answer one question satisfactorily. If you have any pamphlet, or paper, bearing on the subject, which you can spare, I shall be thankful & will forward you copies of everything I print on the subject of Poe. I will remit any pecuniary outlay at once. Don't hesitate to name such. With heartiest sympathy in your noble exertions, I remain, believe me, my dear madam, ever admiringly yours,

John H. Ingram

P.S. What I should like most to be able to disprove is the story of Poe's expulsion from West Point, desertion from the army, and the borrowing the money from a lady, *re.* Dr. Francis, &c.—of the publishing a book of a certain Captain Brown, as his own original work, on conchology— see Griswold's "Memoir." Do you know if the poems of E. C. Pinckney are now procurable?[9]

J.H.I.

1. *Edgar Poe and His Critics* (New York: Rudd & Carleton, 1860; rpt. New Brunswick, N.J.: Rutgers Univ. Press, 1949).

2. Samuel Austin Allibone, *A Critical Dictionary of English Literature and British and American Authors* . . . , 3 vols. (Philadelphia: J. B. Lippincott & Co., 1872). See II, 1614–15, for his sketch of Poe's career.

3. Thomas Cottrell Clarke (d. 1874) was owner and editor of the *Philadelphia Saturday Museum.* In 1842 he had agreed to provide the money necessary to start Poe's long-dreamed-of magazine, the *Stylus,* but he later withdrew his offer.

4. *The Works of the Late Edgar Allan Poe,* ed. Rufus W. Griswold, 4 vols. (New York: J. S. Redfield, 1850–56). Griswold's "Memoir" prefaced Vol. III, but was moved to Vol. I in 1853. Redfield sold his copyright on the edition to W. J. Widdleton ca. 1863, and after printing many editions, Widdleton resold it to A. C. Armstrong, who replaced Griswold's "Memoir" with Ingram's.

5. Thomas Powell (1809–1887) was born in London and came to the United States in 1849. He published *Living Authors of England* (New York: Appleton, 1849) and *Living Authors of America,* 1st ser. (New York: Stringer and Townsend, 1850). See pp. 108–34 for his article about Poe.

6. Thomas Dunn English (1819–1902) was a medical doctor, a lawyer, and an author. His most popular ballad was "Sweet Alice, Ben Bolt." For brief accounts of his relationship and quarrels with Poe, see either Arthur Hobson Quinn, *Edgar Allan Poe: A Critical Biography* (New York: D. Appleton--Century Co., 1941), pp. 503–6, or James A. Harrison, ed., *The Complete Works of Edgar Allan Poe,* 17 vols. (New York: T. Y. Crowell & Co., 1902), IV, 233–58.

7. Nathan Covington Brooks was editor and owner, with Dr. Joseph Evans Snodgrass, of the *American Museum of Science, Literature, and the Arts* in Baltimore. Poe contributed tales and articles to his magazine from its beginning in Sept. 1838 through its concluding issue in June 1839.

8. And stop it he did. He proved that Charles D. Gardette had admitted authorship of the hoax in his book *The Fire Fiend and Other Poems* (New York, 1866). Ingram took the whole subject to the cleaners in his edition of *The Raven* (London: George Redway, 1885). The verses had been published, deadpan, in the *Southern Literary Messenger,* 23 (July 1863), 397–98, as "The Fire Legend—a Nightmare. From an unpublished MS. of the Late Edgar A. Poe."

9. Edward Coote Pinckney, *Poems* (Baltimore: Joseph Robinson, 1825).

Providence, Rhode Island
January 13 1874

Dear Sir

I have this morning received thro'
Mr Carleton your letter of Dec 20.
While I am gratified to know that you
are preparing a memoir of the great genius
whose character has been hitherto chiefly
known thro' Griswold's distorted narrative
&, while I shall be most happy to assist you
in any way which you may suggest, I cannot
but fear that you will find the facts of
his life so elusive, the dates so contradictory
the details so perverted by relentless enemies
& injudicious friends that you will have a very
difficult task before you. Have you seen
in Harper's Monthly for September 1872 an
article entitled Edgar Allan Poe? It is not
very satisfactory & has not much in it
that is new. Portions of it, especially
the opening paragraphs on Poe's parents
& ancestry are taken almost verbatim
from "Edgar Poe & his Critics," though

Page 1 of Mrs. Whitman's first letter to Ingram, Jan. 13, 1874. (Courtesy University of Virginia Library.)

2. *Sarah Helen Whitman to John H. Ingram.* Item 115

Providence, Rhode Island
Dear Sir: Jan. 13, 1874

I have this morning received thro' Mr. Carleton your letter of Dec. 20.

While I am gratified to know that you are preparing a memoir of the great genius whose character has been hitherto chiefly known thro' Griswold's distorted narrative, &, while I shall be most happy to assist you in any way which you may suggest, I cannot but fear that you will find the *facts* of his life so elusive, the dates so contradictory, the details so perverted by relentless enemies & injudicious friends that you will have a very difficult task before you. Have you seen in *Harper's Monthly* for September 1872 an article entitled "Edgar Allan Poe"?[1] It is not very satisfactory & has not much in it that is new. Portions of it, especially the opening paragraphs on Poe's parentage & ancestry, are taken almost verbatim from *Edgar Poe & His Critics* though without any reference throughout the article to the little book or its author. The article was written by Mr. R. H. Stoddard & I learn that he has been revising it for the new London Edition of Poe by Routledge & Sons. Have you seen it or do you know anything of it? In the article as published in *Harper's*, he introduced from my brochure, without quotation, an anecdote about Poe's love for the mother of one of his schoolmates, & adds, "The memory of this lady is said to have suggested the lines beginning, 'Helen, thy beauty is to me'—& *may* have done so, though I am not aware that Poe himself ever countenanced the idea." Now, since he copied the anecdote from my book, he *must* have known that I had quoted, in connection with it & in confirmation of it, passages from a letter written to me by Mr. Poe within a twelvemonth of his death.

On reading his article in *Harper's*, which seemed to me on its first perusal candid & rather friendly in its spirit, I wrote to him to say that though pleased with the general tone of his article, I was pained to find that he had expressed doubt of Poe's having countenanced a statement for which I had given his letter as authority. He replied that so many months had elapsed since he wrote the article (just published in *Harper's*), that he was "unable to remember" what he *had* said in it! This seemed to me a palpable evasion of the matter in question. He declared however that he had no *intention* to discredit any statement that I had made in *Edgar Poe & His Critics*, & if he had done so, he asked my forgiveness. He then went on to say—

The more I looked into Poe's life the more I doubted the truth of any statement about him in print; Griswold I gave up before I began, yet I had to trust him to a certain or rather *un*certain extent. The first puzzle I encountered was the year of Poe's birth, which Griswold says Poe told him was 1811 *&* 1813. From evidence furnished me by a gentleman of Baltimore I came to the conclusion that 1809 was the correct year. Mr. Wertenbaker's letter corroborates this statement.

I had said in my letter to Stoddard that I had evidence in my possession that Poe was *not* expelled from the University. To prove this I *sent* him copies of two letters written in *May* (I think) 1860; one from Dr. Stephen Maupin, president of the University, & one from Mr. *Wertenbaker*, the secretary, written at the *request* of Dr. Maupin.[2] They contained a record of the date of Poe's entrance into the University & of his age as entered by himself in the matriculation book of the college. He entered the University in Feb. 1826 & gave his age as 17.

The record states that he was not at that time intemperate but was known to have a passion for cards which had not however drawn upon him any censure from the faculty. I suffered Mr. Stoddard to *retain* these copies of letters hoping that he would use them at some time to clear up at least one stain on the record of the unfortunate poet. Perhaps I can obtain them or copies of them. Before writing to Stoddard I wrote an article for the Providence *Journal* in which I commented favourably on his article but regretted his repetition of the slander about Poe's expulsion. I enclose to you this printed article which I should like to have you preserve & at some time return to me.

I also in my first letter to Mr. Stoddard offered to place in his hands letters which were written to me by Mr. Poe which would show that I had not spoken without authority in what I had said of the lines about the mother of one of his schoolmates. But all this I must leave for the present because I am anxious to let you know *at once* that I have duly received your letter. I will try then to answer some of your questions briefly, in the order in which you present them.

About Mr. T. C. Clarke. I presume it is the Mr. Clarke who was to have been associated with Mr. Poe as *publisher* of the *Stylus*. I saw him for the first & only time in New York in the autumn of 1859. It was just after it had been announced in the Philadelphia papers that Rudd & Carleton were about to publish *Edgar Poe & His Critics*, by Mrs. Whitman. He came to New York, sought out my address, & came to see me. He had a long talk with me, expressed great pleasure in learning that I was about to protest against the injustice of Griswold—he evinced an affectionate & admiring interest in Mr. Poe, as a man & an acquaintance. Mr. Clarke was a plain, honest man, apparently, & without much literary culture—at least such was my impression. He told me of his own projected work, asked for my assistance respecting certain particulars of my personal acquaintance with Poe—of my engagement & the cause & manner of its dissolution. He wrote me one or two letters the following spring, & then I heard little or nothing more of him until some three months ago a young gentleman by the name of Wm. F. Gill, a partner in the publishing house of Gill & Shepard, Boston, having been in correspondence with me for the last two or three months, in relation to a lecture which he was proposing to write on E.A.P. (in which he intended to introduce readings & recitations from the poems) told me that he was in hopes of inducing Mr. Clarke to make over to him the facts which he had been so long storing up for publication.[3] Mr. Clarke is, I should think, quite an old man.

I have not heard from Mr. Gill very lately but saw it stated in one of the Boston papers that he was thinking of the stage as a profession. I fancy that his genius is rather too versatile for him to succeed as an author.

You ask if I can point to any one anecdote of Griswold's which has been publicly refuted or even *denied* in print.

In the New York *Tribune* for June 7th 1852 you will find a letter to the editor from Wm. J. Pabodie of Providence in direct & specific denial of the account published by Griswold of outrages committed in the house of a New England lady on the evening of the appointed marriage.[4]

Mr. Griswold on seeing this printed denial wrote a *savage* & unmanly letter to Mr. Pabodie threatening if he did not withdraw it to do dreadful things.

Mr. Pabodie not only did not withdraw it but in a printed letter to Griswold brought forward incontrovertible proofs of other & greater falsifications indulged in by the irate Doctor in his "Memoir." From that time he was discreetly silent.

I will mail to you this evening if possible a copy of *Edgar Poe & His Critics,* & if I can obtain it, a copy of Stoddard's article in the magazine of Sept. 1872. I shall be *very* glad to receive a copy of your magazine article on Poe, your "prelude." You see that I am getting very tired. I will attend to some of your other questions soon. I have never seen Miss Rosalie Poe. Mrs. Clemm, who was an occasional correspondent of mine until within a year of her death, never mentioned her to me. Mr. Poe once, when speaking of the loneliness of his life, said in reply to a question I asked about his sister, that there had long been a coolness or estrangement between them. I have heard through the papers that she was very destitute. There is, I think, a Mr. Neilson Poe, who was a cousin of theirs, but whether in Baltimore or Richmond, I have forgotten.[5]

It was not Mrs. Macready but Mr. Macready who sent "The Fire Fiend" to the *Star.* I enclose you a fragment of it, sent to me anonymously some years ago. I knew at once that it was a forgery, & am glad that you recognized it as such.

Any letter addressed to me at Providence, Rhode Island, will duly reach me.

Yours cordially,
Sarah Helen Whitman

I shall be anxious to know that my letter reaches you safely.

I *may* not be able to send the *Critics* tonight, but if not, will do so soon.

Mr. Carleton's present address, should you ever have occasion to write to him again, is G. W. Carleton & Co., publishers, Madison Square, New York.

If any one of the biographical dictionaries speaks of my having written of E.A.P. elsewhere than in "The Critics," it must allude to to a vol. of poems, a small edition of which was published by a Providence publisher, by his own request, in 1853.[6] If you would like to see it, I will send you a volume.

1. R. H. Stoddard, "Edgar Allan Poe," *Harper's New Monthly Magazine*, 45 (1872), 557–58. Many references to this article and its author, none of them complimentary, are ahead. Richard Henry Stoddard (1825–1903) was a poet, reviewer, and an editor of merit, despite Ingram's unrelentingly savage estimates of him. Stoddard had met Poe and later, as editor of the *Broadway Journal*, Poe had refused, in print, to accept for publication Stoddard's poem "The Grecian Flute." After that, Stoddard understandably disliked Poe; he never did really understand or appreciate Poe's own writings, even though he wrote much about him from 1853 until the end of his own life.

2. Dr. Socrates (not Stephen) Maupin, presiding officer of the University of Virginia faculty, directed William Wertenbaker, librarian and former classmate of Poe's, to draw up a statement on May 12, 1860, about Poe's scholarship and acceptable behavior at the university, denying that Poe had been expelled, apparently in answers to the many inquiries beginning to reach the university authorities. Dr. Maupin appended a note to Wertenbaker's statement on May 22, 1860, attesting to its validity. See Item 92 in the Ingram Poe Collection.

3. William Fearing Gill (1844–1917) was an impulsive, erratic, but apparently sincere admirer of Poe and his writings. He published a hastily and badly written biography of Poe in 1877, which has value simply because it contains some new materials about Poe. He continued to lecture and write about Poe for the remainder of his life; he became a bitter vocal enemy of John Ingram's; and he broke faith with Mrs. Whitman by publishing portions of Poe's letters to her which she had allowed him to read but had expressly forbidden him to publish.

4. William J. Pabodie of Providence, R.I., was educated as a lawyer but chose to spend his life as an occasional poet and a full-time dilettante. He was a close friend and neighbor of Mrs. Whitman's and, on occasions, Poe's host when Poe visited Providence to see Mrs. Whitman. After Poe's death Pabodie wrote articles in the *Tribune* in his defense. Pabodie committed suicide in 1870.

5. Neilson Poe (1809–1884) was a cousin of Edgar's who married Josephine Emily, daughter of William and Harriet Clemm. In Virginia and in Maryland his first name was pronounced "Nelson," and Mrs. Whitman and Ingram regularly spelled it so.

6. Sarah Helen Whitman, *Hours of Life and Other Poems* (Providence: George H. Whitney, 1853).

3. *John H. Ingram to Sarah Helen Whitman*

My dear Mrs. Whitman, 26 Jan. 1874
   By the same post I received today both your beautiful little book,
and your most interesting letter [Jan. 13], and, instead of waiting to
reflect & comment fully upon either, hasten to acknowledge them, and
by the same post forward you two copies of the *Mirror*, containing
an *introductory* paper on Edgar Poe.[1] The *Mirror*, though only a
weekly, is written for by some of our best known writers, & has a large
circulation so that the series of papers which I am about to publish in
it—and which I will forward you as they appear—will go before some
thousands of readers. The Feby. no. of *Temple Bar* magazine will be
out in a few days, & I will forward a copy to you directly it appears: *it*
circulates in the U. States &, indeed, wherever the English language is
spoken. Feby. no. contains a paper on "Edgar Poe" by myself, shewing
the falsity, or improbability, of Griswold's statements. Do not be
disappointed with it. Future papers in the *Mirror* &c. will disprove
nearly every accusation of Griswold's. I believe that I have much
information, derived from old American papers, that you do not know
of. The anecdotes that I wish most to disprove now are about the
"Conchology" book by Brown—of this I think I have a clue to, & the
borrowing money, of a lady & then refusing to pay &c. &c. till forced
by fear of chastisement from lady's brother to acknowledge the debt.[2]
Dr. Francis, of New York, recently dead, was said to have conveyed
Poe's apologies to the injured family—*vide* "Memoir."[3] This much said
I will proceed to a running commentary upon your letter, & reserve
other things till later. First as to difficulty of information—for me, in
England, 'tis difficult to get at the truth but I'll leave no stone
unturned to do my best. I'm not wealthy & my time is officially
engaged, or I would take a trip to the States. I may someday—as I
have already seen a good deal of the finest European scenery. I see a
great many American papers &c. in the British Museum Library—what
I want most, that they have not got, is *Graham's Magazine* from its
commencement about Nov. 1840 to end of 1842. *Harper's Monthly* for
Sep. 1872 I have *not* seen but will try & get. Mr. Stoddard, after what
you say, I shall not much rely on. I did not know that Routledge
projected a new edition. One, pretending to be complete, was
published by the late J. Hotten, known for his reprinting American
books & works on which he had no copyright to pay: it contained about
one third of Griswold's collection & yet is *our* most complete edition.[4]
But the poems & selections from the tales are being continually
reprinted & Poe is deemed by our first critics the finest poet America
has produced—*vide Encyclopaedia Brittanica, Chambers's
Encyclopaedia* &c. His fame is far higher here, & in France, than in his

native country, but everywhere is Griswold's beastly story accepted as
gospel. In England we bury a man's misdeeds with him & remember
only the good, whilst during his life—why! we *literati* are far *too
lenient*—are a regular mutual admiration society & would scorn to
publish a *personal* line about anyone—however disliked. The slightest
departure from this rule would be severely criticised. But I am
straying. Reverting to Hotten's collection, it gave some new
information about Poe's school in England—'tis but ten minutes from
where I live—& a translation from the French of Baudelaire—of
essays on Poe's life & genius. Nothing new in them but they—whilst
accepting Griswold's story as true—consign the Doctor to "immortal
infamy." Your book I will review separately for the *Mirror* & your
poems too, if you will kindly send them. I enclose you two of my
juvenile poems inspired by Poe, written & published soon after I had
entered my teens & reprinted in a little vol. published under my
boyhood's *nom de plume* of "Dalton Stone."[5] They are very boyish & I
suppressed the book after it had received several favorable notices
from the press—but I send these verses to show you how long I have
been under the weird influence of Poe. I will forward you a book of
mine on flowers—not as a specimen of my literary skill, but as a proof
that I have made a good-sized book: it will follow in course of a day or
so.[6] I must get a copy from the publisher. Is there any chance of getting
a copy of the 1st, 2nd, or 3rd editions of Poe's poems, do you think? Or
even written copies of *variorum* readings? I'd pay anything in reason
for them. Next week the *Mirror* will contain a poem from Poe's
Broadway Journal, which I believe he wrote—"To Isadore."[7] Do you
know it? Do you know real date of his early poems' publication? You
will see that I have doubted date of birth, in *Temple Bar* &c.
Information about the school is valuable to me. I will return all the
printed slips as soon as I copy what I require. As regards "The Fire
Fiend," *it was Mrs. Macready*, the reader, & not Macready (whose
family we know well), who sent it to the *Star*, where I read it. I have
the whole of it (sent to me by the same literary friend who now edits
the *Mirror* & who is an intense admirer of Poe) & know that in
America Macready is always given for Mrs. Macready—'tis rather a
strange affair—she said Mrs. Clemm gave it to her—or rather, hinted
so—whereas it was written by a Mr. C. Gardette—an American who
has since acknowledged the circumstance & published it in a vol. of
verse as his own.

As regards Mr. Clarke—if I can arrange with him I should be glad,
for purchase of the Poe papers; but I must be certain that they are what
I do not possess & then must rely upon a publisher, as I am not, as
before stated, wealthy. I was born in luxury, but unfortunate

circumstances, which I need not trouble you with, have brought us from "our high estate," & I only have—for my mother, sisters, & self, what my official position & literary labours produce. But for this, my Poe papers would have been produced earlier. The New York *Tribune* I will see for denial of the anecdote you speak of. I have not yet heard from Miss Poe. Thomas Powell, in his *Living Authors of America*, says she was also adopted by Mr. Allan, who was, says a German encyclopedia, Poe's godfather? I know several foreign languages &, as you perceive, have not rested satisfied with native accounts. I was but a child when I first read an account of Poe in *Chambers's Journal* (Edinburgh & London), & have ever since adored him & have longed to write his life.[8] No sooner did I get the "Memoir" than I began to see its unaccountable differences, & it is by putting one against the other that I shall show many of Griswold's audacious fabrications. Why! Even in his life of Mrs. Osgood—his dear friend—he cannot quote a date accurately.[9] Had Poe been an Englishman, a thousand pens, ere this, would have worked in his defense. Had he been *all* that Griswold has painted, we would have deemed his genius & his troubles a cloak as inclusive as charity to hide his faults. Let me have your poems, if you can spare a copy. It was in Allibone's immense dictionary of English & American literature that I saw you spoken of as an admirer & defender of Poe &, fancied from the wording, in other works than *Edgar Poe & His Critics*. I have left much for future correspondence, but wished to at once acknowledge your letter, books, &c. In England, where Griswold's title of Dr. (whence obtained, I wonder?) & his evident assumption of knowing Poe & being his friend, have always caused his story to be accepted as a record of facts (save in Mr. Moy Thomas's letter), & I have often been laughed at by friends—literary & otherwise—for doubting the "Memoir."[10] English people do not comprehend the amenities of American *literati*. Forgive my saying this but, although no warmer admirer of America & her institutions lives than myself, her press, I must persist, affords license for much that the most rotten old despotism of Europe would blush to acknowledge. Pardon this—help me in my endeavours—trust to my honour— anything which you *merely lend*, believe me, I will return as quickly as possible. I may keep this book though—may I not? You have not autographed it. I could not get a copy anywhere in England—saw it only in British Museum under heading of Poe. Many well-known, distinguished English *literati* are anxious to learn results of my researches. Must catch today's post, but fear that I have said much that I need not have said, & have omitted much that I would have said. *En passant*, how did Poe pronounce his name? 'Tis fashionable here to say Poë: is that correct? And now, respite from worrying you, but believe ever, my dear madam, henceforth your name will be coupled with the name of Edgar Poe in the memory of your ever faithful friend—

John H. Ingram

A portrait of Poe, different from the collections, cannot, I suppose, be obtained. Would you mind lending me any scrap of his [writing] to get copied for *facsimile*? It should be religiously guarded & returned. *Flora Symbolica*, my book on flowers, will follow in a day or so.

J.H.I.

1. This article, "New Facts about Edgar Poe," was published in the London *Mirror*, Jan. 24, 1874; no known copy survives.

2. For an acceptable but inconclusive account of Poe's part in the composition of *The Conchologist's First Book* and the portions contributed by Captain Brown and Professor Wyatt, see Quinn, pp. 275–77, 528–29.

3. Dr. John Francis Ward (1789–1861) was a popular New York physician and a very close friend of Rufus Griswold's. Ward died Feb. 8, 1861. The New York *Times* printed a long obituary for him on the eleventh.

4. John Camden Hotten (1832–1873) was a London publisher who had issued in 1872 a selection of Poe's writings called *The Works of Edgar Allan Poe, with a Study of His Life and Writings, from the French of Baudelaire.*

5. *Poems by Dalton Stone*. Ingram had this little book published in 1863, and, imitating Poe in this, as he did in many other ways, later claimed he had suppressed it, as Poe claimed he had suppressed *Tamerlane*. Ingram's book is listed in *Lippincott's Pronouncing Biographical Dictionary* (Philadelphia: Joseph Thomas, 1930).

6. John H. Ingram, *Flora Symbolica; or the Language and Sentiment of Flowers, Including Floral Poetry, Original and Selected* (London: F. W. Warne & Co.; New York: Scribner, Welford & Co., 1869).

7. "To Isadore" was written by A. M. Ide, Jr., a seventeen-year-old would-be poet from South Attleboro, Mass., who sent it to Poe for possible publication in the *Broadway Journal*. Poe probably retouched the lines before printing them on Oct. 25, 1845. Albert Pike, an American poet of sorts, also wrote a poem named "Isadore."

8. This article was first printed in *Chambers's Journal*, 19 (1853), and reprinted in *Littell's Living Age*, 38 (Apr. 16, 1853), 157–61, as "The Life and Poetry of Edgar Poe."

9. Griswold's essay "Frances Sargent Osgood" appeared in *The Memorial*, a souvenir volume of poems and articles in honor of Mrs. Osgood, edited by Mrs. Mary E. Hewitt (New York: George P. Putnam, 1851), pp. 13–30.

10. W. Moy Thomas had published an article, "Edgar Allen [*sic*] Poe," in the *Train*, 3 (Apr. 1857), 193–98, in which he defended Poe's character and suggested that perhaps Griswold had tampered with Poe's letters and papers. See Item 523 in the Ingram Poe Collection.

4. *John H. Ingram to Sarah Helen Whitman*

Dear Mrs. Whitman,   28 Jan. 1874

I am troubling you with another epistle close upon my reply to your very welcome one. I am very desirous of collecting all possible information respecting Edgar Poe as quickly as I can, and, therefore, after a few preliminary remarks will give you a regular series of questions, and, if you can and will answer any one of them I shall be thankful. I have sent you a copy of my *Flora Symbolica* by registered post, and hope you'll get it safely, and like it: if you have inclination to review it anywhere I should feel flattered. With one exception it has been favorably noticed by our leading publications. The *Times* downwards: daily to quarterly all spoke well. There are some of my dear lost sister's verses in it—Ella Ingram.

I look for your poems: all that I have seen of yours—save "The Portrait"—was in Duyckinck's *Cyclopedia*. My notice in *Temple Bar* is delayed until March: it is not what I would have liked but I dare not offer to alter it again; my threefold revision having delayed it. But in the interim the *Mirror* will appear & shall follow with poem "To Isadore." I shall, however, meantime collect every possible reference for a complete biography, including & duly acknowledging all your information. I want to collect all the writings, I can, of Poe's, not included in the 4 vols. You quote a marginal note that I did not know of his: was a separate collection of "Marginalia" ever published, do you know? An American said he thought Lowell had edited one. What I chiefly want & cannot get here is *Graham's Magazine* from its commencement in (Nov. 1840?) to end of 1842. My *Mirror* papers may contain some things unknown to you even. Meanwhile, if there are any of the following questions you can & will answer, I shall be thankful.

1. Is there anyone to apply to at Baltimore, for precise date of Poe's birth; anecdotes of childhood or family?

2. 1816 to England & 1822 departure to U. States: are these dates correct?

3. *Were the Allans kind to him*? Did they leave him in England, or stay here? Was Allan his godfather & was Edgar's 2nd name Allan?

4. Any anecdotes of his *childhood, school days*, University life, or adventures in Europe, Russia, &c. from friends, &c.?

5. Do you know if Ebenezer Burling, who Powell says was to accompany him to Greece, is alive?

6. When first collection of poems was published? 1827? If any poems therein not reprinted?

7. Mr. Allan's 2nd wife is said—when Allan died—to have refused Poe his books?

8. Military Academy—date of entry &c.—any fellow students known?

9. When he married?

10. *Burton's Gentleman's Magazine*—about 1838–39—any nos. to be had?

11. Prize for "Gold Bug"—in what publication?

12. *Broadway [Journal]*—can I procure any nos.? From Oct. [18]45 to Jan. [18]46, Poe had it alone—Briggs was out.

13. *"Literati* of New York"—do you know that they are not properly reprinted in Griswold's collection, but are garbled &c.? See case of English. Did you know anything of the libel suit gained by Poe against English? The letter by English appeared in New York *Mirror*, 23rd June, 1846: the letter has been abstracted, or not sent with remainder of the newspaper to British Museum.

14. Is there any reliable account of his last moments?

15. Are the Lewis family to be got at? Griswold says they were his dear friends.

16. Do you know anything of the Brown "Conchology" story? His enlistment in & desertion from the army?

I have asked these questions hurriedly & apparently coldly & businesslike, but you must not deem that I am unsympathetic, or want the information for mercantile purposes. I admire & reverence Edgar Poe to an extent that makes me quite a scoff amongst the many, who think I am somewhat crazy on the point: but you, & those who study him with kindred feeling, cannot avoid the glamour of his masterly influence.

Had I been wealthy, long ere this I'd have properly investigated the whole subject and have published the result, but alas! the *res augusta domi* of late years have cramped & enfeebled my exertions. Still, if Mr. T. Clarke, or Mr. Gill, have any real information & will part with it for any sum within reason, I will do my best to meet them with what is needed.

Do you know who was author of that vile paper in the *S.L. Messenger?* Griswold calls it "an Eulogium." I *believe*, strictly *sub rosa—entre nous*, that it was J. M. Daniel, Editor of the Richmond *Examiner*; the same, I suppose, you speak of at page 43 of *E.P. & His Critics*.[1] The author of that cruel paper in the *North American Review* was, I believe, a certain "Rev. A. Lamson." Do you know him?

And now I have bored you enough for the nonce, and will desist, relying upon your kind aid towards placing the name & fame of our admired poet in that position which it deserves to be in, and hoping that you will not misunderstand my motives & that you will trust me to return any papers, cuttings, MSS., &c. when required, I remain, believe me, ever faithfully yours,

John H. Ingram

P.S. Do you know if E. C. Pinckney's poems are to be got? Are there any friends of Edgar Poe, besides yourself, to whom I might apply? May I keep "The Portrait"? 2 slips returned: more to follow. Is there anything I can procure you?

1. John Moncure Daniel (1825–1865), journalist and editor of the Richmond *Examiner*, 1847–53, 1861–65, published an article on Poe, which *he* called a "Eulogium," in the *Southern Literary Messenger*, 16 (Mar. 1850), 172–87. For a synopsis and analysis of this covert attack on Poe, see Quinn, p. 666.

5. *John H. Ingram to Sarah Helen Whitman*

Dear Mrs. Whitman,   3 Feb. 1874
   I am going to trouble you with another letter. I have seen Mr. Stoddard's paper in the *Harper's Monthly*: I saw it at the British Museum Library, but I cannot purchase, or even order a copy here, because it contains copyright English works & must not be imported by publishers: if you can procure me a copy I shall be glad. The paper furnishes fresh information about Poe's family &c., but it is very incorrect in some particulars, *as I can prove.* You allude to Longfellow's remarks on Poe in the *S.L. Messenger*, but I cannot find them.[1] The British Museum copy only comes down to the middle of 1851. I have seen Mr. Pabodie's letter to the *Tribune*, of June 1852, but could not find the further correspondence you allude to. I have a *proof* copy of my paper on "Edgar Poe" for *Temple Bar* Maga., and if you can dispose of it for me, & will do so, to some respectable monthly, I will gladly forward it: you can get it in advance of its publication—and the money received for it—we do not get less, ever, than 16 guineas the sheet—you could credit me with & expend it in obtaining me books & papers relative to Poe: that is, if you do not mind the trouble. *I'll forward proof in a few days* but rely upon your honour not to let it become public, or known, save in the manner I have suggested, until the middle of March. Can you find out Mr. Clarke's address? I am presuming always that you will not object to aid my endeavours towards clearing the fame of our hero. Perhaps Mr. Clarke would not mind letting you know what he would take for his collection of Poe papers & would give you some idea as to what they consisted of— whether letters, MSS., facts, or unreprinted writings. *Copies* of any unprinted letters of Poe's I should value: perhaps you have some you would not mind furnishing me with: I would always acknowledge my authority. I enclose you copy of "To Isadore": do you know it? The poem "To Helen" which you include in *E.P. & His Critics* is a great favourite in England. What became of all the letters & papers of Poe's Redfield, the publisher, or Griswold, obtained, do you know? *I'll write to Mr. Gill. E.P. & His Critics* has become one of my best friends: I read, & reread it continually. I have nearly all the books mentioned in

the "Usher" library. Do you know Gresset's "Ver Vert"?² 'Tis very good.
I fancy Poe believed firmly in the sentience of *all things,* including
that of the globe itself. His *Eureka* has not been published in England:
I hope to edit it: it influenced me when I read it (as a boy) immensely,
but my views have so grown of late years that I fancy a reperusal
would not have the same effect. Can you get me the *Graham
Magazines,* or copies of Poe's papers therein, on *Autography,
Cryptology,* &c. Strictly *entre nous,* I want to edit all his works not
reprinted in England and prefix *the* life: the collection, need I remark,
shall be inscribed to you—it is necessary *to be before* Mr. Stoddard &
Messrs. Routledge, to be sure of success. Can you *lend* me an
autograph of Poe's to get a *facsimile* made? A daguerreotype, or photo.
copy of a portrait cannot be procured I suppose. Time you see is an
object. If Routledges' bring out a collection with Mr. Stoddard's
information, I fear that I shall not succeed in getting another publisher
to take my edition out unless I have something *very different* to say &
give. My real wish is to clear Poe's fame but to succeed I must, as you
well know, come before the world with something fresh, clear, and
attractive. Tomorrow, I will forward you another *Mirror* with some
information that you may not know of. My mother knows the Irish
Powers by name: her father assisted one of them out of a convent in
Portugal, during the Peninsula War. I shall be glad to see your poems:
"The Sleeping Beauty" & "Cinderella" I have heard of.³ I shall send
"The Portrait" to the *Mirror.* Hoping to hear from you soon, I remain,
believe me, yours in sympathy.

John H. Ingram

[*Written above the salutation on page 1:*] I'll return the cuttings in my
next.

J.H.I.

1. Mrs. Whitman had written in her book *Edgar Poe and His Critics,* p. 25, "Mr. Long-fellow has very generously said, in a letter to the editor of the Literary Messenger: 'The harshness of his criticisms I have always attributed to the irritation of a sensitive nature chafed by some indefinite sense of wrong.'" The letter referred to had been addressed to John Reuben Thompson, ca. Oct. 1849, and the remarks were printed by Thompson in the *Messenger* in Nov. 1849.
2. Poe had placed Jean Baptiste Louis Gresset's poem "Ver-Vert," written in 1734, in Roderick Usher's library in "The Fall of the House of Usher," *Burton's Gentleman's Magazine,* Sept. 1839.
3. These poems by Mrs. Whitman and her sister, Susan Anna Power, were first printed in the *Union Magazine,* Oct. 1848.

6.   *John H. Ingram to Sarah Helen Whitman*

Dear Mrs. Whitman,   11 Feb. 1874
    I am again troubling you with a letter, but, as you will see, more
with the object of making you the medium of other letters to other
people: I hope I shall not tire you out, but now that I've got a real clue
to the long hidden mystery of Poe's life, I am anxious to unravel the
whole story. The various letters enclosed are open to your inspection &
if you will kindly try and forward them to their proper destinations,
you will indeed, be conferring a favour on me. If you do not know the
address of Mr. Thos. C. Clarke, probably Messrs. J. B. Lippincott & Co.
of Philadelphia, do. Do you object to anything I have said in my letter
to Mr. Clarke? Do you mind becoming the medium of a transaction
between us? I could trust to you to receive my money & not to pay it
for valueless matter: but I know nothing of Mr. Clarke—whether he is
author, publisher, or what. Do you know anything of the
"Autobiography" alluded to? In *Edgar Poe & His Critics* you speak of a
paper by J. Wood Davidson, in *Russell's Magazine,* but I cannot *see* or
get that publication in London: is a copy of the paper obtainable by
you?[1] The paper in the *North A. Review* was by a "Mrs. Vale Smith," I
believe, not by Mr. Lamson.[2] I find the "Fire Fiend" affair was
thoroughly shewn up in *Notes & Queries,* but I did not see the account
until Saturday last. You may emphatically deny that Macready had
anything to do with it. See *N&Q* for 1864–5. Wallace's *Literary
Criticisms* have you seen? I have not, but if they are by D. Ross
Wallace, I dare say they are favourable to Poe.[3] The *Edinburgh Review*
paper *I'll cut up* at the first opportunity: it is shameful, but of course
thoroughly influenced by the "Memoir." I hope to have the paper out
this evening in the *Mirror* & will forward at once. Let all your literary
friends see it. I will gladly send more copies. Are there any papers in
America you would like to receive copies?
    I enclose letters for Dr. Lowell & Bayard Taylor. Can you get them
forwarded? I don't know their addresses. The former, *I fancy,* resides
in Boston, & the latter in New York—but I'm not certain—
    There! I hope you are not sick of me. Forgive my troubling you so
much & believe me to be

                                                        Faithfully yours,
                                                        John H. Ingram

P.S. I have paper *re.* "Edgar Poe" coming out in both *Temple Bar* &
Belgravia but I have not sent advance sheets of former because I'm not
quite sure Ed. would approve.
    Do you know whether Poe had any English correspondents? I fancy
that he got no further than England on his Greek expedition. Can you

throw *any* light on the subject? The Russian affair, I fancy, was a complete mirage—what do you think?

Wm. Gilmore Simms, who, I believe, is dead, was a very old friend of Poe's: Perhaps his family have letters which they would allow to be copied: do you know their residence? I fear not, as it is, most likely, in the South.

Who wrote "Edge Hill"?[4] I do not know the work. Griswold alludes to it.

I shall not send B. Taylor's letter this post.

[Enclosure: John H. Ingram to Thomas Cottrell Clarke]

Dear Sir,   11 Feby. 1874

You may have heard of me from Mrs. S. H. Whitman, as the author of some magazine papers on Edgar Poe, and as the collector of material towards a new biography of the poet. For fifteen years past I have been gathering information towards a new life of Poe but I have not been so industrious as I should otherwise have been in the matter, because of seeing, from time to time, announcements of your intention to produce a biography of America's great poet. From what I have lately heard, however, I presume you have relinquished your intention and are willing to dispose of your collection of papers relating to Poe to some one able & willing to do justice to his memory. As regards this latter necessity I think Mrs. Whitman, Providence, Rhode Island will satisfy you, whilst, if you are willing to see [*sic*] your collection, I will buy it if you can be contented with a reasonable price. I am not rich & cannot be sure of regaining what I expend in the matter but will do my best—even if only as a labour of love—to give the world a fair and correct life of Edgar Poe. If you will sell & have something worth buying perhaps you will, at your earliest convenience, kindly forward me your terms & state what it is you have to dispose of—Whether letters, or *copies of letters, unpublished MSS.*, unreprinted papers, corrected dates, reminiscences & so forth—I dare say Mrs. Whitman will not object to be the medium of the transaction. If I send her the money, you can let her see the collection & receive the needful per her. If, however, you have disposed of your papers, or still purpose publishing a life kindly inform me, so that I may have the gratification of obtaining the work. Have you published anything about Poe? If so, perhaps you can kindly forward me a copy & I will send you copies of my magazine papers in exchange. I am sending this through Mrs. Whitman not knowing your address. Did you see Mr. Stoddard's paper in *Harper's Monthly*? It is not very satisfactory, repeating, as it does, much of Griswold's fabulous "Memoir," and evidently annoyed about a boyish ode to a Flute having been rejected by Poe![5] Did any number of his projected *Stylus* appear? I suppose not. Are the old numbers of *Graham's Magazine*, 1840–2—

or of *Burton's Gentleman's Mag.* 1838–9—procurable? I would give a
fair price for them, as for anything connected with Poe. Do you know
what *noms de plume* he assumed? "Lyttleton Barry" was what he
wrote under, sometimes in the *Broadway Journal.* Poe published his
"Autobiography," I fancy: is it obtainable? Was it in Brooks's *Museum?*[6]
In 1833–4 Poe must have written a good deal—doubtless in the
Baltimore papers—is any portion of it to be had? Anything of his—or
copies of it—not contained in Griswold's 4-vol. collection would be
very acceptable—poems especially—have you, or can you obtain any
one of the earlier collections? *Prior to 1845.* Kindly write & tell me
your intentions. I do not want to lose further time but to get out, as
quickly as possible, a faithful work on the life & correspondence of
Edgar Poe. By the way, did he ever go to Russia? My information
would lead me to think not, but you may know. I will not trouble you
with any more questions now, but hoping soon to hear from you,
remain, believe me,

Yours truly,
John H. Ingram

1. James Wood Davidson (1829–1905), a New York author and editor, formerly of
South Carolina, had printed a defense of Poe, "Edgar Allan Poe," in *Russell's Magazine*,
2 (Nov. 1857), 161–73. Item 525 in the Ingram Poe Collection. He later published *Living
Writers of the South* (New York: Carleton & Co., 1869).
2. There is an article, "Edgar Allan Poe," by Mrs. E. V. Smith in the *North American
Review*, 84 (Oct. 1856), 427–55.
3. This reference is almost certainly to Horace Binney Wallace (1817–1852), whose
Literary Criticism and Other Papers was posthumously published (Philadelphia: Parry
and McMillan, 1856).
4. *Edge-Hill, or The Family of the Fitzroyals. By a Virginian* (Richmond: T. W. White,
1828). This novel was written by James Ewell Heath (1792–1862), sometime editorial
adviser to T. W. White (1788–1843), printer, publisher, and founder of the *Southern Literary Messenger* in 1834.
5. Poe's refusal of Stoddard's poem was printed in the *Broadway Journal*, Aug. 2,
1845, without mentioning the author's name: "We doubt the originality of the 'Grecian
Flute,' for the reason that it is *too good* at some points to be so bad at others. Unless the
author can re-assure us, we decline it." Ingram's expressed contempt for Stoddard took
many forms, among them calling the poem "The Grecian Fiddlestick."
6. Poe contributed "Ligeia" to the first number of N. C. Brooks's *American Museum*,
Sept. 1838. Poe did not write an autobiography, as we know. It is generally accepted as
fact that he did contribute to Henry B. Hirst's biographical sketch of himself that appeared, with a portrait, in the Philadelphia *Saturday Museum*, Feb. 25, 1843.

7. *Sarah Helen Whitman to John H. Ingram.* Item 119

My dear Mr. Ingram, Feb. 11, 1874
Yesterday morning came your welcome letter [Jan. 26] & today the

papers & poems. I glanced first at the poems & read with unwonted
pleasure & surprise their fresh & fervid utterance of genuine poetic
feeling. *Why* I should have felt *surprise*, I can hardly tell you. Perhaps
I had unconsciously inferred from the directness of your letters & their
indication of methodical habits of thought that it was the analytical &
purely intellectual elements of Poe's genius that had most attracted
you.

Through these early poems of yours I have come to know you better.
They appeal almost exclusively to the *imagination*—a faculty of all
others least appreciated by the *professional* critics of poetry. I thank
you for sending them; but why not send more? Why not the whole of
the lines on the 7th page?

> Call up him who left half told
> The story of Cambuscan bold.

The Old English Baron first introduced me to the realms of romance. I
was eight years old at the time, yet I have never forgotten it.

I must tell you how well I like the matter & *manner* of your "New
Facts" in the *Mirror*.[1] More about that presently. But, *now*, to your
questions. I have told what I know of the "Conchology" story on
another page. I wonder if it will agree with the "clue" you spoke of.

The story about the borrowing of money from "a distinguished
woman of South Carolina" with all the atrocious incidents connected
with it, is so *incredible*, as it stands, that I *could* not believe it—not if
"forty thousand brothers" should swear to it on the faith of their
fraternal fealty & the word of their knightly honor! But I have not yet
heard that *any*-body has sworn to it. I believe it stands on the word of
Dr. Griswold alone & with his character for veracity we need not waste
much time in seeking for the slender & tangled thread of truth to lead
us out of this dark labyrinth of fiction.[2]

*Some*thing there *was* which caused much scandal & gossip at the
time & which doubtless served as the foundation or rather as the
nebulous nucleus out of which this story was evolved. Certain
benevolent ladies, friends of the invalid wife, were in the habit of
visiting her in her last illness & of ministering to the comfort of the
family. An open note, or letter, from Mrs. Osgood chanced to be seen
by one of the ladies & was thought to call for their interference.[3] A
committee was appointed to call on the poetess & to remonstrate with
her against the imprudence of such a correspondence. Mrs. Osgood, in
consequence of their representations, consented that they should act
in her behalf and demand the return of her letters. Margaret Fuller—
the late Countess d'Ossoli, was, I believe, one of the ladies who acted
on the occasion, & Miss Anne C. Lynch, now Mrs. Botta, was another.[4]

It was from the latter that I received in the summer of [18]48 the version which I have given you. But "the distinguished woman from South Carolina" was the acknowledged *instigator* & Grand Inquisitor of the movement.[5]

The ladies repaired to Fordham, presented their credentials & made their demand. The poor Raven, driven to desperation, ruffled his black plumage—called the fair embassadrisses "Busy-bodies!" & added injury to insult by saying that Mrs. ——— had better come & "look after her *own* letters." Now this was very indiscreet in him & *very* reprehensible, and no one knew this better than himself. But you shall hear what he himself says about it in a letter dated Nov. 24, 1848:

Stung to madness by the grossness of the injury which her jealousy prompted her to inflict upon *all of us*—upon both families—I permitted myself to say what I should not have said. I had no sooner uttered the words than I *felt* their dishonor, I felt, too, that although *she* must be conscious of her own baseness, she would still have a right to reproach me for having betrayed under *any* circumstances, her confidence. Full of these thoughts, & terrified lest I should again, in a moment of madness be similarly tempted, I went immediately to my secretary (when those two ladies left me) made a package of her letters, addressed them to her, and, with my own hands, left them at her door. Now, Helen, you *can*not be prepared for the diabolical malignity which followed. Instead of feeling that I had done all I could to repair an unpremeditated wrong—instead of feeling that almost any other person would have retained the letters to make good (if occasion required) the assertion that I possessed them—instead of this, she urged her brothers & brother-in-law to *demand of me the letters*. The position in which she thus placed me you may imagine. Is it any wonder that I was driven *mad* by the intolerable sense of wrong? If you value your happiness, Helen, beware of this woman! She did not cease her persecutions here. My poor Virginia was continually tortured (although not deceived) by her anonymous letters & on her deathbed declared that Mrs. ——— had been her murderer.

The extract quoted above is from the same letter, a portion of which is introduced on the 74th page of *Edgar Poe & His Critics*.

You will perceive that neither this letter nor the account which I have given you can be publicly used in refutation of Dr. Griswold's story. I rely on your discretion, therefore, for holding it as *strictly confidential*. If you can meet the charge by saying that, so far as you can learn, the story rests solely on the authority of Griswold, it might be well, perhaps, to do so. If you could say after your own manner something like what I have said in the paragraphs marked with a blue pencil mark, for instance.

It is *possible* that the "distinguished lady" *may* have advanced money to *Mrs. Clemm* & *may*, after Poe's aggressive allusion to "*her own letters*," have called on him for an acknowledgment of the obligation. But I have never heard of anything of the kind except in Griswold's "Memoir."

Speaking of "Isadore," you say you think it was written by Poe. In the two bound vols. of the *Broadway Journal*, now in my possession, every anonymous article or paragraph written by him has the pencilled letter P. appended to it. He added these letters in giving me the volume[s]. Turning to the poem, I find no initial affixed to it, & *therefore* think it not *his*, though it has much of his style & many of his favorite phrases. Have you any other reason for thinking so than the resemblance of style? Do not return any of the printed slips I send you unless I specially request you to do so. The article on "Dry Facts & Traditionary History" you may *preserve* for me, as I may want it, but not for several months.

I wish to send you a corrected copy of "The Portrait." I never liked the opening line, "Slowly I raised the purple folds" etc. *After long years* is simpler & more suggestive, don't you think so?[6]

I am trying to obtain a photograph for you from a daguerre of Poe taken in this city. It was taken after a wild distracted night (of which I will tell you the story hereafter)—when

> He had wandered home but newly
> From an ultimate dim Thule—
>   A wild, weird clime,
>   Out of space, out of time.

And all the stormy grandeur of that via Dolorosa had left its sullen shadow on his brow. But it was *very* fine. Another, taken a few days after, is sweet & serene in expression, but so *faded* that I fear nothing can be done with it. I wish you would send me a reflection of yourself. Won't you?

You will see from Stoddard's article in *Harper's* (a copy of which I shall mail with my letter this evening) that Poe's age is given in a note differently from either of the dates in Griswold. Mrs. Clemm wrote me that Poe never knew anything about dates, but always had to appeal to *her*. I doubt if her own memory was more reliable. He has however assured me (vaguely) that he was older than I imagined. I think that he had, moreover, a morbid love of mystification, as had Byron, & that he sometimes purposely evaded the collectors of statistical information.

You ask for an autograph—something of his writing from which to obtain a printed facsimile. The difficulty will be to find even a paragraph that is not *personal*. Still I will *try*. I will make inquiries for the reviews & magazines which you require but can only send you *Harper's* today. You ask about earlier versions or editions of the poems too. Perhaps I may find some among my papers. If I can do so I will enclose them with the printed matter.

There is one piece of important evidence in relation to the private life of Poe, which I have been trying to obtain for you. I sent the only (printed) copy of it to Mr. Wm. F. Gill, the publisher of whom I told you. He seemed to consider it very important and I gave thinking that he would use it in the lecture he was preparing. I hear nothing further of the proposed lecture, & last week I wrote to him to ask him to *lend* me the copy I gave him. But as yet he has not sent it. I believe he is very busy just now republishing one of Wilkie Collins's lectures. While I think of it I will give you the address of *Shepard & Gill, Publishers, 151 Washington St., Boston.* The article I allude to was in the New York *Evening Mail,* Dec. 10, 1870. It contained an article occupying more than two columns & consisting of Mr. Gowans' (Wm. Gowans') recollections of authors with whom he had been personally acquainted.[7] It was sent me from New York by Mr. T. C. Latto, a Scotch gentleman who has always felt a deep interest in Poe.[8] I enclose to you some leaves from letters on Mr. Gowans' testimony, which contain the substance of what I cut from the paper & gave to Mr. Gill. I have marked with a red pencil the parts to which I would call your attention. *You need not return the letters.*

If I am to mail my letter tonight I must close & leave many things unsaid. But I will write again in a few days if possible. And I will send you some of the *poems* of which you were kind enough to say that you would write a notice. I should certainly be glad to have you speak of them, or of the little book I sent you which of course I intended for *you.* I will send you some of the notices of the poems if I can find them. But of this hereafter. I shall have something to say of Stoddard, too, & his article in *Harper's Monthly.*

With cordial & sincere regard
Sarah Helen Whitman

I have written on the margin of "The Portrait" something which you can cut off & paste on a fly leaf of *the book* if you like. I am sorry I did not write it in the book myself.

P.S. About the work on "Conchology" I will tell you what I know, & what I *infer* from the few facts in my possession. Whether they concur with the "clue" of which you speak I shall be glad to learn from you. Some time after the publication of R.W.G.'s "Memoir," an Englishman by the name of Wyatt called on me in Providence.[9]

I think he had seen the article by W. J. Pabodie in the *Tribune* & had called on me as a friend of Edgar Poe to express to me his indignation at the injustice done to his memory in the "Memoir." It was this gentleman who told me what I have referred to on the 75th page of my book. He assured me that having for years known Poe intimately & having often been near him in his states of utter mental delirium &

desolation he had never heard from him a coarse or brutal word, never an expression that would have done discredit to his heart or brought reproach on his honor. He apparently felt for him, as did Mr. T. C. Clarke, a most affectionate & friendly sympathy & regard. Some years after this interview I saw in the *Home Journal* a communication in reference to the charge about the work on "Conchology." It stated that "Prof. Wyatt" who had published a series of articles on natural history in *Graham's Mag.* was also the *compiler* of several works on Natural History selected from English authors; that one of these works was a work on "Conchology" in which he had been assisted by Poe & to which he had asked him to lend the prestige of his name, offering for the use of it a share in the profits. I preserved a copy of the article in the *Home Journal* for a long time but I cannot find it among my papers, nor can I remember the exact *year* of its appearance. I think it was in 58 or 9.

The transaction was not one altogether unknown to the *literati* of those days, I imagine, & perhaps not *entirely* so to those of our own.

P.S. No. 2. Mr. James Wood Davidson, the author of *Living Writers of the South*, a gentleman of fine culture & scholarship, in a review of the *Poetical Works of Poe*, published by Redfield in 1859, with an "Original Memoir," touches some points of interest, which I will copy for you from the *Courant*, a literary weekly published at Columbia, South Carolina, in 1859:

The anonymous memoirist takes occasion to indorse in a general way Dr. Griswold's "Memoir." He has gone a step farther, he has repeated some of his misstatements & among them the story of Poe's engagement to "an accomplished literary lady of Rhode Island" & the dissolution of the engagement: we quote the statement before us: "The day was appointed for their marriage; & to disentangle himself from this engagement, he visited the house of his affianced bride where he conducted himself with such indecent violence that the aid of the police had to be called in to expel him." Griswold's "Memoir" appeared in 1850. In April, 1852, the statement was repeated in *Tait's Magazine* (British) and in reference to this, in a letter to the New York *Tribune* in June of the same year, William J. Pabodie, Esq. of Providence, says: "Mr. Poe was frequently my guest during his stay in Providence: In his several visits to the city I was with him daily. I was acquainted with the circumstances of his engagement & with the causes which led to its dissolution. I am authorized to say, not only from my personal knowledge, but also from the statements of all who were conversant with the affair that there exists not a shadow of foundation for the stories above alluded to." Mr. Pabodie is a native & citizen of Providence, a lawyer & a man of letters, occupying a position in society that entitles him to an audience under any circumstances. The anonymous memorialist before us with a carelessness that might be called unscrupulous, has ignored Mr. Pabodie's testimony &

gravely repeats what the friends of Poe might be excused for considering a malignant falsehood. Yet we infer from the general tone of the memoir that the writer though careless was not guilty of intentional wrong. . . . The anonymous memoirist farther intimates that all personal difficulties & business misunderstandings in which Poe was a party, necessarily originated with him. Poe had business engagements with Graham, Godey, & Burton, of Philadelphia. At first the broad announcement was made that Poe had quarrelled with all &, therefore, the fault must be with him. Let us see. As to Graham, we commend to the ghost of Griswold a perusal of Graham's notorious *Letter*. As to Godey, that gentleman himself wrote to the *Knickerbocker* of Jan. 1857, that the story is untrue, & that Poe's conduct to him "was in all respects honorable & unblameworthy." Two out of three against the charge & in acquittal of Poe.

J.W.D.

Mr. G. W. Eveleth, the gentleman who, according to Griswold, was mentioned by Poe in the last letter quoted from him as "a Yankee impertinent" etc., etc., has apparently placed so little confidence in the authenticity of this letter, so maliciously published, that he has continued to the present day one of Poe's warmest & most efficient defenders.[10] Mr. Eveleth is a man of much curious learning—a mathematician & a man of science. He is not a *Yankee* but a Marylander, though living for many years in New England. This fact *Poe of course knew*, though Griswold may have supposed him to be "a Yankee." Poe would have been very unlikely to have called him "a Yankee" & the whole letter, with its postscript, looks very much like a fabrication.

As an instance of Griswold's unreliability, Mr. Eveleth wrote to me in a letter dated April 5, 1854, that Mr. J. P. Kennedy & Mr. J. H. B. Latrobe, Esqrs., of Baltimore, assured him, in answer to his inquiries on the subject, that "the prize spoken of in Griswold's memoir of Poe was not awarded by them (as Committee) *under anything like the circumstances* recorded by Griswold."[11]

1. This was "New Facts about Edgar Allan Poe."

2. Griswold had written the following in his "Memoir," pp. xxiii–xxiv: "On one occasion Poe borrowed fifty dollars from a distinguished literary woman of South Carolina, promising to return it in a few days, and when he failed to do so, and was asked for a written acknowledgment of the debt that might be exhibited to the husband of the friend who had thus served him, he denied all knowledge of it, and threatened to exhibit a correspondence which he said would make the woman infamous, if she said any more on the subject. Of course there had never been any such correspondence, but when Poe heard that a brother of the slandered party was in quest of him for the purpose of taking the satisfaction supposed to be due in such cases, he sent for Dr. Francis and induced him to carry to the gentleman his retraction and apology, with a statement which seemed true enough at the moment, that Poe was 'out of his head.' It is an ungracious duty to

describe such conduct in a person of Poe's unquestionable genius and capacities of greatness, but those who are familiar with the career of this extraordinary creature can recall but too many similar anecdotes; and as to his intemperance, they perfectly well understand that its pathology was like that of nine-nine of every hundred cases of the disease."

3. Frances Sargent Locke Osgood (1811–1850) was an attractive and prominent member of the New York literati and the wife of Samuel Stillman Osgood (1808–1885), the artist who painted the portraits of Poe, Frances Osgood, and Griswold that now hang in the New-York Historical Society's rooms. Poe admired and extravagantly praised Mrs. Osgood and her writings, and she returned his compliments. Griswold wrote her obituary in which he quoted from her last poem, "Israfel," but he changed her masculine pronouns to feminine.

4. Sarah Margaret Fuller d'Ossoli (1810–1850) was a journalist and a social reformer, associated with the New England intellectuals. She married Marquis Angelo d'Ossoli in Rome in 1847. Poe did not like her.

5. Mrs. Anne Charlotte Lynch Botta (1815–1891), another member of the New York literati, lived in Waverly Place in New York City and was hostess of the first American literary salon. Poe knew her as Miss Anne Lynch; she married Professor Vincenzo Botta in 1855.

6. Mrs. Whitman's poems "The Portrait" and "Resurgemus" were written after her engagement to Poe was broken; both are concerned with their former relationship. They were published in her volumes *Hours of Life and Other Poems* (Providence: Geo. H. Whitney, 1853) and *Poems* (Boston: Houghton, Osgood & Co., 1879).

7. This "distinguished literary woman of South Carolina" was Mrs. Elizabeth Frieze Lummis Ellet (1818–1877), a sentimental poet and translator who had left Columbia, S.C., in 1849 to live in New York City, where she, too, became a member of the New York literati. She was at one time an ardent admirer of Poe but later became one of his bitterest and most relentless enemies.

8. William Gowans (1803–1870) was a Scotch bibliophile who boarded with the Poe family in New York City in 1837. Many years later, in his *Catalogue of American Books*, No. 28, 1870, Gowans wrote a strong defense of Poe.

9. Thomas C. Latto of New York wrote Mrs. Whitman of his conversations with William Gowans, who described to him Poe's uniformly quiet, gentlemanly behavior, with not the slightest trace of intoxication or dissipation.

10. Professor Thomas Wyatt was the author of *A Manual of Conchology* (New York: Harpers, 1838).

11. George W. Eveleth of Phillips and Lewiston, Maine, corresponded with Poe between 1846 and 1849. Poe was apparently amused and pleased enough with Eveleth's brashness to respond at length to his pointed questions, fortunately for us. Eveleth copied all of this correspondence and that he had with other persons about Poe and sent all of it to Ingram in 1878. It is reproduced in my book *Building Poe Biography* (Baton Rouge: Louisiana State Univ. Press, 1977), pp. 195–234. After Poe's death Eveleth wrote articles for the Portland *Transcript*, June 8 and July 6, 1850, defending Poe against charges of intoxication and he again came to Poe's defense in an article, "Poe and His Biographer Griswold," the *Old Guard*, June 1866.

12. John Pendleton Kennedy (1795–1870), biographer, novelist, and eminent Baltimore lawyer, helped Poe get his job with the *Southern Literary Messenger* in 1835 and proved in many other ways to be a true benefactor and friend. John Hazlehurst Boneval Latrobe (1803–1891) was a lawyer, inventor, and one of the judges, as was J. P. Kennedy, who awarded to Poe in 1833 the prize of $50 offered by the *Baltimore Saturday Visiter* for the best tale submitted.

8. *Sarah Helen Whitman to John H. Ingram.   Item 121*

My dear Mr. Ingram,   Feb. 16, 1874
    I have just received yours of Jan. 28. I will consider all your
questions on another page. On the 13th I mailed to you a letter & copy
of *Harper's*, Sept. No. 1872. In that letter I told you what I suppose to
have been the origin of the story about "a distinguished woman of S.
Carolina." The lady was Mrs. Ellet, whose name you will find in Poe's
"Literati." I do not know why Dr. Griswold called her a lady of
Carolina, unless he wished to divert inquiry from the actual facts of the
case.[1] Perhaps she was not altogether so evil & perfidious as Poe
seemed to think in the extract from his letter which I sent you. There
may have been extenuating circumstances on her part. I will at some
time copy for you the whole of this letter & you will understand why
he spoke with so much intensity, fearing that she would seek to
interrupt the relations then subsisting between us.
    I believe I told you that Mr. Stoddard on receiving my first letter
expressed regret at having *unintentionally* appeared to question any
statement made by me in *Edgar Poe and His Critics* and said that he
should be glad to see any of Mr. Poe's letters that I might be willing to
send him & would send me the correspondence in relation to him
[Poe] which had been drawn out by his "imperfect sketch." The tenor
of his article seemed lenient & not unfriendly; though on a *subsequent*
reading I could not but feel that its tone was one of depreciation rather
than of admiration or genuine sympathy. Believing in his general
friendliness & candor of feeling toward Poe, I sent him two or three of
his letters "written (as he himself says & as I implicitly believe) at the
most earnest epoch" of his life.
    When Mr. Stoddard returned the letters his only remark concerning
them was "the letters are curious, very curious indeed. The fact is that
the more I read about Poe the less I understand him. I am too
commonplace a person to understand unusual developments of
genius."
    Certainly Stoddard ought to know best about this. I am half inclined
to think he was right. Many persons seem to think, that with the other
writers who immediately succeeded Poe, he was jealous of his high &
increasing reputation. At any rate, he has never sent me the promised
correspondence.
    The woodcut of the cottage at Fordham is typical of the spirit of the
article. I have been there but should not have recognized it, although
its *outlines* are not unlike. It looks very much as if the artist had tried
to make it look as petite as possible. I begin to distrust the spirit of the

whole article. I do not see that the account given by S[toddard] as to the last days of Poe has anything more than a very improbable rumor for its basis.

I believe I have not told you that Mr. Carleton told me, in announcing his acceptance of my MS., that it had been read by Mr. Stoddard & very highly praised by him. Mr. Aldrich also read it, as I have been told, & was supposed to have written a lengthy notice of it, but no notice was ever published by either of these gentlemen.[2] *This sub rosa.*

The letter which I sent to S[toddard] in evidence of my authority to say what I *did* about the lines to Helen (Mrs. H[elen] S[tanard]) was one in which Poe had explained to me the motives which had induced him to seek my acquaintance & the feelings which prompted him to write the lines to Helen *first* quoted by Griswold in the article signed Ludwig, (but omitted until the next issue of the *Tribune* for want of room) &, *afterwards* in his "Memoir."[3] In relation to the scandalous & injurious story which Griswold has associated with his quotation of the poem in the "Memoir," I will write you a few words of denial which you may use in any way you like. I will write it on a separate page & send by the next mail. And now, to revert to your questions. I cannot answer any of your inquiries till we come to the 9th. When was he married? Turning to a letter from Mrs. Clemm written from Alexandria [Virginia], April 14, 1859, I find that in answer to my inquiries, she says, "Edgar and Virginia were married at Richmond in 1836. Judge Stanard & his son Robert were among the first who called on us."[4] But you must remember that Mrs. Clemm was not considered infallible in the matters of dates.

About the *Broadway Journal.* I have the two bound vols. of that *Journal*, as I told you in my last letter. I do not think there can be much of importance to you that is not already republished. I should be willing to lend them to you, but I think it would hardly repay you for the trouble.

Do I know that the articles in the "Literati" are not properly reprinted? I have had reason to *think* so, but I cannot now remember on what grounds; perhaps I shall recall them. I do not know anything about the libel suit, gained by Poe against English, save what Mr. Poe says in a letter which I will perhaps copy for you in a few days. The Lewis family? They saw much of him I imagine during the two or three last years of his life. In the winter & spring of 1858 Mrs. Clemm resided for a time with Mr. & Mrs. Lewis in Lafayette Place (I think) in New York. Mr. and Mrs. Lewis separated soon after, & Mrs. Clemm, having, I believe, taken part with Mr. Lewis against the lady, was made very uncomfortable & wrote me that her situation as a guest in the house was becoming very embarrassing. She left them soon after & Mrs. Lewis went abroad. Some eight or nine years ago the *Home Journal* announced her approaching marriage with (I think) a French nobleman. Since then I have not heard anything about the family. Soon after Mrs. Clemm left, while visiting friends in New York, I received a card from Mrs. Lewis to attend one of her receptions, but, mistaking the evening, found no one at home. I have never met her.

I do not think there is any reliable account of Poe's last moments.

Some of the questions which you have asked are answered (authoritatively or not, I cannot say) by Stoddard. I think I have heard that J. M. Daniel was suspected of being the author of "The Eulogium" in the *Messenger*.

I will inquire about Pinckney's poems. I enclose Mr. Davidson's reply to my inquiries about Graham, etc. If you write to him, I can assure you a prompt reply. He at one time thought of writing a life of Poe, but all the valuable papers which he had collected for that purpose were burnt with his library, etc., at the burning of Columbia, South Carolina, during the war. He is a most honorable & high-minded gentleman. He is now in New York. His address is James Wood Davidson, Box 567, New York City.

I had not finished writing the above when the penny post brought me your letter of Feb. 3rd, with the richly illustrated & exquisite volume. I have only had time to see how rare a treasure of *poetry* & painting & tradition it is.

I must defer any reply to your letter till the next mail.

I will only say in relation to a disposal of the advance sheets of your article that I am utterly & entirely ignorant of all transactions with publishers. I have no relations with any publishers & never made a contract in my life. I wonder if you would consent to my asking Mr. Davidson to act for you? I suppose whatever is to be done should be done at once & I am afraid there will not be time to hear from you on the subject. I would most gladly procure & send the works you need *myself,* but have been like all the *children* of *Providence,* so cramped in resources by the failure of the *Great Sprague Manufacturing Company* (which has crippled so many of our city banks), that it was with difficulty we could meet the heavy taxes of the year.

I have seen the account in the *Home Journal* about the engagement with the "Maiden named Alice." Of course it is "a fiction."

I am going to inclose to you in this letter a letter from E.A.P. from which you may if *you think best* have a facsimile taken of the lines I have inclosed in pencil.

Be *very careful of this letter* & return it as soon as possible. If you allude to it in your reply, do it on a separate piece of paper, for my

sister is so unwilling that I should part with any of these letters even
for a day that she would be sure to remonstrate.

Very gratefully & sincerely,

Your friend,
Sarah Helen Whitman

[Enclosure: James W. Davidson's letter, Apr. 23, 1858. Item 88 in the
Ingram Poe Collection.]

    1. Mrs. Ellet had lived in Columbia, S.C., where her husband, Dr. William H. Ellet,
held a professorship from 1835 to 1849.

    2. Thomas Bailey Aldrich (1836–1907) was, in his time, an important author and edi-
tor of the New York *Evening Mirror*, the New York *Home Journal*, and the *Atlantic
Monthly*.

    3. Jane Stith Stanard (d. Apr. 28, 1824) was the mother of Poe's schoolmate and close
friend Robert Stanard and was said by Poe to have been his inspiration when he wrote
the first "To Helen." Mrs. Whitman and Mrs. Clemm regularly spelled her name "Stan-
nard." Griswold's obituary of Poe, signed "Ludwig," was printed in the evening edition
of the New York *Tribune* on Oct. 9, 1849, the day after Poe was buried in Baltimore.

    4. This letter was first printed in full, along with other materials, in an article by
James A. Harrison and Charlotte F. Dailey in the *Century Magazine*, 55 (Jan. 1909), 439–
52.

9. *Sarah Helen Whitman to John H. Ingram.*   *Item 122*

My dear Mr. Ingram,   Feb. 19, 1874
    I mailed you on the 17th a letter & some printed papers to go by the
steamer that left New York on the 18th.

    I wrote hurriedly & while suffering from intense neuralgic pain in
my eyes. The printed matter consisted simply of a page copied from
Poe's article on autographs—*where* printed, I have forgotten, & of
some pages from *Russell's Mag.* sent me, years ago, by Mr. Davidson,
containing versions of some of the earlier poems. If I were in your
place, I should *omit* in copying the earlier version of "Lenore" all but
the three verses which I have indicated. Those erased by a blue pencil
mark have some weak lines in them & I think could hardly do justice
to him. It is my earnest wish that you print only these 3, in case you
wish to reproduce them. The other poem, "The Valley of Nis," I think
might be printed in full. Do not think, however, that I wish to *dictate*
to you in this matter, only *earnestly* to *suggest*. You asked me about my
quotation of a passage from "Marginalia," which you say you do not
find. A part of the passage quoted is from some comments in
"Marginalia" on *Undine* in the Redfield edition, & *a part* from one of
the stories. I have been looking for it in such of the stories as
"Eleonora," "Morella," "Berenice," "Ligeia," etc. As yet I have not
found it, but if I have time & my eyes are not *too tired*, I will look
again before I close my letter. I know it is there.

Sarah Helen Whitman in 1869, age sixty-six. From a painting by John G. Arnold. (Photograph courtesy Brown University Library.)

In quoting the passage from *Poe's letter* (the one I sent you), I added *another* from *another* letter, without separating them by separate quotation marks. It may interest you to know that on a flyleaf of one of the vols. of the *Broadway Journal* Poe marked in pencil, as among his favourite compositions, "Ligeia," "Valdemar," "Tell-Tale Heart," "Ragged Mountains," "Domain of Arnheim," "Morella."

I will send you these vols. if you *wish*, but then you would have to send them back, & I am afraid it would not compensate you for the trouble. If I die soon, *very soon*, as I often think I *may*, I will certainly order them sent to you. I have access to all the vols. of the *Southern Literary Messenger* & almost all the English & American reviews & periodicals. If you tell me of anything in any of these, I could perhaps have the articles or facts copied for you. The Providence Athenaeum & the University Library have very extensive collections. *Graham's*, I have not yet been able to obtain. Have I not seen your signature to an article on *poetry* or *fiction*, recently, in one of the English monthlies? I recollect an article which seemed to me original & striking & a name with which I was unacquainted, which as I vaguely recall it now seems like *yours*.

About disposing of the advance sheets of the article in *Temple Bar* & at the same time to keep your secret—it seems to me that it would be *very difficult*. The *Atlantic* loses no opportunity to disparage Poe's genius. I could apply to *Harper's*, through Geo. Wm. Curtis, but he is not the editor, though he writes what intellectual people regard as the best part of *Harper's*, "The Easy Chair."[1] *Old & New* is very uncertain as to the *time* of it appearance, & still more as to the *pay*.[2] There is not a person in Providence to whom I could look for aid. Though called the wealthiest city of its size in the Union, it has no magazine or other literary periodical. If you had named the *Tribune* as a medium, perhaps I might have disposed of the article *to them*. Mr. Whitelaw Reid wrote to me three years ago to request me to furnish an article for the *Tribune* on a given subject, saying that Mr. Greeley had told him that he "knew of nobody who could do it so well." John Hay, one of the editors, was a correspondent of mine & a warm admirer of Poe. But I do not know that it would suit your views to offer it to them. I did not write the article requested, having been absent from home & very much out of health at the time. Since then I have had no communication with them. I earnestly wish to aid you in this, but feel very incompetent to act in the matter.

You asked for my poems. I send the volume noticed in Duyckinck. I have marked for you in the index the poems which specially refer to Poe. I have marked, too, some of the others which I specially like, with a blue pencil. Those which relate to E.A.P., I have marked with a *red* pencil. All of these were written after his death, with the exception of

"A Night in August," "Arcturus written in October," & "Our Island of Dreams." The *four* verses of this poem marked with a *red* pencil were published before his death under the title of "Stanzas for Music." I will tell you the *history* of this poem by & by. It, undoubtedly, *suggested* the poem of "Annabel Lee," although I am *well assured* that the author of the so-called "Original Memoir" had no authority for saying that the poem was "addressed" to me. This "Memoir" was published by Redfield in 1858 as a preface to the large illustrated edition of *the poems*, afterwards brought out in a small volume of Blue & Gold.[3]

With the exception of these three poems & a few verses of "The Raven," written at the request of Miss Anne C. Lynch for a valentine party given to the *literati* of New York in the winter of 1848, the poems in relation to him were all written since his death.

"Resurgemus" was first published in a volume published as a Memorial to Mrs. Osgood in 1850 (I think).[4] The volume was reviewed by Mr. E. P. Whipple, who then furnished the literary notices for *Graham's*.[5] The poem then, I think, had no other title than a quotation from the angel Israfel. The critic speaks of it as you will see in an extract on the printed slip enclosed from the Providence *Journal*.

I will indicate with a red pencil the lines in "The Raven" which appeared in the anonymous valentine, which he refers to in a letter which you shall see hereafter. The volume of poems which I shall try to mail tonight shall be supplemented by another one in a *binding*, by another mail.

Mr. Geo. Ripley, who wrote the *Tribune* notice inclosed in the book, is a critic of high authority, as you perhaps know.[6] Do not think me egotistic, dear Mr. Ingram, in telling you these things. Among the poems published since the volume was published, I like above all others "Proserpina to Pluto," "The Venus of Milo," "A Pansy from the Grave of Keats," and "Our Last Walk." I will send you more of them another time. Remember that I am to send you a *better copy of the poems soon*. My friends think that I should prepare, before it is too late, a volume containing the later poems. I will copy for you what Poe said of the poems in a lecture delivered at Lowell in the summer of 1848, on the poetesses of America. It is very high praise, but it was left out from Griswold's copy of that lecture, & I imagine *not* without Poe's consent. He was angry with me at the time. I had not answered a letter which he wrote to me after our separation. I will tell you about it another time. I inclose a notice of *Edgar Poe & His Critics* from the Yorkville *Enquirer*, by Mr. Davidson. Keep it as long as you please (till I ask for it), but don't destroy it.

I think I shall be able to send you some photographs of Poe next time. The artist told me he would have them ready for me by the middle of next week.

I send copies of "Sleeping Beauty" & "Cinderella," revised for preservation & private circulation, preparatory to an illustrated copy at a convenient season. My sister has had proposals from a publisher who wished to purchase the copyright, but not being satisfied with the style of the illustrations contemplated by him, she declined.

I have so many things to say, but if I would take advantage of the mail, I must close at once.

With sincerest sympathy & regard,

                                                              Sarah Helen Whitman

I am not sure that I have sent "The Pansy from the Grave of Keats." If not, I will send it next time.

I want you to remark what Curtis says of the sonnets in the page from *Putnam's Magazine*, & have patience with all my "egoism." I want you to *know* me.

1. George William Curtis (1824–1892) was a member of the Brook Farm Community in 1842–43, chancellor of New York State University, as well as being at various times a member of the editorial staffs of the New York *Tribune* and *Harper's Weekly Magazine*.

2. *Old & New* began publication in 1870 under Edward Everett Hale's editorship, but it was never successful, and in 1875 it merged with *Scribner's Monthly*.

3. *The Poetical Works of Edgar A. Poe, with Original Memoir* (New York: J. S. Redfield, 1858). Illustrated by F. R. Pickersgill, John Tenniel, Birket Foster, Felix Darley, Jasper Cropsey, P. Dugan, Percival Skelton, and A. M. Madot. The *Blue and Gold* edition was brought out in 1859.

4. See p. 12, n. 9.

5. Edwin Percy Whipple (1819–1886) was an author and lecturer, as well as an important critic.

6. George Ripley (1802–1880) was a Harvard mathematics professor, Unitarian minister, editor, reformer, and critic. He founded the Brook Farm Community and its transcendental magazine, the *Dial*.

10. *Sarah Helen Whitman to John H. Ingram.   Item 123*

Dear Mr. Ingram,   Feb. 20, 1874

I mailed a letter & book of poems to you last evening, forgetting that it could not leave New York before Saturday. This will go by the same steamer. You will remember that *facts & dates* in Poe's life were very elusive. I believe I told you that Mrs. Clemm wrote me that he was married in [18]36. Mr. Stoddard, as you will perceive, says that he entered the University in 1825. This is a mistake; he entered it in [18]26. A history of the University published about a year ago in *Harper's Monthly*, I think, shows that the first term of the college commenced in [18]26, corroborating Mr. Wertenbaker's report, & proving that Poe could not have entered in [18]25.[1]

You asked if his name was Edgar *Allan*. It *was*, & Mr. Allan was his godfather.[2] The name was not called Poë here, but undoubtedly it is one of the derivatives from the French name of Pois or Poix, as is the name of Poer or Power. Poey is another. But if I touch upon this subject I shall never stop.

About the lines entitled originally "Stanzas for Music," but in the volume of poems "Our Island of Dreams." I will tell you their history, for it seems to imply a fatality—a prophetic instinct of the soul, apart from the conscious reason—something which overrules our voluntary actions & gives to them an unforeseen significance.

I had promised to furnish something for a new magazine to be called the *American Metropolitan* (of which only two numbers were issued).[3] Poe, who was engaged to write the literary notices for the periodical, wished me to send the "Lines to Arcturus" (written in October), & had himself carefully copied them for this purpose. After the rupture of our brief engagement, I withheld them, thinking their interior meaning might be apparent to many & give further notoriety to events whose publicity was already sufficiently painful. Urged by the publisher to fulfill my promise for the February number, if only by sending half a dozen lines, & too ill, at the time, to write, I sought among my neglected manuscripts for something available, when I found *three* verses of an *unfinished song*, written four or five years before for an Italian gentleman to accompany a wild, monotonous, dirge-like air which he had composed for the guitar. I had not seen them for years, but as I now read them, they sounded so strangely weird & mournful, so eloquent of all that I would have wished to express in reply to a letter which I had received from Edgar Poe soon after our final separation, a letter which I had not *dared* to answer, that I added the last verse & sent them without venturing to give myself time for reflection or hesitation. Of course they elicited a good deal of comment & conjecture, but *I never regretted sending* them. In his letter he [Poe] had urged me to write, if but one line, to assure him that *I* had not countenanced the cruel reports about the causes which led to our separation which had been so widely circulated. I had suffered so much through the opposition of my friends & family to the contemplated marriage that I dared not incur the repetition of the terrible scenes I had passed through by any *direct* communication with him.

I sent the stanzas to the publisher & they appeared in the February number, which I think was not issued until the middle of March, when the publisher failed & the magazine was discontinued.

In the interval, Mr. Poe had, I have reason to think, felt himself deeply wounded & aggrieved by my silence. It was during this interval that he prepared the review of Griswold & the poets, a portion of which was first published in the *Literary Messenger*. In that notice he introduces my name only as among the most *accomplished* of the ladies quoted by Griswold. In a lecture on the female poets of America which Mr. Poe delivered in Lowell in the summer of 1848, he made a different estimate. He brought me the MS. of the lecture and read me the portion extracted in Mr. Atkinson's notice. He said that he intended to *re*write the lecture when Griswold's book on the female poets was out, & should then have very much more to say on the subject. But when his notice of Griswold's book came out in the Review, as copied into the "Literati," I saw only the cold & incidental allusion to my poems, which you may perhaps have seen there. This notice was already in *print* before my poem was published.

After that, no word ever passed between us, nor had I any indication from any source of his feeling toward me, until I heard of his death.

Yet, I cannot doubt that he accepted my "Stanzas for Music" as a peace offering, nor can I doubt that in writing "Annabel Lee," the vague, sweet fantasy, so charming in its vagueness & obscurity, that he intended that *I* should read in it the veiled expression (visible to no eyes but mine) of his undying remembrance. Griswold, I think, has intimated that it had reference to his Rhode Island betrothal. Most assuredly, Poe never would have told him so. I think when you see in his letters the ingenuity & subtlety of his methods of conveying his thoughts without directly expressing them, you will understand my view of the subject & will not think it fanciful. Notice in his poem the repetition of the words *The wind came out of the cloud by night* & compare them with the words of my song—*The night wind blew cold on my desolate heart.*

But all this is for *you* & not for the *world*. Do you remember what the writer in the London *Morning Chronicle* for October 1, 1853, says about "Annabel Lee" in a review of James Hannay's *Life of Poe*?[4]

Can you tell me when the beautiful book you sent me was published? I find no date on the title page.[5]

You ask if I have any anecdotes of his school or college days. I had a letter from one of his schoolfellows (written in reply to inquiries), from a "Mr. John Willis of Orange County, Virginia." He was a classmate of Poe's, & though very slightly acquainted with him, expressed great admiration for his genius, & asserted that whatever he might since have become, he was at that time possessed of the most honorable sentiments, etc., etc. The letter was written not far from the date of the letters from the faculty of Virginia College [University of Virginia].

I gave the letter to Mr. Gill, which I now deeply regret, for I am afraid he is too careless to make any use of the information which he sought from me. I have heard nothing from him, though I have written twice for the printed report of Mr. Gowans' recollections of Poe, of which I spoke in a former letter. Perhaps he has been tampered with by some of Poe's enemies. I have been looking for a letter every day for the last three weeks. I shall get some friend to call on him at his place of business. I cannot now remember about Longfellow's words to the Editor of the *Literary Messenger*, but they *must* be there. I will look for them.

You say you found Mr. Pabodie's letter to the *Tribune*. The "further correspondence" was not *printed*. I will try to procure it for you; that is, I will try to send you copies of it. Mr. Gill has *seen* the letters, but has returned them. I will look them over & see what can be done.

You will find Mr. Clarke's address in Allibone's *Dictionary*. I am quite sure it is in Philadelphia.

The photographs I shall try to get according to the promise of the artist, by the middle of next week, & will mail them at once. I hope that Poe's letter which I inclosed to you will reach you safely. I have lost so many of these letters that I dread to part with them.

I trust *you* implicitly, but fear the chances & accidents of its transportation. Here is a note which Mr. Savage wrote to Hiram Fuller, a *soi disant* friend of mine & Mrs. Osgood's.[6] Mr. Fuller gave it to me just after my book was published. He is not a man to understand Poe. I mean *Savage* is not. Fuller of *course* is not. But I am so tired with writing this long postscript to my last night's letter that I can only tell you how sincerely & earnestly I share your hopes & desire your success.

S.H.W.

1. This "history" was an article, "Mr. Jefferson's Pet," *Harper's New Monthly Magazine*, 44 (May 1872), 815–26; an engraving of the western aspect of the university is on p. 817.

2. Edgar Poe's name was never legally "Allan," and Mr. Allan was not his godfather, certainly not as we understand the term.

3. The *American Metropolitan*, edited by William Landon, New York, in Jan. and Feb. 1849.

4. James Hannay, *The Poetical Works of Edgar Allan Poe, with a Notice of His Life and Genius* (London: Addey and Co., 1853).

5. See p. 12, n. 6.

6. John Savage (1828–1888), journalist and dramatist, attempted to defend Poe's reputation against Griswold's "Memoir" in an article entitled "Edgar Allan Poe," which appeared in installments in *United States Magazine and Democratic Review*, 27 (Dec. 1850), 542–44, 28 (Jan. 1851), 66–69, (Feb. 1851), 162–72. Item 515 in the Ingram Poe Collection. Hiram Fuller (1814–1880) was a journalist and editor of the New York *Mirror*. Poe sued him in 1846 for reprinting Thomas Dunn English's defamatory attack and was awarded $225 in damages.

11.   Sarah Helen Whitman to John H. Ingram.   Item 124

My dear Mr. Ingram,   Feb. 24, 1874
    I mailed in time for the steamer that sailed on the 18th two letters,
one enclosing *an autograph letter.* Be very careful of this & return it to
me after you have taken a facsimile of such portions as you desire.
    I shall send by tomorrow's steamer two *cartes* from the daguerre
taken in this city under the circumstances which I described in a
former letter, when the poet had wandered home but newly from that
"Ultimate dim Thule." The one in the oval is direct from the original,
the other has gone through modifications & ameliorating processes.
Neither of them give[s] an adequate idea of the stern & sombre
grandeur of the original. I have left with the photographer the one
which was taken for *me* a few days *after* this first sitting which has an
entirely different character & is serene & elevated. The artist thinks
that he can *reproduce* it, though the picture was injured by remaining
too long in the camera. If he succeeds, I will send you a copy as soon
as I can obtain one.
    I believe I told you that I had written twice to Mr. Gill, but had
received nothing from him for several weeks. This morning a letter
arrived which I will transcribe for you:

                                                            Boston
Dear Mrs. Whitman,   Feb. 23, [18]74
    Your letter came while I was away with Mr. Wilkie Collins. Since the
second letter I have been under pressure of unusual business & excitement.
The Gowans paragraph is not at hand. I will send it in a day or two. I enclose
the Griswold piece. The Poe lecture will be given next month, if I live. Have
mislaid your letter, which I was to introduce, (in the long time that has
elapsed) but still hope to find it.
    Trusting this will find you well, I am

                                                    Yours sincerely,
                                                    Wm. F. Gill

    In this letter he says nothing of a letter from Mr. Griswold which I
lent him. It was written in the autumn of [18]49, after Poe's death. In it
Griswold asked if Mr. Poe's letters had been returned to me—said that
Mrs. Clemm told him they had *all been returned to me*; he had asked
her for them, he said, in *order* to return them. He cautioned me to be
very careful what I said to Mrs. Clemm, who was, he said, not *my*
friend, nor *anybody's* friend. The letter was full of virulence &
bitterness against her. I had not *asked* for my letters, nor even *desired*
their return; nor had Poe, in the only letter which I received from him,
after our last parting, asked me for *his own.* I believe that these letters,
in their simplicity & directness & in the pure passion of their

eloquence, contain more of his soul's strange inner life than anything that remains of his correspondence.

The first letter contains twelve closely written pages, the longest letter, as he assured me, that he had ever written, & from what I have learned from Mrs. Clemm & Mrs. Osgood on this subject, I cannot doubt that it was so. But I can only write you very briefly now. I have been ill & my time has been unavoidably occupied by various & pressing engagements. I intended simply to speak of Griswold's letter as an unauthorized attempt to advise me in a matter about which I had sought no advice & to prejudice me against one whose name I had never mentioned to him, and this too at a very early stage of his literary executorship. Could it be that he assumed this office for the sake of gratifying some private enmity, while professing to do so under the guise of friendship? You ask about the correspondence that passed between Mr. Pabodie & Dr. Griswold, after the publication of Pabodie's article in the *Tribune*. The day after its appearance, Dr. Griswold wrote a very intemperate & unmanly letter to Pabodie, threatening that if the letter was not withdrawn he would do very dreadful things— that he would not suffer any assertion of facts made in his "Memoir" to be contradicted with impunity, etc., etc. Mr. Pabodie corroborated his *Tribune* article by so simple & plain a statement (not only in relation to the charge answered in the *Tribune*, but to the story of an alleged conversation held with a New York lady, which is associated with the story of outrages committed at the house of a New England lady, &c.) that Dr. Griswold was silenced & remained thereafter discreetly passive and non-resistant.

I would send you the correspondence, but the charges made against Mrs. Clemm in G[riswold]'s letter are so monstrous & so malevolent that I should be sorry to have them seen by one who knew her only through this scandalous letter.

Judge Parsons directed my attention to the enclosed extract from a leading authority in a work on Medical Jurisprudence, Philadelphia, 1855.

[*Letter is incomplete*]

[Enclosure]

Wharton & Stille cite "The Murders in the Rue Morgue" & "The Mystery of Marie Rogêt" as the most remarkable illustrations in our literature of the value of the inductive process as applied to the work of drawing from mechanical & physical indices the truth which underlies them & regard the early death of the author & the causes which diverted his genius from the severer branches of study as a serious national loss.

12.   Sarah Helen Whitman to John H. Ingram.   Item 125

My dear Mr. Ingram,   Feb. 27, 1874
   I wrote the enclosed in a great hurry. I hope to send the photographs tonight.
   I have been very unwell & greatly pressed for time for the last few days. I have not yet received the article in the *Mirror* of which you speak in your letter of 11th instant—but suppose I shall do so soon. I have found *N&Q* in the Athenaeum ("The Fire Fiend" exposé). Thank you for pointing it out to me. It must be ranked with the Persian origin of "The Raven,"—The Shaver story of "Manuscript Found in a Barn," etc., etc.[1] I have heard that the article in the *North American Review* was by a Mrs. Vale Smith, but I do not know whether there is such a person or whether it is an assumed name. I am inclined to think that it is. Mr. Davidson's article would not enlighten you much on facts. I had it long among my papers on this subject, but it is missing. I doubt if Mr. Davidson himself has a copy. He lost his books & MSS. in the Columbia fire, during the war—but I will ask him. Poe autographs are *very* scarce. With the exception of my own letters & papers, I know of none save a few in collections of autographs.
   I gave away a letter of his written to Mr. Pabodie to Mr. Latto. I will write to him about it. It is simply a letter of thanks to Mr. Pabodie for his hospitality to him during a visit to this city in November, I think. I shall feeling [*sic*] anxious about the autograph letter I sent to you nearly a fortnight ago (I think) until I hear of its having reached you.
   In speaking of the manner in which Poe "denounces any imputation upon himself," he had reference to a passage of a letter which he read during the long evening spent with me in Providence, & which I will copy for you, perhaps to send by the next mail. I have been quite prostrated by neuralgia for the last few days. Do not fear to *trouble me by questions*. I shall be most happy to answer any question that you may put to me & do not think that I shall regard any question *as an intrusion*. Everything which you have written either in your letters to me or in the published writings, which you have sent me, assures me of your competence & of your earnestness. *I trust you implicitly.* I wish that I had sooner known of your purpose; so much that would have been valuable to you has been lost or given away.
   It is very strange that so little is know of "the expedition to Greece." It seems strange to me that I never spoke with him on the subject.
   Mr. Gill told me that Mr. Clarke says that he *did* go to Greece, or did leave the country with that intention. And, in a letter written in the summer of 1859 by Mrs. Anna Cora Mowatt (then Mrs. Ritchie) to my friend & hers, Mrs. Julia Deane Freeman, Mrs. Ritchie says that having recently met Mr. J. R. Thompson at a party in Richmond, he

told her that soon after Poe's return from West Point to Richmond he became enamoured of Miss Royster (afterwards Mrs. Shelton), &, it was said, was engaged to her.[2] Mr. Allan opposed the marriage & he and Poe had a violent quarrel which ended in Poe's departure for Greece. On his return by way of England Mr. Allan was reconciled to him. Miss Royster was married to Mr. Shelton. Mr. Allan had some time before married "a beautiful Miss Patterson of Baltimore," the lady who is now his widow.[3] "Poe," Mrs. Ritchie writes,

who had by this time fallen under the baneful influence which wrought his ruin, again quarreled with his benefactor. Mr. Thompson is not certain of the cause of the quarrel—nothing is really known, though there are scandalous tales afloat, for which there does not seem, so far as I can learn, *any foundations*. Mr. Thompson became acquainted with Poe in the summer of [18]47 or [18]48. (I cannot trust my memory as to the year.) Poe came to his office, introduced himself, talked in the calmest manner of his faults, & finally engaged to write for the *Messenger*. He & Thompson became quite intimate, & Mr. Thompson has a full appreciation of the fine points of his character. Mr. Shelton had died, leaving a will depriving his widow of all his property if she married again ⟨ He left one child, a boy ten years of age—SHW ⟩. Report says that Poe courted her in spite of this barrier. Mr. Thompson says that he knew nothing of this from Poe, never having heard him speak of the lady. One day in [18]47 or [18]48, (I think it was but you must not rely on me for the date) Poe came into the office in a great state of excitement, sat down & wrote a challenge of which he requested Thompson to be the bearer. In explanation, Poe handed him a paragraph cut from the *Examiner*, then edited by Mr. Daniel, publishing Poe's reported marriage with Mrs. Whitman of Providence, & making some comment on the lady's temerity. Poe said he did not care what Daniel might say of himself, but Mrs. Whitman's name should not be dragged in. Thompson refused point-blank to carry the challenge. Poe sought an interview with Daniel, & the offensive paragraph was withdrawn. The following winter came a story of Poe's having appeared in church only a few days before his appointed marriage with Mrs. W. was to take place in such a state of intoxication as led to his consequent rejection by the lady. Poe returned to Richmond the following summer & led a more desperate life than ever. He left for Baltimore on Thursday, had an attack of delirium, was carried to the hospital & died there on Sunday. The first telegraphic dispatch Mr. Thompson ever received was an account of his friend's death. Mrs. Shelton went into widow's mourning—everyone believed that she was engaged to him & that the marriage was shortly to take place. This is an outline of what Mr. Thompson told me. Pray soften any harsh word that I may have said, in recounting it to Mrs. Whitman.

I was then in New York preparing & revising the pages which Carleton published at the close of that year. Mrs. Ritchie had years before been a friend & correspondent of mine. Mrs. Freeman, who knew that I was anxious to obtain some authentic information about Poe's last days in Richmond, wrote to Mrs. Ritchie, who was then in that city, on the subject, & the above extract was received by her in reply.

There is some confusion of dates in her report; it must have been in the summer of [18]48 that he wrote the challenge to Daniel, I think. I was not at that time personally acquainted with Mr. Poe. He had seen me, but I had no acquaintance with him until the September following. In December of the same year occurred the rupture of our betrothal, under circumstances very different from those reported by Thompson or by Griswold, which you shall hear from me hereafter. It is true, as Dr. Griswold says, that our names had been often mentioned together. Mr. Poe, before going South, had delivered the lecture on the poetesses of America (from which I sent you an extract) in Lowell, & had spoken much of me to his friends in Lowell, New York, & Richmond. This must in some way have led to the obnoxious paragraph in the *Examiner*. It was in the summer of 1849 that the rumor of his engagement with Mrs. Shelton was first circulated. I will tell you what I know of this another time. I have seen the letters which he wrote to Mrs. Clemm during the brief period of his engagement to that lady. She sent them to me in 1859, that I might know all that could be known of his feelings and views in entering upon this engagement. At the same time, Mrs. Clemm asked me to give her an autograph of his writings to send to Mrs. S[helton], that lady having informed her that she had not a line of his writing in her possession, & wished greatly to obtain one. This seemed very strange, & if true, the engagement between them must have been of very short duration. An inextricable difficulty seems to attend every attempt to get at the precise facts & dates of Poe's history. I send you a minute which I have just found, which I wrote down from the letters of Dr. Maupin & Mr. Wertenbaker. Mr. W. says Poe wrote his age in the matriculation books of the college in Feb. 1826, "Born Feb. 19, 1809."

I wish I had time to tell you how much I enjoyed the *Symbolica*. I took up the book at a late hour a few nights ago, when very tired, & was held by it till past midnight. I have no strength & no time now to tell you how it fascinated me. I will write soon, by the next steamer if possible.

For the present I can only say may heaven prosper you in all things,

Sincerely your friend,
Sarah Helen Whitman

Friday, Feb. 27

I enclose an article from the *Journal* for its allusion to Gautier's allusion to Poe. Do not return it.

I am disappointed again in getting the first unmodified copy from the daguerre tonight. Will send it if possible next week. The one in the oval is taken from the same original, the "Thule"—but, as I said, is modified. The other is from the faded picture which was taken for me a few days after.

It is the best the artist could get from it.

1. Ingram refers to this story on p. 84 of *The Raven* (London: George Redway, 1885), remarking that among the most self-evidently absurd fabrications of the origin of Poe's poem was a story that had found its way to England, after running the rounds of the American press, and had been republished in the London *Star* in the summer of 1864 to the effect that Mr. Lang, the well-known Oriental traveler, had discovered that Poe had translated, almost literally, "The Raven" from the Persian. On July 29, 1870, the New York *Tribune* reprinted a letter from the New Orleans *Times*, July 22, 1870, in which the Rev. J. Shaver called attention to a paragraph in *Littell's Living Age*, July 8, 1870, p. 105, which stated that a manuscript found in an old barn in a New Jersey village was that of a letter written by Poe to a Mr. Daniels of Philadelphia on Sept. 29, 1849, in which Poe confessed to have stolen "The Raven" from a contributor, Samuel Fenwick, of New York. Item 550 in the Ingram Poe Collection.

2. Mrs. Anna Cora Ogden Mowatt Ritchie (1819–1870), actress and writer, married James Mowatt in 1834 and William Ritchie in 1854.

John Reuben Thompson (1823–1873) was a poet, journalist, as well as owner and editor of the *Southern Literary Messenger* from 1847 to 1860. He was acquainted with Poe and after Poe's death liked to pose as his rescuer, in a lecture he delivered here and there, "The Genius and Character of Edgar Allan Poe." Thompson certainly is responsible for some of the more sordid stories about Poe's behavior. His lecture was edited by J. H. Whitty and J. H. Rindfleisch in 1929; 150 copies were published by Garrett and Massie in Richmond.

Mrs. Sarah Elmira Royster Shelton (b. 1810 or 1811, d. 1888) is generally regarded as having been Poe's boyhood sweetheart in Richmond. When they met and parted again in 1849, almost certainly they were engaged to be married, a fact Mrs. Shelton denied for many years; as Poe's fame grew, her reticence about their last relationship decreased.

3. Mrs. Louisa Gabriella Patterson Allan (d. 1881) of Elizabeth, N.J., and Richmond became the second wife of John Allan on Oct. 5, 1830.

13. *John H. Ingram to Sarah Helen Whitman*

My dear Mrs. Whitman,   27 Feb. 1874

On my return home from official duty I had the pleasure of finding your most interesting and welcome letter [Feb. 11]; its enclosures, and *Harper's Monthly*. I was just going off to a dinner party, and had only time to skim over its contents, *en route*, but having reread it since, twice, I will now try to reply to its friendly contents *seriatim*.

As regards my boyish verses, it is, of course, kind of you to speak of them, but I have thought it necessary to relinquish poesy for ten long years, finding that I had not the "elegant leisure" Griswold speaks of, to devote to what would otherwise have been the impassioned occupation of my life. I never have, *I know it*, written anything in rhyme worth preservation, but had my life run on in the same pleasant paths in which it began, I feel that I could have done something the world would not willingly let die. Your words have touched a secret spring and the hopes & aspirations—long since crushed down, fettered under a heavy weight of woe—gush forth anew. But alas! I fear the day is gone for me! I have loved—I do love poesy with an idolatrous adoration! But enough of these "forbidden things"! If I can find some more titles of the unbound vol. you shall have them, but I am ashamed to send them. I should have cut those two pieces out: they were only to show you how long I had worshipped Poe. I have, I fancy, only one bound copy, and that I want to preserve: it is full of corrections, printer's errors, &c. In "Lauralie," I see, they have "as" for "has"—that was not my fault. You shall have the "half told story" but it *scarcely* comes up to Chaucer! As regards No. 1 of "New Facts" title, *en passant,* [it] was not mine—it was cut up & pulled out mercifully [*sic*] by Ed. of *Mirror* to suit his ideas, but No. 2 is my own, as a rule. I sent you copy at once & enclose another.[1] *Temple Bar* has again been deferred—'tis too bad! Hope deferred, with me, makes the heart sick. As regards the "Conchology" clue, it turned out nothing. I had been referred to the *International* (American) *Magazine* for Sept. 1850, and when I looked there I found only Griswold's "Memoir" with the note you know of: the "Memoir" must, therefore, have appeared there before it was prefixed to the collection.[2] By the way, my collection [of Griswold's edition of Poe's works], in 4 vols., was published in 1863 by Widdleton, New York, and now I see, in Allibone, that later editions have some 200 or 300 more pages. What date is yours? If the more recent ones contain more matter, I must get them. I know my edition does not contain a great deal that Edgar Poe wrote: some of his "Marginalia," his papers on "Autography," "Cryptology," &c. are absent. *Mais, revenez a nos moutons*—"Conchology" affair I will work out satisfactorily now, I don't doubt.

As regards the South Carolina lady, I can manage without any particulars—it will, perhaps, be as well for me to return that portion of your letter, but I don't like parting with your writing. You are now, & forever, enwound in my mind with Israfel—and I treasure every scrap of yours. "The trees which grow around a temple soon grow dear as the temple's self." I hope we may both be spared for me to some day come to speak my thoughts to you *viva voce.* "To Isadore" struck me as the style & manner of Poe: it was unsigned but then so are some of his earlier pieces & I *felt* sure it was his: others think so too. Most of the scraps & cuttings, I have already returned, having copied them, but will retain everything else you do not ask for. I will review *E.P. & His C.* in the *Mirror* & send it to you. I published "The Portrait" therein, as also a note. I will forward it in next letter. If I can reprint it elsewhere, emendation shall be made. Did you get *Flora Symbolica?* Don't accept it as a fair specimen of my skill. It was written under pressure of terrible grief chiefly, indeed to occupy my mind—years ago—before I was 20. I wrote several tales in which *Imagination* had full sway—I rewrote one or two, and wrote some others based entirely upon my studies of Poe & Hawthorne, & had arranged with a publisher for their publication in a vol. & in sending them from one of his warehouses to the other the MSS. were lost! They refused me any compensation—not that that could soften the loss of my hopes and aims—and I have now placed the matter in my solicitor's hands, but do not think that I shall get a penny from the firm because they are too wealthy & the head of it is a canting humbug. My poor stories! They would have given you a better idea of my imaginative powers than a *mere book*, as *Flora Symbolica* is.

Your *Via Dolorosa* recalled the *Via Mala* to my mind: have you traversed it? from Chur to Splügen. That is a spot for poets to see & almost despair over, but even it is not so terrifically grand as the Splügen Pass. As yet I have only just had a glimpse of *la bella Italia* & now my heart longs for it as the "hart pants for the water brooks"—My photo! Well, you shall have it soon, but I have not a single copy left. My last & best *carto* was taken in Germany & I am just going to send for some & will forward as soon as they arrive & perhaps you will not deem me impertinent if I ask for an exchange? You will not mind sending me your face, will you? Talking of Germany reminds me of a letter just received from America from some acquaintances made there (*i.e.,* in Germany) a few years ago: knowing my want of information as regards my hero, they have just sent me a sketch of the life & character of E.A. Poe written by a professor of Baltimore. I need scarcely quote one sentence to prove its *value*—"he had three wives, the last of whom was the beautiful Virginia Clemm" &c., &c. It is shameful to see such ignorance of their greatest author in America.

As regards Stoddard's paper—by the way, how am I to recompense you for your kindness? Do you want any English publications? To Stoddard—I am savage with him. His paper is little more than a compilation of your book *E.P. & His C.,* Griswold's "Memoir," and Powell's life in *The Living Authors of America.* This last was written *just after Poe's death* & is *very kind*—only one cruel statement, *i.e.,* his expulsion from the University. Powell (an Englishman) shewed himself a great admirer of Poe & was, consequently, secretly defamed by Griswold: do you know his book? Stoddard did surprise me in saying that Poe shewed no trace of classic education in his works! Either Powell is no judge or he [Stoddard?] has not read Poe's works. His "Grecian Fiddlestick" has [poisoned?] him against the subject of his sketch. Where Poe went to school is not like description in "William

Wilson," but the opposite house resembles his description. The calligraphy story I have shewn the falsity of in "New Facts" & in *Temple Bar* paper. I have copy of a long letter by Poe to J. Kennedy & expect some more. Poe *was dismissed* from West Point but the enclosed scrap will explain why.[3] Russia, I fancy, he never saw. Mr. E. Schuyler, Secretary of your Legation, has kindly had books of the Embassy & Consulate searched & not an allusion in either.[4] General Cullum, I fancy, is wrong about early vol. being dedicated to Bulwer. Bulwer's son, the present Lord Lytton, is almost sure that his father never heard of the dedication, or from Poe. Was the B— Ebenezer Burling, who was to have accompanied Poe to Greece? Do you know anything of Mrs. M. St. Leon Loud?[5] *Thereby hangs a tale, I ween.* I have copies, *now*, of many of the poems, as published in 1831—"To F.S.O.," quoted in "New Facts" No. 1, appeared in 1836 to "Eliza"— the name of "Helen" occurs frequently. Was there anything in the story of "Alice" think you? Poor Mrs. Clemm did no good, I fancy, with her reminiscences. I'll write to Mr. Gill. As for Gilfillan, he is already forgotten in England.[6] I can prove other falsehoods of Griswold's besides those mentioned: he was so careless, that I can easily disprove many allegations. I'll wind off for post, but more information next time.

Ever yours faithfully,
John H. Ingram

P.S. The photograph from Poe's portrait would be invaluable in my eyes.

---

1. Ingram's "More New Facts about Edgar Allan Poe," reprinted following this letter, survives in only one known copy: three pages which Ingram clipped for his own files, now in the Ingram Poe Collection. The London *Mirror* for 1872–74 was published in four volumes; of these only one copy of Vol. IV is extant and is now in the Library Company of Philadelphia. This article shows how quickly and in what fashion Ingram used the materials Mrs. Whitman had sent to him in the foregoing letters. Here one can get a fully characteristic view of Ingram's tone and attitude as he attacked Griswold's "Memoir"; one can also observe Ingram's style, with its slipshod grammar, awkward sentence structures and repetitions, none of which Ingram changed in his writings about Poe over the next forty-five years.

2. Griswold's "Memoir" of Poe did appear in the *International Magazine*, Oct. 1, 1850.

3. Robert W. Hall, U.S. Military Academy, West Point, wrote Ingram on Feb. 3, 1874, that the records of the academy showed that Poe had been admitted as a cadet on July 1, 1830; the following Jan. he had been tried by a general court martial and his dismissal had taken place on the following Mar. 6. Item 117 in the Ingram Poe Collection.

4. Eugene Schuyler, secretary of the U.S. Legation, St. Petersburg, Russia, had written Ingram on Feb. 2, 1874, that a search of the Legation papers from 1820 to 1830 showed nothing relating to Edgar A. Poe. On Feb. 6, 1874, Schuyler had written again to say that he had searched the books of the U.S. Consulate and that he had found no record whatever of Edgar A. Poe having been detained. Items 116 and 118 in the Ingram Poe Collection.

5. Mrs. Margaret Barstow St. Leon Loud was a minor poet of Philadelphia whose husband, John, had offered Poe $100 to edit his wife's poems by Christmas of 1849.

6. In early 1854 the Rev. George Gilfillan (1813–1878) published a rancorous sketch of Poe's life and career in the London *Critic*, in which he quite outdid Griswold. This article was republished in both the *Southern Literary Messenger* and *Littell's Living Age* Apr. 1854, and in Gilfillan's *Third Gallery of Portraits* (New York: Sheldon, Lamport, and Blakeman, 1855), V, 325–38.

14. "More New Facts about Edgar Allan Poe," by John H. Ingram, London Mirror; A Weekly Magazine and Review of Literature, the Drama, Science and Art, *Feb. 21, 1874. Item 570*

More New Facts about Edgar Allan Poe

LOGICALLY SPEAKING a chain is no stronger than its weakest link; and, acting upon this truth, we are justified in regarding the whole of Griswold's "Memoir of Edgar Poe" with doubt, if we discover a single falsehood, or one *evidently wilful* misstatement. How much stronger, then, is our case for the defence if we are enabled to show—as well as lapse of time and distance from sources of investigation will permit—that nearly all the accusations brought against the deceased poet by his biographer can be proved to be utterly false, or gross perversions of the truth.

Although a very large number of names are introduced into the "Memoir" by Griswold, as if to set at rest any doubt as to its correctness, upon careful analysis they are, almost invariably, discovered to be either those of people who died before the work was published, or of persons totally foreign to the purpose. In one instance—that of Mr. George R. Graham—Griswold was too hasty. Mr. Graham was not dead, nor was *he* to be cowed into silence by the American Zoilos, and he protested against the "Memoir," the only source of every biography of Edgar Poe yet published in England.

The first stumbling-block we encounter is the date of the poet's birth. Griswold, in the "Memoir," and every other biographist copying him, says that Poe was born in January, 1811, although elsewhere he avers that the poet wrote to correct this into 1813. We disbelieve that correction, the more especially as we have the subject of the "Memoir's" own authority for stating that he was born in 1809, a far more probable date. Edgar accompanied his adopted parents, Mr. and Mrs. Allan, to England in 1816, and, after passing five years in the Manor House School, Churchstreet, Stoke Newington, returned to the United States in 1822. In his twelfth year he entered an academy at Richmond, Virginia, and here he would seem to have studied until the close of 1825. His reverend biographer states that he only spent "a few months" there, and then "entered the University at Charlottesville, where he led a very dissipated life. The manners which then prevailed there were extremely dissolute, and he was known as the wildest and most reckless student of his class. . . . His gambling, intemperance, and *other vices*, induced his expulsion from the university." The mere fact that at this time Poe, on Griswold's showing, was but eleven years of age, should have made biographers careful about crediting such testimony. What were the real facts? Lying before us we have copies of two letters written in May, 1860—one from Dr. Stephen Maupin, president of the university, and one from Mr. Wertenbecker, the secretary, which certify that Edgar Poe entered the university in February, 1826, and that he himself recorded his age in the matriculation book of his college as seventeen; that "he spent but one session, that of 1826, at the institution, and *at no time* did he fall under the censure of the Faculty;" and, it is added, "he was not at that time addicted to drinking."

Instead of having been expelled, Edgar Poe left the university with the boyish idea of assisting the Greeks in their revolutionary movements against their Turkish oppressors. He left home in 1827. What he did in Europe, and how he did it, no one seems to know; but at the end of a twelvemonth he turned up at St. Petersburg, where, says the charitable Griswold, "our minister was summoned one morning to save him from penalties incurred in a drunken debauch." On turning to Dr. Lowell's notice of the poet, we find it stated that the poor orphan boy—he was but eighteen—"got into difficulties in St. Petersburg through want of a passport, from which he was rescued by the American consul, and sent home." Other biographers tell a similar story, [1] as did even Griswold himself in his other works, whilst Powell remarks that Poe had a narrow escape in Russia "from the fangs of that brutal Government, in consequence of an irregularity in his passport. The exertions of the consul saved him from the consequences of the error, and through his friendship he returned to America."

On his return home the young poet wished to enter the army, and Mr. Allan procured his adopted son an appointment to a scholarship in the Military Academy at West Point. Before the young cadet had passed a twelvemonth at West Point he received the unwelcome intelligence of his adopted father's second marriage with a girl young enough to be her husband's granddaughter. Reverting to the "Memoir," we find Griswold, indeed, remarking that "it has been erroneously stated by all Poe's biographers that Mr. Allan was now sixty-five years of age, and that Miss Paterson, to whom he was married afterwards, was young enough to be his granddaughter. Mr. Allan was in his forty-eighth year, and the difference between his age and that of his second wife was not so great as justly to attract any observation." Many might deem a sufficient reply to this statement to be found in the following paragraph of the famous

1. The "Eulogium" confesses its inability to state whether "lust or lucre" was the cause of his detention.

"Ludwig"-Griswold letter to the *Tribune*. "Mr. Allan," it remarks, "was sixty-five years of age, and the lady was young." The author of the "Eulogium," who lived in the same city with Mr. Allan, gives his age as sixty-five at the date of the second marriage, and he is corroborated by Powell.

In 1827, Poe, when barely eighteen, had published a volume of poems, including "Al Aaraaf," "Tamerlane," and other shorter pieces, some of which, as "Poems Written in Youth," are still reprinted *verbatim*, whilst others are totally ignored, or, having been recast, are to be found in the later collections, under new titles. Two years later a second edition,[2] or collection rather, was published, and in 1830 the third edition, "revised and improved." The author of the "Memoir," although thoroughly conversant with these dates, declares that "this small volume of verse" was not printed until after Poe left West Point, in 1831, following in this statement the writer of the "Eulogium;" "and," continues the reverend gentleman, "I *believe* there is no evidence that anything of his, which has been published, was written before he left the university."

Notwithstanding this accurate biographist's belief, we are able to state that not only was Poe correct in the dates *he furnished* Griswold with, but that that gentleman himself has left the "evidence" he attempted to ignore. On the thirty-seventh page of the "Memoir" he gives 1829 as the original date of the publication, whilst elsewhere, during the poet's lifetime, and as lately as in the pseudonymous letter to the *Tribune*, he quotes 1827! In fact, in his eagerness to depreciate the poet's abilities, he frequently defeats his object, and only manifests his own inveterate hatred towards him. Were such errors, however, merely the results of carelessness, they would deteriorate from the value of the book as an authority, and should make us hesitate about placing implicit faith in its author's statements. Lowell, in his notice of Edgar Poe, published in *Graham's Magazine*, and the Countess d'Ossoli (Margaret Fuller) in the *Tribune*, both, and both more reliable authorities, give 1827 as the date of the first publication; and the latter states that some of these poems were composed when their author was eight or ten years old. Poe himself says that he wrote "Al Aaraaf" when he was only ten. Probably no one cares to know that in the opinion of the impartial Griswold these "verses do not seem to evince, all things considered, a very remarkable precosity." Margaret Fuller thought otherwise, as did also James Hannay. Lowell calls them "the most remarkable boyish poems that we have ever read. We know of none that can compare with them for maturity of purpose, and a nice understanding of the effects of language and metre. . . . John Neal himself, a man of genius, and whose lyre has been too long capriciously silent, appreciated the high merit of these and similar passages, and drew a proud horoscope for their author."

2. "Poems." Baltimore: Hatch and Dunning, 1829.

Page by page, and paragraph after paragraph of his so-called "Memoir" have we sifted and put to the touchstone of truth, and testimony after testimony have we succeeded in obtaining of the falsity or improbability of its author's allegations against Edgar Poe; but having proceeded thus far in our investigations, we must forego a system that would require a whole number of the *Mirror* to work out thoroughly, and henceforth only draw attention to one or two of the more glaring discrepancies between the real facts of the case and the fictitious ones of Rufus Griswold.

In 1833, poor Poe having, upon the strength of his poetical successes, adopted literature for a profession, is found to have been literally starving. A local paper having offered two prizes for the best tale and the best poem, both prizes were awarded to Poe, on account, Griswold positively affirms, of his beautiful and distinct caligraphy. One of the adjudicators, having been attracted by Poe's handwriting, selected his papers for the premium, avers the biographer, and thereupon "it was unanimously decided that the prizes should be paid to 'the first of geniuses who had written legibly.' Not another MS. was unfolded." Everybody appears to have accepted this story, and never to have doubted that a committee, including the Honourable J. P. Kennedy and other well-known persons, should have hesitated at such a dishonourable course of proceeding. Fortunately for the credit of all concerned we are enabled to disprove the entire story, having succeeded in unearthing the published award. We therein read that "Amongst the prose articles *were many of various and distinguished merit*; but the singular force and beauty of those sent by the author of 'The Tales of the Folio Club' leave us no room for hesitation. . . . We have accordingly awarded the premium to a tale entitled 'The MS. Found in a Bottle.' It would hardly be doing justice to the writer of this collection to say that the tale we have chosen is the best of the six offered by him. We cannot refrain from saying that the author owes it to his own reputation, as well as to the gratification of the community, to publish the entire volume. These tales are eminently distinguished by a wild, vigorous, and poetical imagination, a rich style, a fertile invention, and varied and curious learning." Then follow the signatures of the committee. That Griswold had read this award is morally certain, as he even refers to its terms.

Professors Anthon, Henry, and Hawkes having offered Poe a more advantageous engagement on the *New York Review*, he, in January, 1837, resigned the editorship of the *Southern Literary Messenger*, the circulation of which high-priced magazine had, during the one year of his clever supervision, increased from seven hundred to nearly five thousand. According to the "Memoir," however, Poe's severance from the *Messenger* was caused by his irregularities; his continual drunkenness having "frequently interrupted the kindness, and finally exhausted the patience, of his generous though methodical employer," the *late* Mr. White. Griswold then quotes the editor's valedictory address; but suppresses the proprietor's note which follows it, and which could not fail to create a doubt as to the authenticity of a letter purporting to have been written by this late Mr. White to Poe, and quoted in the "Memoir" to the effect that "*all engagements* on my part cease the moment you get drunk." Mr. White, after alluding to the able manner in which Poe had performed his editorial duties during the past year, during which period, indeed, he had *monthly* written the chief portion of the magazine, and adds, "Mr. Poe, however, will continue to furnish its columns, from time to time, with the effusions of his vigorous and popular pen," &c. And Poe did write for the *Messenger* until a few weeks before his death.

About this time Poe wrote "Arthur Gordon Pym." Says his editor: "It is his longest work, and is not without some sort of merit, but it received little attention. The publishers sent one hundred copies to England, and being mistaken at first for a narrative of real experience, it was advertised to be reprinted, but a discovery of its character, *I believe*, prevented such a result." We have already had examples of this reverend gentleman's belief, and are not, therefore surprised to find that it was *twice* reprinted within a very short space of time in England.

In May, 1839, Poe, after having been for some time a contributor to, became editor of the *Gentleman's Magazine*, belonging to the late Mr. Burton, a well-known comedian. The account given by the "Memoir" is that Poe held this post until June, 1840; that Mr. Burton would willingly have retained him in his editorial position, but that "he was so unsteady of purpose and unreliable that the actor was never sure when he left the city that his business would be cared for. On one occasion, returning after the regular day of publication, he found the number unfinished, and Poe incapable of duty." The very good-natured proprietor, however, so runs this legend, "prepared the necessary copy himself, published the magazine, and was proceeding with arrangements for another month when he received a letter from his assistant, of which the tone may be inferred from the answer," which answer, as its quoted by Griswold, apparently does not contain a single allusion to its recipient's presumed drunkenness; but whilst differing from Poe's supposed views of criticising, advises him, as his troubles have given a morbid tone to his feelings, to "use more exercise, write when feelings prompt, and be assured of my friendship." So Poe continue in his editorial office for several more months when, taking advantage of Mr. Burton's prolonged absence, says this reliable "Memoir," he obtains lists of the magazine subscribers; prepares the prospectus of a new monthly to supplant the *Gentleman's*; and when encountered by "his associate late in the evening, at one of his accustomed haunts," in response to Mr. Burton's request to give him his manuscripts, responds: "Who are you that presume to address me in this manner? Burton, I am—the editor—of the *Penn Magazine*—and you are—hiccup—a fool!'" "Of course this ended his relations with the *Gentleman's*," gravely adds Griswold. Unfortunately for the reverend biographer's veracity, it did nothing of the sort! Whether this ridiculous anecdote was evolved out of the imagination of the "Memoir's" author, or was really told to him by one of the mischief-makers who, he acknowledges, continually sowed dissension between Poe and himself, we know not, but its disproof is found in the fact that Poe *retained* his editorial post for two years longer, during which time the *Gentleman's* passed into the hands of Mr. George R. Graham, and, under the title of *Graham's Magazine*, became one of the best—if not the best—magazine in America.

Poe continued for more than two years—not eighteen months, as stated by Griswold—the editorial guidance of *Graham's Magazine*, and the value of his services may be gathered from the fact that during this period its circulation rose from five to fifty-two thousand. Turning to the "Memoir," its author tells us that "the infirmities which induced his separation from Mr. White and from Mr. Burton at length compelled Mr. Graham to seek for another editor." Another editor was found in the person of Rufus W. Griswold, and it is interesting to learn, on the authority of Duyckinck's "Cyclopedia of American Literature," that he conducted it with great success, in consequence of obtaining "the contributions of some of the best authors of the country, who found liberal remuneration, then a novelty in American literature, from the generous policy of the *proprietor*." The very first man to deny the truth of Griswold's characterization of Poe was George R. Graham. He designated it as "The fancy sketch of a jaundiced vision"—"an immortal infamy," and, probably knowing better than any man the position in which the two authors stood to each other, declared that there existed "*a long, intense, and implacable hatred between Poe and Griswold*, which disqualified him for the office of his biographer!" All that Griswold could reply was that Mr. Graham's letter was "sophomorical and trashy," "poor fustian," its writer, his late employer, "a silly and ambitious person," and, in italics, the audacious remark that for "*four or five years not a line by Poe was purchased for Graham's Magazine*"—that is to say, whilst he (Griswold) was the editor! Such a piece of impudence is, probably, unparalleled in the history of literature, unless, indeed, our next sample of his skill does not surpass it.

In May, 1846, Poe commenced a series of critiques on the "New York Literati," in Godey's *Lady's Book*. They were immensely successful, but the caustic style of some of them produced terrible commotion in the ranks of mediocrity, as may be learnt from the proprietor's notes to his readers, respecting the anonymous and other letters he receives concerning them. "We are not to be intimidated," he remarks, "by a threat of the loss of friends, or turned from our purpose by honied words. Our course is onwards. . . . Many attempts have been made and are making by various persons to forestall public opinion. *We have the name of one person.* Others are busy with reports of Mr. Poe's illness. Mr. Poe has been ill, but we have letters from him of very recent dates, also a new batch of the 'Literati,' which show anything but feebleness either of body or mind. Amost every paper that we exchange with has praised our new enterprise, and spoken in high terms of Mr. Poe's opinion." A Dunn English, or Dunn Brown, for he is duplicately named, dissatisfied with the manner in which his literary shortcomings had been reviewed by Poe, "retaliated in a personal newspaper article," says Duyckinck, and "the communication was reprinted in the *Evening Mirror*, in New York, whereupon Poe instituted a libel suit against that journal, and recovered several hundred dollars." Griswold's account is that Dunn English "chose to evince his resentment of the critic's unfairness by the publication of a card in which he painted strongly the infirmities of Poe's life and character." "Poe's article," he continues, "was entirely false in what purported to be its facts. The statement of Dr. English appeared in the New York *Mirror* of the 23rd June and on the 27th.[3] Mr. Poe sent to Mr. Godey for publication in the *Lady's Book* his rejoinder, which Mr. Godey very properly declined to print." This led, asserts the biographer, "to a disgraceful quarrel," and to the "*premature conclusion*" of the "Literati." This review of English, *alias* Brown, appeared in the second or June number of the "Literati," and from our knowledge of Griswold's usual inaccuracy, we were not surprised to find, upon reference, that the sketches ran their stipulated course until October, and, after that date, Poe still continuing a contributor to the *Lady's Book*, but what did startle us was to discover that *the whole of the personalities* of the supposed critique by Poe on English, as included in the collection *edited by Griswold*, were absent from the real critique published in the *Lady's Book*. It is impossible to reproduce the whole of this audacious fabrication, or its prototype, but a comparison between some passages of Poe's review in the *Lady's Book* and the article in Griswold's collection will convince the most sceptical that, since the days of Ireland or Psalmanazar, no more shameless imposition has apparently been foisted on the public. "Brief poems" are changed into "scraps of verse." "Barry Cornwall and others of the *bizarre* school are his especial favourites" is transformed into "When Barry Cornwall, for example, sings about a 'dainty rhythm,' Mr. Brown forthwith, in B flat, hoots about it too." "I learn," says Poe's paper, "that Mr. Brown is not without talent, but the fate of the 'Aristi-

3. This number, strange to relate, has either been abstracted from or never bound up with the file of this newspaper in the British Museum Library.

dean' should indicate to him the necessity of applying himself to study;" but this is altered to "Mr. Brown has at least that amount of talent which would enable him to succeed in his father's profession—that of a ferry-man on the Schuylkill; but the fate of the 'Aristidean,' should indicate to him that, to prosper in any higher walk of life, he must apply himself to study."

The whole of the personal, grossly personal, and badly-worded portion, beginning at, "Were I writing," down to "Mr. Brown had for the motto on his magazine cover, the words of Richelieu:

> "'——Men call me cruel.
> I am not: I am *just.*'

Here the two monosyllables, *an ass*, should have been appended. They were no doubt omitted through 'one of those d——d typographical blunders' which, through life, have been at once the bane and the antidote of Mr. Brown." The whole of this, we reiterate, as well as some other portions of equal coarseness, are absent from Poe's critique.

But the grossest accusation which his biographer brings against Poe is the oft-told incident of his engagement to be married to "one of the most brilliant women of New England," and the method adopted by the poet of breaking the engagement, "which," says Griswold, "affords a striking illustration of his character." According to the veracious author of the "Memoir," Poe, in the evening before what should have been the bridal morn, committed such drunken outrages at the house of his affianced bride, that it was found necessary to summon the police to eject him, which, of course, ended the engagement. This misstatement being brought under the notice of the parties concerned, Mr. William Pabodie, of Providence, Rhode Island, wrote a direct and specific denial of it to the *New York Tribune*, and that paper published it on the 7th June, 1852. "I am authorized to say," remarks Mr. Pabodie, "not only from my personal knowledge, but also from the statement of ALL who were conversant with the affair, that there exists not a shadow of foundation for the story above alluded to." The same letter goes on to state that its writer knew Poe well, and at the time alluded to "was with him daily. I was acquainted with the circumstances of his engagement, and with the causes which led to its dissolution," continues Mr. Pabodie, and he concludes his letter with an earnest appeal to Griswold to do all that lies in his power "to remove an undeserved stigma from the memory of the departed." An honourable man would have confessed the incorrectness of his information, and have done his best to obviate the consequences. Not so the rev. gentleman—he wrote a savage letter to Mr. Pabodie, threatening if he did not withdraw his he would take a dreadful revenge. Mr. Pabodie *did not withdraw*, but in another letter to Griswold brought forward incontrovertible proofs of other falsifications indulged in by the author of the "Memoir," who henceforth remained discreetly silent.

This disgraceful affair needs no further comment. We have not the space or we could continue our *exposé*. The incredulous reader may find the publications we have named in the British Museum Library, [4] and all the charges against the victim of Griswold's insatiable malice, we are prepared to prove to the world, as we have proved to our own satisfaction, are as unfounded as they are cruel and dastardly.

As regards his estimate of Poe's genius, were he even an impartial witness, it would go for naught. The world has judged for itself, nor cares that Rufus Griswold can only perceive "ingenuity" and "art" in the poems, "dexterity in the dissection of sentences" in the critiques, or deems that "the analytical subtlety has frequently been over-estimated" of the tales of Edgar Poe.[5]

John H. Ingram

4. Godey's *Lady's Book*, and the "Literati," by Edgar A. Poe.
5. In taking leave of this subject for the present, it is but just that we should tender our hearty thanks to Mrs. Sarah H. Whitman, the never faltering friend of the deceased poet, for her kind assistance in furnishing us with evidence towards the elucidation of Poe's university career, and the date of his birth.

15. *John H. Ingram to Sarah Helen Whitman*

My dear Mrs. Whitman,   2 March 1874
I hasten to acknowledge the receipt of your very interesting letter of the 16th Ultimo, and of its enclosures. In order to make certain of getting my reply off today I shall not attempt to indulge in any flights of imagination, but keep my Pegasus well curbed, and only resort to the apparent "methodical habits of thought." In the first place, let me tell you what I am doing towards increasing my material. I have written to Peabody Institute, Baltimore, for copies of letters by Poe to Mr. *Kennedy*, left by that gentleman. Did you see Tuckerman's *Life of J. P. Kennedy*? I wish I knew how to get at Tuckerman, to give him "New Facts"—he repeats Griswold's words as to the prize award, &c., but quotes a very interesting letter from Poe & "notes" *re.* him, from Kennedy's diary.[1] I shall embody them in a new paper that I'm going to write. *Temple Bar* has not used my paper *yet*: the moment it appears you shall have a copy sent, but so much fresh matter has come to my knowledge since, that you will not, I fancy, think much of it, save, perhaps, from its *tone*. Of course I do not leave a stain on him. But *what is better*—I have just engaged with a quarterly—our highest

style of periodical—for a complete biography of Edgar Poe. Before July
it cannot appear. I did not send advance sheets of *Temple Bar*, but will
try & arrange thro' Mr. J. W. Davidson, or someone, for its
simultaneous appearance in both countries. I want to get all the
correspondence of Poe's that I can by beginning of April—I have
written University at Charlottesville, *re.* E. Burling &c.² I told you, I
fancy, that I had heard from Russia. I fancy Poe wrote to Charles
Dickens *re. Barnaby Rudge*, but neither young Dickens, or John
Forster, can find any trace of letter. I have written Robert Browning,
who is, I believe, in Italy, for copies of letters to Mrs. Browning.
Bayard Taylor says Poe was the means of introducing her works (thro'
Graham's Maga.) into America. Lord Lytton tells me that he does not
think his father (Bulwer) ever *knew* of a book being dedicated to him
by Poe, of whom, *of course, as a poet* ("Owen Meredith") he is an
admirer. I am going to spend the evening next Friday with an
American, whose father was intimately acquainted with the Geo. R.
Graham I speak of, & who,—*entre nous*—went to the bad. Mr. Gowans
published some annual books that *may* throw some light on my
theories—I've not got to see them yet. I have discovered a book by
Wyatt—*A Manual of Conchology*, pubd. (I think, but have not date
with me) in 1838, in *Philadelphia*. On this first edition, Poe's name
does not appear. The other papers mentioned in your letter (save
Knickerbocker's Maga.) are not in British Museum. A file of the *Home
Journal* might give some information, but *that* is not in British
Museum—I have looked thro' *tons* of papers for any scrap of
information! I'll write to Mr. Davidson at once. I have had the name of
a New York bookseller given me where I *may* get some of the
publications I named. And now to your letter—Oh! in the first place,
please write to my official address until you hear again. In about a
fortnight I am going to remove my *Lares et Penates*, but will give my
new *locale* as soon as I am settled down. *Nos moutons!* *Harper's* I have
acknowledged receipt of & given you my opinion of—the article is
what its author terms himself "commonplace" & as I have told you [is]
made up of your book, Griswold's "Memoir," & T. Powell's pleasant
biography in his *Living Authors of America.* "The Grecian
Fiddlestick" & the utterly improbable conclusion are original,
apparently. The picture of Fordham, I did not think so bad, but it has
been long known in England, appearing in Hotten's collection (or
rather Selection from) of Poe's works, as does also, if memory fails me
not, the *facsimile* given in *Harper's.* I have seen another *facsimile*—in
Tuckerman's collection of autographs—which gives Poe's signature in
full. I shall try & get *that* copied. I *fancied* that Mrs. Ellet might be the
lady, but saw that she did not come from South Carolina. You may rely
on my delicate manipulation of the story. You speak of copies of other

letters of Poe's—cannot you give me copies of any, or *of paragraphs* like those you gave Mr. Stoddard? If suitable for publication, which I presume they are, having been lent to Mr. Stoddard. Mr. Aldrich is likely to have some sore feelings toward Poe, *vide* plagiarism in Vol. 3 of Poe's works[3]—that letter *re.* Mrs. Helen S[tanard] must have been *very* interesting—cannot any more of it be published? Nearly all Poe's *earlier* versions of his poems mention "Helen." If you could kindly let me have a few lines of "personal reminiscence," I need scarcely remark how valuable they would be, for any quarterly paper, which should be the basis of my biography & contain the germ of it. Poor Mrs. Clemm's evidence is rather shaky, I fear, but I'll see how the date of marriage comes out with other facts. *En passant*, I think I told you that I was authorized to contradict statement of "The Fire Fiend" having been endorsed by Macready's name—it was a *hoax*. The *Broadway* is useful, but, as I can *see* it here, I do not care to trouble you to lend it, but, if you knew of a copy for sale, I'd buy. It is useful thus: to prove Poe's gratitude, *i.e.*, his remarks on Mr. T. White's death; to disprove Griswold's story *re. changeable* criticism on Jones—see Poe's explanation, &c., &c. *Literati*, see my "New Facts No. 2," comparing Griswold's with Godey's publications; libel suit, *see my footnote* to "New Facts." The Lewis family, I must give up. On your advice, I am quite content to let Mr. Davidson act for me with regard to advance sheets, but I must hear what the quarterly people say. Mr. D. is doubtless acquainted with publishing matters. I get, on the average, 8 guineas per sheet of 16 pps. (say 33 or 34 dollars?). I shall be glad to see your other poems—some, I see, were written in conjunction with a sister. "Cinderella" & "Sleeping Beauty," probably? You may be sure that if life, health, & *mind* are spared, an exhaustive biography of E. Poe will be brought out by yours very faithfully,

John H. Ingram

The precious enclosure was safely received; shall be religiously preserved, and returned, as speedily as possible, by *registered* post. I almost wonder that you can let it out of your possession, but, as far as I am concerned, you may rely upon its sanctity.

Yours,
J. H. Ingram

1. Henry Theodore Tuckerman (1813–1871), critic, essayist, poet. Among many books, he published *The Life of John Pendleton Kennedy* (New York: G. P. Putnam & Sons, 1871), which has an account of Kennedy's associations with Poe, pp. 373–77.

2. Ebenezer Burling was a friend and classmate of Poe's who may have accompanied him as far as Norfolk when Poe left John Allan's house in 1827.

3. Poe brought Aldrich's name prominently into his "Mr. Longfellow and Other Plagiarists," *Works*, ed. Griswold, III, 292–354.

16.   Sarah Helen Whitman to John H. Ingram.   Item 126

Dear Mr. Ingram,   March 3, [18]74
   I sent you by Saturday's steamer a letter enclosing two photographs.
I will send the more *direct copy* of which I spoke in the steamer that
sails next Saturday. It will not be ready sooner.
   I have this morning received from Mr. Gill the article from the
Evening Mail containing Mr. Gowans' reminiscences of literary men, &
among others, of Edgar Poe. His testimony is very important in making
up an estimate of Poe's habitual character in private life. I sent it to Mr.
Gill with a request that he would preserve and return it. If he writes
the lecture which he proposes, he will undoubtedly use it, but that
need not prevent you from doing so, if you think it advisable. Keep it
as long as you like, or keep it until I *ask* you for it.[1]
   Thinking that you might like to see the remainder of the article from
which I cut the portion enclosed in my letter, I have sent it with the
printed matter by the same steamer. I hope to hear something about
Graham's Magazine soon. The number containing Lowell's article was
Feb., 1845.
   I have much to say to you, but am suffering from severe pain in my
eyes today. Will write soon.
                                                    S. H. Whitman

   I find among my papers portions of Savage's article in the
Democratic Review. His note to Fuller in relation to my little book, I
have mislaid. I think he said the title page & the genealogical part
were the most significant things in it to him, & he thought somebody
might take it up & make a goodsized, saleable book out of it. I think
Mr. Savage is dead within the last year or two, but I am not sure.[2]
   I wonder if he is the son of the old gentleman with whom I had *a
passage at arms*, as reported in the letter about Dry Facts which I sent
you.
   I fancy he is an Irishman by the manner in which he speaks of poor
Clarence Mangan, whose life was so sad & strange. I see that you, too,
are an admirer of Horne's *Orion*. The history of that neglected volume
shows that popular poetry is popular for something in it that is not
necessarily or essentially *poetry*.
   I am glad that you said good words about *Paracelsus*.[3] I think you & I
have many parallel attractions in literature. It is a genuine bond of
sympathy to like the same books & the same authors—is it not?
                                                    S.H.W.

   1. This paragraph contains the basis for William F. Gill claiming that Ingram had used
materials in his biographies that had been previously assigned to him. When Gill forced
W. J. Widdleton, the New York publisher who had bought the copyright to J. S. Redfield's

edition of Griswold's volumes on Poe, to insert a statement to the effect that Ingram had done so, Ingram angrily replied in a widely published "Disclaimer," Gill with a "Reply," and Ingram again with a "Rejoinder." All of these are ahead.

   2. John Savage lived until 1888.

   3. These references to Horne and Browning raise the possibility that a letter is missing, for in the letters above Ingram has not mentioned *Orion* or *Paracelsus*. Another surmise is that such remarks could have been on a page that she returned to Ingram later in order to prove a point.

17. *Sarah Helen Whitman to John H. Ingram.* *Item 127*

Dear Mr. Ingram,   March 4, 1874
   In writing to you yesterday I neglected among other things to answer your question about my quotations from "Marginalia."
   You say you do not find the passages cited. Perhaps you allude to something I said on the 55th page [of *Edgar Poe and His Critics*] about a *thought* in his notice of *Undine* in note CVI of "Marginalia." See his allusion to Fouqué's "personal opinions on the subject of second marriages,"—to his assumed belief that "the *mere death* of a beloved wife does not imply a separation so final or so complete as to justify an union with another." Note these expressions & the quotation from Fouqué which follows: "The fisherman had loved Undine with exceeding tenderness & it was a doubtful conclusion to his mind that the mere *disappearance* of his beloved child could be properly viewed as her death."
   I find no other allusion to the "Marginalia," unless it be one at the foot of page 70, beginning, "I regard these visions, even as they arise," etc.,—which you will find in note XVI.
   It has been the fashion of late with some of our New England magazines & weekly periodicals to undervalue Poe's critical ability, &, doubtless, his judgments were at times greatly influenced by personal feeling, yet in looking over his notes on books & authors in the "Marginalia" yesterday (not having recurred to them before for many years) I was astonished to perceive in contrast to the usual falsetto blandishments & personal asperities of contemporary criticism, how genuine, racy, & pertinent were all his critical annotations.
   I enclose the *Ultima Thule* photograph.*
   In haste,

                                    Yours most cordially,
                                       S. H. Whitman

*This picture is very valuable—Mr. Coleman himself took the negative from the original daguerre, which is *lost*. He has given away but one copy—years ago, before the art of bringing out the negative had attained its present perfection—& has produced these copies expressly for me. The one I sent you before was *lithographed* from the original daguerre & the copy I sent you was from the lithograph taken in 1857 or 1858.

You can send back *one* of the portraits marked on the back with a pencilled cross—keeping the one you like best. Have you copies of the *Broadway Journal* in the library? If so & there is any copy which you wish particularly to see, I will tear it out & send it, or if the volumes themselves are very important, let me know & I will send them.

S.H.W.

18. *Sarah Helen Whitman to John H. Ingram.* *Item 128*

[*Penciled note in Mrs. Whitman's script:*] Introductory to the letters which you shall see hereafter.

March 6, 1874

In the early summer of 1848 I received through the post a poem in the handwriting of Mr. Poe commencing—"I saw thee once— only once—years ago:" There was no signature to the poem, nor any title.[1] I knew the handwriting, because I had previously received another anonymous offering from him & had been told by a gentleman from New York who was present when I received it that the direction was in Poe's handwriting. Soon after I received the poem, an English lady, Miss Anna Blackwell, who knew Mr. Poe in New York & who had come to spend the summer in Providence, told me that she had recently received a letter from him expressing great interest in me— telling her that he had once seen me, etc., etc. Miss Blackwell did not answer the letter, but gave it to me to do as I liked with it.[2] It was not until August, or late in July, that I heard anything further in relation to him—I mean anything *directly* in relation to him. Mr. Griswold, who was then preparing to bring out his *Female Poets of America*, had visited me to say that he wished to obtain my consent to publish some of my poems. I had not at that time published any collection of poems, but I gave my consent that he should use anything of mine which pleased him.

He spoke of Poe's interest in my writings & said that he [Poe] had been delivering a lecture on the poetesses of America in Lowell, & he thought would visit Providence during the summer.

I asked him how it was that Poe had incurred the enmity of so many of the literary men of New York. He said it certainly was not that he had done anything exceptionably wrong to *deserve* it—that he had *always* said Poe was not so much to blame in his literary embroilments as were his enemies. He seemed to speak with great earnestness. It was not until after Poe's death that I discovered the rancor of his feelings toward him.

Soon after Griswold's visit to Providence, Miss Maria J. McIntosh, the authoress of several popular works published by the Harpers, being on a visit to our city, came to spend an evening with me, &, in the course of conversation, told me that she had recently spent an evening with her friend Mr. Lindsey at Fordham & had had the pleasure of meeting there that wonderful genius Edgar Poe.[3]

I listened with profound interest to all that she said of him, & especially when she told me that on learning she was about to visit Providence, he had spoken of me, of my writings, etc., in terms which gratified & charmed me.

She apparently knew nothing of the poem which he had sent me earlier in the summer, nor did I speak of it to her.

After listening to her report of him, I began to feel that it must seem very ungracious in me to make *no* acknowledgement of the beautiful lines that he had addressed to me, & regarding his interest in me as a purely intellectual one, I wrote six lines, without title or signature, which I directed to him & addressed to *Fordham*.

They reached him at Richmond, Va.

On receiving the lines, which I intended only as a gracious & playful acknowledgment of his beautiful poem, he returned at once to New York & after obtaining a letter of introduction to me from my friend Miss McIntosh, he came to Providence & presented it in person.

The lines which I enclosed to him were the last stanza of a poem called "A Night in August."[4]

Out of this stanza was evolved the poem printed under that title in the *Home Journal*, which after several alterations took the form which you will find in the volume.

You shall hear the result of this visit another time.

S.H.W.

1. Mrs. Whitman had sent this manuscript of Poe's second "To Helen" to Dr. J. R. Buchanan in Louisville, Ky., for a psychometic reading, but he never returned it.

2. Miss Anna Blackwell, an English poet who had boarded with the Poes in 1847 during several weeks of her visit to the United States, wrote Poe ca. May 24, 1848, to ask his help in getting a volume of her poems published in America. He replied to her on June 14, 1848, regretting that he could not help her. When John Ingram wrote to Miss Blackwell in France in early 1877 asking for her reminiscences of Poe, she replied on Feb. 12, 1877, that she had seen Poe but twice and knew nothing of him.

3. Miss Maria J. McIntosh (1803–1878) was a member of the New York literati. It was she who gave Poe the letter of introduction to Mrs. Whitman in 1848.

4. The lines below are the last stanza of Mrs. Whitman's poem "A Night in August," as published in her 1853 volume, *Hours of Life and Other Poems*:

A low, bewildering melody
Seems murmuring in my ear—
Tones such as in the twilight wood,
The aspen thrills to hear,
When Faunus slumbers on the hill,
And all the entrancèd boughs are still.

19. *John H. Ingram to Sarah Helen Whitman*

My dear Mrs. Whitman,   6 March 1874

In the first place, I have not yet received the vol. of poems mentioned in your kind letters of the 19th & 20th of Feb. I shall institute inquiries in the Foreign Dept. of our G.P.O. & let you know the result in this epistle: if the book arrives safely, I will write at once. In future, when I send any valuable enclosure, I shall register it. I need not tell you how precious your letters are to me, but I cannot help feeling that I have been disturbing your repose—perhaps endangering your health & rest by my troubling you. Pray forgive me, and, although *every letter contains something of value* to me, do not let me cause you to risk health, or happiness, in writing so much & upon, doubtless, so agitating a subject. As regards my wretched boyish verses, pray do not trouble with them; if you begin to amend, you'll never cease: I see you correct a grammatical error in "Lauralie," but it is not worth *your* while. I will just trouble you with a short autobiographical reminiscence & then drop that subject. As a child—before I could read—I determined, as I looked at my father's great books & saw how they interested him, to become an author, & by the time I could spell words of one syllable, I began to write, but in prose—one night when I was still a boy, I went into my own room, and for the five-hundredth time, began to read out of Routledge's little vol. of Edgar Poe's poems. Suddenly, something stirred me till I shuddered & quivered with intense excitement. "I felt as if a star had burst within my brain." I fell on my knees and prayed as I only could pray then, and thanked my Creator for having made me a poet! I seized a pencil & wrote a wild lyric, "The Imprisoned Soul." For months after that—amid all the miseries of life—I trod on air. I knew that I was a poet & that recompensed me for all the terrible trials I was then enduring. Day after day I wrote & wrote. At night, I kept lucifers & a candle, pencil and paper by my side, because I continually composed verses & fragments of what I thought *in my sleep*. At last I thought of publishing

John H. Ingram in ca. 1873, age ca. thirty-one. Item 485 in the Ingram Poe Collection. (Courtesy University of Virginia Library.)

these pieces. I began by sending them to our best magazines. To my
horror they were "declined with thanks"! Not daunted, I tried oft &
o'er, but always with the same result. At last a small monthly magazine
was started, for verse only. I sent my latest piece, together with one by
my eldest sister (without her knowledge, though)—she had written
from childhood. The editor wrote accepting my darling sister's poem
("The Lake" it was called; you shall have a copy in my next), but
asking me to send something else because, although my thoughts were
good, my metre was bad. Metre! I had never thought of that! I had
thought poets breathed their poems as flowers did perfume! Rhyme
was always ready, but rhythm & metre I never thought of! I now
knew—so I thought—why my poems came back. To work I went and
counted my syllables on my fingers with the precision of a pendulum.
I sent said editor some pieces which he published (he is now Ed. of
Cassell's Maga.). Thus cheered, I sent to one of the cheap journals—
under a *nom de plume* of "Dalton Stone," rendered necessary by
certain circumstances. The editor (now Ed. of the *Mirror*) pubd. them.
For five years I wrote bushels of verses which were always printed by
the cheap journals—sometimes, two or three complete pieces a day—
"Lauralie" was written in half-an-hour (I remember it well!) & "Hebe"
in less time. *I never corrected a word*, but sent them "with all their
errors thick upon them" to print. For all these verses I never received
a single penny—nor, indeed, for some weird stories which were
published before my 20th year. I selected some of the verses & made
them into a little book—friends took about 100 copies—8 or 9 kind
reviews appeared, & one unfriendly one, for which I wrote a sharp
letter to the Ed.! Some months after I was introduced to him (he is
dead now) but fortunately in my own name, & I had written to him as
"Dalton." Ten years ago & the world's cruelty crushed my heart to
atoms, & in a pathetic "Farewell to Poesy" I parted from the dearest
hope of my life. *That piece* you shall have if I can find a copy. Since
then I have never published any verses save one or two of my boyhood
pieces. An earnest "Recall" was soon after printed in same journal as
the "Farewell." I wrote to its unknown author—an Irishman—we met
subsequently. Soon after he went to America—but I cannot hear of him
now—he married. My darling sister—my only literary friend—I mean
friend with very deepest meaning—died. Do not speak of her to me,
for I cannot bear it, but you will find a few of her pieces in *Flora
Symbolica*. If you like to ever review that commonplace book, do
notice them, but don't say anything in your letters. *Flora Symbolica*
was written some years ago, but published in October, 1869. I am now
31—write much & am paid.[1] But my heart is not in it. My favourite
stories have been lost by a careless publisher, before I could get them

published. There! you know all you can possibly wish to know of me! I'll send a photo as soon as I get some copies from Germany.

And now something more important. First—if you can only get someone to copy such paragraphs of Poe's letters as you do not object to be published—you speak of some shown to Mr. Stoddard, &c. I will pay therefore, as I feel assured 'tis too much for you to write out so much. *Your* reminiscences, if you can write them without wearying your eyes would be valuable. The *Broadway Journal* I have spoken of. Don't talk so sadly of dying—*you must live* till I can cross the Atlantic to see you! Mr. Gill I have written to & asked him to let me have copies of letters &c., and I will forward remittance. I hope he'll reply. If you have a friend in Boston, a personal visit might be better than all the letters. Every scrap of printed matter shall be carefully preserved & I shall be glad to return them, feeling as if I were holding property not my own. Some I must copy, however. Give me your candid opinion about "Isadore": do you think Poe wrote it? I cannot quote it without feeling sure. As regards the "Lenore" poem—I had already quoted it in full in a magazine paper, but will suppress part. *Your* wishes in these subjects are *laws*. I quoted an earlier version, but had to piece it out with the *Southern Lit. Mess.* copy—not having the verse mentioning "Helen." I have early versions of many of the poems—the 1831 collection—that is, copies of them–not the vol. itself. "Poe's morbid love of mystification" I fully recognize. Do you think he really was 17 when he entered Charlottesville? Rules of West Point do not admit cadets after they are 21.

New York *Evening Mail* (10 Dec. 1870), *Home Journal*, &c., I cannot see in London. If I can only obtain your poems, I will review at once, but should prefer not reviewing *E.P. & His Critics* just yet, as I shall extract (with due acknowledgment) its most biographical portions in my Quarterly paper. Some of the separate poems you mention did not come in letter, *i.e.*, "Pansy from the Grave of Keats," "Sleeping Beauty," nor "Cinderella." I did not want any secrecy about the *Temple Bar* paper, only did not want it to appear sooner in U.S. than in England. I was mistaken about Mrs. Ellet; it was not her but someone else I thought of. I shall work out the story of "Conchology" all right. Did you ever hear of Dr. Shelton MacKenzie? I fancy English *by birth*.[2] Allibone's quotes his opinion of Griswold: it is very severe & unfavourable to Griswold. Clarke's address is not in Allibone, I'm nearly sure—merely Philadelphia. I've written to Allibone—was Clarke a publisher? I wrote Mr. J. W. Davidson. I think I had better send him some money to get books & papers with. We are just raising money for E. Poe's sister, who is very badly off. Shall perhaps get a ($1000) thousand dollars. Thanks for speaking of Poe's notes in

Broadway: [*illegible*] is not so good as others though. I don't know whether you have seen any paper of mine. My boyish *nom de plume* "Dalton Stone" was much better known, I fancy, than is my own name—not amongst *literati*, but popularly. Further news for next letter. No news of the book.

Yours every faithfully,
John H. Ingram

1. Ingram here tells the truth about his age. He was born on Nov. 16, 1842, as is attested to by a copy of his birth certificate he supplied to the Civil Service Commission authorities when he received his commission in 1868. Later, after his articles on Poe and his edition of Poe's works made him eligible to be listed in a forerunner of *Who's Who*, he adopted as his birthdate Oct. 7, 1849, which is of course Poe's deathdate. Apparently thinking better of the business, he reverted to Nov. 16, 1849, and that date is still the one listed for him in all reference books and most library card catalogues. See my article "The Birthdate of John Henry Ingram," *Poe Studies*, 7 (June 1974), 24.

2. Dr. R. Shelton Mackenzie was born in Ireland in 1809. He never practiced medicine but became a distinguished author and editor.

20. *Sarah Helen Whitman to John H. Ingram.* Item 129

My dear Mr. Ingram,   March 10, [18]74
    Yesterday morning I received the *Mirror* for February.
    Your article is admirable—*incontrovertible* in most of the points touched upon by you.[1]
    I have only time now to tell you how much I like it & to thank you for your generous ardor in the defense of one who has been so deeply wronged. I have done what I can for the furtherance of your wishes as to *Graham's*, etc. Having entrusted your commissions to Mr. Davidson, I am waiting anxiously for a letter from him. I sent by last Saturday's steamer letters & photographs.
    I think you must have the *autograph letter* I sent you ere this. I hope soon to hear of its due arrival. Let me know as soon as possible if you wish for the *Broadway Journal* & if it should be sent by mail or express.
    In the Providence *Journal* of this morning I find the announcement of an illustrated poem by Mr. Gill, which I enclose.
    I have heard nothing from him by letter since I last wrote you.
    There are one or two trifling mistakes, which I will point out, in your articles. James Russell Lowell is not, I think, *Dr.* Lowell. At least he is not called so here. Mr. Wertenbaker's name is Wertenbaker & not *becker*, although a misprint in the letter—the printed letter—I sent you led you to think so. Mr. Pabodie's name was *Wm.* J. Pabodie. He is mentioned in the Appendix to Griswold's *American Poets*, I think. But these errors are of little consequence.

I enclosed in my last letter a fragment of a letter from Mr. T. C. Latto in relation to the relentless enmity of Briggs & English.[2] The letter was written three years ago, but I presume their hatred still survives. You need not return this or anything I send you without I expressly request its return.

Don't touch upon the private history I gave you of the story about borrowed money, or, if you *do*, do it lightly & vaguely, without introducing names.

Mrs. Botta (Miss Anne C. Lynch) is very much afraid of being compromised socially, & likes to keep the peace with everybody. Mrs. Ellet still lives, & would doubtless be implacable towards anybody who should tell the true story of the affair. I imagine, however, that her interest in the matter, her *interference*, was simply a point of *literary* rivalry, rather than *personal*.[3]

If I copy for you the letters of E.A.P. of which I spoke in my last, you will see in one of them another allusion to this matter.

In the vol. of poems which I sent you there are three sonnets addressed to Mrs. Browning, the 2nd & 3rd of which [contain] allusions to her poem of the "Fugitive Slave," published soon after the passing of the Fugitive Slave Bill in the U.S. Congress in the summer of 1850.

The whole North was roused by the aggressions of the slave-holding power, and it was in allusion to *her* poem & to the passage of this law that the last of the three sonnets was written. The thought in the sonnet is not clearly expressed, as it stands; after the first seven lines, it should read:

> That Gorgon terror chills them into stone,
> Yet, while they prate & patter, thy great heart,
>   Serene in love's own light & woman's ruth—
> Loyal to God & to God's living truth—
>   Hath uttered words whose fulgent rays shall dart
> Like sunbeams through our realm's Tartarean gloom
>   Till love's own holy light its Stygian depth illume.

I like the sonnets so well that I would have them as clear in meaning as I can make them.

And now I must once more thank you & bless you for the words you have spoken—

S. H. Whitman

I send you copies of two printed articles which may interest you through their allusion to names with which you are already acquainted. I will write by Saturday's steamer.

Mr. Poe's article on Wm. Ellery Channing was not less amusing than true.[4] Yet you will see that I can appreciate the poet, while I cannot but laugh with his critic. Poe made a mistake in thinking that the Wm. Ellery of whom he speaks was the *son* of the distinguished clergyman of that name. He was *his nephew*, the son of his *cousin*, the late Dr. Walter Channing of Boston. The poet married the sister of Margaret Fuller, but the marriage was not a happy one & they separated after a few troubled years. He has lately written his recollections of *Thoreau*, with selections from his writings.[5] He once addressed a poem to S.H.W., which is very characteristic.

1. The article referred to is "More New Facts about Edgar Allan Poe," reprinted on pages 47–55.
2. Charles Frederick Briggs (1804–1877) was a journalist and author who had founded the *Broadway Journal* in New York in 1844. After Poe became a partner and for a brief time sole owner and editor of the *Journal*, Briggs, who was a close friend of James Russell Lowell's, joined the ranks of Poe's relentless defamers and enemies.
3. If Mrs. Ellet's interference was not personal at the time of her instigation of the defamation of Poe, it shortly thereafter became intensely so.
4. *Graham's Magazine*, Aug. 1843. See *Works*, ed. Harrison, XI, 174–90.
5. William Ellery Channing, *Thoreau: The Poet Naturalist with Memorial Verses* (Boston: Roberts Brothers, 1873).

21. *John H. Ingram to Sarah Helen Whitman*

My dear Mrs. Whitman,   11 March 1874
   Your last letter [Feb. 19] containing your "Pansy" has come safely to hand but I am dreadfully put out about your book: it has not yet arrived, nor do I think it ever reached England. I have made searching inquiries here—will you kindly do so in America. I am looking forward to a treat, but don't send me reviews of *your* books unless they bear, in any way, upon the subject of Edgar Poe: no reviewer ever affected my mind & I can admire and appreciate you without depriving you of extracts that must be valuable to you; in fact, the miscarriage of your book makes me nervous about anything going wrong. I shall register anything that could not be replaced if lost. There are a great many things of yours in my possession which I will copy (when needed) & return. As regards the "Pansy" which "needs no bush," I am going to be audacious and make a few critical remarks, not as a critic but to show you how I have read it and appreciate its beauty—it is an amaranthine flower & deserves to be a "joy for ever." May I use it in the *Mirror*? If I may dare suggest a change, I would ask why not—in 26th line—have "a fading flush"? The alliterative sound would be improved & would not *flush* be more accordant with "morning gold" than *blush* which is [*illegible*]? *I fancy I should also rather read "The*

silver blaring trumpets blow"—the alliteration is as good, & "snarling" seems scarcely so fit an adjective for the representative of a trumpet's sound. The last line but one—the penultimate—is weakened by the inversion—you know how Poe railed against such forms—and even at the risk of identical rhymes, I almost fancy—unless you find another rhyme such as "nought will sever," which is weak—I should read it "Lives the charmed life that lives for ever, A Beauty and a Joy forever." No! I don't like that—so let it remain a beauty and a joy that ne'er will wane to me.

As you are kind enough to read my boyish lines, I have looked up quite a lot of my verses & will send them by book post. I enclose my "Farewell" & "The Recall," mentioned in my last. Since that was written, I have published a few pieces but they were only those written previously. *Poems by Dalton Stone* was published in 1863, although I suffered the printer to persuade me into putting, or rather, allow him to put [18]64. My friends took somewhere about one hundred copies & a few were sent out for review—one bound & a dozen unbound I kept, & the rest I told the publisher to destroy, not wishing such immature, badly printed, & frequently incorrectly printed verses to get into circulation.

Returning to your letters: I cannot comprehend the behaviour of such men as Messrs. Gill & Stoddard—their negligence appears to me quite criminal. To the former I have written but not to the latter—nor do I think I shall—I am not gratified by his paper. I have written to Messrs. Eveleth, Davidson, President of Peabody Institute, Baltimore, to a friend of Miss Rosalie Poe, to Mr. Allibone (who does not seem too friendly either to Poe or to England), & to others. Mr. Gowans' "Reminiscences" *would be valuable*, but copies of Poe's letters are what I now chiefly want. I daresay some of his letters are in New-York Historical Society's hands. I have asked Mr. Davidson to look them up. As regards Miss Poe, she is very badly off & I am trying to get her a little assistance in England & France. Alfred Tennyson, Swinburne, W. Rossetti, & others have promised me their aid. Her brother's name is a tower of strength in England. You should see the letters I get even about my "New Facts," which were, indeed, *new* in England. The paper in *Temple Bar* does not contain anything new to you but as it may not appear this month—they have so much in hand—I will therefore send you my proofs in a day or two, but you must not let them go out of your hands or be *seen by anyone* who can make use of them until you receive the magazine with my article in, when of course, the more who see it, the better. You will see that said article was written before "New Facts" were known even to me. If there be *anything* you *strongly object* to in *Temple Bar* paper let me know at once, as I might yet be in time to alter again, but it can only be for aught very important.

I must copy a portion of one of Mr. Swinburne, the poet's letters, and ask *your advice* for my reply to any similar question:

Amongst all his poisonous {i.e., Griswold's} assertions there was but one—I hardly like to allude to it—which has always seemed to me, if one were compelled to believe it, inexplicable and intolerable—the rest, even if true, would not be damning accusations, or, however lamentable, beyond all excuse or comprehension of charity: I refer, of course, to the foul allegation of an attempt to extort money from a woman by threats of defamation in return for relief received, which were afterwards retracted under a counter threat of chastisement. Incredible as this vile story is, I have looked eagerly for a full & *unanswerable* refutation of it, point-by-point, which I hope you will be able to give; I do not find it touched upon in your present or first article. . . . I wish, indeed, that poor Baudelaire were alive to see his own instinctive contradiction of Griswold's villainies confirmed by evidence, & to give the help it would have rejoiced him to offer to the poor lady who remains to represent the name which he honoured and made famous throughout France by his own labours. . . . I am writing to Mr. Morris {the poet} & have commended the matter to him as to one of Poe's truest & warmest admirers. . . . With best wishes for your success & sincere congratulations on the good work you have already done for the long & grievously outraged memory of the first true & great genius of America, believe me, yours very truly, {Signed} A. C. Swinburne.

In reply, I protested against acceptance of any tale told by Griswold, but added, *as he might elsewhere hear*, that like many of the doctor's slanders, it might have had a slight basis of rumour to go upon—this being a story well known to American *literati* of Poe's time—but that I could avow thus much, that in it the lady concerned was not a South Carolina lady,* did not lend Poe money, who did not threaten to publish any letters of her, & that altogether there was really nothing dishonorable to Poe in the affair.

Swinburne seems satisfied—have I said too much? Must I retreat into mere generalities? Without your consent not a word further. I have so much to say & ask that cannot be got thro' by correspondence. Oh, "that I had the wings of a dove," to get across the Atlantic & hear all that you would choose to impart. Cannot you get someone to copy such portions of the letters in your hands you will let me have—'tis too trying for you—mark out what I may publish & what's only *entre nous*, but give the dates, if you can. As for the portraits, they will be invaluable. How can I repay you for such kind aid? I am, I fancy, in your pecuinary debt & must forward a remittance. Would I were rich!

---

*Do you know that Mrs. E[llet] (is she alive?) lived several years in S. Carolina?

My portrait may be some time, so in my next, I must send you, *pro tem*, the only copy we have at home & which you should have had already but 'tis disfigured—how & by what sad means you shall someday hear. By the way, in about a fortnight we expect to be in our new home—proper address in my next.

Copy of letter about E.A.P. from his schoolmate Mr. Willis would be valuable: the more witnesses for the defence the better.

With regard to "Resurgemus," I must know the poem before I can say *emus* or *amus*, but I should think the latter not probable. 'Tis third conjugation. I have made up a packet of scraps for you: do not bother to read, or at all events, correct them—they are full of errors—printers' & others. Your poetical "call up him who left half told" in the real state of affairs might be more appropriately said: "Like the story of the Cat & Fiddle, begun & broke (*sic*) off in the middle." I've some better pieces somewhere you shall have. Don't trouble about Griswold's letters. I don't wish to see anything of his—my opinion of poor old Mrs. Clemm or of anyone else not a word of his would alter. I see Allibone gives more pps. of the collected edition of Poe's works than my 4 vols. contain— what year is your edition? Mine is 1863. You may rely upon receiving all my information some day in an exhaustive biography of our hero.

Ever faithfully yours,

J. H. Ingram

22. *John H. Ingram to Sarah Helen Whitman*

My very kind friend,   11 March 1874

Although I have today sent you a long scrawl, I am, perforce, compelled to send you another letter in order to acknowledge the safe arrival of the portraits. I was almost frightened to look at them at first, and now that I have gazed "long and deep," I feel that I must have seen them before! Have either been printed? Perhaps it was in Duyckinck. I refer on Saturday at the Museum. I have not the work in my own library. The portrait, or rather a gross copy of it, of Griswold's 4-vol. collection, appears in Hotten's *Edgar Poe* & Stoddard's portrait is the same as in S. Lowe & Co.'s *Poems of E. Poe*, with the so called "*original* Memoir" written, I fancy, by Briggs of the *Broadway Journal*. I must have both these portraits engraved for *my* biography, as well as the one in Stoddard's. You allow this, I presume.

The *Temple Bar* paper's publication may be some time yet before it appears. I therefore send you the proofs but, as already pointed out, they must not be published in America till they have appeared here, or

Edgar Allan Poe, Sept. 1848. From a daguerreotype taken in Providence, R.I. Mrs. Whitman called this the "Ultima Thule" photograph. (Photograph courtesy Brown University Library.)

till I give the word. This paper was written before I had heard from you, which explains some of its discrepancies. I have marked various parts as follows, please preserve it until you get it again in *Temple Bar* for fear of any accident. 1st query—Mr. Powell, who is (or was) English, although resident in the States, is my authority for the adoption of Rosalie by the Allans. Poe's reminiscences of Mrs. H[elen] S[tanard] would seem to shew that the Allans were not kind. I am not quite certain of Poe's birth date—*now*—even. Born 19th Feb. 1809 as entered by Poe in University matriculation book, but he did not enter West Point Academy until 1 July 1830, the authorities tell me. Now I believe the rules are that no cadets be admitted after they have attained 21. Perhaps Mr. Allan's influence got this point overruled. "Five years residence in England" I am not sure was quite so long, but all these matters of detail, I shall eventually work out with the precision of a mathematical axiom. "Various academies": do you know if Powell is right? The name of *any one* might help me. I would write to Richmond about it. His skill as draughtsman: did you ever see or hear of any drawing of his? I think he knew something of everything. I fancy we must forego "the first honours"—we spell it with the "u." Dr. Maupin does not allude to it. As for St. Petersburg, I do not recollect a single allusion to it in Poe's works, and Mr. Eugene Schuyler, Secretary to your Legation, has kindly had the books and papers of both Legation & Consulate searched without result. The Legation during the whole time "Mr. Middleton was Minister from 1820–30," and the Consulate for 1828–29.

Was Mrs. Allan kind? If Mrs. S[tanard]'s kindness had such effect, Mrs. A[llan] could not have been very demonstrative. I always picture "in my mind's eye" Mr. A[llan] as a rather vulgar, purse-proud despot. I have no authority, therefore, should not say so, but I *do* feel it. Is a child of Mr. Allan alive, I wonder? I can scarcely ask Mrs. Allan anything, I fancy, *even if alive*. See my remarks about Poe's books— Powell is my authority. Do you think it probable? Date of return on visit to Baltimore? Now Poe was dismissed West Point on 6th March 1831, and, according to Powell, was going to help the Poles. I cannot hear of him till autumn of 1833, when he was in Baltimore. Can you give anything between those dates? 'Tis important, because of Griswold's story of the enlistment & desertion. I should like to reduce *that* to an improbability. Refer to Griswold's "Memoir" & see what he says about Poe's editorship of *S. Literary Messenger*. It deceived me (*i.e.*, Griswold's reference). Can't you "shew it up" in Providence *Journal*? He, Griswold, says, "In the next number of the *Messenger* Mr. White announced that Poe was its editor, &c." & then proceeds to *prove Mr. White a liar*.[1] It is a specimen of Griswold's *criminal* carelessness, for, had he gone through the *Messenger* with the slightest care, he would have discovered that it was not Poe who was appointed, but a gentleman who subsequently resigned, and Poe was not appointed until Sept. My notes are in another room. I quote from memory, but I think you will find it was announced as an "Editorial" in Sept. Griswold says at 500 dollars per annum. I have a copy of letter from Poe to Kennedy, saying 520. Griswold never is correct. Mrs. Clemm says (*vide* your letter) that E.P. & V. Clemm were married in 1836, in Richmond. I should like to get the *month*—it might make the letter quoted by Griswold more improbable. "Gold Bug" was published in *Dollar Magazine*, says Allibone—but I am not sure of year yet. Dunn English, I hear is alive & very prosperous. I wonder whether he really wrote "Don't you remember Sweet Alice, Ben Bolt"? See *Broadway Journal* & Poe's defence of English. I have an American song book edited by Howard Paul in which authorship is given elsewhere. That reminds me—there is a pretty poem by Mrs. M. St. Leon Loud. I think there is a sneer at her in the "Eulogium" in *Messenger*. Allibone gives a short notice of her & says "see Poe's autobiography." I know nothing of this autobiography—it may be important. I have written to Allibone & asked him (*En passant*, I always send No. 2 of "New Facts" when I write to Americans). Griswold speaks of Poe's life written by himself for Brooks's *Museum* & quotes a so-called portion of it. Do you know or can you hear of this publication? I can not see it, or hear of it. Fordham cottage, was it little? Duyckinck says it was furnished by means of the damages got from English for the libel. "Reminiscences of Poe" in the *extinct Sixpenny Magazine*—I wrote to Ed. twice & sent stamps for reply, asking author's name, or, if he'd forward letter, but got no reply.[2] This was years ago. Now I would *force* a reply. Do you know the paper at all? 'Tis very interesting & speaks of visits to Fordham & of conversations with Poe. If you don't know it, I'll forward it, but shall want it for *much* use in the life—it appears very friendly. Do you think I am correct about Mrs. Osgood's aid & her sheltering Mrs. Clemm? I fancy 'tis not so. Your letters have not denied it, however. The Lewis family are made the aiders in Griswold, apparently. The *Home Journal* story, I gather from your previous letters, was the Wyatt "Conchology" story. Wyatt published the *Conchology* book with his own name in 1838. Poe's name must have appeared later. Brown's book, says Griswold's note, 1833—but *it* passed through 2 or 3 editions, I think. I am quoting entirely from memory, which is very good, however, on these points. How about the portrait [*illegible*] at the end? Do you object to this? The "Eulogium" copied Griswold without due acknowledgment—that explains that, but if J. M. Daniel wrote it, he did not acknowledge his authorities in full. I must leave that paragraph. You will perceive I had written paper before I learned to know you. In *my* "Life" I shall not only give honour where 'tis due but shall be able to give something very different to this paper in *Temple Bar*. Still you will see *my tone* is faithful to my subject. There! no more tonight—'tis past 12—will send off early tomorrow & with heartfelt thanks for all your kindness, I remain, ever believe me, yours most devotedly,

John H. Ingram

1. Thomas Willis White (1788–1843) was a printer and publisher in Richmond before he founded the *Southern Literary Messenger* in 1834. He apparently recognized his own lack of editorial abilities, for at one time or another he employed or sought editorial advice from James E. Heath, Edward V. Sparhawk, Lucian Minor, Judge Beverley Tucker, and, of course, Poe.

2. Mrs. Mary Gove Nichols published "Reminiscences of Edgar Allan Poe" in the *Sixpenny Magazine*, Feb. 1863. The Union Square Book Shop, New York, reprinted a private edition of 450 copies of her article, with an Introductory Letter by Thomas Ollive Mabbott, in 1931.

23. *Sarah Helen Whitman to John H. Ingram.   Item 131*

My dear Mr. Ingram,   March 13, [18]74
    Your interesting letter of Feb. 27 came this morning, & with it the enclosed pages from Mr. Davidson of March 11th, which will show you the result of our enquiries, after Mr. Clarke up to the present date.

    I send fragments of one or two letters from him [Davidson], written in the early years of my acquaintance with him when he contemplated writing a memoir of Mr. Poe. They are not of much importance, but as they touch upon some things of which we have already spoken, I send them with his letter of March 11th.

    I have been prevented from writing today by unexpected interruptions, but will write by the next mail. I am anxious to hear about Mrs. *St. Leon Loud*, of whom I know only the name as reported in connection with his [Poe's] return from Richmond shortly before his death.

    The story of the *three wives* is quite "a new fact." About as true, probably, is this about Elizabeth Arnold as a widow, which I enclose.[1] I knew from Mr. Poe himself that he allowed the lines to Eliza to be published to F[rances] S[argent] O[sgood]—I think it was at her request, but of this I am not quite sure. They were written to Miss Lizzy White, the daughter of Mr. White, the publisher.

    But I must not say more tonight.
    Yours sincerely and gratefully,

S. H. Whitman

1. Elizabeth Arnold Hopkins was a widow when she married David Poe, Jr., in 1806. She had married Charles Hopkins, an actor, in Baltimore between June 12 and Aug. 11, 1802. Hopkins died on Oct. 26, 1805. See Quinn, p.12. See also p. 466, n.2, this volume.

24.   *Sarah Helen Whitman to John H. Ingram.*   Item 133

My dear Mr. Ingram,   March 16, [18]74
    I acknowledged by Saturday's post your very interesting letter of Feb. 27. Yesterday morning came a note from Mr. Gill, a copy of which I enclose. I fancy he has received a letter from you which has in some way given an impulse to his energies. I have not yet replied to his note. I hardly know what to think of him. I am afraid that his ambition outruns his ability. What do you think?
    I am *so* sorry about the loss of your stories! There can be *no* compensation, no consolation for such things unless, indeed, one can believe (as I devoutly do) that a beneficent destiny shapes our lives to finer issues than we know, & that *all* our losses are gains.
    No, I have not travelled to *Via Mala*—not the *Via Mala* of which you speak (though many another, doubtless, quite as desolate & sombre), nor have I seen the Splügen Pass, nor Italy, nor Eldorado, nor Atlantis, nor the Happy Islands. I am content to see these beautiful things thro' the eyes of poets & prophets—content to remember & to dream.
    And you will send me your photograph. I am so *glad* & *grateful*.
    By this time you have received the *Ultima Thule* picture. I thought it was *good* when I first looked at it—at Coleman's copy, I mean. It recalled to me, then, so vividly the sombre gloom of the *original daguerre*. But as I became more familiar with it, the *memory* of the original faded out of it, & it had an unnatural, *galvanized* look about it. I am sorry I sent you either of the copies from that picture,

> We cannot see thy features right,
> They mix with hollow masks of night.

    I think the one he had taken for me is far better, though neither is capable of suggesting to one who had never seen him the unrivalled beauty & nobility of his face in its serener mood & aspects. Both of those portraits were taken, as you must remember, when he had just been passing through the terrible excitements to which he alluded in the autograph letter I sent you. "The agonies which I have lately endured *have passed my soul through fire.*"
    The photograph taken for me was taken on the 13th or 14th of November, just as he was about to leave Providence after his third visit to the city. During this visit he had sought to persuade me, as he did in

Edgar Allan Poe, Nov. 13 or 14, 1848. From a daguerreotype taken in Providence, R.I., at Mrs. Whitman's request. (Photograph courtesy Brown University Library.)

all his letters, that his happiness & welfare in time & in eternity depended upon me, & after many sad & stormy experiences he had won from me a promise that nothing should cause me to break my plighted troth to him but his own infirmity of purpose. Just before we parted he had said something to me about Arcturus which I promised to remember in looking at it.

An hour or two after he had left the city certain representations were made to my family in relation to the imprudence of the conditional engagement subsisting between us which augmented almost to phrenzy my mother's opposition to the relation. During the painful scenes which followed, I chanced to look toward the western horizon & saw there *Arcturus* shining resplendently through a rift in the clouds, while *Ophiuchus*, or a star which I believed to be Ophiuchus, in the head of "the serpent," was faintly glimmering through the gathering darkness with a pale & sickly lustre.

To my excited imagination everything at that time seemed a portent or an omen. I had been subjected to terrible mental conflicts & was but imperfectly recovered from a painful & enervating illness.

That night, an hour after midnight, I wrote under a strange accession of prophetic exaltation the lines "To Arcturus," beginning "star of resplendent front." The words from Virgil "*Nec morti esse locum*," etc. were prefixed to them, through why I should *then* have thought them appropriate I cannot tell. I only remember that as I repeated the Latin words they had a sound so majestic, so exultant, so full of solemn & triumphant augury that the remembrance of it, even now, fills me with a mysterious joy. You will better understand through this account the references in the *autograph letter* of E.A.P. the 13th of November. This puzzled me very much for a time when I recollected that I had discovered soon after the lines were written that Arcturus & *Ophiuchus* must have been below the horizon when I thought I saw them thro' the western clouds & that it must have been some other stars that I mistook for them.

When the poem was printed in my volume of poems it was therefore dated as if written in *October*. But I forget that you have not yet seen the poem.

I will send you some little things of *myself* soon.

Faithfully your friend,
S. H. Whitman

I was greatly perplexed to know whether you wished your 2nd no. of "New Facts" to be circulated in the papers or whether the danger of their being *appropriated* by others would interfere with such a wish.

I wish that I had some literary friend at hand who could advise one how to forward best your purposes. I am afraid that Davidson is very busy. He lost nearly everything in the War of the Rebellion, & is, I fear, not "in funds." I have not heard from him since I sent him a copy of your paper.

I have found that an oval about the size of the one I enclose may be placed over the photograph of Poe, the one taken for *me*, & greatly improve it. The lower curve of the oval should go just below the *shadow* of the shirt bosom & just above the buttonhole of the coat. The photo might be placed on a larger card & an oval of the size or a little larger than the one I enclose placed over it.

I will send you something finished in this way soon. This picture of mine has been hidden away all these years because I thought it did not represent him truly, but many persons who have seen it lately think it has the best expression of any picture yet taken of him.

I sent notices of my poems from *Putnam's* & from the *Tribune* & a copy in a Newport paper of Poe's comparative estimate of three New England poets—Mrs. Osgood, Miss Lynch, & S.H.W. Were they sent between the pages of the book & lost with it, I wonder, or did you receive them?

I feel sure that "Isadore" was not Poe's. Others may not know this & I shall say nothing to anyone but you. It was very like him.

25. *John H. Ingram to Sarah Helen Whitman*

Howard House,
Stoke Newington Green
16 March 1874

My dear Mrs. Whitman,

I am going to commence another letter to you today, although I may not finish it for another day or so, being so busy preparing to move into the above *new* residence—or rather, I should say *old*—the house being, I fancy, quite two hundred years old, and having room in its many ingles & angles for a whole regiment of ghosts.

To my everlasting questioning, however. You give me Poe's birth date as 17 Feby. 1809: in my last, I pointed out that this would bring his age higher than the maximum allowed by West Point Academy—it also throws out other dates—as for instance if he returned from his English schooling in 1823, it would make his age 13 and alter the date of his tuition at the Richmond Academy—when he first met Mrs. Helen S[tanard]. By the way, although the version of "Lenore" printed in *S.L. Messenger* in 1835 mentions the name of Helen—as "Helen, thy soul is riven," an earlier version, that of the vol. of poems published in 1831, omits the name, reading "Thy life & love are riven." Now it is a question whether the earlier vols. of 1827 & [18]29 read it

thus. 1827, I rather fancy, is merely an imaginary volume. Have you
ever seen it, or know any one who has? On page 70 of *E. Poe & His
Critics* you give an interesting "pencilled note" referring to "later
poems"—do you refer to any particular poems or the whole collection?

You must not think I trouble you needlessly about dates, &c. Every
question has a bearing on some point or the other, although I do not
explain each one more fully. I must be particular about my dates—in
fact—work them all out with mathematical precision, otherwise, every
critic who can detect the slightest act of omission or commission on my
part will have the whole reputation of my purposed work at his mercy.
Almost every publication I have asked to buy is merely for verification
of dates, & if I can get these dates without buying the books, so much
the better—although there are still a few I would like to purchase,
such as the early editions of the poems, &c. Perhaps you can see in
your institutions *Graham's* & *Burton's Gentleman's* magazines. The
former—I want date of first number & the date of Poe's leaving,
probably at end of 1842—& of the second—date of Poe's leaving, if he
did leave before the amalgamation in Nov. 1840 with Graham's *Casket*.
1st no. of *Graham's*, in Nov. 1840 (?) would probably mention Poe.
None of these publications, unfortunately, in the British Museum. If
they could be got at, I might settle the story of Burton & the *Penn
Magazine* recorded in Griswold's "Memoir." I wish I could ascertain
whether Poe published a vol. of "Marginalia" during his life. It is not
mentioned in any list of American publications, but in the 3rd vol. of
Griswold's collection Poe is frequently made to refer to it as if it were a
published book. You sometimes speak of publications, not mentioned
in Griswold, for which Poe wrote. I should like to get the names of
said publications & particulars of what he did for them. Reviews,
editing, or what? What did he write for the *American Metropolitan*, for
instance? Mr. Gowans' "Recollections" I *must* get—they will fill a gap
in the life. Do you know what Miss Royster's (*i.e.*, Mrs. Shelton's)
Christian name was? May I make use of Mrs. Ritchie's information?
Do you know anything of Dr. Shelton Mackenzie, whose unfavourable
opinion of Griswold is given in Allibone? W. R. Wallace's *Literary
Criticisms* may be in your institution—he speaks of Poe, and probably
favorably, as Poe spoke highly of him in the "Literati." When did Mr.
Pabodie first make Poe's acquaintance? Is he alive & if so, could and
would he give a few words of reminiscence? You, I rely upon to do so
for the book. I shall try & submit proof sheets to you when I go to
print. Do you know Baudelaire's exalted critiques on Poe?
B[audelaire] spent several years of his life in making Poe's works
known in France. Do you know anything of Mrs. M. St. Leon Loud
(née Barstow) or of her connection with Poe? In *E.P. & His Critics* you
quote a notice of Willis on the illustrated poems of Poe. I do not know

it. The *Home Journal* I cannot get here—does the notice give any
reminiscence or allusion to Poe's life? Amongst your letters I see you
had one alluding to the English libel suit. I should be thankful for
copies of any parts you would allow me to see, but would not ask you
to send me the originals, after the unaccountable non-arrival of your
much-looked-for book. I shall not send anything valuable without
registering. Can you think of anyone likely to have letters from Poe
from whom I might ask for copies? I live in hopes of getting much from
the South shortly. I shall be anxious to hear from Mr. Clarke. I fancy he
knows more & can give more information about Poe's early & middle
period of life than anyone. If he has sold his facts to Mr. Gill, I should
think that gentleman would dispose of copies to me. I don't want
originals & should not interfere with his elocutionary projects. He
appears to me, from your letters, well meaning, but careless thro' press
of other matters. Is not that your opinion? As for Mr. Stoddard, I think
his paper as bad almost as Griswold's "Memoir." On rereading your
first letter, I perceived that only Mr. Pabodie's first letter was printed:
you will see that I was careful in my "New Facts" No. 2 not to commit
myself. What do you think of "New Facts"? Every letter I write to
America I send a copy with it. You I have sent three. In a subscription
I am trying to raise for Miss R. M. Poe, I have found "New Facts"
useful because they are quite *new* in England. I have sent away some
dozen of them already.

My dear Mrs. Whitman,
     Yours of the 3rd Instant just arrived with the cuttings—some of
which seem very useful. Mr. Gowans' are good, but not so valuable as
those recorded in Mr. Latto's letter, but each separate paper of real
personal evidence shall be made use of. The paper on Willis in the
Northern Monthly, Jany. 1868, is very good for our purpose. Can you
not give me the writer's name?[1] It would be invaluable: he styles
himself a publisher, & as having given a gold medal prize for a poem
in 1826! Is he alive, think you? He says Poe was associated with him in
the editorial conduct of a paper *previous* to his introduction to Messrs.
Morris & Willis—that is to say before 1845. Then, as you have deeply
scored, he adds, "I published a life of Mr. Poe, with a portrait from a
daguerreotype," &c. This is most important. The author's name would
be a clue to get the book, in all probability, & then what evidence may
await us! I will try & ascertain if the *Northern Monthly* is alive & write
its editor for name of author of this paper on Willis—& may I trouble
you to do your best for me? I am ashamed of throwing so much on you,
but hope to repay your labours by the production of such a life of our
hero as *even you shall* be satisfied with. Poe's fame is yearly
increasing, whilst that of nearly all his contemporaries in the States is

gradually fading. In a century, it requires no prophet to foretell, whilst Edgar Poe's name & fame will have made him a star of the first magnitude, the other writers of his generation will have gone down below the horizon. I do not mean that Bryant, Longfellow, Emerson, *Hawthorne*, & one or two others will not be remembered but, save the last, they will be emphatically *of the past*. This is not my own sole opinion, but the prevalent idea of "the coming men."

As for Horne's "Orion"—whose *farthing* (½ cent?) edition of the poem I have—his epic is slowly regaining its forgotten fame—its author is again in England & recently republished "Orion" at—fancy—three dollars. I was writing to him a day or two ago at the suggestion of Mr. Swinburne, who alluded to Poe's eulogy on the poem, to ask him to help me on behalf of Miss Poe. How the whirligig of time veers round!

En passant, Mr. Gowans' reminiscences include a few lines on Howard Payne, of whom I mean to write a short sketch some day to vindicate his claim to "Home Sweet Home," but *he* was not much as a poet & must wait.

As to Mr. Savage's paper in the *Democratic*: he must be an Irishman—there is no doubt of that. There are just a few scraps of information, but only a few, not in Griswold & those are the same as some of Thomas Powell's life in *The Living Authors of America*.

Do you know anything of Mangan's writings? Mr. Savage repeats his countryman Mitchell's absurd theory that Mangan was as good a poet as Poe. I need scarcely say that that is utterly absurd. Not one literary man in a thousand, in England, knows Mangan's name, and, need I remark, no amount of literary prejudice would create that amount of ignorance if the poems, after having appeared in widely circulated publications, as Mangan's have, were valuable. My acquaintance with the poetic literature of Europe is most extensive &, therefore, I have read the works of James Clarence Mangan, published with "Memoir" in New York; & his *Anthologia Germania*, published in Ireland; & his *Poets of Munster*, & some few stray pieces not included in the above.[2] About three months ago I wrote a sketch of Mangan's life, including one or two of the best peoms I could find of his. I offered it to *Temple Bar*, but they said they did not think the subject suitable, & they accepted my paper on Edgar Poe before it was written! Of course that does not prove anything. Publishers & their *advisers* are often bad judges, but in this case I think they would have the true connoisseurs with them. As for Poe copying Mangan's *style* of poetry, does bright Hesperus extract its silver beams from a gasjet? What I have said proves that Mangan's style *is not* "well known in the British Isles." I have utterly failed to discover in all our English publications more than two allusions to him; one, a very severe notice of his *German*

Anthology, when it appeared, & a reprinted poem in Carpenter's *Penny Readings*, in the usual short biographical sketch appended to which it is stated that Mangan is alive & holds a government appointment in Newcastle! So much for the poor fellow's fame! He died in 1849 & never was in England. I have spoken to several well-educated Irishmen about him & they have never heard of him & will have that I must mean Dr. Wm. Maginn, a much more talented man.[3] See Dr. Shelton Mackenzie's sketch of *him*, reviewed in *Knickerbocker* for 1857. When I publish my sketch of Mangan you shall see it. But there, enough of that! I do get annoyed that literary men will talk such humbug!

To return to Mr. Savage's paper: he states that Poe wrote a work on "Phases of American Literature." Have you ever heard of it? I have not. Mr. M. A. Daly is his authority. Do you know anything of that Irish-named gentleman? What could have become of Poe's MSS.? He must have left a large quantity. Mrs. Clemm probably had them but must have disposed of them to some one. Oh, if Poe had only left a child to defend his fame & preserve his writings! Were I not stuck like a limpet on "our old home," I should have visited America long ere this, *chiefly* to gain all the information I could about Poe & his works but for the fist of Fate. My annual leave of absence cannot be expanded into more than five weeks, but I hope in course of a year or so to get some chance of visiting you. Meanwhile, my book shall appear & if anything valuable "turns up" subsequently I can use it in a later edition.

For the present, then my dear Mrs. Whitman, gratefully & faithfully, I am yours,

John H. Ingram

P.S. Can you give me any idea of the charge for a few advertisements in good, well-circulated American papers for information & copies of Poe's letters? You doubt Mr. Gowans' remark about Poe being engaged on *A. G. Pym* at the time he knew Poe. Have you any reason for so doing? A portion of it appeared in *S. Lit. Messenger* in Jany. & Feby. 1837. Early in 1838 Poe was in New York & in June (?) 1838 Harper's published the complete work. Who did write that paper on Willis? I *must* learn. The medical extract you include must be the one which my doctor told me a few days ago first introduced the name of Poe to him! About *Graham's Magazine*—have told you in this letter the dates of most importance, but it will be useful if it can be shewn that the 4-vol. edition with notice of Poe by Lowell contained any *really important* "alterations & omissions," or, indeed, any great deviations, either in story of life, or estimate of genius to the paper in *Graham's* of Feby. 1845. In the spring of 1843 Poe obtained the 100 dollar prize for "The Gold Bug," given by the *Dollar Magazine*. Do you know anything of that publication, or where it appeared?[4]

I throw out all these hints, as perhaps one may give a clue to you to something new. My skeleton framework of a memoir is gradually filling in. "The Mystery of Marie Rogêt" was published in November 1842. Was it in *Graham's*?[5] If so, *another* disproof of Griswold is made. Oh, for Mr. Graham's letter! So often spoken of. Mr. G. R. Graham—*entre nous*—went to the bad & died of destitution.[6] "The Purloined Letter" followed soon after—was that in *Graham's*![7] Did you know the *Columbian Magazine*? *Previous* to Nov. 1845 "Mesmeric Revelation" appeared in that.[8] Do you think Mr. Stoddard correct in saying that Poe only got ten dollars for "The Raven"?! Is the Life alluded to by writer on Willis the "autobiography" mentioned by Allibone & spoken of by Griswold? I fancy it may be.

I greatly fear your sight has suffered through writing so much lately; if it be so, at all risks discontinue for a time, although by so doing you deprive me of so much pleasure, as well as valuable information. Perhaps you can get some young friend to help you. I am grieved at the non-arrival of your poems. Poe's autograph letter shall be registered when returned—for goodness sake do not trust another to the mercies of the post, but only send copies. Yours ever,

J. H. Ingram

I am going over some old Baltimore papers in hopes of proving date of Poe's birth, but fear *that* is lost labour.

1. "The Late N. P. Willis, and Literary Men Forty Years Ago," *Northern Monthly Magazine*, 2 (Jan. 1868), 234–42. Item 544 in the Ingram Poe Collection. The author of this article quotes from Willis' writings sentences that reveal his working relationship with and his respect for Poe. In letters ahead Ingram will write that he believes the author to be Thomas C. Clarke, a statement disputed by the late Professor T. O. Mabbott who, in 1965, filed a letter with this item in the Ingram Poe Collection, stating his belief that Ingram and Miller were both wrong, that Maj. Mordacai M. Noah (1785–1851) was the author. Professor Mabbott did not, however, attempt to account for the fact that seventeen years passed after the Major Noah's death before this article was published. Perhaps, too, he forgot that my job in preparing the bibliographical calendar of the Ingram Poe Collection was to report the materials in the collection.

2. James Clarence Mangan (1803–1849), *The Works of . . .* Biographical Introduction by John Mitchell (New York: P. M. Haverty, 1859); *Anthologia Germania* (Dublin: W. Curry, Jr. & Co., 1845); *The Poets and Poetry of Munster* (Dublin: J. O'Daly, 1849).

3. Dr. William Maginn (1793–1842), poet, journalist, founder in 1830 of *Fraser's Magazine*.

4. The *Dollar Magazine* was published in New York, with N. P. Willis as one of the editors, from Jan. 1841 to Dec. 1842.

5. Poe's "Mystery of Marie Rogêt" was first printed in *Snowden's Ladies' Companion*, Nov. and Dec. 1842, Feb. 1843.

6. George Rex Graham (1813–1894) was editor, publisher, and owner of *Graham's Magazine* in Philadelphia. He was Poe's employer and longtime good friend during Poe's lifetime; after Poe's death he published in his magazine, Mar. 1850, a long letter to N. P. Willis in defense of Poe. In the letters ahead Ingram and Mrs. Whitman will refer

many times to Graham's death; as they were writing, Graham had nearly twenty more years to live.

7. "The Purloined Letter" appeared first in *The Gift* for 1845.

8. "Mesmeric Revelation" had appeared in the *Columbian: Household Monthly*, Aug. 1844.

26. *Sarah Helen Whitman to John H. Ingram. Item 134*

My dear Mr. Ingram,   March 17, [18]74
    I send you this note—this fragment of a note [from Poe's letter of Nov. 14, 1848], written at an epoch memorable alike to both of us, because it shows the conflict of his tortured spirit with the relentless doom that awaited it—and because I *know* that it cannot but awaken in a heart like *yours* the tenderest & most compassionate sympathy.

    The next time I write I will try to tell you something of the letters, etc. which followed that first visit to Providence in Sept.

    There is so much that is strange & almost incredible in our brief acquaintance that it must seem to one not acquainted with the private history of this epoch of his life apocryphal. It is for your *private* satisfaction that I shall write it.

                                                            S.H.W.

27. *John H. Ingram to Sarah Helen Whitman*

                                                    Howard House
                                                    Stoke Newington Green
My dear Mrs. Whitman,   19 March 1874
    Above will be my address in future: we remove on Saturday next. I have received yours of the 4th Instant, containing 2 more photos of Edgar Poe, and herewith return the marked one as desired. Two of the others I hope I may retain altogether & one other for the present. Two of these I hope to get properly & artistically engraved. I am now negotiating with one of our very first publishing firms for a complete edition of the entire works of Edgar Poe in about 6 library volumes, *with* "Memoir" by self. This, mind, is strictly *entre nous*. There is little doubt that if this edition be brought out, & I foresee no impediment, it will become the standard edition & its life, the standard biography of Poe. Meanwhile, I have arranged with the *New Quarterly Magazine* for a life of Poe, to run to about 30 pps. to appear in July number. The simultaneous publication in an American publication will be neither

necessary nor permitted, as editor informs me that he is gradually obtaining a good circulation there.

On 21st Ultimo I sent you No. 2 of "New Facts," since then, have sent you two more copies. Many thousands have circulated in England & will help to pave the way for a new estimate of the poet's character.

I must devote another letter to my opinions about the photos, when I get settled down in my new abode. I have sent you the injured photo of myself, but I fear it is too mutilated for you to get a fair idea of your correspondent from. I hope to get some new copies from Germany soon.

En passant, do not believe what you hear of Swinburne. You know how things are falsified.

As regards the *Broadway Journal*, do not think of sending that or any portion of it, as I can see it at the [British]Museum—the first few nos. are missing—& will have copied the things I require. Many thanks for the sheet of "Autography"—2 papers of which appeared in *S.L. Messenger*, & the remainder, I believe, in *Graham's Magazine*. The *Illustrated News* (of New York) for 1853 is not in the Museum. I must try & get the rest of the papers on "Autography" to reprint in the complete edition—every scrap I can obtain of Poe's writings must be included.

ᴊ shall be anxious to hear from the South, where I have written to several people. You shall learn the results. More information as to Poe's earlier years will be acceptable. Your reminiscences in your last letter are most interesting, but break off at a most exciting moment. You do not say whether I may use these reminiscences—doubtless you rely upon my good taste to manipulate all this material with delicacy & tact—is it not so?

Do not trust any more original papers of Poe's to the mercies of the post. I am so anxious about your vol. of poems which has not yet been heard of—several poems also which you say you have sent have not arrived—were they in the vol.? "Cinderella" & "The Sleeping Beauty" &c.

That Dunn English, I hear, is a somebody in the States. I am surprised, however, Mr. Latto could not tackle him. It does not matter! When all *that* small fry has been forgotten for ages the bright star of Poe's fame will be a Pharos in the history of literature.

I am sorry you have taken such trouble about the "Marginalia." What I alluded to was on the page 9 (?) of quotations, "With these keys we may partially unlock the mystery." That is what I could not recollect the place of, or having read. The "Undine" note I well know, as my darling sister had pointed it out as an illustration of the theory which *she first* propounded to me, of Poe's dread of remarriage. You may imagine its double interest to me. I am very fond of the "Marginalia," and fancy they display Poe's mind better than much of his other writings. In my complete life of him, you will find that I shall quote from them largely.

As regards the opinions of those magazines, you cannot be swayed by them.

I shall break off now & remain in hopes of soon getting copies, or extracts from others of Poe's letters, & hoping & *believing* that I shall ever retain your sympathy & good will, I am, & ever shall be, believe me, most faithfully yours,

John H. Ingram

P.S. Let me know what you think of the *Temple Bar* paper.

Since reading your "Pansy" I see Keats was the author of the "snarling," but that, of course, does not alter *my* opinion.

P.S. I send you the only portrait left on condition that when I get some from Germany you get a perfect copy—& now send me your own—as you are & not as you were in the enchanted garden.

About the portraits of Poe, I must write more fully another time. I have not realized the possession of them yet. I have waited a reply from *Quarterly re.* taking facsimile, but if do not hear in day or so will get it done myself, so as to return letter quickly. May I use in "Life" the portion criticising "To Arcturus"? Oh, that I could talk to you! Three weeks each time for an answer. Never mind—be assured I shall accomplish my book & as you would like to see it done.

28. *Sarah Helen Whitman to John H. Ingram.* Item 135

My dear Mr. Ingram, March 20, [18]74

Your letter of March 2 reached me last evening, that of March 6 this morning. I have *so* much to say, but must, in order to avail myself of tomorrow's steamer, write *very* briefly. What you tell me of your mental history in the last thrilled me with strange sympathy. I had suspected, nay, I had felt *assured* that you had passed through some such experience. But I must not dwell on this now. I have many questions to answer & many things to say. I am not sorry that the book was lost, since I should be sorry to have you review it without suggesting some changes in relation to several things; I *am* sorry on one account. It makes me apprehensive about sending *other* books. But for this, I would send you *tonight* the [two volumes of the] *Broadway Journal*, which you can keep till I ask you for them, which will not probably be before the opening of "the seventh seal." I wish to consult with some friends about the safest way of sending them.

I did not mean to speak "sadly" of the great event of death. To me it is the culminating hour of life—the hour of triumph & enfranchisement. It *may* not be so near as I imagine, for I am always flattering myself that it is at hand, & yet I have stayed *so long* & know that it has all been *well*.

You ask about Tuckerman. He died not long ago. I was invited to meet him one evening some ten or twelve years ago at Mrs. Botta's. I *liked* him, but we did not speak of E.P. I have not seen his book on Kennedy, but will try to get it.

I intended to have copied for you the letter speaking of Mrs. H[elen] S[tanard]. It was a mere allusion. The letter contained no matter for the biographer, but, as a psychological relic—as a revelation of the poet's tender heart & impassioned soul—it is, to the poet & the man of genius, a rare & priceless record. I am sure *you* will regard it as such. Yet it has nothing, I imagine, that can be revealed to the public. Perhaps the *next* letter, which I will send with it, or soon *after*, may have a *few passages of publishable matter*. About the autograph letter which I sent you. I hope you will not think from the erased words, which I have supplied in pencil, that my family were harsh or ungracious to him. They were, *at times*, even ready to place implicit trust in his power to retrieve his destiny. *No* person could be long near him in his healthier moods, without loving him & putting faith in the sweetness & goodness of his nature & feeling that he had a reserved power of self-control that needed only favoring circumstances to bring his fine qualities of heart & mind into perfect equipoise. But after seeing the morbid sensitiveness of his nature & finding how slight a wound could disturb his serenity, how trivial a disappointment could unbalance his whole being, no one could feel assured of his perseverance in the thorny paths of self-denial & endurance. My mother did say more than once in his presence that my death would not be regarded by her so great an evil as my marriage under circumstances of such ominous import. For myself, I had *no* thought but for *his* happiness & for my *mother's*. I had a firm conviction that we should soon be separated by death, & that it was *my* death & not *his* that was to part us. I had *no* fears about the results of such an imprudent union, because I believed that its earthly tenure would be of very brief duration.

I allowed Stoddard to see this letter, partly to show him that I had not spoken unadvisedly in what I said of H[elen] S[tanard], & partly because my last hope of seeing some competent writer speak in defense of Edgar Poe was that S[toddard] might at some future day write out a fuller & more truthful life of him than had yet been attempted. I thought that the perusal of these letters, which he assured me should not be shown to others, would awaken a chord of sympathy in his heart for the writer & show him that he was utterly incapable of the brutality & coarseness which G[riswold] had ascribed to him.

I send with this hurried letter a German sketch of Poe, with a translation of "The Raven."[1] It has Poe's autograph & a crude copy of Sartain's mezzotint from Osgood's portrait. I have the original of this mezzotint in the two vols. of prose & poetry published by Redfield in 1850. If you have not got it & would like to see it, I will cut it out of my copy & send it to you.

S.H.W.

I seem, now, distinctly to remember having asked Edgar about "Isadore," believing it to have been his. I cannot remember his answer, but if he had said that it *was* his, I could never have forgotten it, & he would most certainly have subscribed it with the "P," as in the other cases [in the two volumes of the *Broadway Journal*].

What a singular case that was about a claim to the authorship of one of Hood's poems in *Temple Bar* some time ago. What do you think about it?

1. This translation was very likely "Der Rabe," by Carl Theodor Eben, published in Philadelphia in 1869. Ingram reproduced it in his edition of *The Raven*, pp. 59–65.

29.   *Sarah Helen Whitman to John H. Ingram.   Item 136*

My dear Mr. Ingram,   March 23, [18]74
I acknowledged your deeply interesting letter of March 6th by Saturday's steamer. Before I speak further of its contents, I will copy for you the letter containing the allusion to Mrs. H[elen] S[tanard]—I mean that I will copy from it such passages as I can find *time* to copy today. You shall at some future day see the whole letter. I dare not yet trust it to the uncertainty & risks of an ocean steamer. When I sent it to Stoddard, it was entrusted to the care of an intimate personal friend—a friend of mine & of Stoddard's who was responsible for its safe return to me through his own hands.[1] You will not find in it (as I told you before) anything that can be used to quote from. At least not during my life, but you will find in this & the other letters of which I spoke indications of character which will enable you to understand, as nothing else could do, the singular & complex elements of his nature— the intense superstition; the haunting dread of evil; the tender, remorseful love; the prophetic imagination, now proud & exultant, now melancholy & ominous; the keen susceptibility to blame; the sorrowful & indignant protest against injustice [and] reproach.

Notwithstanding its poetic exaltation of feeling in the pure passion of its eloquence, its simplicity & its directness, the enclosed letter cannot fail, I think, to command the sympathy of every unprejudiced reader.

You will see that during his first visit to me in Sept. 1848, he had avowed a love for me to which for many reasons I dared not respond.

In bidding him farewell, I promised to write to him & explain to him many things which I could not impart to him in conversation. This first letter of his is in answer to the one he received from me. By the next steamer I may be able to send you something which you *can* use, if you think it expedient to do so.

I have written a somewhat peremptory letter to Mr. Gill, & hope to get from him in a day or two copies of the letters of Mr. Wertenbaker & Dr. Maupin, & the address of Mr. Clarke. He is very careless of these papers, of which I long ago requested a copy. Yesterday I had a note from him asking me if I could tell him *where* Mrs. Osgood's reminiscences of Poe were to be found! He cannot have read Griswold's "Memoir," yet is writing a *refutation* of all his calumnies! I am at a loss what to make of him. I am afraid if he gets hold of your last paper in the *Mirror*, he will adopt it without crediting you as his authority. But perhaps I do him an injustice in this.

This must suffice for tonight. There were only a few words more, & I am *very* tired. Keep this, but hold it sacred, for his sake & for mine.

I know that *you* will not say of it—that it is "curious, very curious indeed [as Stoddard did]."

S.H.W.

1. This friend was William Whitman Bailey (1843–1914), assistant librarian in the Providence Athenaeum Library, later a professor in Brown University.

30. John H. Ingram to Sarah Helen Whitman

My dear Mrs. Whitman,   24 March 1874

I am glad you like the "New Facts," as it was *made up* under pressure of events not likely to admit of much literary excellence. Thinking the paper I had originally written for the *Mirror* too *closely* trenched upon *Temple Bar* article, I had it back & cut out & put in, some parts as I deemed requisite—then I had the good fortune to obtain the correspondence of S.H.W.! Again, I had the paper home & again went to work with the scissors—by this time, I saw the whole thing required rewriting, but before I could commence an imperative demand for its return came from Ed. of the *Mirror* & it had to appear with all its "errors thick upon it." Those errors are more than you point out. To one of yours, however, I must plead not guilty—J. R. Lowell, is,

I have seen it authoritatively stated, "Dr." I will look out my authority. So little is the fact known, however, that the *Mirror* called him "Mr." in either the same, or next number. Mr. Wertenbaker's name was spelt correctly in my MS. & proof, from your letter, but in my hurry of correcting proof, I inadvertently altered it. Mr. Pabodie's name, &c. I copied, & I fancy *verbatim*, from the *Tribune*. All these matters of detail, *which it is important should be accurate*, will be very carefully looked after in my "Life of E.A.P." I have sent you my proof of *Temple Bar* article & hope you will like it, but since it was written *your kindly aid* & my own discoveries have let in a flood of light on the subject.

I have engaged to write a "Life of Poe"—to extend to 30 pps. or so— for the *New Quarterly Magazine*: copy to be ready by end of April for publication in July next. This *on dit* had better be *sub rosa*. Besides this, I am in treaty with one of our best publishing firms for the publication of Poe's complete works in so many (4 to 6) vols. with "Memoir" prefixed, portraits, &c. The "Memoir" to extend to about 150 pps. If this treaty be only carried out you may expect, *this year*, to see a *standard* life & collection of Poe's works. But I must ask you to keep this treaty quite secret for the present. Publishers are slippery people, & these negotiations *may* fall through; if not, you shall learn the result immediately it is arrived at. To induce them to close I have written today offering to accept £25 (or say 100 dollars) *less than they offer* for first edition & *if that does not sell out, to forego all remuneration*. The collection is not proposed to be quite complete. To bring it within due compass, a large portion of Vol. 3 must be omitted, & some portions, I fear, of Vol. 4. The "Literati" includes few names known to English readers, save one or two like myself, who study *American* literature closely, & may nearly all be left out, in the circumstances. There are a few things in Vol. 4 which, even you, I fancy, can relinquish without regret.

You will have received my acknowledgment of the autograph letter long before this. I wish I could notify arrival of your anxiously expected vol. of poems. Thanks for the cuttings—they are interesting to me & will be carefully preserved & some day, all carefully returned. In one of my letters I have asked you not to send any more notices of *E.P. & His Critics* unless they throw additional light upon the subject of our researches. You will not misunderstand me—what I meant was, no review whatever will affect my favorable opinion, one way or another, of the beautiful little work.

If copies of the papers on cryptology, ciphers, &c. which appeared in *Graham's* could be obtained, I might get them inserted in the collection, but the papers on "Autography," I fear, must be omitted. If you can kindly let me have copies of letters, or portions thereof, written by Poe, I shall be thankful, but, as you see, time presses for them. As soon as I settle with publishers, I must get the "Memoir" filled in, as *it* must accompany first vol. *Can you point out any letter or letters from or even to Poe in Griswold's* "Memoir" *that is* authentic? Those to Willis of course are. Can Mrs. Botta, or any literary friend of Poe's, with whom you are acquainted, give me *copies* of any portion of a letter of his? I have requested Mr. Davidson to kindly try. Part of Griswold's books & *papers* went to the New-York Historical Society—they might include some of Poe's letters—*the slightest scrap* would be useful. I am hoping to hear from the South in a day or two. Even a commonplace letter to Mr. Pabodie would be useful for my Life.

You may confidently rely upon my most careful manipulation of the "South Carolina lady" affair. Neither Mrs. E[llet]'s dignity nor Mrs. B[otta]'s love of keeping the peace shall be infringed. I was hoping to hear the sequel to your former reminiscences—why am I kept from hearing the result of the first interview, as promised? Anything that is confidential, do kindly mark, as otherwise, I may be debarred from using what you would permit me to use & which might be of importance.

Believe me ever to be yours most faithfully,

John H. Ingram

P.S. I think I shall most likely scratch both Dunn English & Briggs in my Life.

J.H.I.

31. *John H. Ingram to Sarah Helen Whitman*

My dear Mrs. Whitman,   25 March 1874

This is the only result obtainable in England, from my inquiries after your book; it is probably, therefore, still in America.[1] Could it have been stopped on account of any writing inside, or on the newspaper cuttings? *E.P. & His Critics* when received had had the cover nearly torn off, as if to see whether containing any writing.

Faithfully yours,

J. H. Ingram

P.S. I hope you have received all my letters & printed papers safely. I believe I have received everything but this book, although some poems mentioned by you as sent were not in letter.

1. Ingram enclosed a copy of a letter to himself, dated Mar. 24, 1874, from John Tilley, secretary, General Post Office, saying that all possible inquiries for a missing packet addressed to Ingram had been made, without success, and adding that the U.S. Post

Office Department did not make searches for missing letters or packets which had not been registered.

32. *Sarah Helen Whitman to John H. Ingram. Item 137*

My dear Mr. Ingram,   March 27, [18]74
I have just received your two letters of March 11th & 12th, with the *photograph*.[1] It is younger than I thought you, but all the complex elements of character are shewn in it which I have found in your letters & writings—the concentrated energy & self-reliance, indicated in the contour & pose of the head; the intensity of purpose; the clear penetration & faintly indicated power of sarcasm, in the eyes; the tender, sensitive, poetic soul in the lips and brow. I have only time to tell you how glad I am thus to know you through the magic of the sunbeams.

I shall send you by tonight's mail, for tomorrow's steamer, the two volumes of the *Broadway Journal*. There are in them one of two marginal notes in pencil by E.A.P. One of them requires or *suggests* explanation: you will remember that in my little book on Poe the following passage occurs on page 70: "All that I have here expressed was actually present with me. Remember the mental condition which gave rise to 'Ligeia,' etc., & observe the coincidence."

When I wrote these words I was spending the summer in New York, preparing & *revising* the essay, which I had been writing during the preceding year, for publication. I had left my letters & papers in Providence. Just before putting the last touches to the MS., I remembered a passage in one of Poe's *letters* or *appended to some poem* (as I then thought) about the poem "To Helen" having been written (as "Ligeia" was also written) after a vivid & lifelike *dream* which occurred to him soon after he knew me or recognized me *thro'* *Mrs. Osgood's description*.

But I looked for the passage among my papers in vain. I knew that he had told me this in conversation & with other details, but I also *knew* that I had some *pencilled lines* of his on the subject. In this uncertainty, I recalled as well as I could the substance of the pencilled lines & the *viva voce* explanation of the poem, & inserted it as illustrative of his mental idiosyncrasies. Still I could not find the pencilled lines nor remember on what letter or MS. they were inscribed. I began to think I had *read them in a dream* when, three or four years after the publication on the little book, I chanced to find them in the *Broadway Journal*, which I had not opened for years.

Subsequently, when urged by a friend for a single line, for even three or four words of his writing, I cut off the first two lines, & *then*, repenting, cut out & gave him, I think, two or three *words*, & only three days ago found between the leaves of the *Journal* the lines which I had cut off, & replaced them as you will find them. Perhaps I did not give him even these *few words*, but left them between the leaves of the book. If so, you will find them there. I have made quite a long story about a trivial matter, but I want you to understand the discrepancy between the printed allusion to the matter in the book & the words as they stand on the margin of the *Journal*.

And now, let me say to you, while I remember to do so, that you *owe me nothing*. I wish my ability to serve you were equal to my wishes.

You *cannot* have seen anything like the photograph from the daguerre taken for *me on the 13th of November*. It was never out of my hands till I left it with Coleman in order that a copy might, if possible, be taken from it for you. Coleman occupies now the very room in which this & the Ultima Thule portraits were taken 25 years ago. His copy is better than I had dared to hope, from the faded look of the original. The *other* (since the original has been stolen, or is presumed to have been stolen) *may* have been copied.

I have not yet seen Powell's book, but will try to find it. I do not know about the many or various academies. His skill in drawing? Mr. John Willis, a classmate whose letter I gave Mr. Gill, spoke of passing an evening in his room just before the close of the term, & finding the walls covered with drawings executed by him. I will try to get a copy of the letter at least.

I told you that I had written Mr. Gill an imperative letter, & he has responded very frankly & good-naturedly. He excuses his apparent negligence & returns papers, etc., but does not give me Mr. Clarke's address.

He has had the letters of Mr. Wertenbaker & Dr. Maupin *copied* for me, & I enclose the copies. Mr. Latto has also sent me a letter which Mr. Poe wrote to Pabodie in acknowledgement of his kindness to him. This has his *autograph*. You can have it—the letter—copied if you like, but must be very careful of it & return it as soon as possible. When Mr. Pabodie died in 1870, he left me this letter & other papers, & I gave the letter to Mr. Latto, who had given me from time to time much information about Poe, & who was deeply interested in his genius and his history. His address is T. C. Latto, 16 Utica Avenue, Brooklyn, New York. He has written (years ago) something for *Blackwood's Mag.*, a poem I think on Scott, & one on Cooper, published in *Harper's* in the summer of 1870, with his signature. He is a most estimable gentleman—a man of much taste & good sense, but not (I fancy) of much literary influence. He was employed for a long time in the publishing house of Iverson & *somebody*, New York. They speak of him in high terms as a gentleman of fine social qualities &

great integrity. He is about 55 years old, I think. I am sorry that the letter to Pabodie is so stained & disfigured. It was in this state when I received it from him [Pabodie], or rather, from his executors.

I was much interested in Mr. Swinburne's letter. I have always been an admirer of his *Atalanta in Calydon* (is that the name? I have forgotten), & of certain things in the Mary Queen of Scots drama, & some of the lyrics.[2] I can never remember names & dates without a painful & determinate effort. His "Garden of Proserpine," too, is a great favorite with me.

Certainly Mrs. E[llet] lived for a year or two, perhaps several years, in S. Carolina. She is *alive*, & once (I think in 1851 or 2 or 3) commenced a correspondence with me, ostensibly on the subject of the spiritual phenomena of which she had some experience. I wrote cautiously & reservedly, fearing she had sought my acquaintance in order to prejudice me against Poe, & the correspondence soon dropped. I have never seen her. I cannot tell you more of her than I did in my former letter. I fancy she would resent anything that looked like a personal attack on her. She is said to be implacable toward Poe, but I fancy it is for his slighting allusion to her writings. Still, I do not *know*. Certainly he never borrowed money of her & refused to pay. I am as sure of it as of my own existence. Yet I should treat the subject in a very general way, as if the proven mendacity of Griswold placed such a story utterly out of the range of serious criticism. We may have the terrible "brothers" down upon us, & then what will become of us! Remember that discretion is the better part of valor, & who knows what tigress we may start up out of *this jungle of rank weeds*.

My latest edition of Poe is the same as yours. I have not seen the one of which Allibone speaks.

Poe spoke of the first Mrs. Allan with the tenderest affection, of the second with admiration of her beauty & an avowed feeling that the marriage was one of great discrepancy. *Entre nous*, Mr. Allan was represented, to me, by him, as a man of a gross & brutal temperament, though *indulgent* to *him* & at *times* profusely lavish in the matter of money—at others, penurious & parsimonious. Do not speak *of this to any one*. I never heard him speak of any difficulty with the second Mrs. Allan.

I think he told me that his sister was adopted by them, the Allans or *some* one, & placed at the school of a Mrs. McKinsey in Baltimore or Richmond. He added that they had seen but little of each other & were of very opposite temperaments, etc., etc. Do not speak of this.

I do not know if any child of the Allans' still lives.

Can I give anything between the dates of 1831 & 1833? I am afraid not, but will try. I imagine there was no foundation of Griswold's story of enlistment & desertion. One hardly needs to disprove a slander like that stated only on Griswold's authority, *n'est ce pas*? Tell me about Mrs. St. Leon Loud in relation to whom you said there was a story to be told.

Allibone speaks of *Poe's autobiography*, you say. I have never seen it, never *heard* of it, I think, before. I will try to find out about Brooks's *Museum*.

I can find what Duyckinck says about reminiscences of Poe in the extinct *Sixpenny Mag.*. I will look at it tomorrow. I do not know exactly what you refer to when you say, "*If you do not know it*, I will forward it." I can *find* it, if it is in Duyckinck; otherwise, I do not know it, & shall be glad to see it.

You ask me about Mrs. Osgood's aid & her sheltering Mrs. Clemm. I have not yet seen your account of it, not having received your proofs of the *Temple Bar* article. Mrs. Osgood & Mrs. Clemm had no love for each other, I imagine. I will tell you more about this another time. All I *know* is from Mrs. Osgood. You say my letters have not denied it. I must then have lost some letter or *published article* of yours, or mis*laid* it. Where did you speak of it? Was it in any number of the *Mirror*? I am very anxious about it. Have you sent me more than three several articles in the *Mirror*?

But now I must close, with a thousand things unsaid. Shall send *Broadway Journal* tonight.

May you succeed in your noble work. It is full of difficulties, but all will end well, I trust. May the good gods help you.

Your friend, most cordially & gratefully,

S. H. Whitman

About the "Pansy." Certainly, you may use it, only let the printer be careful about misprints. I am sensitive on that point. I had thought of your word in the line, "A fading flush of morning gold." If *you* like it better, *I* like it as *well*. So, with "the silver-*blaring* trumpets." I think I should certainly have chosen it, if "silver-*snarling*" had not been the word used by Keats & often quoted. You can do as you think best about it. I cannot tell you how much I value your praise, your sympathy. Praise is not always welcome, but *your* praise is priceless.

I sent poems & papers in the last book. I am not sure what were in the book & what in the letter. Was there a printed letter giving an account of an interview with Walter Savage Landor, & an extract from Edgar Poe's notice in his Lowell lecture? And were the poems of "Proserpine to Pluto" & the "Venus of Milo," etc. in the letter?

Thanks for the "Rhododaphne."[3] I had long been curious about it.

1. The date March 12 is an error; Ingram wrote two letters dated March 11.

The photograph (reproduced in this volume on page 63) was taken when Ingram was thirty-one years old.

2. Algernon Charles Swinburne, *Atalanta in Calydon: A Tragedy* (London: Edward Moxon & Co., 1865); *Mary Stuart: A Tragedy* (London: Chatto & Windus, 1881).

3. "Rhododaphne: or, the Thessalian Spell," a poem by Thomas Love Peacock (1785–1866). Poe, in his "Marginalia," CLXXVIII, the *Democratic Review*, Dec. 1844, says of it, "'Rhododaphne' is brim-full of music" and quotes five lines.

33. *Sarah Helen Whitman to John H. Ingram.*   *Item 138*

My dear Mr. Ingram,   March 30, [18]74
I sent off a hurried letter with the *Broadway Journal* by Saturday's steamer, leaving many things I wished to say unsaid.

I wanted to thank you for the "Farewell." There is such a strange & exquisite simplicity in it—such genuine & heart-breaking pathos, that I could hardly keep back my tears while I read it.

I am so glad to *know* you through the photograph you sent. I can speak to you now more unreservedly than ever before. I trust implicitly your heart & your intellect. I fear, only, your impetuosity & your *impulsiveness*. Don't claim *too much* for our poet—be wary & keep cool and don't be *too sarcastic*. Your "Grecian fiddlestick," for instance. Not Merlin's wand could evoke a fiercer storm.

Don't be troubled about the loss of the poems. What I most regret is a charming little photograph from Le Jenne's Cinderella, prefixed to my sister's poem. It has just been discovered that a number of letters & packages mailed here to be sent away have been opened & rifled by a young clerk in the Post Office. This may account for the loss of the poems.

I want you to tell me what poems & papers were in the letters sent by the same mail with the book—some were sent in the *book* & some in the letters. You need not send anything back, unless I ask. I should like to have you *preserve* for me the printed notice from *Putnam's* for Nov. 1853, by George Wm. Curtis, if, indeed, it was not lost in the book. I will send for it if I need it. I shall probably, if my health is equal to the supervision of it, republish, or *prepare* for republication after my departure, the volume published already, including the poems since written. Mr. Whitney, the publisher, surrendered to me the copyright before he gave up business as bookseller & publisher. Mr. Carleton also gave up to me his copyright of *Edgar Poe & His Critics*.

I want to correct something I said about Mrs. Lewis. I believe I told you that in the summer of 1858 when she sent me a card to one of her receptions, she was living in Lafayette Place. I gave you the name of her residence from memory only. I now distinctly remember that it was

Irving Place. Mr. Davidson, who visited New York for the first time that summer, went with me to call on her. But I had lost her card, & mistaking the evening, did not find her. On enquiring for Mrs. Clemm who, I had heard, was residing with Mrs. Lewis, I learned that she had left her for another home in Brooklyn.

I tell you doubtless many things that may seem irrelevant, but having spoken of the lady's residence at that time, I want to be accurate about it.

I have been recurring to Mrs. Clemm's letter about the date of the marriage. I find that she does not mention the *month*. Her memory seems to be utterly at fault in nearly everything pertaining to dates & places. In a letter dated April 14, 1859, she says, *"Eddie was not in Richmond 'twice.' We left there* in 1837 *& he never visited it again since the death of Virginia until 1849."* Now Mrs. Clemm could have had no motive for *concealing the fact of his* having been in Richmond in August, 1848. But her *forgetfulness* of the fact shows how *utterly* unreliable was her memory of past events. She wrote to Mr. Davidson that Poe "never was in Europe 'twice'," but her statement is of no weight, after her forgetfulness of his having been for two successive summers in Richmond at a much more recent period. I will enclose the letter. Keep *the annotations sacred & preserve the letter*.

You can use the lines about Arcturus if you see fit. Perhaps I will send you another letter or copy of another soon. I must think about the pros & cons.

You say you want to see everything Poe has ever published. Do you know there was another verse to "Ulalume" until it was republished in Providence in the autumn of 1848, when, at my suggestion, he left out the last verse?

I used to have the original copy, but have lost it. Perhaps I may obtain another for you if you would like to see it. The letter to Pabodie was written at my suggestion. I knew that he wanted an autograph of Poe that he could show, & I asked Poe to write one with his full signature.

Mr. Latto prizes it very much, so be careful of it & return it soon.

Sarah Helen Whitman

One o'clock p.m.

The proofs have just arrived.[1]

The paper is masterly in its refutation of Griswold's rash & reckless statements. It is admirable too, in tone & manner—earnest, energetic, & evidently springing from a profound & passionate conviction of the essential truth of its statements & the incontrovertible character of its evidence.

The paragraph at the bottom of page 11, about Mrs. Osgood, *leave out by all means if not too late.* I will tell you more another time. Mrs. Osgood was much under the influence of Griswold during the last year of her life, & saw nothing of Poe or of Mrs. Clemm. Though not important in *itself*, the paragraph will tend to throw discredit, I fear, on other statements.

I do not think Poe had consumptive tendencies. I have never heard any such theory advanced. Unquestionably his death was caused by inflammation of the brain.

I don't quite like the intimation that Poe's family lost *caste* through the marriage of his father with *an actress* & his adoption of the stage as a profession. It seems to undervalue a vocation much more consonant to the tastes of a young man of genius than the routine of the law could have been—*n'est ce pas*?

In speaking of Miss Rosalie Poe, I should prefer to say, "Of this *lady* we learn no more, etc." than of this *girl*. But these last remarks are, perhaps, hypercritical & unimportant.

I enclose the first letter I ever received from Mrs. Clemm. It is dated from Lowell, & was written 19 days after Edgar's death.[2] She was then visiting Mrs. Charles Richmond in Lowell. When I next heard from her she was in New York, but returned, I think, the following winter to Lowell. She subsequently passed some time, I think, in the family of Mr. W. Strong, Milford, Conn. Some years afterward she lived for a time with Mrs. Lewis.

But before I close, let me speak of your *poems* which came with the proofs. They are *exquisite*—filled with the rarest & most ineffable aroma of poetry—even their faults add to the impression of their strange beauty & pathos by showing their unstudied & spontaneous creation. "Death in the Dwelling," "The Unknown Captive," "The Pool of Death," "Autumnal," "My Childhood Home," "October," "In Venice," "The Old Stone Well," & "Our Garden Gate," are all *brimfull* of poetic beauty. "The Garden Gate" is *perfect* in its way. It has such an indescribable naivete, such a sweet, unwonted freshness, & the close is *so* felicitious! I cannot begin to tell you how it charmed me. I only wanted to change *one* word, to make the "freed branch" the "bended branch," & to alter the *closing* line of the next-to-the-last verse, "Returned to our Garden Gate" to something more rhythmical.

I *dare* not read any more of the poems, lest I should be too late with my letter—I resolutely lay them aside for the time. But their fragrance & tenderness enfolds me & will not be put aside.

One more word about the proofs. The use you make of the "Eulogium" on the last page is very telling. It brings your summing up of evidence to a climax. Nothing could be better managed.

I wish that I had a good magazinist or journalist to do my bidding. But I cannot well do anything myself—first, because I am quoted in

the article, & second, because I have almost blinded myself with
writing, & fear every day that I shall be remanded to a dark room &
wet bandages.

May I republish "The Garden Gate"? Will you let me make the
changes I suggested, or will *you* make the changes, if you agree with
me that it might be improved in these trifling particulars?

I don't see how that objectionable line in the "Pansy"—"Waneth
never"—*can* be improved. It troubled me at first, but I have got to
liking it better. But goodbye for tonight.

S.H.W.

1. These were apparently first proofs of Ingram's forthcoming *Temple Bar* article. Of
the various revisions suggested by Mrs. Whitman in this letter, Ingram only continued
to promise that he would make them. The article is reprinted on pages 168–80.

2. This letter, dated Oct. 26, 1849, is printed in full in *Building Poe Biography*, pp.
33–34.

34. *John H. Ingram to Sarah Helen Whitman*

My dear Mrs. Whitman,   31 March 1874
I am getting settled in my new residence whither yours of the 16th
has just arrived, but amid a chaos of books and papers, have been
pursuing my writings marked "Important." I personally packed &
carried all my E.A.P. papers from one house to the other, amid the
scarcely suppressed astonishment of my people, who fancy that I am
tinged with the eccentricity of literature.

Your letters stir up strong emotions in my mind & in responding to
them I find it difficult to restrain from indulging in personal &
autobiographical feelings instead of confining myself to researches into
the life, etc. of Edgar Poe. I fear, frequently, that I am not acting a
friendly part to you "in stirring from their long repose" memories of
yore—if so, forbear—but do not cease to be my correspondent. Your
letters have become a joy to me, that I should be grieved to lose
entirely. You cannot dream of the sad disasters which have haunted me
thro' life, nor of the terrible thoughts & intense depression of spirits
which I am sometimes the prey of. What more than all adds anguish to
my agony is my mental loneliness. I have a loving mother & kind
sisters, but no one to comprehend me, or sympathize with me *now*.
The *res augusta domi* have been but a small portion of our domestic
troubles. It was terrible to lose worldly wealth & all the comforts
which it brings, but that was slight compared with our other
calamities. I have already confided to you thoughts & things untold to
anyone else, and, therefore, dare tell you, what is not unknown, alas,

but to too many—the terrible hereditary curse which over-hangs our devoted house & which is, indeed, the only thing I tremble before. It is insanity. Four near & dear relatives have, one after the other, succumbed to it. First one aunt & then another, & then my poor noble father, & now, within the last twelve months, one of my surviving sisters—a girl of but 24, has fallen under the curse & has had to be removed from home. My own mind is as clear & acute as possible & the family curse appears unlikely to descend upon me, especially if my worldly affairs jog along composedly, but still the *mere knowledge* of the taint in the blood *is* terrible. But there! I will not worry you any more just now on those matters, but return to Poe's works & life.

Whilst I think of it, do you know, or have you noticed any discrepancies between the printed copies of the poems? The *facsimile* in *Harper's*—I suppose it is a veritable *facsimile*—contains several differences to the poem of "Annabel Lee" in the 4-vol. collection. I am in the city & speak from memory. *Harper*—Stoddard's paper— concludes the verse, "In her tomb by the side of the sea" & in the 4-vol. collection it reads, "In *the* tomb by the *sounding* sea." 4-vol. collection p. 19, has poem "To — —". Should not last line but one, the penultimate, read "empurpled," & not "unpurpled," as there printed? *En passant*, my edition is full of printer's errors. Do you know to whom this poem was written? To one whose name was formed of "Two foreign soft dissylables." You remember the poem "To One in Paradise"? Originally there was another verse, which I shall restore, as it more fully explains why the hero of "The Assignantion," in which story it appears, should be deemed an Englishman. Do you know who "M.L.S." is to whom the poem on page 111 is inscribed, but who is described as being dead? Do you think that Mrs. Helen S[tanard] had a daughter "Mary"? Poe published a poem in the *South. Lit. Messenger*, "To Mary". You know the one, "Beloved, amid the early woes," &c. Who was Mary?

By the way, I found those words of Longfellow's you quote, in Mr. J. Thompson's notice of Poe's death—he had so written amongst other matters to Mr. Thompson. Do you know of any sketch, or pictures, that could be got, or copies, of any place connected with Poe, besides the Fordham view in *Harper's*? It would be useful in the collected edition I am trying to arrange for, & in which, or rather, from which, I shall omit some minor *literati* & insert a few unknown pieces. Have you heard of, or seen anything of, the "Cryptology" papers yet? I have written to Mr. W. G. Simms. I cannot get any replies from the South, although I have written to several people. If Miss R. Poe would answer—even by proxy—I might raise a nice little sum for her. It is strange no notice is taken. As for Dr. Porteous! I don't suppose he can be *anybody* here. There was a celebrated Porteous, a bishop, I fancy, who died ages ago & whose theological works, I expect, are still saleable, & this man probably trades on his name. It is quite amusing to read in American papers allusion to "celebrated" somebodies who are indeed unknown in England. I don't say that Dr. Porteous is one of these men, but it is not probable. I never heard of him, nor have one or two I have asked. He may be a Scotchman.

As for Mr. Gill, I wrote to him & offered to purchase anything he might have disposable of Poe's, especially for copies of letters. I sent him "New Facts" from the *Mirror*, as I thought it might be useful for his lectures, but it is very crude & not very valuable. Directly my quarterly paper appears (in July) there will be something to work upon & I shall be glad for him to see it. I don't know what to make of his abilities, or intentions, but if he really wishes to aid in giving a better view of Poe, he is heartily welcome to everything I can supply him with. If he answers me, I shall be able to judge better what his *intentions* are. If he has not obtained Mr. Clarke's collection, I should like to obtain it. How strange that his address cannot be obtained. Mr. Gill, probably, knows it. I have asked him.

You will have received my letters about non-arrival of your vol. of poems—it is most annoying. I do hope you will recover it—it could not have reached the British Post Office. Mr. Davidson did not appear to have gained much information when he wrote the letters enclosed in yours of the 13th date. Mr. Thompson's allusion to the Brownings is interesting, but Powell is very unreliable, both in his authors of England & America. I much doubt whether he met the people he speaks of, or even knew the circumstances he relates. His life of Poe is wildly fictitious, although so friendly. Stoddard's paper & quotations are made up entirely (save the last few columns) of your book, Powell's, Griswold's, & the Eulogium—word for word in many cases without the inverted commas, or any reference, save to Griswold. 'Tis no less than downright robbery. To Mr. Davidson's letters again—he is right about H. B. Wallace. I thought it was W. Ross Wallace who wrote the "Literary Criticisms." He does not, however, mention what they do say—only, I presume, the usual generalities.

What is that about "Landor's Cottage"? I did not ask. As for Mrs. Clemm's assertion that Poe never left America after his return from Dr. Bransby's school—which, by the way, is only a few minutes walk from my residence—do you think it reliable—probable? Russia, I feel assured he did not reach, but other parts of Europe, I *believe*, were visited. By the way, in your *Broadway Journal*, is the story of "Why the little Frenchman wears his hand in a Sling" marked as by Poe? "Lyttleton Barry," I suppose, was a *nom de plume*? It is so inferior to his other stories.

The extract about "the widow" came this morning & not in former letter, as stated. I suppose it is utterly fictitious. I *must* send you the paper about "3 wives"—have not got it with me. Many thanks for the copy of a note—that will be strictly private. I keep all my Edgar Poe papers together & *should anything happen to me* they will all be carefully packed & sent to you. I should be troubled to think a single fact or link should be lost. However, I hope to be able to live to complete my appointed task—my labour of love—& a great many other things *in futuro*. As for my poor stories—that was a misfortune for me. I should have had them all published long ago, had they been taken care of. There was one called "Mortmere," of which I possess a rough sketch, that I fancy was so strongly & unconsciously permeated with the *spirit* of "The House of Usher" & its owner, that I'm certain the critics would have founded a charge of plagiarism upon it. And yet, the imitation was entirely unconscious. I have not had the autograph letter facsimiled—that is to say the paragraph—but will get it done quickly & return it. I feel it a burden on my mind. I thought the publisher might like to have it done in some particular way, but as they take so much time over their settlements, I had better get it done & return it quickly. I have so much that I might say, but will leave off just for the nonce, remaining ever, believe me, yours most faithfully,

John H. Ingram

P.S. Don't you want to know anything about any English or other European books or authors? I should like to do *something* for you.

J.H.I.

35. *Sarah Helen Whitman to John H. Ingram.*   Item 140

My dear Mr. Ingram,   April 2, 1874
I have just received your two letters of March 16. I envy you your *new* home in the *old* house which has so many a "coigne of vantage" for the accommodation of ghostly visitors. I never have seen a ghost, though I once saw a beautiful luminous hand that wrote for me three initial letters, which I still preserve & look upon with awe & wonder! It was in a *private house*, & in the presence of the master of the house, my cousin, Wm. Power Blodget, and the celebrated medium Charles Foster.

But, to our *dry facts*. I cannot reconcile the discrepancy in dates of which you speak. You will have seen before you get this letter the copy of Mr. Wertenbaker's letter, which I obtained from Mr. Gill, & there I must leave the evidence. If *any*body can arrive at certainty on these matters, *you* can. But I do not know how I can help you. I will *try*, however.

I was deeply impressed by what Poe told me of his interview with Mrs. Stanard, of the effect which her gentle words had on him, & of his sorrow at her death, & his repeated solitary vigils by her grave.

When, in the spring of 1859, I wrote to Mrs. Clemm for the date of her [Mrs. Stanard's] death & other particulars of the incidents connected with this subject she wrote me in reply the letter which I enclose to you.[1] I could not reconcile her statements with my own impression of what he had said to me on the subject—an impression which, though somewhat vague as to *details*, was profound & indelible as to the leading facts of the story.

He told me that when he heard of her death he was overwhelmed with sorrow, & that being at the time either at some academy or at the University (I cannot distinctly remember which), he was in the habit of letting himself out at a certain window of the establishment & going to the cemetery where she was entombed, & that on stormy & dreary nights he went most often—that he could not endure to think of her lying there forsaken & forgotten. I *know* that his report was *essentially* true. I cannot feel sure about anything else.

I know nothing of the early editions of poems, nor do I know anyone of whom I could be likely to obtain information. You may perhaps learn something from Davidson. I sent him your article in the *Mirror*. I have not since heard from him. I am afraid he must be ill. I think—indeed I am quite sure, that no vol. of "Marginalia" was published during Poe's life. Poe's references to it were probably to the magazine publishments. Did he speak of it as a volume?

Only two numbers of the *American Metropolitan* were published. Poe was *engaged* to write the literary notices. I cannot *remember* that he wrote anything for them. I had the numbers *once*, but have not seen them for years. The only thing *I* wrote for it was the lines of which I spoke, called "Stanzas for Music." They were cut out & sent with the new verses to the printer under the title of "Our Island of Dreams," when my poems were collected in 1853. I will enclose a copy of the four *original verses*.

You ask if I know what was Mrs. Shelton's Christian name? I do *not*, but I have fancied that the last lines in Griswold's collection of the poems were addressed *to her*. I have never asked anyone nor have I ever heard anyone speak on the subject. They had not *appeared* I think in any previous collection, & were probably written after his engagement to her in [18]49. Yet Griswold, I think, has spoken of "Annabel Lee" as *the last*. I should like very much to learn the date of these lines to M.L.S. I am curious, too, to learn something of Mrs. St. Leon Loud. Won't you tell me what you know of her?

Certainly you may make use of Mrs. [Anna Cora Mowatt] Ritchie's letter, if you think proper to do so. In copying her letter, I did not preserve the date. It must have been a month or six weeks earlier than I had supposed, because in an extract from one of Davidson's letters which I sent you he alludes to it, & his letter, I think, was written in April.

You allude to Wallace's literary criticisms. I will look for them at once in our Athenaeum Library. Poe first met Mr. Pabodie at my mother's house in the autumn of 1848.

April 3, 1874

Last evening came your letter of March 19. Have already sent the *Broadway Journal*. It is *yours*. Last evening I received a letter (note) from Mr. Davidson [dated March 31, 1874] which I enclose, & one from Mrs. Clemm, written to me while I was preparing the work published by Carleton. It will not add much to your collection of *facts*, but may serve to illustrate other points. Preserve it for me. I may want it, though it is not likely.

The passages from Poe's letter of Oct. 18—*those marked with a blue pencil*—you can use if you think best to do so. I have not yet been able to hear of any copies of *Graham's Mag*. Perhaps I may be able to answer some of your questions next week. I have just read Powell's paper on Poe.

Maunsell B. Field, a relative of the great Cyrus, has just got out a rambling, gossiping collection of *Memories of Many Men and Some Women*, published by Harper & Brothers, 1874. Have you seen it?

I quote what he says of Poe, though you may perhaps already have seen it:

Edgar A. Poe I remember seeing on a single occasion. He announced a lecture to be delivered at the Society Library building on Broadway, under the title of the "Universe." It was a stormy night & there were not more than sixty persons present in the lecture room.

I have seen no portrait of Poe that does justice to his pale, delicate, intellectual face & magnificent eyes. His lecture was a rhapsody of the most intense brilliancy. He appeared inspired, & his inspiration affected the scant audience almost painfully.

He wore his coat tightly buttoned across his slender chest; his eyes seemed to glow like those of his own Raven, & he kept us entranced for two hours & a half.

The late Mr. Putnam, the publisher, told me that the next day the wayward, luckless poet presented himself to him with the MS of the "Universe." He told Putnam that in it he had solved the whole problem of life; that it would immortalize the publisher as well as the author, & bring him the fortune he had so long been vainly seeking. Mr. Putnam, while an admirer of genius, was also a cool, calculating man of business. As such, he could not see the matter as Poe did, & the result was that he lent Poe a shilling to take him back to Fordham.

An ingenious climax, but not true, I fancy, to the *dry facts* of the case, since it took *four shillings* of New York money to get from New York to Fordham, & would the cool, calculating man of business have wasted so much money on the improvident prose-poet of "The Universe"?

I confess I have always liked Swinburne since I read in the *Galaxy* of March 15, 1867, an article on him, written by Mr. Winwood Reade of Harvard College, on the social & intellectual proclivities of "the pagan poet." I made an extract from it for the [Providence] *Journal*, from which extract I quote a paragraph, which I headed, "*Interesting to Ladies*, & specially interesting to *Old Ladies*."

Mr. Swinburne affects the society of artists, but maintains that women are the only fit company for a man of intellect, & that those *mythical enchantresses*, *old* women, are the best.

He is, says Reade, the most passionate lover of intellect I ever met. He admires intensely Landor, Baudelaire, & Balzac. He declares that Ezekiel intoxicates him. Isaiah he regards as an inferior poet. He considers Edgar Poe *the* literary genius of America, & praises especially "The Raven," "The Bells," & some of the tales, etc.

I believe the words "mythical enchantresses" are my *own*, & not Mr. Reade's, but I gave him the credit for them. I like the "Ave atque Vale" above all things, & now, once more, to *you*, "Ave atque Vale."

S.H. Whitman

1. This letter, dated Apr. 14, 1859, is printed in full in *Building Poe Biography*, pp. 41–44. The original letter is now in the Lilly Library, Indiana University, Bloomington.

36. *John H. Ingram to Sarah Helen Whitman*

My dear Mrs. Whitman,   2 April 1874
Your letter dated [Mar.] 20th safely to hand & by following post the German brochure. Many thanks, indeed! Do you wish this translation back again? I have only just glanced over it yet but am very pleased with it & shall probably get it inserted with a few biographical words of Poe, in a German publication. In many climes & languages, I hope, eventually to extend his fame. This translation, so far as I have looked into it, seems very good—in some cases the triplicate rhymes even are preserved. You, of course, understand German. Who is the Mr. Whitman to whom the book is inscribed, may I ask?

I do not think "The Raven" could be translated into French, or even well into Italian, but I fancy it might be done in Spanish. I shall try some day. How poor that ballad of Byron's looks after the majestic gloom of the Raven & the mournful sway of the "Haunted Palace."

Thanks for the suggestion as to the setting of the portrait—at present, however, I am keeping it (*i.e.*, them) *perdue*. I want them engraved.

Never mind who makes use of, or how widely spread are, any *printed* papers of mine on E. A. Poe. I mean any *published* papers. I only wish secrecy about projected & unpublished matters.

As regards the *Broadway Journal*, as I have already said, I can see that (a few early numbers are missing) at the British Museum; therefore there is no necessity for the risk & expense of sending it. If there be anything of Poe's *written in it*, any note or remark, perhaps you can kindly copy it & let me know. Is there anything *you* can point out in it, such as any paper worth republication not in the 4-vol. edition? Do you know of any "Marginalia" elsewhere? I have found some in the *S. Lit. Messenger* in Mr. Thompson's time. Was "Littleton Barry" Poe's *nom de plume*? Some of the stories in the *Broadway* have that appended. I suppose the tale "Why the little Frenchman wears his hand in a Sling" *is* his? I don't think it worthy of Poe. Can you point out anything not in the 4 vols.?

Kindly let me have any extract from or portion of his letters *that I may publish*, at once, can you? And any reminiscence that may be published. The publishers I hope to arrange with have written today for my MS. "Memoir." I shall have to send them a portion & the rest as soon as possible. Anything that comes to light subsequently must wait for another edition. I dare say I shall be shortly able to announce that arrangements for publication are complete. The advantage of bringing out the "Memoir" prefixed to the works is very great, as you will perceive. I shall incorporate all that I possibly can of *E.P. & His Critics*, duly acknowledging my indebtedness.

I have so much to say but neither time nor method just now for saying it, but I dare say you think I give you quite enough to read—but what a boon a personal chat would be! We may have it some day, but I want *to say & ask everything* at once. I am fearfully impatient & yet, strange to say, doggedly persevering. Never let go a matter which I have set my heart upon. Some day I *must* give you a short biographical sketch of myself, not for egotistic motives, but that you may know & thoroughly trust me.

As for my poor faith—alas! I fear that—well, no—I am not like Lucretius, & yet—dare I tell *you*? My researches have ended in making me believe *all things possible but nothing certain*. I hope— hope—hope, & that is the most *I* can do.

To your letter: I *am* sorry that your book miscarried, because I longed to make it & its thoughts mine. The sonnets came with "The Raven"— of them more hereafter. The notice from *Putnam's* of the Lecture on

the Female Poets (*vide* Atkinson) came safely—*Harper's*?—but not
from the *Tribune*, I fancy. I am at office & must look through your
papers again this evening. The *Tribune* could not have come—I could
not forget it.

Don't get Tuckerman's *Life of Kennedy*. There is not much about
Edgar Poe. First an extract from Griswold of the prize story—
acknowledged as from Griswold—then copy of a note & a letter from
Poe & and a few kindly remarks from Mr. Kennedy's diary about him.
All this you will find in my "Memoir" & made the very utmost use of.
Kennedy says he had *many* letters from Poe & by his will he left two
bound volumes of autograph letters from eminent men to the Peabody
Institute, Baltimore. I sent a letter to the President of the Institute
asking him to kindly favour me with copies of any letters of E.A.P. that
might be there. Answer could have come more than a week ago, but no
reply. Nor can I get any reply from the South from people I have
written to. If Miss Rosalie Poe would only acknowledge my letters or
get someone to I could help her materially, but no letter comes. I have
not heard from Mr. Gill. I sent him No. 2 of "New Facts" to use if he
liked & asked about Mr. Clarke's collection. If that could only be got.
I'd send the money at once, although for a week or two I shall not have
any spare cash. I owe you a good bit, I'm sure, & will duly remit it. You
can dispose of it—if you don't want it—in buying something of Poe's
for me. I should like to get either of the earlier collections of poems, or
even the 1845 collection. The 1829 & 1831 were *privately* circulated
only, I believe. The first at Baltimore published by Hatch & Dunning,
84 pps., & the 2nd at New York by E. Bliss, 124 pps.

[*The last page of this letter has its corners torn off and the fragments
lost; both sides of the page are fragmented. That below is all that
could be salvaged.*]

I want to make use of some of the earlier versions & will only quote
the better portion, but I should be glad if you would let me use nearly
all "The Paean." If you still say no, of course I will not, but except the
verse about a "costly 'broidered pall," I do not think there is a thing to
be withheld—but I await your decision.

The 1827 edition, I fear, was a "mystification," and I had better not
say too much about it.

One moment reverting to Tuckerman. I like his works frequently,
but he is wearisome with surplus energy [*illegible*] of his critiques. Do
you know his paper on Leopardi, my favorite Italian after Dante?
There were some allusions in that German work you have just sent me,
very interesting *to me*, i.e., to Lenau, the German; to Mangan (who is
quite unknown in England); to Alfred de Musset, etc. Oh, what talks

we could have! Why are we so wide apart? That book will supply the autograph; it is a good one, I think, because in the British Museum I have just discovered a work edited, I fancy, by Tuckerman with autographs of American writers, extracts from each of Poe's, an extract from [*illegible*] critique, or rather eulogy of Mrs. Osgood.

Can you tell me the name of the writer on that paper on Willis—'tis really important—& to guess is no good.

Poor Mr. Davidson. I have suffered too much myself not to feel for him, although I am thankful to say I am emerging from my troubles of that class. Oh, that I could help all who need it—my heart is thoroughly sore with grieving for those who want help, but whom I cannot assist.

As for "Isadore," I cannot help feeling that Poe must have had a hand in it, but I may be wrong. Don't withhold your belief from any one on my account. I fear no man's opinion. I told the editor that I had no certainty of it being Poe's, but he was only too glad to get it on suspicion. You see what he says. Swinburne, who is enthusiastic about Poe, says, "I don't think it is by Poe, but by a disciple of his," or words to that effect.

37. John H. Ingram to Sarah Helen Whitman

My dear Mrs. Whitman,   4 April 1874
I am at the British Museum waiting for books & whilst I wait will try & send you a few queries which have occurred to me since my last letter. First with respect to *E.P. & His Critics*—on pps. 21–22 you say that in the autumn of 1845 Poe recited "The Raven" at Waverley Place, "a few weeks previous to its publication." Now it was published in Feb. 1845 in Colton's *American Review* & in the *Evening Mirror* for 30 Jany. 1845. You *must* mean 1844. Again, on p. 16, should not "autumn of 1847" be of 1844? Page 70, to MS. of which "later poems" do you refer? "Ulalume"? Again, I do not think it was the spring but in the summer that Poe moved to Fordham. Can you say positively? I am now anxious to get as many queries settled as possible because my "Memoir" must be ready for the publishers to look at speedily. My rough draft is finished up to 1847. I have just been looking out Mr. Savage in Allibone. He is an Irishman & not a son of *your* Savage. He has had a varied life, and most probably knew Mangan personally— hence his exaggerated critique.

Have you received *Temple Bar* proofs or heard anything of your book?

                                                              7 April 1874
I have just received your last letter [Mar. 17] & the enclosed copy of

Poe's letter, and it has, for the moment, so unnerved me that I cannot think of the many things I wanted to say. It makes me tremble to come under *the power of words*. If he could write *so*, what must his language have been! I do not wonder at the impression he made on those who came under his magic spells. I cannot devote any words to speak of this weird letter now—writing as I am in the midst of official turmoil, but will reread it in the solitude of my study where I may, for a while, resign myself to its glamourie. *If* ever a man could *compel* "spirits from the vasty deep" it was he. What a "Faust" he could have written. But, avaunt! I *must* run into the commonplace grooves of my pros & cons. Some day what talks we *will* have, if only on paper.

I must throw my queries in this time, at least, quite helter-skelter. In the first place, I have discovered some particulars of the unknown writings of Poe. In Lowell's notice in Jany. or Feby. no. of *Graham's Maga.*, reprinted in *Evening Mirror*, allusion *is* made to Poe's work on *Conchology*; to a translation & digest of Lemonnier's *Natural History*; & to contributions to *French & English* Reviews! Another note speaks (in *Eve. Mirror*) of a tale called "The Elk"—it probably appeared in *Graham's* between 1840 & 1843—if not, perhaps in *Burton's Gentleman's Maga.* prior to that date, of course.[1] I rather fancy Mr. Burton *is alive*. I will ask Mr. Davidson, who has written today & will write again—'tis only an acknowledgment of mine. I'll send him a small note in a day or so, to cover his expenses. Oh, for Mr. Clarke's address! This story of "The Elk" I would give something for! I have looked through the *Broadway* & have found out that "Isadore" was written by "A. Ide"—Poe omitted name in hurry of printing! There are no new stories, I fancy, *there*—one or two reviews, perhaps, worth extract & some "Editorial notes." I am going carefully through the *Southern Lit. Messenger* & *may* find something there. No. 20 (of *Broadway Journal*) *en passant*, has a review on "Old English Poetry" I may use. Do you think "Peter Snook" in No. 23 is Poe's? Kindly say. Review of Hood in 2nd vol. I may, perhaps, wish to include—in nos. 5 & 8. No. 9, "The Little Frenchman," I suppose is Poe's? The *Gentleman's Maga.* aforementioned, I fancy, had several not reprinted contributions of Poe—in 1839 one on "Gymnastics." Have you the *Northern Monthly* (or *Newark Maga.*) at your institutions? The index to the 3rd (? 2nd) vol. will, probably, contain the name of the author of the paper on Willis, in Jany. 1868. Can you kindly learn?

Returning to *E.P. & His Critics*: p. 22. Was letter from E. B. Browning written *to Poe*? p. 30. Who is the English writer who passed several weeks at Fordham? p. 36. Of Griswold's "Memoir" by— "Society Library"' does G[riswold] mean the library of New-York Historical Society? The portrait prefixed to Redfield's 2-vol. collection—is that not same as the one to G[riswold]'s 4-vol.

collection? I want to have two portraits engraved & if you think *that* a better one than that prefixed to the German translation, or to Gris's collection, I should like to borrow it, if you do not mind its being cut out, & the probable risk of [its] being injured. One at least of the photos, will be used. Is the Fordham cottage still in existence? Perhaps Mr. Davidson could get it photoed for me? I should be glad of any print, or view, or picture, of any place connected with Poe, for use in my collection. I am going to have a photo taken of his school—the frontage is the same as of yore—& will send you a copy. Not a trace can I get of his ever having been there. I'm just going to advertise. I suppose there is not a chance of getting any portrait or view of anyone or thing connected with his younger days? Perhaps a view of Charlottesville University—of his college—might be got? What do you think? I cannot get any reply from the South. Is it not strange? I would obtain material aid for Miss Poe. Do you know anyone in Baltimore? What a light Miss Poe might, if she would, throw on matters—at any rate, I should be glad to help her.

Can you obtain a copy of title pages, indices, & dedications, of any of Poe's books: *i.e.*, of the "Conchology" work, published by "Barrington & Co." & by "I. Bell"; of *The Tales*, published by Wiley & Putnam, & of *The Tales of the Grotesque & Arabesque* 2 vols., printed, I fancy, twice—one by Lea & Blanchard, Philadelphia, 1840, and once by Harper & Bros. The poems of the early editions were privately published only. Can you see or hear anything of an annual called *The Gift*, published under Miss Eliza Leslie's editorship? I fancy the "MS. Found in a Bottle" first appeared in that & perhaps in 1831—between '31 & '35. I should be thankful to know. The *Saturday Visiter* affair I would explain. If you can, do kindly find out. Perhaps a prize was given by *The Gift*?

Never mind Mr. Gill's use of my *Mirror*; he is welcome to it & to its contents to do as he pleases with. I sent him a copy. I only want to get Mr. Clarke's budget—that is, a copy of it.

By the way, in your first letter you said that Routledge & Co. were preparing an edition of Poe's works. Can you remember the source of your information? *It may be important to me to know this.* There! I fear I have wearied you quite enough for this once. Pray forgive me, & believe me to be, ever yours faithfully,

John H. Ingram

I should be glad of the promised *publishable* reminiscences, or, indeed, or any that may be incorporated in the "Memoir."

J.H.I.

Appleton's Monthly, Vol. 7, p. 104, I'm told, had something about Poe's grave, of interest. Can you see that at the Institute? 'Tis not at

British Museum & an American acquaintance had it but has lost that
very part.[2]

J.H.I.

1. "The Elk," or "Morning on the Wissahiccon," a sketch of the river, was first published in *The Opal* for 1844, edited by Mrs. Sarah Josepha Hale.

2. This article, "The Grave of Poe," was in the Jan. 1872 number of *Appleton's*. It is
perhaps a column and a half of mostly maudlin memories of Eugene Didier's having
attended Maria Clemm's funeral "last winter," Mrs. Clemm having died Feb. 16, 1871.
Didier reports his conversations with her, a description of Edgar Poe's personal appearance, and his habits of composition. "His custom was to walk up and down his library. . . .
He never sat down to write until he had arranged the plot, the characters, and even the
language, he was to use." Didier's account of Poe's death is reluctantly accepted by this
writer as more plausible than the story of "cooping" that Ingram, through Dr. William
Hand Browne, of The Johns Hopkins University, was shortly to introduce into Poe biography. Didier claims that on his way home from Richmond to Fordham, Poe missed
the Philadelphia train in Baltimore, met some old friends from West Point, accepted
their invitation to a champagne supper, and after refusing and then taking a glass, got
wildly drunk, wandered off from his friends, was robbed and beaten by ruffians, and left
insensible in the street.

38.   Sarah Helen Whitman to John H. Ingram.   Item 141

My dear Mr. Ingram,   April 7, 1874
    I am so sorry that I have no more definite answers to give to your
many questions. Perhaps by the next mail I may be able to do better. I
have made fruitless inquiries for old numbers of *Graham's Magazine*,
and not until last night could come upon any trace of them. Last
evening, Mrs. Latham (sister of Senator Sprague) promised to send me
a set of *Graham's* running through a year, but what year I could not
ascertain.
    I have, so far, looked over tons of old magazines without avail.
    I will *try* to obtain for you the papers on "Autography".
    I enclose a letter—portions of a letter, from the same friend who
entrusted to me the original letters of Dr. Maupin & Mr.
Wertenbaker—a friend whose sad history I dare not *now* tell you.[1] In a
passage of the letter, marked with my blue pencil lines, there is
something about his West Point career which I fear can now, alas,
never be verified.
    About *dates*. I remember to have learned in some way that the date
of Mrs. Allan's death as given by Griswold was not the correct date. I
forget on what authority I heard this, but I well remember that I made
a note of the date given as the true one. Perhaps I may find it, but I
fear not. If somebody could examine her tombstone.
    I speak of this as important, in reference to what you said about the

record of Poe's age on the books of the University as *throwing out of order* other dates. I have not myself given much attention to these matters because, like poor Mrs. Clemm, I have an inherent incapacity in that direction, & only yesterday dated a letter as April 6, 1863!!— which however I discovered in time to bring my figures *up* to time.

I have been looking through & through the "Marginalia" for those "keys"—have not yet found them, but am sure that I saw them there not many weeks ago. I shall find them sooner or later, rest assured. I think you have Mr. Eveleth's address in a letter of Davidson's which I sent you. I enclose you a letter written in [18]66, which may have something of interest for you.[2]

I send you also a slip which I began to write & left unfinished, on reading James Parton's sketch of Poe in the New York *Ledger* some time ago, containing anecdotes from Griswold, whom he stigmatizes as a writer utterly unreliable—though without naming him.

I once saw a copy of a Richmond paper (I have forgotten the name of the paper) containing an account of this feat of swimming, with several names of Poe's classmates attached to it.

I send you a few of the poems which contain allusions to the Raven [Poe]. "Arcturus," I have told you about. The poems which contain allusions I have spoken of are indicated by the blue pencil marks.

But—"Ave atque Vale." I must leave many things for another time.

Sarah Helen Whitman

Tell me about the old house & its ghostly chambers.

I send by the same mail an answer to your question about "Cinderella" & "Sleeping Beauty". Will send my own volume soon.

Mr. Parton quotes from Rufus W. Griswold, though without quoting his authority, the story of a marvellous feat of swimming performed by Mr. Poe while at the University at Charlottesville. Mr. Parton stigmatises the biographer who relates this story as a notorious falsifier, & utterly discredits the story. "Neither Byron, nor Leander, nor any of the great swimmers, could," he says, "have performed such a feat as this." Yet on the authority of this very biographer, Mr. Parton proceeds to repeat the story of Mr. Poe's expulsion from the University. No such expulsion ever took place.

You ask if "Cinderella" & "The Sleeping Beauty" were in my volume. They were *not*, with the exception of two extracts from the latter, exclusively my own.

When the ballads first appeared in Mrs. Kirkland's *Union Magazine* (nos. for August & December, 1848), the names of my sister & myself were prefixed to them.[3] Her name coming first in the "Cinderella", & mine in "The Sleeping Beauty." She wrote half of "The Sleeping Beauty" & two-thirds of the "Cinderella."

Griswold introduced the former among my poems in his *Female*

Poets of America with a note signifying that the poem was "a joint production of Mrs. Whitman & her sister Miss Power, as before stated"—alluding to his introductory remarks.

In 1867 & [18]68 a few copies of these ballads, improved & revised, were reprinted in pamphlet form for preservation, in view of a future illustrated edition. It was these revised copies that I sent you.

Griswold having given undue precedence to my name in connection with the two poems, in these later reprints my sister's name alone appeared on the title page with Griswold's note appended at the foot of the first page. Confidential—you may have inferred that there is in my life *a power* behind the throne. Say a pleasant word about the ballads for my sake. I speak of them as *hers*.

1. This "friend" was S.E.R. (Sallie Elizabeth Robins), the young girl from Putnam, Ohio, who planned as early as 1861 to write a complete vindication of Poe's reputation and to whom Mrs. Whitman sent items of biographical interest. It was she who invited Mrs. Clemm to live in her Ohio home and serve as a primary source of information about Poe. Mrs. Clemm accepted the invitation eagerly, for she had worn out her welcome in many homes in the Baltimore and New York area; she moved to Ohio in mid–1861. For some reason, certainly not divorced from the difficulties of Poe biography, Miss Robins was shortly thereafter confined in a nearby mental institution, leaving Mrs. Clemm stranded during the winter of 1861–62 in a strange household, on no member of which had she the slightest claim. The beginning of the Civil War made traveling back to Baltimore difficult, but Mrs. Clemm overcame that, as she had so many other obstacles. See, in *Building Poe Biography*, a letter dated June 29, 1861, pp. 54–55, from Mrs. Clemm to Annie Richmond in Lowell, Mass., and the editorial commentary following for a summary of Mrs. Clemm's uncomfortable situation in Ohio.

2. In this letter, dated Dec. 30, 1866, George Eveleth tells Mrs. Whitman that if she is to be the memorialist of either of the forthcoming editions of Poe's works, he is willing to furnish for her use Poe's "Rejoinder" to Thomas Dunn English, a letter from Poe about the Poe-English quarrel, and Poe's statement about the conclusion of "The Mystery of Marie Rogêt."

3. Mrs. Caroline Matilda Stansbury Kirkland (1801–1864) wrote early popular books and edited or assisted with editing the *Union Magazine* from 1847 through 1851.

39. *Sarah Helen Whitman to John H. Ingram.*   Item 143

My dear Mr. Ingram,   April 10, 1874
     I cannot let tomorrow's steamer go without taking you a brief word from me, though I have nothing new of importance. I have not yet received the copies of *Graham's* of which I spoke in my last letter.
     I have written to Wm. D. O'Connor, who wrote the notice of my little book in the Philadelphia *Post*, about "the *Northern Monthly*" & have sent him your paper in the *Mirror*. He has more literary influence than

any other writer of like *independence* that I know. He knows, too, & is known by, many English writers of the period, especially those who have taken much interest in his eccentric friend, Walt Whitman. O'Connor wrote an eloquent defence of him under the title of *The Good Grey Poet*, which received high praise. I wish you would write to him. He is terribly oppressed by his work in the Treasury Department, but he *may* be able to help you. He is a near & dear friend of mine, & if his health permits, I think he will do so. His address is: Wm. D. O'Connor, Treasury Department, Lighthouse Board, Washington, D.C.[1]

The only reason that I did not write to him sooner is that I have heard from his brother-in-law, Dr. Wm. Channing, son of the celebrated clergyman of that name, that O'C was very unwell & greatly out of spirits.

A few years after Poe's death, while he was a young man of 19, he sought my acquaintance, & we have since been the nearest & dearest of friends.

Pabodie is dead, as you will have seen from a former letter. I hope Mr. Latto's letter from Poe, which I gave him & which I mailed to you, has long ere this arrived safely, with the copies of the *Broadway Journal*. It will be too bad if anything should prevent. Let me know as soon as possible. I am anxious to know if the printed letter describing a conversation with [Walter] Savage Landor reached you, & the printed notice of S.H.W., Mrs. Osgood, & Miss Lynch, from Poe's lecture on the New England or American poetesses in Lowell.

I shall have much to tell you hereafter, which I cannot now speak of—oh, I found the "keys" for which I had been hunting: they were in the 220th note (CCXX) [of Poe's "Marginalia"], about DeFoe's *Crusoe*.

Poor Pabodie committed suicide just after he had, through the death of a brother, come into possession of a hundred thousand dollars. He died in Oct. 1870.

5 p.m.—I have just got your letters of 24th & 25th March. I am curious to know about Allibone's "sanctimonious remarks"—curious to know whatever *you* know about Mrs. St. Leon Loud.

The Boston *Commonwealth* of Saturday has the following item: "Mr. William F. Gill will give a special course of dramatic readings at Parker Memorial Hall on Wednesday, April 15 & 22." Our friend still lives, but I fancy has not yet completed his lecture on Poe. Meantime, a young gentleman who sought an introduction to me as a friend of Mr. Gill's, spent an evening with me night before last & spoke of his friend in the most exalted terms as a young man of wonderful genius & an enthusiastic believer in the great poet.

I confess my heart warmed toward him and I was almost persuaded to believe in the possibility that he would someday set to work, as he says, on his defence [of Poe].

I send you two or three slips from O'Connor's letters that you may judge something of his calibre. If anything he has said of Poe will be of any use to you, I can authorize you to use or quote it. He did not know Poe personally, but I doubt not was often unconsciously inspired by him. His devotion to me seems hardly intelligible on any other grounds.

Good night.

S.H.W.

I do not know whether you are acquainted with the last verse of "Ulalume" as originally printed. Poe omitted it at my suggestion, in a copy which he prepared for publication in the Providence *Journal*, with the above heading, & it is so printed in all the subsequent collections. He agreed with me that the penultimate verse made a more effective ending.

Yesterday I went to the Providence Athenaeum Library & found the original version in the *American Whig Review*, edited by Colton. I copied from it the verse, in pencil, for you. At the bottom of the page I found Poe's autograph in pencil. It recalled to me a circumstance which I had entirely forgotten.

"Ulalume" was published without signature & an anonymous copy had floated to me in some newspaper. I was strangely impressed with its weird imagery & vainly questioned everybody likely to have heard of it. One morning, being with Poe at the Athenaeum, I asked him if he had ever seen the poem & could tell me who wrote it. To my infinite surprise, he told me that he himself was the author. Turning to a bound volume of the *Review* which was in the alcove where we were sitting, he wrote his name at the bottom, and I saw it again yesterday, after an interval of more than 24 years.

> "Said we, then—the two, then: "Ah, can it
>   Have been that the woodlandish ghouls—
>   The pitiful, the merciful ghouls—
> To bar up our way and to ban it
>   From the secret that lies in these wolds—
>   From the thing that lies hidden in these wolds—
> Have drawn up the spectre of a planet
>   From the limbo of lunary souls—
> This sinfully scintillant planet
>   From the Hell of the planetary souls?"
> "Ulalume," a Ballad   Colton's *American Whig Review*
>   December, 1847

The Athenaeum has been enlarged since those days & the *Whig*

Reviews are now in a remote corner of the building, on an upper gallery; otherwise the autograph might have been abstracted.

1. William Douglas O'Connor (1832–1889) was an occasional author who spent most of his career as an editor of the *Saturday Evening Post*, and later in various Washington bureaucratic jobs, rising finally to the post of librarian in the U.S. Treasury Department. His strong defense of Walt Whitman, *The Good Grey Poet, a Vindication* (New York: Bunce & Huntingdon) was published in 1866. So "near and dear a friend" did he remain to Mrs. Whitman that when she wrote out her autograph will on May 30, 1878, she left to him the sum of $100, "for his sole use forever."

40. *Sarah Helen Whitman to John H. Ingram. Item 144*

My dear Mr. Ingram,   April 14, [18]74
    I hoped when I last wrote you that I should be able to give in my next definite answers to some of your questions. I think I told you that I had written to my friend Wm. D. O'Connor. Yesterday morning I received the enclosed lines from him, promising that he would write "fully on Sunday." I looked anxiously for his Sunday letter, hoping that it might contain something of interest for you that I might be able to forward in the present letter. But it has not yet come. If you had only a little more time! I spoke in my last [Apr. 10] of O'Connor's friendship for Walt Whitman, who is so much admired by Tennyson, Rossetti, & some other of the English poets. He is not of my husband's family (as you may have supposed), & I had at one time a great repugnance to his writings, but after becoming personally acquainted with him during his visit to the Channings in this city, I learned in a measure to conquer my repugnance, in view of his noble qualities of mind & heart. Still, from a copy of his poems, which he gave me, I have torn out ruthlessly a third of the book.
    Yesterday, in looking for some notice of O'Connor's *Good Grey Poet*, which is mentioned, I find, only in a notice of W.W.'s writings, I turned to Allibone's notice of Poe. It was certainly contributed by some deadly enemy. And his reference to his engagement with "a New England lady," which I had only read carelessly before (if, indeed, I had read it at *all*, which I begin to doubt), was more venomous & insulting than even Griswold's gross fabrication. I remember, now, that Mr. Latto alluded to this passage (quoting it) in one of his letters, & regretted that some one who knew me had not furnished him with a more reliable notice.
    In my next letter I will try to give you an account of our last interview, & you will then see how *great* an injustice has been done to *him*—how gratuitous and unmanly an insult to me! I wish it were

possible to discover the author of this libel. But I must try to be calm till this sad story is elucidated—so far, at least, as my words have the power to elucidate it.

Don't neglect to return Mr. Latto's letter—the *autograph* letter from Poe to Pabodie, as soon as convenient. Did I tell you that you might use the portion of Poe's letter about "Arcturus" if you thought proper to do so?

You ask me to send you a photograph. The only photographs I ever sat for were some little profile views, unskillfully printed, which were taken in 1862 at an establishment in Broadway. On my return to Providence, my sister chanced to see them, & finding that I was about to destroy them on account of an unshapely bonnet, which, after the fashion of the period, was worn far back on the head, she begged me to let her costume the head so as to hide the bonnet, which she did with such success by a coiffure of crowns, helmets, & cowls, as to please so many of my friends that I was induced to have them reprinted with these adornments cut from illustrated newspapers & magazines, etc. I send you one of these, which you will perceive is a piece of composite art.

> What seems its head
> The likeness of a kingly crown has on.

If you care to keep either of them, send me back the one you don't want. There are two fine oil paintings of me, one by C. G. Thompson, a brother-in-law of Mrs. Ritchie, & somewhat overpraised by Hawthorne in his Italian Notes as the finest painter of character in America. There is also another more recently taken—perhaps good photographs can be taken from them—we will see.[1]

But now, for the present, "Vale"

S.H.W.

---

1. The painting of Mrs. Whitman by Cephas Giovanni Thompson (1809–1888) was executed in 1838, when she was thirty-five years old. At her death she willed it to Brown University. The second portrait was painted by John Nelson Arnold (1834–1909) in 1868–69, in Mrs. Whitman's sixty-sixth year, and willed by her to be presented at her executors' discretion to either the Providence Athenaeum Library or the Rhode Island Historical Society. Through error her executors, Caleb Fiske Harris and Dr. William F. Channing, sent the Thompson painting to the Athenaeum Library in 1884, where it now hangs in a frame which came from Gilbert Stuart, in their Art Room, beautiful to see. The Arnold painting, after hanging in the artist's studio in Providence for nearly forty years after its completion, was given to Brown University, and it now hangs in the Caleb Fiske Harris Room of the John Hay Special Collections Library of the Brown University Library. Neither library has seen fit to correct the error made so long ago, and well might each be content with the painting it now has.

41. John H. Ingram to Sarah Helen Whitman

My dear Mrs. Whitman,   14 April 1874
   Even whilst I was writing my last of the 7th to you, I was very
unwell. I came home ill & went to bed where I have been nearly ever
since. My medical adviser forbids pen & ink for some days, but I must
just send you a few lines to acknowledge your letters dated 27th March
& 30th, together with the enclosures, in one of autograph letter of
Poe's (to Mr. Pabodie) & copy of Mr. Wertenbaker & Dr. Maupin's
testimonial; & in other, 3 of Mrs. Clemm's letters. *All* of these
enclosures are valuable & shall be quickly returned.
   The University account will be most valuable for my complete
"Memoir," which is roughly drafted to 1847 only. Any *authentic* record
of Poe's earlier days is so valuable, but so scarce. Mr. Willis's letter will
be useful if you can get copy from Mr. Gill. Mr. G. was advertised last
autumn in New York to deliver lecture on "The Romance of E.P.'s
Life," but I suppose it never came off. The *Home Journal* said he was
well thought of at Boston & that he had some original information
about Poe (? yours or Mr. Clarke's?). I fancy an *amusing* anecdote, I
tell another time, of Mr. G. of Boston refers to his father, a reporter. Oh,
if Mr. Robert Stanard were alive! I fancy he was Poe's prime "chum" &
doubtless classmate at Charlottesville—see note, p. 26 of the
"Memoir," about swimming feat—but this *may* have been earlier than
the University. Did Mrs. Stanard come, think you, from New York? In
the "Marginalia," Poe mentions a few good conversationalists—one a
Mrs. S———d, formerly of New York.
   I have only received three poems yet: "The Pansy," "The Portrait,"
& "The Raven"—the two latter I have had printed in *Mirror* & will
forward you them, if you like. "The Portrait" was printed before your
emendations came to hand. "Recollections of Landor" came & is
herewith returned, as is also 2 notices of your dear little book, as I am
glad to be able to return something—the *autograph* letters will be
registered when I return them. The only notices of your poems that
reached me were *Putnam's* & Providence *Journal* (Mr. Anthony's). The
sonnets "all coloured with the fame of one" have also arrived.
   The autograph is beautiful. The *Broadway Journal* is safe at the
office—locked up till I return. It will be useful in many ways—of
which hereafter—be duly cared & returned carefully. Don't fear about
"the South Carolina Rose." I shall allude to the story in the most
general & slightest way.
   Mrs. St. Leon Loud. I meant to ask *if there were any story?* There
must be something *sub rosa*, from the slighting allusion in the
"Eulogium" & Allibone's remark. I have seen a very pretty poem by
this lady.

The *Sixpenny Maga.* "Reminiscences" are *not* in Duyckinck. What could I have said to make you think so? 'Tis long out of print, so cannot get copy & I want to use several pps. for the "Memoir." 'Tis visits & *talks* at Fordham with Poe. I don't quite believe all of it. I wrote editor of [*Sixpenny Magazine*] twice, whilst it existed, & sent stamps, but he never replied to my questions as to author, &c. Shall send it to you when I've used the parts I want.

Only 3 *Mirrors* sent. I've muddled somehow about Mrs. Osgood. I'll try & get that altered in *Temple Bar*, p. 11, if possible, but I'm not certain 'tis not too late. Slighting the stage was not intended—context explains why "Rosalie" was styled a girl—Edgar, "the boy." Extract from Lowell notice I have acknowledged. The poems not mentioned not to hand. Mrs. Clemm's letters shall be strictly private. Shall send a perfect photo of self soon.

Am amused that you find something in my verses to admire. I thought that I was the only one who could care for them *now*. I've turned to "The Garden Gate," & find last line to penultimate verse corrected to "Returned *unto* our Garden Gate." "Bended" is a great improvement, & now, if you can get anyone to republish do so with this or any of mine. If I did not think you saw thro' friendship's *couleur de rose* specs, I should feel encouraged in my rash intention of some day collecting & publishing a little volume of boyish pieces, including a few of those in this vol. of "Dalton Stone." 'Tis full of errors—some most stupid—"The Unknown Captive," p. 3, "dear" for "drear" twice, &c. You have hit off some of my weaknesses to a "t."

I fear that I am much to blame in having so continually trespassed on your good nature—how I grieve for having injured—most unintentionally though it was—your sight. Do take rest. I've done nothing for a week—dare not—have worked too hard & must rest, perforce—& then *Excelsior*!

Mr. Davidson has sent me Mrs. Lewis's address in London. I wrote & she answered most cordially & I am to see her when she has recovered from an attack of influenza![1] She says she *can* help me—but I shall be *very careful* with her. What do you advise?

Oh, my poor head. Must say goodbye. Yours, ever faithfully,

John H. Ingram

1. Mrs. Sarah Anna Robinson Lewis (1824–1880), minor poet and wife of Sylvanus D. Lewis, a Brooklyn lawyer, had trouble deciding at various stages of her literary "fame" which name best suited, Estelle Anna or Stella Anna, but finally settled on Stella, during which process her husband paid Griswold to make changes in his *Female Poets of America*, and later her changes in her name were to cause bibliographical perplexities, especially between Caleb Fiske Harris and John Ingram. Poe did not like her, but she did furnish money and hospitality to both Poe and Mrs. Clemm, obviously in a bid for Poe's favorable reviews of her verse, which she got. Mrs. Clemm was a "guest" for long periods

in the Lewis household in the 1850s, but when Mr. and Mrs. Lewis were divorced in 1858, and Mrs. Clemm had made herself uncomfortable and her presence unwanted by taking Mr. Lewis' side in an argument with his wife, which he lost, it was necessary for Mrs. Clemm to find other quarters.

42. *Sarah Helen Whitman to John H. Ingram.* Item 145

My dear Mr. Ingram,   April 17, [18]74
     In my last hurried letter [Apr. 14] I neglected to advert to your questions about the possibility of obtaining autographs of letters etc. They are *very rare.* Three years ago, Mrs. Botta, in aid of some great national charity, got up a costly & valuable collection of autographs & portraits of distinguished people. While it was in preparation, she wrote to me earnestly entreating me to let her have a fragment, if no more, of one of Poe's letters or poems. I was obliged to decline doing so, and, when the catalogue of the collection was published, I observed that, in connection with the announcement of an autograph of E. A. Poe, the words were affixed, *"very rare."* Mrs. Botta has unrivalled enterprise in the pursuit of any desired object, & she would not have appealed to me so *earnestly* & *repeatedly* if it had not been exceedingly difficult to obtain one elsewhere. The last fragment of his writing which I gave away—I mean the last addressed to *me*, was a brief postcript, cut from a letter & signed only by his first name. I gave it to James T. Fields, the Boston publisher & *litterateur*, ten years ago. Mr. Fields would never have applied to *me* (since he has never been friendly to Poe, I hear), had he been able to have obtained his autograph from any other source. In reply to your next question—I can*not* point out any letter in Griswold's "Memoir" as authentic. I have reason to think that many of them were *not* authentic, but it might be difficult for me now to *prove* this.
     You will see from the copies of the letters of Poe which I have sent you that it would be difficult to find in his letters to *me* lines or sentences sufficiently impersonal to use.
     You say in your last letter, "I was hoping to hear the sequel of your former reminiscences—why am I kept from hearing the result of the [*Letter breaks off*]
     I must leave this story for another letter. No time today.
                                                                     S.H.W.

My dear Mr. Ingram,   April 21st,
     Your letters of April 2nd & 7th received. You do not say anything of having received mine of March 17th, with a copy of a note written by E.A.P. on board one of the Long Island Sound steamers. Have I lost one of your letters, or have you lost one of mine, or did you in your

hurry forget to announce its reception? You speak of one of *later* date, but not of *that*, which makes me a little anxious. And now to our dry facts again. I will take up the questions in yours of April 2nd *first*. You ask about the German "Raven." I do not want you to return it. I know nothing of the Mr. Whitman to whom the book is inscribed. The pamphlet was sent me by a young lawyer of New York, Franklin Burdge, who graduated at Brown University in Providence. I have distributed all the copies of "New Facts" which you have sent me. You speak of *other mistakes* than those I pointed out. Do you refer to anything relating to the Dunn English article? I fancy that some things left out in Godey's article are to be found in *Broadway Journal*. Is it not so? I hope that the *Broadway* reached you safely. I sent with it a letter containing an *autograph* letter of Poe's, & copies of the Wertenbaker & Maupin letters, on March 27th. March 30th, I sent comments on proof of *Temple Bar* article. I hope it will not reach you too late for alteration of the paragraph about Mrs. Osgood's kindness to Mrs. Clemm—ninety-nine readers in a hundred might not notice it, but it might be criticized by those who knew about it.

Mr. Latto wrote to me a few days ago to ask if the pictures which I described as hanging in a quiet parlor in New York—the pictures of Poe & Mrs. Osgood, were not seen by me in the house of Mrs. Osgood!

Everybody in New York understood by "that fragrant & delicious Clover-nook" I meant the home of Phoebe & Alice Cary. Alice had written a volume of stories called *Clovernook*, praised by the critics as better than Miss Mitford's stories of *Our Village*.[1] I did not agree with them. The pictures belonged to Griswold & were lent by him to the Carys. Even if you *could* get a reply from Miss Rosalie Poe, I doubt if you could obtain any particulars of interest from her, for the reasons which I have stated before. However, I have never seen her, nor do I know anyone who knows her. It is only through a paragraph in the papers that I have heard of her destitution. I will try to find out through O'Connor. I know no one in Richmond. I should not know where to obtain for you the earlier collections of the poems. The 1845 collection published in the Wiley & Putnam series called "Library of American Books," I have. It was given to me by Edgar Poe & has his autograph, etc. on the fly-leaf. I cannot part with it, but I can give you the titles. On the first title page, "Wiley & Putnam's Library of American Books. The Raven & Other Poems." On the following page,

The Raven & Other Poems
by
Edgar A. Poe
New York
Wiley & Putnam, 161 Broadway
1845

Then, after the poems, another title page, "Wiley & Putnam's Library of American Books. Poe's Tales."

I shall cut out the Preface & Index & enclose them in my letter. You need not return. They are published in the editions issued after his death. Certainly I cannot object to your using such parts of "The Paean" as you think best. I only tell you my own view of the matter. But if *you* think they will not injure his reputation, by all means print them, especially if you think they will be of interest to his friends. I am glad that you found the German pamphlet likely to be of use. Do you know that I am an admirer of Clarence Mangan, though I thought Savage could know little about Poe, to say that *his* grief was superficial or assumed, while Mangan's was real & heartfelt. They had *both* only too much knowledge of "the burden & the mystery of all this unintelligible world."

There can be no doubt of the genuineness of the autograph in Stoddard's article—the lines from "Annabel Lee." Did I understand you rightly as saying that you doubted them? The *mezzotint* in my volumes *is* the same as that in the four-vol. edition of [18]56, if *that* is a copy of Osgood's painting.

I have just received a letter from O'Connor. He cannot tell me the name of the writer of that paper on Willis—thinks the magazine continued only through a few numbers—will try to find out & let me know.

And now, after these brief & imperfect replies to your letter of April 2 (which came yesterday), I will take up yours of the 7th, which came this morning. My allusion to the reading of "The Raven," before the appearance of the poem in the autumn of 1845, at one of Miss Lynch's soirées, must of course be regarded as an anachronism. I have been looking over the letters of that lady, but find the one in which she described Poe's reading of "The Raven" at her house *is missing*. I know that she spoke of it in one of her letters of that winter, 1844 or perhaps 1845, but can find no letter of hers earlier than May 20, 1845, in which she says nothing of the reading. I must leave it. "Some one has blundered," as the Laureate sings. It is very much more likely to be me than anybody else. I think that I can guess how it happened. A Providence lady passed that winter or the next with Miss Lynch & described to me the effect of the reading upon the assembled company. Perhaps I referred to *her* for the date after the letter was lost, & it *might* have been given me incorrectly by her. I *now* think that the reading must have been given early in January of 1845. Again, I *may* have been misled in thinking the reading was *before* the publication of the poem. I think in my next edition (?) I shall have to leave out "a few weeks." etc.

Certainly, on p. 16, should have been 1844 instead of 1847. I thought

I corrected it in the book I sent you, did I not? And will you make the correction for me in the copy in the British Museum? It was a misprint, which I pointed out to Carleton at the time. It should have been corrected in the list of errata—but I believe this would begin & end the "list."

I knew that *you* would feel the truth & fervor & passionate sincerity of that wonderful letter. It is an utterance of love so profoundly *real, yet so divinely ideal,* that it has to me the deathless fragrance of an immortal flower.

Burton is dead. Has been dead many years.[2] I will look for "The Elk." It *may* have been in the summer that Poe moved to Fordham, but I am *quite sure* that he told me that he took Virginia out there in the spring of the year to see the cottage, & that it was half-buried in fruit trees, which were then all in blossom. That she was charmed with the little place, which was rented for a very trifling sum. They may not have gone there to live immediately, however, but I thought from what he said that they *did*. I saw the place in March, 1856. I went there with some friends. The cottage was occupied by a Mr. Pond, a composer and professor of music. We were permitted to enter the house, which was then kept in nice order, and everything remained much as it did in the time of its celebrated inmate. The neighborhood was then very picturesque—there were groves of trees which extended for a long distance on either side of the road, through which the beautiful little river, called the Bronx, wandered deviously, now seen on one side of the road & now on the other. But everything is changed now, & the city of New York, once 14 miles from Fordham, now reaches almost to the quiet little village. The lady who spent several weeks there in the early autumn of 1847 was Miss Anna Blackwell. She was in very delicate health at the time, & a friend of hers who chanced to know Mrs. Clemm prevailed upon that lady to receive her as a boarder for a few weeks. She was charmed with the exquisite neatness & quiet of the household & the delicious repasts, prepared for her by Mrs. Clemm. She was not much acquainted with Poe & saw but little of him during her stay there, but spoke of him as a courteous & gentlemanly person. She came to Providence for magnetic treatment in the summer of 1848, & returned to England in the fall. There is in a no. of *Harper's Monthly,* quite recent, a view of the University at Charlottesville & an account of its early history. You will find it within the last two years.[3]

I don't know how I can find out about *The Gift.* I have one annual of that name, but no year. No date. It contains "William Wilson."[4] But I must stop now.

1. Alice Cary (1820–1871) and her sister Phoebe (1824–1871) were both popular poets and members of the New York literati; both were especially good friends with Rufus

Griswold. Mary Russell Mitford (1787–1855) had published in 5 volumes between 1824–32 *Our Village: Sketches of Rural Character and Scenery* (London: G. and W. B. Whittaker). Alice Cary had published *Clovernook; or Recollections of Our Neighborhood in the West* (New York: J. S. Redfield, 1852).

2. William Evans Burton, born in London on Sept. 24, 1804, had emigrated to the United States in 1834 where he became a popular actor and author, as well as publisher of *Burton's Gentleman's Magazine* in Philadelphia from 1837 to 1840, with Poe as his editor for part of that time. He died in New York City on Feb. 10, 1860.

3. *Harper's New Monthly Magazine*, 44 (May 1872), 815–26.

4. "William Wilson" was published first in *The Gift* for 1840.

43. *John H. Ingram to Sarah Helen Whitman*

My dear Mrs. Whitman,   21 April 1874
   You will have received my last letter [Apr. 14] telling you of my illness—today, the first time in a fortnight I have been out. It is summer—summer has burst her swelling sheath & bloomed upon us here in a single day—& me—I am suffering under a languor of body & mind—unable to read. I have just been turning over the pages of George Curtis's *Lotus Eating* merely to look listlessly at Kensett's beautiful little vignettes.[1] I could not read, but still named—*words* (& you know the power of words!) therein have recalled "the tender grace of a day that is fled," that *can* "never come back to me." And your letter, too, which arrived today, enclosing those of Mr. O'Connor, have stirred "thoughts too deep for words."

> And I would that my pen could utter
> The thoughts that arise in me.

But, alas, I can today only talk what you will call nonsense. My nerves are all unstrung! I do not know what jealousy is—still, I felt a twinge at reading those letters of Mr. O'C's. I have been so selfish with you & grown to look forward so eagerly for your letters that I began to think I had nearly monopolized all your leisure thoughts &—well, I find you have a nearer & a dearer & a more tangible friend. Oh, that I had the wings of a dove! When will science find a speedier path across the Atlantic's foam, so that England & America may hear the beating of each other's hearts? But there! Forgive all my bombast today, for I am out of sorts with everything. A few more hours & Richard will be himself again.

   I cannot write much today, although I have so much to answer & so much to say. Firstly, speaking of what came almost last—that extract from *Chambers's Journal*. Why that very article was the first one that introduced me—a boy of about twelve—to a knowledge of Edgar Poe![2] Hence forth & for ever he has been a guiding star to me. The hours I,

& one *who is not*, have spent over that very paper. I may well ask by what "strange alchemy of brain" you should think of sending that to me. I send the half, all that remains of the original paper—the paper that first altered the entire structure of my mental life! I will retain your copy for a short time. I keep every scrap you send me together, so you may rely upon getting everything back again when you need it.

As for the *Broadway Journals* which are still locked up (unseen by me, as yet) at the office, I feel that I cannot so far impose upon your kindness as to accept as a gift. I will make a careful use of them, & then, quite as gratefully, return them to you. I feel that I have already so over-used your kindness—so imposed upon your good will & liberality that I am quite ashamed of myself. My dear Mrs. Whitman, what can you think of me? I really don't know how to repay your kindly aid. A little while, however—a little patience, & you will see the results of your help. Be I spared a few more years & the name of Edgar Poe—freed from the polluting daub of Griswold's touch—shall be honoured from John O'Groats to Land's End. A few weeks & you will begin to receive my papers on Edgar Poe. I have written a review of his 1831 vol. of poems & in deference to your wish have omitted some of "The Paean," but not so much as you scored out—you will not mind this—will you? Wait till you get the paper & read my views. 'Tis coming out in the *Gentleman's*—the oldest, *by far*, of our monthlies.[3] All these short papers & magazine sketches are to prepare the public for the "Memoir."

I will do justice to Miss Power's ballads. Why not have them republished in England? "Cinderella" would just suit Warner, the publisher of *Flora Symbolica*. They would be sure to give something for the copyright. What does Miss Power say to this?

A few words, by the way, I have long wanted to speak, on the *Flora Symbolica* subject—on another sheet you'll find them. On another page you will see some remarks about C[hristina] Rossetti—ten, or more years ago, we twain were constant correspondents, & I have just "turned up" a MS. I then wrote, for a magazine that died too soon, about Jean Ingelow, C.R., &c.,[3] and I find these words—"The following very beautiful poem, 'At Home,' contains much that would have pleased the congenial taste of Edgar Poe—the most original of all modern poets": & then follows the lyric of which—on another page—I have copied the first & weakest verse. Wm. Rossetti, whose editing of Shelley so upset Mr. O'Connor, is an intense admirer of Poe & I could shew you a bushel of letters from him about my forthcoming "Memoir." W.R. is on his bridal tour & a few days ago was in the south of France. I rather worried him about the extra stanza to "Ulalume"— he quoted it in a collection of American poetry & I challenged him as to his authority. He could not remember at first, but we unearthed it in Griswold—in an old edition—at last.

I enclose for your perusal & return one and one-half letters *re*. Poe; one from Lord Lytton, & half a one of Swinburne's *re*. help for Miss R. Poe—the other half I find is not very ladylike. I trust to you not to let these letters be seen by anyone who would publish anything in them—let them be strictly *entre nous* & when read, please return to me—I value them.

Do you know anything of Mr. Whistler, *vide* Swinburne's remark?

I cannot find the song book with poem by Mrs. Loud, née Barstow. When I can I will send it—as also Allibone's letter, or rather note—it was pure "fudge"!

Mrs. Lewis asked me to call last Saturday, but I was too ill to leave the house. I have asked her to name another day. You will speedily learn the result. Mr. Eveleth never answered my letter, nor have several Americans. I will write to Mr. O'Connor, as soon as I can, but I have to complete a paper of 30 pps. for the *Quarterly* on Edgar Poe, in which I shall not use all my information. I am pressed by the publishers for a portion of the "Memoir" & yet have only a rough draft of it, and on the other hand, the doctor protests against me writing, or *even thinking* for some time to come. I will resume tomorrow, because there are things in your letters that I cannot leave unanswered any longer, & then may be silent for several days—every spare effort for my MSS.

22 April 1874

Firstly, the poems came safely & although I regret the vol., still, they have afforded me pleasure & will assist my work. I dare not linger to say what I want to about them, however, now. I shall devote an entire letter soon to them & the sonnets.

Poe's notice of the 3 Female Poets of New England, I will copy & return in course of a post or two. I have found Allibone's note. The cards with texts, &c. & about waste of time, I gave away at once. The note is on a printed paper I want, about indexing, so copy first half— 2nd half is about books (quite foreign to our purpose). S. A. Allibone is writing:

Dear Mr. Ingram:

It would be difficult to answer one half of your queries *re*. Poe. The best plan, I think, would be for you to draw up a series of questions numbered, and advertise them in the *Atlantic Monthly*, and *The Nation* (both at New York), requesting answers to be sent directly to you. As it may save you trouble, I return the letter to me, &c., &c.

Faithfully yours,
S. Austin Allibone

This is all very well, but what I pointedly asked for most was some information about Poe's "Autobiography," *nowhere else alluded to* than in this account of Mrs. St. Leon Loud. In the so-called "Eulogium," March 1850, *S. Lit. Messenger*, you will see an allusion to her. When my books are all unpacked—I have so many—I shall be able to find & send you Mrs. Loud's poem of "The Deserted Homestead," or some such name.

I enclose you a critique on Poe by E. Benson you may like to see, & the *Home Journal* story of "The Raven," *re.* Alice, &c. On the other side of the slip you will see something about Mr. Gill & his "Romance of E. Poe."[4]

My illness has so upset me that I am not sure what I have answered & what is to answer. I regret the little photo of Cinderella, *re.* yours of the 30th Ulto. Perhaps the thief discovered in Providence Post Office may be able to restore it & the book. I have told you what poems I had received. The sonnets came happily to hand. I number all your letters & in most cases keep the enclosures in them, making a *précis* of contents for reference, but, as I generally reread them every now & then, that is scarcely necessary. Everything of yours shall be returned when the "Memoir" is in print.

The "Ultima dim Thule" photo is in the publishers' hands for engraving, & the two letters of Poe for autograph & facsimile. I suppose there is no better view of Fordham come-at-able than *Harper's Monthly*? Perhaps Mrs. Lewis can help me to get photo or view of Poe's grave, or the cemetery, or of the hospital where he died, or of the Virginia university, or of the Academy where he went to school in Richmond—I don't know its name. Perhaps Mr. Davidson could get me view of West Point, or of Poe's residence in New York, or Fordham? I have just sent him a few hurried lines, but will write him again soon & send him a remittance in case he can do so, or get me anything—"Autography," &c.

An account of our old house in another letter to follow.

I've no faith in ghosts *or spirits* out of literature. I believe in poesy, in nature, in intellect, in beauty, in woman & —well that is all just at present. Spiritualism, *as such*, is a myth & a sham, I am certain.

I am thankful for those passages from Poe's letter of Oct. 18, 1848, & for copy of Charlottesville document—they are most valuable & will only appear in the "Memoir."

Never mind the dates—I believe I have got them all in "apple pie order." The last lines in Griswold's collection could scarcely be to Mrs. Shelton because, says Poe, "These weak lines are written by him—By him who, as he pens them, thrills to think his spirit is communing with an angel's." Evidently, therefore, with some one dead. In the *S.L. Mess.*, July 1835, he addressed "To Mary" the lines, "Mary, amid the cares—the woes," &c. afterwards altered & inscribed "To F——," p. 53 of collection. Poem "To One in Paradise" is all right in "The Assignation"—last verse & all complete. You compare with p. 33, Vol. 2 of collection. It was not Wm. R. Wallace who wrote the criticisms, I find from Mr. Davidson's letter, so, perhaps, it *may* not be good. I shall not allude to the *Eureka* publication story.

Accept all you hear of Swinburne—good or bad—*cum grano salis.*

Au revoir, dear friend,

John H. Ingram

1. George William Curtis, *Lotus Eating: A Summer Book*, illustrated by Kensett (New York: Harper & Brothers, 1852). John Frederick Kensett (1826–1872) was a landscape painter and engraver of the "Hudson River School."

2. The clipping was "The Life and Poetry of Edgar Poe," reprinted in the *Living Age*, Apr. 16, 1853, pp. 157–61, from *Chambers's Edinburgh Journal*, 19 (Feb. 26, 1853), 137–40. If John Ingram read this article when he was "a boy of about twelve," it is added proof, if any be needed, that his true birthday was 1842. This newsclipping is Item 518 in the Ingram Poe Collection.

3. Jean Ingelow (1820–1897) was a member of Christina Rossetti's circle and a poet thought by her public to be of high merit.

4. This newsclipping was almost certainly Eugene Benson's summing-up of Poe as a critic in *The Season*, Aug. 1871. Item 556 in the Ingram Poe Collection describes a one-half column clipping which is believed to be a portion of this article, "The American Critic."

44. Sarah Helen Whitman to John H. Ingram.   Item 147

My dear Mr. Ingram,   April 24, 1874

Your strangely interesting letter of March 31 has only reached me today, though your letters of April 2 & April 7 were received three & four days ago.

This will explain to you why I feared that a letter might have been lost.

What you tell me of the mournful heritage of your house filled me with unutterable awe & sorrow. There is, then, a closer bond of sympathy between us than I had yet dreamed. How sad & strange it all seems. My own life has been filled with constant anxiety by the fluctuating mental moods of one nearest & dearest to me—one gifted with noble intellectual powers & admirable moral qualities, but warped through & through by a naturally haughty and dominant temper which from early years could brook no constraint & no opposition. This hereditary temper once, under circumstances of unusual excitement, developed into acute mania, which yielded, after a few weeks of retirement & hospital treatment, to an accustomed state of health. But the constitutional temperament still remains, often compelling me to either lead a life of comparative seclusion, or obstructing & complicating all my social relations. It has been the mission of my life to harmonize & soothe this haughty & perverse spirit, united, as it is, with so much that is exceptionally original, witty, sagacious, & brilliant—nor this alone, but so much that is intrinsically *good, sincere,* & *generous.* It is this blending of good & perverse qualities that has made my life *so* difficult. The fear of all fears, to me, has been that this noble nature might become permanently overthrown by some unlooked-for disturbance of its ever treacherous serenity.[1] But, let us clasp hands in tenderest sympathy over these abysms of sorrow & trust that death will leave on the loved ones, so afflicted on earth, "only the beautiful." *Do* not yield to depression—do not feel that your spirit can ever be *alone.*

I cannot write another word today. I had intended to have sketched for you the progress of my story, "left half told," that you might see how rudely such chroniclers as Allibone, *et. al.* have profaned it by their touch—but not today.

I have had another letter from O'Connor, who says he was *"intensely* interested in your paper in the *Mirror."* I did not tell him that you were thinking of getting out a new edition of the works. I send you some of the pages of his letter. You need not return them. I think he will write to you. I copied for him what you said of Stoddard & what you said of Swinburne & part of Swinburne's note to you.

O'Connor has *great genius,* but not a very *marketable* kind of genius. He is eccentric & original & intense—& has no enterprise, & though he has had some fine opportunities of distinguishing himself in journalism, offered him by leading New York papers, he cannot put his Pegasus into harness, & so lives on a salary & slaves for daily bread. But *good night* & *good morrow,* & heartfelt wishes for your best welfare.

S.H.W.

You ask if I have noticed the discrepancy in the facsimile of the last verse of "Annabel Lee" to the usual line? I believe it is stated that Poe made two versions of that line. I have seen something in print about it, but I have forgotten where & when.

I do *not* know whose name is intended in the "two foreign, soft, disyllables." I have never heard any suggestion on the subject.

You ask who is M.L.S.? I have asked *you* the same question in a recent letter. Mr. Eveleth, from whom I had a letter last week, says Mrs. Shelton's name was Sarah. I had before supposed the lines might have been addressed to her. I do not think Mrs. Stanard had a daughter Mary, but I may be mistaken.

I will try to find out in what number of *Harper's Monthly* I saw an engraving of the University of Virginia. It was since the number containing Stoddard's article, I am quite sure. I think it must have been in the winter of '72–3.

About "Landor's Cottage" I am anxious to know *when* & *where* the paper first appeared. Because the last time Poe was in Providence, one day in praising the simple but effective arrangement of some articles of furniture in the room where we were sitting, he said, "I intend, Helen, to write *a pendant* to 'The Domain of Arnheim,' in which I shall speak of beautiful effects attainable by inexpensive means."

When I saw the article "Landor's Cottage" in the collection published after his death, I noticed that he had described the exact pattern of the paper on the room where we sat together.

Nobody has been able to tell me when & where this article was first published. I *long to know*.[2]

Oh! that I could have seen your "Mortmere"! What a suggestive name for such a story.

S.H.W.

1. The person here referred to was Mrs. Whitman's sister, Susan Anna Power, born Feb. 1, 1813, ten years after Sarah Helen.

2. "Landor's Cottage" was first published in the *Flag of Our Union*, June 9, 1849. This weekly family newspaper had been established in 1846 by Frederick Gleason and Martin Murray Ballou; by 1850 its circulation was 100,000; it was merged in 1871 with the *American Union*. All files of the *Flag* were thought to be destroyed in a fire in 1872 or 1873, but in 1909 Professor Killis Campbell of the University of Texas discovered a complete set for 1849 in the Library of Congress.

45. *John H. Ingram to Sarah Helen Whitman*

My dear Mrs. Whitman,   28 April 1874

Although every extra word I now write is an extra pang of pain, I cannot forbear from writing to you, and answering questions, settling queries & telling tales. There is so much to say, however, that the difficulty is where to begin. In the first place, your photos—I have kept one & herewith return two—but they are not good—they are too small &, in my opinion, "the kingly crown" is *not* ornamental. Why not a good vignette of you as you are?

You say it is a pity that I am in such haste about Poe's life. Now it is a most providential thing that I have been in such haste, leaving everything on one side, & neglecting pecuniary & literary engagements, in order to get the "Memoir" ready for the press, for now I feel, what with bodily & mental languor, that had I not roughly drafted out my references, &c., &c., I should have had to place the work on one side for an indefinite time. Literary labor, & all work exercising the brain, creates quite a fever in my poor weary head. My "Memoir" for the *Quarterly* is nearly complete & should be finished this week, & the entire life for the collection cannot take me long. I had purposed 200 pps. for its length, but the publishers will not allow it to exceed 100 pps. In present circumstances, this is just as well, as I can embody all real information in that space & it will still allow me to go on collecting information & copies of letters for either further editions, or, perhaps, ultimately for a separate biography. It is not improbable that some day—ere very long—I may contrive a visit to America, where I shall necessarily be able to gather much more information.

While I think of it, for a week or so, do not let any one know of my intended publication of the works, or some piratical publishers will be anticipating me. Last month a few lines appeared in the *Mirror* stating that "our readers will be pleased to learn that Mr. John H. Ingram is engaged upon an entirely new life of Edgar Allan Poe," &c., &c. Yesterday I received a letter from the editor requesting my reply to a letter he enclosed from some London bookselling firm asking who John H. Ingram was & who was to publish the life of Poe, as *a New York correspondent had asked them.* I declined to give any information without further particulars. You shall learn the result, if any, when I know. Perhaps it was Mr. Stoddard? Friend or foe of Poe's will matter little when once the work is published.

While I think of it, in your *E. Poe & His Critics* you say Mrs. Poe was buried in "a neighboring cemetery" by Fordham. This is not quite correct—there was no cemetery—she was buried in the family vault of a neighbor who allowed her to be interred there. This is interesting as corresponding with the terms of "Ulalume."

I have at last got the *Broadway Journal* & *looked* through it & found much of interest, but I still feel your writing in 2nd vol. notwithstanding, that you cannot part with these books, and that much as I value them, I dare not so impose upon your great kindness as to retain them.[1] I know it would be too great a pang for you to part with them. Their use will be valuable to me & there are many things in them, not in the 4-vol. collection, that I can reprint. There was a prospectus of the *Stylus* in 1st vol. Did you know that? I can quote some words from it.

And now a few words *entre nous* & the proverbial post. When speaking of myself it matters little what I say because I only am concerned, & although in writing to you of others, you may retain *sub rosa* what should be so, still, *as you know*, letters most sacred, & only intended for one pair of eyes, may someday come to light & wound &

anger those who see their contents; therefore, you will comprehend that sometimes there are things which I could say to you—*viva voce*—which I cannot entrust to the accidents of a letter.

In my last I told you that Mrs. Lewis was in town & that I expected to call on her. She invited me the Saturday before last, but I was too ill to go, but had the pleasure of calling last Saturday. She admires Poe immensely & shewed me several *short* notes from him, but not one containing anything sufficiently interesting for publication—her longer letters, she tells me, have been lost, &c. She has the MS. of Poe's critique on her, but I do not think I care for any of it for facsimile—it is much garbled, it appears, in Griswold's collection. Mrs. Lewis has a very bad opinion both of Griswold & *Mrs. Clemm*, but does not seem able to give me the slightest item of publishable interest. She is very kindly disposed, but I cannot see that she is able to help me. She has a magnificent portrait—a daguerreotype—of Poe, as fresh as if just taken, & if I had not placed the "Ultima dim Thule" portrait in the engraver's hands, should have like to use it.[2] If anything of interest comes from this quarter, you shall duly learn it.

As the miscellaneous writings will be in the last monthly volume, there is still some time to recover the papers on "Cryptology," &c. I have written to Mr. Davidson *re.* the papers on "Autography" which were reprinted in the New York *Illustrated News* in 1853. Mr. Eveleth has never replied to my letter—the conclusion of "Marie Rogêt" & the "Dunn English letter"—which he said he had—would have been useful—very useful.

I am told that I should put my name and address *outside* letters uncertain of reaching their destination, as with my first to you, otherwise, unlike with us, they will not be returned from America.

I return the Shaver story. I am simply disgusted with such absurd & vile lies & only wonder that newspapers can be found to insert such rubbish. Mr. Field's recollections I have not heard or seen anything of, save from you. The European sale for the book, I should say, is a vision of the authors or publishers.

As regards Walt Whitman, I am not in a position to judge of his merits. I saw a most eulogistic notice of his works some years ago, & at once ordered a copy of *Leaves of Grass*, or some such title, but my bookseller could not get it without sending to America, so I let the matter drop—since then I have frequently seen & heard of him—opinions of the most divergent hue, & a few weeks ago the *Academy*, my favorite literary journal, in a notice of Bryant, written by a Mr. George Saintsbury, said that America's only two original poets were Edgar Poe & W. Whitman. I have only seen a few extracts from Whitman's works—reviewers seem shy of quoting him—& I must say that they have not taken me by storm. Some day I will try again to get something of his complete & judge him fairly. Tell it not in Gath, but really the few detached sentences I had seen seemed only the work of a superior—a nature's Martin Tupper & of all the insufferable twaddle that was ever written, the Proverbial Philosophy is the worst. I would as soon read a vol. of MS. sermons by a place-hunting parson. I daresay Whitman is better than I think. I would not misjudge a true poet for my good right hand, but I will not endure any imposters in my realms of Poesy. I can be cruel on such subjects & some of these days I may turn my hands to deeds of war.

There is a curious incident told me by Mrs. Lewis which I may surely tell & which may interest you. Mrs. Lewis dreamed that Edgar Poe appeared to her & said, "I have much to tell you," & thereupon, began saying something which, with the usual indistinctness of dreams, was blurred and unrememberable when she awoke. The following day my letter reached her & she at once thought Poe had been telling her of me! There is a curious coincidence for you. This morning I dreamed (the first time for weeks) & dreamed that my paper on "Poe's Early Poems," which will appear this week in the *Gentleman's Magazine*, was out, & that I was being "pitched into" about it by the reviewers. I was preparing a withering reply when my irrepressible scorn woke me up. I hope this nonsense won't weary you when we have so much else to discuss.

By the way, Poe did do that swim, only Grisworld, as usual, enlarged on the performance—it was 6 & not 7–½ miles. Poe declared he could swim the English Channel—22 miles. There is nothing so wonderful in the swimming 6 or 7 miles. I have a married brother who could have done that a year or two ago—but the wonder was *against the strong tide*—one of the strongest, Poe *declared*, ever known in the river. So much for Mr. Parton's scepticism!

Tomorrow I will send you *Gentleman's Magazine* for May with my notice of "Poe's Early Poems."[3] I trust there is nothing in it to annoy you. I shall be very anxious to know—it was written very hurriedly, as I have scarcely dared to snatch a moment from the life, & you will scarcely credit the amount of labour that has required for the adjustment of dates, &c. I have foregone many things—I can assure you—to carry that out properly. Some day, however, I hope to get more information for a new edition. I do not think I shall be able to go to press *before* June.

Mr. Latto's letter gave you a faithful report of Allibone's story, which is where you had read it before, probably. Mr. Latto's autograph letter is with the publishers. It will be duly returned by registered post.

You had said that I might use the lines about "Arcturus." I shall duly notice Miss Powell's [Power's] ballads & in another number your poems & the *E.P. & His Critics*, but you will not think it neglect if you do not get the notices for some weeks. I must strain every nerve to get the "Memoir" finished. Were another collection of Poe's works, with "an original Memoir" again, perhaps written by a foe, to appear before mine, I should never get the publishers to proceed with present edition, besides, I am relinquishing so much—both in bodily exercise & pecuinary engagements that I must "get along" quickly now. Happily my rough draft is almost complete.

I have looked all through the *Broadway* & am so pleased with it— there is much that will be useful. *Graham's* or the *Gentleman's* with such personal supervision would have redoubled our good fortune. "The Elk" I am anxious to get a clue to.

And now, for the present, I will conclude my scrawl with my very kindest & most admiringly sympathetic good wishes as yours ever,

John H. Ingram

1. But he did retain them, at least until 1886, when he sold them at a bookseller's auction in London. They are now in the Huntington Library, San Marino, Calif.

2. Poe had given this daguerreotype to Mrs. Lewis about 1848. After allowing a commercial photographer to reproduce for sale hundreds of copies, she allowed Ingram to use a copy for Vol. I of his 1880 *Life of Poe*, and she left it to Ingram at her death in 1880. It came to the University of Virginia Library with Ingram's other Poe papers in 1921, and I used it as a frontispiece for *Building Poe Biography*.

3. This article is reprinted immediately following.

46. "Edgar Allan Poe's Early Poems," by John H. Ingram, London Gentleman's Magazine, 12 (May 1874), 580–86

Edgar Allan Poe's Early Poems

John H. Ingram

"I HAVE OFTEN THOUGHT," says Edgar Poe, in his essay on "The Philosophy of Composition," "how interesting a magazine paper might be written by an author who would detail, step by step, the processes by which any one of his compositions attained its ultimate point of completion"; and he suggests autorial vanity as the reason why such a paper has never been executed. "Most writers, poets in especial," he continues, "prefer having it understood that they compose by a species of fine frenzy—an ecstatic intuition—and would positively shudder at letting the public take a peep behind the scenes." The author of "The Raven" has, for his own part, he assures us, no sympathy with this repugnance, and he describes in curious detail how his best known poetical work "proceeded, step by step, to its completion with the precision and rigid consequence of a mathematical problem." Having his own words for justification, I will not hesitate to lay before the public what cannot fail to be deeply interesting: the boyish poems of Poe, as they originally appeared.

Many of his biographers speak of a volume of verse published as early as 1827–and I believe the poet countenanced that date—but if this is correct, the volume disappeared without leaving any trace, unless the delicate little poem "To Helen," and the lines from "Al Aaraaf," quoted by Lowell, may be accepted as genuine remains of the booklet. In 1829, according to Dr. Duyckinck, another little volume was published, but it does not appear possible now to obtain a copy.[1] In 1821, whilst Poe was a cadet at West Point Military Academy, the third collection (accepting the publication of the 1827 edition as proven), appeared under this description: "*Poems* by Edgar A. Poe. '*Tout le monde a Raison.*' Rochefoucauld. Second edition."[2] This volume, like its predecessors, was for private circulation only, is the one which I propose to analyse. It is dedicated to "The United States Corps of Cadets," and the dedication, it appears, drew upon its author the ridicule of his fellow students. An unfortunate, a ludicrous passage was picked out for jest, and although the little book contained some of his most exquisite fancies, and poems which have won the warmest commendations of the critics of both continents, it could only excite mirth in the minds of the dedicatees. Says General George W. Cullum, a brother cadet, "These verses were the source of great merriment with us boys, who considered the author cracked, and the verses ridiculous doggerel." "Even after the lapse of forty years," continues the veteran, "I can now recall these absurd lines from 'Isabel':—

> "And this ray is a *fairy* ray—
> Did you not say so, Isabel?
> How fantastically it fell,
> With a spiral twist and a swell,
> And over the wet grass rippled away
> With a tinkling like a bell!"

Detached from the reminder of the poem, it must be candidly confessed that these lines do not show much promise, but when it is found that this boyish book contained many poems since reprinted almost *verbatim* amongst the poet's matured works, and as such deemed by the finest critics worthy of the greatest lyrists, the judgment of "us boys" does not count for much. That they deemed "the author cracked" is not so unreasonable: as long ago as the days of Horace, *poet* and *madman* were considered synonymous terms—*aut insanit homo, aut versus facit*— and we have pretty positive proof that there was a vein of insanity in Poe.

1. *Poems*—Hatch and Dunning, Baltimore, 1829—81 pp.
2. Elam Bliss, New York, 1831—124 pp.

Dated West Point, 1831, these tentative verses were introduced by a prefatory letter of seventeen pages, addressed to a certain mystical B———. General Cullum supposes "B———" to have been intended for Bulwer, but the tone of the letter seems to negative this supposition, although undoubtedly Poe had a boyish admiration for the subsequent Lord Lytton, and a few years later we find him publishing a eulogistic review of one of the recently printed works of the author of "Pelham." Be this as it may, this introductory epistle contains some paragraphs not unnoteworthy, especially as coming from so young an author as Poe then was. He will not admit the fact that "a good critique on a poem may be written by one who is no poet himself." This, he remarks to the unknown B———, "according to *your* idea and *mine* of poetry, I feel to be false—the less poetical the critic, the less just the critique, and the converse." He then proceeds to combat the belief that popularity is any evidence of a book's intrinsic value; and remarks: "You are aware of the great barrier in the path of an American writer. He is read, if at all, in preference to the combined and established wit of the world. I say established; for it is with literature as with law or empire—an established name is an estate in tenure, or a throne in possession. Besides, one might suppose that books, like their authors, improve by travel,—their having crossed the sea is, with us, so great a distinction." Especially, it might be added, when there is no copyright to pay.

Poe also avers that it is a vulgar error to suppose that a poet cannot form a correct estimate of his own writings. "Whatever should be deducted on the score of self-love," he suggests, "might be replaced on account of his intimate acquaintance with the subject; in short, we have more instances of false criticism than of just, where one's own writings are the test, simply because we have more bad poets than good." Referring to traditional evidence contradictory to his proposition, he remarks: "By what trivial circumstances men are often led to assert what they do not really believe! Perhaps an inadvertent word has descended to posterity." And, alluding to Milton's averred preference for his later work, Poe asserts that "Paradise Regained" is little, if at all, inferior to the "Paradise Lost," and is only supposed so to be because men do not like epics, whatever they may say to the contrary, and reading those of Milton in their natural order, are too much wearied with the first to derive any pleasure from the second. "I dare say Milton preferred 'Comus' to either—if so, justly," he adds, and probably not without sympathisers.

He next directs the arrows of his sarcasm against "the heresy of the Lake school," and with all the petulance of a boy declares: "*Some years ago* I might have been induced, by an occasion like the present, to attempt a formal refutation of their doctrine." He proceeds to demonstrate that the end of our existence is happiness, not instruction: "*Ceteris paribus*, he who pleases is of more importance to his fellow men than he who instructs, since utility is happiness, and pleasure is the end already obtained which instruction is merely the means of obtaining."

"Against the subtleties which would make poetry a study—not a passion," pursues the fiery-hearted lad, "it becomes the metaphysician to reason—but the poet to protest"; and protest he does, "that learning has little to do with the imagination—intellect with the passions—or age with poetry." Reverting to the Lake school: "As to Wordsworth," says Poe, "I have no faith in him. That he had in youth the feelings of a poet, I believe—for there are glimpses of extreme delicacy in his writings— (and delicacy is the poet's own kingdom—his *El Dorado*)—but they have the appearance of a better day recollected." He was to blame in wearing away his youth in contemplation" is the shrewd comment of this boy critic. He cannot speak of Coleridge, however, "but with reverence," although he deems "it is lamentable to think that such a mind should be buried in metaphysics, and, like the Nyotanthes, waste its perfume upon the night along." "In reading his poetry, I tremble like one who stands upon a volcano," says our cadet, "conscious, from the very darkness bursting from the crater, of the fire and light that are weltering below."

"What is poetry?" exclaims Poe. "Poetry! that Proteus-like idea, with as many appellations as the nine-titled Corcyra! 'Give me,' I demánded of a scholar some time ago—'give me a definition of poetry.' 'Tres volontiers,' and he proceeded to his library, brought me a Dr. Johnson, and overwhelmed me with a definition. Shade of the immortal Shakespeare! I imagine to myself the scowl of your spiritual eye upon the profanity of that Ursa Major. Think of poetry, dear B——, think of poetry; and then think of Dr. Samuel Johnson! Think of all that is airy and fairy-like, and then of all that is hideous and unwieldy; think of his huge bulk, the Elephant! and then—think of the 'Tempest'—the 'Midsummer Night's Dream'—Prospero—Oberon—and Titania!"

The most remarkable paragraph of this precocious critic's long-winded Introduction is, probably, the next, wherein he proclaims what a poem, in his opinion, is; and it must be confessed, in nothing that he afterwards said or did, is there aught that belies his boyish ideal. "A poem," he says, "is opposed to a work of science by having, for its *immediate* object, pleasure, not truth; to romance, by having for its object an *indefinite* instead of a *definite* pleasure—being a poem only so far as this object is attained; romance presenting perceptible images with definite poetry, with *indefinite* sensations, to which end music is an *essential,* since the comprehension of sweet sound is our most indefinite conception. Music, when combined with a pleasurable idea, is poetry; music without the idea is simply music; the idea, without the music, is prose, from its very definiteness." Our paradoxical young poet sums up the confession of his poetic faith, and with it, his prose introduction, by remarking that "I have, dear B——, what you, no doubt, perceive, for the metaphysical poets, *as* poets, the most sovereign contempt. That they have followers," he concludes, "proves nothing":

> "No Indian Prince has to his palace
> More followers than a thief to the gallows."

Having concluded his prose, Poe favours his readers, if he had any, with a poetical *introduction* of sixty-six lines: a portion of this is included in the general collection of poems written in youth under the title of "Romance." The following lines are a portion of the cancelled version:

> For, being an idle boy lang syne,
> Who read Anacreon, and drank wine,
> I early found Anacreon rhymes
> Were almost passionate sometimes—
> And by strange alchemy of brain
> His pleasures always turned to pain—
> His naïveté to wild desire—
> His wit to love—his wine to fire—
> And so being young and dipt in folly
> I fell in love with melancholy,
> And used to throw my earthly rest
> And quiet all away in jest—
> I could not love except where Death
> Was mingling his with Beauty's breath—
> Or Hymen, Time, and Destiny
> Were stalking between her and me.

To the few who have a knowledge of the true story of Edgar Poe's life—not the many who know him merely from the slanderous stories set afloat by his implacable enemy, Griswold—these, and other omitted portions, have a strange biographical interest: they hint at something more than mere rhymes. In all these early verses, too, the student of his poems may detect the same idiosyncrasies of rhythm, punctuation, rhyme, and everything which distinguished the work of his maturity, save the refrain, which is a prominent trait of his latest composition.

"Israfel"—the melodious—next attracts our attention, in this little book: it has received several finishing touches—each an improvement— has been expanded by seven additional lines, and is now included amongst the later poems. Increased strength has been given to several lines by altering the position of the words, but the modifications are scarcely sufficient to warrant the quotation of the poem as it originally stood. The piece now called "The City in the Sea" next appears in the book, and under the title of "The Doomed City." Many and many felicitious changes have taken place in this fine poem; enough, Poe deemed, to abstract it from its place amongst the juvenile poems; as it now reads it is five lines shorter than formerly, and its conclusion has gained considerably by the suppression of these two concluding lines:—

> And Death to some more happy clime
> Shall give his undivided time.

We now arrive at "Fairy Land," the verse which so excited the merriment of Poe's fellow cadets, and which they considered "ridiculous doggerel." As this poem now stands it is replete with imagination—the soul of poesy; but, it must be confessed, the cancelled portions *are* weak, very weak for so delicately, so morbidly particular a poet as was Edgar Poe, and, although containing some really poetic fantasies, it is only worthy preservation as a relic, and as such I quote a portion:—

> Sit down beside me, Isabel,
> Here, dearest, where the moonbeams fell
> Just now so fairy-like and well.
> Now thou art dress'd for Paradise!
> I am star-stricken with thine eyes!
>   . . . . .
> In my own country all the way
> We can discover a moon ray,
> Which through some tatter'd curtain pries
> Into the darkness of a room,
> Is by (the very source of gloom)
> The motes, and dust, and flies,
> On which it trembles and lies,
> Like joy upon sorrow!

"Irene," the next poem, having been altered and abridged from seventy-four to sixty-one lines, under the title of "The Sleeper," was relegated to the poems of manhood. The changes are many and various, and all testify to the taste and discernment of their maker. For those desirous of collating the lines with the present version I quote those that have undergone the greatest change:—

> I stand beneath thy soaring moon
> At midnight in the month of June.
> An influence dewy, drowsy, dim,
> Is dripping from yon golden rim.
> Grey towers are mouldering into rest,
> Wrapping the fog around their breast.
> Looking like Lethe, see! the lake
> A conscious slumber seems to take,
> And would not for the world awake.
> The rosemary sleeps upon the grave,
> The lily lolls upon the wave,
> And million cedars to and fro
> Are rocking lullabies as they go
> To the lone oak that nodding hangs

Above yon cataract of Serangs.
All Beauty sleeps!—And lo! where lies
With casement open to the skies
Irene, with her destinies!
And hark the sounds, so low yet clear
(Like music of another sphere),
Which steal within the slumberer's ear,
Or so appear—or so appear!
Oh, lady sweet, how camest thou here?
Strange are thine eyelids! strange thy dress!
And strange thy glorious length of tress!
Sure thou art come o'er far-off seas
A wanderer to our desert trees!
Some gentle wind hath thought it right
To ope thy window to the night,
And wanton airs from the tree top
Laughing through the lattice drop,
And wave this crimson canopy,
So fitfully, so fearfully,
As a banner o'er thy dreaming eye
That o'er the floor and down the wall,
Like ghosts the shadows rise and fall—
Then, for thine own all radiant sake,
Lady, awake! awake! awake! . . .

"A Paean" follows next: as "Lenore" it subsequently reappeared in the later collections, but greatly improved in form and rhythm. The name of "Lenore" was undoubtedly an afterthought of the poet, but it gives a richer and more melodious tone to the flowing verse. This solemn dirge was, I have good authority for declaring, like so much of Poe's poetry, autobiographical: two or three persons, perchance, know, or rather guess at, the event to which it refers, but the full secret is, doubtless, a mystery, and, like the "Hortulus Animae" of Grünniger, *es lasst sich lesen*. The verses were divided in the following manner originally:—

How shall the burial rite be read—
    The solemn song be sung!—
A paean for the loveliest dead
    That ever died so young.

Her friends are gazing on her,
    And on her gaudy bier,
And weep!—Oh! to dishonour
    Dead beauty with a tear!

. . . . .
Thus on her coffin loud and long
    I strike—the murmur sent

Through the grey chambers to my song
    Shall be the accompaniment.

Thou died'st—in thy life's June—
    But thou didst not die too fair:
Thou didst not die too soon,
    Nor with too calm an air.

From more than friends on earth
    Thy life and love are given,
To join the untainted mirth
    Of more than thrones in heaven.

Therefore, to thee this night
    I will no requiem raise,
But waft thee on thy flight,
    With a paean of old days.

This is followed by "The Valley Nis," subsequently reduced to half its original length, and then re-christened "The Valley of Unrest." The excisions are so many, and so important, that I feel justified in quoting the whole poem as it read formerly:—

Far away—far away—
Far away—as far at least
Lies that valley as the day
Down within the golden East—
All things lovely are they,
One and all, too far away?
It is called the Valley Nis;
And a Syriac tale there is
Thereabout which Time hath said
Shall not be interpreted:
Something about Satan's dart—
Something about angel wings—
Much about a broken heart—
All about unhappy things.
But the Valley Nis at best
Means the Valley of Unrest.
Once it smiled a silent dell
Where the people did not dwell,
Having gone unto the wars;
And the sly, mysterious stars,
With a visage full of meaning,
O'er th' unguarded flowers were leaning,
Or the sun ray dripped all red
Through tall tulips overhead,
Then grew paler as it fell
On the quiet Asphodel.
Now each visitor shall confess

Nothing there is motionless—
Nothing save the airs that brood
O'er the enchanted solitude:
Save the stars with pinions furled,
That slumber o'er that valley world.
No wind in Heaven, and lo! the trees
Do roll like seas in northern breeze
Around the stormy Hebrides—
No wind in Heaven, and clouds do fly,
Rustling everlastingly,
Through the terror stricken sky,
Rolling like a waterfall
O'er th' horizon's fiery wall—
And Helen, like thy human eye,
Low crouched on Earth some violets lie,
And nearer Heaven some lilies wave,
All banner like, above a grave.
And one by one from out their tops
Eternal dews come down in drops,
And one by one from off their stems
Eternal dews come down in gems!

Introduced by the sonnet now styled "To Science," follows "Al Aaraaf"—it has been denuded of about one hundred lines. "Tamerlane" also, which appears in the volume, has been shortened.

Such, then, is the little collection of Poe's earliest efforts. Valuable as an index to the precocity of his genius, and the care with which he elaborated to their ultimate perfection the poems he has left us, they also prove how his genius grew with his years, and cause us to lament that "events not to be controlled" prevented America's greatest and most original poet from continuing his efforts "in what, under happier circumstances, would have been the field of his choice." Unfettered by sordid cares and domestic wants, Edgar Allan Poe might have left the world a volume unsurpassed, perhaps unequalled, by that of any lyric poet that ever lived. But, alas! "the paltry compensations," if not "the more paltry commendations of mankind," are necessary for subsistence, even to the author of "The Raven," and we have to rest and be thankful for the half dozen or so poems which were all that the *res augusta domi* permitted his riper manhood to produce.

47. *Sarah Helen Whitman to John H. Ingram.* Item 149

My dear Mr. Ingram, May 1, 1874
Your letter of March 31 [Apr. 14], received yesterday, filled me with anxiety. *Do* not, I implore you, allow yourself to become excited over

your work. Leave everything till you are quite well again. I shall be *so* anxious till I hear from you again. I have been anxious from the *first*— fearing that the perplexing contradictions, which I knew you would be likely to meet with, would discourage & worry you. I am glad to know that you are to see Mrs. Lewis—since she has lived in Baltimore, where so much of his life was passed, she *must* be able to throw light on many points. Why do you say that you shall receive with caution what she tells you? Have you any reason to think that she is unfriendly to E.A.P.? Of course she will not be likely to speak favorably of Mrs. Clemm, but I have heard nothing to her discredit from any other source. Mrs. Clemm says that she was very uncomfortable with her, but she was, I fancy, apt to find trouble in *all* her homes, save perhaps that of Mrs. Annie Richmond in Lowell, & even there, she could not be contented to remain after the first winter. Mr. Davidson wrote me many years ago that he had *seen*, or had had, letters from Mrs. Lewis, & that she had told him, or told someone, that "Annabel Lee" was addressed to her. I fancy, from a piece of gossip which was detailed to me by a friend of Mrs. Osgood's, that Mrs. Clemm had *told* Mrs. L[ewis] that it *was*. Indeed, I think my informant stated that she was *present* when Mrs. Clemm told Mrs. Lewis that "Edgar had written the poem for her." I had asked my informant why Mrs. Osgood had said in her contribution to Griswold's narrative that the lines were in memory of Virginia, & she told me, in reply, that Mrs. Osgood, indignant at what Mrs. Clemm had said, had written what she did "to put Mrs. Lewis down." I had suspected some such motive from the tone of Mrs. Osgood's allusion to the ballad. "You may imagine how Fanny's lip curled," said my correspondent, "when I reported to her what Mrs. Clemm had said." I doubt whether Mrs. Clemm knew any more of the matter than most other people.

I think many of Mrs. Lewis's poems very fine. I long to know how she impresses you & whether she can throw light on the story of Mrs. E[llet] & the "borrowed money," etc. I sincerely hope that she can. I have heard Poe speak of Mrs. Lewis, & it was with interest and appreciation, though I inferred that he was not at the time (1848) in habits of frequent & friendly intercourse with her.

Whatever claim others have as the the inspiration of "Annabel Lee," *I* cannot doubt that the beautiful fantasie was *suggested* by the printed lines which I enclose, the four verses originally published under the title of "Stanzas for Music."

The name of "Annabel Lee," responding, as it does, to the burden of the song, "the kingdom by the sea," was, I think, chosen for this correspondence, and the repetition of the words, "the wind came out of the cloud," etc. was, I doubt not, suggested by the third & fourth lines of my stanzas.

I will give you a few of my reasons; others, more impressive, I do not now dare to give you.

Recollect—we were to be married in a few days. Poe had at last prevailed upon me to consent to an immediate union. He had written to Dr. Crocker to publish "the banns of marriage" between us. He had written to Mrs. Clemm to announce our arrival on [*sic*] New York early in the following week, when it came to my knowledge & the knowledge of my friends, that he had already broken the solemn pledge so lately given by taking wine or something stronger than wine at the bar of his hotel. No token of this infringement of his promise was visible in his appearance or his manner, but I was at last convinced that it would be in vain longer to hope against hope. I knew that he had irrevocably lost the power of self-recovery.

Gathering together some papers which he had entrusted to my keeping, I placed them in his hands without a word of explanation or reproach, and, utterly worn out & exhausted by the mental conflicts & anxieties & responsibilities of the last few days, I drenched my handkerchief with ether & threw myself on a sofa, hoping to lose myself in utter unconsciousness. Sinking on his knees beside me, he entreated me to speak to him—to speak—one word, *but one word*. At last I responded, almost inaudibly, "What *can* I say?" "Say that you love me, Helen." "*I love you.*"

Those three words were the last I ever spoke to him. He remonstrated & explained & expostulated. But I had sunk from a violent ague fit into a cold and death-like torpor. He brought shawls & covered me with them, & then lifting me in his arms, bore me to a lounge near the fire, where he remained on his knees beside me, chafing my hands & invoking me, by all tenderest names & epithets, to speak to him again, *one* word. A merciful apathy was now stealing over my senses, & though I vaguely heard all, or much, that was said, I spoke no word, nor gave any sign of life. My mother & sister & another friend were in the room. I heard my mother remonstrating with him & urging his departure. Then Mr. Pabodie entered the room & joined my mother in entreaties that he would leave me. Her last words I did not hear, but I heard him haughtily & angrily reply, "Mr. Pabodie, you hear how I am insulted." These were his last words, & the door closed behind him forever. His letter I did not dare to answer. Exaggerated & humiliating stories were in circulation. He entreated me to deny them, to say that I at least had not authorized them. I never answered the letter. But I sent to the publisher of the *Metropolitan* the "Stanzas for Music." Meantime, he had doubtless felt aggrieved & deeply wounded & had, perhaps, said & done some things which would, if known, place an inseparable gulf between us. I imagine that the notice of Griswold's *Female Poets*, which was published in the *Southern Literary*

Messenger, was prepared before he saw my verses. *After* he had seen them, I believe that, knowing all earthly reconciliation between us impossible, he sought to express to me his undying love & remembrance in the most beautiful & tender & spiritually imaginative of all his poems.

I send you the photograph from a picture painted by J. N. Arnold, in which the drapery of the robe is copied from the picture taken so long ago by Thompson. The picture which Poe thought was so like Robert Stanard. There was more dignity & nobility in that, & many prefer it to this, but while that is not *always* recognized, this *is*, even by persons who have known me only within the last ten years. It is more youthful in expression than the one taken so long ago. This was taken in the winter of 1838–39.[1] But now I must stop talking about myself.

Goodbye, & may the good angels guard & keep you. Remember what I said, "keep cool."

Sarah Helen Whitman

P.S. All that I have written is (at least for the present) *for you alone*. I hope my letter of April 3, sent in the *Atlas*, arrived safely. It contained a copy of a portion of one of Poe's which might be quotable.

Miss Anna Blackwell is now I believe in Paris. I do not know her address, but she is an acquaintance of Mr. Daniel Home, the medium. If you know anyone who knows him, you could obtain it from him.[2]

1. J. N. Arnold painted this picture of Mrs. Whitman in the winter of 1868–69. See also p. 118, n. 1.

2. Daniel Dunglas Home (1833–1886) was a Scottish medium who won fame of a sort as an exponent of table-turning and levitation in America in 1850, and in London by 1855. Robert Browning lampooned him in 1864 in his "Sludge, the Medium," and Mrs. Whitman, who had met Home and was very favorably impressed by his "powers," published an article, "Mr. Home, the Medium," in the Providence *Journal*, May 24, 1865.

48. *Sarah Helen Whitman to John H. Ingram.*   *Item 150*

My dear Mr. Ingram,   May 4, [1874]

Two or three weeks ago I wrote you that a sister of Senator Sprague had promised to obtain for me from a friend one or two volumes of *Graham's Magazine*. She did not know of what *date*, but would ask her friend to loan me such as she might happen to have.

This afternoon she brought me two bound volumes, one containing the numbers from Jan. to June, 1842; and one from Jan. to June, 1850. In the March number of the vol. for 1850, I found the long-sought-for letter of George Graham to Willis! It is in "The Editor's Table," &

occupies three closely printed pages. It is eloquent & forcible, & contains some important facts in proof of Poe's integrity & fair dealing with publishers, etc.

How strange it is that so little use has been made of this letter!

I shall try to see Mrs. Lattimer this evening. If I cannot obtain permission to abstract these two pages, I will *copy* them for you verbatim & send them by the next mail. I will tell you about the contents of the other volume another time.

There are two articles in the 1850 vol. by the Thomas A. Wyatt, M.A., who is connected with the "Conchology" book.

To think that this letter should be placed, as it were, in my hands by the beneficent "princes & powers of the air," when *no*body could give me any, the slightest, clew as to its whereabouts!

I take it as a good omen for your success.

You have had infinite trouble in looking up facts & authorities, but I will commend to you the motto of my forefathers—*Per crucrum ad coronam.*

Ever your friend,

S.H.W.

49. *John H. Ingram to Sarah Helen Whitman*

My dear Mrs. Whitman,   5 May 1874
Yours of the 17th & 21st April to [hand?].¹ The enclosure about Hood many thanks for. When [*illegible*] I will duly return, as also the Index &c. of Poe's [*illegible*]. That collection, I fancy, they have in Museum. I [will] look for it, as I want to copy the Dedication to [Mrs.] E. B. Browning. I will also see about altering "1847" to "1844" in copy of *E.P. & His Critics* therein. Th[ere is] a black mark in my copy which may or may n[ot be an] alteration. You allude to another edition being p[ublished]. If you have *many* copies on hand, you m[ay] find it worth while to send some to an En[glish] publisher. I would galdly look out a respectable one. But if you have only a few 'tis not worth the trouble. Should you think seriously of a new edition you might arrange for a publisher in London (here). For a new edition, I might be able to suggest a few *slight* additions or changes, if you would not mind. Very slight—but I will hear your views first.

I will ask Mr. Davidson to get that no. of *Harper's* [*illegible*] have seen it (looked it out in Museum) [*illegible*] might probably get the view of Charlottesville engraved. I don't think Miss Poe could do [very] much, but she could, doubtless, confirm [*illegible*] time & place

of her brother's birth & know something of his boyhood, journey to
England, &c. Mrs. Lewis [did not] give me the slightest publishable
information, though very friendly & willing. In fact we do not talk
much about Poe—strictly *entre nous*, I don't think she can understand
him as we do, but she has a warm sympathy for him & a scorn [for his]
traducers. I should like to hear your opinion of Mrs. Clemm, as *I do
not wish to misjudge her*. Do *you* think she was a bad woman? Did
you ever see her? I doubt not that [she] was given to begging, but that
may have been [through] misfortune & not fault. While I think of it,
Dunn English is dead, I am told.[2] [Briggs] I shall not mention *by name*.
[*illegible*] nameless in my "Memoir" will doubtless be [*illegible*] to
remain so.

I have just completed "The [True] Story of Edgar Poe's Life" for the
Quarterly, & [now] for the full life! I had to allude to your engagement
with Poe, to refute Griswold. I told it nearly as in "New Facts," merely
adding, that probably the rupture was neither occasioned by either
Mrs. W. or Poe. Was that right so to say? I send another copy of "New
Facts"—not that I fancy them of any account. The mistakes will all be
corrected in the "True Story." Do not trouble or bother about anything
in the way of discrepancy that I point our in *E.P. & His Critics*, unless
I specially ask for replies.

I have not had time to write to Mr. O'Connor yet. I am doing too
much as it is, but I cannot rest now until I have finished this life of
Poe. Mr. O'Connor's review of *E.P. & His Critics* is the only one I kept
back, as I thought it better than the others, but I will return it shortly. I
don't think there is anything that I can use in it. I like Mangan, too,
although crusty about his being compared with Poe. You will see my
paper on him some day.[3]

En passant, my mother tells of a Miss Power (of Ireland) rescued by
her father & his brother officers, from a convent in Portugal, during the
Peninsula War, she having been detained against her will.

I have written to our Consul at Baltimore—to fly from one subject to
another—about Miss Poe, as I cannot get replies from any Americans
south—not one has answered. No answers received either from Mr.
Gill, Lowell, Eveleth, Simms, Miss Poe, or her helper, Rev. G. Powell.
Nor from President of Peabody Institute, &c., &c. You can comprehend
how this cripples me. I write & hope for some answer & wait patiently
three or four weeks, & then have to go all over the ground again. What
a *Providence* that I chanced to find you out. I shall begin to believe in
"secret affinities." We were bound & fated, I shall think, to get
acquainted. Would that I could get to have a *viva voce* instead of a
spiritual interview!

Don't trouble any more about autographs. The publishers have that of Mr. Latto's, than which none could be better. Mrs. Lewis has several, but none equal to the Pabodie letter.

The *Broadway Journal* contains much of value—much that I hope to reprint. It will help too, to supply & correct Griswold's garbled reviews. If you find it unpleasant, or grieves you, to continue the history of your personal acquaintance with Poe, do not distress youself. It could not be published, so do not let me intrude upon its sanctity any further.

Many thanks for the German "Raven," &c., but I can return it eventually, only I want the engravers to have the portrait for use & I think I may get the translations reprinted in a German paper when I get time to carry out my ideas on the subject. My grand difficulty is time—time—time. It will fly so! I have some idea—time permitting—to get up a book wholly & solely about "Raven" literature—this is *entre nous*—to contain Poe's "Raven," a collection of the parodies & translations, history of the poem, &c. I do not think you can have any idea of the great number of parodies & imitations, in England and America, of "The Raven."[4] This translation would then be useful. Eventually everything shall be returned to you. I do not care to have & hold other people's property & will duly "render unto Ceasar," &c.

Paper on Dunn English in *Godey's* was not written until after *Broadway* had been given up, so there is nothing there about it.[5]

I think I shall get Mrs. Osgood's name out of *Temple Bar* article, & fancy I should alter it to Mrs. Lewis? At all events, it is only given as a belief. Alice & Phoebe Cary's poems, I *love. Clovernook* I knew by name, but have not read it.[6] I am going—when *time* comes—to write a paper on them in my series of biographical literary sketches, such as Mangan, &c. If you have any information, or interesting letter, &c. of or from them, perhaps you can kindly lend it or them to me? Nothing, however, will cause me to deviate from Edgar Poe's "Memoir," which I hope to complete by end of this, or beginning of next month. The extract in *Harper's Monthly*, from Poe's "Annabel Lee," as I believe I pointed out to you, differs in some words from the written version in the 4-vol. collection. Do you think a complete version of Stoddard's copy could be obtained? I am rather afraid, however, to ask him, as I do not want him to know of my purposed collection until it is ready for publication, so perhaps I had better let *that* alone. With the publication of this said "Memoir" of mine, I do not mean to relinquish my efforts to obtain more information about Poe for further editions or, perhaps, a separate life. Only it will be a starting point &, at the same time, a resting place. It even may elicit something.

Thanks for *your* picturesque view of Fordham. Do you know anything of the interior of the house? Mrs. Lewis differs from a printed account I have & which must be *in*correct in its description of number of rooms, &c. Mrs. Lewis says two bedrooms above, & sitting room below, with kind of cellar or kitchen underneath: 'tis not of much consequence, but it shakes my confidence in the *Sixpenny Magazine* paper to find it so incorrect about a simple thing—& yet one so easy to verify.

Mrs. Lewis does not think Poe ever crossed the Atlantic, but his account of his school is too exact: he painted Stoke Newington *as it was* photographically—with pre-Raphaelite minuteness.

I must conclude. I hope you'll get the *Gentleman's Magazine*. I am very anxious for fear that you may not like it. I hope you will. I would not on any account, do or say anything to annoy *you on this subject*. It was written under extreme pressure. In the "Memoir" I do not think you will be able to find a single thought or sentence objectionable. By the way, I duly received that copy of Poe's note written on the steamboat. I must have alluded to it in one of my letters, I feel certain, although it came when I was so unwell. It may interest your friend Mr. O'Connor to hear that his friend Walt Whitman—whose writings I really *must* examine some day—is said to be very popular in Denmark & a new translation & favourable review of *Leaves of Grass* has just been brought out there. But, doubtless, he knows it. If you come across a poem of W.W.'s, perhaps you could kindly send it for my opinion.

Cannot I send you anything? I send you another copy of "New Facts." I have circulated four dozen copies amongst our *literati* & some are getting very curious about my "Memoir."

A very kind letter from Mr. Davidson today, but no information yet.

In haste, yours, ever the same,

John H. Ingram

P.S. Before reviewing Miss Power's ballads, I should like to know if she would like to get them published here.

1. Through the years this letter has been fragmented by the paper crumbling; the right hand side of page 1 and the left hand side of page 2 are mutilated.

2. Thomas Dunn English did not die until 1902.

3. A brief note in the London *Athenaeum*, Nov. 17, 1877, announces that a critical and biographical article on Mangan, written by John H. Ingram, will appear in the Dec. issue of *Dublin University Magazine*.

4. And he did just that. *The Raven by Edgar Allan Poe, with Literary and Historical Commentary by John H. Ingram* was published in London in 1885 (George Redway).

5. Louis Antoine Godey (1804–1878) was publisher and proprietor, with Charles Alexander, of *Godey's Lady's Book* from 1830 until 1877. He published reviews by Poe as well as Poe's controversial "The Literati of New York City," beginning in May and ending in October, 1846.

6. See p. 124–25, n. 1.

50. *Sarah Helen Whitman to John H. Ingram.* Item 152

My dear Mr. Ingram,   May 6, 1874
    I mailed a hurried letter to you last evening to tell you that I had
found George Graham's letter.
    In the evening I saw again the lady who sent me the volume
containing it, and I asked her if I might hope to obtain the volume or
the pages containing the *letter*, but she seemed unwilling to ask her
friend, thinking she would be very unwilling to part with it. So I had
to content myself with copying it. I made one or two trifling elisions
where the writer weakened the effect of his statements by repetition or
introducing irrelevant reflections.
    I think it is a most *valuable* & *eloquent* & *truehearted statement*. It
is incomprehensible to me how I could have missed seeing this letter
when it was first published. Some of the paragraphs which I have
indicated by a blue pencil mark are so well expressed that I cannot
help thinking they were of more than mortal phrasing—were inspired
utterances. I wish I had known the writer.
    A circumstance which I forgot to tell you in speaking of my
interview with Mr. Clarke in December, 1859—the missing
publisher—(I think he will yet come to light), I now recall with
singular interest. I was residing at the corner of 36th St. & Madison
Avenue, in the upper part of the city, & Mr. Clarke told me in his long
ride from the lower part of the city, George Graham had accompanied
him. He said that Graham expressed great pleasure at the
announcement of my little book, & told him that it was a disgrace to
the American Litterateurs—to American *Literature*, that such a
shameless desecration of the dead should have gone so long
unrebuked. I did not know then how kindly & tenderly Graham had
written about Poe, or I should in some way have sought his
acquaintance.
    But was it not a singular coincidence that the two should have been
accidentally thrown together in one of the New York omnibuses on
that particular occasion, & that I should then for the first time have
heard of Graham's indignation against Griswold?
    I have only time to send the enclosed & will tell you more about the
volume for 1842 in which are some of Poe's articles—but only an
appendix to the two papers on autographs, which must have appeared
in the autumn of 1841.
    You were ill when I last heard from you, and I am very anxious.
    Do let me hear as soon as you *can*, and *do* be careful of your health.
                                                            S. H. Whitman

51. Sarah Helen Whitman to John H. Ingram.   Item 153

My dear Mr. Ingram,   May 11, 1874
    I have been very anxious about your health—almost afraid to
write—lest anything I might say should feed the intense action of your
mind, which so much needs rest. I know the fine temper of the steel,
but I fear the wearing of the scabbard. For *my* sake—for the sake of all
who love you—for your *work's* sake, do not overtask your mind. Do not
fear that anything which can be written on the subject can forestall
your work.
    I do not think Stoddard intends anything more than a republication
of his article in *Harper's*, perhaps in the *Bric-a-Brac Series*, which I
saw for the first time announced in this morning's *Journal*. I enclose
the advertisement. Of course Poe & Hawthorne will be among his
"famous people." By the way, that extract from the *Season*, over the
signature of Eugene Benson, is only a *part* of an article published in
the *Galaxy*, December 1868, entitled "Poe & Hawthorne."[1] It is a
subtle & admirable analysis of the comparative attributes & merits of
the two writers. I will quote for you a few sentences:

> Poe & Hawthorne are two brilliant exceptions in American literature.
> Among Americans they are the only two literary men who have had the sense
> of beauty & the artist's conscience in a supreme degree. They belonged to the
> haughty & reserved aristocracy of letters. Hawthorne was like a magician
> hidden from the world, creating his beautiful phantasms: Poe was like a
> banished spirit, abased among men, exercising an intellect, & drawing upon a
> memory, that implied a clearer & higher state of being than that of material &
> common life. His mental perspicacity & unerringness suggest a super-mortal
> quality, & make the simple narrative of "The Gold Bug" appalling; for you
> will remark that the sentiment of strangeness & terror which it begets is
> excited without any of Poe's usual resources—that is, of death or murder in
> any form. One is appalled by the *precision* of the intellect revealed, which is
> unmatched by any English story writer. But is because of the *beauty* that Poe
> created, because of his admirable style, the pure & strange elements of his
> nature, his general & minute method, rather than because of his puzzles, or
> curious intellectual *inventions*, that he is a type of exquisite & brilliant genius.
> The interest of his inventions would be exhausted at the first reading, if they
> were not set before us with a fine literary art that charms even while it is the
> medium of the exceptional, & often of the repugnant.
>   Very few persons have a definite idea of the difference between the unique
> & unrivalled genius of these two men, Poe & Hawthorne, who still had,
> positive, if hidden, bonds of sympathy with each other, while they were
> radically different in their work & in the springs of their beings. Both had an
> exquisite sense of the music of thought; both loved the mysterious & the

bizarre; both labored to paint the exceptional & dominate our intellects with an intimate sense of the spiritual & the unseen. They were alike splendidly endowed with imagination, but Poe had more invention—in fact a most marvellous faculty of invention—& he was the more purely intellectual of the two. His intellect was direct, inevitable, & unerring; Hawthorne's was indirect, easily turned from its object, & seemingly purposeless; Poe's always seemed instinct with intense purpose. Hawthorne would have preferred to hide all his processes of creation, happy in evoking beautiful figures, but with no desire to let you see how he did it. Poe, like all inventors, took pains to let you see the process of his mind; he laid bare his mechanism, took his listener, step by step, with him, well aware that he *must* admire a skill & ingenuity so superior to all he had known.

I will try to get the magazine for you.

I told you that in my next letter that I would tell you what I had to say about the volume of *Graham's* for 1842. There is no title page to the first six numbers of the year 1842—nothing to show the name or names of the editors, but in the title page of the last six, from July to Jan. the name of Griswold appears with that of Graham. The only articles bearing Poe's name in the vol. are "Autographs: an Appendix," "A Few Words About Brainard," "To One Departed," "Life in Death" (a story I had not before seen, very fine in weird, descriptive power), "The Masque of the Red Death," & "The Poetry of Rufus Dawes." The Appendix to "Autographs" is the same as the one I sent you.

Do not fear that anything you have written to me will ever be seen by another. No eyes but mine have seen a single line of your letters, with the exception of a *list* of questions, which I sent to Davidson & which he asked leave to retain until he could make further inquiries.

Whenever there is anything in your letters which I think will interest my sister, I read it to her, but she has never read any of your letters. When I asked you to say something pleasant about "Cinderella" & "Sleeping Beauty," it was with no idea of your saying anything about them to the public, but simply in your letter to *me*. She is very jealous of her claim to these poems, which she thinks has been made subsidiary to mine.

Yet, when I read to her what you said about them, & about noticing them at some future time in some paper or magazine, she said if you should ever do so, she wished to have *my* name associated with *hers*, but hers ought to come first—to which I assented most heartily. It is difficult to give entire satisfaction, & yet I have tried *so* hard to do so.

All this *entre nous* & the proverbial post.

2 o'clock p.m.
Just after commencing the foregoing pages I received yours of the

28th Ultimo. You have seen Mrs. Lewis. Oh, how I wish you could obtain from her permission to copy the daguerreotype, even though it may be too late for the volume, the first edition of the Life. Is it a full or a three-quarter view, & has it ever been photographed? Did she tell you when it was taken, in what city? I wish you could obtain her permission to have it photographed.

You say that she does not like Mrs. Clemm. Did she tell you *why*? Did you ask her about Dunn English & the libel suit, & about Mrs. Ellet? Or was her acquaintance with Poe of a more recent date? Did she know anything of Mrs. Shelton, or of Poe's sister? Don't answer my questions while you are so busy—don't ever write *at all*, if it is "a pain & a weariness."

I hope you will get my copy of Geo. Graham's "Letter to Willis" in time to use it. I think it is, as a faithful indication of character, worth all that has been said of him from those who knew him personally, more genuine, earnest, & *true-hearted* even, than the sketches of Willis & Mrs. Osgood, both of which had a savor of self-glorification in them. This of Graham's is evidently warm from the heart. Mr. Gill told me that the publisher of a Boston paper who had had business relations with Poe told him that Poe was always true to his word; he used some very forcible current phrase, which I have forgotten, to express his sense of Poe's honorable dealing in money matters. I have heard nothing of late from Mr. Gill & despair of getting back Mr. Willis' letter, which I gave him. I suppose that he has not answered your letter.

Mr. Eveleth has not answered the letter I wrote in reply to his first letter announcing a letter from you. I fancy it would be difficult for him to get at his papers, which he left at home in Phillips [Maine].

You say that Mrs. Lewis's letters from Poe were short. I think he was not in the habit of writing long letters. He told me that he had never in his life written letters so long as those he had written to me. And soon after Mrs. Osgood learned from some of Poe's friends in New York that we were engaged, she came to Providence on purpose to see me & learn the truth of the rumor. She was deeply interested in him, but they had had no intercourse with each other either by letter or otherwise, after the affair of which I told you, the demand for a return of letters.

In her interview with me, she told me that she had always known that we, he & I, should once meet, the influence of each on the other would be inevitable & enduring. She threw herself at my feet & covered my hands with tears & kisses; she told me all the enthusiasm that she had felt for him & her unchanged & unchanging interest in him & his best welfare. In answer to her questions, I told her of the poem which he had sent me of his visit to Providence, of his letters, & of all that she wished to know. When I spoke of the letters of ten or twelve pages, she seemed almost incredulous. She said his letters to her were all very brief, were in fact mere notes filled with expressions of devoted friendship & admiration, but very brief. I have longed to know if he ever wrote to another as he has written to me. Mrs. Clemm wrote me that Mrs. Shelton had not in her possession any fragment of his writing. If Mrs. Lewis & Mrs. Osgood had not, I must believe that he departed from his usual habit in writing as he did to me.

I told him all that Mrs. Osgood had said in his praise, told him of her confession of mingled joy & sorrow in hearing of our engagement.

After our parting & estrangement I think he turned with grateful remembrance to her image, and I think he wrote of her in such words of emphatic praise in his notice of Griswold's *Female Poets*, & of me in terms of such cold negation, to show his gratitude to her & his indifference to me.

I know, too, how this act of petulance must, afterwards, have reproached him when he saw my verses and have prompted him to convey to me the expression of his reconciliation & remembrance in the poem of "Annabel Lee." But, as I told you before, this assurance is for you alone.

It was on his second or third visit to Providence that he brought with him the MS. of the lecture delivered in Lowell, & called my attention to the passage in relation to Mrs. Osgood, Miss Lynch, & Mrs. Whitman. I asked him for a copy, which he gave me, saying, "I shall have something much better than this to say, Helen, when my notice of Griswold's book comes out."

In that notice I was classed with three or four others, I think, as among the most "accomplished."

And now I bid you once more remember, dear friend, to take time and rest.

Do not fear that anybody can forestall your destined & appointed work. You have done nobly, & *must* succeed.

Tell me if you like my "Proserpine."

Goodbye.

Sarah Helen Whitman

P.S. *Harper's Monthly*, March 1872, has woodcuts of Virginia University. If you can see it & think they would be useful, I will try to procure a copy.

I knew about the "tomb," but thought it was in a cemetery. I have been reading the "Eulogium" again. The *critical* part is admirable, I think.

1. Eugene Benson, "Poe and Hawthorne," *Galaxy*, 7 (1868), 742–48.

52. *Sarah Helen Whitman to John H. Ingram.*   Item 154

My dear Mr. Ingram,   May 14, [18]74
   Your proofs came this evening. The article is all that I could have
wished—better, far better, than I had dared to hope. You have treated
the subject *admirably* & like a *master*. I am delighted. There is
nothing in it like patronage or partisanship. It is impartial,
appreciative, & full of kindly sympathy & clear apprehension. I have
not a fault to find with it. I congratulate you, from my inmost heart.[1]
   That you may not be anxious about anything you have spoken to me
in confidence, I return you the page which you requested me to
burn—with the letters of L[ewis] & S[winburne]. The "Life & Death"
in *Graham's* is "The Oval Portrait," a little altered, I find.
   I am so anxious about your health. That is my *only* anxiety, now. I
hope you will try to obtain a copy of Mrs. L[ewis]'s daguerreotype.
   Do not fear that I shall want the *Broadway Journal* again. I must
soon leave them behind me, and I would rather leave them to *you*,
with you, than with any other whom I know. There are copies of
Eureka, & the Wiley & Putnam edition, with his writing on the fly leaf,
which I wish you to have. And—but we will talk of that another time.
   I have a lock of his hair, too, which, if you like, you shall share with
me. He sent it to me in the letter of which I copied so large a portion
for you—the one written after his first visit to Providence.
   Is it not astonishing that such absurd stories as that of the "MS.
Found in a Barn" should be circulated & copied in respectable
journals? But it shows the interest evoked by his name, even when
associated with such palpable falsehoods.
   I am glad to find that you read and like the *Academy*. I have not,
however, chanced to see Mr. Saintsbury's article.
   You are mistaken in thinking there is the faintest resemblance
between Walt Whitman & the immortal Tupper.
   I can*not* read our "dear, dear Don Quixote" in the original. But he
translates into my heart nevertheless. I do not know Christina
Rossetti's poems well enough to retain any of them in my memory, but
I will look for the lines you like so well. Name to me, when you have
time, some more of the "glorious & beautiful" poems you like in her
volume.
   In your penultimate letter you say that, for the present, you believe
only "in nature, in intellect, in beauty, etc." If you had added to the
belief in these divine things a faith in an all-pervading, all-controlling
spirit of Love & Wisdom—in "the Love that reigneth & ruleth," I
should have asked no more. Do not think for an instant, from the words
& phrases used in some of the sonnets, that I believe in the dogmas of
theology—of the churches. I believe in redeeming Love, but it is in a

redemption as inevitable & universal as creation itself. As for "Spiritualism," it is not a matter of belief, but a matter of knowledge, with those who have carefully studied its alleged phenomena. It came to *me* without my seeking, & there may come a time for *you* to believe it, if it is best for you to do so.

S.H.W.

I write these hurried lines, my dear Mr. Ingram, simply to acknowledge your *proofs*. I was greatly interested in the letters you sent me, which I return.

Have you read Lord Lytton's *Ring of Amasis*, and is it good? I bought it a day or two ago, but have not had time to look at it.[2] The subject is one strangely attractive to me. His poetical writings have so much that *approaches* poetry in them, & yet are so far from attaining it that they affect me painfully. I cannot analyze the feeling. There is the machinery, but the soul is wanting.

When I avow my interest in the spiritual phenomena, you must not imagine that it implies a belief in all the charlantry practised in the name of spiritualism. But I must not speak to you on this subject, nor would I have you believe in it at present if I could.

I saw today in the *Contemporary Magazine* or *Quarterly* for April some interesting papers—letters & extracts of letters from Mrs. Browning to R. H. Horne, the author of "Orion."[3] Have you seen the articles?

But goodbye for tonight. You see I am getting very tired. Our first sultry days came on so suddenly, after the long, cold Spring, that they take away all my vitality.

Sarah Helen Whitman

1. These were apparently revised proofs of Ingram's long-delayed article "Edgar Poe," which was published in *Temple Bar* in June and reprinted in the *Eclectic Magazine*, 20 (Aug. 1874), 203–10. It is here reprinted on pages 168–80.

2. Edward Robert Bulwer, first Earl of Lytton [Owen Meredith] *Ring of Amasis* (London: Chapman & Hall, 1863). The first American edition was published in New York by Harper & Brothers in 1863.

3. The two volumes of this correspondence were not published until 1877. See p. 462, n. 1.

53. *John H. Ingram to Sarah Helen Whitman*

My dear Mrs. Whitman, 10 [19] May 1874
I hope you will attribute my long silence to its true cause—illness. For ten days I have been ill in bed with rheumatic fever & have not been allowed even to be moved out of bed to have the bed remade, &

even now, when I have got rid of my pains, the doctor is very severe, saying that the slightest thing may cause a relapse. I am trying to scribble this in bed. I hope you will make it out—'tis difficult for me to write, although I have written you endless mental epistles during my illness but you can't get them—we've not discovered mental telepathy yet.

I'm tired already & fear I cannot tell you a tithe of what I wanted to. First, however, I wrote to Mr. Eveleth, but got no reply, but you said that he had written to you. Do you think you could induce him to give me a copy of the remaining portion of "The Mystery of Marie Rogêt" which he once wrote you was in his possession? I have kept that, & its two connecting tales, out of the first vol. of my collection in hopes of getting his conclusion. Do kindly try.

How lucky that letter of Graham's should have turned up & how you must have slaved to write it out for me so quickly. It is invaluable. I could not believe my eyes when I read that it had turned up. The whole affair of Poe's life since I commenced writing it has been one series of almost supernatural surprises. For years have I sought for Graham's letter & never could get the slightest clue to it—now, just as its appearance was imperative—eh, presto! 'tis here. Poor Graham! I have met an American in London who knew him well—said he was most gentlemanly but that having been drawn into drunken habits by two assistants, he got ruined—they got the business & Graham died of poverty & drink! Does *Graham's Magazine* still continue, do you know?[1] Mrs. Lewis was positive that Griswold never edited *Graham's*. This worried me because you know I made such use of it in "New Facts." Looking through 2nd vol. of the *Broadway*, I there discovered not only that he was editor but that he was concerned in & knew all about Poe's sharp notice of Jones, the critic, & therefore knew well when he [Griswold] wrote—towards the end of the "Memoir" about Poe's variable judgments that, in this instance, he (Griswold) was telling a gross & deliberate lie! I'll have him on the hip! 'Twas just the same with the Laughton Osborne allusion on the same page. He was an unmitigated rascal. I must rest again now.

As regards Miss Blackwell—I'll write. A friend of mine in our office knows Home. Don't expect she'll know much. Mrs. Lewis, even, cannot give any printable information. She thinks Edgar Poe was an angel—too good for this world & would not believe that he ever drank even. Told me of the "Annabel Lee" being for her, but I did not make a single comment. You can't nail her to any explanation of Griswold's stories. 'Tis enough for her that they are untrue & further, she did not seem to care to investigate. I don't think I pressed her on the matter of "The South Carolina Lady," but I asked her if she knew anything of Mrs. E[llet]. Her reply is on another sheet of paper.

Did you get the *Gentleman's Magazine* & how did you like the
paper? Mr. Davidson has been very kind & working very hard for me.
Has got me the 2 vols. of *Graham's* which I most wanted & made up
the rest of the "Autography" papers from the N.Y. *Illustrated News.*
Graham's are at my office, but expect them home tonight. Don't know
if they contain the papers on "Cryptology" which I want. I want to find
the story of "The Elk" & the "Life & Death," two tales I know nothing
of.[2] I know when nearly all Poe's tales appeared, but not "Landor's
Cottage." It has always had great interest for me, because my dear
sister, who is no more, was fond of it & by sketching a ground plan of
the cottage, told me that all the doors opened into one room—strange
to say, I have never sought to verify this, but she was so exact I doubt
not but that she was right.

Mr. Davidson sent me an offer from Ed. of the *International* to write
a life of Poe for him—partly critical & partly biographical. I shall be
glad to.

I have just heard from poor Miss Poe & from Mr. Davidson
respecting her. I cannot sent her letter as I may have to shew it, but
will copy some of it. Poor old lady! I do pity her & will do my best for
her at once. Perhaps among your friends you may get a little aid. I am
in hopes to get enough to buy her a small annuity. It would do no good
to place much money in her hands at once. Mr. Powell (Rev. G. Powell,
127 N. Broadway, Baltimore) writing to Mr. Davidson, says,

Miss Poe is very destitute. I have given her about $60 this winter from a
lecture I delivered on the life of her brother. This is the only money of any
account she has received for years. She is 62 years of age & very feeble. I have
seen her almost weekly during the last six months and she has always
appeared in the same thin cheap calico dress. She is a good old lady but
simple. I would not advise a large quantity of money being sent her, for she is
no financier; she lost what little money she had during the war & since then
she has been so destitute that I fear money would have an intoxicating effect.
Her condition today is a disgrace to the American nation. I am glad my
countrymen are doing something for her, &c. P.S. Miss Poe has a cousin in
Baltimore, but I am sorry to say he takes no interest in her whatever. Poor
Edgar's grave is level with the ground, not a stone marks the spot where his
body crumbles. Shame.

That is the substance of Mr. Powell's letter: he, I presume, is a
Britisher. Now, presently for Miss Poe's letter, but I'm so tired & have
so much else to say. Your letter containing your portrait was so
welcome that I seemed to revive ever since it arrived. My dear mother
was going to write to you for me, but quite knocked herself up over me
& is now ill in bed.

I cannot tell how that letter of mine was delayed. I try & post them
all myself, to be sure. In my next I want to send you Baudelaire's

Essais on Poe. Your letter of 4th came today & yours dated 6th, but Providence post mark of 5th, came yesterday. This is singular. Much remains to say in my next in a few days. We must find out Mr. Clarke. How strange that Mr. Gill won't answer—has he sent you copy of Mr. J. Willis's letter?—I mean of Edgar Poe's schoolmate—Miss Poe, I fear, cannot give any information, but she speaks of having lived with her brother at one time. I wonder when—we shall see soon, I suppose. Miss R. M. Poe's letter—copy—Extracts:

Never living with my brother until a few years before his death—I did not know I had a brother or brothers, I may say until I was a good sized girl. I took your letter, as I was advised, to my cousin Neilson Poe, who is a lawyer in Baltimore. He replied that with my permission he would answer it & at the same time said there is money coming to you concerning this.

Miss Poe asked N[eilson] P[oe] to write, as she could give me no information about "my poor brother's life." Miss Poe says that when I wrote to Mr. Powell her cousin refused to give any information & to silence her said that I had now published my books & therefore required no more information. This Neilson Poe is a disgrace to his name. Miss Poe has a home but no means of getting food or clothing. She says, "I am 64—I am two years younger than my brother." [3] This doubtless is wrong. I will do my best for her as soon as I can. It had better go to Mr. Powell, I suppose.

Can you say how you found out that Poe was descended from Le Poers? The Powers I know well.

And now, my dear friend, quite worn out, I conclude as yours ever faithfully,

John H. Ingram

As regards Mrs. E[llet]—I'm so tired but will try & tell Mrs. Lewis's story & when you have read this please burn it because although Mrs. Lewis did not say it was private, still our conversation was. Mrs. E. called on Mrs. L. at her lodgings in London. I forget if they had met before. Mrs. E. pretended to be very friendly & asked to be allowed to copy something of Mrs. L's. Whilst she was copying it Mrs. L. left the room to order luncheon for two & by a series of events which I need not record was absent half an hour. On her return saw that Mrs. E. had not got any further with her copying than when she had left the room but did not think anything of that. So they lunched & soon after Mrs. E. said she must go. She went & after her departure Mrs. L. discovered that she had ransacked her large writing desk & that a publisher's letter, which would have been worth $600 to Mrs. L. was gone! It never came back & she lost the money! Mrs. L. says, "I blame myself only, for having received such a viper after all the things I had heard of her."

I don't think Poe ever spoke of her to Mrs. L. Mrs. L. says he never spoke ill of a soul. Mrs. L., I fancy, must have been led to believe that Poe cared more for her than he really did. Gratitude for her kindness was undoubtedly his sole feeling towards her. Mrs. Clemm used to taunt her, she says, by declaring Poe had written her long affectionate epistles, but that she, Mrs. C. had intercepted and destroyed them. Mrs. L. is inveterate against Mrs. C., whom she thinks all one with Griswold. Mrs. L. says when Poe died a large trunk full of his papers was brought to her house, at, she understood, his dying request. But in a day or two Griswold came & produced an order from Mrs. Clemm for all the papers, & Mrs. C. personally confirming this order, Mrs. L. gave up everything.

This side *re*. Mrs. E. I rely upon you to destroy—

I wonder who that other friend was who was present when you parted from E. Poe? Do you think she or he could have originated the rumours—*some one who must have known* the truth recounted the story.

J.H.I.

1. In letters to follow Ingram and Mrs. Whitman will continue to speculate about Graham's death, but when this letter was written Graham actually had more than twenty years left to live. He had gone bankrupt in 1853, but he did not die until July 13, 1894. The first issue of *Graham's Magazine* came out in Jan. 1826; the last in Dec. 1858.

2. "Life in Death," later called "The Oval Portrait," was first published in *Graham's Magazine*, Apr. 1842.

3. Two of Rosalie Poe's letters to Ingram are reproduced in full in *Building Poe Biography*, pp. 60–63.

54. Sarah Helen Whitman to John H. Ingram.   Item 156

My dear Mr. Ingram,   June 2, 1874
    Your anxiously looked-for letter [May 19] has just reached me & leaves me still more anxious. I knew before I opened it that it would tell me of your illness. I had made three attempts to answer your letter of May 5th, but was unequal to the effort. I, too, have been ill— prostrated by the effects of ivy poisoning. On the 17th of May, I ignorantly gathered a spray of ivy, thinking it woodbine, & held it for a long time in my hand. The poison seemed to produce a universal feeling of languor & inertia, from which I am very slowly recovering. Oh, I *hope* you are quite well now—but I shall be so anxious till I know that you are.
    I will write to Mr. Eveleth today about the continuation of the "Marie Rogêt" story. I cannot think that anything further on the subject

has ever been published. There was a *paragraph* in "The Round Table," written by Mr. Eveleth, giving an explanation about the story, from a letter of Poe's to Eveleth—very *brief*.[1] I think this must be what Eveleth alluded to.

Graham's Magazine, I think, was discontinued about the time when *Harper's* commenced.[2] In your last letter you asked me about the cottage in Fordham. I was inside the house. There was a parlor with two windows in front. An entry & stairway with a small bedroom behind them, and a room used as a dining room, which you descended two steps to reach. It may also have been used as a kitchen. It was in the addition to the left of the house, as you see it in the woodcut in *Harper's*. It had a window in front & behind, I think. Upstairs there was a room over the bedroom, & one over the parlor. There *may* have been a kitchen also in the basement, as Mrs. Lewis described it, but I think not. When I was there, there was, I believe, a window to the north, opposite the two front windows. Miss Blackwell told me that there was a straw matting on the parlor floor, two small pine tables, made by Mr. Poe, & very neatly & tastefully covered by him with fine green baize nailed down with two rows of brass-headed nails. The window curtains of white muslin were of snowy purity & delicacy, & the effect of the whole charming in its simplicity & neatness.

Mrs. Locke of Lowell, also, told me much of the neatness & comfort of the cottage *menage*. Mrs. Locke passed a day there in the summer of 1848. It was in the month of June.[3]

I am so glad that anything you may have found in the *Broadway Journal* will enable you to refute Griswold. Poor Griswold! I wonder how he feels about it all now. I wonder if it is true that Mrs. Osgood endorsed his estimate of Poe as regards Poe's intercourse with *men*. Griswold asserts that she did. But his assertion proves nothing. If she *did* read & approve this, she could not have been a loyal & true friend to Poe.

Mr. Davidson writes that he has found & mailed to you the *Graham's* vol. for 1850. I am glad that he is helping you. You will have learned from my last letter that the "Life in Death" story is the same with "The Oval Portrait." You will have seen, too, how much I liked your notice of the poems. Could Mrs. Lewis, do you think, tell you *when* & *where* "Landor's Cottage" first appeared? How much I long to know more of the sister you loved so well!

What you tell me of Mr. Powell's account of Miss Poe is certainly very sad. But if Mr. Powell is to be her agent in the matter, would it not be well to obtain some reliable information about *him*? Or have you already done so?

I cannot but think there is a mistake about Miss Poe's having lived with her brother "within a few years of his death." It could not have been after he removed to New York. Does Mr. Davidson know anything of Mr. Powell? Miss Poe's letter is dated from Washington at the Epiphany Church Home. Has she found a permanent asylum there, I wonder?

What you have quoted from Miss Poe's letter about her not having known that she had "a brother, or brothers, until she was a good-sized girl" seems very, *very* strange! Where had the poor child been, then, & with whom? Mrs. Clemm, I have been *told*, professed to believe that she was not the child of her brother, but of the nurse who had the charge of Rosalie in her infancy. Don't speak of this.

It is all very strange, but Mrs. Clemm is herself an enigma.

You ask me what I think of Mrs. Clemm. I have no reason to think ill of her, yet I cannot say that she inspired me with confidence in her sincerity. I felt that she loved Poe devotedly, and that *he*, at least, believed in her. He often spoke of her kind & tender care of Virginia in her illness, & of her self-sacrificing & more than motherly devotion to both of them. I think she could love & hate with great intensity. I should accept *cum grano salis* the impressions of Mrs. Lewis with regard to her; doubtless there was blame on both sides.

I did not understand the *motive* of Mrs. E[llet] in abstracting the letter, which would have been so valuable to Mrs. L[ewis]. Could Mrs. E[llet] have used it herself, or did she take it simply to annoy the other lady? Did you ascertain to what motive the act was ascribed?

I must not write another line today, for I have still to write to Mr. Eveleth about "Marie Rogêt," but I fear it will be of no avail.

I shall be delighted to receive Baudelaire's *Essays* on Poe.[4] A gentleman who was in Paris three years ago vainly sought to procure them for me.

I am very tired & will answer other portions of your letter as soon as I am strong enough. I have so much to say & ask, but goodbye now & take rest & get well soon.

Ever & gratefully your friend,

S.H.W.

1. Poe's letter to George W. Eveleth, dated New York, Jan. 4, 1848, can be found in John Ward Ostrom, ed., *The Letters of Edgar Allan Poe*, 2 vols. (Cambridge, Mass.: Harvard Univ. Press, 1948), II, 355–56. The *Round Table* paragraph was published in Vol. 5, Jan. 26, 1867, p. 62.

2. *Harper's New Monthly Magazine* began in June 1850; *Graham's Magazine* stopped with the Dec. number, 1858.

3. Mrs. Jane Ermina Locke (d. ca. 1859) was a minor poet of Lowell, Mass. She was instrumental in having Poe invited to deliver a lecture in Lowell on July 10, 1848, and expected to be his hostess at her home, Wamesit Cottage, during his visit. On the night of his lecture, Poe met Mrs. Nancy Locke Heywood Richmond, a relative by marriage of Mrs. Locke's, as Mrs. Frances Osgood was also her cousin by marriage. After meeting Mrs. Richmond and finishing his lecture, Poe transferred his baggage and person to Mrs.

Richmond's home that night. Mrs. Locke never forgave him, and she became, if it is possible to measure enmity by rank and degree, perhaps next after Griswold and Mrs. Ellet, Poe's bitterest enemy.

4. Charles Pierre Baudelaire, *Histoires Extraordinaires* (Paris: Michel Lévy Frères, 1865).

55. *John H. Ingram to Sarah Helen Whitman*

My dear Mrs. Whitman,   15 June 1874
   You cannot credit with what anxiety I have waited for your next letter. I have grown to watch for and prize your communications, apart even from their connection with Edgar Poe, with strange & inexplicable interest—and now—as I had feared—I hear from yours dated the 2nd & just received that you have also been ill. What a singular illness—poisoning by Ivy. I fancy the plant must be more virulent with you than with us, although I must confess it has a most stupifying, enervating &, at the same time, repulsive odour for me. I trust most sincerely that the effects have now worn off with you. As for me, I am almost myself again but my long illness and its consequent idleness have almost unfitted me for writing. I have been daily wishing to write to & hear from you, but could neither do the one thing or get the other. Although I have been able, for some days past, to get out & about, I am still suffering from bodily pains—rheumatic— & I may add mental—for my neglected work has worried me greatly. Tomorrow I leave town for the Isle of Wight for a week or two for change of air. Today I can only just send these few scrawled lines. I have not been able to write to you, from sheer inanity, but your letter has just stirred me up enough to a simple & doubtless incoherent acknowledgment. Oh, that I could have a *viva voce* interview instead of this dull, sluggish method.
   I have not seen Mrs. Lewis since the second interview, although again invited during my illness. Really, with all the will in the world she can give no information. She left Baltimore when quite young, & so many years ago, that she cannot remember anything of its inhabitants, & she says that it was not until about the last year of his life that she had any real intimate knowledge of Poe. She thinks he was superhuman—almost an angel—& said she did not believe anything alleged against him—not even the drunkenness. She had your little book, *E.P. & His Critics*, on the table at my first visit, but seemed disinclined to allude to it—but I *fancy* there were notes (pencil) in it. Mrs. Lewis is *very eccentric*—doubtless much changed since she lived in America, & I fancy, from being, perhaps, without relatives or very near friends in the world, has grown—*entre nous*—

very singular. Her *heart* is in the right place, however, I feel assured. I dare say I shall be able to get her to let me have the portrait copied & then will send you a copy.

By the way, I have just returned the proofs of the engravings of E. Poe for *our* life. I think it is very successful & *feel* that it is like. I shall be proud of the day when I can forward to you the vol. containing it. I am not superstitious—although not quite so sceptical as a former letter led you to imagine—but I do really feel as if I were marked out & certain to write Poe's life—indeed, were I to die this moment, there is a complete life—an abridged one—written for the *Quarterly* that would serve my purpose. The publishers are getting on so rapidly with Vol. 1 that I must somehow shorten the "Memoir" & let them have it as complete as time will admit of. All of importance *yet known* will be incorporated. The *Quarterly* paper will not appear in July. I was behind time through my illness & as it was only an abridgment of the "Memoir" could not appear next October, as the Vol. 1 is expected out earlier. Editor seems sorry & I am to call on him. You shall hear the story of it another time.

Mr. Davidson has been very kind—sent 2 vols. of *Graham's*—1841–2 (2nd & 3rd of Poe's editorship). Am still minus Vol. 1 (that is Vol. 18). Mr. D. also sent the number with Graham's letter & *Harper's*, with the University article—same as you sent. "Autography" from which I shall omit a few names—and "Cryptology" papers were in *Graham's*. "Life in Death," I saw at once was "The Oval Portrait," but I shall use the omitted portion.

There is much of Poe's writing still uncollected, I am sure. Much of the "Marginalia," &c., & I dare say Griswold suppressed much for his own & his *customers'* sake. Poe wrote for the Philadelphia *Saturday Evening Post*. His paper on ciphers appeared in *Graham's* June 1841 & in it he speaks of having written papers on an analagous subject 18 months earlier, in a "weekly paper of this city,"—*i.e.*, Philadelphia. Again of his *prospective* review of *Barnaby Rudge* in *Sat. E. Post* of May 1, 1841—see Works Vol. 3, p. 474. What has become of the letter of C. Dickens to Poe—see "Philosophy of Composition"—neither young Dickens, or John Forster, know anything of the correspondence. You see there is much still much to learn for a future edition.

The *Gentleman's Magazine* will throw some light if it ever turns up.

Miss R. Poe cannot, I fancy, do anything. I believe her home is permanent but does not provide food or clothes. My illness has delayed my efforts on her behalf, but Mr. Davidson writes me as if he knew Mr. Powell—not that I shall trust a single shilling to him. Meanwhile I wrote to our Consul at Baltimore. He says, "Mr. Powell has been to see me & will write you in a few days giving you some information, such as you require, also that he could give a great deal if he had the time at his disposal to do so, & that he could put his hand on many letters (never published) of the late E. A. Poe." Then, speaking of Miss Poe, he repeats the information of Mr. Powell, who seems the ruler of the old lady, adding, "he (Mr. Powell) showed me a letter from her . . . I would judge from Miss Poe's letter that she is by no means a person of much intelligence:—penury & hardship may, however, have something to do with this." Mr. Powell says Miss Poe must not have much money given her at this time, or it would be too much for her reason—this to Mr. Davidson. She has not answered me. He says she has worn one thin dress all the winter to his knowledge & yet tells Mr. D. that he gave her over 60 dollars—see scrap enclosed, sent me by Moncure Conway. Mr. Powell I cannot trust without knowing more of him. I fancy letters, &c. soon shew who may & who may not be trusted.

From her letters I cannot say that I care for Mrs. Clemm—they seemed to me, working upon your feelings for money. I can not say that I feel very admiringly disposed towards her. I must leave much for next & future letters—

Let me remark that I did thoroughly agree with Mr. O'Connor's remarks on Stoddard's paper in the *Harper's Monthly*—it was so mean & little.

I have always kept your letters sacred, but I read out your judgment on me, from my imperfect portrait, to my mother, only suppressing the too flattering finale, & she said it was admirable—that if you had known me for years, personally, you could not have told my character better. I don't know that I quite agree. Your picture is so pleasant to me. At home they say, "It looks such a good face & that the eyes must be very fine."

I see in last week's *Mirror* declined as unsuitable something styled "Griswold's Punishment." I wonder what it—this something—is like! I enclose you the only two notices I have of the *Temple Bar* & *Gentleman's* articles. They are from two of our best literary papers.

I send you with Baudelaire's notice of Poe, the *Temple Bar* article. Unfortunately, 'tis published from the first proof & not like the later one you have. I cannot account for this. You will see the errors. They have altered the name of Mrs. Osgood to Mrs. Lewis, at my request. Mrs. O[sgood], I think there is little doubt, *was quite under Griswold's control* at last, but she could not forget Poe & the last poem of the collection published just before her death was to the *adored* "Israfel." Do you know it? What a beautiful handwriting was hers! One collection of her poems in British Museum is a presentation copy to Rufus W. Griswold. I don't think even Griswold's great hold on the poor woman would have made her false to Poe—doubtless Griswold "cooked up" her reminiscences.

Again referring to Mrs. Clemm, Graham in the 1850 letter states that what money Poe received from him "went directly into the hands of his mother-in-law for family comforts"—and Mrs. Lewis deems that Mrs. Clemm got Poe into disrepute by begging & borrowing & receiving all his earnings & wasting the money—in some things—Mrs. L[ewis] says she was very extravagant. I cannot make anything out of this riddle & shall not try. I do not want to misjudge Mrs. C[lemm], or judge her without firmer testimony.

My remarks about my previous letters was not fearing you might repeat, or show anything that were better private, but not knowing into whose hands they might someday pass—but there! I do not think any of the letters we have yet exchanged would injure us at any day of judgment.

I could not understand myself the motive of Mrs. E[llet] in abstracting the letter. It appeared she could not get the money herself, but only prevent Mrs. L[ewis] from getting it: mere petty malice, so far as I could comprehend. Mrs. L[ewis] is not very clear in her rambling chatter. No pinning her into a corner.

I fancy Baudelaire wrote more about Poe than I this day forward by book post, but that is all known in England. I'll try for the others.

Thanks for the enclosures. By the way, I liked "Proserpine" better than any of the other poems—better than Jean Ingelow's "Persephone."

Oh! I've so much to leave over. I was too hasty with the Shaver Barn extract—lend it to me again some day—it will do for the book of "The Raven" I told you of. *All* your papers shall be returned when my "Memoir" is in print.

And now goodbye, & get well,—quite well & through all, ever & ever, believe me, my very dear friend, to be yours most faithfully.

John H. Ingram

[Enclosure: Newspaper clipping from the London *Academy,* June 6, 1874.   Item 577]

In *Temple Bar* for this month there is an article on Poe, exposing the bad faith of the life by Griswold, which is still treated in England as a trustworthy authority. In the *Gentleman's Magazine* for May there is an interesting article on an early collection of Poe's poems, printed for private circulation in 1831, when he was a cadet at West Point. There are copious extracts which have both a bibliographical and literary interest.

[Enclosure: Newspaper clipping from the London *Examiner,* June 6, 1874]

In *Temple Bar*, there is a valuable paper on Edgar Poe, by Mr. John H. Ingram. Mr. Ingram inpugns the accuracy of Dr. Griswold's account of the poet, from which the prevailing notions about him are derived, and adduces evidence to prove that when this standard biography was called "the fancy sketch of a jaundiced vision," nothing more was said than the literal truth. Dr. Griswold is charged with malicious omission, and fabulous insertion; and Mr. Ingram makes it quite clear that, if we are not to modify our notions about Poe's debauchery and irregularities, we must at least cease to credit many of the disreputable anecdotes which Dr. Griswold has accumulated around his name.

56. "Edgar Poe," by John H. Ingram, Temple Bar, *41 (June 1874),* 375–87

Edgar Poe

John H. Ingram

UNTIL THE PRESENT moment Dr. Griswold's "Memoir" of Edgar Poe has been accepted, almost unquestioned, in Europe: in America its correctness has been frequently and authoritatively impugned. Baudelaire in France, and Mr. Moy Thomas in England it is true, have ventured to question the truth of the reverend gentleman's account of Poe's life,[1] but, twenty-four years after the poet's decease, we still find ourselves the first in this country to appear before the public with any proofs of the thorough untrustworthiness of the said "Memoir." The present is not an occasion for a full and critical examination of the biography by Dr. Griswold, but we confidently believe that enough evidence can be adduced here to prove that when Mr. Graham styled it "the fancy sketch of a jaundiced vision," he was but giving utterance to the truth. Writers in search of a sensational subject are prone to resort to Poe's life for a point to their moral; but we must content ourselves with the barest and most unsophisticated narration of his career, as gathered from fresh evidence, merely pointing out on our course his biographer's more palpable deviations from the fact.

Edgar Poe could boast of gentle lineage; a fact, probably, of little value, save that it explains to some extent the delicacy of his feelings and fancies. Descended from the old Norman family of the Le Poers, the race would appear to have retained its position in society until our hero's father forsook jurisprudence to elope with an actress. After having "donned the sock" himself for a few years, David Poe died, and within a few weeks of his youthful bride, leaving three children, Henry, Edgar, and Rosalie, utterly destitute. Mr. John Allan, a wealthy merchant, and a friend of the family, having no children of his own, following a com-

1. "The Train Magazine," No. 16, vol. iii, pp. 193 &c.

mon American custom, adopted the boy Edgar and his sister Rosalie. Of
this girl we learn no more, save that she is still alive and in a state of
utter destitution.[2]

Edgar Poe was born in Baltimore, but when is still doubtful. Griswold, and other biographers copying him, say in January, 1811, and this
date is alleged to have been taken from a letter of the poet's, but those
who have investigated the "Memoir" will probably be inclined to question its correctness. Poe, in his wonderful story of "William Wilson,"
speaks of passing the third lustrum of his life at Dr. Bransby's, and if that
might be accepted as a fact it would, by antedating his birth some few
years, get rid of several singular anomalies in his biography. Griswold
frequently overlooks the necessity of being accurate in his dates. On the
very first page of his "Memoir," in order to avail himself of a ridiculous
anecdote communicated to him by "an eminent and estimable gentleman," of Poe's conduct at a school in Richmond, Virginia, when he "was
only six or seven years of age," he disregards the fact that, according to
his own account, his hero was then and had been for two years past in
England.

Accepting the date recorded by all his biographers, his adopted parents brought Poe to England in 1816, and placed him at the Manor
House School, Church Street, Stoke Newington. The school was then
kept by the Rev. Dr. Bransby and would appear to have been situated
in grounds of considerable extent, although now sadly shorn of their
proportions. The poet's description of the place must be taken *cum
grano salis*, and the oft quoted recollections of "William Wilson" may
well be referred to the usually exaggerated dimensions of childhood's
reminiscences. In 1822, after a residence of five years in England, he
returned to the United States, and, says Griswold, "after passing a few
months at an academy in Richmond, entered the University at Charlottesville, Virginia, where he led a very dissipated life. The manners
which then prevailed there were extremely dissolute, and he was known
as the wildest and most reckless student of his class; but his unusual
opportunities, and the remarkable ease with which he mastered the
most difficult studies, kept him all the while in the first rank for scholarship." The "gambling, intemperance, and other vices," which "induced," says this biographer, "his expulsion from the university," must
have been the result of extraordinary precocity, because, if this authority
is reliable in his dates, Poe was now in the eleventh or twelfth year of
his age!

If the "William Wilson" theory may be accepted, and the statement of
Mr. Powell, in his sketches of "The Authors of America," that Poe went
to "various academies" previous to entering the Charlottesville Univer-

2. Rosalie, Edgar Poe's sister and only surviving relative, is stated to be now living at
Hicks' Landing, in Virginia, in the most necessitous circumstances.

sity, be borne in mind, the poet's age would be from fifteen to twenty during his collegiate career. Notwithstanding his alleged dissoluteness, this precocious boy, according to his more reliable biographers, actually found means to obtain the first honors of his college, and at the conclusion of his university career, instead of being expelled, as Griswold asserts, left *alma mater* with the intention of aiding the Greeks in their struggles for independence. A mere boy, Poe would appear to have joined in the various pastimes of his fellow students, but that he made himself notorious by "his gambling, intemperance, and *other* vices," would appear to be in direct contradiction to all unprejudiced evidence now obtainable. Griswold admits that at this period Poe was noted for feats of hardihood, strength and activity, and that "on one occasion, in a hot day of June, he swam from Richmond to Warwick, seven miles and a half, against a tide running probably from two to three miles an hour." Certainly a wonderful performance for a dissolute youth, and one that if not vouched for on good authority, might well have been relegated to the depths of the Doctor's imagination. Apart from his athletic feats, Poe's great abilities enabled him to maintain a respectable position in the eyes of the professors. "His time," remarks Powell, "was divided between lectures, debating societies, rambles in the Blue Ridge mountains, and in making caricatures of his tutors and the heads of the colleges." He was a clever draughtsman, and is stated to have had the habit of covering the walls of his dormitory with rough, charcoal sketches. "Rousing himself," adds Powell, "from this desultory course of life, he took the first honors of the college, and returned home."

Poe left the Charlottesville University with the intention of emulating Byron in his efforts on behalf of the Greeks. In conjunction with an acquaintance, Ebenezer Burling, the future poet purposed proceeding to Greece to take part in the struggle against the Turks, but his companion's heart failing him, Poe had to undertake the perilous journey alone. This act of chivalry on the part of the youthful adventurer was undertaken in 1827, when, according to his biographers, he had attained the prematurely mature age of sixteen! The would-be warrior got no further than St. Petersburg, where he was arrested in consequence of an irregularity in his passport, and was only saved from further difficulty through the exertions of the American consul, by whose friendly assistance he was, moreover, enabled to return to his native land, the recognition of Greece by the allied powers rendering *his* aid no longer necessary. It should be noted that Griswold states his young countryman's troubles at St. Petersburg arose "from penalties incurred in a drunken debauch;" but this allegation was denied directly it appeared in print; its author never attempted to support it by evidence of any description, and every other native biographer gives the story as we have told it.

On his return home poor Poe found a sad change. Mrs. Allan, who seems to have acted a mother's part to him, and whom he would appear to have regarded with deep affection, was dead. He was too late even to take a last farewell of his only friend, her funeral having taken place the day before he reached Richmond. Mrs. Allan died on the 27th of February, 1829, and from that day his biographers very justly date all his misfortunes. Mr. Allan, who does not appear to have manifested much pleasure at his adopted son's return, when Poe declared his resolution of devoting himself to a military life, seems to have assisted him in obtaining an appointment in West Point Military Academy. "Here he entered upon his new studies and duties," remarks Powell, "with characteristic energy, and an honorable career was opened to him; but the fates willed it that Mr. Allan should marry a girl young enough to be her husband's grand-daughter;" and this event, Poe was soon made to feel as a death-blow to his hopes of succeeding to his adopted father's property, in accordance with that person's oft-expressed intention. Here again it is necessary to revert to Dr. Griswold's "Memoir" to contradict his emphatic statement that Mr. Allan, on his second marriage, so far from being sixty-five years of age, as "stated by all Poe's biographers . . . was in his forty-eight year." He seems to have re-married in a twelve-month after his first wife's death, and yet the careless recorder of the event, forgetting on the very next page his declaration of the "forty-eight year," allows him to die in the spring of 1834, or barely four years later, at fifty-four instead of fifty-two years of age.[3] The point is hardly worth quibbling over save that it is another specimen of Griswold's want of accuracy. Common sense would show that a man who had been so long married and so hopeless of offspring as to have adopted two non-related children in 1814–15 was more likely to be nearer sixty-five than forty-eight in 1830.

Whether the truth lies with all the other biographers or with the Doctor, as regards this circumstance, matters little; it suffices to say that Poe but too speedily discovered, after Mr. Allan's second marriage, that affairs had altered to his detriment at home. The birth of a son to his adopted father was made the means of completely alienating that man from his hitherto reputed heir, and poor Edgar found all his pecuniary prospects suddenly blighted. The unfortunate cadet's allowance being entirely withdrawn he was compelled to leave West Point, and resolved to proceed to Poland, to aid the patriots of that nation in their struggle to shake off the Russian yoke. Here again it is requisite to refer to a statement of Griswold's, to the effect that Poe parted in anger from Mr. Allan, who refused in any way to assist him further, because, "according

3. In his account of Poe's death, Griswold himself stated Mr. Allan to have been sixty-five.

to Poe's own statement, he ridiculed the marriage of his *"patron"* with Miss Paterson and had a quarrel with her;[4] but a different story, scarcely suitable for repetition here, was told by the friends of the other party." The different story is then referred to in a note as hinted at by the writer of an "Eulogium" upon the life and genius of Mr. Poe, in the "Southern Literary Messenger," for March, 1850. To this "Eulogium" and its author, we shall again refer, merely contenting ourselves now with stating that this tale can only be spoken of as unsupported by a tittle of evidence.

On the 6th of September, 1831, the unequal conflict in Poland was ended by the fall of Warsaw. The news reached the chivalric poet in time to prevent his departure, but left him once more aimless and almost resourceless. In 1827, in happier times, Poe had published a small volume of poems, which ran through three editions—a fact Dr. Griswold forgets to mention—and which appears to have received the warm commendations of local critics. Griswold asserts that it included "Al Aaraaf" and "Tamerlane," pieces since republished in the collected edition; but this would not appear to have been the case; and the poet's own reference to those poems being "reprinted *verbatim* from the original edition"—as if to refute his biographer's suggestion that they had been constantly revised—applies to the volume of 1830–31. Of the former work the only poem preserved would appear to be the sweet little lyric "To Helen," embalmed by Lowell in his sympathetic sketch of its author. Encouraged by this illusory success, Poe started for Baltimore, where he turned to literature as a means of subsistence. He quickly found that the waters of Helicon were anything but Pactolian; and although some of his finest stories were written at this time, and accepted by the magazines, they were scarcely ever paid for, and at last the unfortunate man was absolutely and literally *starving*.

At this period of the terrible tale, as frightful as the most dramatic of his own stories, Poe, according to Griswold, enlisted as a private soldier, was recognised by some officers who had known him at West Point, and who made efforts, with prospects of success, to obtain a commission for him, when it was discovered by his friends that he had deserted. About the whole of this story there is that air of improbability which the reverend doctor is so fond of. Of the many lives of the poet, by friends and foes, published in America, Griswold alone mentions the circumstance, and as his "Memoir" has been authoritatively stigmatised by Mrs. Sarah Whitman, and others, for containing anecdotes which "are utterly fabulous," it must be regarded with grave suspicion. There is one fact which renders it very improbable: Poe went to Baltimore in 1830, and was in that city in 1833. Griswold places the affair between those dates, stating, "how long he remained in the service I have not been able to ascertain." Is it likely that a man so well known as Poe was would have enlisted,

4. The italics are ours.

deserted, and yet have remained in a place where he was so generally known? or that his friends would not have encouraged him to remain in the army to wait the result of their exertions?

In 1833, the proprietor of the "Baltimore Saturday Visiter" offered premiums for the best prose story and the best poem, and to adjudicate upon the mass of papers sent in three well known men were obtained. The committee included the Honorable John P. Kennedy, author of the well known fiction, "Horse-Shoe Robinson." "The umpires," remarks Powell, "were men of taste and ability, and after a *careful consideration* of the productions, they decided that Poe was undoubtedly entitled to both prizes. As Poe was entirely unknown to them, this was a genuine tribute to his superior merit." The poem sent was "The Coliseum," and it was accompanied by six stories for selection; "not content with awarding the premium, they" (i.e. the committee) "declared that the worst of the six tales referred to was better than the best of the other competitors." Griswold, enlarging upon the "Eulogium" already referred to, tells the story of the award in the following manner. We leave our reader to judge the value of Dr. Griswold's "Memoir" by this fact alone, if he will compare the extract we now give with the official report given below: "Such matters are usually disposed of in a very off-hand way. Committees to award literary prizes drink to the payer's health in good wines, over unexamined MSS, which they submit to the discretion of publishers, with permisssion to use their names in such a way as to promote the publisher's advantage. So, perhaps, it would have been in this case, but that one of the committee, taking up a little book remarkably beautiful and distinct in caligraphy, was tempted to read several pages; and becoming interested, he summoned the attention of the company to the half dozen compositions it contained. It was unanimously decided that the prizes should be paid to 'the first of geniuses who had written legibly.' Not another MS. was unfolded. Immediately the 'confidential envelope' was opened, and the successful competitor was found to bear the scarcely known name of Poe."

Thus runs the printed report of the committee, published with the award on the 12th of October, 1833, and republished in the "Southern Literary Messenger," previous to Poe's assuming the editorial management of that magazine:

"Amongst the prose articles were many of various and distinguished merit, but the singular force and beauty of those sent by the author of 'The Tales of the Folio Club,' leave us no room for hesitation in that department. We have accordingly awarded the premium to a tale entitled the 'MS. found in a Bottle.' It would hardly be doing justice to the writer of this collection to say that the tale we have chosen is the best of the six offered by him. We cannot refrain from saying that the author owes it to his own reputation as well as to the gratification of the community, to publish the entire volume ('Tales of the Folio Club'). These tales are eminently distinguished by a wild, vigorous, and poetical imagination, a rich style, a fertile invention, and varied and curious learning.

Signed   "JOHN P. KENNEDY,
              "J.H.B. LATROBE, and
              "JAMES H. MILLER."

Comment on this is needless.

From this time Poe's affairs mended, and his writings were not only sought after but paid for by the publishers. In the spring of the year following (1834) Mr. Allan died, and of his property, to quote the elegant words of Griswold, "not a mill was bequeathed to Poe," and, it is alleged, the widow of his adopted father "even refused him his own books." Early in 1835, the poet began to contribute poems, tales and reviews to the "Southern Literary Messenger," a newly established monthly magazine. Mr. Kennedy, after a year and a half's friendship with Poe, had advised him to forward a paper to Mr. White, the proprietor of the above publication. He did so; became a regular contributor, and in May, 1835, he was made editor, at a salary of five hundred dollars per annum. The accession of the new editor worked wonders in the "Southern Literary Messenger," in a short time raising its circulation from four hundred to three thousand. Its success was partially due to the originality and fascination of Poe's stories, and partially owing to the fearlessness of his trenchant critiques. He was no respecter of persons, and already began to rouse the small fry bookmakers by his crucial dissection of their mediocrities. "He had a scorn," says Powell, "of the respectable level trash which has too long brooded over American literature. Poe did not like tamely to submit to the dethronement of genius. . . . What gods and men abhor, according to Horace, a certain class of critics and readers in America adore." Amongst the best of his productions at this period was the "Adventure of Hans Pfaal," which appeared in the "Literary Messenger" three weeks previous to the appearance of Mr. Richard Lock's "Moon Story," which indeed it probably suggested, although from the way in which Griswold alludes to "Hans Pfaal" being "in some respects very similar to Mr. Lock's" story, one is led to believe our poet the copier instead of the copied.

In September, 1835, Poe, who had hitherto performed his editorial duties at a distance, found it necessary to leave Baltimore for Richmond, where the "Messenger" was published. Again amongst his kindred, he met his cousin Virginia Clemm, a girl in years, and already manifesting signs of consumption; but undeterred by this or by their poverty, the poor poet was wedded to his kinswoman. He continued the direction of the "Messenger" until January, 1837, when he left it for the more lucrative employment of assisting Professors Anthon, Hawkes, and Henry, in the management of the "New York Quarterly Review." Griswold, it is true, states that he was dismissed from the "Messenger" on account of his irregularities, and he quotes a goodly letter from its *deceased* proprietor, upbraiding him for getting drunk, but promising to allow him to "again become an assistant in my office" on condition that he forswore the bottle. Unsupported by other evidence, we should doubt the truth of this extract. Undated, addressed to a gentleman who has raised his publication to a profitable and famous circulation, and who would appear at this time to have been married, is it probable that Poe would have been termed "an assistant in my office," and offered "quarters in my house," by Mr. White, who, like all the authorities referred to by this biographer in corroboration of his allegations, save the writer of the aforementioned "Eulogium," unfortunately dies before the charge is brought?

In 1837, Poe wrote some of his slashing critiques for the "New York Review," and by them, says Powell, "made many enemies." In July of the same year, he also completed and published his wonderful narrative of "Arthur Gordon Pym." Griswold displays his usual animus by stating that "it received little attention," and that in England, "being mistaken at first for a narrative of real experiences, it was advertised to be reprinted, but a discovery of its character, I believe, prevented such a result." In truth it was in a short interval twice reprinted in England, and did obtain considerable notice, "the air of truth" which, it is suggested, was only in the attempt, having excited much interest in the book.

The heavy "Review" work was not in Poe's line, and at the end of a year he left New York for Philadelphia, where he was engaged on the "Gentleman's Magazine," since merged into "Graham's." In May, 1839, he was appointed editor of this publication, and, as usual, "came down pretty freely with his critical axe." At the same time he contributed tales and papers to various other magazines, so that, although obliged to labor severely, he began to get a fair livelihood. In the autumn of this year he published a collection of his best stories, in two volumes, under the title of "Tales of the Grotesque and Arabesque."

Poe edited the "Gentleman's" until June, 1840, when it changed hands and became known as "Graham's Magazine." Griswold states that Mr. Burton, the former proprietor of the publication, found the poet so unreliable that he "was never sure when he left the city that his business would be cared for," and sometimes had to perform the editorial duties himself. Wonderful to relate, however, Poe was retained in his post until the last moment, when the following scene is alleged to have occurred: (somebody, of course, had taken shorthand notes of the conversation). Mr. Burton is supposed to have been absent for a fortnight, and, on his return, to have learned that his editor has not only not furnished the printers with any copy for the forthcoming number of the

Magazine, but has availed himself of the time to prepare the prospectus of a new monthly, to supplant that he is now editing. Burton meets "his associate late in the evening at one of his accustomed haunts," and says, "'Mr. Poe, I am astonished!—Give me my manuscripts, so that I can attend to the duties you have so shamefully neglected, and when you are sober we will settle.' Poe interrupted him with 'Who are you that presume to address me in this manner! Burton—I am—the editor—of the 'Penn Magazine'—and you are—hiccup—a fool.'" Such absurd anecdotes are not worthy refutation, but an almost certain proof of their incredibility is furnished by the fact that not only did Mr. George R. Graham engage Poe to continue the editorial duties of the said magazine, but he was also the first to denounce Griswold's "Memoir" of the poet, as "the fancy sketch of a jaundiced vision," and as "an immortal infamy."

Poe retained the editorship of "Graham's Magazine" for about two years, during which period some of his finest analytical tales were produced. In 1843, not 1848, as stated by his inaccurate biographer, he obtained the one hundred dollar prize for his story of "The Gold Bug;" a story written in connection with his theory that human ingenuity could not construct any cryptograph which human ingenuity could not decipher. Tested by several correspondents with difficult samples of their skill, the poet took the trouble to examine and solve them in triumphant proof of his theory.

In the autumn of 1844, Poe removed to New York, where, in literary circles, his fame had already preceded him. He speedily found employment on the "New York Mirror," and Willis, who was one of the proprietors of that paper, has left us a highly interesting portraiture of the poet at this epoch of his life.

"Apropos of the disparaging portion of Dr. Griswold's sketch, which appeared at Poe's death," he remarks, "let us truthfully say, some four or five years since Mr. Poe was employed by us for several months as critic and sub-editor. He resided with his wife and mother at Fordham, a few miles out of town, but was at his desk in the office from nine in the morning till the evening paper went to press. With the highest admiration for his genius, and a willingness to let it atone for more than ordinary irregularity, we were led by common report to expect a very capricious attention to his duties. Time went on, however, and he was invariably punctual and industrious. With his pale, beautiful, and intellectual face, as a reminder of what genius was in him, it was impossible, of course, not to treat him always with deferential courtesy . . . With a prospect of taking the lead in another periodical, he, at last, voluntarily gave up his employment with us, and, through all this considerable period, we had seen but one presentment of the man—a quiet, patient, industrious, and most gentlemanly person, commanding the utmost respect and good feeling by his unvarying deportment and ability.

"Residing as he did in the country, we never met Mr. Poe in hours of leisure; but he frequently called on us afterwards at our place of business, and we met him often in the street—invariably the same sad-mannered, winning and refined gentleman, such as we had always known him. It was by rumor only, up to the day of his death, that we knew of any other development of manner of character. . . . Such only he has invariably seemed to us in all we have happened personally to know of him through a friendship of *five or six years*. And so much easier is it to believe what we have seen and known, than what we *hear* of only, that we remember him but with admiration and respect."

Poe left the "Mirror" in order to take part in the "Broadway Journal," and in October, 1845, he was enabled to buy his partner out, and to obtain the entire possession of this periodical. Under his control it became, probably, the best work of the kind ever issued, but, from the very nature of its contents, must have appealed to too small though select a class to make it remunerative. Accordingly the poor poet had to relinquish its publication, and on the 3rd of January, 1846, the last number was issued. What he did for the next few months heaven only knows; but in the May number of the "Lady's Book" he commenced a series of articles on "The Literati of New York City," in which "he professed," remarks Griswold, with the wonted sneer, "to give some honest opinions at random respecting their autorial merits, with occasional words of personality." The papers seem to have made the literary quacks of New York shake in their shoes. One unfortunate who came under the lash, unable to bear his castigation quietly, retorted in no measured terms; in fact, instead of waiting, as Griswold did, for Poe's death—when every ass could have its kick at the dead lion—this Dr. Dunn Brown, or Dunn English, for both names are given, in a personal newspaper article, referred to the alleged infirmities of the poet. The communication being inserted in the "Evening Mirror," on the 23rd of June, 1843, Poe instituted a libel suit, and recovered several hundred dollars for defamation of character. Let anyone who has the slightest belief in Griswold's impartiality now turn to his garbled account of this dispute. He never mentions the suit for libel or its results; indeed, his *suppressio veri* is an iniquitous as his *suggestio falsi*.

In the autumn of this year Poe was residing in a little cottage at Fordham, near New York. The household comprised the poet, his wife, a confirmed invalid, and her devoted and never-to-be-forgotten mother, Mrs. Clemm, whose name will ever be linked with that of her unfortunate son-in-law. His wife was dying of a long, lingering decline, and the poet himself was ill, and, paralyzed by poverty, scarcely able to labor. "Mr. Poe wrote," says Willis, "with fastidious difficulty, and in a style too much above the popular level to be well paid. He was always in pecuniary difficulties, and, with his sick wife, frequently in want of the merest necessaries of life." A most interesting description of the poet's *menage* at this bitter period of his existence is afforded by a paper which appeared in a London periodical, as "Reminiscences of Edgar Poe."[5] The writer gives a circumstantial account of the homely abode and its occupants, and his description of the family's poverty-stricken condition is heartrending.

"The autumn came," says the writer, detailing his second visit, "and Mrs. Poe sank rapidly in consumption, and I saw her in her bedchamber. Everything here was so neat, so purely clean, so scant and poverty-stricken, that I saw the sufferer with such a heartache as the poor feel for the poor. There was no clothing on the bed, which was only straw, but a snow white spread and sheets. The weather was cold, and the sick lady had the dreadful chills that accompany the hectic fever of consumption. She lay on the straw bed, wrapped in her husband's great-coat, with a large cat in her bosom. . . . The coat and the cat were the sufferer's only means of warmth, except as her husband held her hands and her mother her feet."

These circumstances being made known by the writer of the above, a paragraph appeared in the "New York Express," to the effect that "Edgar Poe and his wife are both dangerously ill with consumption, and that the hand of misfortune lies heavy upon their temporal affairs. We are sorry to mention the fact that they are so far reduced as to be barely able to obtain the necessaries of life. This is, indeed, a hard lot, and we hope that the friends and admirers of Mr. Poe will come promptly to his assistance in his bitterest hour of need." This appeal was followed by an article from Willis in the "Home Journal," adverting to the dangerous illness of the poet and his wife, and their consequent sufferings for want of the commonest necessaries of life, and evidencing their case as a proof of a hospital being required for educated and refined objects of charity. "Here," he urges, "is one of the finest scholars, one of the most original men of genius, and one of the most industrious of the literary men of our country, whose temporary suspension of labor, from bodily illness, drops him immediately to a level with the common objects of public charity."

The effect of this appeal was to bring instant aid to the poor suffering family; Poe's many friends reading it in a different spirit to that of his biographer, who avers that the article by Willis was only "an ingenious apology for Mr. Poe's infirmities," and that the manly letter to its author from Poe, announcing his own gradual recovery from a long and dangerous illness, but his wife's hopeless condition, "was written for effect. He had not been ill a great while," continued his ruthless assailant, "nor

5. "The Sixpenny Magazine," No. xx. February, 1863. NEW SERIES—Vol. XX, No. 2.

dangerously at all. There was no literary or personal abuse of him in the journals," he adds, alluding to a paragraph in the poet's sad letter to Willis, to the effect that his wife's sufferings had been heightened by the receipt of an anonymous letter containing "those published calumnies of Messrs.————, for which," says Poe, "I yet hope to find redress in a court of justice."

This letter, which, according to Griswold, "was written for effect," is dated 30th of December, 1846, and was followed in a few weeks by his wife's death. Mrs. Poe's last moments were soothed and her wants administered to, we believe, by the poet's good and noble friend, Mrs. Lewis, in whose hospitable home, when the poet himself died, Mrs. Clemm is said to have found shelter. It is needless to follow the adventures of the poet through the labyrinth of errors in which his biographer has enveloped them. On the 9th of February, 1848, he delivered a lecture in New York on the Cosmogony of the Universe. This was the substance of his greatest work, and which was subsequently published under the title of "Eureka, a Prose Poem." It has never been reprinted in England.

From this time to the day of his death Poe steadily worked with his pen and as a lecturer, to obtain a livelihood. And he succeeded. But consumption had long been sapping his system, and enfeebled as it was by long suffering, constant and harassing literary labor, and more than all, *want*, it was ready to succumb; and on the evening of Sunday, the 7th of October, 1849, he died, if the correct date of his birth is given, in the thirty-eighth year of his age.

The present opportunity does not admit of a complete analysis of the "Memoir" by Griswold—the memoir on which every English life of Edgar Poe had been founded; but it is believed that enough has been said to prove the biographer's animus. Mrs. Whitman, in her clever little brochure of "Poe and his Critics," states that "some of the most injurious of these anecdotes" (i.e. in the "Memoir") "were disproved, during the life of Dr. Griswold, in the New York 'Tribune' and other leading journals, without eliciting from him any public statement or apology." Quite recently we have had, through the columns of the "Home Journal," the refutation of another calumnious story, which for ten years had been going the round of the English and American periodicals. "Moreover," adds Mrs. Whitman, "we have authority for stating that many of the disgraceful anecdotes, so industriously collected by Dr. Griswold, are *utterly fabulous*, while others are perversions of the truth, more injurious in their effects than unmitigated fiction."

When Edgar Poe died a long account of his life and writings appeared in the New York "Tribune," signed "Ludwig." Dr. Rufus Griswold was subsequently obliged to acknowledge himself the author of it. It is the well-known paper beginning "Edgar Allan Poe is dead. This announcement will startle many, but *few will be grieved by it . . . he had few or no friends.*" In November following the poet's death, a kindly notice of him and his writings was furnished to the "Southern Literary Messenger" by Mr. John R. Thompson, his successor in the editorship of that magazine. It did not contain an unkind or disparaging word. A month or two later appeared a collection of Poe's works in two volumes, and it was most depreciatingly reviewed in the "Tribune" by a writer whose style is easily recognisable, and who signed himself "R."—(Rufus). In March, 1850, appeared an extremely lengthy review of this same collection in the "Literary Messenger;" it is the so-called, by Griswold, "Eulogium," and beginning: "These half-told tales and broken poems are the only records of a wild, hard life. . . . Among all his poems there are only two or three which are not execrably bad." It then proceeds to vilify Willis and Lowell for their tributes to the memory of Poe, the latter of the two, it avers, belonging to that "minute species of literary insect which is plentifully produced by the soil and climate of Boston." The writer then administers a gentle reprimand to Griswold, and forthwith proceeds to detail a life of Edgar Poe. Now comes the strange part of the story. Nearly the whole of this very lengthy life and critique was subsequently embodied in the "Memoir" by Griswold as original matter, without any acknowledgement or inverted commas, save for the paragraph relating to the poet's quarrel with Mr. Allan's second wife; we have, therefore, this conclusion before us: either Dr. Griswold openly plagiarized wholesale from the recently published but anonymous article, or *he himself was the author of the paper in question.*

57. *Sarah Helen Whitman to John H. Ingram.   Item 159*

My dear Mr. Ingram,   June 16, [18]74
   I have not had a line from you since your letter of May 19, written when you were still in bed from the effects of rheumatic fever. Your mother, too, you said, was ill. I cannot tell you how anxious I have been about you. I have myself been too unwell to write, though I had so much to say to you & ask of you.
   I hope I shall be better soon—well enough, at least, to answer the questions put to me in yours of May 5th.
   Do, if you continue ill, get some friend to write a brief word to me.
   I will write very soon, if able, but now with heartfelt wishes for your health & welfare, I must say goodnight.
   I had so eagerly looked for a letter this morning!
                                                                 S.H.W.

   I have not seen the article on Poe's poems [Ingram's "Edgar Allan Poe's Early Poems"], but have sent to Boston for the paper.[1]
                                                                 S.H.W.

1. Ingram wrote that he sent her a copy of this article on Apr. 29 (see page 134); Mrs. Whitman apparently never received it. The piece was reprinted in *Every Saturday*, NS 1 (June 13, 1874), 659–62.

58. *Sarah Helen Whitman to John H. Ingram.* Item 160

My dear Mr. Ingram,   June 30, 1874

I cannot tell you with what "wondering, unbelieving, joy" I received yesterday your letter of June 15. Your letter of May 19, written in pencil while you were ill in bed, filled me with terrible forebodings, & twenty-nine interminable days of waiting made me *sure*, quite *sure*, that I should never hear from you again. I resigned myself, as I have long, long ago learned to resign myself, to the inevitable, but my heart was heavy as lead. Not that I should have found the certainty of your death insupportable, for death (as our Milesian cousins might say) I have always looked upon as the best thing in life—but I feared for you lingering illness & the exhaustion of mind & body that so often succeeds to a prolonged mental strain, in temperaments like yours.

Oh, I am so glad that you are getting better & that you have gone away for a time of rest & recuperation to the Isle of Wight.

For myself, I have been utterly nerveless & good for nothing since I was stung by the venomous poison ivy. Perhaps it may be doing for me the gracious service which the "aspic" that stung Cleopatra did for that "Serpent of old Nile." I doubt if you have this species of ivy in England.

I wrote you a hurried note about a fortnight ago, entreating you if you were too unwell to write, to let some friend send me a word. You had not received this when you wrote, I believe. I enclosed a paragraph from the Boston *Commonwealth* about an article in *Every Saturday* on Poe's early poems. I did not *then* know that it was yours, published there *without* signature, but credited to the *Gentleman's Magazine*. As soon as I received your letter I copied the notices from the *Academy* & the *Examiner* & sent them to the [Providence] *Journal*. I send you a copy of the *Journal's* reprint, which came out in the editorial columns of this morning's paper. I would have added something about the forthcoming work, but was not sure what you would like to have said about it & thought it would be best to let the paragraphs appear as an editorial gleaning from English papers.

I wrote to Davidson a few days ago to enquire if he had heard from you. His answer came this morning & would have added to my anxiety, if I had not previously received your letter. In reply to a question about Dr. Powell, he says, "I do not know Dr. Powell beyond what he himself writes me, & an occasional notice in the newspapers."

This morning came *Temple Bar* & Baudelaire, both of which I am delighted to receive, though I have not yet had time to look at them.

I do not wonder that Mrs. Lewis thinks Poe was "an angel." In spite of his "irregularities" (that is the harshest word which I could ever find in my heart to apply to him), I have always *felt* that he was essentially *noble, gentle, & good,* beyond any other person I have ever known, but I have hardly dared to say I *think* so. Do you understand this?

You will see that in copying the *Examiner's* notice, I have left out the word associated with "irregularities." It gives a false idea of his excesses, such as they were. Perhaps I am too fastidious about words, but I do not like to see the one omitted associated with his name.

In reply to a letter of enquiry which I wrote recently to Mr. Eveleth, he says,

> Touching *the continuation of "The Mystery of Marie Rogêt,"* I am at a loss to know what suggestion I started in that "fragment" of one of my letters to you which you sent to Mr. Ingram. When was that letter written? My recollection is that "The Mystery," as it first appeared in a magazine, broke suddenly off at an interesting point, & a note, *as if* by the editor of the magazine, was inserted within brackets. I think I enquired of Poe something about that, & that he said something about its having been intended to mystify the reader. *Where can you find John Neal's letter?* Have you tried Neal himself? The copy which I have, or had, among my papers, I think was obtained from him, &c., &c.

I have written to Neal this morning.[1] While I was so anxious about you, I had not the heart to write.

I think this is all there is to tell about "The Mystery."

Your notice of the Talmud, etc. was admirably done. I remember with what interest I groped through the article in the *Quarterly* one hot summer day in 18 something—I forget whether 71 or 2.

You ask how I know, or how I found out, that Poe was descended from the Le Poers. I "found it out," in the first place, much the same way that Falstaff discovered "the true Prince"—by *instinct*. I am as sure of it as if his descent in a direct line from "the high & mighty Baron" with whom I claim kinship had been traced out for him at the Herald's office by Sir Bernard Burke himself, but I *know* about it only what I am going to tell you. One evening he had been speaking of the strange sympathies & correspondence in our tastes, feelings, & habits of thought, when I said suddenly, "Do you know, I think we must be related & that your name, like my own, was once spelled le Poer." He looked up with a surprised & radiant look, & said, "Helen, you startle me! I know that certain members of my grandfather's family *did* so spell their name." The names of John Poe, & John Poer or Power were common in both our families.

My father is said, by some of my relatives who knew Mr. George Poe of Georgetown, the cousin of Poe's father, to have resembled him in feature & expression as closely as if he had been his twin brother.[2] Mr. Poe was a very rich but a stern & misanthropic old man who cared nothing for his wonderfully gifted relative. I think he is no longer living.

Thierry, in his *History of the Norman Conquest*, says, "The desperate fortunes of Strongbow's followers in the invasion of Ireland may be inferred from the surnames of some of these adventurers: Raymond (or Roger) Le Pauvri, without altering that casual appellation or soubriquet, became a high & mighty baron on the eastern coast of Ireland," & Poer or Power is still the name of a noble family in Ireland.[3]

Thierry seems to be ignorant of the fact that the name of this "adventurer," Roger le Poer was the name that nearly half a century earlier became so illustrious in England in the person of Roger le Poer, the Norman Chaplin of Henry the First.

But I must not tire you with my hobby—I am *very tired* myself. I have so much to say & to ask. But now goodnight. My heart's blessing follows you in your excursion to the beautiful island.

Don't trouble yourself to write to me when you are weary. Only let me get a brief word from you at least fortnightly, if you can. I will write again soon.

I will send you soon perhaps another briefer letter of Poe's which may show you something of the great things which he hoped to achieve in literature.

Be very careful of Mr. Latto's letter & return it as soon as it has been used.

Try to get a copy of Mrs. Lewis's photograph.

Ever & forever, your friend,

S.H.W.

I shall send copies of the notices in this morning's *Journal* to all my correspondents.

O'Connor has been very ill, or he would have written to you.

Mr. Eveleth asks for all the copies of the *Mirror* containing your articles.

I do not wonder that you feel you were appointed for the work you are doing. (Nobody *could* have done what you have done, & done it so well.) I have often thought, "Can a man be so wronged as Poe has been & no voice raised to defend him?"

And now at the right time, & in the right place, you have come, so admirably equipped & trained for the championship, as no other ever was or could be. Ave!

You asked if I had many copies of *Poe & His Critics* left. I have but

five remaining & there are none to be bought anywhere. I will send
you a volume of poems soon.

   1. John Neal (1793–1876) of Portland, Maine, was a novelist as well as editor of the
Yankee. He reviewed Poe's early poems encouragingly, and Poe dedicated *Tamerlane* to
him in 1827.
   2. George Poe was the brother of "General" David Poe and grandfather to Neilson
Poe.
   3. Jacques Nicolas Augustin Thierry (1795–1856), *History of the Conquest of England by the Normans*, trans. William Hazlitt (London: H. G. Bohn, 1856).

59. *John H. Ingram to Sarah Helen Whitman*

My dear Mrs. Whitman,   6 July 1874
   I have received your short pencil note [June 16] which is some
comfort, although I *do* miss your nice long letters which you were so
regular with & which always made a sunshine in the shadiest place.
   You will have received my letter [June 15] announcing that the worst
of my illness was over & that I was thinking of leaving town. I left for
the Isle of Wight—our "Garden Isle"—and returned a few days since,
doubtless better in health, although I was very ill whilst away. Had a
fainting fit in the night & must have been in a swoon for some long
time. I have returned to my official duties but still feel weak and
almost aimless. This latter feeling will probably soon wear off, but it
unnerves me & renders me less fitted to complete my allotted tasks.
   I think I told you in my last that I was a few days late with my article
for the *New Quarterly* & that the MS. was returned me, as I had
stipulated for the appearance of the said article not later than July. I
thought—I still think—the editor behaved shabbily, but he has written
me a long apology.
   Blacks will publish the first vol. of Poe's Works on the 1st of October,
but have it all printed & write to me for the "Memoir" to complete the
volume. I am not, I *feel*, competent at the present moment to write the
work as it should be written, but not to delay, I have cut up & added to
the life I wrote for the *Quarterly*, & so hope to get something done at
once. This "Memoir" will embody all the information I have received
from you & something more & will thoroughly refute the Griswold
fabric. I shall, however, still persevere in collecting material for
another life, & perhaps, in a year or so, if alive, shall be able to bring
out another & a separate life, with new letters, &c. This *entre nous* for
the present. My life to the world is that prefixed to Black's edition.
   Mr. Gill has at last written to say that my letter had only just reached
him, having been mislaid by his secretary. He does not give Mr.

Clarke's address but says he (Mr. C[larke]) cannot give any information not contained in *the* collection which Mr. Gill has purchased & will sell if I *much* wish to buy it. If not, Mr. Gill will write a life, &c., &c. Now *you know* that I do much desire any information (reliable), but I feel that Mr. Gill is not acting honestly & candidly & that now, having made all the use *he* is able to of Mr. Clarke's collection wishes to make me pay for it. I am now writing to tell him that my life is written, but that I am still prepared to purchase anything of real interest for the chance of a future edition, but I do not much care to trust to Mr. G[ill] & think that I shall ask Mr. Davidson to intervene, if I get a satisfactory reply.

I have so much to say but must defer continuation until tomorrow.

I have got the whole of "Autography" (thro' Mr. Davidson) in *Graham's*, so send you two papers of it—one you sent me. I also enclose you a cutting from a paper—a temperance publication—*re.* E. A. Poe. I wrote this letter in reply to one of the usual lives founded on Griswold's story. It was written whilst unwell & is not much, but it contradicts some of the slanders, & lets the temperance folk know that there is a different account of Poe extant. [Lamons?] was doubtless an American.

7 July 1874

I resume, but have so much to say that I feel all my thoughts crowded into a chaotic mass. First, Mrs. Lewis, whom I am to visit this evening, has promised me a copy or two of the portrait, so you will be able to get a copy of that. I am sorry I did not know of it in time for the collection, but the engraver has made a very good portrait, &, I fancy, very like, from the "Ultima dim Thule" one, as you will see some of these days. Mrs. Lewis, I fear cannot afford much information— nothing definite.

Did you get the Baudelaire *Essais* & the *Temple Bar* article safely? In my next, I shall probably be enabled to return Mr. Latto's letter & your own. The printer has *facsimiled* the whole of Mr. Pabodie's letter in error, so I shall publish it, as well as the paragraph from yours.

I have not been able to do anything further with Miss Poe's matter, but must now set to work at once. She has written again to me, as has also the Provost of Peabody Institute *re.* Poe's letters to Mr. Kennedy.[1] Latter says that Neilson Poe can give me information & that he has written, but I've not received any letter & fancy that he is only trying to stifle inquiry, but I am just going to write to him. Also to a Mr. Valentine, a young sculptor, a cousin of the first Mrs. Allan.[2] I believe we shall yet rake up something & I shall not relax my efforts.

Mr. Davidson has been very kind, & I am just going to write to him. He obtained 2 vols. of *Graham's* for me—also the no. containing

Graham's letter, so I shall return your MS. copy, as you may like to
have it by you.

   I shall be glad to hear what is said in the *Every Saturday* on "Poe's
Poems." But all this time I have been overlooking the fact that you
have been ill. I hope it is *have* been. I shall be so glad to hear of your
recovery. You cannot possibly credit how eagerly I look for your letters
& what an invigorating influence they seen to have upon me. I cannot
help feeling that you *must* be good & do not doubt but that your
influence has been much wider and greater with many than you can
imagine or ever know. I do not speak from any foolish wish to flatter,
but from my heart what I feel, so, whenever not too weary, write to me,
and believe that when you do you are doing good to one wayward &
tempest-tost mortal—but write—only write the veriest
commonplaces—questions & answers—or what you will—all will be
acceptable.

   I am scribbling this amid official din, & not having your letters here,
scarcely know what I have to ask about, or answer. My edition of Poe,
in 4 vols., will be very complete. The "Autography"—omitting one or
two names, such as Griswold's, Mrs. Ellet's, &c. This latter, by the way,
I hear is very intimate with a literary lady here whose receptions I
have attended. This said lady is "at home" every Monday, so I shall
drop in & hear what she has to say *re*. Mrs. E[llet]. I have also
recovered a paper on "Cryptology," some more "Marginalia," &
reviews & an article styled "Pinakidia," which is an early series of
"Marginalia." I have also reprinted the omitted portion of "The Oval
Portrait." I thought that I knew all Poe's works by heart, but really I get
quite excited at reading the proofs & forgetting my task of correction,
go reading away till I am pulled up by a sudden remembrance. *Arthur
Gordon Pym* I have not a duplicate copy of, & when I get to the end of
my proof I feel quite disappointed at not being able to continue its
exciting perusal. I keep thinking that it must be real—true—it affects
me far more powerfully than when I first read it. When I sent the copy
to the publisher, they wrote to say that it would be well to insert a note
in the vol. saying what portion of the narrative was by Poe and what
portion was really written by Mr. A. G. Pym!! They were deceived by
Poe's wonderful powers—I was quite pleased at this, because Blacks
are well-educated, talented men. They write me that Professor Nichols
of Glasgow, the author of an article on "American literature" in the
forthcoming edition of the *Encyclopaedia Britannica*—a magnificent
& truly national work—speaks very highly of "A. G. Pym."[3]

   Griswold's critique will have little avail now-a-days. A few years,
and I hope & trust Griswold & his "Memoir" will be consigned to
oblivion. Poe's name will gradually arise great & grand & purified from
all the gross stains the implacable malice of Griswold has cast upon it.

It is a delight to me to feel that I shall have assisted in the goodly task, but it is to you—you, more than any other human being, that this result will be due.

In making out my pages on Poe's ancestry & going over various heraldic & genealogical works, I could not clearly trace the connection between the Poes & the La Poers. The latter & the Powers is clear, but not the Poes. Can you afford *any* light? Two branches of the Poës are still landholders in Killarny, but though favoured with genealogical trees do not claim relationship with the Poers, or the Powers.

I much fear that my "Memoir" of Poe will contain very little unknown to you, but that you must forgive—to the British, probably to the Americans—the facts will be new—beyond my papers, such as you know of—nothing has been *demonstrated* against Griswold here, & he has been accepted as gospel truth.

I know nothing, as yet, of "Landor's Cottage." Were I only in America I am certain that I could recover, not only much of biographical interest, but even much valuable of Poe's writings now lost. What a pity that I cannot rescue these things. Every year the task will be more difficult.

Mr. Davidson is very kind, but I dare say tires, & once or twice has overlooked most singularly & unaccountably—things of value.

Well! I think I must wind up this scrawl. When my "Memoir" is really printed I shall be able, 'tis to be hoped—to write you something more connected & reasonable. My illness threw me out so fearfully that I told them at home that I thought Griswold's ghost must have been racking my bones to stop the exposure of his infamies. I shall be too strong for him yet!

There! Daily hoping to hear from you, I remain, believe me, my very dear & much prized friend, ever most faithfully yours,

John H. Ingram

1. Nathaniel Holmes Morison (1815–1890), provost of Peabody Institute, Baltimore, was a friend and close associate of Neilson Poe. He informed Ingram in his first letter, June 6, 1874, that Poe's letters to John P. Kennedy would come to the Institute on Mrs. Kennedy's death. Later, Morison served Ingram well, and Poe biography, by copying many letters from Mrs. Clemm to Neilson Poe, letters that Neilson was apparently too indolent to copy himself. This valuable correspondence from Morison continued to reach Ingram until 1880, and it is worth remarking that at no time did Ingram ever attempt to reprimand or quarrel with this particular contributor to the building of Poe biography.

2. Edward Virginius Valentine (1838–1930) proved to be one of Ingram's staunchest helpers in his efforts to build Poe's biography. A native of Richmond, he was a friend of the second Mrs. John Allan and an important sculptor. Two of his best known works are the recumbent marble figure of Gen. Robert E. Lee in the Memorial Chapel at Washington and Lee University, Lexington, and the bronze figure of Gen. Thomas J. "Stonewall" Jackson at Virginia Military Institute.

3. This possibly refers to Professor John Gough Nichols (1806–1873), at one time editor of the London *Gentleman's Magazine*.

60. *John H. Ingram to Sarah Helen Whitman*

My very dear Friend,   14 July 1874
   Your welcome letter dated 30 June is to hand safely which, coupled with the fact that the publishers have just returned the autograph letters to me, *compel* me to write at once.
                                                                          15 July 1874
   Urgent matters compelled me to defer my letter till today & now, I am so pressed for time that, while there is much—very much to say—I shall have to postpone the chief portion for a few days.
   Firstly, let me say whilst I think of it, that I have spent another evening with Mrs. Lewis but without gaining information *re.* Poe. She has promised copies of Poe's portrait & is very sorry that I did not have it for the collection, but I think now that I am glad that I used yours—the engraver has made a very good portrait from it, as I believe you will say, something very different to the gross caricatures hitherto known. I asked Mrs. L[ewis] about Mrs. E[llet] again & am told she is known to but not liked by an English literary lady whose receptions I attend, a Miss Kortright, a great friend of the Hawthornes. I *may* call there next Mondy if feeling well enough, for I am still very queer, although I am engaged out today and Friday to garden parties & am going to try & attend. To return to Mrs. E[llet]—the *purloined letter*, says Mrs. Lewis, was taken on behalf of Mr. Lewis, in whose pay Mrs. E[llet] is supposed to have been.[1] Mrs. E[llet] is declared by Mrs. L[ewis] to have goaded & worried Griswold to death—if it were so it was, indeed, a just retribution. Mrs. Lewis only knew Poe quite at the end of his life & *knows nothing of his history* & believes *everything* told of him *fictitious.*
   I am just now so unnerved & so *strange* in my head—weary & forgetful—that I do not feel equal to write you a long letter. I will write again soon. Thanks for Providence *Journal* notice. *Every Saturday* might have acknowledged same, but does not matter. I would prefer them to have copied *Temple Bar* paper. I do want to write to Mr. Davidson, &c. My trip, I fancy, did not do me much good. I wish I could forswear literature for a few months. In September I leave town for a month or so & must look forward to that.
   Poe's Works progress rapidly.—Vol. 1 is in print all but "Memoir" & the first proof of that came yesterday. I hope to send the rest of MS. about Tuesday next. I have shortened it greatly—it will not be more

than 80 pps. When prospectus appears you shall have copy. Vol. 1 is to appear on 1st Oct.

I do trust you are getting better from the poison. Mentally I lean upon you for support & encouragement. Your letters are the "best medicine to a mind diseased" that I know of at present. By the way, do you know that the "serpent of Old Nile" did not die from the bite of an asp? Dear old Sir Thomas Browne exploded that vulgar error two centuries ago.[2]

Thanks for the Providence notice. Providence! *omen bonum.* I am glad you omitted that *nasty* & unnecessary word. I will send extracts from the *Mirror* in my next for Mr. Eveleth & perhaps, some for you. I always thought "The Mystery of Marie Rogêt" was complete, until you sent me Mr. Eveleth's remark. John Neal's letter would be very interesting, but too late for this edition. I thought Neal was dead years ago—he must be very old. I saw J. R. Lowell again styled "Dr." in the *Academy* a week or two ago. He is going back to Harvard College in October. That Mr. George Poe is new to me. If alive, I presume no information could be got from him. Let me know directly you get the autograph letters. I will register them, but shall be anxious to hear of their arrival. Thank Mr. Latto for his kind loan of his, even though only lent to you.

And now goodbye for a while, & forever, believe me to be most faithfully yours—

John H. Ingram

Entre nous—can you recommend any really good tales for an American collection? I do not know any of Neal's, save one poor one. Do you think Simms' "Martin Faver" is obtainable in America? 'Tis not here. Only first rate & short stories, such as Irving's, Poe's, Hawthorne's. Of course, they cannot be equalled, but authors of minor note, sometimes, write one or more really fine magazine stories. No hurry, but you may think of something. Did you ever write any tale? *Au revoir.*

Poe made out a strong case against Aldrich & Hood's "Death Bed" piece. A certain Irish writer—I forget his name—has tried to get the credit of Campbell's "Exile of Erin." "Woodman, Spare that Tree," is in dispute. You will see some fine lines by Mr. R. Wilde, quoted in 1 or 2 vol. of *S.L. Messenger* which have been claimed as by "O'Daly" & by [illegible], & so forth *ad infinitum.* By the way, I did not know of the "MS. Found in a Barn"—was it worth any [sic]? I know all about the spirit poems of Miss Lizzie something-or-the-other.[3] I have written a cruel paper on them—'tis with the *Mirror* & will appear some day, I suppose. You shall have everything I write in any way relating to Poe, that is published.

But there! I won't bother you any more now, only, say that, if you can spare me the time, do kindly send me any extracts, &c. that may be published at your earliest convenience & forgive me for saying so after all your kindness to yours unforgetfully & ever faithfully,

John H. Ingram

P.S. Someday you shall have better letters from me than the hurried scrawls I now send. I send a blue envelope because I fancy 'tis seen better & becomes better known in the post.

J.H.I.

1. Sylvanus D. Lewis, lawyer in Brooklyn, N.Y. was divorced from Stella Lewis in 1858. Friendly to Poe, he also helped Mrs. Clemm when Poe's sister, Rosalie, tried to claim Poe's entire "estate."

2. Sir Thomas Browne (1605–1682) *suggested* that Cleopatra might have died in another way. See *The Works of Sir Thomas Browne*, ed. Geoffrey Keynes, 4 vols., Vol. II, *Pseudodoxia Epidemica* (Chicago: Univ. of Chicago Press, 1964) pp. 363–64.

3. Miss Lizzie Doten, a medium of sorts, professed to believe that she was on occasions inspired by important poets to deliver their posthumous poems. In a volume called *Poems from the Inner Life*, published before Dec. 19, 1863 (Boston: Colby & Rich), she published five poems supposedly dictated to her by Edgar Poe; in later editions she added still another. For three of these "spirit poems," see Items 97 and 561 in the Ingram Poe Collection. As late as 1872 Miss Doten was still delivering publicly her inspired poems.

61. *Sarah Helen Whitman to John H. Ingram.*   *Item 163*

My dear Mr. Ingram,   July 21, 1874

Your letter of July 6 came yesterday & made my heart so glad, but what you tell me of your illness in the Isle of Wight makes me still very anxious. Had you ever such an attack before your last illness?

I have been suffering greatly from languor since I wrote you, but your letters always bring me back to life. A letter from O'C[onnor] this morning, the first received from him in three weeks, asks if this Erl-King of the skies, the comet, with his "crown & tail," has anything to do with this extraordinary weather which so prostrates & paralyses everybody. He has read your *Temple Bar* article in the *Eclectic* & likes it, "as far as it goes," but thinks you are not savage enough on "Griswold's villainies." But O'Connor, with the blood of Brian Born & Roderick O'Connor, "King of all Ireland," in his veins, is too intensely belligerent and too fond of a free fight to be a safe critic in such matters. He is *deeply* interested in your work. He will try to find out something about Miss Rosalie Poe & Mr. Powell. He has been very ill, & greatly confined by his duties as librarian, famished among books which he has no time to read. Mr. Gill, it seems, by the cutting from the *Commonwealth*, is again "fairly at work," as he wrote me last spring, when he hoped to complete his lecture in fifteen days. Rather surprising, is it not, that your letter written so long ago should have just turned up?

You may remember that Emerson, in his poem of Uriel, speaks of a word, or

> A look that solved the sphere
> And stirred the devils everywhere.

So will it be, I fancy, with your book. Griswold's ghost may, as you surmise, still be brewing mischief. Yesterday a young M.D. who worships Poe, as all young men of culture & imagination do, sent me a copy of the New York *Commercial Advertiser* showing that the demons are greatly stirred in Baltimore. Strange that three editors should be thus roused by the renewed interest in their great poet. Perhaps they only represent the three heads of one surly Cerberus. Could it be the Mr. Neilson Poe, who still represents the family of "De la Poer" in Baltimore? Did I tell you in my last letter that Poe told me, in speaking of his family name, that the relative of whom his grandfather spoke was called the Chevalier L'Poer in some family record & was there or *elsewhere*, spoken of as a friend of the Marquis de Grammont?

I have a memory which vaguely retains dates & statistics—the *letter* is apt to escape me, but the *spirit* is indelible. Now, when convinced of my relationship to Poe, I endowed him with all my ancestral honors.

I believe I told you of the strange resemblance which my father's sister, Mrs. Rebecca Power Tillinghast, wife of the Hon. J. L. Tillinghast, M.C., saw to my father in the face of Mr. George Poe of Georgetown, D.C., & during the spring of 1849, when my mother once saw me in the dress of an Albanian chief, worn for a tableau, she was so appalled by my resemblance to Poe that she would not remain in the room or give me a second look. Everyone who had seen Poe remarked the resemblance. The aid of a burnt cork to the eyebrows & applied as a mustache on the upper lip, transformed me. The resemblance was magical.

Do you remember Byron's lines

> The wild Albanian kirtled to the knee
> With shawl-girt head & ornamented gun
> And gold-embroidered garments, fair to see.

Have you read an article in *Saint Paul's* in Nov. & Dec., 1873, on "Byron & his Times," by Roden Noel? Very just & noble I think in its critical & moral estimate of the man & the poet. Who is Roden Noel?[1]

Last Wednesday I saw for the first time a copy of the edition of Poe's poems for 1831. How does it happen, I wonder, that in the three verses which I marked in the poem *now* called "Lenore," the word "Helen" occurs, while in the edition of 1831, from which you quote "The Paean," it does not occur. I do not remember whether the poems, as quoted in the pages of a *Southern Review* which I sent you, gave the *date* of the edition. Can you tell me?

The copy which I saw for the first time last week was shown me by Mr. Harris, who had obtained it after much search at a booksale in New York. He has sought for many years for the edition said to be published in 1827, but can find, as yet, no trace of it.

He distinctly recollects having seen somewhere an incidental allusion to a vol. of poems called *Tamerlane*, published in Boston by "a Bostonian," in 1827. He thinks that this must be *the* edition of 1827, it being unlikely that two editions of Poe's poems should be published the same year. I gave him the proof sheets of your article on the poems in *The Gentleman's Magazine*, as I had another copy in the *Every Saturday*. I also gave him your address. He is an ardent & indefatigable collector of American poetry—a man of wealth & culture & with a superabundance of leisure.[2]

He is just about to leave the city for the mountains & may be absent til September. He brought me a copy of James Hannay's *Poetical Works of E.A.P., with a Notice of his Life & Writings*. I had seen extracts from the *Life*, but had never seen the volume. Of course you have seen it, as it was published in London in 1853. I like much of the life, especially the two last pages of his critique on Poe's writings. Some of the illustrations, too, are very good, but "Helen" in the garden is very—conventional & commonplace. Don't you think so? But not so bad as Pickersgill's in the Illustrated Redfield of 1858.[3]

Mr. Harris had never seen the Wiley & Putnam edition of *Tales & Poems* published in 1845, from which I cut the Index & Preface for you. This is a copy of an edition he has been long anxious to possess, but which is, it seems, difficult to obtain. I told him that I had cut from the book the Index & Preface, which you were to return to me after using. At this he opened his eyes in such undisguised amazement & reproach that I recognized the infatuation of a book collector, as never before: "This book—a gift from Poe—a presentation copy—containing his autograph—and I had cut out a leaf!!" To appease him, I promised to *give* him the book that he might preserve it from further spoiliation. So when you can, you will return me the page I sent you & I will then place the book in his hands for safe keeping. All this sprang from his seeing in the Providence *Journal* the paragraph about your books from the *Examiner* and *Academy*.

I found in *Appleton's Journal of Literature, Science, & Art,* for July 18, an article with an illustration about Poe's house at Fordham, by M. J. Lamb.[4] I shall mail the *Journal* to you with my letter this evening. This morning I received a copy of the *Journal* from Davidson, but no letter. He is apparently very busy. I think the writer is wrong about the *four* windows to the parlor. You said in one of your later letters that in case I should ever republish *Edgar Poe & His Critics* you would like to suggest to me a few alterations & omissions. I should be *very* glad to receive any suggestion from *you* on the subject. Be *sure* to tell me when you write.

On the 93rd page of *Appleton's Journal* you will find among the literary notes a quotation from Leslie Stephen in *Fraser's* about Poe & Hawthorne, suggested I fancy by Eugene Benson's article in the *Galaxy,* a portion of which I copied for you. But the author in this case praises Hawthorne & disparages Poe, in a way which looks like *malice prepense.* Read it. Who is Leslie Stephen?[5]

I think I foresee that stories of Poe, anecdotes, fabulous & otherwise, will abound for some time to come.

Your answer to the Temperance man is well done, but I think your denial of the cause of separation between us, as stated by Griswold, is rather too strongly stated. If I had never seen Poe intoxicated, I should never have consented to marry him; had he kept his promise never again to taste wine, I should never have broken the engagement.

I wrote you not long before your illness an account of the scenes & incidents referred to in Poe's letter, "The agonies which I have lately endured, etc.," but pressing questions from you which required immediate answers caused me to leave the story unfinished. Some day I will resume it & you will understand what I mean by saying had I never seen him intoxicated I should never have consented to marry him, but goodbye now.

Your friend ever & forever,

S.H.W.

1. Roden Berkeley Wriothesley Noel (1834–1894), an English poet and relative of Lord Byron, published *Life of Byron* in 1870 as part of the Great Writers Series.

2. Caleb Fiske Harris (1818–1881) was a merchant, ardent bibliophile, neighbor, and devoted friend as well as literary executor to Mrs. Whitman. He drowned in Moosehead Lake, Maine, on Oct. 2, 1881, and his large and very important collection of rare books, including many first editions of early American poetry and drama, eventually came to the Brown University Library.

3. For Pickersgill see p. 34, n. 3.

4. "Poe's House at Fordham," *Appleton's,* 12 (1874), 75–77. Item 579 in the Ingram Poe Collection.

5. Leslie Stephen (1832–1904), English critic, biographer, and editor of *Cornhill Magazine* in 1871. He edited the first twenty-six volumes of the *Dictionary of National*

Biography (1885–1891), conjointly with Sir Sidney Lee, beginning in 1890. Virginia Woolf was one of his two daughters.

62. *Sarah Helen Whitman to John H. Ingram.*   Item 164

My dear Mr. Ingram,   [July 27, 1874]
    Washington papers containing the announcement of Rosalie Poe's death were recd. from O'Connor this morning.
    You kind efforts in her behalf must be a heartfelt satisfaction. I will write tomorrow if possible. Ever your friend
                                                      S.H.W.

    I doubt not that the thought that you were interesting yourself for her cheered her last moments, even though she was mercifully spared the need of further aid. I write in great haste on a slip of paper which I intended to enclose in my next letter.[1]
                                                      S.H.W.

[Enclosure: Newspaper clipping from the Washington, D.C., *Evening Star*, July 22, 1874.   Item 582]

POE. At the Epiphany Church Home in this city, this morning, in the 68th year of her age. Miss ROSE POE, the last surviving sister of the late Edgar Allen [*sic*] Poe. Funeral from the Church Home, Thursday morning, at 9 o'clock.

[Enclosure: Newspaper clipping from the Washington, D.C., *Daily Critic*, July 23, 1874.   Item 583]

DEATH OF THE SISTER OF EDGAR ALLEN [*sic*] POE.—Miss Rose Poe, the last surviving sister of the late Edgar Allen Poe, died yesterday morning after a lingering illness at the Epiphany Church Home, on H Street, near Fourteenth, in the 68th year of her age. She came to this institution from Baltimore, where she had been living for some time with distant relatives, on the 1st of March last, and was at the time in very delicate health. A week ago yesterday she had a violent attack of congestive chills, and though every effort was made to strengthen her she sank visibly, and expired quietly and without pain, as above stated. Her funeral took place from the Home this morning, and the remains were interred in the Rock Creek Cemetery. In the death of Miss Poe it is believed that the last of the family, and indeed, of the immediate relatives of the gifted young poet, Edgar Allen Poe, has passed away.

    1. The slip of paper contains a newsclipping pasted in the center and around which this letter is written; the clipping announces articles in the August number of the *Eclectic*, among which is listed "an interesting account of Edgar Poe taken from *Temple Bar*."

63. *Sarah Helen Whitman to John H. Ingram.   Item 165*

My dear Mr. Ingram,   July 31, [18]74
    I need not tell you how happy I was made by your letter of July 15,
which came yesterday when I had just completed three or four pages
of a letter to you, which I have, for the present, thrown aside to reply to
your last. I am so glad you are better & that you are going to take a
long rest in September. I received from Washington last Monday, July
27, two papers containing notices of the death of Miss Rosalie Poe. I
mailed them to you on the same evening, to go by a steamer that sailed
for Queenstown on Tuesday. It must be pleasant to you to know that
your kind intentions toward her must have cheered her last moments. I
wish I could learn something of her true history. Mrs. Clemm never
named her in any of her letters to me. You speak in your letter of July 7
of having received "another letter" from her. What did she say in it?
Did she speak of being ill?
    To revert to your last letter, what was the *subject* of Mrs. Ellet's
grievance against Griswold & about what did she pursue him to his
grave? Did you understand? Did you find out when & where the
portrait Mrs. L[ewis] has of Poe was taken? I enclosed with the
cuttings from the Washington papers a paragraph from the Boston
Commonwealth naming, as among the papers in the last *Eclectic*, "an

The grave of Rosalie Poe, Rock Creek Cemetery, Washington, D.C. She was born in
1810, not 1812.

interesting article on Edgar Poe from *Temple Bar*." I hope you will
have received duly the copy of *Appleton's Journal* with a sketch of the
Fordham cottage. I will try to find out whether the signature attached
to it is a genuine one. On Tuesday I received two hurried lines from
Davidson enclosing an extract from the *Commercial Advertiser*—the
same which I had enclosed to you & which I told you was sent to me
by Col. Dwight, a dear friend of mine who left college at the
commencement of the Civil War to take command of a Rhode Island
battery, & who passed through all the great battles of Bull Run,
Fredericksburg, Gettysburg, Antietam, etc. without a scar, ever in the
hottest of the fight. At Gettysburg he had a horse shot under him & lay
for a while amid floundering horses & dying comrades, weltering in
their blood, yet received not even a bruise or a single scratch. He
passed the dreadful summer of [18]63 in the fatal swamps of
Chickahominy, where so many of our bravest soldiers died of malaria,
yet suffered no loss of health or strength. Yet now, after all these perils,
he is slowly dying of consumption, in the prime of his manhood. He
studied medicine in Paris & Germany & passed last winter with his
young wife travelling from place to place in search of health, which
ever eludes him.

He had for Poe an interest amounting to infatuation, & when in Paris
a few years ago, sought everywhere for Baudelaire's translation of the
poems to send to me, but could not find them. As I said before, he sent
me the article which I enclosed to you. He has been too ill to see me
since his return, but in sending it, he said:

I was greatly pleased, dear St. Helena, with the Poe article in *Temple Bar*,
as you well know I should be with anything tending to change or impugn
Griswold's delineation. In our three weeks at Ems this spring, Mrs. Dwight
was unable during the whole time to find Poe's works in the circulating
library. The librarian told her they were *never* in, so popular is he among the
Germans.

I enclose Mr. Neal's answer to my note. When I last saw him he was
a most noble looking old man with hair as white as wool, but without
any of the apparent infirmities of age, but he must be between eighty
& ninety, I think. I saw him last in 1868. He addressed a large
audience in this city on the question of woman suffrage, which he
eloquently advocated.

I believe Mr. George Poe is dead. It was in 1865 that my aunt saw
him in Georgetown, & he was then an old man. I think he had an
unmarried daughter who attended with her father the Episcopal
church in that city, of which my cousin, Nicholas Power Tillinghast,
was then pastor. Mr. Poe was rich & misanthropic.

In one of your last letters you asked me about Alice Cary—if I had
any letters of hers, & if I knew her intimately? I have no letters of hers,

& I did not know her intimately. I know so many of her intimate friends, and she was herself a person so easily known & understood that I, nevertheless, *seem* to have known her well. She called on me, & I returned her call, & she invited a small party to meet me on the evening of which I have spoken in *E.A.P. & His Critics* (don't forget to tell me of the alterations which you would suggest in the book, in case it is ever republished). They were, Alice & Phoebe, enthusiastic spiritualists—"mediums," their friends said—& late in the evening the conversation turned on that subject. They talked of what might be their possible occupation in that dimly-discovered country from which so many travellers were beginning to return. Alice asked me what life I aspired to, & I playfully said I wished to live in a haunted castle like those evoked by Mrs. Radcliffe, with echoing corridors & a North Tower which had not been explored within the memory of man, a moat & a drawbridge & a bower-window & troubadours & wandering minstrels to beguile the melancholy time during my knight's absence in the Holy Land. "Good," said Alice, "and *I* should like to be your dairymaid & look after your cows." "I engage you in that capacity," I said, "and feel confident that my cows will always live in clover & that the milking songs of my dairymaid will be the sweetest in all the land."

Have you read Mrs. Mary Clemmer Ames's book about Alice & Phoebe Cary?[1] She tells a singular story about a vision which all the family had of two sisters, seen in the *daytime*, standing in the door of their new house a few months before the death[s] of the two. Strangely enough, Mrs. Ames says nothing of Griswold, who was, to the last, one of their most constant visitors. He was there on the evening of which I speak, but I did not know it until he was gone! I will tell you about it sometime when I am stronger. I will think about the stories which might seem attractive enough for your collection.

Do you like Bret Harte? In a number of *Temple Bar* that I read lately, there was an article on his stories, and special praise given to one called "How Santa Claus Came to Simpson's Bar." The writer of the article praised it for its *pathos*, & said it was "in itself sufficient to make a reputation." The story had certainly fine elements in it, the *ride* was unquestionably stirring & spirited, but my sister & I thought the "pathos" was slightly overstrained & factitious. So that in response to Bret Harte's invocation, "Sing, oh Muse, the ride of Richard Bullen, I must fain follow him, in prose, afoot!" we commenced in ballad style "Dick Bullen's Ride," which had great success & wide circulation. I send you a copy of our "Condensed Ballad." I suppose you have seen Bret Harte's "Condensed Novels." The ballad should be read in connection with the story "How Santa Claus Came to Simpson's Bar." My sister asked me to send it to you, thinking it might amuse you if you are familiar with the original, published in the *Atlantic* for March, 1872.

I am so glad to know that you have faith in me & like to receive my letters, on condition that I don't "moralize," & preach "no sermons."[2]

Have I *ever* moralized or preached sermons to you? It is not my vocation. I have implicit faith in you & like you, ever so much, *just as you are!*—sure that at *some* time, we shall meet in "our own order of star," & become friends, near & dear friends, through the never-ending cycles of eternity. And so, good night, till morrow.

S.H.W.

You say that Davidson has omitted to answer some important questions. Perhaps *I* can help you in the matter.

[Enclosure: John Neal to Sarah Helen Whitman.   Item 161]

Portland, Maine
My dear Mrs. Whitman,   July 6, 1874

I am sorry that I cannot answer you satisfactorily. Not remembering the year, nor in which journal or paper my "protest" appeared, I am unable to trace it.

Nor indeed can I distinctly recall the nature of my protestation, though my wife has some recollection of it, without being able to say when or where it was published.

Truly & heartily your friend & well-wisher,

John Neal

[*Mrs. Whitman continued her letter to Ingram, on the back of Neal's:*]

I am so glad to know that you are satisfied with the engraving from the photograph I sent you. I could not bear to think that by using it you had missed the chance of a better. It was taken at the rooms of Masury, the original daguerre, I mean.

[*Pasted beneath the above lines is a newsclipping from the Providence Journal, July 11, 1874 announcing the death of Samuel Masury.*]

1. Mary Clemmer Ames (1839–1884) published *A Memorial of Alice and Phoebe Cary* (New York: Hurd & Houghton, 1873).

2. It would appear that a letter from Ingram is missing, for no such injunction to Mrs. Whitman appears in the preceding correspondence; such a tart remark from him could have been on a page returned to him, as she did on occasions.

64. *John H. Ingram to Sarah Helen Whitman*

My dear Mrs. Whitman,   3 August 1874

If I do not acknowledge your most welcome letter [July 21] *at once* I feel that I may not be able to nerve myself to reply for some days. I am in a feverish state of anxiety to do something and yet am scarcely able to do anything unless it be put directly before me. My correspondence—a large portion from old valued friends—has accumulated to an unanswerable extent. Many pressing & imperative letters are waiting replies & I cannot rouse myself to answer them. I cannot comprehend my lassitude. I no longer seem to take pleasure in anything & all my aspirations have shrunk into a dreamy carelessness.

The "Memoir" of Poe, that is to precede his works, is all printed and does not give me any satisfaction. I feel that so much better a life *should* have been written—*could* have been written even by me—and I know not what the world will say of it—what *you* will say of it. Oh! that something would stir me up! I feel that I could thankfully accept any kind of excitement so that it could arouse me from this lethargy. But enough! I will forego this egotism and *try* to discourse of something more to the purpose, merely remarking *en passant* that though I frequently fainted as a youth that I never previously had such an attack as I had in the Isle of Wight.

And you are suffering from languor—do you think it merely arises from sultry weather, or do you ascribe it to the remains of the ivy poisoning, or to any other cause? Let me forego all the kind things I would say and *do feel*, for while, and comment upon the subjects of your letter *seriatim.*

As regards the Comet just gone or the comet just coming, I do not think much can be said. *Entre nous*—I do not believe in these distant bodies exercising any influence on our bodies, whatever they may on our minds. You remember Poe's "Conversation of Eiros & Charmion" on the comet? The London *Mirror* is just going to publish it, as 'tis unknown in England. Two & a half vols., out of four, of Poe's works, of my edition, are in print, but the 1st vol. will not appear before the 1st of October. There will be illustrations by Sambourne (of *Punch*, &c.).

By the way, Mrs. Lewis has promised me some copies of her portrait of Poe, but she is out of town just now so I suppose I shall not get them till "the fall." Her name reminds me of Griswold, whom Mr. O'Connor thinks I have not been savage enough with. It strikes me that Griswold got a very good share of the punishment he deserved before he left this life. I can *now* believe what Mrs. Lewis said—that Mrs. Ellet hastened G[riswold]'s death—and *all that Poe said of that woman.* In the British Museum I have just seen Griswold's printed letter about *his bigamous* marriage (do you know the story?) and therein he calls Mrs. E[llet] everything, & *a great deal more*, than Poe did &, I think, pretty well proves her to be unfit to be admitted into any decent house, or to be known by any decent person. No word is too severe for such a creature! But Griswold proves himself, *I think*, equally (or nearly so) as bad. What a horrid nest of villains! For goodness sake never come in contact with or have anything to do with Mrs. E[llet]. I believe she prejudiced several English people, when she was in England, against Poe. The Misses Kortwrights have suspended (*protem*) their receptions. I fancy Mrs. E[llet] prejudiced *them* from what I hear, but when I can call there again I shall "a tale unfold," &c.

The *Temple Bar* paper, as printed, was really only the result of intuition—when written I scarcely had any proofs against Griswold—besides, our English press will not print, even when I write it, stronger language than that you have seen. Many hard words of mine, on this subject, have been deleted &, I believe, rightly. More credit is given to a calm, severe, summing-up, than all the fierce invectives of the English language, with *the Irish* into the bargain, to back it! You see I can *think* prudently *sometimes*.

I am glad, however, that even the *Temple Bar* article is being republished in America, as it will do something. All the deficiencies of *The Templar* [*sic*] letter I at once admit. 'Twas written off, on the spur of the moment, from the Isle of Wight. I was too unwell to reason logically & *without proper references*—so forgive it.

As for poor Miss Poe, I am ashamed of myself—after having obtained promises of support from so many, I have dropped the matter, but I *must* take it up *at once* & do my best for her.

I have been utterly used up in my mind since my illness. The name of Gill I have often seen in American papers as *always coming* but I cannot see that he ever comes anywhere. His letter, strange to say, I did answer.

The three editors I fancy are too poor fry for a *decent* pen; otherwise, I should like to do as Emerson's *word* & "stir the devils everywhere." A free fight all round just now would do me good—"will any gentleman just tread on the tail of my coat"—I am up for mischief.

Mr. Neilson Poe—oh, "by the pricking of my thumbs" (mentally understood), I instinctively feel there is mischief *there*. I feel assured that Mr. N.P. was & is no friend of Edgar Poe. What think you?

Of the Chevalier & his friend de Grammont you speak in your book, *E.Poe & His Critics*, of which more at some future time. At leisure I will jot down a few *memoranda* for the new edition which I yet hope to see.

I did not see the paper on Byron in *St. Paul's* by Roden Noel. I remember this name but know its owner not—it may be a *nom de plume*—the Noels are relatives of Byron by marriage.

And you have *seen* a copy of the 1831 edition of Poe! I would give something only to see it—is that impossible? I suppose Mr. Harris would not lend it to me for a few days per registered post? If not, *could I have a faithful MS. copy of it*? *Do* try & hear what he says. "The

Paean" in the 1831 copy does not mention the name of "Helen," does it? I'm not sure of my copy being quite exact but I believe it to be. Your copy is from the *Southern Lit. Messenger*, where Poe republished it with a few slight changes, including the name of "Helen" being inserted—doubtless, after the death of Mrs. Stanard—who appears to have died in 1831–2? Lowell mentions 1827—Duyckinck 1829—as the early edition. This latter was published by Hatch & Dunning, Baltimore—see my printed papers. Will Mr. Harris write to me? Perhaps I can do something for him here. I have a very large knowledge of American poets of the past generation & collect *American* editions. Can he tell me where to get the Poems of Ed. C. Pinckney—they are—or rather a small collection of them—is in the British Museum. I also want "Martin Faber," by Wm. G. Simms.[1]

I know Hannay's edition of Poe well—some of my friends were great friends of Hannay. I have never seen a single illustration of Poe's works that I cared about.

I shall leave town next month for five weeks, but you will—I trust— hear from me again before I leave & whilst I am away. I had forgotten about the Index of the *Tales* & *Poems* of the 1845 edition. I return it herewith, as also the notice of Poe's Lowell lecture, which I fancied I had sent back before. I am looking up a lot of letters from Messrs. O'Connor, Davidson, Latto, & from Mrs. Clemm belonging to you & will return them, as also several cuttings, &c.

The early version of "The Paean," is in *Russell's Magazine* (from S. *Literary Messenger*) as also is the "The Valley Nis." I suppose you never got the letter or a copy thereof of Mr. John Willis, Poe's fellow student at Charlottesville? I will send some *Mirror* cuttings for Mr. Eveleth—if he has the Dunn-English letter, or any letter or paper by Poe, I should be thankful for a *copy*. I have never been able to get "The Elk." Mr. Davidson—to whom I *must* write tomorrow—has been *very kind* but he is not *so up* to Poe matters as I am & is liable to overlook his writings. I shall never clear up matters, or get all the works until I visit America. "The Elk" was probably in the *Gentleman's Magazine* of Philadelphia. That & Brooks's *Museum* (of Baltimore) would have, doubtless, *unknown* writings of Poe. *The Gift* (1831? &c.), edited by Eliza Leslie, might have early & unknown tales.

I have discovered a quantity of "Marginalia." The copy of *Appleton's* you spoke of did not arrive, but Mr. Davidson has kindly sent a copy. I shall write the editor to tell him that "The Raven" was not written at Fordham but in New York City. How can people continue to tell such things without any authority? I wish poor Poe had been born in Europe. How differently would his name & fame have been treated. Forgive me for saying so *to you*, but then all the world is *our* stage. How glad I am though that we can converse in the same language.

The paper on Hawthorne by Leslie Stephen was first published in the *Cornhill*, but is now in a book of essays styled *Hours in a Library* or some such title.[2] Some of Mr. Stephen's essays are very good & some very *bad*—notably, one on Balzac. His paper on Hawthorne & Poe is beneath contempt. *Appleton's* extract is but a portion. I know nothing of Mr. S[tephen?]. I sent you a piece of Eugene Benson's article in the *Galaxy*. I kept no copy & only what you sent me. The whole article is I suppose not available?

No more at present. As I have Graham's letter, I will return your MS. copy. Did you get the "Autography" papers? I will send the paper on Poe in the *Sixpenny* which kindly return (when perused) with comments. Will you do this—as I am doubtful about the author's correct[ness]. No more—no more—my ever dear friend from yours ever & ever faithfully,

John H. Ingram

1. William Gilmore Simms (1806–1870) published *Martin Faber; the Story of a Criminal* (New York: J. & J. Harper, 1833).
2. Leslie Stephen republished his paper on Hawthorne in *Hours in a Library*, I (London: Smith Elder & Co., 1874), 256–98.

65. *Sarah Helen Whitman to John H. Ingram.* Item 166

My dear Mr. Ingram,   Aug. 7, [18]74
    Miss Rose F. Peckham, who is an intimate friend of mine, is going to sail for Europe next week in the *Parthia*. She will be in London for a few days before going to Paris, where she will probably pass the winter for the purpose of cultivating her taste in art. She has chosen to enter the profession of an artist from a genuine & disinterested love of the pursuit. She has already done some fine work in portrait painting, but her last & most successful effort was a fine head of Sappho, nobly conceived & executed with a fine sense of the tragic grandeur of her ideal. She is a born artist, but feels that she has much to learn. Her father, Dr. S. F. Peckham, is a physician of Providence, a man of wealth & ability, widely known & respected. She goes abroad in company with a lady from Boston, also an artist.
    Soon after I became acquainted with her, she told me of her great interest in Poe, as a *school-girl*, & of her desire to know me, springing from this cause. She told me that one of her early compositions was on the subject of his life & genius, & at my request gave me the MS., two pages of which I enclose, that you may know that there is on this subject at least a bond of sympathy between you. Since I have known

her, that is, for the last three or four years, we have been warm friends.

I have much to say, but must wait til next week. It is pleasant to think of you as enjoying yourself these beautiful summer days at "garden parties."

I hope that for you the gardens may be all "enchanted."

And so, goodbye for tonight.

Sarah Helen Whitman

Mr. Latto has received his autograph letter & tells me that he has been waiting to notice the recent papers on Poe until the "City of Churches" shall have a respite from the all-absorbing clerical scandal.

You must not tell Miss Peckham that I sent you her school-girl composition. I am afraid it might not meet with her approval. I saw her last evening for the first time after an interval of several months; she has been passing the summer at their summer home in Putnam, while I have remained in Providence.

I send you some lines written to the wife of one of our poets, Geo. S. Burleigh, with whom I passed pleasant months by the sea shore two or three years ago.

You will see that I have marked for you some of [my] favorite lines in Victor Hugo, etc.

66.   *Sarah Helen Whitman to John H. Ingram.*   Item 168

My dear Mr. Ingram,   Aug. 18, 1874

The days when I receive your letters are marked with a white stone in my calendar. Yesterday was such a day. I cannot wonder at the languor of which you complain. After such prolonged & intense mental action, it is but natural & will be, I trust, restorative. Do not trouble yourself to return any papers & letters which I send you, unless I *expressly* ask you to do so. My copy of Graham's letter (if you have introduced the *printed* letter in your book), I do not care for. I shall have it in the book. I would send you Eugene Benson's article on Poe & Hawthorne if I did not fear that it might be lost, as was the copy of *Appleton's Journal.* I am also afraid that you may have left home before another mail arrives. I will try to get a duplicate of the *Galaxy* number which contains it. I think that I copied *nearly* all that was not in the printed slip that you sent me. I am sorry my copy of *Appleton's* miscarried, as I had made some pencil notes on the margin—not of much importance, however, I fancy. About the influence of the stars, etc., you say, "I do not believe in those distant bodies exercising any influence on our *bodies*, whatever they may do on our *minds*." I thought that it was an admitted fact that whatever influences the mind has a reflex influence on the body. Is it not? I am inclined to believe in the stars. I have a conviction not to be shaken that the occult sciences covered great truths, dimly discerned & obscured by superstition, doubtless, but nevertheless truths.

I recollect reading with an interest which few persons will understand a work by Cornelius Agrippa on *Occult Philosophy*, which has been edited by Morley.[1] He believes in the power of words, the power of names, & the significance of anagrams.

Did I ever tell you of an anagram which can be made from the words

S a r a h   H e l e n   P o e r ?

3 6 5 1 2   8 4 9 1011   7 121413

If not, place the letters in the order in which I have numbered them.[2]

I was strangely thrilled when I saw the result, & you, I think, will admit that it was at least curious. By the way, what does the initial letter "H" in your name stand for?

You excite my curiosity by what you tell me about Griswold & Mrs. Ellet & the printed letter about Griswold's marriage. I know that he married a lady, thinking her to be an heiress & behaved very scandalously toward her. At least that was the story, but I do not remember anything about a charge of bigamy imputed to him.[3] If I ever heard it, I have forgotten it. The *Temple Bar* article has, I imagine, been read with great interest & without any adverse criticism. Mr. Eveleth writes me that "the *Southern Maga.* for August has an article on Poe in which reference is made to two French commentators—high appreciation of the poet's genius."[4] He said he had, when he wrote, merely glanced at the article. I think he told me that the letter of Dunn English was among papers in a distant city, not at the time accessible to him.

I do not think the *Southern Magazine* is taken in this city. I cannot learn whether English is still living on the planet. Did you not write me that he had taken his departure?

Strange to relate, I received with *your* letter a letter from Mr. Gill containing the enclosed program of his intentions in the lecturing field. With the letter came an elegant printed little vol. called *The Martyred Church*, consisting of some verses by Mr. Gill & elaborate illustrations drawn by Hammatt Billings, the whole dedicated to the Rev. Phillips Brooks, D.D., who has lately been preaching at St. Paul's, London.[5] Mr. Brooks was the pastor of the "martyred church," or the Church of the Trinity, destroyed by fire Nov. 9, 1872, when half Boston was destroyed. Mr. Gill's dedication of the poem to Mr. Brooks is quite characteristic: "To Rev. Phillips Brooks, who a witness of the incident here described has kindly encouraged the author by his warm approval of the verses, etc., etc."

The little book was issued by Shepard & Gill last winter, but I only now have seen a copy. Mr. Gill says in his letter that he looks forward to meeting me again ere long & that he should have sent me a copy of his verses, but for a criticism which had naturally made him sensitive about doing so. He says he had been charged with the resemblance of his poems to some verses of mine—a translation of Uhland's *Lost Church*, to be found in a vol. which I gave him last fall.

He says he had not read my poem at the time of publishing his verses, etc., etc. (which I can readily believe & which I could as readily condone, if he *had*.) On having his attention called to the resemblance, he feared that I, too, should regard him as a trespasser, etc., etc. He thinks I will at least be pleased with the *illustrations*, & sends me, as he says, one of his lecture circulars, to show me that he has not given up the defence of Poe. I shall of course write at once to assure him of my cordial approbation of his little book & my utter freedom from any suspicions or fears in relation to plagiarism, etc. I will tell him that I shall be glad to have him return the letter of Mr. Willis, if he does not care to use it.

I hope you will have an interview with my friend Miss Rose Peckham before you leave the city. Mr. Harris (Caleb Fiske Harris) will be absent from his home for five or six weeks longer; when he returns, I will tell him what you say. I do not know his present address, as he is travelling from place to place. You say you have never seen a *single* illustration of Poe's works that you like. Do you not, then, like Birket Foster's "July Midnight" in the "enchanted garden," of the Revised Edition of [18]68, Palmer's "Haunted Palace" & "City of the Sea," in Widdleton's of 1870?[6] I think these & a few others are fine, though my witty friend Col. Dwight (of whom I wrote you in a recent letter) says the "Haunted Palace" looks like a railroad depot, with a frantic crowd of excursionists rushing from the platform. Nevertheless, *I* think it is a weird & splendid picture.

How I wish you could have heard Poe's voice! To have heard his reading of "Ulalume" or "The Bridal Ballad" is a never-to-be-forgotten memory!

I entirely agree with you that "a calm, severe, summing up" is better, far better, than any vehemence of [*sic*] denunciation. I have not had a line from O'Connor since he sent me the papers containing the news of Miss Poe's death. I fear he must be *very* unwell.

Of my own health, I will only say that I have been very ill with neuralgic spasms in the head—intense & agonising. I am much better for the last week, but the malady is lying in wait, I know well, to seize on me with renewed virulence at the first unfavorable change of weather. Yet I am enjoying this summer beyond any summer of my life, that is, so far as my sense of the beauty of nature can make life serene & beautiful. And never before had I such a sweet, enduring sense, such unmistakable *tokens* of the presence of loved ones ever near and in sympathy with all my inmost hopes & aspirations. I dare not speak to *you* of things which make life to *me* so transcendently & mysteriously beautiful. I do not care to *see* the presences that surround me; I *know* that they are near. I could tell you strange things, but you are not yet ready to hear them.

Is this "preaching"? I hope not, because I wish to obey your injunction *not* to preach. But good night, and may the "High Gods" guard & bless you!

S.H.W.

1. *Cornelius Agrippa* [1486?–1535]: *The Life of Henry Cornelius Agrippa von Nettesheim; doctor and knight, commonly known as a magician*, ed. Henry Morley (London: Chapman & Hall, 1856).

2. Mrs. Whitman had printed this anagram of her name in the New York *Evening Post* sometime in the 1860s; along with it she had published an anagram formed from Edgar Poe's name: "A God Peer."

3. Joy Bayless handles thoroughly the enmity between Griswold and Mrs. Ellet, the charge of bigamy against Griswold, the relationships between Poe and Griswold, as well as other controversies that swirled around Griswold. See chapters 6, 7, and 8 of *Rufus Wilmot Griswold, Poe's Literary Executor* (Nashville: Vanderbilt Univ. Press, 1943).

4. W. Baird, "Edgar Allan Poe," *Southern Magazine*, 15 (1874), 190–203. The commentators were Baudelaire and Gautier.

5. This book of Gill's consists of fourteen pages and is dated 1874.

6. For Birket Foster see p. 34, n. 3.

67. *John H. Ingram to Sarah Helen Whitman*

My dear Mrs. Whitman,   4 Sept. 1874

Although I may not be able to complete this letter today, I will try my best as I have so much to reply to, so much to say, and have remained so long silent—indeed, I believe that I have three letters to answer—yours of the 31st July, 7 Augt., [18]th of Augt. Perhaps I have answered the first, but my memory is so very treacherous at the present moment that I am not certain on the point. Before, however, taking up the thread of your story, let me tell what small amount of news I may have to retail.

In the first place, I have seen Miss Peckham and had a chat with her and find her a very nice girl so far as first impressions go, & expect to have the pleasure of escorting her and her companions to the Crystal Palace tomorrow. I await her reply. Unfortunately, all my family are away just now so that I cannot offer her an English welcome, but when she returns from Paris, I hope to be able to do so. In a few days I mean to leave town, and shall, perhaps, take Paris in my way so that I may hear how she is getting on there. I need scarcely remark how affectionately she spoke of you. She seems already rather homesick. She sketched off my profile for you, but I was not a very patient model, so don't rely on its exactness.[1]

Two days ago the enclosed reached me from the Virginia University, with a letter from the Chairman or President. Mr. Wertenbaker is still living and labouring in the University as librarian! It is gratifying to know that Poe is so read and liked by the students. I should liked [*sic*] to have used more of *the* letter in "Memoir," but think I have the substance of it—derived from the extract you sent me.[2]

Poor Miss Poe! How sad a life! But for my illness I might have done something for her. You cannot think how grieved I felt at having raised her expectations & then never have really done anything for her. And so many were willing to help. Her death came like a blow to me & made me feel so miserable—but I was powerless, through my illness, to carry out my scheme on her behalf. I put a short notice of her in the *Mirror* and it was copied into various papers.[3] Mr. Davidson, who is always kind, although I have seemed to neglect him as I have everybody lately, sent me a paragraph from an American paper stating that Miss Poe was eighty-eight & died at Baltimore, &c. So much for newspaper information! Many thanks for you sending me the cuttings. There did seem something strange about the poor lady. Mrs. Lewis told me some wonderful story about her not being Poe's sister, but I fancy 'twas only an idle rumour. Miss Poe's second & last letter to me was only a few lines asking me whether I was doing anything for her, and stated that she was unwell, but not in a way to make me think seriously of her illness.[4] I do so repent that I did not get someone to reply for me.

As to portrait of Poe belonging to Mrs. Lewis—she has promised me copies & says it was taken only three months before his death—and, I fancy, at New York. But I seem to think that I have already mentioned this—as also about Mrs. Ellet & Griswold. The latter married a Jewess with money and (so I hear) because she would not assign her property to him, would not take her as his wife—they lived apart, but this 2nd Mrs. G., being charitable, adopted G's daughters. G[riswold] hearing of a wealthy widow tried to get a divorce from his wife and upon a false affidavit (so I'm told) succeeded, in a Southern court. He at once got married to the widow lady & lived with her some long time. Now Mrs. E[llet] would seem to come to the fore. I fancy she had been very intimate with Poe & very jealous of Mrs. Osgood. She afterwards became *very* intimate with Griswold, and in his printed letter he unmistakably says—I must say so—improperly so. They quarrelled & Mrs. Ellet set herself to work to ruin Griswold. She investigated the divorce case—probably knew something of it—wrote *anonymous* letters—so G[riswold] says, to everyone about it—wrote to his second living wife & her relatives—& got them to take her & her children away. Stirred up the Jewess & her relatives to prosecute—proved the forged statement—got the divorce annulled &, I hear, even turned his own children against him. Ruined & disgraced, he died quite young. Mrs. E[llet], the demon that did him to death—his partner in crime— still survives—a very devil in strength to do & conceive villainy. You can believe poor Poe's remarks now—can you not? Griswold especially insists upon her writing anonymous letters—he doubtless knew her capabilities well.[5]

Sept. 13, Sunday

My very dear friend, I begin anew with no real prospect of finishing this tonight as I am very tired & out of sorts. First, however, my news. I had the pleasure of accompanying Miss Peckham & three acquaintances to the Crystal Palace, but through incorrect information got there too late for the fireworks or to see the grounds. Miss P[eckham] is very nice. I never met a girl I liked better & am grateful for your introduction—her opinion of me you will doubtless receive earlier than this. She very kindly sketched me a portrait of you, & although in "a dim religious light," I *feel* is something like you. I am going to Paris in a few days & hope to see my American acquaintances there. I like to talk to Miss P[eckham] of you—you seem so old a friend of mine now that I scarcely can comprehend that there was a time when I knew you not.

I have not been at my office for some days, having begun my annual vacation with a few days hard work at home—clearing up matters and arranging the *fourth* vol. of Poe's works for the printer. Vol. 1 I hope to see published next month & rely upon good critiques on the "Memoir"—but that "Memoir," for the reasons already stated, is but tentative. I shall go on—if spared—in life & health—(mental & physical) with my collection of material for a larger & exhaustive "Life & Letters."

Appleton's Journal came from Mr. Davidson. Did you notice that Fordham was therein represented as the house where Poe wrote "The Raven"? It was, of course, written and published before he went to Fordham. I do not think—referring to yours of 31st July, that Baudelaire translated Poe's *poems* save the sonnet to Mrs. Clemm— which I sent you—nor have I seen *them* in French.

I was surprised to hear that John Neal was still alive. I suppose he would not remember anything of Poe's early poems for which, says Lowell in his notice of Poe, prefixed to Griswold's 4-vol. collection, "John Neal drew a proud horoscope for their author." Lowell refers to 1827.

Re. Edgar Poe & His Critics I must write again. Events have
overstrained my memory, but I would advise no reliance upon J. M.
Daniel in his "Eulogium" (in *S. Lit. Messenger*) *vide* pps. 16 & 17
beginning "one who knew him at *this period* of his life," when Daniel
did not meet [him] till 1848–9, & you refer to 1844, & not in N. York
but Richmond, & again at p. 43 you refer to his characterization of Poe.
Why his slanders against Poe are the foundation for Griswold's—*re.*
second Mrs. Allan, &c. By the way, Griswold's "Memoir of E.P." seems
to have appeared in the *International Magazine*, New York, previous
to its prefixing the collection.[6]

While I think of it, if you ever come across the *data* or any
particulars of the "Conchology" story & its refutation in the *Home
Journal*, I shall be thankful for it.

Reverting to *E.P. & His Critics*, I really do not know that I can
suggest anything of note. The unfavourable reviews you therein name
have passed into oblivion & are hardly worth recalling by name—they
were mere *ephemera*. P. 35, the *Edinburgh Review*, in that most
scandalous review speaking of "Ver-Vert" shows his own ignorance of
that singular poem by calling it more than once "Vert-Vert." There is
only one *t* in it. In my library are most of the works Poe alludes to—
many very curious—one quite rare & from which, *entre nous*, he drew
many of his most repeated quotations, is very pretty. 'Tis the *Grey Cap
for a Green Head*.[7] In your Preface you say an "English critic" has
assumed "Poe had no friends." I do not know the English critic, but of
course Griswold said it in his obituary of Poe in the *Tribune*. In my
"Memoir" I speak of Griswold's statement that Poe was *ingenious only
in appearance*, as he invented the enigmas he unravelled (this has
been copied by all biographers) and I have shewn its falsity—this you
might also shew in reprinting—you might also strengthen my view by
referring to Poe's skill in unravelling cryptographs sent him to
decipher. These are all trifles but others may occur to you when you
get my book. By the way, I disprove Griswold's charge of plagiarism—
have you seen "Vivenzio," *vide* Griswold p. xlviii? I could send it to
you. You have, in a note in Providence *Journal*, deemed Poe liable to
charge of plagiarism. I stick up for his originality in all. I republish
nearly all Graham's letter—you might use some of that. But, perhaps,
the book might be as it is—& not increased in bulk—only you should
have a fair price for its publication.

Thanks! *re.* Carys—I cannot but love some of their poems—they
were favourites with my darling sister. I have not read Mrs. Ames'
book about them, but read a review of it & some extracts, I fancy. Many
thanks to Miss Powell [Power] for kindly thinking of me with respect
to the condensed ballad! I was going to ask permission to reproduce it
in the *Mirror* but, unfortunately, that paper will stop publication next

week. This is a great loss to me. I have written much for them lately &
their discontinuance will be a loss to me—for a while at least—of more
than 500 dollars per annum—a good bit for me, who am not rich &
have many chiefly relying upon me. But I dare say I shall ere long
make it up elsewhere. But it upset me, last night, to hear the news from
the editor, who is an old friend of mine, & did what he could for me—
the proprietor is rich—but, I fancy, could not make the *Mirror* pay.
They have several papers of mine written for them & they will have to
come home like prodigal sons. *Mais c'est assez!* I wish, however, I had
reviewed Miss Power's two long poems before the stoppage. I'll try
them elsewhere.

Of course, I like to hear from you—'tis one of the pleasures of a
much over-shadowed life—the story of which I *may*, some day, inflict
upon you—and as for sermons, why I could gladly listen to them or
anything else *from you.* How I long to see you in this life as well as in
the misty one to come. And I fancy I shall yet. I live & hope.

Never mind questions Davidson has not looked up—he is very kind
& I have plenty of people now to write to. I have had a long letter from
a Mr. Wm. Hand Browne, which I send for your perusal, but which
please return to me.[8] I have written him a very long letter. That & three
or four to Miss Peckham filled up the time meant for you—but you'll
forgive me, won't you? I hope to be a better correspondent hereafter.
I'll return Miss P[eckham]'s essay on Poe, which, of course, I did not
mention.

Mr. Gill has written again, but nothing of note—says "no time to
arrange material" which is chiefly "of a peculiarly personal nature in
the form of notes taken down when conversing with Geo. R. Graham &
others who knew Poe intimately," &c., &c.

By the way, Daniel, I should have said, contradicts himself in the
"Eulogium" & I fancy knew nothing of Poe really.

Yours of the 7th August & poems enclosed—many thanks for latter
for which more some day. Enclosed from a Scotch paper *re.* Miss Poe
condensed from my notice in the *Mirror.* Yours of the 19th (with Mr.
Gill's handsome portrait) for tomorrow. Is he so good looking?

14 Sept. 1874

I must abridge my chatter, as I do not wish to keep you without a
letter. Never mind the *Galaxy* number, but I am sorry that your
annotated *Appleton* miscarried. I do hope your friend will let me have
a copy of Poe's early poems in MS. The prose introduction also. My
paper in the *Gentleman's* was made up from fragments. The rest of the
poetic "introduction," the cancelled portions of *Tamerlane, Al Aaraaf,*
&c., I have never seen. As regards the paper mentioned by Mr. W. H.
Browne, it has not arrived.

With you, I believe that "the occult sciences covered great truths," but, as a rule, I fancy, quite unknown & even unguessed at by their professors. By the "influence of the stars on the mind" I meant only through the imagination. But I do not think we can go into that matter on paper just now.

As regards anagrams, I look upon them only as play of fancy— amusing but of no value beyond the usual value of mere amusement. Looking at the anagram you form from "S. H. Poer"—"Ah, Seraph Lenore"—I must confess that *I* do not see anything peculiar in it. Forgive me for so saying, but I must tell the truth—look at the probabilities. What could *not* be found in "S. H. Poer Power Whitman"? As regards *my* name now—one of the oldest unchanged names of Europe. You *can*, perhaps see a curious coincidence in that when I point out that without any anagram being needed, "Ingram" means ('tis Teutonic) "akin to, or, the son of, the Raven"! "Ing" has the force of "Mac" or "O" in the Gaelic, & "Ram" is the Raven. Ingram—of the Raven. My second Christian name, by the way, is "Henry," but I generally call myself in accordance with family matters, John *Hyden-Ingram.*

I have retailed the Griswold scandal as above. I don't think he was ever *tried* for bigamy, but so closely did it resemble bigamy that the 2nd living wife went home & would not meet him again.

The two French commentators mentioned in *Southern Maga.* may be Baudelaire & Gautier, but 'tis uncertain. Poe is now a popular *French* author. A new translation with very original illustrations is appearing (of the tales) in the *Musée Universal.*

Thos. Dunn English is dead. Mother Ellet & Briggs are, it is presumed, still alive.[9] Mr. Gill might give a copy of letter from Mr. J. Willis, but, *entre nous,* he does not seem careful. Don't forget Mr. C. F. Harris & the copy. As regards illustrations to Poe—I don't mean that some are not good pictures but that, as they naturally fall far below what they are intended to illustrate, they only detract instead of add to the beauty. As I could not hear Poe's voice, I live in hopes of hearing yours, which is, I'm told, music itself—& I believe it.

I hope your forebodings as to winter's tortures may prove unfounded. But "tide, tide, whate'er betide" ever & ever, in whatever state of *sentient* being I may be, believe that I shall regard you as the dearest & most endeared of friends & that, while Reason holds her own, your friendship will glitter like a pure gleaming star in the dark sky unto your most devoted

John H. Ingram

1. This sketch of Ingram was reproduced in Caroline Ticknor's "Ingram—Discoura-ger of Poe Biographies," *New York Bookman,* 44 (Sept. 1916), 13, and in my article

"Father John Banister Tabb's Defense of Edgar Allan Poe," *Virginia Cavalcade*, Spring 1975, pp. 156–63.

2. This was a copy of a note by Dr. Socrates Maupin, presiding officer of the University of Virginia, of May 22, 1860, appended to William Wertenbaker's letter of May 12, 1860, attesting to Poe's commendable scholarship and behavior at the university.

3. This obituary, "Miss Rosalie Poe," was published after July 25, 1874, in the London *Mirror*, but no copy has survived.

4. For a discussion of Rosalie Poe's paternity, see my article "Poe's Sister Rosalie," *Tennessee Studies in Literature*, 8 (1963), 107–17.

5. Again, this controversy is more capably handled by Joy Bayless. See p. 206, n. 3.

6. This "Memoir" did appear in the *International*, edited by Griswold, on Oct. 1, 1850.

7. James Puckle (1667?–1724) wrote *The Club, or a Grey-Cap for a Green-Head* (London, 1723; rpt. Philadelphia: Samuel Longcope, 1796), a dialogue between father and son.

8. William Hand Browne (1828–1912), author, editor, professor in The Johns Hopkins University, became an eager and resourceful helper of Ingram's in building true Poe biography. With his learning, mild good humor, and his broad knowledge of both literature and Baltimore, his contributions to our knowledge of Poe deserve more attention and gratitude than they have heretofore received; Ingram, at least, never attempted to criticize or cross him.

9. Thomas Dunn English lived until 1902. Mrs. Ellet and Briggs were to die in 1877.

68. *Sarah Helen Whitman to John H. Ingram.* Item 172

Sept. 29, [18]74

My dear "Sir John the Graeme," alias, MacRaven!

I am so glad that I have at last found a mystical significance, or synonym in your name affiliating you with the Raven!!! I have tried so long in vain. But you are a tyro in the sublime science of telling fortunes by names & numbers if you think that the name which a married woman receives from her husband is to be taken into account in the evolution of an anagram that shall reveal the secrets of her destiny. That would be entirely out of rule.

I am so glad that you & my friend Rose know & like each other so well. I had a charming note from her on the 15th, in which she promised to write again soon. I should have written at once, but I was very ill when I received her letter, & have been growing worse daily. A cough & fever, accompanied with a severe stricture on the lungs, is making rapid inroads on my fragile health.

The Harrises have not yet returned. They are expected to-night; but though they are my near neighbors, it is doubtful when I shall be well enough to see them. I will try to let Mr. Harris know your wish for a copy of the early poems. Would it not be well for *you* to write to him?

I am so glad that you have now met someone who can speak to me of you. It brings us so much nearer. And yet from the time I read your early poems I have felt that we were very near. Don't forget to tell me the promised story of your life, & tell it *soon*.

Thanks for the dear & kind words at the close of your letters. I shall cherish them in my heart of hearts. Thanks, too, for your kind advice about my *Critics*. I do not propose to enlarge it or make other changes, than the correction of mistakes. I think I could easily manage about the first quotation from Daniel by leaving out the words "at this period," &, in relation to the latter one, I might say, "one who saw much of him during the last *year* of his life" instead of "the last *years*."

I know well that Daniel had not love for Poe, but for this very reason his powerful & graphic delineation seemed to me the more valuable. I am glad to know about "Ver Vert." I wish to prepare the book for publication after my death, with the new edition of the poems which my friends often urge me to bring out—but if I prepare them for publication, I am unwilling to have them *appear* until after my translation.

I am well satisfied with *E.A.P. & His Critics* just as it is. I like it better & better as the years go by. Its significance as throwing light on one dominant phase of Poe's genius will be better understood in the near future than it has ever yet been. I only wish I knew something more of Mrs. Helen Stanard. Have you obtained any light in that direction?

I had a letter today from Mr. Gill in which he seemed to fear that your "Memoir" would be likely to take the wind out of his sails, & said he had thought seriously of delivering his lecture this winter in London. I am inclined to think he has already too much wind in his sails for his amount of ballast. His programme speaks well for him, but I do not understand how he could have been "fairly at work" in his defence of Poe, when he had evidently never seen Griswold's "Memoir." About Griswold & his second marriage: I once saw the little Jewess & her rich aunt at the house of my aunt, Mrs. Tillinghast. She was a *petite* brunette, not attractive in appearance. Soon after this Mr. Griswold obtained from Mrs. Tillinghast an introduction to these ladies, & immediately devoted himself to the little heiress. I heard that on finding the aunt held the purse strings he made a great rumpus & a separation ensured, the little Jewess living with her aunt at the South & coming on with some of her aunt's gold every year to New York or Philadelphia to see her husband & keep up appearances. Finally, having an opportunity to make a better *parti*, he sought a divorce, etc. All *this* I had heard, but nothing of Mrs. Ellet's connection with the matter. What a revelation of character & motive!

I think Griswold was about 50 when he died of consumption. He was so wrapt up about the throat & so altered in appearance when I met him at Alice Cary's that I did not recognize him. When he came to Providence to see me in the summer of '48, he was very handsome & looked not more than thirty. I was told that on seeing me at the Carys', he turned away in evident confusion.

I shall enclose a few lines to Rose, because I cannot make out the address she gave me. You will perhaps forward them to her.

Sept. 30

I was very much exhausted when I ceased writing to you last evening, but I cannot close without thanking you for Mr. Wertenbaker's statement. Shall I keep it or return it to you? How thoroughly it refutes the story of Poe's dissolute habits & expulsion from a dissolute University, so carelessly repeated by Stoddard, when the facts were so accessible to all who might take the trouble to enquire. Even after I had furnished Stoddard with copies of the essential points of Mr. Wertenbaker's statement, he made no use of them, but brought out, in the *Aldine*, papers to show that Poe's statement that the Wiley & Putnam edition of poems was a *verbatim* reprint from the earlier printed versions was *untrue*, showing plainly his secret hostility to Poe.[1]

In Mr. Gill's letter of Sept. 17 he wrote, "I have a magazine article very strong against Griswold now ready. I shall take it to New York tonight. Shall you be at home Thursday or Friday of next week, & if so, may I hope to call upon you?" I wrote in reply that I would certainly see him if well enough to do so, but have heard nothing further from him. I cannot help thinking that *your* articles may have helped him in preparing his "strong magazine article against G."

Once more, don't return *anything* I send you unless I request you to do so.

And now I must for the present say goodbye. I will write again when I am able to write without so much pain; and do you write only when it is pleasant & quite convenient to your sincere friend

Sarah Helen Poer

Of course you know that I found "Sir John the Graeme" in the notes to Scott's "Lady of the Lake." You are a Scotchman then, & first cousin to an Irishman. Good!

My dear Mr. Ingram,   Oct. 1

I had a note from Mr. Gill this morning in which he says, "I have been working unceasingly at my biography of Poe—there seemed to be no end to the items of information that kept coming to me, & months after I met you I got from Mr. George R. Graham (to find whom, I walked six miles over hilly roads) some especially important & fresh information most damaging to Dr. Griswold. The subject has never been out of my mind, etc." I was *very* much surprised to learn that Graham, another *Graeme*, perhaps, was still living. Are not you? Or did you know of it before?

Of course when I say that I am well satisfied with my essay on Poe, you will understand me as being satisfied with having done well what I *attempted* to do. I knew well that I could make a more popular book, but I sought briefly & earnestly to throw light on an obscure phase of his genius which no one else would be likely so well to understand. I send you an extract from an article by Ben Lane Posey, an eloquent writer (a friend of Madame Octavia Le Vert) well known at the South, who wrote long eulogistic notices of my book for the New Orleans & Mobile papers. Send me back the printed scrap, & destroy anything which I may send you that you do *not care to keep*, unless I ask you at the *time* of sending it to preserve or return.

Once more, dear friend, Vale atque Vale,

S.H.W.

1. There is indeed an article, "Poe's Early Poems," in the *Aldine, a Typographic Art Journal*, 6 (May 1873), 101, in which the author calls Poe "a liar" for saying that he printed in the 1829 volume, his first, poems he had written and printed before: "They are printed *verbatim* from the original *edition*, the date of which is too remote to be judiciously acknowledged." The author of the article adds, "But they were *not* printed verbatim." This article is signed with the name "Frank Jocelyn."

69. *John H. Ingram to Sarah Helen Whitman*

My very dear friend, 7 Oct. 1874
"Hope deferred maketh the heart sick"—For weeks I have waited, but waited in vain, to hear from you & begin sadly to dread that all is not well. Oh, I do so long to hear from you; if not able to write, do let someone send me a line—a word to say that all is well.

Since my last long letter & its various enclosures was sent off, I have had a sad, sad loss. Just as I had my traps packed for my annual trip & all arrangements for a visit to Paris through Normandy, a letter arrived to say that a very dear friend, my best & kindest, & related by marriage, was dangerously ill at the town in South Devon coast, where he was staying with his wife & three little boys. I was for going to him at once but, persuaded to call on his brother, found that he had just received a telegram to come at once with the family doctor. I need not give you further details; suffice to say that in four days my friend was no more of this life. I cannot express how unspeakably wretched this sad event has made me. My friend was one of the truest & noblest men who ever lived, &, I sincerely believe, never imagined, much less did, a mean thing. He was only 39 & rising rapidly in his profession as a

barrister. Again a perfect blank seems to have usurped the future—
hope seems folly, & but that others are dependent upon my well
being, I feel that I could gladly & cheerfully go down to my grave
"where the weary are at rest." I know that time does & will bring a
nepenthé for such sorrows, but that does not ease the wound in its
newness. But I will turn to different matters.

I have told you how well I got on with Miss Peckham. I looked
forward to meeting her again in Paris & having some pleasant hours
together, but my holiday has been broken up & I am back at my office
again. I desired to go back, because the daily routine & the constant
contact with careless or heartless people are the best salves for such
sores; continual irritation wears out the pain. I had a long chat with
Miss Peckham about the poisonous ivy, & what she said makes me very
anxious about your health—& your sister, Miss Power, was also ill, was
she not?

I have not much by way of news. I have just received a letter from an
English acquaintance, resident in New York, in which he answers my
inquiries about the Poe family by saying that a friend in Baltimore
"knew the surviving members of Poe's family quite intimately," but
that "he could not succeed in enlisting the sympathies of the Poes in
the matter, that they were very reticent," and that they asserted that *I*
was "in correspondence with one of them & that he had given you
⟨ *i.e., me* ⟩ all they cared to say relative to the poet." This seems to
show that Neilson Poe is not the sole survivor & it confirms my
suspicion that efforts are being made to stifle inquiry. Neilson Poe, I
have learned from three correspondents, has said that he has written to
me & that I have written to him. This latter assertion is incorrect, or
was until yesterday, when I sent off a letter to him. I need scarcely
remark that I have never received any communication from him. I
hope for some information from Mr. Hand Browne's investigations. I
hope you received his letter safely, with the other enclosures I sent
you early last month.

Vol. 1 of Poe's works is not out yet. Of course a copy will be sent to
you at the earliest moment. We have been waiting for Mr. Linley
Sambourne's illustrations, but I have desired Messrs. Blacks not to
wait. I have not heard for some days from them, but expect to by every
post. I do long for you to get my "Memoir"—tentative though it be—&
get your opinion on it, on the portrait, &c.

I have no news & only wait & wait for your next letter, meanwhile
remaining now, & forever, most affectionately yours,

John H. Ingram

P.S. This is a stupid letter but better than silence, *n'est ce pas?*

Oct. 13: Post by post I have waited to hear from [you] & thankful I indeed am to at last get your kind & ever dear handwriting, [Sept. 29]. I would not lose a scrap of it.

Miss Peckham's letter shall go off at once as she is also anxious at not hearing of or from you.

I return your slip of *Edgar Poe & His C.*. I think you should preserve all these notices—(I fancy I still have some—Mr. O'Connor's, &c.)—reprint them at the end of the book, or selections from them. You'll see what I have said, & what use I have made, of *E.P. & His C.* in the "Memoir." I long for its appearance & for you to get it. Dear little book that yours is, I should not like it altered more than the few slight things you mention. 'Tis a friend that—although *I know every word of it*, I often consult.

Whilst I think of Mr. O'Connor, last week's *Academy* had a review of W. Whitman's *Leaves of Grass*—very favourable—by George Saintsbury, a fine critic, who will, I believe, review my edition of Poe. Same number had a long paragraph *re.* my forthcoming "Memoir" & the Works. H. F. Curwen, who translated Baudelaire's *Essais* for Hotten's ed. of Poe, has a book announced for early issue, entitled *Sorrow & Song*, taking as representatives of both, Poe, Petöfi, &c. You know Petöfi, the great Hungarian poet? I have written Curwen *re.* Poe, but hope that he has done him justice. Several papers announce my book as preparing. Routledge announce cheap ed. of Poe's poems as edited by Stoddard. I'll get it & see what he says.

So Mr. Gill is nervous! Never mind, all will help to bring Griswold *v.* E. Poe before the world. I don't fancy Mr. G[ill] will do me any harm. I hope he'll fight well, as he is on the right side. I wish he kept a little nearer the truth.

The Ed. of the *International* (through Davidson) has engaged me to write a life of Poe & I am getting on with it quickly, but don't mention to anyone or Gill *might* spoil *that*.

Thanks for Mr. Dwight's note, but I think there's a mistake. In "The Balloon Hoax" Poe speaks of "the guide rope" as the invention of Green the aëronaut & I fancy he was right. I know it has been used a long time here.

The Poes seem determined to stop the E. Poe Memorial—as if *they* could cast *his* name into oblivion! 'Tis like Mrs. Partington sweeping back the Atlantic with her broom.

Well, I suppose I am "a tyro in the sublime science!" Let us hope—we can do no more—that some day all may be clear. *Do* keep me informed of your health. Your account is alarming: don't injure yourself by long letters, but send me a line once a fortnight at least. It does certainly seem to bring us nearer, & more palpably real, to have found a mutual friend, but you are near & dear to me without any other links being needed.

As for the story of my life—*it* depends upon my mood—'tis a sad tragedy. I have, indeed, been as "the bird's unhappy master, whom unmerciful disaster, followed fast," through life. I know troubles *do* affect me more & their impressions last longer, than with many, but my pangs have not been imaginary, or mere sentiment. My life since childhood has been one continual sacrifice—still is—& but for those dependent upon me, I would gladly go to my eternal rest. Why wait for *your* translation? Let the books appear unless you have some deep objection.

I also long to know more of the Stanard family &, perhaps, my investigations may bring something to light. Griswold, I fancy, was 42 when he died. Keep Mr. Wertenbaker's statement. Did I not say they sent me two copies? I'm not Scotch, but supposed to be descended from Scotch family—The Ingrams, *Viscounts* Irving, &c., &c.!! G. R. Graham is dead & has *been some time*, I firmly believe. Mrs. H. L. Williams who told me, & who is in London, knew him well & told me the whole story of his life & death. You may be *quite satisfied* with your book—it *will* last.

Yesterday came a kind letter from E. V. Valentine, a relative of Mrs. Allan (the 1st), as you know. A cousin of his father's accompanied the Allans when they brought Poe to Europe to school. E.V.V.'s brother *heard* Poe lecture & recite "The Raven" & Hood's "Bridge of Sighs."

He speaks of the pallor which overspread his face contrasted with the dark hair which fell on the summit of his forehead, with an inclination to curl. His brow was fine & expressive—his eyes dark and restless—in the mouth firmness mingled with an element of scorn and discontent. Firm and erect gait, but nervous and emphatic manner. Man of fine address and cordial in his intercourse with his friends, but looked as though he rarely smiled from joy, to which Poe seemed to be a stranger, and which might be partly attributable to the great struggle for self-control in which he seemed to be constantly engaged. There was little variation & much sadness in the intonations of his voice—yet this very sadness was so completely in harmony with his history as to excite on the part of this community a deep interest in him both as a lecturer & reader. . . . My brother, who is an accomplished reader, imitates his rendering of "The Raven," and read in Berlin, Prussia, a German translation of the poem. . . . I have a souvenir of Poe presented to me by my kind friend, the late J. R. Thompson. It is a portion of Poe's MS & I prize it. . . . I will make inquiries & try & collect material regarding Poe which may be of interest. This, I will send you.

That is very nice & kind & may lead to something.[1]

Today came letter from E. L. Didier, Baltimore, saying that, besides other things,

Mrs. Clemm was a friend of mine, *from her* I ascertained the exact day &
place of his birth. It was neither Baltimore nor Richmond. Poe's brother was
adopted by my uncle, Henry Didier. I know something about him (Henry
Poe) in connection with Greece, &c. I know the name of the lady to whom
Poe was engaged after his engagement with Mrs. Whitman was broken off;
also the lady Helen S——— & how tenderly Poe cherished her memory, &c.
. . . My grandfather's family & P's family were next door neighbors in the city
60 years ago. I have some interesting facts about his father as an amateur actor
& also an account of his marriage with Miss Arnold, an English actress—
E.A.P.'s mother. . . . my father-in-law, Col. Northrop, was a classmate of Poe's
at West Point. He has furnished me with the facts concerning Poe there &
why he left. . . . The true story of Poe's death has never been published. . . . I
have in my possession a MS poem of Poe's which has never been printed. P.
wrote it in a lady's album in this city, from which I copied it. It is dated March
17, 1829 & signed E. A. Poe. . . . I have an interesting description of P.'s lovely
young wife, V[irginia] C[lemm] . . . the exact date of her death, &c. . . . I
know (*almost certainly*) where P. was in [18]31–2–3. . . . Mrs. Clemm
furnished me with a description of his appearance, &c., &c. . . . You will
perceive that I have information about Poe of great value. I will furnish to you
including the unpublished poem alluded to above for $100:£20. E. L. Didier
(late private secretary to Chief Justice Chase). For 5 or 6 years I have been
collecting materials for a correct life of Poe.[2]

Now some of this certainly seems valuable *to me*, but Mrs. Clemm's
news I am shy of. Of Mrs. H. Stanard I am anxious to hear, but it
strikes me Mr. Didier only knows what you said to Mrs. Clemm &
published in your book. Miss Royster also we know name of (Mrs.
Shelton). Poe's father & mother may only be Stoddard over again. West
Point expulsion *cannot be shaken*—my "Memoir" makes the best of
that. Poe's death is best left alone unless Neilson Poe will speak. The
MS. poem, I fancy, is the one to E[liza] White, after changed for Mrs.
Osgood. Poe's life from Jany. 1831 to Oct. 1833 would be valuable &
might disprove the desertion story! £20 I could not afford, but must
hear what Mr. D[idier] says in his reply to what I shall write him.
English publishers won't pay much, save to one or two writers, & I
shall have to do all at my own risk. I may not get a penny for my
forthcoming 4-vol. collection! This *entre nous*. Blacks I *believe* are
honest & so I *may* get some remuneration, but little for time & energy
expended, were it a mere work-done-account, but you know that it is
not that. So you see I must only pay what is absolutely necessary.
You'll hear the result, in due course, of my correspondence with Mr.
D[idier].

And now—not farewell—but *au revoir* from your ever faithful &
affectionate friend.

John H. Ingram

1. It led to a great deal, even though Valentine had no success in inducing Mrs. Allan to mention Poe's name, much less discuss him.
2. Didier's letter to Ingram, Oct. 1, 1874, is Item 174 in the Ingram Poe Collection.

70. Sarah Helen Whitman to John H. Ingram.   Item 175

My dear Mr. Ingram,   Oct. 22, 1874

Though still suffering from the painful symptoms of which I spoke in my last letter, I cannot defer telling you that I have had an interview with Mr. Harris, the first since his return to the city. He wrote to ask if I would receive him last Saturday evening, and mindful of your request about the early poems, I consented to do so. He expressed much interest about your forthcoming work and asked many questions in relation to it. In reply to what I told him about your desire to see the copy of the 1831 edition, belonging to him, he said that I might say to you, from him, that, some time this fall he was intending to send a package of books to his London bookbinder for binding and rebinding, etc. and that he would send *with them* the copy of poems, with directions that it should be forwarded to your address. He thinks this would be the safer plan. After you have inspected the work, he suggests that you return it to the bookbinder in time to have it sent back with the other books. He thought this would probably meet your wishes, since it must be now too late for you to make use of the copy for the present edition of your work.

I forgot to tell him all that you said about Pinckney's poems, etc. but have copied out that portion of your letter for him, & will let you know what he says about it soon.

I have had but one letter from Rose, the one of which I spoke in my last to you. Her father gave me pleasant news of her. I have much to say to her & to *you*, but I must wait for the health & strength that comes not yet.

I contradicted myself when I asked you in my last letter to write your *story*, & write it *"soon"*—then, in concluding my letter, asked you to write only when "quite convenient & pleasant to you."

I shall not try to reconcile the discrepancy, which you can doubtless interpret.

I long to see your first volume, & am ever & ever your most faithful friend

                                                          Sarah H. Whitman

71. *Sarah Helen Whitman to John H. Ingram. Item 179*

My dear Mr. Ingram,   Nov. 6, 1874
   Your long & interesting letter of Oct. 13th made my heart glad, even
though it recorded an event which brought you so much sorrow. I
found it last Friday morning lying in the letter box side by side with a
letter from Rose—*dear* Rose, to whom I hoped long ago to have
written! Her letter was mailed from Paris on the 15th, & yours from
London on the 16th. I should like to send you a long quotation from
her letter, which I know would gratify you, but perhaps this would be a
breach of confidence, so I virtuously withstand the temptation, & will
only tell you that *I* was delighted with it.
   Under the head of "Foreign Literature & Notes on English
Publications," a correspondent of last Saturday's *Tribune*, G.W.S.
(Stedman, I think), introduced Messrs. Black's announcement of a new
& complete edition of Poe's works, including his hitherto unknown
writings, edited with a "Memoir," by John H. Ingram.[1] Then followed a
description of the manner in which the books were to be brought out,
etc.

   Thus will be brought together, says Messrs. Black, for the first time, the
whole of Poe's known writings. If this be accurate, & if no similar American
edition is to appear contemporaneously, the fact is a remarkable one. It is no
ordinary tribute to Poe's genius that his writings should thus first be collected
completely in a foreign country. In his genius there was no doubt something
alien to that of his own land, & even to that of any land where English is
spoken. He has always been popular with the French, who take delight in
many poems of the grotesque, & who have borrowed many a *conte
fantastique* from the Rhineland and elsewhere. Whether there be a German
edition of Poe, I don't recollect. His English publishers, aptly enough,
announce the present edition as uniform with De Quincey's works.

   Perhaps I am too suspicious, but I seem to detect, under this
Tribune notice, the crafty hand under the velvet glove. After the
treatment which Poe has received from American reviewers &
litterateurs, who can help doubting the sincerity of their cold &
qualified praises?
   Mr. Harris feels *sure* that there was an edition of the early poems
published in 1827—that he shall be able to *find* that edition—a copy of
it—& that it will be found that the Wiley & Putnam edition *is* a
verbatim copy of it. This I doubt. But I am glad to see him so zealously
interested in getting at the truth. He did, in fact, give me some cogent
reasons for thinking that the article in the *Aldine* was a conscious
misrepresentation of the truth, & that it was written with malign intent.
I asked him to write out his argument for you, & this he said he would

endeavor to do, after he had thoroughly investigated the subject & made further search for the missing edition. *This, strictly entre nous.*

Have you read Spielhagen's essay on the genius & writings of Poe? I saw it mentioned in a note to the translator's preface to his novel, *Problematic Characters*, but his essays are not to be found in our libraries.[2] The "Mr. Lyman," to whose note about the balloon matter you refer, is the Col. Lyman *Dwight* who told me of the interest felt by the German students in the writings of Poe. He told me that even those who were very imperfectly acquainted with the English language would pore over his stories with patient & exhaustless interest.

I had many things to say, but must wait for another mail.

If you should chance to be consulting the files of the New York *Tribune* in any further researches, you may find in the *Daily* for Nov. 14, 1853, a notice by Ripley of the lost volume of poems I sent you last spring & of which I will soon send you another copy. It was very well done. I sent you a copy of it in the book that was lost. The only remaining one is pasted in a volume of printed notices.

If you write to Rose, tell her that I have a thousand things to say to her & will try to get well enough to write to her soon.

I have not yet seen the copy of the *Academy* which has a paragraph about your book. It will arrive here next week, probably—it is *always* late.

And now, goodbye for tonight. I trust all will go well with you & your work. A dio.

                                                    S. H. Whitman

1. This correspondent to the *Tribune* could not have been the Stedman who later became a Poe scholar and editor, for his name was Edmund Clarence.

2. Friedrich Spielhagen (1829–1911), *Problematic Characters*, from the German, by Professor Schele DeVere (New York: Leypoldt & Holt, 1869). Spielhagen's essay must have been his "Amerikanische Lyriker: W. C. Bryant, E. A. Poe . . . ," *Vermischte Schriften*, I (Berlin: n. p., 1864), 259–320.

72. *John H. Ingram to Sarah Helen Whitman*

My very dear Friend,   10 Nov. 1874

I just send a few words to acknowledge yours dated 22nd Ulto. *re.* Mr. Harris's kind offer & to recount my usual little budget. First, let me convey my sincere thanks to Mr. Harris for promising me a sight of the 1831 edition of Poe's Works. I shall not need the copy many days & will take every care of it. If Mr. Harris wants anything done in London will you mind asking him to rely upon me—it will be a pleasure to do my best for him. I wish I could have seen the book some months ago, but, better late than never.

I am grieved to have so poor an account of your health, and shall look forward all the more eagerly for your dear letters—but don't over-exert yourself—send me a few lines at the time. I'm unwell, depressed & sad. The loss of that dear friend I have told you of has been a sad blow—often when walking the streets, or when alone, in bed at nights, the tears start to my eyes & utter dreariness comes over me. Alas! the prizes of this life are so mean, and the winners of them so much meaner, that I often wonder what is the use of striving for them—were I not goaded on by the knowledge that others rely upon *my* exertions, I feel that I could *so* gladly put my head on the pillow & pass away to "that bourne whence no traveller returns." But let me not weary you with my dreary platitudes.

Have you received either, or both, of the copies I sent you of Vol. 1 of Poe's Works? I hope, I long for & yet fear to hear your verdict. It seems that I have made so much cry about such little wool. And yet, I do believe I have succeeded in giving a different view of Poe's character to his English admirers, & that is something. Never mind the inartistic style. I have already, I believe, told how, at the last moment, this "Memoir" was patched up & strung together—how my illness had upset everything. However, if life & mind are spared we may hope that someday I shall produce a life of Edgar Poe which shall be worthy of him. I send you two copies because you may have some dear friend you would like to give one copy to. I shall also shortly send you, per Mr. Davidson, two copies of Poe's portrait, not cut down to the book size but suitable for framing. I send them unframed because of the glass &c. getting broken. What do you think of the likeness—is it good? Give me your candid opinion & *suggestions* on all points.

While I think of it—*If you do not want it*, could you let me have the slip I sent you from E. Benson's critique on Poe & Hawthorne? I *might* have a use for it some day. Don't trouble if you've not got it, or can't find it.

I enclose a review from the *Echo*—'tis only a ½ penny paper, but has a very large circulation. Will try to send also a notice from the *Civil Service Review*—a notice that may do much good. I sent you copy of the *Scotsman* & will try & get copy of the *Edinburgh Daily Review*, which had a still longer critique. You will see that they all accept my version as incontrovertible. Hope in a few days to get the leading London views of the subject.

J. Hewitt Key, who was Mathematical master at Virginia University in 1826, is alive & Head Master of London University School. He answers my inquiry, "I *do not recollect* whether he ⟨ Poe ⟩ attended my classes. . . . Dr. Blattermann has been dead many years. Mr. George

Long {Professor of Ancient Languages} is still alive and, I believe in hearty health. He lives near"———a name I cannot make out, but his London bookseller will give it.[1]

I hope you'll be able to alter your mind about deferring the new edition of *E.P. & His Critics* until after you have been translated. These things can be done so much better by oneself than by unsympathizing people. Page 27, I notice you say Mrs. Poe (Virginia) died a year (it should be quite *two* years) before "The Raven" was published.

It is a great disappointment to hear that this edition of the Works cannot be sold in United States. Black's agent in Boston says the American copyright extends first for 28 years & then to the publisher's family for 14 more years. Do you know anything of this? I'll send you some prospectuses for friends. Mr. Campbell, bookseller, Toronto, has copies. The price is little over half the American edition—only about 5 dollars.

When last I heard of Miss Peckham, she was about to move to more convenient quarters.

Kindly distribute the prospectuses. I will send you the various English reviews of the book & shall be glad to see any American ones. I shall see that in the *Home Journal*. I shall be anxious for your private opinion, but don't tire yourself to write a long letter. My correspondence on the matter of Poe's works is truly enormous. I am now expecting to hear from the South again.

How is your sister, Miss Power? Does she suffer still from the effects of the ivy poison?

Did I not once tell you that two branches of the Poë family still held landed estates in Ireland? I was informed a few days ago that one of the family bore the name of "Edgar."

I am anxious to hear Swinburne's idea of my "Memoir."

I fancy we shall *unearth* some real information in the South some of these days. If I live I shall make a pilgrimage to America to gather information.

For two Saturdays I have been making a pilgrimage over some spots sacred to me—the places I had last visited with my late friend, and last Saturday I took his three dear little boys with me to the Zoological Gardens.

Harry Curwen, who edited Hotten's selection from Poe, has written me some nice letters. He has a vol. in the press, *Sorrow & Song*, taking Poe, Petöfi, Munger, &c. as representatives. I'm trying to *convert* him to our views. He never liked Griswold's, but does not think my "Memoir" will quite convert him, but we shall see. I've sent him a copy. Miss Fanny Kortright, a friend of the Hawthorne's, & *who knows Mrs. E[llet]*, has had a terrible idea of Poe, but I think she's coming over. Oh, my dear, dear friend, thanks to your kindness, more than anything else, I shall prove my case. Never mind if I am a little "passionate," there will be time to cool down hereafter, when, in the coming times, a noble name shall have been rescued from infamy, and replaced in its honorable niche in the Temple of Fame by the combined action of one who proudly & affectionately presumes to couple his name with yours, and by you. Ever my friend I shall hold you to be—ever be the friend of yours in all sympathy.

John H. Ingram

P.S. Do you know anything of a Mrs. Nichols?—now in England, and professing to have been a friend of Poe's & desirous of seeing justice done to his character. I'm going to write to her.[2]

J.H.I.

1. J. Hewitt Key's letter to Ingram of Nov. 6, 1874, is Item 180 in the Ingram Poe Collection.

2. This was Mrs. Mary Sargeant Neal Gove Nichols (1810–1884), author, water-cure physician, mesmerist, spiritualist, Fourierist, advocate of temperance and dress reform, and a vegetarian, who knew the Poes in Fordham in 1847. Poe wrote about her in his "Literati" in 1846. She married for the second time in 1848, and she and her husband, Thomas Low Nichols (1815–1901), left America for England at the beginning of the Civil War.

73. *Sarah Helen Whitman to John H. Ingram.*   *Item 181*

My dear Mr. Ingram,   Nov. 13, 1874
    I have just received The Book, and though I have in consequence of many interruptions only had time to give a hurried reading to the "Memoir," I must write you a word of *heartfelt congratulations.*
    You have done *nobly*—far, far better than I had dared to hope, writing as you do under so many difficulties, so much uncertainty as to dates & details. The story is told by you with such apparent ease, such simple sincerity of narrative, that it cannot fail to carry with it all the refutation that is needed of Griswold's fabrications.
    More hereafter.
    In the interval since I received it, one of my friends who has been greatly interested in your work, Mr. Arnold, the artist who painted the picture [of Mrs. Whitman] from which my photograph was taken, came in just as I was opening the volume, and expressed great admiration of the portrait. Thought it the *best* he had ever seen of Poe, and pronounced the character of the head & the execution of the portrait alike excellent. It is true that he had never *seen* Poe, but he thought it an "exquisite" ideal characterization.

Senator Anthony, also, who happened to cut the string & take the book out of its wrappings for me, turned at once to the portrait & pronounced it "good, very good." And he *knew Poe*. He said he must have the book.

I have only time to send this off before the mail closes. It must go by tomorrow's steamer.

I will write again in a day or two. The protrait is much more like E.A.P. than the photograph from which it was taken. How could that happen?

But good night & au revoir

Sarah H. Whitman

The engraving of the cottage is charming.

I am so glad that you had the portrait taken from *this* copy, rather than the one which I call the *Ultima Thule* one.

You have told the story of Poe's life in a manner which displays fine tact & temper, as well as having made it very interesting.

But goodbye for the present.

74. *Sarah Helen Whitman to John H. Ingram.   Item 182*

My dear Mr. Ingram,   Nov. 24, 1874

Since I wrote you on the 13th to acknowledge the receipt of your beautiful book, I have received the copy of *The Scotsman* which you sent me, & think its notice in many respects admirably just & candid, yet it is not a little singular that while O'Connor regarded your papers in the *Mirror* as too lenient toward Griswold, the wary "Scotsman" thinks you too passionate in your defense of Poe! I do not agree with him. I think the general tone & temper of your "Memoir" is not less ingenious & impartial than it is brave & chivalrous. Strange that after the lapse of 25 years a young Englishman should be the first to present to the world an earnest protest & an effectual refutation of many of the disgraceful charges with which the unfortunate poet's memory has been relentlessly stained & clouded!

I have a few criticisms to make & a few changes to suggest, in case the "Memoir" should be reprinted. They are not very important, however. I dare say I am responsible for the mistake—if it is a mistake—about the burning of Davidson's papers mentioned in the Preface. It was at the burning of *Columbia*, & not the "Siege of Charleston," that the papers were destroyed, as I think, unless *he* told you that it was Charleston.

Pabodie was not "eminent" as a lawyer. He studied law, had a law office, & was a justice of the peace for several years, but he had an utter aversion to business, &, not being dependent on the profession for a support, soon abandoned it. He was a fine *belles lettres* critic, & has written a few very fine poems. Some of his patriotic & occasional odes have been quoted as among the noblest in our American literature. He was rather *super*fine in dress and manners, witty & sarcastic in conversation, very sensitive to the world's praise & blame, & *very* indolent. This will not raise an objection to *your* characterization of him in any other place than Providence.

I object to the "beautiful young widow" & to the "fierce flame," etc. I suppose Mrs. Moulton's notice of one of my poems in her "Literary Notes" for the *Tribune* (a notice in which she referred to my book about Poe) is responsible for that expression, *n'est ce pas?*[1]

Singularly enough, Mrs. Moulton's reference to this book came out almost simultaneously with Stoddard's article about Poe in *Harper's Magazine* for Sept. 1872. I wrote to her to ask her if she knew of Stoddard's article when she spoke of my book in the *Tribune.* She replied that she did *not* but was strongly moved to speak of it as she did, "thinking it but just to me that the fact should be recognized"! *I* think it was "a supernatural soliciting" that moved her to do it.

I am glad that you did not speak of Stoddard in your "Memoir." It was better than any condemnation.

I am writing under *great trials & difficulties from within & without.* My sister's health alarms me. She has been for some weeks nervous & restless beyond anything I have seen in her for years. Do not speak of this in writing to me. I must close abruptly.

May heaven bless & guide you. Affectionately & gratefully,

S.H.W.

1. This was Mrs. Louise Chandler Moulton (1835–1908), novelist, poet, and journalist, who wrote literary reviews and notices for the New York *Tribune* from 1870 to 1876. After Mrs. Whitman's death, Mrs. Moulton wrote a long biographical-critical article about her and her work that was published in the London *Athenaeum,* Dec. 21, 1878.

75. *John H. Ingram to Sarah Helen Whitman*

My very dear friend,   27 Nov. 1874

Your kind acknowledgement of the book is to hand—it is, I presume, the copy I have written in—the other copy will doubtless have reached you a day or two later. Any friends wanting copies, must either get them from England, or from Mr. Campbell, bookseller, Toronto.

I have some portraits of Poe—*i.e.*, the engraving not cut to book size:

two for you, one for Mr. Davidson, & one for Virginia University—but I am undecided how best to send them—by bookpost, or how. I shall hear on Monday.

The vol. Mr. Harris is going to lend me is not yet arrived. I am anxious to see it to confirm my paper in the *Gentleman's Magazine* which was partially founded on a communication to the *Philobiblion*, numbers 2, or 4, published at New York, in 1862—small 4°. This information may be interesting to Mr. Harris. Should he ever get a duplicate or *spare* copy of any of Poe's early writings, prose or verse, I should like to purchase, if anyway reasonable.

I am positive that *some* of Poe's early verses were *not verbatim* from an early edition. I should be glad to hear the 1827 edition established as a fact, having long sought to find out, but the early pieces went through various corrections. Several appeared in the *S. Lit. Messenger* in an earlier & inferior state to that of the 1845 edition.

As regards Miss Peckham, I wrote to her, at her old address, Rue Bonaparte, end of last month & have had no reply—how busy she must be!

That paragraph in the *Tribune* signed "G.W.S." about [the] English edition of Poe was the act of an envious or malicious creature. *You* know that Poe is popular in America (at all events his writings are) & in England he is immensely popular, as the reviews of this new edition testify. Certainly he is popular in France, but that does not prove his genius alien to English-speaking lands. His poetry is especially English but his fame is universal. France *borrows* very little literature from the Rhineland, but is ofttimes borrowed. The allusion to the *contes fantastiques* is to Hoffmann, who was anything but a Rhinelander. There are many German editions of Poe's poems & tales. Will you tell Mr. Harris, please, what I say about the early poems?

I have not seen Spielhagen's essay on E. Poe—but will see it. His *Problematical Characters* was extensively reviewed. I wish you could republish *E.P. & His Critics*—it would take well over *here* just now.

You had a reprint of the *Academy* notice of my *papers*—they have not noticed the book *yet* through a muddle of the editor. He, it seems, arranged with three different people (this *entre nous*—all have written their papers & two (I know) have had them back—hence a muddle & a delay. 'Tis a pity, because it is sure to be a valuable critique. I thought to send you copies of all the reviews but cannot get them all myself, & it does not matter—they are all (about one hundred will appear!) extremely good & all to the same tune—not a doubt as to my theory being correct.

I send you the *Standard* (which is about the shortest & most lukewarm) notice because it mentions your name. The *Morning Advertiser*, because, I fancy, Sawyer (editor of the late *Mirror*) wrote it.

I don't know who writes any of them. And will send *Dundee Advertiser* because it must be written by Gilfillan! & he makes the *amende honorable*! Read it. Some papers acknowledge Poe as unapproachably the chief author of America & others waver between Poe & Hawthorne. No one disputes Poe's supremacy as the first poet of America.

In my last I spoke of Mrs. Gove Nichols—she is coming up to town before Christmas & has promised me a chat. She knew the Poes well—knows you—& has met Mrs. Ellet in society. Read enclosed & *burn* it—don't return it. "M.L.S.," to whom the poem by Poe, is now the wife of Dr. Roland Houghton, who has been associated with Revd. John Hopkins in editing a church (Episcopal) paper in New York. *She* is likely to have many souvenirs of E. A. Poe. . . . Graham *is* dead. Mrs. Hale, once editor of *Godey's Lady's Book*, is a likely person to know of Poe in Philadelphia. Of Mrs. Clemm & her goodness & fidelity to Poe I will tell you when I see you—Mrs. Nichols says thus. Her reminiscences will be delightful. Do you know the address[es] of the people she mentions? Perhaps Mrs. Nichols may know herself.

I'm so pleased you like the book. I've been quite nervous about it. So much cry, so little wool—but you know how it was strung together—by *it*, I mean the "Memoir." *We* shall live, I hope, to see something better, however. I'm glad you like the portrait. Blacks wanted it more idealized. I like it as it is.

You do not say whether you are better. I sincerely trust so—& your sister too—is she?

Can you get me a copy *without much trouble* of Griswold's letter to Mr. Pabodie? I think you once said you could do so. Can you say where Poe stayed in Providence? Was it at Earl's Hotel? This is not of much consequence. You will see from my "Memoir" how much I have still to learn about my hero—his early life especially. But someone—doubtless Neilson Poe—stifles inquiry at Baltimore. N[eilson] P[oe] tells everybody who applies to him that he will write & has written to me, but never a letter can I get from him. This morning, to my pleased surprise, a very nice long letter from Miss Peckham, who seems cheerful & industrious. The book—Vol. 1—the publishers tell me is going off very well. I enclose prospectus *for your* friends. Will you distribute these? It will be cheaper from Toronto than from Edinburgh.

Once upon a time you were going to copy other letters of Poe for me. You know that I shall be glad to see such, but do not attempt to do it unless you feel quite able. I trust the cold weather will not affect you badly: it has turned quite winterly. And now, until our next meeting, ever faithfully am I yours,

John H. Ingram

My dear Mrs. Whitman,   30 Nov. 1874
I reopen my letter to add a few words. On Saturday (28th) a very
good review of Vol. 1 in the *Spectator*, a very high class publication.
Saw Mrs. Lewis, who has agreed to lend her portrait—a daguerreotype
taken 3 months before his death—of Poe to be engraved for Vol. iv.
This will be an acquisition. Vol. ii not yet to hand.

Saw on same day at British Museum a little vol. I had, strangely,
long overlooked—a translation of some of Poe's tales into *Spanish*,
with a critical biographical essay by translator. This volume is the *first*
of a series of Spanish & Foreign books of fame & the publisher's
prospectus says, "We cannot commence this library better than by a
vol. of Edgar Poe's works—his fame being *universal*," &c. I shall try to
get a copy of the book but fear 'tis out of print now—'twas published in
1858.

This morning I have received a letter from Mrs. Gove Nichols who
says she will not spare any trouble to assist me, as *you* approve of my
labours. She speaks in the highest terms of Mrs. Clemm's devotion to
her nephew. She will be in town soon & give me all information in her
power. "M.L.S." was *Mrs. Shew*—she was very good to the Poes
during Virginia's last illness. Mrs. Nichols introduced Poe to her. She
does not know her present address. John Brougham, who was very
intimate with Burton, she thinks might help us. Also Mrs. Botta (Miss
Lynch)—do you think Mrs. Botta could give you any more information,
or *copies* of any letters from Poe?

Today I have also received a *most interesting* letter from Dr. Hand
Browne & a copy of his paper on *Eureka*, &c. published in the *New
Eclectic* magazine.[1] I have not had time to read the essay, but it seems
to coincide strangely, what I've seen of it, with the Spanish essay,
which dwells strongly upon Poe's scientific attainments. This Spanish
article I shall translate—it is so good & favourable. Dr. Browne
encloses copy of a letter from John Neal enclosing short copy of one of
Poe's notes of no great value. In a future letter I shall quote much of
Dr. Browne's letter. He hopes to get much information from Neilson
Poe—who is away just now from Baltimore—& knows *his* son well.
The latter *declares Poe was born in Boston* & alludes to Poe's own
declaration—*vide* Griswold's quotation from *Broadway Journal*—over
the Boston Lyceum affair. Poe was "cooped," he [Browne] reiterates, &
drugged.

Mr. Neal's evidence would seem to support the idea of an 1827
edition of poems.

Mr. Gill has called on Dr. Browne who says of him (Mr. Gill), "I
doubt whether he knows anything of value." Mrs. Oakes Smith is
spoken of as having been a friend of Poe's, & others, whom I shall now

write to.[2] The key to all these mysteries will yet be found by yours ever & aye,

John H. Ingram

1. William Hand Browne, "Poe's 'Eureka' and Recent Scientific Speculations," *New Eclectic*, 5 (Aug. 1869), 190–99.

2. Mrs. Elizabeth Oakes Prince Smith (1806–1893), author, lecturer, and reformer, married the American humorist Seba Smith in 1823. Her letters to Ingram and Mrs. Whitman, her personality, and her articles about Edgar Poe will figure largely in the correspondence ahead, with few of the remarks being complimentary.

76. *Sarah Helen Whitman to John H. Ingram.* Item 186

My dear Mr. Ingram,   Nov. 30, 1874

Since the mailing of my last letter (which I had not time even to direct to you, having hastily written the last lines & entrusted it to a friend to direct & forward), I have been "in a sea of troubles." My sister's state of mind has been so restless, so excitable, & so *exigent* that I have been utterly absorbed & engrossed by it. Yet, singularly enough, as often happens when great demands are made upon our powers of endurance, my strength & health have improved under this season of trial. I told you in my last letter that I had received your beautiful book & the notice in the *Scotsman*, which I greatly liked. Mr. Harris, who read the notice, thought it very ably & judiciously written. My sister too was very much pleased with it, as with the portion of your "Memoir" which she has read. She says it presents Poe's character in a very interesting light. Her opinions & judgments, when in a healthy & normal state of mind, are always just & valuable, but she is subject to exaggerated & causeless antipathies, expecially in her feelings & moods about Poe. Do not allude to anything I may have said on this subject or on the subject of her health, or rather her mental moods. You are mistaken in thinking that she, too, suffered from the poison of the ivy.

On Friday the 27th I received your letter of Nov. 10th containing some noticeable words from the *Echo*. You speak of having sent *two* copies of the book. I have received but *one*. Were they sent at the same time? You also speak of having sent me, through Mr. Davidson, some copies of the engraved photograph. I have not yet received them, nor have I heard from Mr. Davidson for a long time. I shall try to write to him tomorrow, if things go well with me at home. On Saturday I received a copy of the *Home Journal* of November 18, containing a notice of your book, brief but appreciative, introductory to the quotation of your Preface, which was given in full, I think. The paper was mailed to me from the St. James Hotel, New York, by my friend G. Lyman Dwight, who, with his wife, sailed from that city for Nassau on the 27th. He will spend the winter there for his health, which has been rapidly failing for the last two months.

I dined with Mr. & Mrs. Harris on the 27th, in company with Hon. John R. Bartlett, a brother-in-law of Senator Anthony, who feels greatly interested in your literary work & regrets that your defence of Poe cannot be sold in the United States, in connection with the edition which you are bringing out.[1] Mr. Bartlett knew Poe in New York. They lived in the same street during some portion of Poe's residence in the city. Mr. Bartlett was then a partner in the firm of Bartlett & Wellford, booksellers & publishers. Poe was often in their bookstore, & (as Mr. Bartlett tells me) held long conversations on literary subjects with Wellford, with whom he was on terms of familiar intercourse. Mrs. Osgood was an intimate friend of the Bartletts, & Poe often visited them while she was staying with them. Mr. Bartlett has never seen him inspired by any more dangerous stimulant than strong coffee, of which he was very fond & of which [he] drank freely. MacIntosh says that the measure of a man's *brain* is the amount of coffee he can drink with impunity.

Dec. 4

I was prevented, my dear Mr. Ingram, from sending the lines written on the 30th of November by unavoidable delays & interruptions. To return to your letter of Nov. 10. You say you long, yet *fear*, to hear my verdict about the book. You have no cause to fear *any*one's verdict. You have done what no other, with the present known resources for a reliable "Memoir" of Poe's life, *could* or *would* have done. I say this deliberately & with a profound conviction of its truth. You have gathered together and carefully collated every, at present, available fragment of evidence which could serve to free his memory from the unmerited reproach which has rested on it. Doubtless the mystery which enshrouds his life will never be wholly removed. It would hardly be in keeping with the mystery of his rare & complex nature that it should be. But, so far as may be, you have placed him before the world as he is. Your story of Poe's life is told not in the spirit of passionate partisanship, but of a generous & appreciative sympathy, tenderly regardful of the wrongs & sorrows sustained by the great genius whose creations have electrified & enthralled so many hearts.

I see that you have changed the date of Poe's birth to *Jan.* 19. This accords with what he told me as to the day of the month & the *month* itself. He never told me the year. Perhaps he did not himself know.

I hope that a notice of your book will soon appear in the Providence *Journal*. I shall send you copies.

Mr. Harris, in a somewhat hasty reading of your "Memoir," which I lent him for an evening (he is to have it again), seemed to think with the writer of the notice in the *Echo* that there was perhaps a little too much space given to an elucidation of Griswold's perfidies. I do not agree with him, since no new & true estimate of Poe's character can be established until this false foundation be effectually undermined. Again, Mr. H[arris], as a book collector, objected to the statement that Poe had *mistaken* the name of Mrs. Lewis in the sonnet inscribed to her. He, having, as he said, in his possession an edition of her poems published under that name. But, probably, very few of your readers will have seen this edition.

Mr. Harris was under the impression that two copies of Pinckney's poems were in his possession, and told me that if it proved so, that you should have one of them. But as yet he has been unable to find the duplicate copy. He will soon send you the copy of Poe's poems of which I told you. You ask if I can send you the portion of Eugene Benson's article which was republished in a New York paper & which you sent to me. I though I returned it to you when I copied for you a portion of my copy in the *Galaxy*. But I will soon send you my copy, & then you can have it all together.

With so many things unsaid which I *most* wished to say, I must wait a few days longer to say them, & now, *good night.*

S.H.W.

I have not written one word to dear Rose since I received the enclosed letter. I hope I commit no deadly breach of trust in sending you her letter. I want you to know how well she likes you. Tell her I love her & will write soon, but don't tell her I sent you her letter. You may send me back the part about yourself some day & destroy the rest.

1. John Russell Bartlett (1805–1886) was a distinguished Rhode Island author, bibliographer, and state official.

77. *Sarah Helen Whitman to John H. Ingram.* Item 188

My dear Mr. Ingram, Dec. 13, 1874

Yesterday I received your very interesting letter of November 27th & must try to send you a few words in reply by tonight's mail. The papers I read with interest & will refer to hereafter. I will try at least to answer some of your questions tonight. I doubt if Mrs. Botta could furnish you with copies of Poe's notes or letters. She applied to *me*, you know, for an autograph (even a few words) or a signature, simply, for the volume of autographs she has so long been industriously collecting. She *may*, however, give you some interesting information concerning him.

Mrs. Oakes Smith has written a sketch of him which was published in some periodical edited by herself & her son, Appleton Oakes Smith.[1] I believe I have a copy of it, as *re*published in the *Journal of Health*. If I have, I will send it to you. It adds nothing to the *facts*, & introduces some apocryphal conversations which Poe is said to have held with her in relation to the influence which I might have had on him had he known me & herself earlier. I feel *confident* that no such conversation ever took place. Mrs. Smith is very imaginative &, I think, apt to rely on her imagination for her facts. With this exception, there is *much* to love & praise & admire in her. I think in writing of Poe as she did she suffered her fancy to take the place of her memory. I have been looking for her article since I wrote the last lines, but cannot find it. She will send it to you, I doubt not, if you write to her. I will tell you more about our relations another time. I believe she felt hurt with me about a letter which she asked me to write in behalf of her son Appleton, who was charged with some state offense, as engaging in the slave trade. I said to the authorities what she *wished* me to say, with the exception of giving my own testimony to his character as an honorable gentleman, which *I could not do* with truth, as my acquaintance with him was very slight. After that our correspondence, which had been friendly & affectionate (for I sincerely loved her), ceased altogether. I have passed many happy hours in her society. We visited Niagara Falls together, & in 1868 we rode together to the top of Mount Washington on the mountain ponies then used in that perilous ascent.

Speaking of your book with Mr. Bartlett, he gave me for you the address of Mr. Wellford, his former partner of whom I wrote in my last letter. He thinks Mr. Wellford might give you some valuable information in relation to Poe's career in New York.

Mr. Harris is now in New York & intends making a final inquest for the 1827 edition of poems, which he *knows* by authentic evidence *was actually published*. Of this more hereafter.

Don't speak to anyone of what I have said about my "imaginative" friend, E.O.S.

I well remember Mrs. Nichols and her book, *Mary Lindsey*—I think that was the name of the book—in which she speaks of E.A.P.[2] I have not seen her since she came to see me in the winter of 1846, with my eccentric friend, Dr. Max Edgeworth Lazarus.[3] Mrs. Gove was a fine clairvoyant and diagnosed diseases with an almost infallible intuition. She was at that time at the head of a water-cure establishment in New

York. I was greatly impressed by her intuitive or clairvoyant power, & I afterward read her book entitled *Mary Lindsey* with great interest as an autobiographical history. I think she may have it in her power to tell you much of Poe. I am very glad to know what you tell me about the sonnet to M.L.S. having been addressed to Mrs. Houghton. Mrs. Nichols can tell you something about Anna Blackwell, the lady who spent two or three weeks with Mrs. Clemm at Fordham.

How do you think the letters sent to me from Charlottesville came to give the date as Feb. 19, instead of January! Did Poe write it Jan. 19, or did they find it out & alter the record?

Have you seen Stoddard's Preface to the new edition of the poems? It is not altered for the better—certainly not in spirit, & a review of it in the New York *Tribune* is full of venom. Gill in the *Lotus Leaves* has done better than I anticipated. Have you seen it?[4] The portrait prefixed to Stoddard's vol. is very bad—a gross caricature—not so well executed as the one in *Harper's*. Dr. A. H. Okie, who met Poe at my mother's house on the day when he was so much excited, the period to which he refers in the facsimile you have given, said to me yesterday, on seeing the portrait in your book, "It is very good, the best I have seen, but a little rigid & not *so handsome* as Poe was." Yet Dr. Okie saw him when but partially recovered from that "wild weird dream," that "clime, out of space, out of time" which Poe has so well described.

Poe stayed on different visits to the city at *different* hotels. The last was the Earl House. Both have been demolished for new buildings a number of years ago. Who is Dr. Hand Browne? I shall look for the *Academy's* notice. The *Spectator's* I shall not be likely to see.

I must leave much unsaid two or three days longer, when I shall write again. "Great is the truth & it shall prevail." May heaven bless & prosper you. You will see that I am writing in desperate hurry, & overlook all.

Ever your friend.

S.H.W.

1. This is probably inaccurate. The four sons of Seba and Elizabeth Oakes Smith bought *Emerson's United States Magazine* in 1858, changing its name to *Emerson's Magazine and Putnam's Monthly*; Appleton Oakes Smith became publisher, Seba Smith, editor. Financial difficulties forced them to suspend publication, but they started again in January 1859 with the *Great Republic Monthly*, Seba and Elizabeth Oakes Smith listed as editors. That publication lasted only until November 1859.

2. The name of Mrs. Nichols' book was *Mary Lyndon, or Revelations of a Life* (New York: Stringer and Townsend, 1855).

3. Dr. Max Edgeworth Lazarus was author of books on hygiene, Zoroastrianism, and psychology.

4. William Fearing Gill, "Edgar Allan Poe," in *Lotos Leaves* (Boston: W. F. Gill and Co., 1875), pp. 279–306.

78. *John H. Ingram to Sarah Helen Whitman*

My dear Mrs. Whitman,   16 Dec. 1874
   I have to acknowledge your dear letters of the 24th Ulto. & of the 30th, & will reply firstly to the various items thereof.[1] *Vide Scotsman* critique—he is not the only one who deems me to have been dispassionate. See *Daily Review* & *Echo*. *Standard* thinks it was not necessary for Mr. Ingram to criticise Poe's foibles! But all—great & small—speak well of Poe & of his biographer. I send you Gilfillan's *wonderful* critique, part II. You'll see he has not omitted you.
   As regards your remarks & notes on my "Memoir"—do please continue them & "pitch into me" about something or I shall think you are not pleased. There must be so much *you* could suggest for revision, omission, or addition. I'll look up place of burning of Mr. Davidson's library. I fancied he said "Charleston." Pabodie's designation shall be amended. The "beautiful young widow" and the "fierce flame" shall be revised—but Mrs. Moulton is innocent thereof. I alone am guilty. Stoddard I studiously avoided mention of. I am armed cap-a-pie for him.
   Mrs. Gove Nichols expects to be in town soon & will tell me much. She thinks Mrs. Clemm was Poe's guardian angel. At her advice I have written to Mrs. Oakes Smith & "M.L.S" now Mrs. Houghton.
   The pictures have not yet gone off. I cannot learn how best to send & thought of sending copy of Mrs. Lewis's daguerreotype with it but, through no fault of hers, that has been delayed. Perhaps both portraits can go together in a few days.
   I wish Mr. Harris had lent me his book a fortnight ago—Poe's poems. H. Curwen, who edited Hotten's *E. Poe*, has just published 2 vols. of biographical sketches, *viz*. Henri Munger, "Novalis," Petöfi, Balzac, Chénier, & Poe—called *Song & Sorrow*—he has sent me copy for review. He repeats most of Griswold's slanders saying, in preface:

Nothing I have attempted in literature yet has been more painful to me than the composition of my "Life of Poe." I began with a thorough determination to vindicate Poe from the aspersions that Dr. Griswold had so cruelly cast upon his memory. . . . That Dr. Griswold was wrong throughout in feeling & bias is self evident from any one page of his biography. Still, after sifting every item of evidence *I* could lay hands on, for Poe and against Poe, my present monograph has turned out very differently from what I had hoped the facts would have justified me in putting forth. ⟨ And again: ⟩ Mr. John H. Ingram has supplied me with many new *data*, derived from America, as to the life of Poe; but these, with two exceptions, arrived too late for insertion. I regret this the less, as his complete edition of Poe's *Works*, with a new "*Memoir*," will be issued almost as soon as my vols. ⟨ My Vols. 1 & 2 published first ⟩. Still *I fear that no data Mr. Ingram could* supply would materially alter my estimate of Poe's character.

I hope to review the books for the *Academy*.[2] There is nothing new in Curwen's account of Poe but two poems from the 1829 edition—"To ———" and "Spirits of the Dead." If I had Mr. Harris's book I could see if they were therein.

Widdleton, copyright publisher of Poe, has just published *Poe's Poems—new edition with poems not in former editions*—also a "New Life" by R. H. Stoddard. This, says Davidson, is a *recast* of the *Harper's Monthly* Life. I have asked Davidson to get me a copy of the poems *instanter*![3] They are doubtless the juvenile verses. Are we not unearthing the past! Widdleton, *entre [page cut]*

[*On verso:*] therefore, Griswold does *intentionally* occupy much space on my canvas. But my next life of Poe shall rectify this.

Poe *did* mistake the name of Mrs. Lewis. She shewed me his letter— *vide* the "Memoir"—& explained how it was so many thought her name "Sarah A." 'Twas a method of signing "Estella A." like "S—— A." But I should *much like (for a grave reason)* to know the book Mr. Harris saw "S. A. Lewis" appended to.

[*Page cut*] this digression, unexpectedly drawn forth for the first time in my life, in the vague hope of that sympathy which cannot be given, I will reclose the adamantine clasps upon that cavity supposed to contain that portion of our anatomy called "the heart," and return to the unsentimental, or rather the sentimental.

Mr. Morison of Baltimore has been stirring up Neilson Poe on my behalf & I give you the extraction of his communication. He says that N. Poe is very indolent, hence his silence to me & to the world. N.P. married Virginia Clemm's half sister! Mr. Morison's chief information is from two long letters of Mrs. Clemm to N. Poe in 1860. In one she says, "Griswold offered $500 for a certain literary lady's correspondence with Eddie," & fearing poverty might induce her to sell it, she destroyed it! Who was the literary lady? Surely not Mrs. Osgood. Neilson Poe, I *think*, will send me his recollections of Edgar, of whom he states, "a single glass of wine would set his brain on fire & that his only safety was in total abstinence." Mrs. Clemm's first letter says, "Eddie was born in Boston, Mass. on the 19th Jany. 1811. ⊰ should be 1809? This is also confirmed by other evidence. ⊱ When he was 5 weeks old he was taken to Baltimore by his parents & remained there for 6 months." Then to Richmond, Va. where his mother died when Eddie was 2 years old. Then adopted by Mr. Allan & put to Academy at Richmond till he was 7. Mr. & Mrs. A[llan] brought him to England & lived in Russell Square. Eddie went to Dr. Bransby's, but every Friday till Monday spent with his adopted parents! Home to America when only 14—University—West Point. Mrs. C[lemm] often trips, however, as you know. She declares that Poe left W. Point voluntarily, but seems to confuse it with Charlottesville. He never went to Greece or Russia, (but his brother Wm. did to Russia, *on dit*), and Mrs. C[lemm] said that Edgar laughed at the story but did not care to contradict it. She then bears most loving testimony to his goodness—in my next *in extenso*.

Mr. Morison then comments, says Neilson Poe ordered the *destroyed* monument for Edgar's grave, & not being rich, has not ordered another, but one is *going* to be erected. Neilson was born in the same year as Edgar.

Second letter, Mrs. C[lemm] repeats how *faithful* Edgar was to Virginia. Private letters, says Mrs. C[lemm], "I burned as I knew so well Eddie wished"—the *literary* letters confided to Griswold, "he never would return & I cannot get them from his executors. They were all from the most celebrated men living." Poe's letters to her she'd given away. The last two of Poe's autographs she gave to Longfellow, "for he is one of my best friends & constantly writes to me. I spent some time at his house in Cambridge."

In P.S. Mrs. Clemm says to N[eilson] Poe, "Will you get a little book by S. Helen Whitman called *E.P. & His C.*? She knew him *well* & contradicts the assertion made by Griswold relative to herself." Mr. Morrison asserts that Mrs. C[lemm] was very indignant at the story of Poe & the 2nd Mrs. Allan & declared it vilely false. Mrs. Allan lives still in Richmond, Va., & is still bitter against Poe. Virginia was only 14 when first married to Edgar—they were *again married* when she was 15. Name & place specified—Christ's Church, Baltimore, by Revd. (*now* Bishop) John Johns. Those are the chief items, but in my next will try to give Mrs. C[lemm's] letters *in extenso*.

And now—forgive trying your eyes (& your heart? for you feel for me?) & believe me ever *yours*,

John H. Ingram

P.S. Open this just to wish you & Miss Power a happy New Year.

J.H.I.

1. Three-fourths of pages three and four are cut off.
2. Ingram did review Curwen's *Sorrow and Song*. His review was published in March 1875; it is reprinted here on pages 265–66.
3. W. J. Widdleton, New York, brought out Stoddard's new edition of Poe's poems in 1875, with a notation that the book was printed in Great Britain.

79.   *John H. Ingram to Sarah Helen Whitman*

My dear Friend,   28 Dec. 1874
First and foremost do not notice any nonsense which I talked about

in my last letter. And now to reply to your *ever* welcome communication of the 13th Instant.

In the first place, never mind commenting on any of the notices of my "Memoir" I sent you, because it is wasting *your* powers—99 out of 100 reviews are not worth preserving—are written either by friends or foes &, in either case are unreliable—the latter *may* be the better as sometimes they detect a flaw in one's armour, and by pointing it out, teach us how to make all safe.

Some few of the higher class publications have spoken out, and one—the *Saturday Review*—has "pitched into" me slightly—not very severely, however, especially for a journal that lives by paradoxical onslaughts. The *Examiner* has a critique by E. W. Gosse, a young poet & follower of Swinburne—he at once consigns Griswold to the depths of Inferno and your humble servant to Paradise, &c. Probably the *Saturday Sneerer* will prove a more *profitable* paper for me than the other.

I enclose you a cutting from a Scotch paper & sent you the conclusion of Gilfillan's rhapsody. I send you also a prospectus with a few extracts but, as I shall have the best extracts reprinted, you must please wait for any more unless I see aught to interest you specially.[1]

Mrs. Botta may not have letters, but might give something new, or direct to something fresh. Mrs. E. O. Smith I had written to ere yours arrived—many thanks for your useful hints, however. I will try & look up Mr. Wellford, but I have so many channels now open that I can scarcely keep even with them all. Still I do not wish to lose a single chance.

I shall be glad to see the 1831 edition of Mr. Harris. The 1829 edition is in Peabody Institute, Baltimore, & contains some more suppressed poetry—one entire new poem which I will send you copy of. It has just been reprinted in a new book here, *Sorrow & Song*, by Henry Curwen who edited Hotten's ed. of Poe—Mr. Curwen's "Memoir" of Poe repeats all the old lies with a few new exaggerations of his own. I shall review it. In this "Memoir" you are—amongst other qualifications—"one of the wealthiest women" in New England, &c.

I fancy the 1827 vol. must be a very little book. The 1829 vol. only contains 71 pages. Stoddard, I fancy, has some of the suppressed verse in his book.

I have seen some other notices besides the one you send, but they are the old old story. As soon as my "Memoir" gets known in America, Stoddard will be literally "snuffed out."

I am looking forwards to see [*sic*] Mrs. Gove Nichols. M. L. S(hew) was the friend who provided the grave clothes for Mrs. Poe—*not* Mrs. Lewis. Gill's notice I have not seen. I do not place much reliance upon his *steady* perseverance, but would help him for the sake of the good cause. The birth was Jany. 19th, in Charlottesville record as you have seen, & which I think I can *now* prove. Stoddard has followed your copy, as I did. Boston *was* the birthplace, during the winter engagement of his parents at the Theatre. This will all be proved!

While I think of it, did you get your duplicate Vol. 1 & two copies of Vol. ii? I desired Blacks to forward same, but they have muddled the book copies awfully. I hope you have, but you do not say so.

In Jany. or March—*entre nous*—your New York *International* will, I presume, publish my native "Memoir" of Poe.

As regards portraits of Poe, I hoped Blacks would engrave Mrs. Lewis's fine one for Vol. iv. 'Tis in their hands but, I fear, too late. If so, we must content ourselves with photo. copies. Mr. Davidson, who has been most kind, has today sent me official copies of the trial of Cadet E. A. Poe for the West Point affair.[2] He was tried & convicted for disobedience of orders & "gross neglect" of duties beyond all dispute—but his gross neglect consisted not in refusal but neglect to attend church & other parades, & apparently, in being bullied by boys—there is nothing a liberal person can construe into evil. *Eureka!* shall be our motto.

Mr. Valentine has written again from Richmond—he is trying hard to help me. He has met a Dr. Ambler, who was a playmate & fellow swimmer with Poe. Dr. Ambler refers Mr. V[alentine] to another party who can give information "about a debating society on which Poe wrote a satire when quite a child," &c. Dr. A[mbler] will send his recollections of Poe—he knew Ebenezer Burling, Poe's friend. Mr. V[alentine] has received a letter from Mrs. Shelton (née Royster) in which she "regrets that she is not prepared to give *any* information in regard to Mr. Poe's early life," but Mr. V[alentine] will try her again. Mr. Valentine has a "life-size crayon head of Poe from a daguerreotype of Poe which" is supposed to have belonged to Mr. J. R. Thompson.

If ever you get any clue to *the precise date* of the explanation of the "Conchology" story in the *Home Journal*, let me know—as you will see, my explanation in the "Memoir" is very vague. The *Home Journal* is not in the British Museum or I would ferret it out. Griswold said Margaret Fuller reviewed Poe's early (1829) poems in the *Tribune* in 1846. I have looked thro' the whole vol. for 1846 but vainly! Griswold could not, I believe, even when he tried, tell a correct date. I think I've found out the name of the publisher who speaks of Poe (in the *Northern Monthly*) as having been connected with him before he was with Willis on the *Mirror*: *viz.* Lockwood, the publisher of "The Album" & the giver of the gold medal (to Yale College in 1826) won by Willis as a student. I know no more, but that is a clue—can you throw any light on the subject? You will remember & *vide* "Memoir" that he had published a life of Poe & said he could publish some revelations as to the cause of Poe's troubles—therefore a valuable aid to us.

And now for extract, or copies, of Mrs. Clemm's letters in possession of his cousin Neilson Poe. These, mind, are *entre nous at present.* They are written to N. Poe—

Alexandria [Va.] Aug. 19, 1860
Dear Sir . . . my dear Eddie was born in Boston, Mass. on the 19th of Jany 1811 ⊰ 1809 elsewhere stated by Mrs. C. ⊱ when 5 weeks old he was taken to Baltimore by his parents ⊰ ? J.H.I ⊱, and remained there for 6 months. They went to Richmond, Va. His mother died there when Eddie was 2 years old. At that time Mr. Allan adopted him. He went to school until he was 7 in Richmond. Mr. and Mrs. A. then went with him to England & resided in Russells Square, London. Eddie went to school about 5 miles from London to Dr. Bransby returning every Friday to his adopted parents, remaining with them until the following Monday. . . . They ret[urned] to Va. when he was 14. Soon after he went to college at the University. . . . He never went to Russia. . . . I can account for every hour of his life since his return from America. He was domestic in all his habits. Seldom leaving home for one hour unless his darling Virginia or myself were with him. He was truly an affectionate, kind husband, and a devoted son to me. He was impulsive, generous, affectionate, and *noble.* His tastes were very simple, and his admiration for all that was good and beautiful very great. We lived for 5 years at Fordham, in the sweetest little cottage imaginable. It was there our precious Virginia left us to go and dwell with the angels. I then wished to die *too,* but *had* to live to take care of our poor disconsolate Eddie. This I *know* I did do, &, if I had been with him in Baltimore, he would not have died and left me alone in this heartless world. . . . Eddie rarely left his beautiful home. I attended to his literary business, for he, poor fellow, knew nothing about money tranactions. . . . He passed the greater part of the morning in his study, and, after he had finished his task for the day, he worked in our beautiful flower garden, or read & recited poetry to us. Everyone who knew him *intimately* loved him. We had very little society except among the literati. . . . Eddie finished Virginia's education himself &c. I assure you, she was highly cultivated, an excellent linguist, & a perfect musician, and she was very beautiful. . . .

⊰ signed ⊱ Maria Clemm [3]

Neilson Poe married Virginia's half sister (Mrs. Clemm's stepdaughter). And now enough for the present. I fear you will not get through all this. Faithfully ever & ever yours,

John H. Ingram

[*Commenting on Mrs. Clemm's letter, Mrs. Whitman annotated the last page:*] This letter is full of singular mistakes as to dates.

1. Ingram's oft-repeated contempt for reviews notwithstanding, he did indeed have many of the favorable reviews of his 1874–75 edition of Poe's *Works* reprinted: *Extracts*

from Opinions of the British Press on the Memoir of Poe, by John H. Ingram, published with Extracts from Quarterlies, Weeklies, Dailies, etc., followed by Extracts from the American (Southern) Press (London: E. J. Francis and Co., n.d.), 4 pp. A copy of this brochure is in the Sarah Helen Whitman Papers, Brown University Library.

2. The official manuscript copy of Poe's trial was made by the U.S. War Department in 1875. This 14-page document is Item 4 in the Ingram Poe Collection.

3. For complete text of Mrs. Clemm's letter, see *Building Poe Biography*, pp. 46–49.

80. *Sarah Helen Whitman to John H. Ingram.   Item 192*

My dear Mr. Ingram,   Jan. 4, 1875
    I received the last of your ever welcome letters [Dec. 16, 1874] on the evening of the 2nd of the New Year. Its contents were intensely interesting. The notice of Gilfillan was, in spite of its *many* errors & exaggerations, eloquently &, in some respects, admirably written. I hope to quote some portions of it for publication.
    A note from Mr. Davidson this morning tells me that he has sent you Stoddard's revised "Memoir." You will see that it is no way improved in spirit. In publishing the extracts which I sent him from the records at Charlottesville, he adds, "But this is a rosecoloured view of the situation"! and proceeds, or rather *seeks* to neutralize its tints by the introduction of a frivolous conversation reported as having passed between a certain Mr. Gilliet & Mrs. Allan. The "rosecoloured view" has, however, the advantage of documentary evidence, while the story of the "seventeen broad-cloth coats" looks somewhat "murky," and apparently needs corroboration.[1]
    If you review Curwen's *Song & Sorrow*, I should like to see a copy of your notice.
    Mr. Harris, who has been in New York, I saw for the first time since his return on Friday evening—other company being present until a late hour, I had but little chance for conversation. He found a copy of the [18]29 edition of the poems, but did not purchase it. He says he has heard of *one* other copy in Boston, which he intends soon to look up. In the mean time, he employed a copyist to make out a list of the contents of the book. The list is now before me. The book bears the title of *Al Aaraaf, Tamerlane, & Minor Poems*, by Edgar A. Poe, Baltimore: Hatch & Dunning, 1829. Matchett & Woods, printers. Note by the author: "Tamerlane." "This poem was printed for publication in Boston in the year 1827, but suppressed through circumstances of a private nature."
    There *was* an edition printed in 1827. Of this there is other evidence than Poe's assertion, *viz.*, in the catalogue of Kettell.[2] More of this another time.

Mr. Harris thinks Stoddard had seen the [18]29 edition & must have known that Poe spoke the truth in saying there was an *earlier* edition. He is looking into this matter of the early poems very carefully. He was anxious to learn if I had heard from you during his absence, & seemed disappointed that I had not. The very next day your letter came, but I have not since seen him. About the lady's *name*. He said it was given as in Poe's sonnet in an early edition of her poems. Perhaps the one noticed, I think, in *Female Poets of America*, as *Records of the Heart*, but however this may be, I do not think it can affect your statement with the general reader. I think, however, that it might have been as well not to have entered so much into details. Yet in reverting to your volume (which, since writing the last sentence, I have done), I cannot see that you could well avoid the explanation about the name. You ask me to pitch into your "Memoir" or you shall think I don't like it. To prove to you that I *do*—that I not only *like* it but feel it to be a work of great value, I am going to point out some marks of haste & to suggest some omissions & alterations. In speaking of "Ulalume" & my question as to its authorship, you call it the "new" poem. The word *new* is hardly applicable, since the poem had been published in December, 1847, and my question as to its authorship was made in September, 1848. It is not perhaps very important, but it a little impairs the versimilitude of the story. Why not substitute the word "weird" for *new*?

Again, it was not from Mr. Atkinson's *report* of Poe's lecture that this characterization of the poetry of the three New England poetesses was derived, but from Poe's own copy of a leaf from his MS. Mr. Atkinson published it among other notices from other sources, furnished him by me, in noticing the volume of my poems in 1853. Mr. Atkinson lived in Lowell at the time of Poe's lecture; I do not know that he *heard* it. He is related to my mother's family by marriage, and he was, at the time my book was published, editor & proprietor of the Newport paper in which this & other notices of my poems appeared.

You ask me to suggest alterations & omissions. I have hastily written something which, if you ever republish your "Memoir," I should like to have inserted instead of the more detailed narrative which you have given, *if you approve*. You have done so well with the fragmentary materials which I entrusted to you that I do not like to give you trouble or suggest change.

I have been very unwell since the cold weather has become so severe, but think I shall rally in a few days. I want to send you an acknowledgement of your interesting letter by tomorrow's steamer & so have written at a pace that I fear will make my writing unintelligible.

I was interested but greatly surprised by what you tell me of Mrs.

Clemm's letters. I fancy the part relating to Longfellow must be taken *cum grano*, etc. Do tell me more about them.

But now good night, for I am very, very weary. Ever affectionately your friend,

S.H.W.

A suggested alteration for page 73:

In the early summer of 1848, we find Poe delivering a lecture in Lowell, on the Female Poets of America. In this lecture he gave to Mrs. Whitman a high rank among the poetesses of New England, ascribing to her "preeminence in refinement of art, enthusiasm, imagination & genius, properly so called."

It has been said, & not without reason, that Poe's literary estimates were too often influenced by personal feeling; in the present instance, however, whatever personal feeling may have mingled with praise, it will be conceded by all competent critics that it had not warped his judgment.

You will understand that this last clause is to give connection with what follows: In the sentence beginning, "Mrs. Whitman, undoubtedly the finest," I should prefer, "one of the finest."

Then, *after the eight lines* at the foot of page 73, ending with "exalted passion," I should *leave out* the line "Meanwhile the beautiful young widow lived on" etc., and the *whole* of page 74, down to the third line from the bottom, and begin at

In September of this year Mr. Poe obtained an introduction to the lady to whom this noble poem had been addressed, which resulted after a few weeks in the betrothal of the two poets.

The engagement lasted but for a brief period during which Poe entertained the most sanguine hopes of a successful career in literature, dwelling with renewed ardor on his plan of establishing a magazine which should give him supreme control in the intellectual world.

We need not inquire too curiously of the causes which destroyed his wild dream of earthly happiness & earthly triumph.

Was he not a doomed man? Has he not himself told us that to all his aspirations there was but one answer, the answer of never—nevermore?

These are simply suggestions. Do with them what you like—what you *can*.

I do not wonder that you thought some of the things which I told you simply that *you* might understand my story (mine & his) were supposed by you as intended for publication, but I confess that I should rather the "Memoir" had been less personal.

P.S. I am always delighted to hear from you. Do not be afraid of troubling me with questions. When you read the letters which I hope to copy for you (perhaps eventually to intrust to you) you will understand better why I am unable to answer so few questions as to the statistics of Poe's life.

I believe I omitted to send you my "Pansy." I enclose it now. It was published in "The Easy Chair" anonymously, by my friend G. W. Curtis, in August or September, 1859.[3] I think it is one of my very best. I hope you will like it. This copy is from Prov. *Journal.* You will like the first ten lines, I think, from your own charming words about flowers.

Photographs not finished. Will send by Saturday's steamer.

What I told you about "Annabel Lee" was for *yourself* alone, & not with any wish that you should say anything on the subject in writing your "Memoir."

It is far better to leave it, in its vague & mysterious beauty, than to make any claim or advance any theory on this contested question. I shall have some curious things to say to you on the subject when I have time. I see that in copying the third verse of the "Stanzas for Music" that the word "wild" occurs twice in the verse. It would be better to say "storm-beaten shore" rather than "wild ocean shore," don't you think so? About "Resurg*a*mus," is not that a mistake? Should it not be "Resurg*e*mus"? I will write more fully by the next mail. Sincerely and gratefully,

Sarah Helen Whitman

1. See page 318, n.1.

2. Samuel Kettell (1800–1855), *Specimens of American Poetry, with Critical and Biographical Notices*, 3 vols. (Boston: S. G. Goodrich and Co., 1829). " 'Tamerlane and Other Poems,' by a Bostonian. Boston, 1827," appears on page 405 of Vol. III.

3. George William Curtis was editor of *Harper's* "The Easy Chair" in 1859.

81. *Sarah Helen Whitman to John H. Ingram.*   Item 193

My dear Mr. Ingram,   Jan. 7, 1875

I sent you some hurried lines yesterday. Do not be troubled at my criticisms; they were only given as suggestions. I should like to know the author of the article entitled "Reminiscences" of Poe's life at Fordham. I vaguely remember having somewhere seen it, perhaps in the *Home Journal.* It seemed to me *then* a fancy sketch. Do you *know its author*? And can its statements be depended on? It seemed to me to infringe a little upon "that dignity that doth hedge" a poet, as well as a king. Nor can I believe some of its statements. That about the caged quail & the tortured or tormented bird, for instance, and the cat & the straw bed. I am very curious about the authorship of this sketch. *Do tell me, if you know.*[1] Did you write to Miss Blackwell? Mrs. Nichols may be able to tell you about Miss B. It was Mrs. N. who asked Mrs. Clemm to receive her for a few weeks as a boarder. If I had been quoting from the article I think I should have omitted the phrase "and her black dress though old and much worn looked really elegant on her." The description of Poe is *admirable*, with the exception of the word "restless." There was *no* restlessness either in movement or feature, as *I* knew him. There was often fervor & intensity, but always mingled with an almost supernatural calmness of eye & gesture. Like his handwriting, his manner seemed *always* self-controlled & self-poised, in strange contradiction to his disturbed & erratic career—*always*, with *one* exception. I will tell you about it someday. Stoddard's book you will have seen ere this reaches you. But why has he omitted the early stanzas to Helen? It is certainly not a "complete" edition of the poems. He says moreover in speaking of the publication of "The Bells" in *Sartain's Mag.*, 1849 (October, I think), "About this time he wrote stanzas 'For Annie' & 'Annabel Lee.'" Now the stanzas "For Annie" were first published in a Boston paper in the early spring of 1849.[2] They were written after his return or *during* a visit to his friends in Lowell where he had again succumbed to the fatal temptation from which the Death Angel was so soon to deliver him, and where he was tenderly & kindly ministered to by the wife of his host.[3] This lady was the Annie of whose kindness to herself Mrs. Clemm spoke in one of the letters I sent you. What you tell me of Neilson Poe & of the letters written him by Mrs. Clemm greatly surprised & interested me. It would appear, then, that Mrs. Clemm was twice married if Virginia had a half-sister, or perhaps these half-sisters had the same *father*. I have heard that Mrs. Clemm's husband was once Mayor of Richmond, but I do not remember how I heard it.

The story of letters of "the literary lady" for which G[riswold] offered $500, I fancy I can account for. It has been often said that Mrs. C[lemm] either carelessly or intentionally permitted a letter of Mrs. Osgood's to be seen by some visitor. Griswold, acting as the agent of Mrs. O[sgood], might have heard &, perhaps, doubted this story, & might have made some offer for the letter or letters on which this story was based. But "here's a coil" which I cannot attempt to unravel.

The enclosed printed parody on "The Bells" has been going the rounds of the papers &, I fancy, must be a fling at Stoddard's "flute." The *unpublished* lines, perpetrated by an admirer of Poe's genius, *certainly* were so intended. I copy them for your amusement. And will write again by the next mail. Benedicte.

On a Grecian Flute

Lo, the fluter with his flute—
  Grecian Flute!
How long the world has waited
  For its tantalizing toot!
"Unheard melodies are sweetest,"*
  Said the charming poet Keats;
But our pleasure is completest
  When we hear them on the streets;
Or sounding loud & shrill
  Through the homes of Murray Hill—
On the heights of Murray Hill
  Loud & shrill,
Hear the flute, flute, flute,
  Flute, flute, flute.

That wicked *Broadway Journal*
  Whose Editor infernal
Let no trumpet but his own
  Through the market place be blown—
Had the chief not been carousing—
  Had the Raven not been drowsing,
The world had not been waiting,
  Been waiting all in vain,
For that melancholy strain
  Of the flute—
In anxious expectation for the tintinabulation
  Of the flute.

*See "Lines on a Grecian Urn."

1. The author of this article in the *Sixpenny Magazine* was Mrs. Mary Gove Nichols.
2. *Flag of Our Union*, Apr. 28, 1849.
3. Poe's host in Lowell was Charles B. Richmond (d. 1873), a well-to-do paper manufacturer and husband of Nancy Locke Heywood (1820–1898), who became Poe's adored "Annie." After her husband's death, Mrs. Richmond had her name changed legally to Annie Richmond.

82. *Sarah Helen Whitman to John H. Ingram,*   Item 195

Jan. 15, [18]75
  Your very interesting letter of Dec. 28 reached me last evening, my dear Mr. Ingram, & though still very unwell from an attack of

congestion of the heart, I hope to send off a few brief lines of acknowledgment to go by tomorrow's steamer. Mrs. Clemm's letter was very characteristic, illustrating her inaccuracy as to dates & details, & her devoted love for the unfortunate poet, whose character, I am well assured, was truly & faithfully described by her. It was *not five* years, but three that they lived at Fordham, & her assertion that she could account for "every hour of his life, etc." was of course a reckless & exaggerated assumption. But why was she writing this letter to Neilson Poe? Could these families, allied by blood & intermarriage, have been strangers to each other's history?

The *official copies* of the trial of "Cadet E. A. Poe" must be a valuable accession to you. They seem to prove the accuracy of a statement contained in a *fragment* of a letter which I sent you some time ago, without telling you, I think, from whom I had received it. It was a young poetess of independent fortune & great intellectual gifts who became insane while contemplating a new "Memoir" of Poe.[1] I will tell you this sad story hereafter. I hope you have received Stoddard's book. You will see that it is printed in London, England, by *Billing*. I forget the name & number of the street. Mr. Harris, whom I have seen since his return from Boston—he was here last evening, just after I received your letter—says that Stoddard's charge of Poe's mendacity as to the *verbatim* reproduction of the early poems in the 1845 edition was founded on a comparison of the [18]45 with the [18]31 edition. It was Stoddard, he thinks, who wrote the article in the *Philobiblion*. He, Stoddard, had not *then* seen the edition of 1829, which is, I think, with some slight alterations & *transpositions*, a verbatim transcript. Stoddard has *now* seen the [18]29 edition, yet he has not recalled his charge of "mendacity," & still, I think, assumes to doubt the existence of the [18]27 edition.

I think I told you that there was *positive evidence* of this edition in *Kettell's Catalogue*. Kettell, in a note or appendix to his *Collection of American Poetry*, gives a list of unpublished poems which he "has seen" in print. Among the poems named therein is *Tamerlane & Other Poems, by a Bostonian*. Now Mr. Harris *thinks* that Stoddard has *seen* this mention of *Tamerlane* etc., but that he, S[toddard], thinks nobody else interested in the subject would be likely to know of its existence. So he [Mr. Harris] recommends *keeping dark* on the subject of Kettell until some critic shall have said in defence of Poe that Stoddard had not compared Poe's poems of [18]45 with the *first* edition. That Stoddard will *then* say there is no *authority* for the existence of any such edition but Poe's word, & that is worth nothing.

He [Mr. Harris] earnestly advises to keep Kettell in reserve until Stoddard shows his cards. He has taken so much interest in the matter that I earnestly wish to follow his advice. He said he wanted to go over the poems again so as to be sure of his ground & that he would give me the result in writing or write to you himself. In the matter of sending the [18]31 edition, he said that he had been waiting for the return of the books (sent months ago) from England, not liking to forward more to his bookbinder until these were returned, when he would immediately send the volume he promised you. He says the poems added by Stoddard are from the [18]29 edition. He calls them "suppressed poems," but portions of them were in the later editions, transposed & cut up. The "Lines to M.L.S." are printed among the early poems, I believe, but if addressed to Mrs. Shew, must have been among the very latest, apparently.

I asked him about the name of Mrs. L[ewis] affixed to the *Records of the Heart*, & this morning he sent me the enclosed note.

The *Aberdeen* notice was admirable. Has the *Academy* yet published a notice? I could obtain that & the *Saturday Review* from the [Providence] Athenaeum.

Of course, dear Rose will never know that I was so indiscreet as to send you her enthusiastic words of admiration & cordial sympathy. Yet had I dreamed that there was anything in their import that could have given you pain or which it would have been disloyal in me to betray, be assured I would not have sent them.[2] I thought only of giving you pleasure. But forget & forgive.

I have not received the duplicate copy of the 1st vol., nor either of the 2nd, nor have I received the photographs or engravings—but there is time enough for all.

You ask about the date of the *Home Journal* article about the "Conchology" story. I think it must have been sometime in the winter of 1858–9, because when preparing my book for publication in 1859, I wrote to O'Connor to consult him about the question of *introducing* it into my protest against the critics, & he advised me *not* to, unless I could take up all the slanders at once. I followed his advice, & sent it— the *Journal* containing it—to some of the numerous correspondents who have from time to time questioned me about the unjust "Memoir" of Griswold. If Graham is still alive he may know something of Wyatt, who, as I told you, contributed articles on Natural History to the magazine. *You* say Graham is dead. *Gill* says he is alive—but if he *is*, Gill will never tell where he is to be found. I wish I could tell you about his last letter to me in which he says he could weep tears of joy that he has been permitted to be a humble instrument in clearing Poe's memory from obloquy! But he is an enigma & I fancy the solution would not be worth the trouble of looking for it—I say this—but enough for the present. With earnest wishes for your happiness, I am ever & ever your friend,

S.H.W.

[Enclosure]

My dear Mrs. Whitman,
  I find I have the following by Mrs. Lewis:

> *Records of the Heart.* By Mrs. Sarah Anna Lewis, New York, 1844.
> *Child of the Sea, and Other Poems.* By Mrs. S. Anna Lewis, New York,
>   1848.
> *Myths of the Minstrel.* By Estelle Anna Lewis, New York, 1852.
> *Records of the Heart, and Other Poems.* By Estelle Anna Lewis.
>   Illustrated. New York, 1857.

The titles as I give them are *verbatim*, omitting unimportant words,
& I think the list includes all she has published in book form, unless
something quite recent. I hope you are better this bright morning.
Yours most truly,

                                                      C. F. Harris

102 Waterman St.
Friday, Jan. 15, [18]75

  1. This was Sallie E. Robins of Putnam, Ohio. See p. 114, n. 1.
  2. This statement once again implies that either a letter or a portion of one from Ingram is missing.

83. *John H. Ingram to Sarah Helen Whitman*

                                        Engineer-in-Chief's Office
                                        General Post Office
                                        London, England
My very dear Friend,   27 Jan. 1875
  First let me remark *re.* the address. It is on the *tapis*, but very
uncertain, that I *may* have to start on a tour for Government, of two or
more months duration, through Great Britain & Ireland &, if this come
to pass, my letters may find me *some* days earlier than if sent "to
home"—so until you hear again, kindly direct as above.
  In the second place, I feel *very unwell* & seems as if something
wretched were going to happen, but don't mind this. I feel a relief in
disburthening my mind to you—to you who seem so near & yet so
visionary to me—who seem almost like a guardian angel, one whom I
would love to see & yet almost deem it better not to. However, I do
hope yet to see you.
  Before dashing into my business affairs, let me inform you that I
have had a charming letter from Miss Peckham & that I have just
answered her. She growls that *you* do not answer her, but I said you

were unwell & begged her to keep up the correspondence. I *do* trust,
however, that you are better.

And now for your first letter [Jan. 4]. *Re.* Stoddard's "Memoir"—I
have written a letter for the New York papers, & shall send it off in a
few days, *pitching* into Stoddard. Had he confined his mean &
scurrilous insinuations to America I would have overlooked them, but
this "Memoir" is addressed "to English readers." Don't mind what *I*
say. I'm quite able to hold my own against anything Mr. S[toddard] can
say or do—in fact, if he is prudent he won't make much "pother," or I
shall "drop him a hotter one." Pardon my phraseology. I shall send you
a copy of the letter. It only dissects a *portion* of his "original"
"Memoir." There are some plums reserved to sweeten another dose, if
he need it. I wonder how he picked up the name of "Gilliet"? Strange
to say, that is a name given me as a clue to Poe's life in England as a
boy—where the Allans resided here.

I have not had much space in my review of Curwen's *Sorrow & Song*
for Poe, who is only one of six biographies—but will send you the
Academy with it in it. Next Saturday (30th) I expect it out. I have
alluded to you & I don't think you'll [horsewhip me?] for what I've
said. Curwen, for obvious reasons, says Poe was engaged to the
wealthiest woman in New England—and I have taken the liberty of
saying that the lady "to whom he was engaged" (as you will see) "was
not, is not even rich." You don't object to that—do you?

Why did not Mr. Harris buy the [18]29 edition? Can he tell me the
price & the place? *If anything within reason* I should like it. There is
a copy in the Peabody Institute, Baltimore, & I am hoping for a copy in
MS. of it. Curwen quotes the omitted poems included in Stoddard's
complete collection.

Thanks for your kind furnishing of particulars. There was,
undoubtedly, an 1827 volume. Will Mr. Harris lend the 1831 edition?
It is not to hand. Would he like "Rhododaphne" & has he a spare copy
of Pinckney's *Poems? Perhaps* Poe was right about the lady's name. I
spoke on her own authority, but that is not very reliable, I *know*—but I
saw a letter from her husband to Griswold which corroborated her
statement. Nevertheless, Mr. Harris is probably correct—will you tell
him what I say? Only don't mention more names than needful. I'll
fight any number of men but I don't want an *embroglio* with any
ladies. "Details" were given at her request.

I am *thankful* for any criticism *you* will take the trouble to make
about my "Memoir" & shall be only too glad to get any suggestion from
you. You know the work is very different to what I intended & to what
the life shall be. The "Ulalume" I will try & adopt your word, but the
second edition, I fancy, is already printed. Poe's lecture shall be put

right. I will adopt what I can of your corrections, as you know, but I shall not put—*quite as you say it*—about Poe's literary estimates being influenced by personal feeling, but shall have something to say on that point. "The beautiful young widow"—if you desire it—shall be left out & the other matters duly attended to, but a distinct denial of Griswold's story *may* be necessary. I don't know, however, but that I may be able to *entirely ignore* Griswold & the whole fry of insectivorous vermin in *The Life*, & you may be sure that, if possible, I shall do so. I'm sorry that I made the allusions to you more personal than you wished. I thought that I had confined my remarks to *authorised* allusions, but I hope *we shall live, & I think we must*, to see my complete Life. *No one* will ever have the chance to write Poe's life so faithfully, I fancy, as I shall. I have every date & circumstance at my fingers' ends. I only want a short tour through the States to complete my information. You shall not be "one of the finest poets"— the praise is not, in my opinion, high.

Now for your second letter [Jan. 7]. I delayed my reply until I had seen Mrs. Nichols who has just been to London for a couple of days. I have seen her this afternoon & have promised to visit her residence at Malvern. She promises to go to work systematically to help me & will not leave a stone unturned to do so. She had (in compliance with an earnest desire of Mrs. Clemm) written "Reminiscences of Poe" for a series of sketches in the *Leader*, & this article was, apparently, the one reprinted in the *Sixpenny*, but with alterations, I think. Can you return it to me to send Mrs. Nichols? Perhaps it was from Mrs. Nichols & *another* paper.

Miss E. Blackwell is in Paris. I will write to her. But I understand Mrs. Nichols to *state positively*— although old & nearly sightless, *entre nous*, she is very positive—that Miss E. Blackwell never boarded at Fordham & that—this she insists on—the Fordham home was given up by Poe & his mother-in-law long before *his* death. Can you lighten this darkness? *Between us twain* I speak everything *in confidence* of all these witnesses, but to each of them separately, am careful—each one having some bitter enmity for each other. Of you only do all speak well. *En passant*, is Elizabeth Blackwell the Doctor Blackwell?[1] I forgot to ask—but shall have to write soon. Mrs. Nichols asks for Stoddard's "Memoir." She is surprised at him trying to throw stones at Poe & expected something better from him. Griswold, she says, was a man of such infamous character that no one could mention his name in decent society. Stoddard's misstatements *re.* poems go for naught. I have alluded to omission of "To Helen" in my letter. Mrs. Clemm, I fancy, married (once) a widower. Mrs. Nichols, *with great probability*, deems the literary lady, whose correspondence Griswold offered to buy, to be the lady about an error in whose name I have just written

you. This seems feasible. She was well off, & Griswold could doubtless
have got a good sum profit for the letters. Mrs. O's letters, I do not
think Griswold needed—he knew all about her, I fancy? *An American
friend of mine* has sent me a parody on "The Bells" & they are so
apropos to my letter *re.* Stoddard, that I must use two MS. verses in my
letter. You will comprehend, but I do not mention my friend's name for
fear of postal or other mishaps. I told you that I had written to M.L.S.
(Mrs. Houghton) by advice of Mrs. Nichols. I have just received an
answer containing one of Poe's own letters—'tis short. M.L.S. was, says
Mrs. Nichols, like an angel to the Poes. I'm very tired but will copy
Poe's letter for you, but don't give it or show it to any one. I must keep
all private *now*, I fear, for my *Life.*

Kindest—dearest friend—My poor Virginia still lives, although failing fast
and now suffering much pain. May God grant her life until she sees you &
thanks you once again! Her bosom is full to overflowing—like my own—with
a boundless—inexpressible gratitude to you. Lest she never see you more—
she bids me say that she sends you her sweetest kiss of love & will die
blessing you. But come—oh come tomorrow! Yes, I *will* be calm—everything
you so nobly wish to see me. My mother sends you, also, her "warmest love &
thanks." She begs me to ask you, if possible, to make arrangements at home so
that you may stay with us tomorrow night! I enclose the order to the
Postmaster. Heaven bless you & farewell.
Fordham, Jany. 29, 1847.   Edgar A. Poe

Mrs. Houghton (M.L.S.) is going to help all in her power to go over
Griswold's *"Memoir"* & point out the statements "which are not only
cruel & malicious but false."

Do you know any "A. B. Harris"? There is a short account of the Poes
in their worst time at Philadelphia, signed by this A.B.H. in *Hearth &
Home* (New York) a few weeks ago.[2] It is friendlily written. I must get it
confirmed. It gives a terrible account of the miseries of the family at
one time, Poe, wife, & mother.

Unfortunately Blacks cannot get *that* portrait done in time for Vol. iv.
It must do for the Life—if possible. I am savage that you did not get
your other vols. It seems it was thro' Scribner's London house. I'll
send the set next month & the portrait. I send you a spare critique by a
young admirer of Poe's—a clever young fellow who has been in
America. *Favourable* reviews have recently appeared in several more
first class papers—even where the reviewers have had to buy copies.
Blacks are so tardy in sending—& I hear the *Quarterlies* are preparing
long reviews. Griswold will never "make head" in England any more,
I am gratified to say. The *Academy* was the only really not flattering
one & the critic thinks to please me better in noticing the poems.

Do you know anything of F. W. Thomas, author of *Howard Pinckney,*
&c.?[3] Stoddard quotes interesting extracts from letters to him from Poe.

I should like them confirmed. I doubt Stoddard's correctness of quotation—he makes mistakes. I have asked Davidson if he can get anything from Thomas, but I am getting quite ashamed of the trouble I'm giving *him*. And now a short goodbye. I'll tell more anon from the Baltimore letters, from the Mrs. Clemm letters. I am tired out, my dear, dear friend, so *au revoir*.

John H. Ingram

29 Jany. 1875

Through a stupid forgetfulness I did not send your letter forward, so can just reply to yours dated [Jan.] 15th.

In first place, do you think Mr. Harris would mind sending the 1831 edition by post *registered*? This would be as safe as any other mode of transit. I would return it in 2 or 3 days, with postage. Would he like "Rhododaphne"?

The other vols. of my *Works* I am most annoyed about your not getting—'twas through the negligence of Scribner's London agent. Will forward next week.

Had I time to finish my comments on Mrs. Clemm's letters you would have seen why she wrote these things to Neilson Poe—he was thinking of writing a "Memoir" of his cousin & brother-in-law & therefore asked Mrs. Clemm for information. More of this anon.

The official copies of the trial *are* valuable, as they place beyond doubt that absence from parades was *the only charge* made against him at West Point officially. Mr. Davidson is *very kind* indeed.

The fragment of a letter you allude to I felt assured was written by some one not quite mentally right. I have had some sad experience in mental maladies & can see this clearer, perhaps, than the uninitiated.

On reference to Stoddard's book, I see that it was printed in England, but not in London. *I rather fancy* S[toddard] & Curwen have some knowledge of each other. I must be quite assured about the *verbatim* affair before I bring it forward.

Can, & why did not, Mr. Harris procure the 1829 edition? Let me know the price. In the *Philobiblion*—would I could prove it Stoddard's!—"Poe's well-known mendacity" is mentioned. The very words of Stoddard.

Next in *unpleasantness* to the *Academy* notice was the *Saturday Review*, which you say you can see. Did I send you the *Spectator*? Some parts of that were very good. As *praise* from high quarters *to me*, *Daily News, Examiner*, & *School Board Chronicle* may be mentioned.

Forget & forgive my stupid & *uncalled-for remarks* about the letter from R[ose Peckham]. 'Twas very kind of you to let me see it. *I don't think Graham is alive*; only Gill sees the advantage of holding his appearance *in terrorem* over dissenters. Wyatt & the "Conchology" story must be cleared up. I am anxious to see *Lotos Leaves* with Gill's account of Poe—'tis reprinting here. *Entre nous*, I cannot help thinking Gill is— well, never mind. 'Tis all the same. And now, once more, *au revoir*.

John H. Ingram

1. Elizabeth Blackwell (1821–1910) was a pioneer in opening the medical profession to women. She entered the medical school at Geneva, N.Y., in 1847, later studied at La Maternité and Hôtel Dieu, Paris, and St. Bartholomew's, London. She established her medical practice in New York in 1851, founded a hospital, and, in 1867, in conjunction with her sister, Dr. Emily Blackwell, organized Woman's Medical College of New York Infirmary.

2. A. B. Harris, "Edgar A. Poe," *Hearth and Home*, 8 (Jan. 9, 1875), 24. This is a maudlin account of Edgar Poe's pride, deep love for Virginia and Mrs. Clemm, and his inability to control his drinking; of Virginia's youth, beauty, lovely singing voice as well as her lying in a room so small that the ceiling almost touched her head, after she had ruptured a blood vessel in her throat; and of Mrs. Clemm's devotion to the pair of them through all of the sufferings and hardships brought on by their bitter poverty.

3. Frederick William Thomas (1806–1866), journalist, author, and devoted friend of Poe's, tried to help the poet get a government job under the John Tyler administration. Poe reviewed Thomas' first novel, *Clinton Bradshaw, or the Adventures of a Lawyer* (Philadelphia: Carey, Lea & Blanchard, 1835), not very favorably in the *Southern Literary Messenger*, Dec. 1835. See Harrison, ed., *Works*, VIII, 109–10.

84. *Sarah Helen Whitman to John H. Ingram.*   *Item 202*

My dear Mr. Ingram,   Feb. 14, 1875
    Since I last wrote to you the weather has been colder than was ever known in New England since the creation of the world. Yesterday, with the arrival of your welcome letter, it seemed to moderate a little. I was *so* glad to receive it. About Miss Blackwell. It was not *Elizabeth* but *Anna* Blackwell who, as I told you, boarded with Mrs. Clemm for a few weeks at Fordham. She is the sister of Dr. Elizabeth Blackwell. It was Anna Blackwell who translated George Sand's *Jacques*, & who is now a resident in Paris.[1] Mrs. Gove Nichols, I think it was, who commended the Fordham cottage to her as a pleasant place wherein to seek rest & recuperation from the fatigues of her literary work. Did Mrs. Gove Nichols say nothing of this—nothing of Anna? They were once friends—Miss B[lackwell] having been a patient of Mrs. Nichols' when that lady was at the head of a water cure establishment in N.Y. Anna B[lackwell] came to Providence in the spring of 1848 to pass the summer, and often spoke of her visit to Fordham. She was at my mother's house one evening in June, I think, when Miss Maria J. McIntosh happened to be present. It was a bright moonlight night.

Miss M[cIntosh] said, "Mrs. W[hitman], on just such a night as this one month ago I met Mr. Poe for the first time at the house of a gentleman in Fordham—a Mr. Lindsay ⸢I think that was the name⸥ & his whole talk was about you." etc., etc. Miss Blackwell then said that she had received a letter from Poe to much the same effect two or three weeks before, but had not thought to speak of it to me. She afterwards at my request gave me the letter, which she said she had not answered.[2] I do not think that she was altogether friendly to Poe at that time, & when she heard of my engagement to him, seemed still less so. He called on her with me during his first visit to Providence & I invited her to join a party of friends to meet him that evening at my home, but she did not come. I enclose a little note fom her acknowledging the call & invitation. After she went to Paris I had one or two letters from her, but our correspondence soon fell off.

I have seen the notice in the *Examiner* of Dec. 19. *It was admirable.* I also saw the *Saturday Review* of same date. Just what anyone might predict of the *Saturday Review.* The genius of Poe could no more be recognized from the standpoint of that *Review* than could the moons of Jupiter or the ring of Saturn be discerned through a dandy's opera glass. It is essentially pert & flippant & never rises to a higher level than that of the most commonplace intellect. And this if the very secret of its popularity—its "bad eminence."

Undoubtedly Stoddard is in league with Curwen. I have not seen Curwen's article, but I am *sure* of it, nevertheless.

If I can see Mr. Harris before mailing this letter, I will find out about the [18]29 edition. I think Mr. H[arris] has been absent from the city for several weeks. You ask why I did not send you such a letter of denial of Griswold's stories as I sent to Gill. Simply because I had already given him the letter & did not exactly know how to duplicate it by another. He has made some palpable and absurd blunders with his material received from me. For instance, he quotes from Pabodie's letter to Griswold in confirmation of the facts of his *Tribune* statement, the following sentence: "That very morning he [Poe] wrote a note to Dr. Crocker requesting him to publish the intended marriage at the earliest opportunity, & intrusted this note to me with the request that I should *deliver it in person.*" For the words "deliver it in person" Mr. Gill has substituted the closing words of another sentence—"Make oath to it if necessary"—words utterly unmeaning in this connection, their place being at the close of the paragraph "These are the facts as I know them, which I am willing to make oath to if necessary." I called Mr. Gill's attention to this & other mistakes which he promised to correct in a second edition of *Lotus Leaves* now preparing. We shall see.

Don't be troubled about my comments as to your introduction of my name in certain connections. I feel *sure* that you published nothing without my implied authority. I did not myself exactly understand what portions of my material you might choose to publish. I don't like to find any fault with your work—a work which you have done so well & nobly—a work which nobody else could or would have done half so well. You ask me if I can return you the article in the *Sixpenny*. You once *promised* me that you would send it but you did not: at least I never received it, & have seen only such portions of the article as are republished in your book & in *Temple Bar*.

About the time of giving up of the Fordham cottage, I know nothing positive. It is stated in the Redfield Ed. of 1850, you know, that Poe left his residence at Fordham for the last time on June 29, 1849. I have always *thought* Mrs. Clemm remained there until after his death. Mrs. Nichols' information on many points relating to this period of Poe's history must be valuable & interesting, but she may be mistaken as to some particulars.

I have just found the extract from Eugene Benson's *Galaxy* article which you sent me & which I thought I had returned. I think with the portion I copied for you it will comprise the whole article. Your explanation as to Neilson Poe's intention of writing a life of Poe explains many things in his course. Perhaps he thinks his work has been taken out of his hands. I have not seen the article in *Hearth & Home*, & I know nothing of A. B. Harris. If it is written in a friendly spirit, I should like to see it, though I protest against the adjective "friendlily." You have given me an invitation to "pitch into" you, so you must not find fault with me, you know. Show me a precedent for the words "kindlily" and "friendlily." Nay, show me a hundred precedents & I will still protest. See how peremptorily I am exercising the privilege you have extended to me?

Poe's letter to M.L.S. I should have known to have been his—known it to have come direct from his heart, without evidence of handwriting or signature. I do not know anything of the Thomas quoted by Stoddard. I think that there can be little doubt that the *Philobiblion* article was Stoddard's. I did not see the article in the *Spectator*.

If you won't think me too fastidious about trifles, I should like to suggest one or two slight verbal alterations.

On page 30 you speak of the calumnies heaped by Griswold "on the dead man's head." *I* should like it better if you simply said, "No better disproof of Griswold's calumnies could be given," etc.

Remember these are only *suggestions*.

On page 35, I should *omit* from the account quoted from Mr. Latto the words "and he was often consulted by Mrs. Clemm as to the ways & means, as the boarding business did not pay." I should simply say after the words "boarded at that time with Mrs. Clemm," "Mr. Gowans lived with them several months & only left when the household was broken up; he had of course the best opportunity of seeing what kind of life the poet led," etc., etc.

The omitted portion is somewhat irrelevant, & the talk with Mrs. Clemm, &c., I think, weakens the effect of the testimony.

So much is said about Poe's poverty, too, that it does not seem necessary to introduce it here.

Don't think me foolishly fastidious, but, somehow, the words "boarding business" jar on my ear. Don't laugh, if you can help it. I know the words are not *yours*, but Mr. Latto's, or, perhaps, Gowans'.

On page 62, you say in introducing a passage from *E.P. & His Critics*, "Here, *exclaims* Mrs. Whitman," etc. I think *writes* Mrs. W[hitman]—or *says* Mrs. W[hitman]—would be better than *exclaims*, because the quoted passage is a narration rather than exclamation, *n'est-ce-pas?*

On page 63 I should say in the quotation beginning "on this occasion"—"On this occasion I was introduced to the young wife of the poet & to the mother, a tall, dignified lady, then more than sixty years old. Mrs. Poe looked very young" etc. Thus leaving out the dress *"which looked really elegant on her."* I think the lady appears to more advantage without her *dress*,—don't *you?* The phrase underscored sounds too much like a dressmaker's. But this is a woman's criticism, & perhaps would have no weight as an *argumentum ad hominum.* I submit it to your grave consideration, however.

On page 85, after the words "injured no one but himself," you say, "and certainly no one before or since has suffered so severely in character in consequence of it." The structure of the sentence is a little obscure, is it not?

Would it not be better—but I leave it to you to straighten it out, if, indeed, it needs straightening.

I must close this hurried letter and bid you Godspeed in your work. May all good angels help you!

I shall hope to write again soon. I have much to say, but not now.

Ever & ever faithfully and affectionately your friend,

S.H.W.

[*Marginal note:*] You can return Anna Blackwell's notelet.

1. George Sand, *Jacques*, trans. Anna Blackwell, 2d ed. (New York: J. S. Redfield, 1847).

2. Miss Blackwell was later to deny to Ingram that she had ever received a letter from Poe. As we shall see, her denial was a lie that figured largely in the rupture of relations between Mrs. Whitman and Ingram. See Item 315 in the Ingram Poe Collection. For a reproduction of Poe's letter addressed to Miss Blackwell from Fordham, June 14, 1848, see Ostrom, II, 369–71.

85. *Sarah Helen Whitman to John H. Ingram.* Item 204

My dear Mr. Ingram,   March 29 [9], 1875
   Your last most interesting letter was dated Jan. 9 [29], just two months ago today![1] So long an interval has not elapsed, since I knew you, between your letters. Yet, as you spoke of having to start on a tour of one or two months duration, through Great Britain & Ireland, as a possibility, I try to comfort myself by thinking that this is the reason of your silence; & then (aware that you have so many correspondents) I try not be anxious about you. Meantime, the winter has passed with me like a strange dream. The storms have been incessant, the cold unintermitting, and disease & death holding high carnival throughout the country. My friend, G. L. Dwight, who was so much interested about your work on Poe, died without seeing it, at Nassau, New Providence, & a fortnight ago I attended his funeral in Providence.
   I read to Mr. Harris your message about Poe's 1829 edition of poems two days after receiving your letter. He told me that he ordered a friend to buy for him the edition of which I spoke—the one which he saw in New York. But his friend dissuaded him. The price was 50 dollars. He has reason to hope that he may soon obtain the other copy held by a friend of his in Boston. If he does, you shall see it. He told me about a fortnight ago that he had sent you one of his catalogues of American poetry, and he requested me to state to you that he should probably send in a fortnight or three weeks the 1831 edition to his bookbinder in London, & should send it inscribed to your address, that he should not like to entrust it to a registered post, thinking sending it by package to his bookbinder much safer. He thinks there is *no doubt whatever* as to the article in the *Philobiblion* having been written by Stoddard.
   I saw the announcement in the Boston *Commonwealth* of Saturday, March 6, that your article was republished in the *International* for March.[2] The March *Eclectic* republishes the *Saturday Review* critique. I enclose the notices in the *Commonwealth*.
   Rose writes me a charming letter about her Paris life. She thinks there never was such a dismal, doleful climate, & is sometimes desperately homesick. I doubt if she had not been more disconsolate in New England. Certainly nothing could have been worse than our own winter.
   I am going to venture out into the snow & sleet to mail my letter for tomorrow's steamer, & to buy a copy of the *International*.
   I long to hear from you and to know that all is well with you. Mr. Harris says you will understand that his Index, being intended chiefly for his own use, & for private circulation, sacrifices necessarily

something to brevity. Thus he has given S.A. as the initials to all Mrs.
L[ewis]'s poems & editions of poems, because the first was S.A.

May heaven bless & prosper you, and all good angels guard you
until we meet here or hereafter.

S.H.W.

1. This letter was posted on Mar. 9, 1874.

2. Ingram's article "Edgar Allan Poe," in the New York *International Review* (Mar.-
Apr., 1875), 145–72, is but a condensation of the "Memoir" with which he had prefaced
Vol. I of his 1874–75 edition of Poe's works and is therefore easily available.

86. *John H. Ingram to Sarah Helen Whitman*

Howard House
Stoke Newington Green
London, England

My dear Friend,   14 March 1875
By this superscription you will see that I have not yet departed upon
the proposed official tour—nothing is yet settled, and at present it
seems to be a "toss up" whether I go or not. This is just the time of the
year when I always feel sentimentally inclined, but luckily for your
patience I have so very much to talk about that I must, perforce, spare
you a long tirade on my fancies & feelings.

Forgive me that I have so long delayed a letter. I have been unwell
again—in bed two days (and ought to have been there longer) with
influenza, and have been working hard—too hard—and also have had
to go to three dinner parties in one week. My excuses seem too many, I
perceive. Some times I wish that I could "cut" all my friends & start
afresh in "fresh fields & pastures new." What *can* I do in literature?
Imprisoned at my office until 4 o'clock, I get home tired out, &, if not
compelled to go somewhere—and, indeed, it is not from any
encouragement they get from me, that people ask me out—I attempt to
answer my letters, or do something literary. But a few of the things I
project can I ever hope to accomplish—but to my muttons.

Have you heard from Miss Peckham? My last has remained so long
unanswered. Mrs. Oakes Smith wrote me a long rambling letter about
nothing, *entre nous*, & I have not had time to answer it. Many thanks
for E. Benson's comparative views of Poe and Hawthorne.[1] If you want
it back say so and I will copy any part I may want & return it. I return
Miss Blackwell's letter with thanks. I am grieved you never got the
"Recollections of E. Poe" from the *Sixpenny*—it is a great loss. I sent
it, I am certain, and, I fancy, by bookpost, done up with some other
papers relating to Poe. I had only extracted a portion & in my longer

life could have made use of some more of it. The paper would appear
to have been a copy of one contributed by Mrs. Nichols to the *Leader*,
an American paper. Owing to Mrs. Nichols' suggestion, I did not send
my letter *re*. Stoddard's "Memoir" to the New York papers, but I am
now determined to do so, for the following reasons. In the first place, it
is addressed to English readers & has been published here by
Routledge—although, apparently, without being sent to the reviewers.
Secondly, I have received a verbatim copy of the *1829* edition of the
poems, as far as beginning of "Tamerlane"—the remainder to follow—
and find that they are *verbatim* with the later editions. Stoddard
undoubtedly knows this & in calling Poe's note "mendacious" is fully
aware that he lies himself. Mr. Harris is undoubtedly right in deeming
Stoddard the author of the paper in the *Philobiblion*—he was then
writing for it, and "H.R.," by which it is signed, is only "R.H." reversed.
So much for Stoddard! I must get Davidson—who is a real friend—to
send me *Harper's New Monthly* with the account of "Poe at West
Point," for Stoddard it seems suppressed all that was in favour of Poe
in the paper & made it appear to his prejudice.[2]

As regards the Nichols—Mrs. Nichols was very friendly & promised
to write me out a long paper (or rather dictate for me, as her sight is so
bad) on Poe. She was, as I have said, the author of the *Sixpenny Maga*.
paper. Now strictly between ourselves & the post, I cannot rely very
much *upon the accuracy* or *the friendliness* of either the Dr. or his
wife. I trust that I am not misjudging them. But the Dr., I am sure, to
make a point, would not trouble himself about the trustworthiness of
his information. He has written me some information about Griswold
unfit for publication &, indeed, everybody *now* seems to have
discovered that Griswold was a villain of the very deepest dye. For my
part, in my next "Memoir" I hope to be enabled to ignore him
completely. Dr. Nichols has just published a 2nd edition of his *Forty
Years of American Life* & therein "pitches into" everything &
everybody.[3] I have got him a few good reviews. He speaks of Poe as a
gentleman & a genius, &c. but recounts two anecdotes of his drunken
ways. One, that he sold a *hoax* to a paper & when it was brought out as
an "extra" & was selling largely, he (Poe) who had got drunk, went
before the publishing office & told the crowd that it was all a hoax—
that he (Poe) had written it, &c., &c. The 2nd anecdote evidently refers
to Poe's engagement with you—its rupture—& is little different to
Griswold's account.

Curwen's book has been noticed in the chief papers & nearly all of
them compare his account of Poe with my "Memoir" & certainly not to
Curwen's advantage. My review of his book in the *Academy* came out
yesterday.[4] I will send it together with review of my work in the
Athenaeum for fear you should not see them. I expect Moy Thomas

wrote this last—'tis a strange review, but I am very glad to see the way in which it speaks of your book.

I have not been able to see Gill's "Memoir" yet. *Lotos Leaves* has been published in London, but at 21 shillings, and I cannot find for certain that it contains Gill's life. I must wait until I can see it at some store—or the Museum, as the price is too much for a chance. But in truth I've not had time to investigate the matter.

I enclose you a long account of my book, by Moncure Conway, published in Cincinnati. My most important communication, however, has been from "*M.L.S.*"—Mrs. Houghton. I hope on a future occasion to give you fuller particulars, but when I tell you that she has sent me some of Poe's letters & many of Mrs. Clemm's and 44 pages of her own writing, you will see that there was something in it. She has also sent me the original transcript by Poe, written in her presence, of "The Bells" & has sent me two books (which have not yet come to hand) but which I beieve are the 1845 *Poems & Tales*! Her information & assistance will be invaluable. She was with Poe during a long illness & during that time, at his request, *took down in pencil the events of his life*. This account, she hopes to find for me! Also a long unpublished poem which she gave Poe 25 dollars for. She says she offered Griswold $500 not to publish his "Memoir" of Poe, but Mrs. Clemm marred all by her unhappy intervention. Poe's first love was named Mary Star. There is the "Mary" I was seeking for—and the lady is supposed to be still alive & married. She was (M. Star) very kind to Poe during his wife's last illness. He also told Mrs. Shew (now Houghton) of some "Helen," doubtless Mrs. Stanard. I cannot now tell you all as I want to answer your letter, but you will see what new sources I am opening up. O! That I could visit America! I *must* & *will*! I thoroughly rely upon Mrs. Houghton. I can tell that from her letter.[5]

I do believe in chirography as the enclosed proof may give you a humorous example, "Don Felix" being "John Ingram." Only don't tell anyone. I am writing a series & expect to see it republished in America. I wish to preserve my anonymousness at present as it affords me greater freedom of opinion.[6] Whenever I can steal a few moments I shall try & copy some of Mrs. Shew's information for you. And now for your own dear letter.

Godey's present address came in Mrs. Houghton's letter—together with interesting reminiscence of Poe by the Revd. Dr. Hopkins.[7] I would not, however, mention anything of Mrs. Houghton's information at present, until I get her permission. The two books have never arrived from Mrs. H[oughton]. If they are lost it will be a shame. Your other vols. through no fault of mine, or even of Blacks, have never gone off. Blacks sent them to Scribner's agent here in London. They delayed them, & I fancy purposely, & now I cannot discover how to send them save separately by post—& your engraving of Poe too! But, *envente*, I do not seem to get a moment to inquire about, or do anything, save at the risk of leaving something else of importance undone. I shall get into a complete maelström one of these days & "finish off" in a flourish.

Do you know a Mr. —— Fiske Harris? He has sent me a catalogue of his American library of Poetry & the Drama.[8] Perhaps at your suggestion? As soon as I can I will look thru it. Have you seen any American notices of my "Memoir"? Now to your letter—

I should have remembered that it was Anna & *not* Elizabeth Blackwell who boarded at Fordham, but to Mrs. Nichols I merely said Miss Blackwell, so she *might* have recollected, but I certainly understood her to ignore Miss Blackwell's residence at Fordham. I will ask her again in my next. By the way, did not Mrs. Clemm ever mention Mrs. Shew to you? She was very much indebted to Mrs. S[hew], apparently. The letter Miss Blackwell received from Poe, have you now? If so, dare I ask a copy? When I see Gill's account I shall be glad to get any corrections of yours to it. Also I shall always be glad to get your corrections & suggestions *re. my* present & proposed "Memoir." I have seen about 40 reviews of my book & only the *Saturday Review* unfavourable, & that not so bad for it. I fancy the *Spectator* was the best, that is, the most talented. I did not care much for the *Examiner*—but there, I don't believe in reviews.

You speak of the 1850 edition (Redfield's). Is not that the one might Griswold's "Memoir" [*sic*]. I am ending this from home—Oh! of course it is! But I did not seem to recollect that it gave a positive date for Poe's leaving Fordham. Don't trouble to answer this paragraph. All your suggestions are valued & will receive my *most careful* consideration &, doubtless, in many instances be acted upon but, *if not* in all, you will know that only weighty reasons will prevent their use. But my next life of Poe will be an entirely new &, *I feel*, a far better & more literary work. My only dread is that I may not live to complete it.

And now, my ever dear friend, once more a mental shake hands. Never forego sending me a few lines, whenever you can, because you do not think you have anything of importance to tell me. I value every word of yours, it is no flattery but honest truth to say, and look for your letters most longingly. But now, goodbye for the present. I hope to write again soon. And remain, believe me, so long as thought is mine, yours most faithfully & affectionately.

John H. Ingram.

P.S. My paper on Poe has appeared in the New York *International* & I will request Davidson to send you a copy. On looking thro' it, it has occurred to me that you may not like the second paragraph allusion to *ancestry*, but I hope you will not be annoyed—pray forgive me—I did not think of your labours at the moment. In fact the allusion tells as much against me as against anyone. But, perhaps, you will not look at it in an unfavourable light.

J.H.I.

1. For Eugene Benson's "The American Critic," see p. 129, n. 4.

2. "Poe at West Point," *Harper's New Monthly*, 35 (Nov. 1867) 754–56, is unsigned: it was written by Thomas W. Gibson, a classmate of Poe's at the academy. See Item 542 in the Ingram Poe Collection.

3. Thomas Low Nichols, *Forty Years of American Life*, 2d ed. (London: Longmans, Green and Co., 1874). Materials about Poe are on pages 230–31.

4. A reprint follows.

5. Mrs. Marie Louise Barney Shew Houghton (d. Sept. 3, 1877) was truly to be of great help to Ingram in his efforts to build Poe biography. At times she was puzzling, if not actually exasperating, but he never lost faith in her, nor, apparently, she in him. Her letters to him are reproduced in *Building Poe Biography*, pp. 89–145, admittedly incomplete, for, voluminous as they are, they were all written in 1875, and her correspondence certainly continued until her death. Trouble developed between Ingram and her family, aided by Eugene L. Didier of Baltimore, as they attempted to regain the many valuable letters from Poe, manuscripts, books, and the miniature of Poe's mother that Mrs. Houghton had sent to Ingram which he understood to be gifts. The supposition is that Ingram separated from his Poe papers those letters from her that would help to prove his case and they were never replaced.

Daughter and granddaughter of well-known New York physicians, Mrs. Houghton certainly thought of herself as a doctor, too. After her introduction into the Poe household at Fordham by Mrs. Mary Gove Nichols, she nursed Virginia until she died, provided her burial clothes, and after the funeral continued to nurse Edgar through a long sickness that followed, during which time he dictated to her fanciful accounts of a trip he had made to France, a duel he had fought, poems and a story he had written, all of which Mrs. Houghton relayed to Ingram; he in turn muddied the waters of Poe biography with them.

Mrs. Houghton correctly diagnosed Poe's principal physical trouble as a lesion of the brain, and she took him to the famed Dr. Valentine Mott for confirmation. It was she, too, who made the only painting known of Virginia Poe; after Virginia's death they propped her body up in bed, and Mrs. Houghton, who could paint with water colors, made the portrait that is now so well known.

6. In imitation of Poe's "Autography," Ingram began publishing a series of articles called "The Philosophy of Handwriting," by Don Felix de Salamanca, in which he attempted to analyze the characters of contemporary British and American authors as they revealed themselves in their autographs.

7. John Henry Hopkins (1820–1891) was a divinity student in a New York seminary when he met Poe, through Mrs. Shew, and heard him expound his pantheistic ideas. Hopkins was a very close friend of Mrs. Shew's and he was apparently afraid that Poe's ideas and personality would prove to be socially and morally dangerous for her; she, in turn, seemed to be inexplicably afraid of offending Hopkins.

8. This is one of the most incomprehensible sentences in any of Ingram's letters. He had known Caleb Fiske Harris, through Mrs. Whitman, for certainly over a year, had written to him and had borrowed copies of Poe's books from him, as well as seeking his advice and help, and even heeding both sometimes.

87. *Review of Henry Curwen's* Sorrow and Song, *by John H. Ingram,*
London Academy, 7 *(Mar. 13, 1875), 262–63*

Sorrow and Song: Studies of Literary Struggle.
By Henry Curwen.
In Two Volumes. (London: H. S. King & Co., 1874).

MR. CURWEN, if we do not misunderstand his exordium, has written
these six "studies of literary struggle" to prove that Grub Street and its
attendant misery are not things of the past. But of the half-dozen writers
whose stories he adduces, not one, it should be pointed out, is an Englishman, or in other respects confirms the truth of his proposition[. . . .]
    The authors whose lives Mr. Curwen has selected to typify the
suggestively alliterative compound of "sorrow and song" are men whose
stories must be badly told indeed not to prove interesting, even though
the teller have few or no new facts to tell[. . . .]
    In his memoir of Edgar Poe Mr. Curwen seems to have been rather
more desirous to "adorn a tale" than to give the somewhat commonplace
story of the poet's life. In all fairness to Mr. Curwen, however, it must
be acknowledged that the inaccuracies of this life are not so much due
to him as to his American authorities. In reading Griswold's *Memoir of*
Poe, he has, like all impartial persons, naturally been disgusted with the
biographer's open display of hatred for the subject of his story, and, asserts Mr. Curwen, when resolved to write the poet's life, "I began with
a thorough determination to vindicate Poe from the aspersions Dr. Griswold had so cruelly cast upon him." After this assertion it seems strange
to find Mr. Curwen declaring that, "after sifting every item of evidence
I could lay hands on for Poe and against Poe, my present monograph
has turned out very differently from what I had hoped," and that he
should then, notwithstanding the fact that there is scarcely an accusation made against Poe by his biographer but has been frequently refuted
in print, repeat, as matter of fact, almost the whole of Griswold's calumnies! Elsewhere we have shown, upon irrefutable testimony, the utter falsity of Griswold's pseudo–*Memoir of Poe*, and it is neither
necessary nor possible to recapitulate here the facts of the poet's career.
Besides the misstatements, however, which Mr. Curwen has been led to
make through following Griswold and his *alter ego* in the *Southern Lit-*
erary Messenger—this latter, doubtless, from Baudelaire's quotations—
we find a few others new to us. Poe was born in 1809, not 1811, and we
much doubt whether Mr. Curwen can give any authority, other than
Griswold's, for saying that the author of "The Raven" ever gave any
other date. Upon what basis Mr. Curwen has raised his romantic superstructure of Poe's passion for Virginia Clemm having originated in 1822

we know not; but this we can say, if it be true, it is the most wonderful circumstance of Poe's life, the precocious young lady then being in her second year! Poe was first married to Miss Clemm in 1834, but she continued to reside with her mother until 1835, when, being only fifteen, she was again married to Poe, some doubts having been expressed as to the legality of the former ceremony. Poe's expulsion from the University of Virginia the unimpeachable records of the faculty disprove; and the statement, transcending Griswold, "that there was not a vice in the whole catalogue of human sins" that this young Yankee Heliogabalus "did not hasten to commit," is utterly disproved by facts. It is needless, however, to re-tread the weary maze of lies in which Griswold and others involved Poe's history, and which Mr. Curwen, through no fault of his own, has so innocently followed, quoting letters which we do not hesitate to call forgeries, and recounting disgraceful anecdotes which had no foundation in fact. How apt he has been to adopt the idea of Poe's badness is shown by his statement that the poet's first use of the *Broadway Journal* was "to attack his enemies at Boston"—an assertion which reference to the pages of that journal in the British Museum Reading Room would have disproved. That the "Helen" of the poem quoted at page 155, vol. ii, was "one of the wealthiest women" of New England will doubtless surprise the lady to whom Poe wrote the lines. She was not, is not, even rich. The poet's engagement with her was not secret, as stated by Mr. Curwen, nor was it broken off in the way he describes, as reference to the *New York Tribune* for June 7, 1852, will show. But enough has been said to prove that Mr. Curwen has been misled by his authorities with regard to Poe's character; he has dealt with him less leniently than either Hannay or Baudelaire did, and yet doubtless with quite as much desire for veracity as they had. Should *Sorrow and Song* reach a second edition—and we trust it may—it is to be hoped that Mr. Curwen will retell this story of a life which is certainly worth the telling.

John H. Ingram

88. *Sarah Helen Whitman to John H. Ingram.*   *Item 208*

My dear Mr. Ingram,   March 26, [18]75
    Your last letter was dated January 29! I dread to think what may have happened in so long an interval. You spoke of leaving England on a government tour to Ireland & Scotland. I hope you are well & that everything has prospered with you during this long silence. My last letter was mailed to you Feb. 16th [Mar. 9]. Since then I have suffered

unremitting pains in my head & eyes. The two last months have been fearful. Such weather was never known before.

Every week I have tried to write to you—tried in vain—Mr. Harris I saw nearly a fortnight ago after a long interval. He told me he had written to you & had sent some books for you to his bookbinder in London. He directed his letter to Howard House instead of the address you last sent me. I hope it reached you. I confidently expected a letter from you today, & am *so* disappointed. It may come this evening.

Mr. Bartlett brought me the *Athenaeum* containing an admirable notice of your book, and I had from the Prov. Library the *Examiner* of Jan. 27, I think, containing Mr. Gosse's article on the poems. I think his comments on "Ulalume" were rather verdant, & does he not know that "Astarte's bediamonded crescent" was the crescent of *Venus*, the morning star, seen rising through the constellation Denebola! He would appreciate the poem better if he knew the weird symbolism of every line & phrase it contains. I was a good deal stirred by his presumptuous criticism.

I have not yet seen the *International* containing your article, although the book agents here promised to send for it. I have been too ill to attend to anything myself, but I must not say another word *now*, only to give you my heart's blessing & say goodbye.

Have you seen Swinburne's *Bothwell?*[1] It is highly praised by Stedman in the March number of Scribner's *Monthly*. Do you ever see that periodical?

Ever faithfully & affectionately your friend,

S.H.W.

You see how unfitted I am for writing.
Can you tell me anything of Swinburne's *Under the Microscope?*[2]

1. Algernon Charles Swinburne, *Bothwell: A Tragedy* (London: Chatto & Windus, 1874).
2. Algernon Charles Swinburne, *Under the Microscope* (London: D. White, 1872).

89. *Sarah Helen Whitman to John H. Ingram.*   *Item 211*

My dear Mr. Ingram,   March 30, [18]75
Your long-looked-for letter [Mar. 14] came yesterday. I am sorry I told you of my anxiety. I ought to have known how very busy you must be, with so much on your hands. Your letter was intensely interesting, as are all your letters.

Mrs. Clemm never mentioned M.L.S. to me, but the difficulty about Griswold's "Memoir" may have led to permanent estrangement. Did Mrs. Houghton anticipate the malign character of the "Memoir?" Do you know when it was that Poe dictated to her the events of his life? And so Mr. Conway was a cousin of Mr. Daniel & tells the same story of the challenge, etc., that was given by Mrs. Anna Cora Ritchie to my friend Julia Deane Freeman. That is well. I *like* Conway's notice & wonder I had not seen or heard of it before, though I think the word "ardent" as applied to my characterization of Poe is out of place; it almost makes me doubt if he has ever read it [*Edgar Poe and His Critics*]. It might perhaps be called too imaginative or too unreal (which I do not admit, however), & one of my friends always speaks of it as my finest "poem." To this I don't so much object. The ideal is often far truer than the actual.

What Conway says about Poe's being the only man whose life had been made the subject of a mythology is true enough. Do you know Mr. Conway personally?

There was a notice in the *Nation* of last week, or rather a critique, of your "Memoir" & Stoddard's "as indicative of a revived interest in the *genius* of Poe," of which genius of course it has not the faintest idea. The notice could not be called favorable to either, but it was not so *un*favorable as might have been anticipated, from the general character of that paper, which is notoriously dry, caustic, literal, & hard-headed; poetry & romance are words that have no meaning in its vocabulary.

You ask about Anna Blackwell's letter from Poe. I gave the letter many years ago to Mr. John R. Bartlett for his large & valuable collection of autographs. The copy which he made for me is still in my possession. I will copy it *verbatim*, though it contains nothing of special interest except of interest to *me*, & perhaps to *you*, in the passage wherein he speaks of S.H.W. Miss Blackwell was, as you perhaps know, of English birth and parentage.

While I have been copying the enclosed letter, your copy of the *Athenaeum* has been left by the postman. I mean the one containing Moy Thomas's review. It is the one which Mr. Bartlett brought me to read, but I am glad to own it. Thanks.

I hope Mr. Harris's letter, which was mailed a week ago, will duly reach you, & I hope that you will not "cut" *all* your friends, as you expressed a wish to in your last. Yet one may find "three dinner parties a week" too much of a good thing.

And now, my dear Don Felix, good night, & keep cool & don't provoke an open fight with Stoddard. Mrs. Nichols gives good advice.

Ever & ever your friend,

S.H.W.

I will write again soon, but don't think you must answer, & don't mind about my criticisms.

90. *John H. Ingram to Sarah Helen Whitman*

My dear Friend,   7 April 1875
    Your letter dated 26th March is just to hand, and has pained me for two reasons. First, to hear of your suffering, the effect, apparently, of the unusual severity and long duration of this terrible winter, and, secondly, because one of my letters seems to have miscarried.
    As regards your health, I do most sincerely & fervently trust that the arrival of Spring (although the winds *here* are still very inclement) is restoring you. I shall look out anxiously for each fresh letter from you—that is to say, more anxiously than of heretofore.
    I cannot understand about my letters. Between the 29th of Jany. & 1st of this month I sent two letters apparently, & the first you do not seem to have received. Unfortunately, I do not retain dates of all my letters & cannot say precisely when the missing one was sent, nor can I [be] sure whether it contained any enclosures, or matters of importance. I fancy it was sent away about the last week in Feby. or first in March, and was, I think, a very long one & thicker than usual. I am speaking from memory only. If the notelet from Miss Blackwell was not in that of the 1st Instant, it was in the missing letter. I hope it will come to hand, but fear after this long time it is lost—the first, I think, that we have yet lost.

                                                             8 April 1875
    I have received a letter from Mr. Harris *re.* some books he is kindly going to lend me, including the 1831 edition of Poe. I will try & write to him next mail day. I am awfully busy. I think I have informed you of the contents of Mrs. Houghton's letters—she has written me again but nothing of consequence save a note from Dr. Hopkins & one from Dr. Henry saying (the former) that Dunn English was a scoundrel & (the latter) that Poe was not connected with *New York Review*. I hope Davidson sent you the *International*. He tells me Professor Liavitt was pleased with it & told him that it had been very favourably noticed. I mean my sketch of Edgar Poe therein. However, it has aroused Mr. Stoddard apparently. You will have received, I trust, before this the review of his book in the *Civil Service Review* &, doubtless, have seen the review in New York *Nation* of 25 March?[1] Do not be annoyed at this latter, to the editor of which I have sent the *Civil Service Review*

critique for his gratification, & by next post day shall forward him my answer. I hope he will print it but, for fear he does not, I shall take the precaution to forward copies to New York. As you will see, the *Nation* has fearfully misquoted me, but placed themselves entirely in my hands by the nature of their attack—by trying to remove the slanders of Griswold & by styling *me a hater of Americans*!

By next mail I hope to send you copies of prospectus I am printing, of short extracts from each review, referring to the *vindication only*. I notice that with scarcely any exception all *our* reviewers speak of Poe as "the greatest literary genius of America" and this from all kinds of papers—even religious. I hope you got the London *Athenaeum* I sent you—Oh! I see you have seen it. *Entre nous*, I fancy 'twas by Moy Thomas.

Mr. Harris's letter reached me quite safely. Mr. Gosse's paper on the poems was rubbish—he is a *very* young man, I fancy, & has been rather severely handled as a versifier in some quarters. He has invited me to visit him but I have not had time yet.

I wonder these kind of reviews move you to anything but pity for the ignorance, or envy, of their authors. To try & abolish Poe by a review is about equal to Mrs. Partington's attempt to stem the Atlantic with her broom.

I enclose you a reprint of the *C[ivil] S[ervice] Review*. If you know any friend in New York who will republish it in any paper, I shall be glad. The Flute Ode will appear in *C[ivil] S[ervice] Review* on Saturday & you shall have copies; reprint it if you can as from the London *Civil Service Review*.

I seldom see *Scribner's* although published in London. I only know *Bothwell* by reviews. Ditto of *Under the Microscope*. 'Tis, I believe, a very trenchant attack upon certain reviewers, although an American compiler classed it among new scientific works! No time for another *iota*. Ever your faithful friend,

John H. Ingram

P.S. Don't trouble about the letter missing. I have muddled some way—somehow. If you get a letter of any date prior to 1 April that is probably the only letter. In great haste,

J.H.I.

---

1. R. H. Stoddard, *Poems by Edgar Allan Poe, Complete, with an Original Memoir* (New York: Widdleton, 1875). The review, which immediately follows, is unsigned, but the single page from an unidentified magazine found in Mrs. Whitman's papers has "Extracted from The Civil Service Review, 3 April 1875," written across the top of the left-hand column.

91. *Review of R. H. Stoddard's "Original Memoir" in* Poems by
Edgar Allan Poe, *by John H. Ingram, London* Civil Service Review,
Apr. 3, 1875

An Original Memoir
[John H. Ingram]

ANOTHER SO-CALLED "Original Memoir" of Edgar Allan Poe has just
been published in New York. It is mainly a republication of a sketch,
which appeared in *Harper's New Monthly Magazine* in 1872, anonymously, the authorship of which, however, is now acknowledged by Mr.
R. H. Stoddard. This memoir would not have been noticed by us had it
not been expressly submitted "to English readers" by its author, probably in the belief that they have no means of detecting his shortcomings.
The book is heralded by a Preface, in which Griswold, who has, of late,
been so severely handled by Mr. Ingram and others, is held up to scorn
for the "serious literary offense" he committed in writing of Poe in the
manner he did; but the *animus* which Mr. Stoddard himself exhibits
towards the memory of his great countryman—for it is presumed that
Mr. Stoddard is an American—proves that he is as little qualified to
write the poet's life as was his predecessor. That Griswold's work was
compiled in a way to be avoided by "all right-minded biographers" most
people will be ready to admit, as also that it "abounds with blunders;"
but that the worst of these blunders, or indeed any one of them, have
been corrected in the present memoir, as claimed by Mr. Stoddard, we
fail to see. Mr. Stoddard accuses Griswold of having neglected to inform
himself thoroughly in regard to the particulars of Poe's life, he having,
amongst other offenses, misstated the time of the poet's birth: and yet,
strange to relate, this "right minded biographer" himself gives an incorrect date. That Poe was not born on the 19th of February, 1809, Mr.
Stoddard might easily have discovered had he only taken that trouble
which he accuses his predecessor of having shirked: reference to a file
of Boston papers of the date stated would have afforded him information
by means of which he might have avoided, at least in this one instance,
the fate of Griswold.

A complete analysis of the eighty pages of twaddle and quotation
which constitute this "Original Memoir" is, of course, out of the question; but an examination of some few of its reckless assertions may not
prove altogether unprofitable "to English readers." Mr. Stoddard's remark that "I need not say that I have tried to write impartially" is, indeed, a needless one, as no one will charge him with *that*; but when he
asserts, "I have passed no judgment upon this singular man," his words
need confirmation. In our perusal of Mr. Stoddard's short account of *this*

singular man, we noted, *ad passim*, the following autorial comments, and as they really constitute the thread upon which are strung the quotations—acknowledged and otherwise—forming this original work, we think our readers will agree with us that the author need not have been so modest about not having passed any judgment. All the accusations which he levies at Griswold may safely be transferred to Mr. Stoddard himself: were they as true as they are false they would still prove that he misused his testimonies "by using them to Poe's disadvantage solely," and that "the fact is, he took no pains with his work, which abounds with blunders." Even from the preface onwards, this impartial biographer endeavours to prejudice his readers against Poe by sneers, innuendoes, and direct accusations of dishonesty. He remarks, with the proviso "it may be said," that the poet gave two false dates of his birth; but we defy him to adduce evidence of his having given one: he alleges that the note to Poe's "Poems written in Youth" is "mendacious," but omits to give any proof of its mendacity: he strives to discredit Poe's statement that "Tamerlane" was printed in 1827, whereas, if he has that bibliographical knowledge of the subject he pretends to, he must know that the poet's assertion was correct: he repeats a puerile story of Griswold's with a view of proving Poe bad even as an infant, and parades his own ignorance, either of scholarship or of the poet's writing, by remarking that Poe's works show little trace of a classical education, adding, "for my own part I believe that his acquirements were rather in the direction of mathematical than classical learning, and that they were not remarkable in either." On the authority of "a lady" whom Mr. Stoddard, as usual, leaves unnamed, he states that, when a schoolboy, Poe's "inordinate self-esteem often led him to fancy affronts when none were intended," and that parents would not allow their children to play with him as "he was *such* a bad boy."

In some parts of his really original work this "right minded biographer," emulous of Griswold, assumes an intimate knowledge of Poe's innermost thoughts, and assures us that, when a youth, the poet "was clever enough to feign repentance if he did not feel it," and that, "having quickly detected the weak points of his adopted parents, he "took advantage of them, so much so that dissimulation and evasion became habitual with him." In support, apparently, of this charge Mr. Stoddard relates an anecdote that is certainly new to us, and which, it is presumed, is derived from one of those sources he states he can authenticate, but which he almost invariably forgets to. The story runs to the effect that when Poe returned from the University, and just after "an enormous sum of his debts" had been paid, the youth incurred "a bill for quantities of champagne and seventeen broad-cloth coats, which he had gambled away;" and, showing off his habitual evasion, had the audacity to say to his adopted mother, and before a stranger, "I went to see how much of the old man's money I could spend, and I have done it."

Returning to the editorial comments of our impartial biographer, we find his declaration, twice repeated, that Poe "was nothing if not critical;" that he "was too idle to take much pains with anything;" that he "was not a good editor. He lacked catholicity of taste and sweetness of temper;" that "he was dogmatic, insolent, impracticable, and always squabbling;" that "he had the genius of a Celt for creating a row," but that "a revolution was beyond his powers;" that "he provoked literary quarrels;" that "he had no settled standard of criticism, except that *he* was infallible, even when contradictory," and so on, to the end of the Memoir.

A very natural question is, Whence Mr. Stoddard's enmity for Poe— an enmity apparently extending to, and even including the poet's friends? Almost of necessity this must be a mystery to *us*; and, did not our original biographer vouchsafe some kind of an explanation himself, one might almost deem this memoir published in the hopes of gaining its author a little temporary notoriety. Mr. Stoddard, according to his own account, had a weakness common to young men: he "wrote verse and thought it poetry." With becoming *naiveté*, he confesses that a perusal of Keats's "Ode on a Grecian Urn," inspired him to indite an "Ode on a Grecian Flute." This effort of genius was sent to *The Broadway Journal*, then under the editorship of Poe, who actually declined to publish it, under the frivolous pretext that some portions of it were "so bad" (*vide* vol. 2, p. 63), although Mr. Stoddard's memory, being somewhat faulty, causes him to assign a different reason. Utterly astounded at the poet's lack of "catholicity of taste," the young versifier called upon him for an explanation, succeeded in penetrating into the editorial sanctum, when, according to his own story, being threatened by Poe with personal chastisement unless he left at once, he very prudently retired. After this episode one can scarcely be surprised to find Mr. Stoddard deeming the publication, which, like Paradise to the Peri, was "for ever closed to *him*," "the *Saturday Review of Billingsgate*"—a foreign locality evidently known to this writer—nor need we be surprised that he believed its editor "determined to make it as atrocious as he could," and that his critiques "possessed little or no value as criticisms." Neither time nor inclination permit us to reprint any more of Mr. Stoddard's autobiographical adventures, although they will doubtless be valuable when the time arrives for his life to be written; but we cannot take leave of this volume without drawing attention to its editor's unmanly and utterly uncalled for behavior towards his distinguished countrywoman, Mrs. Whitman. After using several pages of that lady's work on *Edgar Poe and his Critics*, but without the slightest acknowledgment, he deliberately, and in the face of her direct assertion—an assertion she confirms by Poe's written testimony—proceeds to question the fact that the poem beginning "Helen, thy beauty is to me"—a poem, by the way, not included in this *complete* edition—was inspired by the memory of a Mrs. H. S———. Probably Mr. Stoddard, in expressing his doubts as to the veracity of Mrs. Whitman, does so upon his usually well authenticated evidence, although without any of that courtesy which foreigners deem accorded to ladies by Americans. But we are sick of this "Original Memoir." we had intended to expose more of its many misstatements as to facts, its garbling and misquotations of testimony in Poe's favour, its manifold impertinences and absurdities; but to do so is needless. Not nearly so cleverly constructed as its prototype, Griswold's libel on a dead man's memory, it is far less likely to injure Poe: it carries its antidote with it, and will be forgotten as speedily as read.

The illustrations, it should be noted, are less original than the memoir, having already done good service in Messrs. Routledge and Sons cheap edition of Poe's poems, and in the above mentioned sketch in Harper's *New Monthly Magazine.*

92. *Sarah Helen Whitman to John H. Ingram.*   Item 216

My dear Mr. Ingram,   April 14, [18]75
    Yours of April 1st [?] came yesterday; and last week the *International*, through Mr. Davidson, &, by the same post, the capital paper of our friend "Don Felix" on the philosophy of handwriting—very ingenious, clever, & amusing. The "Don" has made some capital hits, though in some instances the specimens of autography would hardly suggest the traits which the acute critic finds so characteristic of their writers to any but an expert, as, for instance, that of Matthew Arnold, and perhaps Tennyson. But the article is very piquant & entertaining. I wish the Don would give us an interpretation of J. H. Ingram's autograph, which I have heard very much admired for its self-reliant strength & sustained energy—its manliness, directness, & sincerity.
    I am greatly pleased with the article in the *International*. It is more compact in structure, less fragmentary, and more *impressive* in its nervous concentration. I am perfectly satisfied, *more* than satisfied, *delighted*. It will live while Poe's memory shall endure. You have made the very best of your material, and your allusion to the author of the anonymous letters is full of significance without containing indiscreet revelations. I am glad you have written to Mrs. Shelton. I shall look with interest for her reply. Don't fail to tell *me*.
    If the records & recollections which you are calling out shall prove valuable, you will have matter for a volume. But you will doubtless

find occasion to recast & rewrite much that is put in your hands. You say Mrs. N[ichols] is "fanciful." Have you received a portion of her record?

Don't trouble yourself about the other volumes of your edition of the works.

You will have received ere this Mr. Harris's letter & the books which he forwarded for you to his publisher.

I learned the other day from Miss Kate Peckham, the sister of our Rose, that she has decided to overmaster her *heimweh* & stay abroad another year.

I wish I could tell you & ask of you a thousand things which must wait a serener time.

Meanwhile, my dear Don Felix, I am your grateful friend,

S.H.W.

Mr. Harris has been away for nearly three weeks. I hope his letter arrived safely.

If you see or write R[ose], give her my heart's love. Goodbye for today,

S.H.W.

Tell Rose I have written her a dozen letters which are yet uncommitted to paper. I am suffering from neuralgia & what may aptly be called "social pressure," white-washers & house-cleaners, etc. I have been out once to the Opera House to see Janauscheck, whom I did not like, & who is no more like Rachel "than I to Hecuba."[1] Tell her [Rose] I enjoyed her Paris letter in the *Journal*, & her description of the New Opera House. It had her characteristic felicities & faults, neither of which I would willingly omit.

1. Franziska Magdalena Romance Janauschek (1830–1904), known as "Fanny," was born in Prague and became a famous actress in Germany before making her American debut in 1867; her enthusiastic reception and continued enormous popularity made her decide to remain in the United States.

93. *John H. Ingram to Sarah Helen Whitman*

My dear Mrs. Whitman,   22 April 1875
I am going to try & scribble you off a few irregular jottings. In the first place let me say that I am, as usual, very poorly—more so than I tell my people. I have never got up my strength since my rheumatic attack last year—but there! I am just doing what I did not mean to, talking of self, when I have things of importance to communicate.

The parcel of books belonging to Mr. Harris has now reached the binders, but I have not had time yet—despite my anxiety—to call there again. Did I say that Mrs. Houghton, of whom *much* hereafter, had sent me the 1845 edition of the *Poems & Tales* & that I have had a fine written facsimile of the 1829 ed. of poems sent from Baltimore?

You will have long since received the *Civil Service Review* of Stoddard & the poetic sequel by A Reader. I sent a tremendous reply to the *Nation* which I think they will publish & *criticise*. I hope there will not be anything in it to annoy you. They had better publish my reply & let the matter drop, or they my find me rather too strong for them.

Do you know what Stoddard is like? A man who was, or pretended to be, *lame*, drove to Mrs. Houghton's, gave the name of "Jones," & asked if she had any poems or letters of Poe's she would sell to a publisher!! How they found her out *must* have been thus—Mrs. Nichols could not tell her address so I sent my letter to Davidson, & he sent it, naturally, to her husband, Rev. Dr. Houghton. They are separated. He, I presume, read it & sent it on, but must have spoken of my letter to publishing, or literary acquaintances. Hence the appearance of "Jones" on the scene. But he had gone to the wrong place that time, & was dismissed at once.

If Mrs. Houghton had only preserved her relics of Poe she might have told us nearly all we want to know. I look forward to each successive *long* letter of hers with ever increasing anxiety, so valuable are they. I can not understand how it has been that you never knew her. She was so good to Poe & his wife & is so unworldly that—although, apparently, of not great educational qualifications—I feel I *love her* only second to you, my first dear friend and assistant in this matter.

Whilst I think of it—have you not thought it *shameful* that your other vols. have not arrived. I told you how they had been delayed for a long time. I am now going to send you a set bound in half morocco, crimson—they will, be the Fates willing, leave London next week &, I fear must go by Post. I will pack them as carefully as possible, & register them.

Mrs. E. O. Smith has sent me some voluminous letters—mostly about "Lizzie" White, but, I fancy, there is *nothing* in them I can make use of. I have not had the portrait from Mrs. Lewis yet, but Blacks kept a photo of it for future use. I told you, I think, it was too late for Vol. iv. I cannot hear from Davidson. I hope he is not ill—he is generally so punctual—and I sent him money remittance 18th last month & no reply yet. Mrs. Nichols has not yet sent me her recollections. I fancy, *entre nous*, they will be somewhat imaginative. You would hear from me more frequently had I not so many correspondents to stir up in this affair. I am *obliged* to write very long letters to Mrs. Houghton—do not honour me by being jealous—arising out of her valuable information. I have recently written to Mrs. Shelton, to John P. Poe, Neilson Poe's son, to John Neal, to E. V. Valentine, Dr. Hand Browne, &c., &c. The last has recently sent me some interesting particulars from Col. Scharf's *Chronicles of Baltimore* respecting the Poe family & the friendship of Lafayette, &c.[1] Also a copy of a short note by Poe to John Neal.

But I want to let you know what I can of Mrs. Houghton's information. How to compress it! Some you will see is private. The poem "To M.L.S." I think I explained I placed among juvenile poems because Griswold had it there. Mrs. Houghton has sent it to me—it and one other, to be returned, of course, but the original draft of "The Bells" & 3 letters *to be kept*! The two valentine poems are the most exquisitely written MSS. you ever beheld—I forgot that yours may have been written as beautifully. Have you ever told me the exact date of "To Helen"? "To Mrs. M.L.S." is dated—February 14, 1847. The other poem "To Marie Louise" is the poem beginning "Not long ago, the writer of these lines," &c.!! But Griswold presumedly, has omitted several lines, left out the Christian names & inserted "Italian." I shall have a facsimile made of it. One of the letters sent is to "H. D. Chapin, Esq." (now deceased) & is nearly identical in terms with that sent to Willis in 1848 respecting his (Poe's) idea of starting a magazine of his own.[2] One I have already sent you a copy of (to Mrs. Shew) & the other is a short note asking why Mrs. Shew has not been & so forth. If you wish you shall have copy next time. Mrs. Houghton has also sent me extracts from two of his letters to her—one upbraiding her for giving him up—I extract some of it that *must* interest you. It is written in June 1849, was his last to Mrs. Houghton & betrays evidence, in my opinion, of unsettled reason—"sweet bells harshly jangled." After asserting that he knows it is her last visit although she has not said so, he says (*this is private*):

Oh, Louise, how many sorrows are before you, your ingenuous and sympathetic nature will be constantly wounded in contact with the hollow heartless world, and for me, alas! unless some true and tender and pure womanly love saves me, I shall hardly last a year longer *alive*! A few short months will tell how far my strength (physical and moral) will carry me in life here. How can I believe in Providence when *you* look coldly upon me. Was it not you who renewed my hopes and faith in God? . . . & in humanity?

He alludes to something I am not to mention but of no interest but that he calls himself therein "the madman Poe." He then speaks of their last interview, &c., &c. and of the respect & esteem he has for her, adding,

I place you in my *esteem* in all *solemnity* beside the friend of my boyhood,

the mother of my schoolfellow, of whom I told you, and as I have repeated in
the poem, "The Beloved Physician," as the truest, tenderest, of this world's
most womanly souls, and an angel to my forlorn and darkened nature, . . . and
in life or death, I am ever yours gratefully and devotedly,
June 1849   Edgar A. Poe

Not a word of "the Beloved Physician," please. I believe I told you
Mrs. H[oughton] had paid Poe for it. This long poem—& to think that
in her troubles she has lost or mislaid it!! But is now searching
everywhere & hopes to recover it. One of her sons, who knew a part of
it by heart, may have it. It is to be hoped it will be recovered & prove a
masterpiece.³ You shall know at once, if it be found. You see he alludes
to Mrs. Stanard.
    The other letter is very pretty:

                                                          Sunday night
                                                          May 1848

My dear friend Louise,
Nothing for months has given me so much real pleasure, as your note of last
night. I have been engaged all day on some promised work, otherwise I
should have replied immediately as my heart inclined. I sincerely hope you
may not drift out of my sight before I can thank you. How kind of you to let
me do even *this small service* for you, in return for the great debt I owe
you. . . . I shall have so much pleasure in thinking of you and yours in that
music room and library. Louise—I give you great credit for taste in these
things. During my first call at your house after my Virginia's death, I noticed
the size of all your paintings; the scrolls, instead of set figures—of the
drawing room carpet—the soft effect of the window shades, also the crimson
and gold, and I was charmed to see the harp and piano uncovered. The
pictures of Raphael, and the Cavalier, I shall never forget—their softness and
beauty. The guitar with the blue ribbon, music-stand and antique jars. I
wondered that a little country maiden like you had developed so classic a
taste and atmosphere. Please present my kind regards to your uncle, and say
that I am at his service any, or every day this week, and ask him, please, to
specify time and place. Yours sincerely,
                                                          Edgar A. Poe

    Now, my dear Mrs. Whitman, kindly note that I copy from a copy, &
that copy not too legible, so that, probably, a word or two may not be
verbatim. You must also remember that this charming little view of an
interior was painted after, by years, the "Philosophy of Furniture" was
indited & Poe himself had a *carte blanche* to furnish the room—so far
as I understand—with what gold could procure—"with the baubles
that it may."⁴ I hope I am not wearying you with my small scribble, but
I know—from my own feelings—that *you* will be interested in every
little detail that I can send you. But Mrs. Houghton's budget is very
voluminous—and not always so clear as could be wished. She seems a

regular child of nature—ingenuous, unsophisticated, and (like yourself) too trusting for the human world. I must defer much of her correspondence for a future letter, but want now to tell you what she recounts of Edgar's mother—of whom Virginia liked to talk apparently. I begin to think Poe must have inherited his genius from his mother— *all* great men did. It seems she painted very prettily, & one sketch of hers of Boston Harbour was much admired—says Mrs. Houghton. Reverting to *my* (?) portrait of Poe, [she writes]:

I hope you will forgive me if I say that your picture is not as good as the one in Griswold's. I never saw it before that I remember. It may look as he did the last year (for he was very thin & worn when he went away) but Mr. Poe had curling hair: he wetted ⊰ it ⊱ often to *straighten* it, and probably did so before this sitting (of your photo) but his hair *would curl as soon as* dry, around his ears. He had fine dark curling hair, blue eyes with dark lashes, or bluish gray, his mouth was small, which was his only defect, showing weakness. He was like his mother, who wore her curls low on her forehead, to conceal her broad intellectual forehead, or brain ⊰ Mrs. Houghton, of course, never saw Mrs. Poe. ⊱, which was poor Edgar's inheritance. He had a bundle of his mother's letters written in a round hand very like his own, and two sketches of hers, one in pencil, or indelible ink, the other in water colours, representing Boston Harbour. On the back of this picture was a neatly written description which ended in these words, which I copy from my journal ⊰ Unhappily, most of this journal has been destroyed ⊱, "For my little son Edgar, who should ever love Boston, the place of his birth and where his mother found her *best* and most sympathetic friends.

Mrs. Houghton, at Virginia's request, had these pictures neatly framed, & after Edgar's death hung in Mrs. Clemm's room, who, however, did not value them & must have given them away despite her promise to give them to Mrs. H[oughton] "if they left the family." Perhaps the Poes in Baltimore have them? "Boston Harbour morning 1808" was the water colour.

I understand Mrs. H[oughton] to say that she is sending me a portrait of Edgar's mother, & hopes to find & send me one of him—but her possessions are greatly scattered just now through troubles. She is also sending some lines in Poe's writing but which she (Mrs. H[oughton]) thinks were composed by Mrs. Nichols.

By the way, you will see that Poe & Mrs. H[oughton] were only dear friends & that they never had any other feelings. She befriended Virginia and then nursed him through illness. How can I squeeze all into compass of a letter? Oh! for a chat. There is a long account *from the journal* of a long novel Poe wrote when a young man & an account of how he came to tell Mrs. H[oughton] of it—she being, apparently, of anything but an inquiring mind. Hence his confidence, probably. I cannot tell you all about this novel now, but Mrs. H[oughton] says:

The story, he said, was too much of the yellow covered novel ⸗{French?}⸗ style for him to be proud of, and besides there were scenes and pictures so personal that it would have made him many enemies among his kindred who hated him for his vanity and pride already, and in some respects justly—the fault of his early education. These are his own words.

As all our letters are strictly *entre nous* I may let you know that Mrs. Houghton had let Poe furnish the Library & Music room, after his own fancy. The large painting over the piano was by Albani, & is now at the Theological Seminary, New York, for sale, price $1000. Poe seems to have furnished the rooms after "The Philosophy of Furniture" pattern—carpet, red Bohemian glass, &c.

But now let me answer your dear letter of the 30th Ultimo. That Mrs. Clemm never mentioned Mrs. M.L.S. to you was, doubtless, because of the ungrateful way—so it seems to me—in which she (Mrs. C[lemm]) had treated M.L.S. Mrs. Houghton did anticipate, apparently, Griswold's malignity & tried to pay for the suppression of the "Memoir," but G[riswold] had too many reasons for publishing it to accept her price—he said that Mrs. Clemm was "reconciled" to it. Mrs. C[lemm] evidently received a small income from it for life. Don't mention this as Mrs. Nichols & Mrs. Houghton both wish well to Mrs. C[lemm]'s memory—especially the former & we are much indebted to them for "more light." Poe dictated the events of his life to Mrs. H[oughton] when he was suffering from the illness through which Mrs. H[oughton] befriended him, but I cannot tell just now without a long search whether it was in 1847–8.

I am trying to get all my fresh information into reference shape. I do so fear less [*sic*] I should die with this biography unaccomplished, for I fear no one will ever take it up as I have done.

Moncure Conway is a cousin of Mr. Daniel—of whom I have heard queer tales. I do not suppose Conway ever did read your book. Your friend who calls it a "poem" is right—it is a beautiful sustained poem. I have not met Conway personally, which is my fault; he is the Supplementary Envoy, or rather voluntary representative of the U. States here—all Americans go to see him.

The *Nation's* "revived interest" would be ludicrous were it not so shamelessly impertinent. I have sent the *Nation* a "stinger." I believe Stoddard wrote the review himself. I never said the words attributed to me about Mrs. Osgood & the other quotations are vilely garbled, as a rule, as you can see. I was glad to see the copy of Poe's letter to Miss Blackwell—why the remarks about S.H.W. are most interesting. You see Stoddard's attack appeared before the *C.S. Review*, but "Don Felix" is ready for the fray & has but one flaw in his armour—he cannot & will not appeal to this best & most loved guardian spirits—Mrs. W[hitman] & Mrs. H[oughton].

Am just going to dine with "Lord Dunduary" & some literary & dramatic people in honour of the Bard of Avon's birthday. For 'tis the 24th now. Ever thine, my dear friend,

John H. Ingram

1. Col. John Thomas Scharf (1843–1898), historian of Maryland, published *Chronicles of Baltimore* in 1874 (Baltimore: Turnbull Brothers) and, at William Hand Browne's request, forwarded a copy to Ingram.

2. H. D. Chapin was a close friend of Mrs. Marie Louise Shew Houghton's. For Poe's letter to Chapin, see Ostrom, II, 357–58.

3. The manuscript of this poem was never found. Mrs. Houghton clearly said it was entitled "The Beloved Physician" when she wrote out for Ingram such lines of it as she could remember in 1875. Ingram held back these lines until's Poe's centenary was being celebrated in England and America and from them and Mrs. Houghton's letters he put together an article which he called "Edgar Allan Poe's Lost Poem 'The Beautiful Physician'" and published it in the *New York Bookman*, 28 Jan. 1909, 452–54.

4. All of this information about Poe in this letter and much that followed, equally apocryphal, in Mrs. Houghton's letters, made its way into Poe biography in Ingram's 1880 two-volume *Life of Poe*. He had no qualms whatever about omitting portions of her letters, changing the sequences of paragraphs, or quoting simply parts of sentences as whole ones in instances which, had he quoted exactly, Poe would have appeared in a bad or even doubtful light, in his opinion. All of Mrs. Houghton's letters now in the Ingram Poe Collection have been reproduced in *Building Poe Biography*, but it is obvious and is so stated in that book that she wrote many more letters to Ingram that are so far unlocated.

94. *Sarah Helen Whitman to John H. Ingram. Item 219*

My dear Mr. Ingram,   April 27, [18]75

Last Tuesday I received yours of April 7 with the article on Stoddard's "Original Memoir." It is very pointed & pungent, & strikes, through & through, the thin cloak of candor worn by the author, tearing it to shreds and tatters. Yet, for all that, I wish it had been more guarded & temperate in tone. It will be a firebrand in the enemy's camp, but he will turn it against you, I fear, in ways where you cannot parry his attack. He evidently controls the *Tribune*, whose notice of his "Memoir" was, as you know, a very partial one, and he has doubtless influence in other quarters such as might seriously injure the success of your book in America. Then, I think, you have brought *me* rather too openly into collision with him, when more effect might have been produced by a more specific & temperate statement of the facts. You know he *withdrew* his statement to the effect that he was not aware that Poe had ever countenanced the story of the lines "To Helen" having been addressed to Mrs. H[elen] S[tanard], or rather he *omitted* it from his "Introductory Memoir," so that most readers might look in vain for any such attack on my "veracity," as you have charged him with. But perhaps you did this to call him out & put him on his defence. I think it would puzzle him to make out a case for himself. We shall see what will come of it soon, I suppose.

It would seem from your publication of the two parodies as one that you fancied they were both written by the same person. This cannot be the case. The lines in print were widely circulated before I received the anonymous parody in MS., a copy of which I sent you. Probably the two writers, should they happen to see their "odes" incorporated into one, would not be flattered by the correlation, although if the sin of plagiarism should be attributed to either party, perhaps *neither* would care to prove property.

It appears by your reference to *Broadway Journal* (Vol. 2, p. 63) that Poe had mentioned the unlucky flute in that periodical. I did not know this before. What does he say about it? Is Stoddard introduced by name?[1] I am exceedingly anxious to know. I think the owner of the flute must be astonished to find how familiar you are with American journals.

I am so tortured by neuralgic pains in my head & heart that I hardly know whether my letter will be intelligible to you. If I am ever free from them I shall have so much to say to you.

Mr. Harris has not yet returned, but if you have written, your letter will probably have been forwarded to him. You do not say anything of Anna Blackwell. Have you written to her & have you heard from Mrs. Botta? Let me once more counsel you to keep cool & not be too anxious to provoke a conflict.

& now, dear Don Felix, hail & farewell!

S.H.W.

I long to see your "answer" to the *Nation*.

Here is a tribute from a comrade & messmate of Lieut. Dwight which contains a passing allusion to his interest in E.A.P.

I have not yet seen your notice of Curwen's book. Send me the number of the periodical & I can get it from Prov. Athenaeum.

1. See p. 19, n. 5, for Poe's words in the *Broadway Journal* about his refusal to print Stoddard's "Grecian Flute."

95. *John H. Ingram to Sarah Helen Whitman*

Engineer in Chief's Office
G.P.O., London, England

My very dear Friend,   2 May 1875
I am going to rattle off a few more lines to you today, Sunday. I am,

of course, at home,—my superscription notwithstanding—but I shall not send this off until the 4th (mail day) by which day something new may "turn up." I am going to send one of my usual rambling scrambling budgets, spinning off such things as come first into my pate.

Firstly, I will run through yours of the 14th of April—the only letter yet unanswered. I am glad Davidson sent you the *International,* according to my request, as it seems to prove that he got my letter which contained money, although I have not had any acknowledgement. I sent it on the 18th, I believe, of March, but I have written again. I wrote a letter to the *Nation* which I trust they inserted—their reviewer, perhaps Stoddard?—had *evidently* only read the *International* & not the "Memoir" itself.

As regards Don Felix, his papers have been more for a harmless jest, although not a thoughtless one, & he has judged from letters, frequently from several, & not from a mere autograph. I fear "Don Felix," should he have to judge J.H.I.'s handiwork, will have to be less flattering in his remarks than are you. I think of publishing the whole series in book form—*candidly*—do you think it likely to *take*? If Mrs. Shelton, or anyone writes me aught of interest, you shall hear at once. I am glad you like the *International* paper. The ancestral was, as you might see, aimed at Mr. S[toddard], but subsequently it seemed to me you might not like it—& deem that though aimed at a crow it struck a pigeon! But if you are merciful all is well. What do you think of the *Civil Service Reviewe*r? He wrote, I rather fancy, with the view of provoking a reply. He was, of course, then ignorant of the *Nation's* aimable critique, with its misquotations & untruths.

My material is accumulating largely. *Mrs. Houghton is invaluable—* but everything will be duly weighed & *"recast"* before it is embodied in the biography definitive. My correspondents send me much that is worthless—some think that I only want marvellous anecdotes—some sentimental fancies, & others *their* ideas. Mrs. E. O. Smith has sent me a paper on "E.A. Poe" which contains some striking thoughts & admirable criticisms but, as regards biographical value, not worth a single page of Mrs. Houghton's. *Entre nous* & the post (letter post) I think of embodying all the *personal poems* in the "Memoir," & shall give facsimile of many. When I come to America—as I may before long—*perhaps* you will permit one to be made of the lines "To Helen"? I dare say the work could be done at your house. I talk, you see, of coming to America. I must try to before I complete the Life. Within the last 12 days I have had four invitations, including one from the Society of Alumni's Committee of the Semi-Centennial Celebration of the University of Virginia!! Signed by the leading Visitors, Professors, &c. Is not that gratifying—'twas for June—too early—in fact, I am not sure that I can cross the Atlantic before next year, but I shall try.

Did *I* say Mrs. Houghton was fanciful? Oh, no! I see! Mrs. N[ichols]. Mrs. N[ichols] is very, I fear, but the record has not arrived. I got some pleasant reviews for her husband's book on America, but did not like to review it myself. By the way, did you get my *Academy* review of Curwen? Some papers praised his book & some pitched into [it] because of his cruel attack on Poe & referred him to my "Memoir." If my "Memoir" had not appeared first they would all have accepted his *facts* unquestioned.

Vols. 1 & 2 will go off Tuesday, & Vols. 3 & 4 on Thursday—half morocco bound.

I have got the 1831 edition of Mr. Harris's from the binder—it differs largely from the later copies, but the 1829 is almost verbatim!!

I shall make Miss Rose wait for all those nice things you say of her— *I'm jealous*! And so she is literary & writes letters for the newspapers! I might have guessed it, although I fancied her epistles were too fresh to have been garnered into the dustbin of a paper. Her artistic interiors are charming. I almost thought of a breach of confidence with regards to some paragraphs in her penultimate letter: I thought of publishing them (only I feared *your* Rhode Island Rose might show its thorns) in the *Academy* notes, but after all I might only have been serving up the funeral fragments of her "Paris letter in the *Journal!*" It is too horrible to think of. Miss Rose shall catch it.

3 May 1875

Herewith a copy of the daguerreotype of Poe in possession of Mrs. Lewis. I have only just received two copies. I hope it will not get published, as I wanted it for the life. I suppose this copy is as well as the photographer can make it, but it does not look so good as the original, which is slightly coloured: the colouring, probably, renders the copy less distinct. The original, also, gives more of the shoulders and body, & by balancing the head better makes it more picturesque.

Today I have received from Mrs. Houghton a coloured miniature on ivory of (evidently) Edgar Poe's mother! It is beautifully preserved & agrees with Mrs. H[oughton]'s description, as already sent to you. The eyes are very large, as are the features generally, and the hair is curled all over the forehead, as described by Mrs. H[oughton]. Hair & eyes are both brown—almost chestnut. I shall have it photographed & hope to have it nicely engraved for *the* biography.[1]

The various vols. of Mr. Harris—Poe's, Pinckney's, & *Martin Faber*—are all safely received. I have just purchased a fine engraving, from Northcote's painting, of *Captain* (I do not think there ever was any *Admiral*) Macbride. On the 24th Ultimo, Shakespeare's birthday, I dined at the Savage Club, & there saw Moncure Conway, but before I could get hold of him he had disappeared.

Have you seen the paragraph in the *Athenaeum* (since copied into all the dailies) that "Black's admirable edition of Poe's Works" was set up & printed by women? The first volume work, I believe, of any magnitude, & hence, quite an epoch in printing, so far as Britain is concerned.

A few days ago I had a long letter from George Long, who was Professor of Ancient Languages, at Charlottesville, when Poe was there. He (Long) is still hearty; remembers nothing, but is much interested & gives some names of people able (possibly) to help.[2] Professor Key is also well, & was invited to the Semi-Centennial Celebration with me. I was assured of a hearty welcome, &c. The news has got into our papers & run its round, more or less varied. Have not yet seen *Lotos Leaves*—don't think they will be much good. Graham *is dead.* H. L. Williams, Philadelphia resident in London, is *positive* of this—his father, a publisher, subscribed towards the funeral. This we'll keep to ourselves just now—had we not better?

I am grieved to hear of your neuralgia. I do not think Hell can provide any worse *physical* pain than that, & it is so prevalent. But summer is coming, & you may hope for better times.

The half bound vols. have not arrived. This is most annoying, but I'll get them off tomorrow. I have obtained a large photo from Mrs. Lewis, much better than the smaller, so send both & shall be glad of your opinion. As they are now published, I must seek yet another for *the* life.

And now, a short goodbye from yours ever & ever,

John H. Ingram

1. Ingram did use a reproduction from this miniature, the only known likeness of Elizabeth Arnold Poe, as frontispiece to Vol. II of his 1880 *Life of Poe.* Later, Eugene Didier gleefully joined Mrs. Houghton's family and descendants in their efforts to regain the miniature, manuscripts, and letters she had sent to Ingram, by publishing and republishing articles in which he accused Ingram of literally stealing these things. See Didier's *The Poe Cult* (New York: Broadway Publishing Co., 1909), pp. 140–44, 272–76.

2. George Long's letter to Ingram, Apr. 15, 1875, is Item 217 in the Ingram Poe Collection.

96. Sarah Helen Whitman to John H. Ingram. Item 223

My dear Mr. Ingram,   May 7, 1875
I have just received your interesting letter of April 22. I have time

only for a few words in reply. In relation to your correspondents, I wish
I could talk with you unreservedly. You say you have a long
communication from Mrs. E. Oakes Smith about "Lizzie White."
Probably all that she told *you* about her she told *me*. But I have reason
to think that the story was without foundation, from my knowledge of
her relations with the family up to the date of their removal from
Fordham, or at least to the time of 1848—I mean Miss *White's*
relations.

   You seem surprised that I did not know of Mrs. Shew's intimacy with
the family of Mrs. Clemm & her kindness to them. This I could only
have known from Mrs. Clemm, & she was probably estranged from her
soon after Poe's death. I had no knowledge of the lady until you told
me that she was the M.L.S. about whom I had been so curious (as you
had been informed by Mrs. Nichols). Soon after you wrote me this I
inquired of my friend Mrs. Paulina Davis (wife of the Hon. Thomas
Davis of this city) if she knew or had ever known a lady of whom Mrs.
Nichols had spoken to you as a friend of the Poes & one who would be
likely to give you information about them, *i.e.*, if she knew Mrs.
Houghton, formerly Mrs. Shew. She told me that she knew much of
her from reputation and had once seen her & been very kindly treated
by her at her water cure establishment in the upper part of New York.
Mrs. Shew was not then living with Dr. Shew, but in a house opposite,
a very admirably appointed & luxurious establishment where she
received patients. She was afterwards legally divorced from him &
subsequently married Rev. Dr. Houghton, with whom Mrs. Davis
supposed she was still living, though it was many years since she had
heard anything in relation to her. Mrs. Davis's visit to Mrs. Shew was
about the time of Poe's death, I think. Mrs. Davis spoke of her as a lady
of fine appearance & attractive manners.

   Will you think it unkind or officious in me if I ask you to receive
with careful consideration what you have copied for me from her
copies of Poe's letters. They seem to me to be utterly wanting in Poe's
characteristic style & if published by you—incorporated into your
book—might throw doubts on what *is* true. You know it has been said
that "style is the man." Now, Poe's style is emphatically his *own*, & the
style of the letters copied by you is not his own, though the *substance*
may be. The letters may have been copied from imperfect recollection
of lost originals. It is not the *import* of the letters that I question. The
reference to Mrs. Stanard seems to me especially open to criticism in
expression & allusion, "unless some true & tender & pure womanly
love" etc., etc., to the very close. These expressions are feminine,
diffuse, & utterly unlike the terse compact phrases of E.A.P. Whereas
the note which you copied for me in a former letter expressing his

gratitude & longing for her presence was so unmistakably his own, that I felt his spirit in every word.

I dislike to make this criticism, but you know you have asked me to tell you just what I think about everything connected with your work, & after all, this weakness of style may have depended upon failing health & strength, for they were apparently written near the close of his life.

Remember, I do not doubt Mrs. Houghton's *great* kindness to Poe nor his grateful love towards *her*. It is only the *literal* rendering of his letters that I question.

You say M.L.H. does not like the portrait in your book so well as the one in Griswold's collection. That was a mezzotint copy of Osgood's portrait. The same that was contained in the German translation of "The Raven" that I sent you. I cannot understand how anyone could like that better than this.

But there is no curl to the hair in either of these pictures. The picture in Stoddard's "Memoir" was taken, as I understand Mr. Davidson to say, about ten days before Poe's death, in Richmond, and in that the hair *does curl*. I cannot understand this. Certainly his hair had no inclination to curl when I saw him; it had a free & graceful wave over the forehead, but nothing approaching a curl.

I feel very anxious to know the result of your attack on the *Nation*. I can't help feeling a little nervous lest you should have called down an avalanche on our heads. But keep up a good heart & all will end well and the truth prevail. If your pecuniary success was only secured, I should have no fear about the success of your literary undertaking.

I wish you had some powerful friend to do battle for you on this side the Atlantic with the envious & the timeserving critics who, dressed in a little brief authority, attempt to control the press.

But goodbye, & believe me, with heartfelt blessings, ever your friend,

S. H. Whitman

P.S. I am suffering from a torturing headache which never leaves me, but to make a demonstration in the region of the heart.

Once more, let me urge you not to do anything without deliberation & due caution. Much that is spurious will doubtless be published about Poe and many things will be offered by correspondents which should be duly weighed by you.

What has become of the Southern lady? Are there any further developments in that direction? Have you written to Miss Blackwell? Have you heard from Mrs. Shelton?

A young friend of mine in New York wrote me that she met Mr.

Davidson in the horse cars & feared from his pallor that he was far from well. I have not heard from him for months.

After re-reading this hurried scrawl I fancy it won't do for me to say much about "style." If "style is the woman," wo for your friend,

S. H.W.

97. *Sarah Helen Whitman to John H. Ingram.*   Item 225

My dear Mr. Ingram,   May 11, [18]75

I wrote so hurriedly in my letter of Friday last that I left many of your questions unanswered. I have neither seen nor heard of *any* unfavorable criticism of your "Memoir," with the exception of that in the *Nation,* and that is so palpably unjust that it betrays its animus too plainly to influence an unprejudiced reader. Still I fear the covert malice of the writer may work furtively to injure. About an hour after I had posted my letter, Mr. Harris called on me, having only the day previous returned from his protracted visit in Philadelphia, where he had been unexpectedly detained by the illness of a friend. He told me that he received a letter from you informing him that you had received copies of the 1829 & 1845 editions of the poems, etc., etc. I told him of the *Nation's* appearance in the field (which he had not seen) and showed him the article on the "Original Memoir" which he thought *admirably done,* & evidently wished to see it republished.

I have looked at last week's issue of the *Nation.* The enemy has not yet opened battery, but doubtless lies in ambush for a secret attack. I saw in the *Westminster Quarterly Review* for April, yesterday, a favorable notice of your "Memoir" & a passing allusion to *Lotus Leaves.* I received on Saturday a new & revised copy of the latter volume, sent me by Mr. Gill. I will send you the pages on Poe as they stand in the *first* edition, *with my corrections,* as incorporated in the 2nd, next week. I have heard nothing of an American edition of Poe's works in which the "Memoir" of Griswold has been replaced by Graham's letter.

I am afraid you thought me causelessly anxious & distrustful in what I said about Poe's letters, etc. There is *one* thing of which I feel *no* doubt, & that is of Poe's heartfelt love and gratitude to M.L.S. But what is the meaning of a poem in Poe's handwriting, which is supposed to have been "possibly written by Mrs. Nichols"![1] Is that poem in your possession, & if it is, can you let me see a copy of it? I shall keep strictly private anything that you may *intrust* to me in this connection.

I can hardly explain to you why I am thus anxious; I can only again urge you to investigate carefully & judge calmly all that may come

under your inspection under the name of *unpublished* writings &
letters—all *copies* of such, I mean. Of course there is no mistaking the
handwriting. Do Mrs. N[ichols] & Mrs. H[oughton] corroborate each
other's statements, &, if so, why do you say the former is apparently
"very imaginative"? About the poem to the "B[eloved] P[hysician],"
there is something not quite—what shall I say—*vraisemblable?*
Although I am well aware that the *vrai* is not always the
vraisemblable.

It would take me long to tell you my reasons. I should not dare to say
all this to you did I not believe that you know me well enough to know
that my jealous care of Poe's reputation is the *only* "jealousy" that I
feel in this matter. I cannot quite reconcile myself to the expression
"The Madman Poe." Has Mrs. Nichols ever spoken to you of Miss
Blackwell? I saw yesterday an extract from the report of the London
Dialectical Society on Spiritualism containing an account of certain
phenomena witnessed by Miss Anna Blackwell in presence of Hume.

I am very weary & must say no more tonight. Will try to write by the
next steamer.

Don't let *any*thing I say influence you to distrust your *own*
deliberate judgment—only let it be *deliberate.*

Devotedly your friend,

S.H.W.

Can you tell me *why* you thought that Griswold's "Memoir" had
been withdrawn from a new American edition of Poe's works? I am
anxious to know if this is true.

---

1. Mrs. Nichols had written and sent to Mrs. Shew in 1847 a valentine entitled "Like
All True Souls of Noble Birth." Poe had copied it into Mrs. Houghton's album, from
whence Dora Houghton copied it out and enclosed her copy to Ingram on Apr. 3, 1875.
See Items 39 and 213 in the Ingram Poe Collection and *Building Poe Biography*, p. 122,
for a discussion of this poem.

98. *John H. Ingram to Sarah Helen Whitman*

My dear Mrs. Whitman,   18 May 1875
    This will not go off before Thursday 20th, next mail day, but my
budgets grow so, & so much escapes my mind now-a-days when
writing that I must begin when I can.

I am trying to find some means of sending your books by parcel
instead of having to trust them to the untender mercies of the post.
Although I long for you to have them, I shall be grieved for you to get
them *battered,* or some vol. missing, for I don't think they may all go,

per post, in one parcel. A letter of Poe's to his wife, & a daguerreotype of Poe, both sent by Mrs. Houghton, have not yet reached me, although sent off last March. I do hope & pray that they are not lost. Out of all my correspondence with America, as yet, your vol. of poems is all—bad enough certainly—that I have yet lost. Even the paper in the *Sixpenny*—which I said I had sent you—has "turned up." I had put it, apparently, into a letter of yours that I was answering, & omitted, I suppose, to enclose it.

I am now going through your letters again, & making extracts, & notes into a book, instead of the short précis which I made of the earlier letters. My biography must not omit, or, *if possible*, misstate a single item. The present one, I fear, is but too faulty in many respects.

And my dear, dear friend, I must here speak of something which is on my mind & must off. Doubtless it is only fancy, but I cannot help thinking that you do not write to me quite so confidingly—so affectionately—as of yore. *Do* write & tell me that you *feel* the same to me. It is only my fancy, of course, but I must have *your words to satisfy* me. Have I been indiscreet? Have I said or done *anything* to annoy you? You cannot believe how I cling to you & your good opinion. I have endured mental agonies & real terrible troubles in my little life, enough to overthrow a strong one's reason, & through my desert of existence there have been but few oases—but what I have undergone I *cannot* again undergo. My barque *must* have more pleasant sailing in future. But there! forgive my troublesome meanderings about self, only *don't forget the kindly words*.

I am sorry that your name was ever introduced into the *Civil Service Review* notice, although everyone seemed to think Stoddard's behaviour of [*sic*] you the worst offence of all, especially after all you had suffered through Griswold's slanderous story. But you are mistaken in supposing the readers will look in vain for Stoddard's attack on your veracity. In his "Memoir"—the one addressed to "English readers"— he says, alluding to *your* account of Poe's affection for Mrs. Stanard, "the memory of this lady *is said* to have suggested. . . . *It is far more likely, however*, that she remotely suggested , &c." If that does not attack the veracity of the author of *Edgar Poe & His Critics*, I cannot comprehend English—that is, such as Mr. Stoddard writes. Had Poe been all that Griswold declared him to be, I should have infinitely preferred him, even without his genius, to these scurrilous, belittling, libellers *of all* who dare assert what they at least believe to be truth. But I thoroughly scorn & despise these loathsome reptiles & would rather their enmity than their friendship. *For myself*, I fear no man & defy the world. I could enjoy martyrdom, had I a few who believed in me.

He's a slave who would not be
In the right* with two or three.

*What he *believes* to be the right.

So you see, I shall never make a good American! From childhood upwards, from my *father's* words, my *sister's* love, & my own aspirations, I looked upon America as the land of liberty & her children as *the elect*, but of late, from their own lips, I have been so disabused of my ideas that once or twice I have asked myself, "*Are there any good men in America?*" Swinburne, to whom I put the query, says, these are his exact words, "As to the character of Americans generally, my own impression, (confirmed by experience) is that they are either delightful or detestable—the best & the worst company possible, there is no medium." I suppose they are like women, angels or devils. Only *I* prefer real brimstone devils to sneaking backstair supernumaries. *Mais c'est assez pour cela*!

I think it would be as well for you & *I would wish it*, as you are on friendly terms, to write to Stoddard, & say that *you have not given* any authority for the remarks made in the *Civil Service Review*—he has seen it—and that the use of your name therein was without your sanction, or authority, & that he is at perfect liberty to make use of your words. This may put you right with him & spare you any annoyance. It cannot possibly injure or annoy me, &, as long as I *know* that your *heart* is with me, I do not wish for anything else. In writing to Davidson you might kindly say the same thing. *He is* a friend of Stoddard's & may fear the use of his own name. I am just about writing to him (Davidson) & *shall tell him* that you were sorry to see the use made of your name, &c. *He* is a man & can defend himself so, although I should be sorry to get him any annoyance after his kindness, I need not trouble him with advice. In face, I do not suppose he needs it—he has taken care, & justly, of himself, I doubt not. And now to our own subjects.

Letters from Mrs. Houghton & others follow too fast for me to give you all details. I hope you got the portraits of Poe? What do you think of them? *At last* the Poe family have written. John P. Poe, son of Neilson Poe, thus writes, with promise of further particulars:

It is quite a pleasure to me & to all of us to find that the task of vindicating the life & character of our unfortunate kinsman, already too long delayed, is in such excellent hands, and we will aid you in any way in our power. The article in the *International* we have read with much satisfaction & are gratified to learn that the effect of your publication has been so decided. When you visit this country we will be glad to see you & furnish you with all the additional points we can gather. . . . 1st, there is *no* good reason to suppose that the ancestors of Edgar A. Poe were descended from the Dela Poers ⸂an account of the family from John Poe downward⸃. The portrait of Edgar affixed to your edition is not as good a likeness as one in my possesssion but still resembles him strongly. It is chiefly inferior in not showing his peculiar breadth of forehead, which immediately impressed all who saw him . . . *Mrs. Clemm was only married once.* ⸂Neilson Poe's wife was only daughter-in-law to Mrs. Clemm.⸃ Virginia Clemm was born in Baltimore on the 13th August 1822 and was married to Edgar A. Poe on the 16 May 1836. We have a likeness of her which is said to be a good one. From it it is clear that she was very beautiful. I never saw her.[2]

Now pray do let these various items be *entre nous*, my dear friend, for the present. *Formerly*, I was anxious to impart all information at once to help the good cause, but now will be silent save to you, till all is published. Even that *Gill* (to whom I sent so much information & who would not give any—could not, apparently) information, although, when *Lotos Leaves*, which I have not yet seen, *was on the eve of publication* coolly wrote & offered to sell me his collection—that Gill, it seems, is now going about the country asserting that "Mr. Ingram was *much beholden to him for assistance.*" After that, impudence can no further go. I do not believe that *Lotos Leaves* contains anything but what you & I have told him & the nice little account *derived from George Graham.* Davidson, Mrs. Nichols, & Mrs. Houghton say Graham died several years since, & H. L. Williams, of Philadelphia, says his father subscribed, several years ago, to the funeral. Gill, I suppose, consulted his spirit!

The *Nation*, I suppose, dare not publish my letter. In fact, it was so conclusive of their reviewer's utter untrustworthiness, that they could not have faced it out.[3] I did *not* fancy the two parodies by same author, but the printer altered the arrangement of them. Vol. II of the *Broadway Journal* is with the ed. of the *C. Service Review*. When he returns it, I will give you the exact words of the refusal to insert the "Ode to a Grecian Flute" to the "author" of which it is addressed & *not* to any name. I must get a copy made of my answer to the *Nation* for you. I must *keep one copy.*

I replied to Mr. Harris. Cannot answer *all* my correspondents *now.* Letters come by every mail. You have read of the terrible wreck of the *Schiller?* Some of the mail bags were recovered from the sea & from them I received three letters! Soaked, but dried, & the writing perfectly legible. Have never heard from Mrs. Botta or from Mr. Godey. One of the *Schiller* letters enclosed a letter of John Neal's, with copy of a letter from Poe—but, I fancy, you have had a copy of this. I have not written to Miss Anna Blackwell yet but will soon. Mrs. Nichols has *not* written recently. Call me "Don Felix"—'tis better than cold *Mr.* Ingram. How I do sympathize with you suffering from that terrible neuralgia—it is the worst pain, I believe, ever sent to torment man. My dear friend, Eliza Cook, has lost her reason—'tis feared forever—& I believe through this curse. Do not mention this, *please.*

20 May 1875

My dear Friend, you dear letter of the 7 May came to hand yesterday & I will just answer its few remarks. I am alarmed to hear of your continued ill health. It is still this terrible neuralgia? What do the doctors say? But I have little confidence in them. *What* will compensate us for all our sufferings in this life? We deserve something good. *I* only ask for peace. I shall watch for every letter so eagerly. Would we were not so far apart.

I think you have received my full opinion about the "Lizzie White" & other E. O. Smith matters? They are not only improbable but some impossible, as I have *very politely* pointed out. Mrs. Nichols *did not* think it strange that you knew nothing of Mrs. Shew. Dr. Shew is dead & Mrs. Houghton separated from Dr. Houghton—if not legally, really! I do not expect that Mrs. Houghton was *quite* blameless, but I do not know why women should be judged differently to men because they have to bear the heavier share of guilt or misfortune. Mrs. H[oughton] is not a very highly educated woman—at once explained that she is not literary—but one can see she has *natural* talent for some things, & is thoroughly good-hearted, loving, but independent, & perhaps, somewhat too confiding & eccentric. She *might* worry one's life out to live with, but apart would inspire affection. *I* must like her, but that of course does not prevent me carefully weighing all her evidence. That letter, I have already remarked, betrayed symptoms of unusual excitement but I shall not use it, or any of it without due investigation. *You should* know that nothing would be "unkind or officious in you." What I ask & beg of you is candid feeling. Abuse me, blow me up, anything, but tell me what you think.

Mrs. Houghton's kindness to Poe & his wife & desire to see his memory cleared *is* sincere but, of course, something more than intention is needed. But her letters are so naive & original that I am charmed with them.

I fancy the mezzotint portraits in the earlier edition were much better than the later ones—the plate had doubtless worn out & been retouched, so mine in Griswold's [edition] is not good—but what do you think of those sent? I must learn more about the curled hair. I believe most emphatically, let me say, *en passant*, that you have guessed exactly about *that* letter which I gave you extracts from. Have heard nothing of the *Nation*. I shall let *that* drop. It is forgotten now. Never mind powerful critics on your side of the Atlantic. I shall startle the enemy some day.

Have not heard from Mrs. Shelton, but she had my letter & a Richmond friend will call on her. Lippincott says her name is "*Elmira.*" Have not written to Miss Blackwell. Have heard from Davidson. *I love your* style, I, "*Don Felix!*" *Everything* will be duly weighed, be assured. What "Southern lady" do you allude to? Met Mrs. & the Miss Cleavelands (Greeley's people) yesterday & spent evening with them—made myself most aimable & *entre nous* pleased them, & am *earnestly* asked to call again. I never mentioned Poe matters until Mrs. C[leaveland] brought up the subject. I was *so* careful. She spoke of you so affectionately but (strictly private) said it was a pity you had reduced *E.P. & His Critics*, & *not published it as originally written.* Said you had reduced it greatly & omitted—so I understand—"a spiritualistic theory by which Poe's *eccentricities* were explained." I merely responded, "I regard *E.P. & His Critics* as a poem—a beautiful poem," but I *could* have flourished a tomahawk! The Miss C[leaveland]s are *not* like our Miss P[eckham]. Oh, no! Satyrs to Hyperion! But I should be butchered if the post gave up its secrets!

Au revoir! so much to say to you my dear, dear friend, in my next. Ever yours,

John H. Ingram

P.S. Did Gill return you *the same copy* of Wertenbaker's testimony you sent him, or only a copy? I ask to satisfy my own curiosity & not need [*sic*] any more evidence, having Wertenbaker's original paper now. You may comprehend my drift! What date does Gill give in *Lotos Leaves* of [Poe's] birth?

1. Josephine Emily Clemm Poe, Neilson's wife, was the daughter of William and Harriet Clemm, and therefore was stepdaughter to Maria Clemm.
2. John Prentiss Poe's letter of May 1, 1875, is Item 220 in the Ingram Poe Collection.
3. The *Nation* never did publish Ingram's letter. He later decided to couple it with another and publish them for private circulation, but there is no evidence that he did so.
4. Parker Cleaveland was professor of Geology in Bowdoin College in Maine.

99. *Sarah Helen Whitman to John H. Ingram.   Item 229*

My dear Mr. Ingram,   May 27, [18]75
Though suffering from a more severe attack of neuralgia than I have known for years, I will try to tell you how much I was interested in your last letter [May 2], especially in the invitation from the Alumni of the University of Virginia to their Semi-Centennial celebration. I wish you could have accepted it. It was an honorable and fitting tribute.

Have you heard anything yet from Davidson? Your cowardly critic of the *Nation* still lurks behind masked batteries. Perhaps the *Civil Service* strategy has spiked his guns.

I received last week [May 20] a long letter from Mrs. Houghton, somewhat fragmentary & confused in statement, the ostensible object of which was to obtain information about Mrs. Lewis. It would seem that she imagined *me* to be in some way responsible for what you published about Mrs. Lewis. "Mr. Ingram's mention of Mrs. Lewis as doing *my work* ⧼ says Mrs. Houghton ⧽ was more than my sense of justice could endure & I have spoken out to this noble enthusiastic defender of Poe, although I *might not have done so* in time had not the lady who sent me to the Poes warned him of his mistake."[1] You will see from the lady's letter, my dear friend, why I cautioned you in my last letters to consider carefully the communications submitted to you. I am afraid these "Rival Queens" will get you into trouble with their conflicting claims. It may be difficult to settle the demands of both. I frankly confess that I do not like the tone of Mrs. Houghton's communication. She seems to me to be instigated less by a regard for the reputation of E.A.P., or by friendliness toward Mrs. Clemm, than by other & more questionable motives.

I answered the letter as kindly and discreetly as I could by assuring her that I had no personal acquaintance with Mrs. Lewis & had never corresponded with her, that I believed her to be in England, & that our friend Mr. Ingram, from whom I had heard of her own kindness to the wife & mother of Mr. Poe, could probably furnish her with Mrs. Lewis's present address. Before she received my answer she wrote again much to the same effect.[2] I was glad to learn from her first letter, which I enclose, that Poe's recital to her of the events of his life is referred by her to the period of his illness after his wife's death, *i.e.*, in the spring of [18]47. She says in *one* place that she saw *but little of Mr. Poe during the year 1848*, & in *another* that "Dr. Hopkins & Dr. Houghton of course know that the facts she has communicated to you are *true*, they both having *often met Mr. Poe at my house in 1848* & helped me to serve him in many ways."

Wishing to satisfy myself as to the period of Mrs. Clemm's residence with Mrs. Lewis, I went over all the letters from her in my possession & found proofs which I will give you hereafter of her long residence with that lady. I found, also, what may be of more interest to you just now, a brief letter from Mrs. Clemm, dated New York, Sept. 25, [18]51, in which she says, "write soon & direct to the care of Dr. *Houghton*, Union Square P. Office, New York City." Another letter dated Oct. 10, [18]51, I enclose to you. It is important to you chiefly as agreeing with Mrs. Houghton's statement as to the period of Mrs. Clemm's residence with her. I should like to have you return it to me when convenient. My *next* letter from Mrs. Clemm was dated Lowell, May 6, 1852.[3]

I must not forget to tell you that I have read recently your notice in the *Academy* of Curwen's *Sorrow & Song*. I read it with pride & pleasure. It is *admirable* in *matter* & *manner*.

I have a thousand things to say but am dreadfully tired. Mrs. H[oughton] says nothing to me of the lines which you call a Valentine (*was* it a valentine?)—"To Mary Louise," beginning "not long ago," etc.—& if so, what was its date?

[Letter is unfinished]

Dear Mr. Ingram,

The enclosed [October 10, 1851] is the only letter in which Mrs. Houghton is mentioned, but this may be valuable to us as expressing Mrs. Clemm's sense of the hospitality of her friends. It came to me as a pleasant surprise when I looked among Mrs. Clemm's earlier letters for dates of her residence with Mrs. Lewis. In Dec. 1854 I find a letter from Mrs. MacCready, the actress & elocutionist, who brought credentials to me from Mrs. Clemm in the autumn of that year. She says under date Dec. 8, 1854, "I have passed, since my return, two or three evenings with dear Mrs. Clemm at the house of *Mrs. Lewis.*" etc., etc.

In 1858 Mrs. Clemm was still living with Mrs. Lewis & had only recently left for the home of friends in Alexandria when Mr. Davidson & I called on Mrs. Lewis at her home on Irving Place, New York, but did not find her at home.

I wish to do even justice to the rival claims of these two ladies, Mrs. Houghton & Mrs. Lewis as *benefactresses*, if such a thing is possible.

Affectionately your friend,

S.H.W.

Does not Mrs. MacCready say that she received "The Fire Fiend" from Mrs. Clemm as an unpublished production of Poe's? Poor lady, I am afraid her evidence will have to be ruled out of court!

[Enclosure: Marie Louise Shew Houghton to Sarah Helen Whitman]

Dear Mrs. Whitman   May 20th [18]75
I wish very much to ask you a few questions about Mrs. Clemm, Mrs. Poe's mother, I was absent from N.Y. 10 years, being a sufferer from the war, (having Southern claims rendered worthless by this great calamity) Did you see Mrs Clemm after she went to Lowel the last time? She left my house in the spring of /52, as I removed west at that time. She not wishing to go with us, immediately. Mrs. Clemm spent the winter, and part of the summer of *1850.* with us, and the winter of *1851,* when she went to Lowel again. I have sent her letters and some of Mr Poe's to Mr Ingram and all I can find or recollect of Mr Poe's

antecedents given me during the illness which followed his Virginia's death, and during a *relapse* (*a few weeks after*) partial recovery. I have forgotten very many things and but for my Journal or diary *could not* have brought it clearly to mind. I do not see how you all *could* attribute to that Mrs. Lewis, that sorrowful time in his life, when he needed a congenial friend and generous loving care. If it had only been left anonamous, I should have kept silent, but Mr Ingram's mention of Mrs Lewis, as doing *my work*, was more than my sense of justice could endure, and I have spoken out to this noble, enthusiastic defender of Mr Poe, John H. Ingram; altho I *might not have done so*, in time—had not the lady who sent me to *them* (the Poes) warned him of his mistake. I cannot see why Mrs Clemm should have allowed this. Of course I know she is dead and has been for many years, still it cannot be possible she was so far gone in mind and memory, as to have forgotten the long time it took her unfortunate "Eddie" to even *tolerate* Mrs Lewis. I saw very little of Mr Poe the last year of his life, and Mrs Lewis *may have laid them under obligations* just about the time Edgar went to Richmond, which *obliged* him to write up her works *while on this lamentable tour*, for Mrs. Clemm often made promises for him, which humiliated his soul and to which he made *less resistance* as he begun to break up in *brain power* about this time. Of course the body cannot be sustained upon pride (however true and honourable) and *want* may explain more than any thing else. I was very ill in the spring of 49. and during that summer saw very little of my friends at Fordham yet I went twice by his request taking the Rev. Dr Hopkins with me, to talk over his Eureka and I have sent these letters to Mr. Ingram. I have not seen your book "Edgar Poe and his Critics," only notices of it. I lived in retirement many years, with my two youngest daughters and I am still so unsettled that my books, pictures, and other effects are packed in boxes. I have large amount of correspondence and little time or strength to devote to it, which I offer as an apology for my hurried letter to you. Mr. Ingram says you will like me, and I hope you will forgive me troubling you—and can you tell me with whom Mrs. Clemm died, and who comforted her in her last hours. Sincerely yours,

Marie L. Houghton

[Enclosure: Maria Clemm to Sarah Helen Whitman]

Dear Mrs Whitman   New York, Oct. 10th, [18]51
   On my return from Flushing this morning, I received your kind letter. Most gratefully I thank you for the interest you express for my happiness. Relative to the plan you suggested concerning the books, I have not the power to act. Mr Redfield only allows me as many as I can

dispose of among my friends without interfering with his sale of them. By calling the attention of the public by an "advertisement" would affect him materially. And would on my part appear *dishonorable.* When I can dispose of one or two copies at private sale, I of course receive the money for them, and the publisher places them to my account, and as I have no other resource, of course this is to me a very great convenience—I have with my kind friends here a very pleasant home, and it is their wish for me to make it a permanent one. My proud spirit shrinks from any *pecuniary* favors from them, Therefore when I can dispose of a few copies of the books it prevents me being under obligation to any one. Will you have the goodness to present my warm thanks to Mr Pabodie, and explain to him my reasons for declining his kind offer. But should an opportunity occur when he can (without trouble to himself) dispose of a copy for me, I will feel under great obligations to him for doing so, and will send him on a copy when he chooses to send for it. I sincerely hope I may soon have the pleasure of becoming acquainted with you. I think I would recognize you instantly from the description my darling Eddie gave me of you. My friends think me very like him but I know it is only a family resemblance—My friend Mrs. Houghton often says she can almost fancy he is speaking to her, when I am sad and talking earnestly. Alas I am often sad! oh how sad! when I think of all my dear ones—The only consolation I feel is knowing that I shall soon be with them. Pardon me dear friend for speaking thus, but you know it is just two years since my precious Eddie left me forever, and to a *cold heartless* world—I hope you will soon write to me again. God bless you. Affectionately your friend,

                                                        Maria Clemm

1. The two letters Mrs. Whitman enclosed are here reproduced in full for the first time from holographs; that of May 20, 1875, is in the Lilly Library, Indiana University, Bloomington; that of Oct. 10, 1851, is in the Brown University Library, Providence.

2. This letter is here reproduced in full for the first time from the holograph in Brown University Library:

                                                        "The Chestnuts"
Dear Mrs Whitman   May 24th [1875]
I wrote you a few days since, and amidst several letters sent yours to the Post Office. In clearing out my letters this morning I see that this slip is left in my drawer, and fearing I may have sent you an unintelligible letter I enclose it. Perhaps I have sent you the wrong letter—if so, it is a pity but as I have so much writing and so little time, just now, you must forgive me. Yours truly,

                                                        M. L. Houghton
My address is Whitestone, Queen's County, Long Island.
                                                        (over)
My initials, when Mr. Poe knew me, was M. L. S., and the valentine written in 1847 to Mrs M. L. S. and published by Griswold as a poem of his youth, was written in the

February following Mr Poe's wifes death, and published in the home journal by Mr Willis at that time.

I was married to Dr Roland S. Houghton in November 1850. Dr Houghton was associated with Dr Hopkins in the Church Journal for 17. years, as Editor and Publisher—and, sold out that paper about three years since to the present owners. I am staying now temporarily at Flushing—or Whitestone it is called now, having a claim upon this old homestead, and a suit in chancery about it.

I live alone, with two darling daughters, one of whom is a child of genius, being gifted in music and painting. If you should ever come to Flushing, I trust you call upon us. Yours sincerely,

M. L. Houghton

The valentine to "Mrs M. L. S." was written and sent to me in February 1847, *soon after Mrs Poe's death*. It was published by Willis about that time in the Home Journal

That will tell you in a few eloquent words, Mr Poe's feeling toward me in his most generous and even grateful manner and expression. It speaks for itself—and cannot be gain sayed. I have sent the original to Mr Ingram. I was married to Dr Roland S. Houghton in November 1850. Dr Houghton was one of the Editors of the Church Journal for 17 years after this, and his friend and Partner Dr John H. Hopkins sold the Journal to my husband about six years since, after which Dr. Houghton was Editor and Publisher until about three years ago when Dr. Houghton sold the Church Journal to the present owners. I am now staying at Flushing, or Whitestone is the new name—our place being nearer Whitestone than Flushing.

I am only waiting a decision in Chancery, holding possession of this old homestead until that time. My two youngest children are with me (Mary 11, and Dora 14 years) Dora is a gifted child of genius, being musical and otherwise. She has never been to school and has taught musice for nearly four years. She paints nicely, *having orders* for oil copies of some of my nice originals. She has a wonderful memory and has read thousands of books, having been served with choice books from her father's office many years. If you ever come near us we should like to see you.

Mr. Griswold had reason to dislike me, and put the V[alentine] to Mrs M. L. S. among the poems "written in youth." I went to see this creature Griswold with Mrs Clemm twice, and tried *to bribe him* to leave out his memoir, by paying the cost of those published, but his hatred of Mr. Poe was a passion worthy of a *demon* instead of a man.

M. L. Houghton

Address Whitestone, *Queens Co*. Long Island—Post Office Box 72.

You will misunderstand me I do not wish to injure Mrs Lewis, but she has allowed Mr Ingram to make statements untrue.

Mrs Clemm never mentioned *to me of being at Mrs Lewis's house but she might have been, sometime but my honest opinion is, that Mrs Lewis had no home to offer her Where is this Mrs Lewis*. do you know! *I am curious* because of her audacity.!

M. L.H.

No one knows of my supplying Mr Ingram with these letters and facts.

3. Of the two hitherto unpublished letters reproduced below written by Maria Clemm to Mrs. Whitman, that dated Sept. 25, 1851, is from the holograph in the Brown University Library; the letter dated May 6, 1852, is from the holograph in the Lilly Library, Indiana University.

Dear Madam   New York Sep 25. [18]51

I have been intending so long to write to you, and to request you to use your influence with two or three of your friends to purchase of me each a copy of my darling Eddie's books. The publisher only allows me for the present as many copies as I choose to dispose of, but owing to great delicacy of feeling (on account of that *hateful* and most *untruthful* memoir) I can only avail myself of this privilege through the kindness of my friends. I have heard my poor Eddie speak with so much gratitude of Mr Peabodys *great kindness* to him whilst in Providence, that I think perhaps he will extend that kindness to myself by endeavoring to dispose of one or two copies for me. Will you reply to this as soon as you conveniently can? And please direct to me care of Dr Houghton Union Square Post Office, New York City. How much I would like to become acquainted with you *for my dear Eddie did love you very dearly*. Yours most affectionately

Maria Clemm

Lowell, May 6th 1852

Dear friend,

I received your kind letter some days ago, but have been unable to reply to you, on account of my eyes. I have been almost blind for several months, owing to severe remedies used for violent neuralgia in my head. But thanks to my heavenly Father, I again can see, and think my sight will be restored to me entirely. Oh! how much I have missed my loved ones in this affliction. How much I longed to hear the sweet voice of my darling Virginia. How much I wished to hear my precious Eddie in his dear tender tone speak words of consolation. But alas I shall never hear those beloved voices again.—I sincerely thank you for the enclosure in your letter. I was infinitely more gratified with your kind attention, than (*although so acceptable*) with the money. I have been in Lowell for the last two months. Will you explain to me the cause of my receiving your letter by way of New York? It has strangely puzzled me. I intend some time in June to visit Fall River for a few weeks, and will then call and see you—you little know how much I wish to do so. Will you have the goodness to present my regards to Mr Pabodie, I hope to have the pleasure to thank him in person for his kindness to my poor Eddie. I hope you will write to me often. I must now conclude as I am suffering from the pain in my eyes. Yours affectionately,

Maria Clemm

100. *Sarah Helen Whitman to John H. Ingram.*   Item 231

My dear Don Felix,   June 2, [18]75
    I have just received yours of May 20. I am glad you have seen Mrs. Cleaveland, *very* glad. She is good & truthful, warm-hearted & enthusiastic, not very discriminating, perhaps, but *very* sincere— knows a great many literary people & is well acquainted with the Stoddards. I am glad that our friend D[on] F[elix] exerted himself to be "agreeable." That he succeeded is a matter of course.
    She is mistaken about my having left out anything from *E.P. & His Critics*. She has seen much of the spiritual phenomena & been deeply interested in the subject, though having joined the Romanists & become a good Catholic, she probably now relegates all anti-Catholic miracles to the power of darkness.
    You asked how I liked "the two photographs." I received but one,

probably the envelope had been opened & the smaller one abstracted. If the engraver does as well by this as he did by the one I sent you, it will be a valuable accession to your book. In some respects it is admirable. Still the air of the head does not satisfy me; it lacks spirit, & the face is heavier than in the one taken six months before in Providence. I cannot understand how anyone familiar with Poe's features can speak of his mouth as "weak." His chin, though delicately curved, was marked by symmetry & *strength*, while his mouth was sweet & gracious, or haughty & disdainful, according to his mood. *At no time* had it any trait of *weakness*.

Undoubtedly the prevailing impression with regard to this feature of his face has been derived from Osgood's portrait & the engravings and other copies which have been taken from it.

As to my feelings in relation to the introduction of my name in the article in *Civil Service Review*, you entirely misapprehend me. I am not "on friendly terms with Stoddard." I have no desire (to use your own words) to be "put right with him," nor did I regret it from any selfish fear of personal annoyance, as your words seem to imply.

Forgive me if I am a little stirred by the imputation, & let me try briefly to define my position. When I wrote to Stoddard in relation to his article in *Harper's*, he wrote in reply, Sept. 19, 1872, "My dear Mrs. Whitman, so many months have elapsed since I wrote the paper on Poe about which you write that I am not able to remember what I said in it. I certainly had no intention to discredit any statement that you made in *Edgar Poe & His Critics*, and if I have done so I am sorry for it & ask your forgiveness." etc., etc.

It was evident that he had placed himself in a very uncomfortable predicament. I had no wish to hold him there any longer than was necessary, & frankly accepted his apology. I was willing to believe that he was ready to do Poe justice whenever the truth should be made apparent to him. But when the following spring he inserted an article on Poe's "mendacity" in the *Aldine*, I saw that nothing could be further from his heart than justice to Poe, and I began to put a new interpretation on his conduct toward myself. Still I shrink from insisting on my own rights or animadverting on my own wrongs, especially from one who has so abjectly asked my forgiveness. Doubtless he deserved all that our *Civil Service* friend said of him, and has only received "even justice." That he will trace a portion of the article to me or to my friends speaking *for* me, ought not perhaps to give me pain, and yet I shrink from assuming the role of an avenging angel or even a minister of justice.

You (or your friend of the *C.S. Review*) write in a way to make his heart quail & his hair to stand on end! I almost feel like recommending him to mercy, notwithstanding his ignoble course.

Another letter this morning from Whitestone! Nothing in it about
Poe, but some rash charges against Mrs. L[ewis] & evident distrust of
Mrs. Clemm. I think they did not part as friends & never met after
Mrs. C[lemm] went to Lowell.

Gill's assertion that *he* had furnished you with facts for your
"Memoir" is indeed a bold one.[1] I suppose he justifies, or affects to
justify, the claim on the ground that he returned me *copies* of the
University letter, a copy of which I had sent him, & also the printed
slip containing Mr. Gowans' recollections of Poe, which I had
entrusted to him!! I demanded them of him for the avowed purpose of
sending them to you. I had allowed Stoddard to retain the autograph
letter of Dr. Maupin (which was simply an authentication of the
validity of Mr. Wertenbaker's statement), and a *copy* of Wertenbaker's
statement as furnished me by S. E. Robins. This copy gave *Feb.* as the
month [of Poe's birth]. Where or how this mistake originated, I do not
know. It was certainly not with *me*, for I was (on receiving it)
disappointed to find that it was *not January*, which Poe had told me
was the month of his birth. He did not name the *year*. I had a day of
great suffering yesterday, & it is a weariness to write, but let me
entreat you

[*Letter is incomplete*]

1. This is the cause of the first serious quarrel to develop between John Ingram and
Mrs. Whitman. The letters that follow will make quite clear Ingram's violent reactions
to Gill's claim.

101. *John H. Ingram to Sarah Helen Whitman*

My dearest Friend,   2 June 1875
    Incident, letter, and event, follow event, letter & incident so closely,
that I cannot possibly hope to keep you *au fait* with everything by
means of my hasty scribbles. I enclose you some scrawls which I have
rattled off, from time to time, for your perusal, if you think them worth
it, but things crowd so fast upon me & letters—especially from
America—arrive in such multitudes that I am beginning to give up
answering them. To begin such items as I can think of for the moment,
let me commence with the latest.

    I have today met Miss Peckham at one station, & seen her off to
Liverpool from another en route per *Celtic* for New York! She is
thoroughly homesick & seems to me quite worn out & evidently
requires rest. I fancy she must have been doing too much. I hope
sincerely, & believe, that the scent of the sea breezes which waft her

homeward, & the sight of her native land will quite recuperate her. To you I need not say how deeply interested I feel in her—she is so different to some specimens of Yankeedom I have lately been brought in contact with. *Entre nous*, I fear she has been overtasking *mind* as well as body and, could I get a chance, would bid her father insist upon a thorough and prolonged relaxation from study. Had I been master of my own time I should have straightway taken a ticket & started with her to New York.

En avant—on Monday, 31st, a Mr. O. E. Dodge called on me during my absence from home & I returned the call today—he is London correspondent to the New York *Daily Sun* & professes to have been an old friend of Poe's & proffered me "a grateful welcome as the friend of Truth"—he wrote that he visited me to show "A daguerreotype of the once brilliant & noble-hearted Edgar Allan Poe."[1] "Hearing that you had given my old friend credit ⸨he remarks⸩ for *traits* of character which too many of his own countrymen (and mine) enviously labored for years to deny, I thought—though I have not seen your book—that you would be highly gratified by having an opportunity of examining the *only likeness ever taken* of the author of 'The Bells.' "

I receive all these statements now-a-days with suspicion, but sure enough Mr. Dodge has a beautiful daguerreotype so fresh-looking & handsome of Poe—it is the original of one of the photos you sent me! Not the one the engraving is from but the better of the other two. I shall try & get him to have it copied & send you a copy. Strange that I should discover here in London two such fine daguerreotypes of Poe! Mr. D[odge]'s is much handsomer than Mrs. Lewis's, I think, but, as you know, much smaller. Now don't *you* think that I must be marked out by Fate to champion Poe's memory!

I have told you of my possession of *Politian*—some more of it will "turn up" soon, I fancy.[2]

How do you like the photos I sent? I trust you got them safely. Mrs. Houghton says, "The photograph is very good—. . . . It quite startled me, and at first I did not like it, but it is very like him." I only sent her the smaller size, & have also sent one to John P. Poe, but he has not had time to reply.

I cannot tell you all *now* that Mrs. H[oughton] says. I must like her but, nevertheless, shall have to most carefully weigh & investigate some of her wonderful statements. She tells me:

Mrs. Clemm burned a package of my letters to Mr. Poe, which he had *preserved* carefully. She burned them without opening them, she told me. This was very unwise, for they would *now* be of use, in making dates out, and an angel might have read them. They were from a true & loving friend & deserved a better fate. I wonder, indeed! that what he cared for *so carefully*, should have been *so carelessly* destroyed. I said to her, you might have returned them, & given me the privilege of disposing of what he chose to preserve.[3]

That is all I can now give you of Mrs. H[oughton]'s last two letters— *such long* ones!

En passant, Mr. Dodge said he first saw my name in the *Tribune*, giving some flattering remarks about me & my labours & stating that I had accepted offers to lecture in the United States! I've not seen the offers yet! But have heard of it again today. I shall, however, try to visit America—if possible—this year. Mr. D[odge] said he should have taken me—poor *short* little me—for an American by my appearance.

Entre nous, I saw a note of the Cleavelands saying I had "charmed them"—*c'est bien! n'est ce pas?*

Davidson's last two letters not yet answered—he has sent me over a lot of magazines & cuttings. John Neal has sent me an interesting account of Poe's early letters to him in an editorial capacity.[4] I *can* use this—also a short testimony by a [*sic*] R. C. Ambler in Richmond, "got at" by Valentine.[5] Ambler knew Poe as a boy & used to battle & swim with [him]! Other names are given & Valentine is raking up items. He is a friend of the 2nd Mrs. Allan, but finds it a sore matter with her. Mrs. H[oughton] declares that when Allan died Mrs. Allan wrote to Poe, acknowledging herself cause of the estrangement between Poe & Allan & offered to provide for Poe, but that he was too proud to accept anything—that Virginia kept Mrs. Allan's letters, but Mrs. H[oughton] supposes Griswold had them & returned them! Mrs. Clemm's possessions were all given to Neilson Poe when she died—Davidson proved.

Mrs. M. St. Leon Loud was a Miss Barstow. I cannot find out anything about her, & don't think she would be of much use. Mrs. Shelton does not give any sign. Mrs. Houghton has a neighbor 92 years of age, who lived 60 years in Washington, & who (this Mr. Drake) was Director in a bank with "George Poe, Edgar's uncle." G[eorge] Poe, he says, was wealthy, "a man of culture & a very good man." "He was very proud of his poet nephew & often spoke of him & his beauty & genius. G[eorge] Poe lived in Georgetown, & had some lovely daughters. He does not remember any sons." Now this seems confirmed by what John Neal says & what J. P. Poe also remarks, & you have spoken of G[eorge] Poe. *All* will some day be cleared up—from Alpha to Omega!

I have not written Miss Blackwell yet—must at once. Could not Mrs. Charles ("Annie") Richmond help my efforts think you? Is she alive? Would *Lowell* be sufficient address? Mrs. Locke of Lowell—could not she do something? Mrs. Botta remains silent. Mr. Godey ditto. "A. B. Harris" I must find out.

I have gone all through your letters again, & whilst I find that I have much you should have back, I also see there are some things promised not yet sent. For instance, copy of a briefer letter of Poe's to show me something of the great things which he hoped to achieve in literature. This would be most interesting to *me*. Have not had copy of Pabodie's private letter to Griswold, but that is not of great moment, I suppose. Has Gill ever returned you the letter from John Willis, Poe's fellow student? I should like copy of that, but Gill would never give it to *me*. I have got a real clue, I think, to the "Conchology" story now, but cannot get Wyatt's *Home Journal* letter.

I hope Mr. Harris is not expecting letter from me.

You gave Stoddard to read Poe's letter explaining the motives which induced him (Poe) to seek your acquaintance. Might I not have a copy? All your letters (every word) to me are sacred, & only what you authorise, published. I shall make a different history next time. Might I not introduce carefully & delicately the "Stanzas to Music"? Poe's letter of appeal, after separation, you would not like to send copy of, I suppose? You have never told me what Poe's letters to Mrs. Clemm contained, about "his feelings & views in entering upon his engagement with Mrs. Shelton." All these things—*such as you chose to tell me*—you might kindly send, from time to time, when health & leisure permitted. I enclose a monumental slip looking like progress. I can *prove* that for more than ten years Stoddard has been slandering Poe in papers, *Round Table*, &c. anonymously! The scoundrel! And now having exhausted your patience, I fear, & requesting you to burn the paper so marked in red—sincerely trusting that your health is better & holding over for my next plenty to keep you *au courant* with my researches, I remain, believe me, ever, most devotedly yours,

John H. Ingram

[*The following pages marked in red ink:*] Burn all this.

My very dear friend,

You will see that I am scribbling all kinds of odds & ends to you, at odd intervals. In fact, I am continually finding things I want to ask or tell, & know not how, amid my oppressive need of leisure to make time to write one tithe of what I would write to you. Another thing, I cannot always make up my mind to *write* so unreservedly to you as I would talk, could I but have the felicity of an interview with you. In fact, I think you had better even burn this when you have read it, as it refers to womankind.

Just judge how delicately I am placed! You must wonder why I never tell of Mrs. Lewis & why I never repeat any of her information. In truth, although I frequently see—sometimes take a cup of tea at her house—I dare not rely upon, or print a word of hers about Poe. She is more imaginative than your friend E[lizabeth] O[akes] S[mith]! But I must be friendly with her—in fact, *despite many queer things*, I cannot help liking her & feeling for her in her friendlessness—& it would be madness to quarrel with her—unwittingly, by not accepting an invitation of hers, I offended her, & in revenge, she immediately inserted a *nasty* paragraph in the *Home Journal* (New York) about my "Memoir" of Poe, although in a previous issue she'd spoken well of it! Judge from that! Of course Mr. Harris was right about the name, but believing what she told me (& she offered splendid *circumstantial* evidence), I *undoubtingly* accepted the statement as to Poe having given the wrong name in the poem. Again, I am so useful to Mrs. Lewis that she is *very desirous* of my friendship. She gave me the copies of the daguerreotype, although they, I fancy, *cost* her nothing— but are given her for her having sold right of publishing these photos to the Company. *This & all this* is strictly *entre nous*—she was, doubtless, friendly with Griswold, & had some of Poe's papers, I fancy, from him. She has just given me Poe's MS. copy of *Politian* containing several unpublished scenes, which, though they help out the story a little, are inferior to the published portion, further than which, however, they do not go. I am yet in hopes of her finding & giving me some more of the drama. *I am fully acquainted with the story on which it is founded*— but *the public* might not have seen it so clearly from the published fragment, as from all that I have.

Mrs. E. O. Smith is no good & I am in hopes that I shall be free from her in a friendly manner.

Mrs. Nichols has just recovered her sight after an operation. She tells me that she is preparing *her* "Recollections" of Poe for me, but, I fancy, she'll give too much space to Mrs. Clemm, who she was very fond of. I *may* misjudge *her* but I cannot help deeming that she belongs to the *genus* imaginative. I judge from some letters & one short interview— but we'll see.

Were it not so terrible I should often laugh at my American lady correspondents. Half their time & space is devoted to *slandering each other*—swearing that Poe cared only for them, & that everybody else who lays claim to his friendship is an imposter! That they were only girls (each one says the same) when he knew them & when he died & so could not vindicate him to the world, &c.!! *Entre nous*—they all hate Mrs. Lewis (that makes me think she could not have been so bad) & she returns it with interest. In fact, they all look upon Poe's fame as a convenient peg upon which to hang their own mediocrities where the world may see! For my part I believe Poe only cared for Mrs. Houghton out of the lot of them & he loved her & *clung to her* as a *friend*—& as the friend of his wife, but not in any nearer or dearer way. *I'm sure* Mrs. H[oughton] is most anxious to impress this upon me, as, *apparently, someone* who had the right to be jealous of her was jealous. I do like Mrs. H[oughton] so much *for herself* & not only for her goodness to Poe, but your suggestion as to that copy of a letter upset me greatly—yet it was right, & I am so grateful to you for pointing it out, not but what later on, when I came to weigh matters for publication, I must come to the conclusion I *see* you have. In fact, I wrote, & asked Mrs. H[oughton] whether she had not made some mistakes—which I pointed out—in her copy, & her answer confirms my & *your* views. Fear not—I print nothing that I am not sure about & trust that I shall have the joy of seeing you, & talking over *all* things, before I commence the biography for publication. Mrs. H[oughton] I'm sure loved Poe as a friend & would & will firmly stand for him & *for me* & she is a woman it would be difficult to put down, but she— *I'm sure*—is under a cloud. I fear, however, that having told me all she can remember of Poe she is drifting into the *genus imaginative.* Her reminiscences are so startling & so apt to satisfy one's needs that I cannot help being sceptical.

My dearest friend,

Having just discovered a curiosity of my boyhood's days, I bother you with a copy—a *verbatim* one, I fancy—I believe I once did indulge in some autobiographical reminiscences when writing to you, & just at the present moment (when scores of more profitable ((mentally)) works are awaiting my pen), I feel impelled to intrude some more on your kindness. Few would care for such but *you* might & I can, therefore, confide this to the obscurity of my next letter to you as a psychological curiosity. I believe I told you the story of how I fancied that I had discovered that I had become a poet! From that time for the space of about five or six years I wrote verses continuously— *night* & day—whenever I could get a spare moment, composing some thousands—many thousands—of lines. Owing to the derangement of my poor father's mind, everything had gone wrong with us, & I had to be taken from college, with but a scanty stock of educational lores; parental indulgence, indeed, not having made me make so much of previous opportunities as many at my age would have done. (In fact, my education has been really gained since I left school.) These circumstances had left me so poorly educated, indeed, that not only the grammar was occasionally faulty but the spelling frequently so, of my boyish verses. Hence the strangeness of the following facts. Believing that all I wrote was really poetry, it became a great object with me to preserve every scrap of it. As a rule, as soon as I had *finished*! a piece—and I sometimes produced two or three of these said "pieces" as fast as I could write them (*i.e.*, as fast manually) I sent it off to some journal or paper, & therein it *always* appeared, if the paper was one that did not pay its poetic contributors. This continuous versifying changed my whole being—from babyhood I had always been a dreamy, *imaginative* child, but now I really "lived in a world of things ideal," and so passed through the most terrible afflictions almost with happiness! But the rhyming fits always came on most powerfully when I went to bed. I could versify so composedly in the quietude of the night—and to preserve these compositions (as I fancied) from oblivion, I kept a candle, with matches, with paper & pencil by my bedside to be ready at an instant's need, & I have frequently relit the candle—I could not sleep with it alight—half a dozen times to jot down new verses! I fell asleep almost every night making verses & frequently woke in the morning doing the same thing! Not unnaturally I dreamed & dreamed poetry. I assure you several of my best (if you will allow a superlative here) verses were so composed & many far better I believe to any I have preserved. I often dreamed of the future & when I awoke in the midst of the tantalizing vision seemed to remember the whole. I seized the pencil & began to write the words down, but they gradually faded from my mind. I now send you a copy of all I could write down before they had faded. In writing out these night poems my grammar & orthography always seemed correct & the versification better than my day verses:

Life in Death

(a fragment of a long poem composed in sleep)

In statue-like slumber my poor body lay,
But the soul of that body was floating away.
A raising of palls and a nodding of plumes;
A rushing of wind from the opening of tombs.
The portals of Death were flung wide at my cry—
A spasm—'twas over! I neared the sky.
But still roved my thoughts to that body terrene
And something in common our forms passed between.

How strange to float in ambient air,
    And pitying look down,
    Upon the body lying there
    With nothing living save the hair,
    And nothing human but the frown.

My soul disrobed from that crude clay
    Spreads wide its living wings,
    And longs to soar from earth away—
    To leave all mortal things.
But still some essence, subtile, strong,
    Restrains the longing soul,

And keeps it from the living throng
That sways toward the Goal. . . .

Beneath me lies the placid dead
   So late my prison home—
Ah! am I bound? And to that wed?
And cannot I my soft wings spread
   The sunny skies to roam.
Oh, let me leave this lifeless form!
   My being palpitates
To free itself from earth's deform—
To pass between those gates
Which guard Life's ultimates!

Farewell, to thee, tenebrious tomb!
   Dissolve once more to earth!
My spirit seeks its parent home,
   And thee what gave thee birth.
I live! I breath liquescent air!
   Etherial grow the skies!
Roseate infinity how fair
   Thy incorporeal entities!

How strange to find this future state
   So much the Past resemble!
That spirit hearts still palpitate
   And spirit forms still tremble!

John H. Ingram

I duly received your sweet-scented favour of the 11th Ultimo. The violets are still sweet. I only guessed & do not know whether Griswold's "Memoir" is withdrawn. Widdleton advertises the works & notices on Poe by Lowell, Willis, Graham, & others. I have not seen *Westminster Quarterly Review* yet. Curwen told me he would review there. Nor have seen *Lotos Leaves* yet. The poem to "The B[eloved] Physician" is not discovered yet.

J.H.I.

Like all true souls of noble birth,
   Thou'rt formed of purest porcelain earth,
      And not of common clay;
Love, truth, and mercy made the mould
   Which did thy spirit's form enfold
      Upon its natal day.

Upon that form with wondrous art,
   By teeming brain and tender heart,
      Rare flowers have painted been;

And, heedless of thy streaming tears,
Affliction's furnace, hot and fierce,
Has burned the colours in.

Thus decked with tints that cannot fade,
"A vessel unto honour" made,
My homely verse has shown thee;
To it all thirsting souls may come,
And all the lips that drink therefrom
Say "Blessings be upon thee!"

The above is a copy of the verses in Poe's handwriting, addressed to Mrs. Houghton, and supposed to be by Mrs. Nichols. In writing to the latter lady a few days ago, I forgot to ask her if she knew anything about them. I have not received any of *her* reminiscences yet, nor do I fancy they will much increase our knowledge of the facts of Poe's life. She has been blind for some time but her sight has just been restored through an operation. I trust the change may prove permanent.

1. Ossian Euclid Dodge (1820–1876) wrote music and biography and was London correspondent to the New York *Daily Sun*.
2. This statement instances that Ingram was indeed writing "hasty scribbles," "scrawls . . . rattled off, from time to time." He informs Mrs. Whitman for the first time that he has acquired the manuscript of *Politian* later in *this* letter.
3. Mrs. Houghton's letter was dated May 16, 1875; the complete text appears in *Building Poe Biography*, pp. 136–43.
4. John Neal's letter was dated May 10, 1875, and is Item 224 in the Ingram Poe Collection.
5. Dr. R. C. Ambler's recollections of Poe, promised to Ingram by Edward V. Valentine in his letter of Dec. 10, 1874, Item 187, was finally enclosed in Valentine's letter of May 8, 1875. Item 228 in the Ingram Poe Collection.

102.   *Sarah Helen Whitman to John H. Ingram.*   Item 234

My dear Don Felix,   June 25, 1875
I find in my writing desk a fragment of a letter—two pages & a half—which I wrote on the very day, June 13th, when I received your letter telling me of your interview with the Cleavelands, the letter in which you intimated that you had sent me a rose for my violet! I was too unwell to finish it, & must write now the briefest of acknowledgments. I did not see dear Rose till yesterday. She came to me for a bright, brief half hour, with her sister Kate. She told me of her ride with you in the "handsome" from depot to depot, and evidently likes you, but you must remember that she is only an "American," after all—a good specimen of a *bad lot*, as you & Swinburne have

pronounced us to be. For my own part, I doubt if any distinctive characteristics can properly be ascribed to us. Englishmen, Frenchmen, Germans, & Italians have undoubtedly distinctive national characteristics, but as for Americans, we are too many, too large a lot, to be judged by a few specimen bricks. I have emphatically *no* national prejudices or prepossessions, but I believe that nations & empires, races & republics *move*, and I as devoutly believe that their "march" is "westward."

Rose tells me that you are coming in the fall. I hope you will like us. I know we shall like you.

I send you a cutting from a recent Richmond paper which seems to settle the question about Poe's prowess as a swimmer. Parton, in a sketch in the New York *Ledger* six or seven years ago, in which he repeated the old stories of expulsion from the University, etc., assumed to deny the story of Poe's swimming seven miles under the circumstances recorded, as an *impossible* feat.[1] Be careful of the fragment, as it might be difficult to replace it. Mr. Harris sent it to me last evening. You ask me if he expects you to answer his letter. I understood him to say that you *had* answered it some weeks ago. You asked for a copy of a letter in which Poe spoke of the great things he could yet accomplish in literature under more favorable circumstances. You say it would be "of great use to you." I think you misapprehend its character. It indicates rather an exultant *mood* of mind, rather than any definite plan or purpose.[2] I would send you the letter if I dared to trust it to our treacherous steamboat navigation. I will copy for you the portion referring to this subject on an enclosed sheet. You will see that it will not do for publication. Am I not right? What think you? As an indication of his mental moods, his remorse, his sorrow, his proud exultant sense of power, it is full of profound significance & strange interest, & yet I shrink from the publication of that which so nearly touches my own inmost life.

I must mail this word of acknowledgment for your long & interesting letter tonight. Will try to write again soon.

With sincerest faith & friendship in you, my dear Don Felix, I am ever & ever your friend,

S.H.W.

[*Fragment:*] Mrs. Locke has been dead many years, fortunately, perhaps, for *you*, for she might probably have involved you in a "coil" like that which the ladies H[oughton] & L[ewis] seem to be weaving for you. You may have divined something of this from one of Mrs. Clemm's letters addressed to me from Lowell. I do not know Mrs. Richmond. When Poe was lecturing in Lowell in the summer of 1848, he was the guest of Mr. and Mrs. John Locke. Mrs. L[ocke] introduced him to Mrs. R[ichmond], and the two ladies apparently vied with each other in attentions to their brilliant

[*Fragment:*] of her arrival. Received last week a copy of the *Southern Magazine* for June with a notice of your "Memoir." Good! I perceive the writer feels as I do, however, about certain portions of Mrs. N[ichol]s' account as being "too painful for publication." I felt it so when I read it years ago in some paper—perhaps the *Home Journal.* You say Mrs. Botta remains silent. Mrs. Botta is eminently practical, very enterprising, engrossed with the urgent cares and responsibilities of her active and busy life, *very* prudent, circumspect & cautious. Whatever she might say would be *strictly true*, but if

1. James Parton (1822–1891), a biographer and miscellaneous writer, was a steady contributor to Robert Bonner's New York *Ledger.*
2. This was almost certainly Poe's letter to Mrs. Whitman, dated Oct. 18, 1848. See Ostrom, II, 396. As was her custom, Mrs. Whitman had copied only a portion of the letter previously for Ingram; she never did copy an entire letter for anyone.

103. *John H. Ingram to Sarah Helen Whitman*

My dear Friend,   30 June 1875
   On the 21st Inst. I began & finished three sides of a letter to you, but did not complete the epistle, so begin another & will destroy the old one. I have been far from well—too unwell with face ache for some days to do anything. I am continually being attacked by *semi*-fainting fits—half swoons, which come on suddenly &, after a few instants of weakness, pass away, leaving me feeble &, naturally, nervous. But enough of self-improving prospects & youth will, doubtless, carry me through these failings.
   But about yourself? Cannot you get anything to afford you relief from your neuralgic attacks? Cannot something be got? I look for each of your dear letters so eagerly but fear you will begin to wonder about my long silence. Do not pain yourself by writing long letters to me *nor to Mrs. Houghton*—but just send me a card now & then to say how you are getting on. The new international cards will be very handy.
   Let me see, I have not yet answered yours of the 27 May & 4 [2] June. Shame on me! Let me do so briefly.
   About my proposed visit to America—I was, of course, very gratified with the honor proffered me by the University of Virginia, but I could not, anyhow, have got away, by the time stated. They have just sent me another letter in which they remark, "hope that we may greet you as a guest at some day not far distant." I might get away a few weeks later

on, but do not think I shall visit the United States *this* year, but if all be well, shall *next* year. I am very strongly urged, by reasons manifold & manifest, to make the journey as soon as possible, but prudence says "wait a while." I do not mind owning to *you* & *entre nous*, that one of my strongest reasons for not going now is the cost. A journey to America & back, if done decently, the living & travelling included, would involve a much larger outlay than I feel just now justified in incurring. Had I only myself to think for I would not hesitate for an instant, but, I may confess to you, my dear friend, I have a mother & sisters dependent upon me and, although I have endeavoured to make such provision for them as lay in my power, my loss would deprive them of their chief support—my income of course dying with me, it, therefore behoves me to be very careful of my *little* capital.

Cradled in every luxury, my poor father's insanity & overtrustfulness in others, brought us very low. My hard, laborious exertions, and constant self-denial, have enabled us to retain a respectable position, and now, I am gradually regaining our old post in the world—a world which deems poverty the one unpardonable crime. Trifling as you may think such a journey might be, even that cost would make a great hole in the little capital. There! I have confessed to you my chief obstacle— it is wearisome but *must* be endured as so many worse things have already been. Every year the traces of Poe's career will, of course, grow fainter, and I would so much sooner devote my whole mind to the biography *soon.*—Whilst all the various *data* are so fresh in my mind. Though, whilst reason is spared, I shall *always* be ready to vindicate Poe's fame & name against attack, & always remember the salient features of his story. I am naturally desirous of doing something for Fame myself. I wish to write a biography of Poe that shall be the standard one but, that done, I wish to set to work upon other literary projects which are seething in my brain. I do not fear for death personally, yet dread, like poor Chénier, to die without having wrought out any of my ideals save this one only. Till Poe's life is completed I cannot write anything else but rubbish—which is what I am doing now—*n'est ce pas?*

And so to return to yours of the 27th Ulto. I felt anxious about your not alluding in that letter to mine sent on, I believe, 4th May, with the two photos. I now see you have received the larger but not the smaller one. This is too bad! I am not sure whether the smaller one was in the letter, or, as I fancy, with the large one, but I know it went at same time.

En passant, have I ever thanked you for those sweet violets? Their fragrance endures. The *Nation,* I fancy, alluded to my reply but dared not insert it. I must let you have a copy, but I do not think it worth while reviving the affair by publishing it. What think you? I *must* puzzle them by the knowledge I have of American journalism. Davidson puzzles me. I have to write him at once but I shall not show him any more of my cards. He has been very kind in some things but has *never*—strictly between ourselves—been able to get at a single useful fact for me. Perhaps he is too busy—he has worked hard at getting me papers I wanted—would not betray me knowingly, I *feel assured*, but he is too intimate & too much in the hands of the enemy. Again *quite* private, the *International Review* say they will be glad to receive a paper from me on Petöfi. I proposed the subject. I cannot, however, write it until after my holiday. I am too weak & washed out.

I wrote Mrs. Houghton directly your letter came but, whilst indirectly answering some of her queries, preferred not mentioning that I knew of her letter to you. In her last she tells me of having written to you & in answering I shall not even mention that you have spoken of her letters. But *I do like her*. She is genuine & natural, neither of which is the lady she is so cross about. Mrs. H[oughton] was the *real* friend, I have no doubt—the other received *quid pro quo* favours. Mrs. H[oughton] has her faults as you doubtless know but she is a woman, I *believe*, I could most affectionately admire. After yourself there is no American I wish more to see & meet. You see the deficiencies of her education & perhaps wonder at Poe's liking for her. I do not wonder at all. I can see there was that in her which would attract him most powerfully. I have contrived to inform her how I first heard of Mrs. Lewis, & other things she asks you, without alluding to you. *C'est bien! N'est ce pas?* I do not hesitate one instant between "the rival queens." I do not fancy *any unworthy* motives in Mrs. H[oughton]. You see I know her better than you do. The other woman is *bad*—but useful & affords me a curious specimen of humanity such as I like to *study*, without ever committing myself. Mrs. H[oughton] I can trust—not as I can trust you, but in herself & of herself, *but not about others*, or their secrets. I enclose Mrs. Clemm's letter. Mrs. C[lemm] was not a grateful woman, I *fancy*. That is, she wearied out her friends & then forsook them. As regards Mrs. L[ewis] & Mrs. C[lemm], I can only tell you the whole truth personally. Lines "To Marie Louise" beginning "Not long ago" I will send a true copy soon. It is *un*dated. Caligraphy most exquisite. *Mrs. Clemm* never said she received "The Fire Fiend." *Its author acknowledged that that assertion was as false as the imputed authorship.* I will write to Dr. J. R. Buchanan, Louisville, Kentucky, if you wish it but make another attempt yourself *through a friend first.*[1] *Insist* upon its return. Its retention is pure robbery. I must leave off. I *will* return Mrs. H[oughton]'s letters in my next of a few days & answer your 2nd letter of 4th June.

Trusting you are better—I remain, most faithfully in life & death, yours ever,

John H. Ingram

1. Mrs. Whitman had allowed the spiritualist E. W. Capron to send to Dr. J. R. Buchanan, Louisville, Ky., the manuscript of the second "To Helen," sent to her by Poe, for a psychometric reading. Apparently, she had tried to recover the manuscript before this mention of it in Ingram's letter, but without success. See also pp. 351, 352–53.

104. *John H. Ingram to Sarah Helen Whitman. Postcard*

6 July 1875

Yours of 25th Ulto. to hand. You are misinterpreting Swinburne's words, if not mine. He did not style the *Utopians* "a bad lot" but deemed good & bad specimens of them equally numerous. You are adopting the *Nation's* idea of *my* views, I fear—or are you "poking fun" at me? I see you are engrafting a few thorns from the Rose!

Unlike the races, &c., I do not think I shall move "westward" this year—*vide* my letter of the 1st. Next year I hope to trust myself to "treacherous steamboat navigation"—when I trust to *talk over & decide* so many matters that must remain, as yet, unsettled. If all Columbians were Helens or Roses, I should like them too much.

I gave my account of E.A.P.'s great swim from his own words. I will return the printed paragraph in my next, as I have a copy already, & have written to Colonel Mayo, care of the *friend* who sent it & who knows the Col. Some other of his schoolfellows have written me, but *not* John Willis. Parton's *idea* of the swim *you* sent me.

I did somewhat misapprehend character of the letter of E.A.P. you sent extract from. I thought it would be more of *literary* speculation— but such expressions of his are valuable towards a *perfect* comprehension of his mental history. My biography will aim at a full comprehension of his intellectual, as well as worldly existence.

I must send Mr. Harris a line. *Toujours le votre.*

J. H. Ingram

105. *John H. Ingram to Sarah Helen Whitman*

My dear Friend,   22 July 1875

I am getting anxious to hear from you again as you seem to be unwell, judging from your last letters, that I look forward every mail for some token of your wellbeing. Again, I cannot help thinking your

Rose has miss represented me—would we could meet and make *all* clear!

I am very poorly, weak in body & mind just now, & scarcely know what I said in my last. I find I did not return your extract about the swim, which, as I have a copy, or rather original, I now do. I have written Col. Mayo & he has promised a Virginia correspondent to send me his reminiscences of Poe. His account is valuable, as it corroborates Poe's own account as to distance—*vide* my "Memoir"—& differs from that sent me by a schoolfellow of Poe's & which is too much like Griswold's 7 mile journey. Several of Poe's schoolfellows & boyhood's friends are coming to light.

The journey to Europe—*entre nous*—if not to Greece, seems to have been a *fait accompli*. Did Poe never allude to it to you? Mrs. Clemm & Stoddard, you must remember, are the only contrary evidence as yet. The latter is on the wrong track—his whole sketch I could pick, piece by piece, & tell him where he got it from. As regards Mrs. Clemm, *we* know what her memory was worth. Data and facts of his earlier life accumulate so fast & create such continuous correspondence that I find it impossible to keep you *au fait* with everything.

By the way, did you send *Lotos Leaves*? I have never seen anything of the book—& while I think of it—I want to write to Mr. Wellford, Mr. Bartlett's friend, and, I have, unfortunately, mislaid the little slip with his address. For fear I might not find it, can you get it for me again? I have returned all the books Mr. Harris so kindly lent me to the binder. Amongst those who have been giving my Richmond correspondents evidence is the unknown lady quoted by Stoddard, the originator of *all* the bad legends in the early part of Stoddard's sketch, *i.e.*, the desertion of the father; the habitual evasion & deceit; the so bad that other boys were not allowed to play with him; the friends who thought his early productions trash; & the Mr. Gilliat story of the 17 coats!!! I don't know the lady's name *yet*, but her dates, &c., are so contradictory that I shall be quite prepared to demolish her ladyship notwithstanding her circumstantial air. It is something—is it not?—to have traced such a host of libels to one source?[1]

I begin to clearly discern now why Poe was not cared for by his family—they have not written to me again & my self-respect will not let me write again *direct* but, I fancy, I can put the pressure on *elsewhere*—they could assist greatly.

En passant, the same Richmond lady tries to throw doubts on Miss Rosalie's paternity. I cannot contrive to tell you all or a tithe of the little bits of evidence I am getting together of the early life, but I believe that if I survive to tell the story, Poe's biography will be one of the most interesting & yet truthful ever penned.

A nice long letter from John Neal a short time ago.[2]

Ossian Dodge, who knew Poe in his latter years, spent a few hours at my house last week & when I showed him my store of *original* Poe letters & MSS., was fairly astounded. He said, "For years I have been trying to get an autograph of Poe's, but am still unsuccessful, & here are you, who have never been in America, with all these!" He brought his daguerreotype of Poe, given him by the poet—'twas taken, I think he said, in 1845–6 & is, as if the original of one of those you sent me. I showed him every portrait of Poe I possessed, & before he knew I had had *it* engraved he seized the one you gave me & from which the engraving is taken, & exclaimed, "That is Poe! 'tis the only one portraying him in his best moods!" I was very pleased & at once sent off to you, Mrs. Houghton, Valentine, the sculptor of Richmond, and the University of Virginia, engravings. If you receive yours safely, & wish it for any friend, I can send one more, but I have only two left.

An item—the second Mrs. Allan is, I hear, niece of General Scott & *he* was one of Poe's best friends to the last—that, in itself, is a disproof of the *Southern Lit. Messenger*–Griswold story.

What do you think of the enclosed? It is a copy of the poem offered me for $100. The tone is Poësque, but what do you say to the caligraphy? Don't let it be seen yet.[3]

Since writing the above I have spent *nearly one hour* looking for this copy (I have a copy) & got quite sick & frightened at its disappearance. I must get a change & respite from work *quickly*—sometimes my mind becomes a complete blank on matters that I should be quite *au fait* with & I grow so nervous I don't know what to do. I do so dread softening of the brain. I would rather die a dozen deaths than become insane—but it is too terrible to think about! Forgive me if I am incoherent. I am just now so overworked & worried I don't know what to do & yet I've so much to say.

What do you mean by saying "I cannot quite make you out?" Once upon a time you could make me out to an iota—it is that prickly Rose has been shaking your preconceived opinions.

Did I ever tell you that I had discovered Stoddard's anonymous attacks upon Poe in the *Round Table* (New York) as far back as 1863–4?[4] Or that I had seen a vol. of verses by Mrs. St. Leon Loud called *Wayside Flowers*?[5] They seemed, to my casual glance, *very poor stuff—entre nous*.

A very grand edition of a French translation of "The Raven"—a large square, as large as a table—has appeared & the translator & artist have sent me a copy—'tis now en route—full particulars on its arrival.[6]

I hope you've received my card safely. I cannot attempt to give my views herein of Poe's mental moods, but *all* will be worked out thoroughly in the biography which I *hope* to make not only a *chef d'oeuvre*, but to your *entire* satisfaction.

I asked Browne to send you the *Southern Magazine*. I have not got my copy yet.

Horne is just about to bring out a *very much* revised edition of his *Cosmo di Medici*—it is a *chef d'oeuvre*, indeed.[7] You shall have copy. Since the *Cenci*, 'tis the finest drama to my mind, of this age.

I'm not afraid of "the coil" between rival ladies. You break off about Mrs. Richmond—is she alive? Or any of the Locke family? Do not think I hesitate between Mrs. H[oughton] & Mrs. L[ewis]. I don't. I prefer the former altogether, & I shall thoroughly sift & arrange conflicting claims. Do let me know whether you got any reply about the MS. lines "To Helen." If not, I'll write, but you should get Mr. Harris or some friend to call on the Dr. & *insist*. I saw the Cleavelands again twice & shall probably visit them in Paris—they tell Mrs. Lewis they are charmed with me, but you know how much that goes for. Do you know that Mrs. Nichols is also Catholic—they are perverting [*sic*] in America with a vengeance.

Re. Stoddard—I am grieved to annoy you, but see how difficult it is to speak as I would through the post. I wanted him not in any way to deem you responsible for the *Civil Service* paper, but more of this hereafter. I must get a copy made of my letter to the *Nation* & send you. I defy them to insert it—they dare not, I am assured. As regards Gill, I think he must have sent an incorrect copy of Wertenbaker's letter, knowing it to be shameful—but it is as well to know whom to be cautious of. Does he allude in *Lotos Leaves* to Poe's foreign journey? There is *no doubt* about January being Poe's birth month. I return Mrs. Houghton's letters.

Much left over for my next. This should have gone Saturday—was very poorly—fainting fit yesterday. Yours ever—here & hereafter,

J. H. Ingram

1. Edward V. Valentine had sent to Ingram on July 2, 1875, a copy of a six-page letter addressed by a Mrs. Dixon of Richmond to "Messrs. Editors," in which she, very likely with the collaboration of Mrs. Ellis, wife of John Allan's business partner, had related these stories of Poe's youthful misdeeds. Items 236 and 237 in the Ingram Poe Collection.

2. This was Neal's letter of May 10, 1875, noted on p. 310.

3. We learn later that Ingram did not enclose a copy of a poem (see his letter of Sept. 15, 1875, p. 327). The poem in question was Poe's "Alone," and the handwriting *was* genuine. The copy Ingram had seen was a *photographic* reproduction of the manuscript. For details of the complicated transaction involved, see Irby B. Cauthen, "Poe's *Alone*: Its Background, Source, and Manuscript," *Studies in Bibliography*, 3 (1950–51), 284–91.

Poe had written "Alone" in an album of Miss Lucy Holmes of Baltimore, later wife of Judge Isaiah Balderston. Eugene L. Didier found the lines in the album, owned by Mrs. Balderston's daughter, Mrs. Dawson, in 1875, had them photographed after touching up the manuscript himself by adding the title and a conjectural dateline, "Baltimore, March,

17, 1829," then submitted a reproduction of the lines as "a newly-discovered poem by Edgar A. Poe" to *Scribner's Monthly*. The touched-up poem appeared in that magazine for September 1875. It is reproduced here on page 324.

4. The *Round Table* was a brashly direct, unconventional weekly journal begun in Dec. 1863 in New York. In the beginning R. H. Stoddard was an editorial assistant; later most contributions came from the magazine's nationwide audience. Suspended in July 1864, it was revived in July 1866 with the subtitle "A Saturday Review of Literature, Society, and Art."

5. Mrs. Margaret Barstow St. Leon Loud (1812?–1889) published *Wayside Flowers: A Collection of Poems* (Boston: Ticknor, Reed, and Fields, 1851).

6. *Le Corbeau, Poëme par Edgar Poe*. Traduction Française de Stéphane Mallarmé, avec illustrations par Edouard Manet (Paris: R. Lesclide, 1875).

7. Richard Hengist Horne (1802–1884), *Cosmo de' Medici* (London: G. Rivers, 1875).

106. *Sarah Helen Whitman to John H. Ingram.* Item 241

My dear friend,   August 10, [18]75
    I received the day before yesterday your most welcome letter of July 22. I am grieved to the heart to learn that you have been so unwell. Do not, I entreat you, for the sake of all who love you, do not overtask yourself so much. Take time to rest & recuperate during these sultry August days.
    You are wrong in attributing my silence to your "prickly Rose." She is thoroughly & heartily your friend, although she may sometimes indulge in a prickly kind of persiflage with those to whom she is, at heart, most loyal. She has not been in Providence since the interview of which I told you, & will return to Europe in November. I have been too languid & inert to answer her last piquant letter of July 26, or your post card of July 6. Indeed, I thought by your writing in this diplomatic way & requesting me to answer in the same that you were too much occupied to care for longer letters, even had I been well enough to write them.
    Thanks for the engraving. I was *very glad* to learn that it was selected by Mr. Dodge as the *best* of the portraits. That seems to be the opinion of all who have seen it, with the exception of Mrs. Houghton. I think you told me *she* did not like the portrait with which your "Memoir" is illustrated? You say the daguerre which Mr. Dodge showed you as having been given him by Poe is *apparently* the original of the photographs I sent you, the portraits taken from what I call the *Ultima Thule* portrait, *i.e.*, the daguerreotype taken at the office of Masury & Hartshorn in Providence in November 1848, a few days before the one which you selected for your volume was taken *at the same office for me*. The original "Ultima Thule" daguerre was

Le Corbeau bookplate inscribed to John H. Ingram and autographed by Stéphane Mallarmé and Edouard Manet. Autographic drawing 25.8×28.5 cm. The bookplate probably accompanied Mallarmé's gift of *Le Corbeau* to Ingram. (Courtesy University of Virginia Library.)

framed in a large black walnut frame & remained *for several years on exhibition* in the gallery of the artists by whom it was taken. Mr. Manchester, then in Masury's employ, took these portraits *himself*. He bought out Masury & Hartshorn & had this original portrait (daguerreotype) of Poe in his possession until it mysteriously disappeared some years ago. While in his possession, *Mr. Coleman* took from it the photograph I sent you. I believe I have told you all this before, but I repeat it now to show you that Poe *could* not have given the *original* of this picture to Mr. Dodge, since he lived less than a year from the time it was taken. If you ever come to Providence you can verify what I have told you from the lips of Mr. Coleman & Mr. Edwin Manchester, who are severally at the head of large photograph establishments in the city.

It may well be that a *copy* of the original may have been taken, so like it as to deceive the very artist who took the original. But it is very *unlikely* that Poe could have procured such a copy & given it to Mr. Dodge. If he has a *true copy* of that wonderful daguerreotype, I would give any sum under fifty dollars for a sight of it. *But, if he says Poe gave it to him, & that the daguerre was taken in* [18]*45 or* [18]*46, it cannot, in the nature of things, be the one of which I sent you a photograph as taken by Coleman.* Can you solve this riddle for me?

I wish if you have opportunity in any future notice of Poe & the Poe portraits, you would speak of the two pictures taken in Providence & give the dates of each. When I write out for you the history of that epoch, you will see that the two portraits forcibly illustrate the varying states of his mind at that eventful period of his life. They are, moreover, far the most characteristic that have ever been taken of him. I have made a long story about the Ultima Thule portrait, but I hope you will see the gist of it.

The incidents of Poe's visit to Providence at the time these portraits were taken I was about to write out for you last summer when I received a letter from you saying, "Do not trouble yourself to write me anything more of your personal experiences, etc., since they cannot, as you say, be *published*." Within the last few months you have written to the effect that I do not write so confidentially as formerly. If I do not, it is only because I have feared to encumber you with facts not available for use. I will soon tell you briefly what I know of his Richmond associations, etc., and other things which may interest, even if they may *not* be published during my life.

This moment I have received your postal card of July 28.[1] I am so glad you have found the poem. I do not think I can be mistaken as to its authenticity. I will return it at once.

I have not yet written to Buchanan, I am so hopeless of obtaining the lost MS. Nor is Dr. Buchanan so much to blame as you suppose, since the poem was sent to him voluntarily, & not at his request. You say why not ask Mr. Harris to call on him? But St. Louis is thousands of miles away; nevertheless, I will, to please you, make another attempt.

Mr. Harris & his wife are at the White Mountains, have been away for weeks. I lent him before he went a copy of the *Southern Magazine* for June, with the notice of your book. I will send you the copy, since you have not received one. I see that the London *Quarterly* for July has an article on Poe.[2] I shall receive a copy in a few days.

There is one request I made of you which you have overlooked. It is that you send a transcript of the lines omitted from the poem "To Marie Louise." If you give the line which precedes their introduction, I shall know where to place them. Do not think me unkind towards Mrs. H[oughton] or unduly suspicious in recommending a cautious & careful consideration of all the so-called literary remains of the great genius whose memory you have done so much to illustrate. Do not for a moment distrust my profound interest in your work—my sincere & genuine personal sympathy and affectionate regard for you as a friend. *Do* be careful of your health. Send me, when you can, your letter to the *Nation*. So Mrs. Cleaveland is a friend of Mrs. Lewis, is she? I am glad to know that Stoddard is the author of those dastardly articles in the *Round Table*.

I have not heard from Davidson for months. Have you any reason to doubt his loyalty to the cause we have at heart?

But goodbye now, & believe me ever faithfully & affectionately your friend,

S.H.W.

P.S. I will see Mr. Bartlett soon about Mr. Wellford's address, which I have forgotten. Will also try to send you copy of the article in *Lotus Leaves*. Gill sent you through me an accurate copy of the Wertenbaker letter as he received it from me. He has corrected the date in his later issues. He says nothing of the foreign expedition, the visit to Europe, I think.

I was interested in what you tell me of the large illustrated copy of "The Raven." Tell me more about it when you have seen it.

You see I am getting very tired. I have said nothing of my health, for I am unwilling to weary you with useless details of suffering. I am sometimes very anxious to escape from "this fever called living," and the time seems long—the years of trial & suffering. But I know well that the life which awaits us will make the troubled dream of the present seem lighter than a summer cloud.

1. There is no postcard from Ingram dated July 28, 1875, in Mrs. Whitman's papers.
2. "Edgar Allan Poe," *British Quarterly Review*, 62 (1875), 89–102. Unsigned, but written by Dr. Alexander Hay Japp (1837–1905), a Scotch author and publisher.

107. Sarah Helen Whitman to John H. Ingram.   Item 242

My dear friend,   August 13, 1875
    I wrote you a day or two ago that I saw the announcement of an
article on E.A.P. in a Boston paper as having appeared in the London
Quarterly for July.[1] On enquiry, I found it was not the *London*
Quarterly but the *British Quarterly*. I read the article this morning in
the Athenaeum copy & have just written to the Leonard Scott
Publishing Co. in New York for a copy of the number. It is the best
critique on Poe's life & genius—take it for all in all—that I have yet
seen. It makes honorable mention of your "Memoir," & does even
justice to the idle gossip of the Stoddard fabrications, whose bric-a-
brackish character is well characterized. Of course, you have seen it. I
am very anxious to know the name of the author. Will you tell me in
your next letter or postcard (if that is all the space you can afford me)?
    I would send you by this mail the copy of the *Southern Review* I
promised, but wish to make an extract for which I have no time today. I
am anxious to see the "omitted lines" of which you spoke, and your
answer to the *Nation*, if it will not be too much trouble to copy it.
    The weather is oppressively damp & sultry today. I hope you have
cooler & clearer skies in your London world, if indeed, you have not
flown away to your beautiful Isle of Wight.
    I have always doubted the good-will of Poe's relatives, and am not
surprised at what you tell me of their neglect in writing.
    Ever faithfully your friend,

                                                           S. H. Whitman

    I write these hurried lines only to insure a speedy answer to my
question about the *Quarterly* article. You shall hear from me again
soon.

                                                              S.H.W.

[Note appended, dated August 15, from Rose Peckham:]

Dear Mr. Ingram,
    You owe me a letter, so this is only to say "How do you do?" to
please our dear friend who is a far kinder spirit than I am. I am
spending a few days in the city—the loss of a dear little niece is the
sad occasion. Perhaps I may find a letter from you on my return to East
Putnam. If so, I shall answer at length. Meanwhile, believe me your
fried (summer weather has done it) friend,

                                                              Rose

    1. This letter has survived only in a copy of it that Ingram made for his files. He sent
the original to Dr. A. H. Japp.

AN EARLY POEM BY EDGAR ALLEN POE.

THE following verses, which are given in fac-simile, were written by Edgar A. Poe, shortly after he left West Point in 1829. Poe was then only 19 years old. The fact that these verses were written in the album of a lady of distinguished social position is alone sufficient to contradict the statement of Griswold, that, after leaving West Point, Poe was a homeless and friendless wanderer. He had found a home with his aunt and adopted mother, Mrs. Clemm, who was his first, last, and best friend.   E. L. D.

Alone

From childhood's hour I have not been
As others were — I have not seen
As others saw — I could not bring
My passions from a common spring —
From the same source I have not taken
My sorrow — I could not awaken
My heart to joy at the same tone —
And all I lov'd — I lov'd alone —
Then — in my childhood — in the dawn
Of a most stormy life — was drawn
From ev'ry depth of good & ill
The mystery which binds me still —
From the torrent, or the fountain —
From the red cliff of the mountain —
From the sun that round me roll'd
In its autumn tint of gold —
From the lightning in the sky
As it pass'd me flying by —
From the thunder & the storm —
And the cloud that took the form
(When the rest of Heaven was blue)
Of a demon in my view —

E. A. Poe

Baltimore, March 17, 1829.

Facsimile of Poe's "Alone," published by Eugene L. Didier in *Scribner's Monthly*, 10 (Sept. 1875), 608, with Ingram's notation "not Poe's calligraphy," lower right-hand corner. Item 611 in the Ingram Poe Collection. (Courtesy University of Virginia Library.)

108. *John H. Ingram to Sarah Helen Whitman*

My dearest Friend,   11 Sept. 1875

I am just come home from a month's tour through France & Switzerland, much better, I *believe*, in health.

I am *so* glad to find among my letters two from you. Long replies by next mail. I feared you were too ill to write. Accept my very best & most fervent good wishes. I *won't* postcard you again.

Among letters is one from Widdleton, the publisher of Poe's Works in New York, saying he had written before (his letter never reached me) in reply to mine & asking if I were still willing to carry out my suggestions as to my "Memoir" prefixing Poe's Works!! He adds, "Mr. Gill, of Boston (publisher), to whom I mentioned your kindly offer, asks us not to use your "Memoir" as it covers material taken from his paper on Poe in *Lotos Leaves*." Did you ever hear of such audacity? His own letters to me convict him of falsehood.

Best wishes to Miss Rose, to whom a letter at earliest opportunity. Haste for today's mail. Yours ever & ever the same,

John H. Ingram

P.S. I have *Southern Magazine.*

I've just written to Mrs. Hale: do you know her personally? A note from you might interest her on our behalf. My great aim now is to get Clarke's *Museum* with the sketch of Poe's life (and portrait) therein.[1] I have no correspondent in Philadelphia where so much lies *perdue.* Can you name anyone likely? Godey never answered. Did you ever hear of a tale by Poe called "Siope"? 'Twas published in *Tales of the Grotesque & Arabesque.*[2] Is that in your library? I never saw Burton's letter (about Poe) in answer to Griswold, but expect it will turn up some day. Poe & Burton, I fancy, became partners!!

1. Henry B. Hirst's biographical sketch of Poe, with a portrait, had appeared in the Philadelphia *Saturday Museum* on Feb. 25, 1843. Poe himself had almost certainly furnished Hirst with at least portions of the materials.
2. "Siope," the first version of "Silence—A Fable," was first published in the *Baltimore Book* for 1838.

109. *John H. Ingram to Sarah Helen Whitman*

My dear Friend,   15 Sept. 1875

I am in a perfect chaos of letters & papers, but I am determined to put everything on one side for a few moments' chat with you. In the first place, let me express my intense delight at once more hearing from you after your very lengthy—very cruel—silence of so many weeks. And a ten-page letter too! Quite your old style & not the more recent two or three sides. Oh, *my* dear Providence! would that I could but once clasp your hand & let you know me & see me as I am, instead of through letters, or other folks' eyes—*rose*-colored though they be! *Mais, en avant!*

A month ago and life was a burden to me & a burden that I fancied would not be carried much longer. Ill health & domestic affliction—*that* affliction which is worse than death—distracted me. I put all on one side—ordered all letters & papers to be kept back, and, although feeling almost too broken down to leave home, I started for France. The first night, too ill to cross the Channel, I stayed at the English port, Newhaven. Next day, made an effort and crossed to Dieppe—stayed there three days & thence to Paris—second morning there contrived to faint. (*En passant*, called on the Cleavelands who are there.) Still vainly seeking health, I pursued my way, stopping at various towns en route to Neuchâtel. No better. One day the weather changed to cool—that day I sought out & found some English friends living in the mountains. A magical change took place. I grew almost well in a day! My adventures need not be further detailed. After three days' visit I left my friends & rambled about Switzerland—to Geneva, Chillon, Martiguy, Saxon, Chamouni, &c., & home *via* Paris. I cannot believe the change. I am as sceptical as the old lady who was so shamefully treated by Pedlar Stout & begin to think that "it surely can't be I," so much better in every respect do I feel. I shall yet live, I ween, to do something. And now enough of self, & let me see what there is to answer in your two letters, not replied to in mine of Saturday 11th Instant.

First, yours of the 10th Augt. As regards postcards, I deemed if too unwell to write a letter you could at least send me a line by one of these conveniences. As regards the portrait—Mrs. Houghton afterwards quite unsolicited, somewhat modified her words & said that she grew to like it more & more. Why wish *your* words respecting the "Ultima Thule" portrait verified—*your* words are all in all to me. I think the resemblance of the one in Mr. Dodge's possession marvellous. Did you see a short article on the "Portraits of Poe," in the *Home Journal*, by Chandos Fulton? It is not of much account, but mentions some portraits I am not acquainted with: for instance, a

large photo to be seen in Brady's Portrait Gallery, formerly on Broadway, has been made popular by Anthony's *carte de visite* in his collection of celebrities. This was taken while Poe was editing the *Broadway Journal*. There is much vitality in this portrait. ⊰ also, it continues ⊱ A very "speaking" portrait is a daguerreotype taken of the poet about the same time as the Brady photograph by Mr. Gabriel Harrison, who has presented this & a photograph in color (worked from it) to the Long Island Historical Society. The mouth of the poet was crooked, slanting or running down on the left side: in this portrait, this peculiarity, not always concealed by the moustache which the poet wore in early life & latterly, is in a measure concealed by the poet's holding his head a little sideways, at the suggestion of Mr. Harrison, who was quite well acquainted with him.

I copy for fear you may not have seen this article.[1] I will try for photographic copies. Have only just received the printed slip.

As regards the daguerreotype in possession of Mr. Dodge, I fear he will not sell it to me—he does not seem to want money—but I'll try & get him to allow photographic copies to be made. Perhaps I may send a few words about the Poe portraits to the *Home Journal*, but I have *so* much to do. Remember! only my evenings for literature.

I cannot think how I said such stupid words to you about the unpublishable reminiscences, but I know that I sometimes feared you were overtasking your strength by writing so much. You may be assured that personally I wish to learn every atom of information about Poe. I wish to glean every thought, & word & deed, not merely for publication, but that the man in his entireness may be known to me— that I may gather into one comprehensive form that great & weird mind, the history of which, as well as its carnal covering, I wish to strive to put into a literary shape. And I *will* succeed. Whilst it does not overwork your strength *pray* do give me every jot & tittle of your mental & material memory of our Israfel. Do you see how his name & fame now permeate every American publication: another generation, & he will overtop, by a head, all his literary compeers of your land, in the *public* estimation—scholars acknowledge his preeminence already.

I am sorry I did not enclose you the poem—an editor *forced* it from me & sent it to America for publication, but just as it arrived a copy appeared in *Scribner's Monthly* for Sept.—in *facsimile*. You have, of course, seen it, & will decide with me, that the handwriting is *not* Poe's, but that the style of composition is, or at all events is a splendid imitation. The note in *Scribner's* (by E. L. Didier—*entre nous*) is full of errors, as you will see, as regards dates, &c. Even "Allan" is spelt incorrectly. I have written a letter to the editor, Dr. Holland. Now privately, *entre nous*, the handwriting is as much like Didier's own as is possible to be!![2]

Dr. Buchanan is still to blame, *I* deem. I did not note where he was living, & merely mentioned Mr. Harris or *some* friend, thinking a *personal* visit from a male friend likely to prove more effectual than a letter.

Browne, the editor (a splendid fellow, I fancy) of the *Southern Magazine*, has now sent me a copy.

I told you—did I not?—all about Mrs. Lewis giving me the MS. of

Politian & that it contained some unpublished scenes. I have written an article about it which will appear in the first number of the new *London Magazine*, to appear middle of Oct., with *facsimile* page.[3]

I did not know of the article on Poe in *London Quarterly* for July. I will inquire. There was a review of my "Memoir" in *London Q[uarterly] Review* for, I fancy, April?—but I'll hear tomorrow. The reviewer is a friend of mine. Did you get the *St. James Magazine* for Augt.? I did not like the paper much & arranged with the editor for a note on it in Oct. no. *but forgot all about it whilst abroad*—forgot everything, & now hope he'll let me off. I asked him to send you copy of the magazine.[4]

Herewith *verbatim* copy of the lines "To Marie Louise." I feel positive that Poe & not Griswold made the known version, although G[riswold] *may* have suppressed the names & even put "Italian." Do kindly keep this version *sub rosa* for the present—you see how carefully I must keep my treasures until ready for publication when such harpies as that Gill are about. Did you ever hear of such audacity as his?

That Graham died long since I'm sure, & now T. C. Clarke is dead! He died in Camden, N.J., 23 Dec. 1874, aged 74. He was descended from Dr. John Clarke, of R[hode] Island & Providence fame. I am hoping to unearth *much* about his connection with Poe. It is positively asserted that as the firm of Clarke & Poe they did publish some nos. of the *Stylus* in 1843. The *American Monthly* was published by Dr. R. M. Bird & Clarke. The *Museum* also was published by Clarke. Griswold says Poe wrote his autobiography for the *Museum* in 1843 & the *Northern Monthly* writer is now revealed as T. C. Clarke.[5] I had so imagined &, I believe, suggested it to you, but, for want of evidence (half my information has been first obtained by intuition), and *that* Gill's concealment, could not follow up the clue. Had Gill but *sold* me Clarke's address, what a rich field I might have had, whilst Gill himself could not use it for lack of knowledge.

I will get a few copies of my *Nation* reply printed & send you copy. Mrs. Cleaveland & Mrs. Lewis are bosom friends. It is well to know that Stoddard was the *Round Table* man—it puts us on our guard & diminishes the number of our foes. Davidson is quite true, & most kind, but is a friend of Stoddard's. Mr. Wellford's address is somewhere, but my Poe material has grown to such proportions that I'm wondering how to arrange it all—mentally it is all arranged. I know there is much I have omitted telling from time to time— especially of the boyhood—but you'll know all when the life appears.

Oh, how shameful! You've not had the books yet! Pray, pray forgive me. The four cannot go in one parcel so I'll send 2 vols. tomorrow & 2 Saturday. *Lotos Leaves* I've not yet seen. Will describe *Le Corbeau* hereafter. It emenates from some of Poe's admirers in Paris. *Another* translation of his poems is to appear there. The translator & illustrator have begged my aid.[6] Would you had better news of your own health. I had hoped your long kind letter foretold a restoration to the enjoyments of health.

Yours of the 13th respecting the *British Quarterly*. I had neither seen nor heard of it! I have heard first from America of several English notices, &c.! I'll get it at once and try & discover the author's name. The *Nation's* answer is too long, I fear, to copy at present but will get it done, or printed.

John P. Poe is said to have written a long letter to me but it has not come to hand. I doubt the Poes, although what they say will be facts.

Friend "summer weather" will not get a letter just yet I fear. I enclose a paragraph about *Le Corbeau*—similar notes have been in many English & some American papers, but latter exclude my name. If you don't want it, kindly paste on card & send to my friend Wm. Hand Browne, Esq., *Southern Magazine* Office, Baltimore, Md.

And now, goodbye for a little time, from yours most devotedly,

John H. Ingram

[Enclosure]
Verbatim

To Marie Louise

Not long ago, the writer of these lines,
In the mad pride of intellectuality,
Maintained the "Power of Words"—denied that ever
A thought arose within the human brain
Beyond the utterance of the human tongue:
And now, as if in mockery of that boast,
Two words—two foreign, soft dissyllables—
Two gentle sounds made only to be murmured
By angels dreaming in the moonlit "dew
That hangs like chains of pearl on Hermon hill"
Have stirred from out the abysses of his heart
Unthought-like thoughts—scarcely the shades of thought—
Bewildering fantasies—far richer visions
Than even the Seraph harper, Israfel,
Who "had the sweetest voice of all God's creatures,"
Would hope to utter. Ah, Marie Louise!
In deep humility I own that now
All pride—all thought of power—all hope of fame—
All wish for Heaven—is merged forevermore
Beneath the palpitating tide of passion
Heaped o'er my soul by thee. Its spells are broken—
The pen falls powerless from my shivering hand—

With that dear name as text I *cannot* write—
I cannot speak—I cannot even think—
Alas! I cannot feel; for 'tis *not* feeling
This standing motionless upon the golden
Threshold of the wide-open gate of Dreams,
Gazing, entranced, adown the gorgeous vista,
And thrilling as I see upon the right—
Upon the left—and all the way along,
Amid the clouds of glory, far away
To where the prospect terminates—*thee only.*

Undated and unsigned but the finest specimen of his caligraphy I have seen.

J.H.I.

1. Chandos Fulton, "Portraits of Poe," a newsclipping from the New York *Home Journal*, Mar. 12, 1873. Item 563 in the Ingram Poe Collection.

2. Neither Ingram nor Mrs. Whitman had seen specimens of Poe's handwriting of 1829–30 (see Cauthen, "Poe's *Alone*," p. 289). But Ingram's skepticism was instrumental in forcing Didier's hand in this matter.

3. This article on *Politian* was reprinted by William Hand Browne, editor of the *Southern Review*, 17 (Nov. 1875), 588–94, and is reproduced in this volume on pp. 357-64.

4. John Watson Dalby, "Edgar Allan Poe," *St. James Magazine*, 36 (1875), 473–87. This biographical-critical article was based on Ingram's recently published edition of Poe's works; it suggested changes and omissions to be made in possible future editions. Item 608 in the Ingram Poe Collection.

5. This refers to the article "The Late N. P. Willis, and Literary Men Forty Years Ago." See p. 84, n. 1.

6. The translator and illustrator were, respectively, Mallarmé and Manet.

110. *Sarah Helen Whitman to John H. Ingram.*   *Item 245*

My dear Friend,   Sept. 28, [18]75
    Your welcome letter [Sept. 15] has made me so happy. I had been very anxious about you. You say a month ago life was a burden to you, *I*, too, all through the dog-days seemed possessed by a leaden lethargy, such as I never felt before. I had important letters to answer, but could not write—could not think—have not, even yet, written to Dr. Buchanan. I fancied you might not live to receive the MS., & to me it seemed of little consequence. Were we in *mesmerei rapport*, I wonder? From the date of your note of Sept. 11 I began to feel a marvellous reaction.
    To begin with the "fac-simile" poem—was there ever so audacious

and so palpable a forgery? I think that the *poem* might readily be accepted as genuine. If it had been in Poe's writing, I should not have questioned it even without signature. The introductory note, however, is in *itself* enough to show its fraudulent character. Who is Mr. Didier & how did he get hold of the so-called fac-simile? And this is accepted by the press without question or criticism! Stoddard must have *known* that this was not a facsimile, yet he probably countenanced its publication. At this rate there will soon be a glut in the market! Facsimile poems will flood the press. *Do* be careful of ascribing anything to Poe that comes from such questionable sources. Still, the *poem may* be his, but if so, why was it not given in his own handwriting?

But *have* you seen the October *Scribner's* containing Francis Gerry Fairfield's "Mad Man of Letters," in which Poe is presented as a favorable specimen of the epileptic type![1]

Now for the animus of this medley—this farago of mendacity & metaphysics: *Scribner's* is the publisher of Stoddard's Bric-a-brac-series, & Stoddard doubtless can get anything inserted in the magazine that he likes. Fairfield is an impecunious author who has heretofore made Poe an idol.[2] In 1871 he advertised that he was about to publish "an edition of Poe's masterpieces; to contain also a critical estimate of Poe's claims as the representative of a literary originality *purely American.*" Not finding a publisher ready to undertake his work, he has published within the present year a book called *Ten Years with Spiritual Mediums.* This book assumed all the alleged phenomena of spiritualism to be *true*, & referred all to *epileptic neurosis!* This book received very harsh treatment from professional "alienists" on the one side, who scouted him for accepting the *facts* of spiritualism even though he attributed them to "epileptic nerve auras," & was ridiculed by those who believed in spiritual intervention for declaring that in the presence of a medium he had seen a hand evolve itself out of a nebulous cloud & play one of Mendelssohn's airs on a piano, when no one was in contact with the instrument.

He was next spoken of as having prepared an analysis of Poe's physiological & mental peculiarities & now presents it to the public as a perfect type of the epileptic temperament. Now this article has been six months in the hands of the editors of the magazine & has doubtless been modified to suit his patrons. "One of the masters of the century," as he formerly designated Poe, is now simply "A Mad Man of Letters."

Observe, too, that *Griswold* and *Stoddard* are quoted as "the sole authorities for the facts of Poe's life so far as they are accessible."

I should think even Stoddard must shrink from such a copartnership. I have answered this precious specimen of "epileptic lying," and will send you a copy by the next mail, if the article appears in time. In the meantime, before my reply reaches you I hope you will read the article in *Scribner's*. One must read it to appreciate its audacity.

Thank you for sending me the "Lines to Marie Louise." I think with you that the alteration was unquestionably made by Poe himself, and for reasons which I think I can understand. I will give you my theory about it next time I write. I am very tired now.

I sent to the *Journal* office yesterday the *Appleton's* announcement, & they brought it out this morning in the most conspicuous part of the paper, at the head of the editorial column. I will enclose a copy of it to Mr. Browne tomorrow.

I, too, have little confidence in the goodwill of Neilson Poe, *et. al.* I never supposed *that he* knew anything of his ancestry beyond his immediate progenitors in this country. I have not seen the *St. James*, have no access to it, & seldom see the *Home Journal*.

I am delighted to find that you knew nothing of the origin of the *British Quarterly* article, because it shows what an unprepossessed & unprejudiced writer thought about the question. I never have seen a copy of the *New London Magazine*. Oh, I see the first number is not yet out. Do you know the *date* of *Politian*? I long to know it.

I have seen it announced some time this summer that Gill was to publish one of Stoddard's serial publications! I always knew it was useless to try to get any information out of Gill. More of him next time. I am so sorry that Davidson could not have made out Clarke's address. He must have been living when you first wrote for it. Yes, I *knew* that Clarke was a Rhode Islander; we talked it over when he came to see me in the winter of [18]59–60.

I claimed kinship with him then, I remember, for I believe that like my maternal ancestors he was descended from Walter Clarke, one of the early governors of R[hode] I[sland]. I believe he was an honest, upright man, & he seemed to *love* Poe.

But goodbye for today.

S.H.W.

Is the photo I enclose taken from Harrison? I am ashamed of my hurried letter.

1. Francis Gerry Fairfield, "A Mad Man of Letters," *Scribner's Monthly*, 10 (Oct. 1875), 690–99. Item 628 in the Ingram Poe Collection.

2. As early as Mar. 1866 Fairfield had published two articles: "Poe as an Imaginative Writer" and "Poe's Masterpieces" in the New York *Home Journal*, both highly appreciative of Poe's genius and suggesting a table of contents for a new edition of Poe's masterpieces.

111.   Sarah Helen Whitman to John H. Ingram.   Item 248

My dear Friend,   Oct. 5, [18]75
The books have arrived safely. The 2nd volume came this morning. Receive my grateful acknowledgements. I sent the item about the "Corbeau" etc. to Mr. Browne, with a note referring him to Fairfield's "Mad Man," etc, etc. Also commending to him the article in the *British Quarterly*. By return mail I received a very cordial & kind note from him. He thinks all Americans owe you a debt of gratitude for the disinterested zeal you have shown in clearing the memory of Poe from the "fiendish malice" with which Griswold & his followers have sought to blast the memory of their too illustrious countryman.

Of the *Scribner* article he says, "It scarcely deserves a reply. The writer's evident ignorance & folly put him outside the pale of those who are entitled to hearing & reply." My commentary on the article is still held back, though a polite note from Whitelaw Reid, the editor of the New York *Tribune*, assures me that it is soon to appear. It ought to be out in today's *Tribune*, which I shall have this evening. If it *is* I will enclose a copy of the article.

I have been looking over some of your letters. In one of March 14, [18]75, you say, speaking of intelligence received from Mrs. Houghton, "Poe's first love was named Mary Star; she was very kind to Poe during his wife's illness; she is supposed to be still alive & married." Have you any further light on this matter? Don't fear to trust me with any private matters in relation to Poe's history. I am as loyal to *you*, as mindful of *your* interest in all that appertains to this subject, as I have been loyal to *him* & mindful of *his* reputation.

About the "Lines to M.L.S." In the *published* copy, Poe writes, "With thy dear name as text / *Though bidden by thee*, I cannot write." Now was not *this* the poem for which Mrs. H[oughton] paid him the 25 dollars? *She* had furnished the death shroud for Mrs. Poe. After the wife's death, she attended the *husband* through a dangerous illness. May not her patient, filled with grateful devotion & passionate admiration for his *beloved physician*, have said to her, "How shall I ever repay you for your kindness to Virginia & me?" And may not Mrs. H[oughton], then Mrs. S[hew], have replied, "Write me a poem." I cannot conceive her to have said to him, "Write a poem to me & I will pay you 25 dollars for it."

Undoubtedly *Poe* made the alterations which appear in the published copy. The metaphor involved in the lines "Merged forevermore / Beneath the palpitating tide of passion / Heaped o'er my soul by thee" is forced & somewhat awkward, and in preparing his poems for publication, he may have omitted the four preceding lines to avoid it. Is the *New London Magazine* taken here, I wonder?

When your article on the scenes in *Politian* appears, let me know. Is the *New Eclectic* an English publication? Mr. Browne, in his letter to me, speaks of an article of his in the *New Eclectic* in 1868 or '69 in which he attempted to do some slight justice to the scientific side of Poe's genius.[1] He promised to send me a copy. Perhaps the *New Eclectic* is only the *Eclectic* that I already know so well, probably it *is*. If so, I can find it in our bookstore.

Among the magazine notices which occupied two or three columns of the *Tribune* on the 28th of September was the enclosed notice of Fairfield's book. And on the 2nd of October, *the sonnets*. The animus is so palpable that I am less surprised at the delay of my article than that the ed[itor] should have accepted it *with thanks*.

Stoddard evidently has a purchase on the proprietors. *I*, too, am glad to know that Stoddard was the author of those articles in the *Round Table*. Mr. Eveleth wrote me in 1867, I think, that he had replied to one of those anonymous attacks, but his reply *never appeared*.

I had a postal card from Davidson this morning. It contains only these words, the first received from him for months—"New address, here for the winter. Health good. Greetings. Best wishes. Sincerely always, Jas. Wood Davidson, 819 21st St. N.W., Washington, D.C."

I have written so many letters within the last 24 hours, not all such scratchy scrawls as I favor you with, that I must stop for today. *Lotus Leaves* and other matters next time, *certainly*.

The *Northern Monthly* writer, you say, is now revealed as T. C. Clarke!

You say that Widdleton has expressed his willingness to preface his next edition of the poems with your "Memoir." Can you prevail upon him to give you the name of the author of the first "Original Memoir" prefixed to the 1858 illustrated edition of the poems, & afterwards to the small Blue & Gold edition, both published by J. S. Redfield? This was the "Memoir" which claimed that "Annabel Lee" was addressed to the New England lady whose home Poe had desecrated by his brutal orgies. When Stoddard was in correspondence with me about his article in *Harper's*, I asked the question of him, the question as to the authorship of the article, but in his next letter he either forgot or intentionally omitted to reply to it. You who can find out everything, perhaps can find out this.

And now with heartfelt gratitude to you and with fervent hope & faith in your power to fight the dragons of envy, malice, & all uncharitableness, I am your friend,

S. H. Whitman

Dr. Porteus, who you may remember lectured on Poe to raise money

in behalf of his sister, was drowned on his return from a boating
excursion from Sea Cliff near Brooklyn to Glen Cove, under somewhat
mysterious circumstances.

Don't forget about *Mary Star.*

1. William Hand Browne had written in the *New Eclectic Magazine,* 5 (Aug. 1869),
190–99, that *Eureka* was "a prose poem and one of the boldest speculations conceived
by the brain of man."

112. *John H. Ingram to Sarah Helen Whitman*

My dear Friend,   11 Oct. 1875
Your ever welcome letter [Sept. 28] came to hand this morning
together with one from Mrs. Houghton, who has had much domestic
affliction. In a small space of time I must hurry through all I can.

I do not know whether the photo you enclose is "from Harrison's"
because I have not yet seen that. May I retain this? Mr. Dodge is
coming to take tea with me this week, and I expect to get a copy of his
for you. When I have my set of Poe's portraits complete, & have
published such as I need, I think of presenting them to our National
Portrait Gallery.

London Magazine will not appear till end of the month. *St. James's* I
bought a copy to send you, but editor said he had sent, so I did not, but
will now—'tis not of much account, however. I have not found out
name of the *British Quarterly* reviewer. I wrote editor but got no reply.
He may have forwarded my name to the writer—we shall hear some
day. Sept. no. of the *Dublin University Maga.* contains a review,
dealing chiefly with the poems. It is the best & most valuable critique
on them I have seen, but does not do full justice to the prose.[1] I must
get the number & send you. The writer often coincides with my views:
he says,

Poe's poems seem to me a part of myself—verses from "Ulalume,"
"The Bells," and "One in Paradise" are continually swelling up into my mind
and gushing to my tongue. ⊰{He also remarks:}⊱ ｜Poe is the most remarkable
genius that America has yet given birth to. He was a many sided man, he could
write well about anything.

He quotes some words of Swinburne's about Poe from *Under the
Microscope.* I have read this said pamphlet of S[winburne]'s. There is
only a short *note* regarding Poe therein saying that he is the only
original singer America has yet produced. J. Purves is the name of the
writer in *D[ublin] U[niversity] Mag.,* a name I have seen occasionally

appended to magazine papers, but I know him not. The paragraph about *Le Corbeau* is running all over the world.

About the *facsimile* poem: I wrote to *Scribner's* about it, pointing out at same time the absurd mistakes in the note. If they don't publish my letter, I'll take up the matter in our *Athenaeum* or *Academy.* Didier was, he wrote me, secretary to [Justice] Chase—he has written two or three short paper about matters connected with Poe, but all are worthless—*un*reliable. He offered me the poem & his memoranda for $100, but never answered my letter offering to purchase the poem alone if it proved genuine. A Baltimore correspondent sent me the copy as *facsimiled* in *Scribner's,* but when I *privately* pointed out that it much more resembled Didier's than Poe's [hand]writing, never replied. Didier said his family adopted W. H. L. Poe.

Don't be afraid that I shall accept any forged verse as Poe's. I have had bushels of rubbish sent me but I know at a glance what they are. But this "Alone" I am puzzled about. I do think it is genuine. I'll consult Swinburne.

I've not seen Oct. *Scribner* yet. I'm glad to be *en garde re.* Fairfield, as he may *try* me in *some* way.

I'm afraid that Gill has stopped Widdleton from accepting my offer to *give* him (gratis) a *corrected* copy of my "Memoir" of Poe for publication in America. I have seen *Lotos Leaves*—beyond the few *facts* derived from you, your letters, & my paper in the *Mirror,* I do not see anything Gill can substantiate therein. His assertions are most reckless & easily capable of disproof.

As regards [the] lines "To M. Louise," I can quite comprehend the reason of the alterations. *Appleton's Journal's* London correspondent is the editor of the *London Maga.* & they will do anything for him and, *entre nous,* he for me. Also, *entre nous,* I have given Browne a copy of my *Politian* for his maga. & asked him to send you a copy. I judge *Politian* to have been written between 1831 & '33. *When* my Life appears you'll see some accepted dates upset. *Entre nous,* strictly, I am expecting to publish a separate collection of Poe's poems. If I could only have got at Clarke! I much doubt whether Gill ever bought Clarke's collection, or even saw him. What do you think? I am making every exertion to obtain his publications of 1843—the *Stylus* & the *Museum.* I feel sure Clarke was a friend. His letters &c. would have been so useful. Oh, that we could have found him out in time! I long to reach the States to pursue my inquiries—had I been as well in August as I am now I should have made the trip this year, but I must now restrain my impatience. I am a new being now, and you—you are better, are you not? *Do* write as usual. I'll keep you informed of all matters of interest. Do not mind any of the Stoddard tribe. They will disappear and "leave not a wrack behind" whilst the name & fame of Poe will grow in brilliancy yearly.

By the way, in *Beadle's Monthly* for Feby. 1867 is a shameful paper on Poe by Mrs. E. O. Smith in which she quotes, or pretends to quote from you, these words: Poe "was, it is true, vindictive, revengeful, *unscrupulous in the use of expedients to attain his ends."* [2] Now do tell me that you did not say this.

Can you see any of the following books anywhere? *Tales of the Grotesque & Arabesque*. There is an unknown tale in this book, or with an unknown title, "Siope." Perhaps Mr. Harris may have it. If so, could a MS. copy be made for me? I'll remit cost. Also, can you see any vols. of *The Gift* (Philadelphia: Carey & Hart) from 1830 to 1841, 1844, 1846 to 1850. They contain tales, &c. by Poe. I want a list of the years & papers of each year—[18]42, '43, & '45, I've seen. *Burton's Gentleman's Mag.* I still want, & *Graham's Mag.*, Vols. 18–21, &c. to 1849 inclusive.

You have not yet told me about Poe's introduction to Mrs. Richmond by Mrs. Locke. Do! Cannot I expect any aid in that quarter?

Au revoir, my dear, dear friend. Keep well & rely upon me to carry to a triumphant issue our glorious work. American shall & *will* accept my "Memoir" of Poe eventually. Yours ever,

John H. Ingram

1. James Purves, "Edgar Allan Poe," *Dublin University Magazine*, 85 (Mar. 1875), 336–51.

2. Mrs. Smith did publish these words as having been written to her by Mrs. Whitman. See *Beadle's Monthly, a Magazine of Today*, 3 (Feb. 1867), 148.

113. *Sarah Helen Whitman to John H. Ingram.* Item 249

My dear friend,   Oct. 12 [18]75

I received this morning the 3rd volume of Poe's works, in perfect order, like the others.

You will by this [time] have received my letter about Fairfield's infamous article in *Scribner's Monthly* for October. My answer to it which was accepted with thanks by the editor of the New York *Tribune* has not yet appeared, but a postal card just received from him tells me that it has only been delayed for want of room, the paper being just now crowded with political matter. I shall look for it this week. Meantime, I have had two very pleasant notes from Dr. Wm. Hand Browne (it is *Dr.* Browne, is it not?) in which he says he should like to publish it, in case the *Tribune* does not. Of this, however, there is now no doubt. I like Dr. Browne very much. A card from Davidson informs me that he shall be in Washington for the winter. Perhaps I have already told you this. I must quote for you what a friend from whom I have not had a line before for more than 13 months says about Fairfield's article:

I began to write to you yesterday about Fairfield's infamous article, begging you to answer it, & am glad that you have done so. I shall look feverishly for your rejoinder. I never so bitterly regretted my absorbing official work as when I read that article & knew that I could not possibly find time to answer it as I longed to. I hope you have not forgotten to counter on him about the lamp & the shadow of the Raven. Poe does not say that the shadow of the bird is actually cast, in fact, upon the floor by the lamplight. The last stanza is conceived rather in the spirit of Keats' "Eve of St. Agnes," *i.e.*, there is a transference of the circumstances of the poem, in Keats' poem into an immeasurable past, in Poe's from a dim past into an eternal present of mournful & never dying remembrance, and out of the circumstances of that past, the poet makes for that undying present, a purely imaginary & magical picture significant of his hopeless sorrow. All this is very evident to me, though I suppose I express it imperfectly; but Fairfield, who, in Shelley's phrase, has about as much imagination as a pintpot, does not even suspect it, & treats as a point of fact what is, in truth, a matter of fantasy. And, then his authorities!—Griswold, Prime, whom Mark Twain flagellates so beautifully in the *Innocents Abroad*—and Chauncey Burr, to whom Ananias was truthful & Munchausen moderate![1]

But I wish to send off the article on Poe in *Lotus Leaves*, & must let Fairfield alone for the present. Bear in mind that Mr. Gill had no authority to publish anything of mine but the letter which I wrote him for that purpose & which is quoted by him on pages 302–303. The letters of Pabodie to Griswold & of Griswold to Pabodie were letters which I entrusted to him *at his request* that he might the better understand Griswold's perfidy & insolence. Gowans' description of Poe's domestic life, etc., & the copy of the University letters I gave him to use at his discretion. I exacted from him a promise that he should submit to me, before delivering or printing his lecture on Poe, his MS., that I might make such suggestions or alterations as might seem desirable. I never saw the manuscript & had no idea that he had made copies (garbled copies they were) of the letters which he returned to me.

Certainly if I had seen the MS. or known of his intention to print these letters, I should have prevented their publication. But perhaps it is best that I was not consulted. I endeavored to think so when I saw that he had placed the matter beyond my own control. The most absurdly careless thing in his version was that which he imputes to a "blundering copyist," *i.e.*, the blunder on p. 301 in which Pabodie says,

"Poe intrusted a note to me with a request that I should *make oath to it if necessary*" instead of "*deliver it in person.*"

The former would indeed be the request of a man not in his right mind. Again, the note which Gill has appended to my letter on page 302 assumes that the occasion on which I say Poe, "after a night of wild excitement, before reason had fully recovered its throne," was the "identical one mentioned by Griswold as the occasion of the alleged outrage." This is entirely a mistake. The occasion to which I alluded in my letter to Gill was the occasion to which *Poe* alluded in the lines of which you have given a facsimile on a leaf between the 68th & 69th pages of your "Memoir," lines from his letter of Nov. 24, 1848. I will tell you about this in my next letter & about his visit to Lowell in the autumn of that year. Again, on the last three lines of page 298, Gill commences a very obscure & awkward sentence about certain indecent allusions designed to prejudice Pabodie against Poe & the "Bottling up of unwelcome truths of which Griswold knew the Providence gentleman was aware," etc. etc.

Now, nine out of ten persons who might attempt to attach *any* meaning to these sentences would imagine that the indecent allusions applied to *me*, whereas they were gross insinuations with regard to his relations to his mother-in-law & to assertions which he, Griswold, professed to have found in Poe's letter to his mother (announcing his betrothal to Mrs. Shelton), *i.e.*, that *if* he married her he must contrive to live near enough to another lady to continue his unlawful liason with *her*.

Now you will remember that these last letters of his—the only letters in which he had mentioned his intended marriage to Mrs. Clemm, as she assured me, and as was sufficiently evident from the tenor of the letters themselves—were sent to me by Mrs. Clemm when I was writing my monograph on Poe in 1859. Would Mrs. Clemm have placed these letters in my hands, would she have allowed *Griswold* to see them, if these things had been in them! But I am not dealing with Griswold now.

I pointed out to Mr. Gill the false interpretation to which the sentences on page 298 were liable & he expunged the whole of the matter, which I have erased with blue pencil marks, in his second edition, & inserted the following in their place:

To this insolent & impotent letter which was tesselated with scandalous & irrelevant stories respecting Mr. Poe's relations with some of his most esteemed & valued friends, Mr. Pabodie replied by calmly reiterating his published statement in the New York *Tribune* & by adducing further proof of Griswold's audacious fabrications. ("Edgar Poe & His Biographer," p. 298)

But enough for tonight. In a few days I will write to you again. I

have been very ill since I last wrote & am only able to say how
faithfully I am ever your friend,

                                                    S. H. Whitman

Do not say a word about my strictures on Gill. It won't do to have
too many affairs of the kind on my hands at once.
   I have said to him what I have said now to you and he seems to take
in in good part.
   I shall send Gill's Lotus Leaf article by tonight's mail.

                                                    S.H.W.

1. This letter was written to Mrs. Whitman by William D. O'Connor of Washington,
D.C.

114.   *John H. Ingram to Sarah Helen Whitman*

My dear Friend,   18 Oct. 1875
   Yours of the 5th to hand. You have received the 4 vols. I suppose? I
sent them separately because the post only carries up to 2 lbs.,
English, *now.*
   Today I send you the paper from *St. James Magazine*—the *London*
as soon as it appears (about the 25th), and the *Dublin University* when
I get a copy. The *British Quarterly*, I cannot hear the writer's name—
perhaps Japp. If so, I shall soon hear.
   I have not got the copy of photo from Mr. Dodge, who seems a
shuffler, *entre nous*, but *I'll have it.* I enclose you one of my own, only
just received (after a twelve months' order!) from Germany.
   Black's have just sent me a letter from J. J. Poë, of Riverston, Penagh,
Ireland, who wishes my address, in order to communicate with me, &
on Saturday I received a *polite* note from J. P. Poe, Baltimore,
Neilson's son, saying his delay in writing arose from not being able to
answer *any* of my questions, declining with thanks my offer of a set of
my edition, as his father had already purchased it, saying they should
be glad to see me on my visit to America, & that the Poe Memorial at
Baltimore would be dedicated on the 25th & that I should be
furnished with full particulars.[1]
   I have just received a very nice letter from Stéphane Mallarmé, the
translator of *Le Corbeau*, who is now preparing a complete translation
of Poe's poems.[2] Unfortunately, whilst I was in Paris he was in London
so we missed. He asks for your address as he wishes, I understand, to
send you a *Corbeau*. He corresponds with Swinburne, & quotes in his
letter some of Swinburne's remarks referring to me—these, Mallarmé
will insert in his Preface to the poems. You see we shall have all

Europe with us shortly. Swiss & French papers are continually referring to my "Memoir" & now I must look up the German, etc. But I am *so* engaged! My letters alone are *one* person's work. I cannot reply to all. I have never answered Miss Peckham—is it not too bad? Can you tell her that I am not forgetful? I must write to her.

And now, my dear friend, to the subject matter of yours of the 5th. You may rely upon Browne, but remember, he cannot be popular in the North because he is thoroughly South. With me North & South are all alike. I agree with him that "the *Scribner* article scarcely deserves a reply," but *it circulates here*, & my blood boils when I see such venom vomited forth by these ignorant spiteful asses. If your letter is printed, send me copy *at once*, my dear friend, & I will quote from it & allude to it in *Academy*, or elsewhere, & send you my letter. Stoddard *is* in force in New York. Didier, Snodgrass, & others are his allies. Didier in one of his papers acknowledges this. Snodgrass has furnished Stoddard with the electioneering account. I am on the track of the woman who gave the eleven broadcloth coats, & *all* the childhood's story to Stoddard—that known, & I know whence every paragraph of *his* "Memoir" came. I must publish a pamphlet on Poe's reviewers. I will not endure all this silent sliming process. But this [of] Fairfield's is beneath contempt.

Of Mary Star nothing is *yet* discovered—the Poes never knew such a lady, J. P. Poe says—but my allies are seeking all over the United States & the truth must appear. There *was* some M——— to whom Poe wrote his early poems, & "Alone" *may* have been to her. Oh, for a *viva voce* interview with you!

The poem "To M[arie] L[ouise]" could *not* have been "The Beloved Physician" (in which was this line, "the pulse beats ten then intermits") for many reasons. Why Mrs. H[oughton] gave the 25 dollars for the poem was this (& why, I believe, *entre nous*, Poe altered the poem "with thy dear name as text," to the published form): Mrs. H[oughton], then Mrs. S[hew], was just going to be married to Dr. H[oughton] & the lover-like style (so those who knew not Poe's fervour deemed it) of the lines "To M.L.S." excited comment. Poe showed her, (Mrs. S[hew]), "The B[eloved] P[hysician]" & said that he was to get 20 dollars for it. Mrs. S[hew] saw that it was more fervent than ever—she was rich & Poe was poor, so she asked him to give it to her & she would pay 25 dollars. This was done—does not this seem *la verité*? 'Tis strictly *entre nous*, as Mrs. H[oughton] does not want the world to know of these transactions. The poem was not written for Mrs. H[oughton]'s *money*.

Another poem was written at her bidding though—*i.e.*, "The Bells." He came to her house ill & depressed & said, "I have to write a poem & do not know what to say." (I quote from memory.) He sat at the open window & the sound of church bells—sad & gay—came in & Mrs. H[oughton] suggested them as a subject & Poe wrote the first draft of "The Bells" as given in Stoddard's "Memoir." And on the MS. (the first) wrote, "The Bells by M. L. Shew." *That MS. I have*, so there is no mistake about it.

The *New Eclectic* is or was American, but I'm not sure whether 'tis the same *Eclectic* which reprinted my *Temple Bar* article. I have Browne's article, which is very good, but I fear to risk it by post again, unless you wish greatly to see it, because *he had* trouble to get it & I mean to quote from it some day. I'll send date in my next. Davidson had not sent me his new address, so many thanks. Widdleton did express his intention to accept my free-will offering, but I fear Gill has frightened him off. Ten to one Gill goes over to the Stoddardites! You see—he'll try Stoddard's Iago, innuendo style. I always thought C. Briggs was the "original Memoir" author.[3] I'll see & tell you in my next. *'Twas for that*, I alluded to him (not by name) as I did in my "Memoir" *re. Broadway Journal vide* as one of the two journalists.

Did Dr. Porteus lecture for Poe's sister? Have you misrecollected? He lectured about Poe (you sent me a slip of his lectures) but therein made no allusion to her. A Revd. Powell did, and raised some money for her. He, I fear, was a sham—he could not write English.

And now, my very dear friend & faithful ally, a short goodbye. My physical health is so much better that I feel ready for anything after my long depression & as it is not in my nature to be idle, at least mentally, you may hope for *something* before long. *Au revoir*, and believe me ever yours devotedly,

John H. Ingram

1. John Prentiss Poe's letter, dated Oct. 2, 1875, is Item 247 in the Ingram Poe Collection.
2. *Les Poèmes d'Edgar Poe*, by Stéphane Mallarmé, was finally published in 1888 (Bruxelles: Demond Deman).
3. For Charles Frederick Briggs see p. 68, n.2.

---

115. *Sarah Helen Whitman to John H. Ingram.*   Item 251

My dear friend,   Oct. 22, 1875
    I sent you with my last letter of Oct. 12 a copy of Gill's article on Poe in the first edition of *Lotus Leaves*. I hope it arrived safely. He is now it seems preparing to publish a companion vol. for Christmas to be called *Laurel Leaves*.
    Yesterday he sent me the MS. of another article on Poe which he proposes to contribute to it. I had not heard a word from him before,

since he sent me a copy of the last issue of *Lotus Leaves* in March or April, I think. His new article is entitled "Some New Facts about Edgar Allan Poe." In it he tells the story of his career at West Point rather more fully than I have elsewhere seen it told, & he also gives an interesting account received from Sartain, the Philadelphia publisher, of Poe's state of mind while in that city for the last time—the story of a night passed with him in wandering about the city, when he had found a refuge in the home of the publisher. It is interesting & well told. I think he has seen your book. He publishes all that I gave him before you knew me about the University, Mr. Gowans' account, etc., and publishes the extract which you published from Poe's letter to me of Oct. 18th, defending himself from the charge of want of principle & moral sense. He also publishes another brief extract from the same letter in which Poe speaks of an ideal home to which he had looked forward in his union with me.[1]

When Mr. Gill visited me in Sept. or Oct. 1873, he expressed a wish to copy these passages for publication, & I consented that he should do so. He did not use them, however, at that time, or in his *Lotus Leaves*, probably because he had learned or suspected before he prepared his article last fall that your book was to contain a copy or extracts from the same letter. So he copied other papers, which he had no permission to copy, & whose publication I regretted at that time, but to which I was finally reconciled.

In replying to his letter I alluded to a passage in his MS. in which he says, "I have now before me a portrait of Poe, a full-face photograph taken a year before his death." From his description of the portrait I think it must be the one in your book. I told him so in my letter, written in reply to his of yesterday. I am anxious to hear his answer.

I send a copy of my *Tribune* letter about Fairfield's "Mad Man."[2] It has been endorsed, or rather followed up, by two eminent physicians, Dr. A. H. Okie of Providence & Dr. Fred K. Marvin of New York.[3] The last is regarded as an expert in nervous diseases & has a high reputation.[4] Fairfield replied to my article in the *Tribune* of Monday, Oct. 18th. His article was an insincere attempt to evade the true issue by raising irrelevant questions.

The New York *Evening Post* came out the day but one after my article appeared with words to this effect:

Mr. Francis Gerry Fairfield having demonstrated to his own satisfaction that it was epilepsy that ailed Poe when he wrote "The Raven," "Annabel Lee," & "Ulalume," some of poet's friends manifest a disposition to inquire what it is that ails Mr. Fairfield. There can be little doubt that the mental condition of the poet was never of a prosaically sane sort. He was not at all the kind of person one would think of consulting as to contemplated purchases of real estate. He was manifestly not made for a bank president. . . . Yet if Poe was a madman, his insanity was of a kind which might be cultivated to advantage by a good many distressingly sane poets of the day.

All the books have arrived in good order. I am delighted. By the way, Fairfield shows his cards very transparently. He admits that he once had the Poe fever. During the attack, he sent an article to the present conductor of *Scribner's Monthly*, who sent it back with the word, "Only one man ever wrote like that & he was mad." Whereupon Fairfield appears to have written another article upon that hint, to suit the market.

Have you heard from Dr. Holland in reply to your article about the *Scribner* facsimile poem?

I must conclude this hurried letter if I would send it off by tonight's mail. I am looking anxiously for another letter from you. I long to hear about the *Politian* article. Is there an agency for the *New London Magazine* in America?

With heartfelt wishes for your health & happiness, I am ever your friend,

S. H. Whitman

Will write again in a few days about what I promised in my last.

1. This article appeared in Gill's book *Laurel Leaves* (Boston: William F. Gill & Co., 1876), pp. 359–88.
2. Mrs. Whitman's letter appeared in the New York *Tribune*, Oct. 13, 1875. In it she used the sharpest words she ever employed in an article or letter to be seen by the public.
3. For Okie's and Marvin's support of Mrs. Whitman against Fairfield, see Items 620 and 622 in the Ingram Poe Collection.
4. Fairfield's letter in reply, in which he repents his former admiration of Poe, was printed in the New York *Tribune*, Oct. 18, 1875. See Item 621 in the Ingram Poe Collection.

116.   Sarah Helen Whitman to John H. Ingram.   Item 252

My dear friend,   Oct. 25, 1875

Yours of Oct. 11 just received. I am so glad to know that you are well! You may retain the photograph. I shall find the Sept. number of the *Dublin University Maga.* at the Providence Athenaeum. I think with you that the "Alone" is genuine, the *poem*, not the handwriting. About Fairfield, I think I told you that he said in his *Scribner* article that "the facts of Poe's life, so far as they are accessible, have been thoroughly sifted by his biographer, Mr. Griswold, who knew him well, & Mr. Stoddard, who has tried to find the clue to his irregular perversity in the study of his life & works"!!

I cut down the *Tribune* letter before sending it—having on this last hint commended to him the reading of *your "Memoir."* But on due reflexion, I thought it best not to mix your name up in my reply to his infamous twaddle—for it is nothing else.

I think that he will be likely to receive such a "sifting" ere long as he will not readily forget.

In the *Tribune* of Oct. 18 he attempted an answer in which he very clearly revealed the motives which actuated him.

In the same paper is a critique on Fairfield from Dr. Fred K. Marvin, who endorses my statement about the poems and declares that Poe was in no sense the victim of cerebral epilepsy, and Dr. Marvin is regarded as high authority in nervous diseases.

I sent Fairfield's weak reply & the accompanying article of Dr. Marvin to Dr. Hand Browne last Saturday, requesting him to return them. If I receive them before I post my letter I will enclose them to you.

I think Stoddard will have no reason to be proud of his coadjutor & accomplice, for such he, Fairfield, undoubtedly is.

Have you received the copy of the Lotus Leaf I sent? I shall look anxiously for your paper on *Politian*.

You ask if I think Gill ever saw Clarke? In the MS. he sent me there was a note from Clarke to somebody, but I do not think Gill spoke as if he knew him. Still I read the MS. so hastily that I cannot be sure. He was anxious to have me return it at once, having sent it that I might see what he wished to print from Poe's letter to me in defence of his integrity, which had been impugned by some of his New York associates. I drew my pencil through some of the personal allusions & expressions & it will be published in his article for *Laurel Leaves substantially* as it appears in your book. I had given him leave to copy & use at discretion this & another passage from the same letter, which he wished to extract from it, *before I knew you.*

I hope you *will* publish a vol. of the poems, & if you could give the order of their publication it would be most valuable & interesting. The letters, or letter, which I received from Mr. Clarke after my interview with him in New York, I sent to a friend in Ohio of whom I have spoken to you, one whose fine intellect & rare genius were afterwards hopelessly clouded by insanity.

I have seen Mrs. E. O. Smith's paper on Poe in *Beadle's Monthly*, but I have not seen it for years. I considered it of no value & lost it. I cannot have said anything to her against Poe. Can you tell me in what connexion she assumes it to have been said? Does she not in that paper speak of a conversation with Poe about "Helen" & *herself*, just before he left New York for the last time? I think I told you in speaking of this that she was very *imaginative.*

I have never been able to find any trace of the *Grotesque & Arabesque*. I will enquire again of Mr. Harris. He has just returned to the city. A volume of *The Gift* is in my possession containing the story of "William Wilson," but the vol. has *no date*. It was *given* to me in Sept. 1841. This is the only vol. of that publication that I have ever met with. The only article it contains by Poe is "W.W."[1]

About Mrs. Richmond & Mrs. Locke. When the article about the illness and destitution of Poe & his wife appeared in the *Home Journal*, it appears that Mrs. John Locke (Mrs. Jane Ermina Locke), of Lowell, wrote to the family & proffered assistance. She continued to be an occasional correspondent of Poe's until the summer of 1848 when he went to Lowell to deliver his lecture on the female poets of America. Mrs. L[ocke] was a lady of talent but wanting, I fancy, in tact & discretion. She had visited Mrs. Clemm at Fordham in the spring or early summer of the year. She was a lady of benevolent impulses & of an enterprising, active temperament. When Mr. Poe went to Lowell to lecture he was a guest in the family of the Lockes.

Mrs. Annie Richmond (Mrs. Charles Richmond) of Lowell was an intimate companion of Mrs. Locke's. I have never seen Mrs. Richmond. She was the wife of a manufacturer and, though not herself a lady of literary culture, had an enthusiastic appreciation of it in others. I am giving you Mrs. Locke's estimate of her. Her letters to Mrs. Clemm (sent me, lent me, by that lady to show me the affectionate regard in which she was held by Mrs. R[ichmond]) were creditable to her heart & head. The daughters of General Carpenter of this city were relatives of Mr. Richmond & visited Mrs. R[ichmond] at the time when Mrs. Clemm was staying with her. They mentioned the interview to me to convey to me the affectionate messages sent me by Mrs. Clemm.

When in the autumn of that year Poe visited Lowell he was a guest of the Richmonds. A quarrel, or what the Yankees call an "unpleasantness," had sprung up between the two ladies, & before he left, open hostility was declared.

And now to return for a moment to Poe's letter of Oct. 18, & his indignant protest against my "cruel words." Before I had answered this letter, he came to Providence entreating me to forgive his waywardness & his reproaches & to remember only the reasons which he had urged upon me for entrusting to him my future welfare & happiness. Urging me to defer my decision for a week & exacting a promise from me that I would write to him at Lowell, before he returned from there to New York, implying that his return via Providence would depend upon my answer.

I delayed writing from day to day, unwilling to say the word which might separate us forever, & unable to give him the answer which he besought me to accord him. At last I wrote a brief note, which I felt afterwards must have perplexed & agitated him. He wrote by return mail to say that he should be at Providence on the following evening. He did not come, or rather he did not come to see *me*. He afterwards told me that, agitated by my note, he had taken the cars for Providence via Boston, but had on arriving in Providence taken something at a druggists which bewildered him instead of composing him, that he entered the next train for Boston, & remained there ill & depressed until Monday. On Monday morning he returned to Providence and confessed to me the facts I have told you, reproaching me for so long delaying to send the promised letter, & then sending one so vague & illusive [*sic*].

Mrs. Locke, with whom, as you will see, I afterwards became acquainted, told me that every day during his visit to Lowell on his return from the post office, he seemed nervous & abstracted, & explained his mood to his friends as having been caused by the non-arrival of an important letter which he was expecting.

On his call at an early hour on Monday morning, I felt quite unable to see him, having passed a restless & troubled night on account of his failure to be in Providence on Saturday evening, as he had purposed. I sent word to him by a servant that I would see him at noon. He replied that he had an engagement & must see me at once. He thereupon asked for paper & wrote the following note which I transcribe for you from the slip of paper on which they were written.

Dearest Helen—I have *no* engagement but am very ill, so much so that I must go home if possible, but if you say "stay," I will try to & do so. If you cannot see me, write me *one word* to say that you *do* love me and that, *under all circumstances*, you will be mine.

Remember that these coveted words you have never yet spoken, and, nevertheless, I have not reproached you. If you can see me, even for a few moments, do so, but if not, write or send some message which will comfort me.

I wrote that I would certainly see him at noon. During that & the following day he endeavored with all the eloquence which he could exert with such matchless power to persuade me to marry him *at once*, and return with him to New York. It was at the end of the second day of his stay in Providence that I showed him some letters of remonstrance received from New York containing the passage quoted in his proud letter of indignant self-defence, cited by you on p. 75 of your "Memoir." On the arrival of some casual visitors, he rose to take his departure, & I saw by the expression of his countenance as he held my hand for a moment in taking leave of me that something had strangely moved him. I said, "We shall see you this evening?" He only bowed without replying.

That night was the night to which I have alluded as the "Ultima Thule" night—& the morning *after it* was the morning in which the sombre & tragic portrait was taken, the original of which, or a daguerreotype copy of which, I wish so much to obtain.

In the evening he had sent me a note of renunciation & farewell, saying that if we met again it would be as strangers. The handwriting showed that it was written in a state of great excitement. I have the envelope of the note, with the words written on it by me, "Sent on the evening of Nov. 8th, 1848." The note itself is lost or has been given away.

I supposed that he had taken the evening train for New York via Stonington, & had passed a night of unspeakable anxiety in thinking what might befall him travelling alone in such a state of mental perturbation & excitement. He did *not* return to New York, but passed the night at his hotel in a manner to which I alluded in the extract published from my letter in *Lotus Leaves*.

A Mr. MacFarlane, who had been very kind to Poe during the night & who had become deeply interested in him, persuaded him in the morning to go with him to the office of Masury & Hartshorn to sit for a daguerreotype. Soon after he left the office, he came alone to my mother's house in a state of wild & delirious excitement, calling upon me to save him from some terrible impending doom.

The tones of his voice were appalling & rang through the house. Never have I heard anything so awful, even to sublimity.

It was long before I could nerve myself to see him. My mother was with him more than two hours before I entered the room. He hailed me as an angel sent to save him from perdition. When my mother requested me to have a cup of strong coffee prepared for him, he clung to me so frantically as to tear away a piece of the muslin dress I wore.

In the afternoon he grew more composed, & my mother sent for Dr. A. H. Okie, who, finding symptoms of cerebral congestion, advised his being taken to the house of his friend Wm. J. Pabodie, where he was kindly cared for.

Of course gossip held high carnival over these facts, which were related, doubtless, with every variety of sensational embellishment and illustration. You will see therefore that poor Griswold had ample material to work on; he had only to turn the sympathizing physician into a police officer, & the evening before the betrothal into the evening before the bridal, to make out a plausible story, incidents which after the lapse of two years before he wrote his immortal

"Memoir" may have become so mixed up in his mind that he worked them up to suit his *motif*.

You know already *something* of what happened in the interval between this never-to-be-forgotten day & the evening when the daguerreotype which adorns your "Memoir" was taken, & the note on board the Long Island Sound steamer was written.

To return to Mrs. Locke. In the spring of 1849 I received many notes from that lady expressive of an earnest desire to make my acquaintance & proffering urgent invitations that I should visit her in Lowell. I promised to spend a few days with her, May fixing the probable date of my visit. While there, I began to suspect that she had hoped to pique the Raven by exhibiting me as her guest, or possibly bring about a reconciliation with him, through my intervention. At all events, she told me as an inducement for me to prolong my stay a day or two after the time fixed for my departure, that she had taken care he should hear of my visit, & she had reason to think he would be in Lowell during the time fixed for my stay. My heart thrilled at the thought of seeing him again, but I could not accede to her request. We crossed each other on the road! I did not *know* it until a letter from Mrs. L[ocke] informed me of the fact; but if you were not such a sceptic as to spiritual or magnetic phenomena, I could tell you of a strange experience which happened to me as the two trains rushed past each other between Boston & Lowell.

But I must bring this long letter to a close, if I would have it ready for tomorrow's steamer.

You did not answer my question about Mary Star. Who is Didier?

I have *so* much to say & ask, & now can only say may heaven bless & keep you.

Your faithful friend,

S. H. Whitman

I have read the *Dublin University* [*Magazine*] article. It is fine.[2]

A copy of the New York *Herald* just received contains an interesting letter from Dr. Moran, who was at the head of the institution where Poe died. It contains an account of his last hours, which if not literally correct, is doubtless the best to be had at this late date. But why did it not come before? I will try to get a copy for you & send by tonight's mail.[3]

S.H.W.

1. See p. 125, n. 4.
2. James Purves, "Edgar Allan Poe's Works," *Dublin University Magazine*, 86 (Sept. 1875), 296–306. This article deals with Poe's prose only.
3. Dr. J. J. Moran's account of Poe's last sickness and death is combined with an article

on the history of the attempts to erect a monument over his remains; it appeared in the New York *Herald*, Thursday, Oct. 28, 1875. Item 625 in the Ingram Poe Collection.

117.   Sarah Helen Whitman to John H. Ingram.   Item 255

My dear Rose   Nov. 1, 1875
   Just look at that! Thinking of Rose & wondering what she would think of your long silence, I began my letter, as you see, in a fit of "unconscious cerebration," I suppose we may call it. Now let me take a new departure.

My dear "MacRaven,"
   I have just received your very interesting letter [Oct. 18] with the photograph for which I have been waiting *so* long. I showed Rose the imperfect copy you sent me, and she said it did not begin to—but I remember you once reproved me for betraying confidence, so I leave you to finish the sentence at discretion. As for myself, I am well pleased with it & see no room for improvement.
   I am delighted that Mallarmé wishes to send me *Le Corbeau*. I do hope that I may live to see the realization of his wish. *Le Corbeau*!

> From that wing one purple feather
> Wafted o'er my chamber floor,
> Like a shadow o'er the heather,
> Charms my vagrant fancy more
> Than all the flowers I loved to gather
> On Idalia's velvet shore!

Urge him to send it. I will present it, when I die, to our Athenaeum Library where it shall be embalmed forever, while "Providence reigns & rules." I long to hear the remarks about you which he is to quote in his preface. When will his translation of the poems be issued?
   Browne is thoroughly roused at last about Fairfield's *Scribner* extravaganza. Fairfield attempted a reply in the *Tribune* of Monday, Oct. 18th. Did I mention it in my last to you? His reply only showed his hand & was utterly worthless as a defense. In it he said *Eureka* was "words, words, words." This roused Dr. Browne, & he talks as if he meant to take the unhappy "Alienist" in hand. He had not seen Fairfield's impotent reply until I sent it to him. Dr. Marvin, who approved and endorsed my statements in the same paper, is well & favorably known to him. Everybody thinks I "used him [Fairfield] up." I don't *like* to serve people in that way, but I couldn't help it. Seriously, I am afraid the poor fellow is "not in his perfect mind."
   You ask about Porteus. I do not know that he spoke of Poe's sister in

his lecture, but he caused it to be announced in the papers that the lecture was given in her behalf, & it was said (stated by him) that he *gave* to her, or *applied to her use*, the sixty dollars made by him. I enclose you a copy.

I enclose you a copy of a note which I wrote to Dr. Buchanan in compliance with your suggestion. I have not as yet had any reply.

Last Saturday I received from the Corresponding Secretary of the Monument Committee a very cordial & complimentary invitation to attend the ceremonies, or, if unable to attend, to send something to be read on the occasion. But I have been seriously ill for a week with sore throat, chills & fever, & today cannot speak out of a whisper. An interesting account which I enclose from the New York *Herald* may interest you, though I fancy it must be taken *cum grano*. From this I learn that Gill is to be the orator of the occasion. I don't think he is acting in Stoddard's interest. From the MS. he sent me of his Laurel Leaf, the *spirit* seems frank & fair enough. Doubtless he is afraid of you. He made no reply to the question I put to him about the portrait.

And now, dear friend, goodnight & good morning forever more,

S.H.W.

How will it do for you to send the enclosed as a postscript to Mallarmé?—a P.S. from my letter to *you*.[1]

If you could ascertain the *date* of that first draft of "The Bells," it would be very interesting and might perhaps show that Fairfield was right and that I was wrong about "the Bells" having been written before "Ulalume." In Jan. 1847 Virginia died; in October Poe wrote "Ulalume," and it was published in December 1847. In Feb. 1847, Poe wrote the beautiful "Lines to M.L.S.," published among the early poems. In *1847* (if I am to judge from the dates given me by Mrs. Houghton) Mrs. H[oughton] saw more of him than on any subsequent year. I infer then that it was in that year that he wrote at her suggestion at least the first two stanzas of "The Bells" & the other poems addressed to her. I will give you my reasons presently.

You say that when Mrs. S[hew] gave the 25 dollars for a poem still more impassioned than the "Lines to Marie Louise" that she was just going to be married to Dr. H[oughton], but in one of her letters to me, the one I sent *you*, she says, "I was married to Dr. H[oughton] in November *1850*." Thirteen months after Poe's death. True, she may have been betrothed to him two or three years before, that is to say there might have been an understanding between them that they were to marry whenever she was at liberty to form another marriage.

Again, she tells me in the same letter that *she saw very little of Mr. Poe during the last year of his life* (1849), when his mind seemed to be breaking up. To quote her exact words, "He began to break up in brain power about this time."

Then, as to 1848, she quotes a long letter or note acknowledging one from her that gave him unwonted pleasure. The note, *his* note, was (in your copy) of her copy, dated Sunday, May 1848. He says it gave him more pleasure than anything had done for months, etc., he hopes she will not drift out of his sight before he can thank her for the great debt he owed her, etc., etc. Undoubtedly it is a faithful copy of the note. But I quote it to show that their intercourse at that time was *infrequent*. In the summer, in July & August, he was absent from Fordham, & after his return in September, I was cognizant of his life until the close of the year.

"The Bells," then, I infer, if written under the circumstances described to you by Mrs. Houghton, was apparently written, or at least the two first stanzas, before "Ulalume"! It may be so. Where did *Stoddard* get his facsimile of those two verses? Yet, if the poem, as it now stands, was written at the time when *I* knew Poe, I cannot conceive that he should not have spoken of it to me, with whom he delighted to read & talk about his favorite poems.

But why was Mrs. Shew's name affixed to the copy of "The Bells" in your possession? Was it the original writing that she sent you, & did he affix her name to it with the intention that it should pass as hers? And why did Mrs. Shew, after inducing Poe to sell her a too passionate poem which he had addressed to her (the "B[eloved] P[hysician]") rather than have it published, why did she suppose that it was Griswold & not Poe, himself, who had discreetly omitted the lines which might cause pain to one who afterwards became her husband?

All of this seems strange to an outsider, but as I said before, "le vrai" is not always "le vraisemblable." Don't think me too critical. Important questions sometimes turn upon apparently trifling matters. But I have done with puzzling questions & have only room to bestow upon you a benison adieu.

Did Mrs. Lewis tell you what she knows, or claims to know, about the date of "Annabel Lee"?

Don't fear that I shall betray *anything* that you confide to me.

[Enclosure: Sarah Helen Whitman to Dr. J. R. Buchanan. Item 253]

Oct 25. 1875

Dr. J R Buchanan
Dear sir:

You may remember that many years ago—I think in the summer of 55 or 6—Mr E W Capron sent you with my consent the MS. of a poem To Helen, sent to me by Mr Poe in June 1848. and first published in Graham's Magazine in the autumn of that year.

Mr Capron was anxious to have the MS. which was without signature submitted to one of your psychometric subjects.

After an interval of some months Mr Capron wrote to you reminding you of his request, and I received from you the following note. It is dated April 30th the date of the year being omitted.

Sarah Helen Whitman

Cincinnati

Mrs S H Whitman   April 30.

Mr Capron requests a return of Mr Poe's MS. poem to yourself. I should do so at once but had almost forgotten its being in my possession and cannot just now lay my hands on it.

When found I shall at once return it with a psychometric sketch.

Yours very respectfully
Jos. R. Buchanan

It is with the faintest hope that after the lapse of so many years you will be enabled to supply any information with regard to the missing that I make this late application.

Yours very respectfully
Sarah Helen Whitman

1. On Apr. 4, 1876, Mallarmé wrote Mrs. Whitman: "I trust that the attempt [his Poe translations] will meet your approval, but no possible success of my design in the future could cause you, madame, a satisfaction equal to the joy, vivid and profound and absolute, one of the best that my literary life has yet procured for me—caused by a fragment kindly sent me by M. Ingram from one of your letters in which you express a wish to see a copy of our 'Corbeau' " (quoted in Caroline Ticknor, *Poe's Helen* [New York: Charles Scribner's Sons, 1916], p. 262).

118. *John H. Ingram to Sarah Helen Whitman*

My dear Friend,   4 Nov. 1875

I duly received *Lotos Leaves* (for which many thanks), and have today received your letter of the 22nd Ulto. containing an enclosure which did my heart good, *viz.*, your vigorous & magnificent demolition of "The Mad Magazinist" who will now see that he must seek other sources of income. I looked so eagerly for a *Tribune,* fearing that the powers which be *pro temp* might suppress your letter and feeling ashamed that I had not done *something* in the case, especially as *Scribner* sells in England, & I wish the foe to see that every movement is seen. But you have done the work so much better than I could have hoped to, & it is better for it to be done by a personal friend & countryman. I should have liked to have said a word, however, about the absurdity of basing the alleged mania upon Poe's latest works & quoting (so far as his prose stories are concerned) *his very earliest* tales. But you have done all that is needed & Mr. Fairfield will be careful in future as to how, in suiting his wares to his market, he selects his subject.

I hope Browne has had a copy of the *Tribune*. I deem the editorial remarks very needless, & not friendly, but I think I shall have a screw to put on W.R. one of these days.[1]

Lotos Leaves is very poor—nothing new, save the Griswold stories, which are of no use. Your resumé of *Laurel Leaves* does not look very promising as to its contents.

Beware of Sartain's adventures. I have some of that gentleman's (or his editor's) reminiscences published at Poe's death, & I don't think much of them.[2]

As regards the West Point matters: is it new? More than contained in *Harper's* "Poe at West Point," which Stoddard garbled & misquoted so? *If new*, I shall be glad to see. I don't believe anyone can, however, lighten that darkness so well as I can.

Have I had the passage from Poe's letter referring to the hoped-for ideal home? I have had that relating to Poe's hope of an ideal aristocracy of letters.

You do not mention anything of Poe's second visit to Europe being in Gill's essay. This seems to confirm my theory that he (Gill) neither knew where Clarke was, nor bought his collection! He *may*, however, be keeping this history back for *more* new facts. I think you could honorably ask him why he does not refer to this journey (*without alluding to me*), as he once told you that Clarke informed him (Gill) that Poe did again visit Europe.

The portrait may not be the one in my book—there are so many, & the one belonging to Mrs. Houghton (*which was stolen*) is not to be heard of.

Dr. Holland has *not* replied, so I shall repeat the question thro' *Appleton's*.[3] "Japp" was the name of the writer in the *British Quarterly Review* the ed. writes me. I only know him by name, & as a *great* admirer, & collector of information about, Poe. If you wish to ask or say anything to him I'll forward your letter, or you can send "care of Strahan & Co., Ludgate Hill, London, E.C."

Oh! you've not had the *Dublin Univ. Mag*. I'll get copy & send. I've directed copy of the *London* to be sent you. A note in Providence *Journal* or elsewhere, would please Williams, *if* you can send it. I have given Browne copy of the paper for *Southern Mag*. & asked him to send you copy. I don't think I shall publish any more of *Politian*, as it is not worthy of Poe's fame—what do you say?

I shall not hurry my Life of Poe—it *must* & *shall* be not only exhaustive, but critically good. I have hopes to get it out next year, but if delay will increase its value shall keep back. It *shall* be monument to Poe more enduring than his Baltimore stone! There is scarcely a year of his life now which I cannot give account of. I do hope you will live to read it, & I to write it. That is my chiefest fear—to die without the completion of my labour. But I *must* do it.

I won't worry with longer epistle now. I've written to your Rose & sent her my photo. Not thro' vanity. I've a versifying fit on me—*vide* proof.

Write when you can, & ever believe me, *tout à vous*.

John H. Ingram

1. "W. R." was Whitelaw Reid (1837–1912), editor and chief proprietor of the New York *Tribune* from 1872 to 1905.

2. There was an editorial, "Edgar A. Poe," in *Sartain's Magazine*, 5 (Dec. 1849), 386–87.

3. Dr. Josiah Gilbert Holland (1819–1881) was editor of the Springfield, Mass., *Republican* and a founder of *Scribner's Monthly* (later the *Century Magazine*), which he edited from 1870 to 1881.

119. John H. Ingram to Sarah Helen Whitman. Postcard

4 Nov. 1875

I have today written an acknowledgment of yours of the 22nd Ulto. but find that I have not answered yours of the 12th. Browne was an M.D. once, so is often styled Dr. *L[otos] L[eaves]* I have today acknowledged. I shall *not* refer to G[ill] at all in print, unless he *publishes* anything about me (but he won't), & even then should prefer to keep my dealings with him *perfectly* distinct from yours, so kindly refrain from alluding to me to him [*sic*].

Have had about 20 cuttings referring to the disinterment, from different sources. The act of opening the coffin was shameful.[1]

I long to hear of the *Lowell*. Pardon card & haste to try for post. Always yours,

John H. Ingram

1. In *Notes and Queries*, 5th ser., 5 (May 13, 1876), 386–87, appeared the following note from J. Brander Matthews, the Lotos Club, New York:

"E. A. POE.—Perhaps the subjoined newspaper cutting may be of interest to some English admirers of the American poet:—

"'In the preparation of the foundation for the monument to the poet Edgar A. Poe, in the churchyard of Westminster Church, Baltimore, it was found necessary to remove his remains to a spot near the grave of Mrs. Clemm, the mother of his first wife. The (N.Y.) *Sun* says, "The coffin at first appeared to be sound, but when raised the sides were found to be decayed and fell to pieces. Nothing remained inside the coffin but the skeleton, all the flesh and grave clothes having long since returned to dust. Some hair yet attached to the skull, and the teeth, which appeared to be white and perfect, were shaken out of the jaws and lay on the bottom of the coffin. The old coffin and its contents were placed entire, as exhumed, in a wooden case, and lowered into the new grave and closed up. The stones for the foundation of the monument were put in place, and everything is now prepared for the superstructure."'"

Ingram reacted swiftly and characteristically, his reply appearing in *Notes and Queries*, June 1876, p. 455: "Engravings of his monument have appeared in several of the illustrated papers. The 'newspaper cutting' quoted by MR. MATTHEWS differs from several newspaper reports forwarded to me at the time of the disinterment of Poe's remains, but I should not have called attention to it but from the fact that it alludes to Mrs. Clemm as the mother of the poet's *'first* wife.' Permit me to inform his 'English admirers' that Poe was but once married, and then to his cousin, Virginia Clemm."

120. *John H. Ingram to Sarah Helen Whitman*

My dear Friend,   10 Nov. 1875
    Only just a few lines to notify safe arrival of yours dated 25th Ulto. [postmarked 29th], for I am besides myself with letters, &c. and cannot get to do my literary work. Would that more of my correspondents were like you! Had something to say & said it.
    I see you have seen the *Dublin Univ. Mag.* so I need not send copy. Pray do not think me remiss in not having sent. I hope Williams sent the *London* as he promised—for fear he may not, I'll send one. Browne will republish the paper this month with a few corrections, but without the facsimile page, in the *Southern.*
    Three copies of the *Herald* to hand. One, I presume, but am not certain, from you. I have seen Dr. Moran's account published years ago, in a somewhat shorter & less circumstantial style. I fancy it is like so many others—very imaginative—a modicum of fact 'mid a very large amount of fancy—the conversations are utterly impossible.
    How interesting is your account of your meetings &c. with Poe—this letter fills up gaps I have wanted filled. Would that the whole story of your personal knowledge of him might & could be told!
    I wish I could let you know all that I have gathered together, but it is not possible until *the* Life is ready, but a personal interview would eliminate [*sic*] much information.
    I see Gill is foremost in the monument affair. I have a secret which is only for you *at present.* Widdleton has written to accept with thanks my offer of the *present* "Memoir" for his next forthcoming Memorial edition. I am only afraid that he will print before he can get my much revised & corrected proof. I hope not, as it will make *all* the difference between completely routing the foe, & leaving several weak points

open to attack. Mind, therefore, that this is *sub rosa*. I hope to get my life out in Germany before long. The French "Memoir" will be founded upon it. Widdleton, New York, wrote to publishers of the Paris "Raven" about having Manet's illustrations, but fears, from the specimens sent, they will not suit *his* public—he is right—they will not. I shall leave off now until tomorrow—mail day.

Saturday, 13th Nov.

Am writing at British Museum. Am going to take tea with Stella (Mrs. Lewis). Mrs. Houghton, in a letter of today, thinks of visiting Germany for her daughter's education. Browne has sent me *Southern* with *Politian* in it. It was as well not to refer Fairfield to me. It is better to have two armies in the field: the rebels won't know which side will be attacked next.

Entre nous, Widdleton's publication, if it is not too late for the revised copy, will be carrying the war right into the enemy's camp, both Gill & Stoddard will be "smote on the hips," Gill having been Widdleton's adviser hitherto, apparently! *Re.* Clarke & Gill: in a former letter you say G[ill] said that C[larke] informed him that Poe *did* visit Europe a 2nd time. *He did* (*i.e.*, Poe did) but did C[larke] tell G[ill] is the question? I wish the *Museums* could be got! I can give order of publication of nearly every tale & poem. Can you see, or Mr. Harris, the first edition of *Tales of the Grotesque & Arabesque*? I want to know what "Siope" is. Poe wrote for *The Gift* for years. Mrs. Smith quotes an alleged letter of yours, I fancy, in *Beadle's*. Is Mrs. Richmond still alive? She may have letters. I *must* find her out. Mary Star is not yet found. John P. Poe says in his last letter that the family know nothing of such a lady. Didier was formerly Secretary to [Justice] Chase & knew Mrs. Clemm; he has written various little things about her—he offered me the poem (before *Scribner*) & other information of no seeming importance, for $100. I wrote him but got no reply.

In terrible haste, ever yours,

John H. Ingram

---

121. *"Poe's* Politian," *by John H. Ingram*, Southern Magazine, 17 *(Nov. 1875), 588–94*

Poe's "Politian"
John H. Ingram

THAT EDGAR POE's youthful tragedy *Politian* has attracted less attention than his other poetical works is not strange: unequal in execution, a fragment and a mystery, the public naturally passed it by. Monsieur

Hughes, it is true, when he translated *Politan* into French, spoke of it as a tragedy "*où vivent des caractères vraiment humains*," but he, so far as we know, is the only person who, as yet, has had a good word to say for it. The same writer has also more than once drawn attention to the not unnoteworthy fact that the hero of the play is, to some extent, and in some of his mental idiosyncrasies, a reflex of the author himself. "*Comme tous les grands ecrivains*," says Monsieur Hughes, "*Edgar Poe prête aux personnages qu'il met en scène ses sensations et ses sentiments personnels*." Certain it is that whatever merit the drama may possess has been depreciated in consequence of its fragmentary nature and inexplicable plot, but it is hoped that a fuller share of interest than it has hitherto attracted will now be obtained for it by our supplying some of the missing links of the story, and furnishing *le mot de l'énigme*.

Politian is based upon a tragedy of real life, and upon a tragedy that was enacted upon American soil. A clue to the story was first discovered in Poe's critique on Mr. Hoffmann's *Greyslaer*, a romance, the poet remarks, "based on the well-known murder of Sharp, the solicitor-general of Kentucky, by Beauchampe. . . . The real events were more impressive than are the fictitious ones," adds Poe; and he continues, "the *facts* of this remarkable tragedy, as arranged by actual circumstance, would put to shame the skill of the most consummate artist. Nothing was left to the novelist but the amplification of *character*. . . . The incidents might be better woven into a tragedy."[1] And into his tragedy of *Politian*, a comparison with *Greyslaer* and Gilmore Simms' fine romance of *Beauchampe*, convinced us Poe *had* woven the incidents. But it was not until we obtained possession of the poet's original draft of the drama, a draft containing much unpublished matter, that we were enabled to demonstrate the truth of our theory. The fragment known as "Scenes from Politian: an Unpublished Drama," was first printed in 1845, in a volume dedicated to Mrs. Browning, but the manuscript in our possession appears to have been written as long ago as 1831. It is entitled "Politian: a Tragedy. Scene, Rome in the ——— century." A list of the *dramatis personae* follows, and is interesting from the fact that it not only introduces four new characters, but because it also affords descriptions of those already known but, hitherto, undescribed: thus, Lalage is recorded as "an orphan and the ward of Di Broglio;" Politian as "a young and noble Roman," and Baldazzar as "his friend." The subsequent transformation of the two latter personages into "Earl of Leicester" and "Duke of Surrey," was in no way necessary to, and certainly did not increase the *vraisemblance* of the drama. The printed extracts as known are an almost literal transcript of this, the evidently first rough draft; the erasures are few, and the alterations still fewer.

---

1. Works of Edgar A. Poe, vol. iv, p. 478. Edinburgh, 1875.

The first Act opens (with an unpublished) scene in the Palazzo of the Duke di Broglio, in an apartment strewed with the débris of a protracted revel. Two of the duke's servants, Benito and Ugo—the latter intoxicated—enter, and being joined by Rupert, a third servant, proceed, after the well-known method of theatrical domestics, to introduce the story by talking over the affairs of their employer's family. Whilst Ugo contents himself with seeking out some unemptied wine bottles, the other two discuss the sad alteration in their master's son, Count Castiglione, who was—

> "Not long ago
> A very nobleman in heart and deed."

The most reprehensible act ascribed to him is his base treatment of the beautiful lady Lalage. Rupert asserts—

> "His conduct there has damned him in my eyes.
> O villain! villain! she his plighted wife
> And his own father's ward. I have noticed well
> That we may date his ruin—so I call it—
> His low debaucheries—his gaming habits—
> And all his numerous vices from the time
> Of that most base seduction and abandonment."

Benito acquiesces, deeming—

> "The sin sits heavy on his soul
> And goads him to these courses."

"They say," continues this speaker, the duke pardons his son, but is most wroth with the poor victim of his crime, who remains secluded in her chamber, lost to the world and hope. The domestics then introduce the topic of Castiglione's approaching nuptials with his cousin Alessandra, who was "the bosom friend of the fair lady Lalage ere this mischance." Ugo now interrupting the dialogue, Benito and Rupert retire to bed, and leave the drunkard in possession of the stage. Just as he is about to depart, Jacinta, the serving-maid of Lalage, and whom Ugo is enamored of, enters. Alternately she excites the jealousy and cupidity of her *innamorato* by showing him some valuable jewels, and leading him to suppose that they had been presented to her by his master Count Castiglione. Ultimately she sets his mind at rest by telling him that the jewels had been given to her by her mistress Lalage, "as a free gift and for a marriage present." The exit of this choice couple concludes Scene I.

The second (also an unpublished) scene introduces Castiglione and his evil genius, the Count San Ozzo, in the dressing-room of the former. San Ozzo endeavors by taunts and ridicule to cure Castiglione of his sentimental fit, and in the course of the conversation contrives to allude to the duke's keeping Lalage in seclusion. He hums—

> "Birds of so fine a feather,
>   And of so wanton eye,
> Should be caged—should be caged—
> Should be caged in all weather,
>   Lest they fly."

This insulting allusion rouses even Castiglione's despicable spirit, and he exclaims

> "San Ozzo! you do her wrong—unmanly wrong!
> Never in woman's breast enthroned sat
> A purer heart! If ever woman fell
> With an excuse for falling, it was she!
> If ever plighted vows most sacredly—
> Solemnly—sworn, perfidiously broken,
> Will damn a man, that damned villain am I!
> Young, ardent, beautiful, and loving well—
> And pure as beautiful—how could she think—
> How could she dream, being herself all truth,
> Of my black perfidy? Oh, that I were not
> Castiglione, but some peasant hind;
> The humble tiller of some humble field
> That I might dare be honest!"

"Exceeding fine!" responds San Ozzo:

> "I never heard a better speech in my life.
> Besides, you're right. Oh, honesty's the thing!
> Honesty, poverty, and true content,
> With the unutterable ecstacies
> Of bread, and milk, and water!"

San Ozzo's philosophy is too potent for Castiglione's repentance, and he strives to solace himself with the reflection that these mischances are of frequent occurrence, and that it would never do for him to bring disgrace upon "Di Broglio's haughty and time-honored line," by wedding the discarded Lalage. With this comforting reflection he dismisses the subject, and allows himself to be amused by a practical joke of his boon companion, San Ozzo, and to the account of which sorry jest the remainder of the lengthy scene is devoted.

"A Hall in the Palace" includes the action of the third scene. It is, with some trifling alterations, that now published as the first in the extracts. It introduces Alessandra and Castiglione engaged in conversation; the latter appears inattentive—*distrait*—whilst his betrothed is already seen assuming the authority of a wife to reprimand and reprove. Mentally contrasting his former with his present love, Castiglione unwittingly exclaims, "Sweet, gentle Lalage!" The storm which this excla-

mation threatens to bring down is averted by the timely entrance of the
Duke di Broglio, who comes to announce an anticipated visit to Rome
of Politian, Earl of Leicester.

The second Act introduces Lalage, who is seen sitting at an open window which overlooks the palace garden; she is attended by the pert
Jacinta. Poe's marginal pencil-notes would seem to indicate that he intended this for the first of the published scenes, but subsequently he
wisely altered it to the second. The printed version is accessible to
every one; it is therefore needless to recapitulate more of it than is absolutely necessary for threading the links of the story together. This
scene portrays how the ungrateful serving-maid, deeming that she had
now obtained all that her mistress had to give, takes an opportunity of
insulting and leaving her. Thereafter a monk enters and witnesses Lalage register a mental vow—a vow, we comprehand, of vengeance. "Be-
hold," she cries, drawing a cross handled dagger and raising it on high—

> "Behold the cross wherewith a vow like mine
> Is written in Heaven!"

To which the monk responds—

> "Thy words are madness, daughter,
> And speak purpose unholy—thy lips are livid—
> Thine eyes are wild—tempt not the wrath divine!
> Pause ere too late!—oh be not—be not rash!
> Swear not the oath—oh swear it not!"
>   "'Tis sworn!"

—exclaims Lalage.

The next (another unpublished) scene brings Di Broglio and his son
before us again. Their conversation is about Politian, whom Castiglione
has just met, and whom he acknowledges to be a very different kind of
man from what he had expected. "I always thought the earl a gloomy
man," he remarks, but instead of that "I have found him full of such
humor—such wit—such whim—such flashes of wild merriment." Whilst
they are still discoursing of the strange Englishman, Politian himself
and his friend Baldazzar enter. Castiglione wishes to introduce the two
foreign nobles to his father, but Politian haughtily interrupts him and
retires, leaving his friend to account for his abrupt departure, which Baldazzar does, ascribing it to sudden illness. In the scene which follows,
and which is published as the third in the extracts, Baldazzar is found
striving to arouse Politian from his strange humors. Monsieur Hughes,
in his translation, draws attention to the fact that Politian's words might
well stand for Poe's own response to advising friends: "Command me,
sir!" he says:

> "What wouldst thou have me do?
> At thy behest I will shake off that nature
> Which from my forefathers I did inherit;
> Which with my mother's milk I did imbibe,
> And be no more Politian, but some other."

"Give not thy soul to dreams," advises Baldazzar, and bids him seek befitting occupation in the court or camp. "Speak no more to me," responds Politian, "of thy camps and courts. I am sick, sick, sick, even unto death!" he exclaims, "of the hollow and high sounding vanities of the populous earth." He next intimates that he shall need Baldazzar's aid in a hostile encounter, although "Alas!" cries he—

> "I *cannot* die, having within my heart
> So keen a relish for the beautiful
> As hath been kindled within it."

Their dialogue is broken in upon by a lady's voice, with "sorrow in the tone," singing behind a lattice an English song, whose burden is "Say nay—say nay!"[2] Baldazzar agains entreats his friend to cast his "fancies to the wind," and to descend to the hall where he is awaited, bidding him remember that his "bearing lately savored much of rudeness unto the Duke." Persuaded against his will, Politian is reluctantly about to descend, when he is arrested by the voice of the unseen singer repeating the refrain "Say nay—say nay!" and he finds the words so in unison with his own desires that he stays, sending an apology to the Duke for his absence.

With the next scene the third Act of the manuscript play commences. Lalage and Politian are seen together in the palace gardens. In this, the finest scene of the tragedy, Politian avows his passionate love for the deserted Lalage. "Even for thy woes I love thee," he avers, and when Lalage responds:

> "Alas, proud Earl,
> Thou dost forget thyself, remembering me!
> How, in thy father's halls among the maidens
> Pure and reproachless of thy princely line,
> Could the dishonored Lalage abide?
> Thy wife, and with a tainted memory—
> My seared and blighted name, how would it tally
> With the ancestral honors of thy house,
> And with thy glory?"

Politian replies in words so intensely Poësque, that one might easily fancy the poet speaking in his own behalf:

---

2. It is a stanza from a song by Sir Thomas Wyat.—Ed. S.M.

> "Speak not to me of glory!
> I hate—I loathe the name; I do abhor
> The unsatisfactory and ideal thing.
> Art thou not Lalage and I Politian?
> Do I not love, art thou not beautiful—
> What need we more? Ha! glory! now speak not of it—
> By all I hold most sacred and most solemn—
> By all my wishes now—my fears hereafter—
> By all I scorn on earth and hope in heaven—
> There is no deed I would more glory in,
> Than in thy cause to scoff at this same glory
> And trample it under foot."

Lalage now intimates that there is "a land new found," "by one of Genoa," the air of which "to breathe is happiness now, and will be freedom hereafter;" but to Politian's passionate appeal to her to fly thither with him, she answers: "A deed is to be done—Castiglione lives!" "And he shall die!" exclaims Politian, as he departs.

The next (another unpublished) scene is occupied by preparations for the wedding of Alessandra and Castiglione, and by Jacinta's harsh treatment of Ugo. It does not do much to advance the action of the drama, which is continued more actively, however, in the next—known in the published "scenes" as the fifth. Politian enters, and is followed by Baldazzar, who informs him that Castiglione, knowing no cause of quarrel with the Earl, refuses to accept his cartel. Seeing the Count himself approaching, Politian contrives to get rid of his friend, and awaits Castiglione alone. The Count is about to suggest that some misunderstanding has arisen, but Politian interrupts him with the words, "Draw villain, and prate no more!" Whereupon Castiglione draws his sword, but when Politian cries:

> "Thus to the expiatory tomb
> I do devote thee in the name of Lalage!"

lets his weapon fall, and refuses to fight. Despite all the menaces of the Earl, Castiglione persists in his refusal to fight against so sacred a cause, and Politian departs with the words:

> "Before all Rome I'll taunt thee, villain—I'll taunt thee,
> Dost hear? with *cowardice*—thou *wilt not* fight me?
> Thou liest! thou *shalt!*"

Most lucklessly, a long hiatus now occurs in the manuscript. The whole of the first scene of the fourth Act, in which we learn that Politian again met Castiglione, and—

> "In the public streets
> Called him a coward!"

is missing, as are also the first thirty-seven lines of the succeeding scene between San Ozzo and the foolish Ugo. The latter, apparently dejected by Jacinta's scornful treatment of him, attempts to commit, and fancies he has succeeded in committing suicide. San Ozzo, for purposes of his own, humors Ugo's insane idea, remarking in an aside:

> "I've heard before that such ideas as these
> Have seized on human brains."

He humors the man to the full bent of his fancy, and dismisses him to inform his master Castiglione that he, Ugo, is dead!

The third scene discovers Politian standing alone in the moonlit Coliseum waiting for Lalage. And with a characteristic soliloquy our manuscript ends. Yet, as to how the drama was to have been brought to a conclusion, though a puzzling question, is by no means beyond all conjecture. With our knowledge of the Beauchampe tragedy to guide us, we shall not probably be far wrong in deeming that the poet intended *Politian* to terminate thus: Lalage leaves the palace in order to keep her appointment with the Earl. In the meantime Castiglione, absenting himself from the wedding festivities in order, in a fit of remorse, to seek Lalage and obtain her forgiveness, sees her unattended leaving the palace. He follows her to the Coliseum, and beholds her clasped in the arms of Politian. He discovers himself and taunts the Earl, who, regardless of the fact that Castiglione is unarmed, draws his sword and plunges it into the Count's bosom. Castiglione dies, and Politian is arrested and condemned to death. Lalage visits him in his cell, and acknowledges that she now loves him. She then takes poison, and Politian stabs himself. With his triumphant defiance of death to separate them, the tragedy may be supposed to end.

122. *John H. Ingram to Sarah Helen Whitman*

My dear Providence,   18 Nov. 1875

I am *so* glad to get *your* letters, especially when they are so full of the old *esprit* as this one [Nov. 1] is, although you tell me in it that your heart is [*illegible*] elsewhere. And the tale "begun & broke off in the middle!"[1] Well, I *have* written to your Rose & sent her a copy of my phiz for herself, to criticise & hypercriticise to her heart's content. I suppose she is now en route for the Old World.

And now to the *business* of your letter. I shall certainly send the P.S. to Mallarmé & strongly urge the sending of *Le Corbeau*—in fact, did that when giving your address—but he is forgetful, or lazy, & the P.S. will arouse him. Do not be disappointed with the illustrations. Manet carries the weird to its very uttermost verge—is sometimes in danger of overstepping the one step from the sublime. In the last stanza, for instance, he seems to have taken Poe's allegory for a literal fact, to fancy the material nature absorbed by "the shadow which lies floating on the floor." The complete translation of the poems & select "Marginalia" is, *I fear*, far from ready. I should be glad to hear of its being in printer's hands. The "Memoir," I suppose, will be founded on my *data*. Preface will quote some lines of Swinburne's referring to me. I will try & send them in my next. I wish Browne would do something new about *Eureka*—he is capable & Poe's admirers generally are not. The world that cares [*illegible*].

[If] Dr. Buchanan has not replied when your next arrives, I will send him a few polite lines, having your permission. Secretary of Monumental Committee (which I fancy is "much cry & little wool" & intended for the advertisement of Mr. Child & the glorification of some nobodies) has sent to ask me to give them "some expression of admiration" to be read at the ceremony.[2] Reply had to go at once. I was very busy & bothered & though I replied politely, yet, I fear, my answer was too curt.[3] Can't be helped. Thanks for the N.Y. *Herald*. I have already given you my views about that. Gill will, doubtless, find prudence in dealing with me necessary. *If* he keeps to his present track & does not make public or printed allusions to me, I shall leave him alone. Does he give *full* account of the West Point Court Martial, or anything more than Gibson's paper in *Harper's* about "Poe at West Point"? Which latter Stoddard so misquoted. Do ask him (Gill) why he does not speak of Poe's adventures in Europe.

Gill claims to have first draft of "The Bells"—he doubtless has *Sartain's* copy, from which Stoddard took his, but I have the veritable first. I have in a former letter described to you how "The Bells" was composed, have I not? & why Poe *put the name of M. L. Shew* to it? I am going to give full account to *Appleton's* London correspondent & will see you get early copy. *All is vrai, & I have* the poem in Poe's own MS. I cannot fix the date at this moment but will try & do my best to. It was not—as I received it, to pass in public as Mrs. Shew's, but only playfully ascribed to her by Poe, as she suggested the theme. Mrs. H[oughton] emphatically declares—what is evident—that she is not literary, but loved Poe for his nobleness & gentleness. She has not read his works! I love her only second to yourself. There is only one point you ask about that I cannot answer, *save by word of mouth—viz.*, that Mrs. S[hew], when she gave the 25 dollars for "The Beautiful Physician," was just going to be married. I have, I believe, an explanation, but that may not be right & she may have had a lengthy engagement with Dr. Houghton—but *I believe* in my own views. Latterly, in 1849, I do not think Poe did see much of Mrs. H[oughton],

I fancy, for the reason the poem was suppressed, his intercourse was objected to. All is capable of explanation when *we* meet. Mrs. H[oughton] (who may not recollect these matters so precisely as you do, & she says she has forgotten so much which even these old letters &c. recall) probably deems Griswold omitted the lines from the poem to her out of spite, whereas, I fancy, Poe did it from prudence—*after the publication* of the lines "To M.L.S." had caused comment. Is not that *vraisemblable?* Mrs. L[ewis] knows nothing & is *more* imaginative than Mrs. E[lizabeth] O[akes] Smith.

But now a short goodbye. *All* will be clear & coherent in the "Memoir," so pray that for its completion may live [*illegible*]

John H. Ingram

1. The bottom third of pages 1 and 2 of this holograph have been cut off; the last three lines of pages 4 and 5 have crumbled.

2. George William Childs (1829–1894) was a wealthy Philadelphia publisher and philanthropist. It was he who had contributed the last $650 needed before the contract for the planned monument could be let.

3. Ingram's reply to Miss Sara Sigourney Rice, Baltimore schoolteacher and moving spirit behind the erection of the monument to Poe, was printed in the book she edited about the services held at the unveiling of the monument over Poe's remains on Nov. 17, 1875, *Edgar Allan Poe, a Memorial Volume* (Baltimore: Turnbull Brothers, 1877), p. 89: "I thank you and your Committee for the honor they do me in inviting any expression of my opinion with respect to the object of their labours, but during the last few years my views respecting Edgar Allan Poe have been so frequently brought before the public that I fear a repetition of them upon the present occasion is scarcely likely to prove interesting. I have little faith in 'heaps of stone' as memorials of the great, but must confess that a public expression of admiration for an illustrious son whose memory has been so long overclouded by unmerited obloquy does seem fitting on the part of America."

123. Sarah Helen Whitman to John H. Ingram.   Item 262

My dear friend,   Nov. 20, 1875
    Yours of Nov. 4th, with a postcard of the same date, received yesterday. I am so glad you liked my *Tribune* letter. It has been very warmly received, generally. Curiously enough, a copy of the *Tribune* of Wed. Nov. 17th was sent me yesterday morning containing two long-delayed articles, dated Oct. 18. I will send you a copy of them as soon as I can obtain another paper. The first is a letter from John S. Hart of Philadelphia. I will copy it for you *here:*

"The Bells" & "Annabel Lee"
Original Form of "The Bells"—Alterations
of Both Poems by the Author

To the Editor of the *Tribune.*

Sir: Mr. Fairfield in his letter on the chronological order of Mr. Poe's writings, makes one slight mistake, which it may be well to correct, as the subject is undergoing a careful scrutiny, & especially as there is a curious piece of unwritten history connected with one of these poems. Mr. Fairfield says "The Bells" & "Annabel Lee" were written prior to 1847. "The Bells" was first published in the November number of *Sartain's Magazine,* for 1849, of which periodical I was the editor. The poem, when first left with me for publication, sometime in June or July of that year, consisted of only two short stanzas, as follows:

The Bells—A Song.

The Bells!—hear the bells!
The merry wedding bells!
How fairy-like a melody there swells
From the silver tinkling cells
Of the bells, bells, bells!
Of the bells!

The bells!—ah, the bells!
The heavy iron bells!
Hear the tolling of the bells!
Hear the knells!
How horrible a monody there floats
From their throats—
From their deep-toned throats!
How I shudder at the notes
From the melancholy throats
Of the bells, bells, bells!
Of the bells!

This was the entire poem in its original form, as first offered to *Sartain's Magazine.* It was accepted in that form & put in type, but before its appearance the author enlarged it to nearly its present size & form, & again, before its actual publication, he sent us a second version in the form in which it finally appeared.

The poem of "Annabel Lee" was also sent to me for publication in *Sartain's Magazine* in the latter part of 1849. It was in type ready for publication, but before its appearance in the magazine the author died, whereupon Mr. Griswold, who was Poe's literary administrator, & who probably found a copy of the poem among Poe's manuscripts, forthwith published it in one of the New York papers—The *Tribune,* I believe. The poem, as put forth by Mr. Griswold, appears to have been from Poe's first draft. The copy, which was sold to *Sartain's Magazine,* & which first appeared in that magazine in January, 1850, contained several alterations & improvements by the author, & in this form the poem has found its permanent place in our literature.

Philadelphia, Oct. 18, 1875.   John S. Hart.

The article by Fairfield I enclose. It is another exposition of his folly & weakness. Dr. Marvin (F.K.M.) is as well known to the medical world as any man in the profession. Though I fancy that when Fairfield wrote the impotent reply to him on the very day M[arvin]'s article was published that *he* did not know the initials F.K.M. to be those of Dr. Marvin. As for F.G.F., I think we have spiked his guns.

The same *Tribune* contains a long editorial on Poe—probably by Ripley—in which antagonism is well masked by a good deal of reluctant praise & professed sympathy. In today's *Journal* I find a brief abstract of the ceremonies at the dedication of the monument, which I enclose. The poem by William Winter is exquisitely tender & not more tender than it is superbly imaginative: the fourth & fifth verses in the depth & splendor of their contrasted imagery are wonderfully fine & impressive. Do try to have them republished, with a word of appropriate recognition of the author's genius.[1] I have seen but few of Winter's poems, but the few that I have seen made a profound & indelible impression.

And now to your letter. You ask if you have had the passage from Poe's letter which Gill copied for publication with my consent when he was in Providence two years ago. You have *not*, because I had hoped long ere this to have seen you and allowed you to have made your own selections, but I will copy it for you now & enclose it in my letter. I have shrunk from having my personal relations to the poet unveiled until I should be no longer a dweller on this oblique planet, but as I draw near the time of my enfranchisement, I feel less of this sensitiveness—more as if I had *already* thrown off the mortal coil.

Gill says nothing of Poe's second visit to Europe. Indeed his article is in no sense an attempt at a consecutive life, only a collection of separate facts.

I thought that he had quoted a letter from Clarke about the *Stylus*, but I *now* think that the letter he quoted was a letter or note *to* Clarke about the projected periodical by a Mr. Alexander of St. Louis.

I think there were some particulars about the West Point career that I had not seen before, though it is so long since I saw the article in *Harper's* on that subject that I cannot be sure. Do you remember two satirical verses of Poe's about Joseph Locke, one of the officers at West Point? I *may* have seen them before I saw them in Gill's article, but if so, I had forgotten it.

You ask about Mrs. Hale. I knew her in Boston and she published some early poems of mine in a volume, a collection of poems called *The Ladies Wreath*, published in 1836, I believe. I have been looking for a very kind letter which I received from her four or five years ago in reply to one in which I asked her if she could tell me in what English periodical Lady Blessington had spoken with praise of one of my poems which appeared in that volume. She could not throw any light on the subject & did not know that her volume had been noticed in the English papers. I had never *seen* the article, but two or three persons had spoken to me of seeing it at the Providence Athenaeum in the *Albion* or the *Athenaeum* or some of the English papers taken there. I supposed that Mrs. Hale would know all about it, & addressed her on the subject. Her letter was so very kind that if you write to her & say that I suggested it to you, it might prompt her to additional readiness to give you all the information about Poe in her power. Poe spoke of her as having been very kind & liberal toward him as an editress. If I find her letter I will send it to you.

I have had a letter from Dr. Buchanan under date of Louisville, Nov. 6, [18]75. He says:

My dear Madam,

I greatly regret that you had occasion to write the letter of Nov. 2 which I have just received. My impression was that I found the MS. of Mr. Poe about the year 1860 & forwarded it to you. Owing to removal from my former residence and the War, some of my most valued autographs have been lost. As I believe, I have not seen Poe's autograph for fifteen years. If it is not with you, I fear it is gone beyond recovery. I am almost *positive* as to having Mr. Poe's MS. about 1860, & *designing* to send it to you, & not having it since. I have just examined my repository of treasures without finding any clue to the lost poem. . . .

Little that has been written will live, but Poe is of those that will be longest remembered.

Yours with high respect,

J. R. Buchanan

"Only this & nothing more."

When I receive the *Politian* article in the *London* [*Quarterly*] I will certainly notice it.

I *liked* the *St. James* article.

Ever and ever your faithful friend & ally,

S. H. Whitman

I never heard of "Siope," have never seen the *Tales of the Grotesque & Arabesque*. I see you have already written to Mrs. Hale. If anybody can unearth Clarke's *Museum*, it will be you.

I have marked with a blue pencil that portion of the extract from Edgar's letter which G[ill] has quoted.

Your poem of the "Two Girls" is *charming*. I shall have it republished.

S.H.W.

---

1. William Winter (1836–1917) was an author and a dramatic critic as well as a poet.

124. John H. Ingram to Sarah Helen Whitman

My dear Friend,   25 Nov. 1875
    Just a few lines to tell you that I have written a hurried—very
hurried—letter to the *Tribune* (under cover to Whitelaw Reid) *re.*
Fairfield. What I have chiefly called him [Fairfield] to account for is
his *errata* in dates, & misquotations. My own opinion is that he is an
utterly worthless scamp: you perhaps know less of his Poe papers than
I do. Under the flimsy veil of being friendly to Poe he used, years ago,
to write papers against him, a larger portion of such papers being
stolen from Poe's own writings. He is a wholesale thief—even the
paper in *Scribner's* being full of peculations—but in that, I fancy—I
feel certain—from various sentences that he is only a tool in the hands
of Stoddard. He is the hired writer of the best bidder, but if my letter
be inserted in the *Tribune* he will see some hints in it that will make
him shiver. I have asked Whitelaw Reid to send the letter to you, if
unable to use it, & if it appears, to forward a copy to you. If it does not
appear, let me have it when read & I will correct it more carefully &
print it with my *Nation* letter.
    The *Nation*, I hear, although it did not print my letter, has since
spoken well of me in its pages.
    Fairfield, I fancy, tried to get Widdleton to let him edit or do
something for his edition of Poe; therefore the publication of my
"Memoir" instead of Griswold's will rather startle him.
    You will see something about "The Bells" in *Appleton's Journal*—
letter of London correspondent. First draft of "The Bells" must have
been written after your engagement with Poe had been broken off.
    I do hope Browne will write a new letter *re.* Fairfield v. *Eureka*. I
wish I had time to copy fully for you & for him Fairfield's *former*
remarks on *Eureka*, but I must not part with the originals just now. It
would be well for us to have Browne write, as, just now, it looks as if
we two were the only defenders & worked together.
    Miss Royster (Mrs. Shelton) does not seem to have been the first
love, but a Mary Star.[1] Mrs. S[hew] has herself pointed out the mistake.
Mrs. Nichols, having recovered her eyesight, promises complete
reminiscences. I wish Mrs. Richmond's address could be obtained.
And Mary Star's. But I have learned so much of Poe's mental & worldly
story that I feel fully empowered to grapple with any difficulties which
may arise. I think my letter will shew Messrs. Stoddard, Fairfield &
G[ill] that I know something about [the] American press, as well as the
Poe chronology.
    What has become of Miss Peckham? I send another *London*. The
paper on *Politian*, I am informed, has been very well noticed all over
the country.

With kindest wishes, *tout à vous,*

John H. Ingram

1. Augustus Van Cleef, "Poe's Mary," *Harper's Magazine*, 78 (Mar. 1889) 634–40, purports to quote Mary Starr's reminiscences of Poe's violent attachment to herself. Her married name is not given in this article, but it was Jenning. For details see Thomas Ollive Mabbott, ed., *Collected Works of Edgar Allan Poe*, Vol. I, *Poems* (Cambridge, Mass.: Harvard Univ. Press, 1969), pp. 232–33.

125. *Sarah Helen Whitman to John H. Ingram. Postcard. Item 264*

Nov. 26, 1875

I send tonight some papers, N. York *Tribune*, N. York *Evening Post* (!), Baltimore *Evening News*, etc., with proof copy of an article to appear in tomorrow's *Journal*, Nov. 28 [*sic*]. The extract is from a private letter to S.H.W. by W. D. O'Connor. More by next mail.

Mr. Lewis's statement is interesting but not quite accurate as to dates, as when he says Mrs. C[lemm] made her home with him from the autumn of 1849 to the summer of 1856. We know that at least two or three years of the time were spent with Mrs. H[oughton] & in Lowell.[1] Have not yet had the paper on *Politian*.

S. H. Whitman

1. Sylvanus D. Lewis's account of his associations with Poe and Mrs. Clemm was written for the ceremonies at the unveiling of Poe's monument in the Westminster Churchyard, Baltimore, Nov. 17, 1875, and it was printed in various newspaper accounts of that occasion.

126. *Sarah Helen Whitman to John H. Ingram. Item 265*

My dear friend, Nov. 30, [18]75

Your kind letter received yesterday. On the 19th Inst. I sent letter & papers—no, the *papers*, with a postal card; were mailed on the 26th. I hope the papers will arrive safely.

Gill had nothing to do with the exercises on the 17th save the recitation of "The Raven." You have nothing to fear from him as an antagonist, I fancy. I have not yet seen the *London* [*Quarterly*]. Was the facsimile in his usual finished hand? Dr. Moran's account seems to have been generally received *cum grano*.

Mrs. Richmond is living, I believe. I have never seen her, but heard from a friend who met her at Rye Beach (a Mass. watering place) a few years ago that she asked after me in a friendly spirit, but did not speak of Poe.

I am delighted to know that Widdleton has accepted your offer. I hope he will get your revised & corrected proof. Mr. Eveleth of Thomaston, Maine, wrote me yesterday that he had just read your article in the *International*. He made a few criticisms. One in relation to the *apparent* contradiction in the quotation of the lines pencilled on the margin of the *Broadway Journal* copy of "Ligeia" to the statement that the lines to Helen were written before Poe *knew* her.

I noticed this apparent discrepancy myself, & intended to have called your attention to it.

I explained to Mr. Eveleth that I had been so importuned by friends & strangers for some single line, or even *word*, of Poe's writing that, overpersuaded, I had often clipped two or three words from some fragment of his writing to comply with their wishes. In this instance I had cut from the pencilled lines "The poem I sent you," etc. the words, "through Mrs. O[sgood]'s description," that is, *recognized* you thro' Mrs. *Osgood's* description. I explained to Mr. Eveleth that in sending you the volumes of the *Broadway* I had pointed out to you the unfinished sentence & given you the missing words, but that in hurriedly preparing your notes for the press, you had probably mislaid my letter & had given the lines, without reflecting that in their incomplete meaning they *seemed* to contradict the fact afterwards stated that the poem was written before he had met me. But this can be remedied by giving the whole in a future version.

I am *so* glad to hear that you are to get your *Life* out in Germany, & that the French will be founded upon it.

Do you think Mallarmé will send me his *Raven?*

I must send you the account I received in a private letter from Worthington, about which I will tell you hereafter. I could not help sending a copy to the *Journal*. It was so graphic.

I must close at once, or miss tomorrow's mail.

Goodnight and a thousand blessings till next time.

Your faithful friend,

S. H. Whitman

127. *Sarah Helen Whitman to John H. Ingram.*   *Item 270*

My dear MacRaven,   Dec. 7, [18]75
    Since I wrote to you Nov. 30, I have received two brief but most interesting notes from you, & today came the *London* [*Quarterly*] with your valuable paper on *Politian*. The facsimile is unquestionably a

genuine reproduction, & having been, as it would appear, written nearer the assumed date of the *Scribner* poem than anything else yet presented as a specimen of Poe's writing, a careful examination of the two may throw some light on the genuineness of the *Scribner* writing. I have not yet compared them, but shall do so, so soon as I have dispatched this hurried note. I sent you on the 26th Ulto. a postal card & several papers on the Poe monument. I hope they reached you safely.

I enclose a copy of the monument, etc. from *Harper's Weekly* of Saturday last, which bears date Dec. 11, though issued Dec. 7. It is decidedly the best copy of the daguerre taken ten days before Poe's death that I have seen, and, indeed it is more *like* him, has more of his habitual & characteristic expression, than any known portrait of him. It is from the same original I presume with the engraving prefixed to Stoddard's "Memoir," but how utterly superior. If you could obtain an engraving from this copy it would give great additional interest to your *Life*. Everybody admires it. I must find out its history from Miss Rice. If Poe looked like this only "ten days before his death," there needs no better refutation of the scandal of his enemies.

Even that "loss of brain power," of which Mrs. H[oughton] speaks, cannot be accredited to this sad & noble face, which corresponds in the hopeless melancholy of its expression to the tone of the two letters written to Mrs. Clemm from Richmond during the last days of his stay, the last days of his life on earth.

Did I tell you that the private letter (from which the writer of the *Journal* article quoted a description of the speech of Mr. Latrobe, etc.) was Wm. D. O'Connor. I sent you a *proof* of the article before it came out in print the following day. I laid aside a portion of one of O'Connor's letters to send you. It expressed an affectionate interest in you & in your proposed work of writing a *Life* of Poe, as a separate work. If I cannot find it tonight, I will send it another time. It was O'C[onnor] who intended & still intends to take Fairfield in hand. If two such pitiless critics as you & he fall upon him, may heaven have mercy on his defenceless head. But O'Connor is so overwhelmed with business that he scarcely has time for sleep. I wish I could send you his account of our friend G[ill]'s recitation of "The Raven." It was intensely funny. This is *strictly under the Rose*—so keep my counsel or dread the consequence.

Rose will have told you of our *meeting & parting* before this is read.

I enclose a story which you may have heard before—about Poe's mother having been a daughter of Benedict Arnold, who was a kinsman of my maternal grandmother, Mary Arnold Wilkinson.[1] Perhaps if the story be true, which seems not improbable, it indicates the same attraction of races or families suggested by the name of

Arnold Le Poer. Send back the paragraph about Poe's mother when you have done with it.

And now for a few days & forevermore, peace be with you. Faithfully & affectionately,

S. H. Whitman

I hope I shall soon see your letter to the *Tribune*, but they often keep an article in type for a month, so full are their columns.

O'Connor says, "If habitual lying is a sign of epileptic neurosis, Bedlam's best man is outside limbo in Fairfield."

Where did *you* unearth his [Fairfield's] past sins & infirmities as to the breach of that darkest sin in the decalogue, "Thou shalt not bear false witness"?

1. Item 1031 in the Ingram Poe Collection, an undated clipping from an unidentified newspaper, states that Poe's mother, Elizabeth Arnold, was a natural daughter of Benedict Arnold. Shortly after Mrs. Whitman had mentioned this probability to Ingram, the question came up again, in *Notes and Queries*, 5th ser., 5 (Jan. 29, 1876) 88: "The Utica *Observer* mentions, as a fact which has escaped the notice of all his biographers, that Edgar Allan Poe was the grandson of Benedict Arnold. His mother, who was known before her marriage as Elizabeth Arnold, an English actress, was the natural daughter of the traitor. This statement rests on the concurrent testimony of a number of old actors who knew Elizabeth Arnold well. Poe himself alluded to the matter occasionally in the company of those who knew this chapter in his family history."

128. *Sarah Helen Whitman to John Ingram.*   *Item 272*

My dear friend,   Dec. 14, 1875

I received yesterday from the *Tribune* your capital paper on Fairfield's audacious fabrications. The editor returns it on the ground that "Fairfield's article has already received in the *Tribune* all the attention that it deserves."

Your article is full of valuable material that must be incorporated in any history of Poe's prose & poetical works. You are mistaken in some minor points. It was *Sartain's Magazine*, so says Mr. Hart, in which "The Bells" first appeared. The last issue of the *Union Magazine* was that of December 1848. To what "olden fantasy" do you refer? "Poe's Plagiarisms"? Did Fairfield really write such a paper? I long to know when & where.

I have written something about your article on *Politian* which will appear in a few days. I will send you a copy by the next steamer.

I have seen Swinburne's letter to the Committee of the Monument dedication. It was in *Appleton's Journal* of Saturday the 11th, & very good.[1]

An extract from a delayed letter of Davidson's has also been circulating through the press.

The paragraph which you sent me about the Edinburgh edition having been "set up & printed by women," which I mentioned in a letter to Miss Rice, I see has been going also through all the papers.

I enclose your article, which I hope to see again. Will write soon, but must say goodbye tonight.

Your watchful & ever guardant "Providence"—

S.H.W.

You have seen ere this our Rose & the other roses & lillies that follow in her train.

I hardly know what to think about the *Scribner* facsimile, but incline very much to doubt.

The *Journal* of yesterday says that Proctor, the English star-gazer, & Wm. F. Gill, the Boston lecturer & publisher, were "badly shaken up" by a railroad accident in Westerly, R.I., Sunday night. No bones broken, I believe.

Au revoir

I hope you received the copy of *Harper's Weekly* that contained the woodcut of the last photograph of E.A.P. & that you liked it.

1. Swinburne's letter, dated Nov. 9, 1875, to Miss Sara S. Rice was also reprinted in facsimile, pp. 69–72 of the memorial volume.

129. *Sarah Helen Whitman to John H. Ingram.*   Item 273

My dear MacRaven,   Dec. 21, 1875
I fully expected to mail you a copy of my notice of your article on *Politian* in time for Saturday's steamer, but the notice, though in type, did not appear until this morning, so crowded has the newspaper been with holiday advertisements.

It has a good place & will attract the attention of the "disaffected." Since Stoddard keeps silent under your unpublished letters to the *Nation* & to *Scribner*, it might be a good time for you to state that Kettell, in a list of printed collections of poetry, mentions *Tamerlane & Other Poems*, by a Bostonian, doubtless, the "suppressed" volume published in 1827. At least Mr. Harris was confident of this, & he is a careful observer of dates & bibliographical items & indexes. Have you seen Kettell's Collection of American Poetry? There is a copy in our Athenaeum which I will examine before sealing my letter.

I am glad on the whole that the *Tribune* did *not* publish your valuable letter, because the error in relation to the *Union* [*Magazine*] might have been caught up by the enemy & used to discredit your other statements. I cut from the Boston *Commonwealth* of Dec. 18 the paragraph about Tennyson. It has the look of American manufacture about it. Don't you think so?

I saw in the Baltimore *Elocutional* (a monthly paper sent me by Miss Rice) a copy of Swinburne's letter in full; I had seen an extract only in *Appleton's*. Speaking of the monuments to Poe's genius raised in France, he alludes to "A double homage due to the loyal & loving cooperation of one of the most remarkable younger poets & one of the most powerful leading painters in France, M. Mallarmé & M. Manet." Have you heard anything more about *Le Corbeau*, as to the probability of his winging his flight to our Rhode Island rookeries?

I received this morning from Widdleton a letter announcing his volume, and informing me that he had sent me a copy through the Providence booksellers. I have not yet received it.

I wonder if you have seen the enclosed from the Baltimore *Gazette* of Nov. 18. It is well said; indeed, the *Gazette* gave the best report of the dedication ceremonies that I have seen. It knows how to say *multum in parvo*.

In saying on the first page of my letter, "Since Stoddard keeps silent," etc., I mean, since he has refused to take up the gauntlet you have thrown down to him. Mr. Harris seemed to think that he *would*, but he has had *time* enough, if he had the *will*. Evidently he thinks it more prudent to fight behind masked batteries.

Did you see the roses? The Queen Rose said she intended to ask you to call on them.

I must say goodbye and post my letter at *once*, for the weather clock says, as you will see in the *Journal* of this morning, we are to have snow or rain before nightfall.

                                                                 S. H. Whitman

130.   *John H. Ingram to Sarah Helen Whitman*

My dear Providence,   21 Dec. 1875
I am trying to scrawl off a line to let you know that I am still alive & have received all your dear letters, the papers & postcard safely. I have been working too hard (for Xmas) & am knocked up. Sunday & yesterday quite useless & I have dozens of letters waiting reply. So be patient, my dear friend, & write when you can. I write to you when I do not respond to anyone elsewhere. I saw Miss Peckham & party for a short time. Miss Rose looked better than I had ever seen her before,

but did not think that I looked any better than at our last meeting. I was very tired. They had a terrible voyage.

I enclose the cutting about the Arnolds. I don't place any faith in it—one of the most circumstantial accounts recently received from Baltimore positively asserts Poe's mother was a widow when married to his father. The old story over again. Mrs. Shelton has spoken out—(this is strictly *entre nous*) & says she was not engaged to Poe when he died, although he would not be denied, & does not seem to have been quite refused—more hereafter—when young they were engaged, but their letters intercepted & Poe deeming himself neglected, went off, &c., &c.[1]

I see Gill has already published your letters from Poe in the *Daily Graphic* & more, apparently, than I have had.[2] Why mutilate them at this late date? If ever I get to see you, I shall expect to *see* them in full, & to hear that you will not harden your heart any longer, by keeping them unpublished. *My* life I hope to make a poem—I mean my life of Poe. I have just had a nice letter from Japp, who wrote the *British Quarterly Review* paper—he has made a study of Poe. I have asked him to come after Xmas & see me. I have just been elected to a Club he belongs to.

The Irish Poës have written again & now hope to claim Poe as a scion of their family.[3] They are all in Burke's *Landed Gentry*.

Widdleton now announces my "Vindication" for his Memorial edition of the poems.[4] I have received photo of the Monument & papers continue to arrive. The engraving you send is the best yet to hand—may I keep it? It is, I fancy, from the photo in possession of Neilson Poe's family. I asked them for a copy & they said "Their photo was so like the engraving I sent them (same as in book) that I should not find it (*i.e.*, theirs) of any use."

Perhaps 'tis the one selected for Widdleton's new edition—several papers have given engravings of this [one] engraved by *Harper's Weekly* (as sent by you), but none so well as this.

In haste & headache this is sent off—but *in all*, I am, believe me ever yours most devotedly,

John H. Ingram

P.S. I hope I shall find Japp *nice* because I want a true sympathiser, ready to carry on the work if I should pass away before its completion—but my family motto is "Hope Ingram."

1. Edward V. Valentine mailed to Ingram, Nov. 20 and 22, 1875, several pages of notes he had taken during conversations with Mrs. Shelton (Items 261 and 263 in the Ingram Poe Collection). Ingram used most of this information, without revealing his source, in his *Life*, Vol. II.

2. Under the title "A Poet on His Critics," the New York *Daily Graphic* for Nov. 16,

1875, printed perhaps a quarter of a column containing excerpts from Poe's letter of Oct. 18, 1848, as having been taken "from advance-sheets of Mr. William F. Gill's article on 'New Facts in Regard to Poe,' to be published in 'Laurel Leaves.'"

3. Ingram received two letters from James Jocelyn Poë, Riverston, Penagh, about the genealogy of the Poe family, dated Nov. 17, and Dec. 4, 1875. Items 259 and 269 in the Ingram Poe Collection.

4. W. J. Widdleton brought out *Poems and Essays of Edgar Allan Poe, Memorial Edition* (New York, 1876), replacing Griswold's "Memoir" with Ingram's, as it had appeared in Ingram's 1874–75 edition of Poe's *Works* but appending a statement that William F. Gill had permitted Ingram to use materials previously assigned to him.

131. *Sarah Helen Whitman to John H. Ingram.*   Item 275

My dear "Sir John the Grame,"   Dec. 28, [18]75

I have time but for a few words tonight. I told you in my last [Dec. 21] that Widdleton had sent me a copy of his "Memorial Volume" in which he publishes the dedication ceremonies at the unveiling of the monument, your "Memoir," *Eureka*, etc., etc. with the poems. The book being dedicated to me by *the publisher!* A liberty which he hopes I shall "not disapprove." There is a fine copy of the portrait from your "Memoir." I have not had time to read the volume yet.

At the close of the publisher's "Preparatory Notice," he has inserted, as you perhaps already know, "That it should be stated that a considerable portion of Mr. Ingram's 'Memoir' is gathered from materials previously used by Mr. Wm. F. Gill in his lecture 'The Romance of Edgar A. Poe,' *written* in September 1873!" I fancy the *Romance* was never made public.[1]

Yesterday he sent me a copy of *Laurel Leaves* in which appears the account of Poe's West Point career, of which I told you. More of this next time. Accompanying his article, "Some New Facts about Edgar Poe," there is an engraved portrait copied from the daguerre of which you sent me a copy last summer—I mean the photograph of Mrs. Lewis's portrait. It is engraved by Frederick, & surrounded by some fine vignettes illustrative of the poems, but the portrait filled me with *dismay.* I have no words to express my sense of the wrong it does him.

You will remember that I did not like the photograph you sent me, but this engraving from it is—hideous. There is no other word that can describe it. The expression is weak, nerveless, inane—altogether *unlike* him & *unworthy* of him. Frederick is, judging from what I have seen of his work, a fine artist. What malign spirit inspired him in making this *memento mori*, it is difficult to conceive.

I know that a fine daguerreotype may often be so changed by an engraver as to lose all its characteristic expression. Witness the woodcut prefixed to Stoddard's "Memoir" in *Harper's* which is from the same original with the fine head in *Harper's Weekly,* of which I sent you a copy in my last letter, I think. Did you not like it? The head in *Laurel Leaves* is so bad that I have pasted the wood engraving from the *Weekly* over it.

I had a letter yesterday from Miss Rice in which she tells me that she had received a pleasant letter from you in reply to an invitation to be present at the dedication, but that it came too late to be used. She asks what I know of Mr. Gill, "a gentleman," she says, "who at his own request read 'The Raven' at the Baltimore celebration." This strictly *entre nous.* The announcement in the paper containing Dr. Moran's letter was that he "had been invited to deliver the address," was it not?

I hope you have received a copy of my notice of your article on *Politian.*

What do you know of *Mr.* Lewis? His testimony to Poe's habits & disposition was very creditable to his own feelings, but I wish he had left out the pet phrase, or name, by which Poe addressed his mother. I do not think that every word a man utters in private life should be printed.

I have *so* much to say, but must still wait, & say now only *au revoir.* Your faithful "Providence,"

S.H.W.

1. Widdleton's printed statement that Ingram had been permitted to use in his "Memoir" materials previously used by Gill and Mrs. Whitman's seeming casualness in reporting it to him were to cause much trouble between these two builders of Poe biography. Ingram's violent reaction took the form of a widely distributed "Disclaimer" and a rude, insulting letter to Mrs. Whitman. But the time had not yet come for Mrs. Whitman to break with Ingram, although his "Disclaimer" did bring into the open the long-held and deep-seated hostilities that had existed between Ingram and any would-be American biographer of Poe.

132. *John H. Ingram to Sarah Helen Whitman*

My dear Providence,   29 Dec. 1875

As I have been fearing, for some time past, that I have omitted answering much you have spoken about, I have just *rushed* thro' your last dozen or so letters & jotted down such things as I fancy may still require a reply. Some, perhaps, may already have been responded to.

Hasty & disconnected as usual, now-a-days, I'll begin at your last letter of the 14th inst., bringing back my hurried scrawl to the *Tribune.* 'Twas late in the field 'tis true, but Reid might have used it, as it shows the style of Poe's slanderers. I think I'll print it, together with my letter to the *Nation* & distribute both together, privately. But I've so much to get about. I wish I could clear out of everything & get a twelvemonth *to myself* to work out my "Memoir" calmly. I will not publish 'till it is as it should be—worthy of its theme.

I must look up the *Union Maga.* & "The Bells." I fancied *Sartain's* was another name for the *Union.* I'll put that straight.

You evidently don't know all Mr. Gerry Fairfield's little games! I have lots of his papers on Poe published in 1864 &c., some *coolly compiled* from Poe, & passed off as his (Mr. Gerry's!) own!—one in *Home Journal*, 1864, is on "Poe's Plagiarisms"—the substance of it was in my *Tribune* letter.

I must see Swinburne's letter to the Committee—had not even heard of it. I wonder if *Appleton's Journal* had my remarks to Williams *re.* history of "The Bells." I gave you the full account, did I not? It was written long *after* "Ulalume," but, *perhaps*, before *autumn* of 1848.

Yes! I have seen *your* Rose—as I have told you—looking charming again.

Don't *doubt* about *facsimile* in *Scribner's*, 'tis clearly Didier's, as *Scribner's* know *now*, although Mr. Stoddard won't choose to acknowledge it. A correspondent has spoken to Didier about the caligraphy not being Poe's, suggesting it *might* be a copy, but *he* (Didier) was "rather indignant," & said it was photographed direct from the lady's album, but refuses to give the name of the owner of the book. *I'll force him.*

Harper's Weekly copy of the *photo* was *very* good. We must get a *real* photo copy. What does Miss Rice say? Is it from the daguerreotype in the possession of the Poe family?

Have you heard anything of *Le Corbeau*? Pray forgive me! I've not yet sent the enclosure to Mallarmé, but will at once. Perhaps Miss Peckham may like to see Mallarmé?

Mrs. Shelton's reminiscences are not very full *yet*, but I'm to write & she'll answer fully. Pray don't whisper of this! You shall know more of her *data* in my next. I'm so glad you like Browne—Dr. Browne—but you could not help it. And his friend Valentine—the sculptor—has been invaluable, chiefly with regard to Poe's early days.

Where can all Poe's letters have got to? Many destroyed, & many, doubtless, in collections, public & private. Such collections might be seen & copies made. Do you know *any* possessors of autographs: we might get some letters (copies) from them.

T. C. Clarke, I *know*, could have done more than anyone. Even his present collection must be valuable. Who can have got it? Gill said, in letter to me, that he had bought it, but I doubt him—he would have made some use of it, & he represented it to me as chiefly *verbal* reminiscences, whereas Clarke had, or *knew* of, publications, &c. But I'm working out the clues.

Mrs. Hale has not replied. I do want a correspondent in Philadelphia very badly—there is much to unearth there. How about Mr. J. Hart? Is he there? Have you his address? That letter published by Dr. Brooks (whose testimony I don't value much for *known* reasons), I doubt, & fancy can throw grave suspicions on.

What a world of rogues this is! Dr. Porteus, I'm told, 'tis *sub rosa*, left England to avoid his creditors. I was told he was a rascal & the news of his death was deemed only a hoax to stop pursuit. Poor Miss Poe got little of his lecture proceeds, I fear.

No news of Mary Star. The Poes say they don't know, & Mrs. Shelton says ditto—but then who was the "M——" to whom Poe wrote his early lines? I don't remember having seen the lines (satirical verses) of Poe's about Joseph Locke at West Point, & yet seem to have heard of them. Were they in paper in *Harper's*? *If so*, I have that. It was by Gibson, who was also court-martialled at W. Point, & was favorable to Poe, but Stoddard garbled the paper shamefully. I don't think Gill will ever do much anyway & may go over to the Stoddardites, but he is too weak to do much harm. Is *Laurel Leaves* out? I must get it.

En passant, in former days Fairfield thought *Eureka* magnificent. His words next time. I am afraid your lines "To Helen," *i.e.*, the MS., will never come back from Dr. Buchanan. How shameless his conduct seems—he must have known it had a money value apart from other considerations.

I'm afraid that I'm not giving any news with all my writings this time.

I must find out Mrs. Locke, & *will*, if she be alive. She must have had letters from Poe. Fancy Mr. Lewis alive again! And I've been led to fancy him dead long ago—but it makes no difference—they're of no use—the L[ewise]s.

In my third edition I want to give the dates of *first publication* of *all* the poems & tales. Do you think Mr. Harris could give me any information about the *Museum* for 1842–3 or 4 of Philadelphia, or the *Stylus* of 1843 of same place—or of the *Tales of the Grotesque & Arabesque* for 1839 (with "Siope"). Also of the vols. of *The Gift*.

But now a short respite for you to this scribble. I do pray that your health is better &, with my truest & most sincere wishes, I am, ever yours,

John H. Ingram

P.S. I have not spoken of the New Year, but *you know* that *all* good wishes for your happiness will be fervently wished by me.

I hope you've not put my name to those stupid impromptu "Love Letters" lines. Editor of *Pic. World* did give name in full, to my annoyance, & now they've spread past recall.

Au revoir,

J.H.I.

133.   *Sarah Helen Whitman to John H. Ingram.*   Item 280

My dear friend,   Jan. 4, [18]76

Your interesting letter of Dec. 21 just received. I am sorry to know that you are not well. You *must* not let the sword wear out the scabbard.

About the Benedict Arnold story, I know nothing certain. I first heard it from Mrs. Oakes Smith when "at the mountains" with her in 1858. She *seemed* to credit it. How hard it is to get at *facts* in this world! I have found the letter from Mrs. Smith which she wrote to me about my book. It does not look as if she thought ill of him. Send it back when you write.

The photo which I sent you from *Harper's Weekly is* a copy of the one in possession of Neilson Poe. I cannot understand how he could have declined to send you a copy on the ground that it was "so like" the one in your book that it could be of "no use" to you. It is very *unlike* it in the general character of the expression. Yours is more intellectual, more full of conscious power & purpose, while the other is grave & pensive, at least in the copy I sent you & which I wish you to retain. A good engraving from it would be invaluable for your collection of portraits. Its *date*, too, makes it doubly valuable.

I think I told you that the daguerreotype from which the portrait in your book was engraved was taken on the afternoon before the evening when Poe wrote to me the note of which I sent you a copy, written on board the steamer, only a few days, or a week, perhaps, after the Ultima Thule daguerreotype was taken. I am now convinced that I must have been mistaken as to the time. I have told you that Mrs. Osgood came just after Poe left, on that occasion, & I well remember that I urged her to go with me to the rooms of Masury & Hartshorn (now Coleman & Remington's) to see the portrait, & that she resisted all my entreaties. If I had *then* had the portrait taken for *me*, I should certainly have shown it to her. This impressed itself very strongly on my mind a few days ago, & now I feel *sure* that it was on his *next* visit to Providence, early in December, that this second *Providential* portrait was taken. The mood of mind expressed in it, too, agrees perfectly with the whole tone of his thought & conversation during this visit.

I will try if possible to ascertain the exact date. I dwell more upon this, because I feel that the dates of all these portraits will throw light on this story of his life. The portrait in the Memorial volume, preceding your vindication, is the one in your book, & if possible even more like him, since some of the lines are softened & the cheeks are not so full, the lines between the nose & the corners of the mouth being fainter.

Have you obtained a copy of Dodge's daguerre? And if so, does it resemble the one which you had from Mrs. Lewis? If you had *only* had time to correct some things which I pointed out to you last summer!

The story about the dilapidated state of his "shoes, boots, & gaiters" & the game of "leaping"—& the—

But it is too late now to waste time in regrets. I think his friends at the South felt something of this regret. Dr. Browne, you will remember, says something about "the interesting, but *in part, too painful* reminiscences of this time of suffering at Fordham," etc., and Dr. Moran speaks (as if to offset the impression there given) of Poe's exceptional "elegance" of dress—which is perhaps *overstated*, but which I was glad to see presented as serving to *qualify* the other statement of abject penury.

Perhaps it would be difficult to have left out the parts to which I allude without giving offence to Mrs. Gove Nichols?

Why was the facsimile from Poe's letter, beginning "The agonies which I have lately endured have passed my soul through fire" omitted? It seemed to me full of character & significance.

I am glad to know that you have heard from Mrs. Shelton, but I certainly gathered from Poe's letter to Mrs. Clemm, the *last* of the *two* written within a month of his death, that Mrs. Shelton had *accepted* him, & that the affair was irrevocably fixed. I should like *so* much to see a copy of the letter! If you will confide *it to me I will give my word of honor to breathe no word of it to anyone* & to return you the copy, or destroy it.

I want you to be very careful of those two letters of Mrs. Clemm's to me in 1859 in which she spoke of *Mrs. Shelton, Mrs. Stanard, & Mrs. Richmond.*[1] Mrs. Shelton's account of their early engagement & separation, etc. agrees with what Poe himself told me, in explanation of a passage in his letter to me.

Have you heard from Mrs. Hale? She has just issued a new no. of a magazine.

What you say of Gill's having published letters to me in the *Daily Graphic* surprises me. It is my first notice of his having done so. *Can you tell me the number of the paper?* And was it from advance sheets of *the Laurel Leaves*?² I have asked you so many questions in this hurried script that I am going to underline them with a blue pencil in order to impress them upon your memory.

I hear of pleasant & favorable notices of the Widdleton volume, but have been shut off from everything by the pressure of letters & exhaustion & exacting cares incident to the season.

Miss Rice tells me that "Mr. W. F. Gill volunteered to read 'The Raven' at the dedication of the monument, & that, greatly against her opinion of the unfitness of the time, he prevailed upon Professor or *President* Elliot to consent." This "in dreadful secrecy she did impart," and, in the same spirit, do I impart it to *you.*

I am glad that you are to meet Japp. Ask him—but no, I will not ask any more questions tonight.

What has become of *Le Corbeau?*

And now, for a little, let me commend you to the spirit of seventy-six, & to all good angels. Your faithful

S.H.W.

1. Maria Clemm's letter of Apr. 14, 1859, mentions these ladies. Ingram copied excerpts from the letter and used portions of them in his 1880 *Life;* the entire amount he copied is reproduced in *Building Poe Biography,* pp. 41–44.

2. The article "A Poet on His Critics" contained only a long excerpt from Poe's letter to Mrs. Whitman, not portions of several letters, as Ingram had led her to believe. See p. 377, n. 2.

134. *John H. Ingram to Sarah Helen Whitman*

My dear Mrs. Whitman,   13 Jany. 1876

I cannot express to you the intense disgust with which I heard from you the words relating to Mr. Gill's scandalous charge in the Memorial volume. I have now *just* received the volume itself from Mr. Widdleton, with a copy of his correspondence with Gill & an endeavour to excuse himself for having inserted what *he* knows is a lie. He says he put it in because Gill *is a publisher* & he wished to make peace!

I have written to the *Athenaeum* a short letter detailing the facts of the case, & not referring to anyone but Gill & Mr. Widdleton, extracts from whose correspondence prove that Gill is a most unscrupulous liar. As our publications are honest, this statement is certain to appear, & I shall reprint it, & send copies to such American & European publications as are likely to notice it. I shall send it by Saturday's mail.

If such an impudent scamp as Gill lived in the "Old World" he would be ejected from the abodes of every decent person, but of late I have but too clearly seen that such rogues are not only tolerated but even feared in the United States: even you yourself condone his insults & his lies to you, & appear to deem his conduct quite natural. I fear he is but one of many, and I therefore think I had better wipe my hands of such a crew, for it is hard to touch pitch & not be defiled.

Legitimate difficulties are to me only incentives to labour, but to have my name dragged through the mire by such filthy scum as this detestable Yankee, I will not endure!!!

Only a few days ago a friend & correspondent of yours wrote to me about Gill saying, "Even your grandchildren will curse the day in which your name became connected with that rogue's," and I laughed at what I deemed ridiculous exaggeration, but now too plainly see that he knew the man.

I can now understand why poor Poe found the United States, as Baudelaire remarks, but one large prison. I have had enough of it.

I so gladly sacrificed literary & pecuniary rewards to try & work out this vindication—my health has suffered, & yet I should not have repined, knowing that I had cleared a noble & unfortunate man's fame. I would have fought & have won against all the tricks of your Stoddards, Didiers, Fairfields, and like, but it is quite impossible to sully my name, *which is* untarnished, by having to have it connected with this Gill's. He is an unmitigated scoundrel & yet, as you see, able to do & act as he likes. I see but one course open to me after having disproved his allegations (which are even worse in his letters to Widdleton than any I have *yet* heard of having been made public—he accuses me of deliberate perjury), and that is to give up having any more to do, or say, in connection with Edgar Poe.

If you know of anyone, *whom you know to be honest,* I will deliver to them as a present my own collection & give them headings of the papers belonging to other people which I must return to them, unless they will permit of their delivery to the person named by you.

Do not place any reliance in the "Memoir" in this Memorial volume, as Widdleton says the revised copy came too late, but that he had ventured upon making some alterations in my sketch!! He says he has also substituted *my sketch* (?) for Griswold's in the complete edition of the Works, & asks if I will forward such further material as I may have & he will endeavour to make good use of it. Of course, I shall not condescend to notice this, but return him his Gill correspondence without any remark.

I shall always be glad to hear from you on *any* subject, but you are the only *Northern* person connected with literature whose words I can place any reliance on—*as a rule*!!! I have found my Southern correspondents strictly honorable, not answering questions when they were uncertain. I am thankful that I have *met & known* some honest Americans, or I should deem the nation populated by devils.

Goodbye, my dear friend—may you obtain an abler—a more faithful confederate you cannot obtain than your eternal well wisher,

John H. Ingram

15 Jany. 1876

P.S. I have delayed until today's mail in order to have the "Disclaimer" ready.[1] I shall circulate it widely, through my correspondents, in the United States.

Mr. Widdleton seems ashamed of himself & has sent me his correspondence with this Gill, who does not hesitate to charge me flatly with the most deliberate perjury. I wish I could get at him by law.

I trust that I have not said anything to wound your feelings, but you cannot fail to see that I have been most disgracefully treated.

Ever yours,

John H. Ingram

1. Ingram's "Disclaimer" was published in the London *Athenaeum*. It is reproduced on p. 387 as an illustration, taken from p. 10 of Caroline Ticknor's "Ingram—Discourager of Poe Biographies," *New York Bookman*, 44 (Sept. 1916), pp. 8–14.

135. *John H. Ingram to Sarah Helen Whitman*

My dear Mrs. Whitman,   19 Jany. 1876
I find there are several queries in yours of the 4th instant, & I hasten to answer same.

You did not enclose the letter of Mrs. Oakes Smith as stated & as, I dare say, you have since discovered. What makes you say about her *not* thinking ill of Poe? She always writes as if a great admirer of him: her most unpleasant allusions were those purporting to be an extract from a letter of yours—by the way, you never denied the authorship of that letter.

I have not been able to call on Mr. Dodge again—his portrait does not resemble Mrs. Lewis's.

I had corrected much of my sketch for Mr. Widdleton, as I thought I had told you, but the revised copy did not arrive in time for the Memorial volume, but will, I believe, preface the collected edition. I don't know what copy Mr. Widdleton printed from—not from any I sent him.

The "Reminiscences," in revised copy, *were* greatly revised, but it proves how difficult it is for me to make myself comprehended—even

EDGAR ALLAN POE.

A DISCLAIMER.

From the "ATHENÆUM" *of* 15*th January*, 1876.

The "MEMORIAL VOLUME" of Edgar Poe's Poems, recently alluded to in the *Athenæum*, has now appeared in New York. It includes my vindicatory sketch of the poet, but introduced by the unwarrantable remark that "a considerable portion of Mr. Ingram's Memoir is gathered from material previously used by Mr. W. F. Gill in his lecture, 'The Romance of Edgar A. Poe,' *written* in September, 1873." That *I have never received a single item of information from Mr. Gill respecting Edgar Poe*, or made use of anything *written* by him on the same subject, and that the publisher of the "Memorial Volume" knew this the following extracts will clearly prove. Last August, Mr. Widdleton, publisher of the above book, wrote to me with reference to the proposed republication in America of my sketch,—"Mr. Gill, of Boston, asks us not to use your memoir, as it covers material *taken from his paper on Poe in ' Lotos Leaves.'*" In reply, I not only most emphatically denied ever having made use of any information derived from Mr. Gill, but also pointed out that my sketch was published in October, 1874,* whereas "Lotos Leaves" did not appear until January, 1875. Mr. Widdleton, in acknowledgment, admitted that Mr. Gill was "evidently strangely at fault," and yet he now publishes, without previously referring to me, the above statement respecting an alleged work of September, 1873, the utter unreliability of which I can prove from Mr. Gill's own letters to me. Early in 1874, hearing that Mr. Gill was collecting material for a lecture on Poe, I wrote and asked him whether he had any reliable information about the poet, if so, whether he was willing to dispose of copies of the same to me, and whether he had any intention of writing the poet's memoir. "I do intend to write the life of Poe," he replied, "unless you should much prefer to buy out my material, which I would sell if your preference was for that. As *I have not written any minor articles*, I cannot send any portions of my materials." Responding that I was willing to purchase any reliable information about Poe other than that I already possessed, and requesting further particulars, Mr. Gill answered, but without naming any price for his collection, "Much of my material is of a peculiarly personal nature in the form of notes taken down when conversing with Mr. G. R. Graham and others, and before I could transmit it *I should be obliged to put it carefully into shape before it could be understood by another.* With all willingness to forward any material possible, I cannot, as yet, find opportunity for the necessary preliminary of arranging material." These letters from Mr. Gill are dated 6th June, and 27th August, 1874, respectively ; they contained requests for copies of what I had written about Poe, requests which I complied with, and, in consequence, had the pleasure of seeing my discoveries partially reproduced, even to the extent of an uncorrected error, but without any acknowledgment, in "Lotos Leaves."

This is my case : let Mr. Gill now state where his aptly styled "Romance of Edgar A. Poe" was published, and what portion of it he claims to have been reproduced in my Memoir of Edgar Poe, a work which several friends in England and America know to be the result of twelve years research.

London.   JOHN H. INGRAM.

---

* Prefixed to the first volume of the complete Edition of the Works of Edgar Allan Poe Edinburgh: A. & C. Black.

to you—when I find you deeming that I feared to offend Mrs. Nichols by leaving out parts! Mrs. Nichols is very kind, and did not attempt to impose any conditions, but, whilst I would not knowingly hurt anyone's feelings by inserting matter they wished omitted, I certainly wouldn't insert matter to please anyone, which I deemed better omitted.

As for Poe's friends in the South, they express great pleasure with the sketch as it stands.

My impression of Dr. Moran's reminiscences is that they are pure imaginations as regards conversations, &c.

The *facsimile* was omitted from the letter press in error—not meaning to have Poe's letter to Pabodie *facsimiled* beyond the autograph, & intending to give the extract from your letter as a specimen of Poe's handwriting, the letters were sent to Blacks, & so, not having them at hand, I forgot the extract when writing out the "Memoir," and did not care to omit the *facsimile* when I found out the omission, when the whole "Memoir" was printed.

Mrs. Shelton has *not* written, but merely replied to a friend of mine to such questions as he chose to ask. She speaks in the highest terms of Poe, in every respect, but has refrained from answering before because of the impertinent busybodies who have bothered her.

I have not heard from Mrs. Hale. Mrs. Clemm's letters shall all be carefully returned to you, together with all other papers belonging to you in my possession, as soon as you advise me as to your wishes for their disposal.

Gill published your letters in the *Daily Graphic* in November, most likely the early half.[1] *Your name was not mentioned*, but I knew the letters because you had given me extracts from them, but I was not to publish them. I find this letter thus introduced, as "the following letter by Poe to a woman he loved is taken from advance sheets of Mr. W. F. Gill's article on 'New Facts,' &c. . . to be published in *Laurel Leaves*." I see it speaks of it as *one* letter only & includes the extract you permitted me to publish in the "Memoir," about Poe vindicating himself. It is to be hoped that if you have not given the original to Mr. Gill you have not lent it.

I have written to M. Mallarmé about *Le Corbeau*.

Goodbye. I shall be anxious to hear your directions as to the disposal of such material as I have of yours, and until I get your reply shall not part with anything relating to Poe, or let anyone know of my relinquishing the life.

Ever faithfully yours,

John H. Ingram

P.S. Many thanks for the beautiful "Old Mirror."

I presume that you are aware that the *Daily Graphic* is an organ of

Stoddard's, or rather, for the publication of his writings? I suppose Mr. Gill did not tell you that he had offered to write a life of Poe for Mr. Widdleton, and that his refusal to accept it caused Gill to make a claim to my "Memoir," & consequently delayed Widdleton accepting it sooner &, apparently, taking that of Stoddard's instead. All this is displayed in the correspondence which Mr. Widdleton, in a fit of penitence apparently, has now sent me.

I think I may safely wager you $100 that before another year is out you will receive proof of Gill's collusion with the Stoddard clique. I hope he will answer the "Disclaimer"—it has been sent to most of the chief editors of the chief papers in the United States.[2]

J.H.I.

1. See p. 377, n. 2, and p. 384, n. 2.
2. Gill's "Reply" appeared in February 1876. It is reprinted on pages 396–99.

136.   Sarah Helen Whitman to John H. Ingram.   Item 282

My dear Mr. Ingram,   Feb. 1, [18]76
The tone of your letter of Jan. 13, received last evening, has so profoundly grieved and surprised me that I hardly know how to reply to it.

I can *well* understand your indignation at Gill's presumptuous claim that you were indebted to *him* for a considerable portion of your material! I can*not* understand your assumption that *I* am in any way responsible for his offences. You must strangely have misunderstood my letter, if you thought that I countenanced or *excused* them. I simply attempted to account to you for the antagonism which had induced this preposterous & incredible & *uncredited* claim.

I returned no answer to Mr. Widdleton's letter introductory to the volume (a copy of which I sent you), simply because I would not seem to endorse this statement of Gill's which he, Mr. Widdleton, may have had pecuniary reasons for inserting.

I could not have written anything for publication of the subject without telling a long story & invoking a bitter controversy, & one which would have been attended with a painful notoriety.

Moreover, Mr. Gill's claim to have *written* an *unpublished* Romance, the first complete vindication of Poe from the slanders of Griswold, a part of which he permitted you to use, was not a claim to *injure* you, so preposterous and improbable was it. You exaggerate the importance of the Boston publisher whom you seem to accept as the representative man of "the North"—"one of a crew whom you think it would be better to wipe your hands of, & give up having anything further to do or say in connection with Edgar Poe," in whose attempted vindication you say you have sacrificed time & money & health.

For all this I am sincerely & profoundly grieved; in truth I have been anxious from the beginning. If you will look at my first letter to you, written in reply to yours of December [18]73, asking for information as to the facts of Edgar Poe's life, you will see that I warned you that you had a difficult task before you, that you would find the *facts* of his life singularly elusive & difficult to authenticate.

Since your very first paper on the subject, I have watched your course with interest not unmingled with intense anxiety. You will remember how repeatedly I urged you to "keep cool," to curb your impetuous spirit, & not to believe every new story or resent every supposed wrong or insult. Your success has surpassed my most sanguine hopes.

I will not say how earnestly I have sought to further your wishes in everything that lay in my power, & now that you are about to wipe your hands of all your Northern friends, I shall not cease to care for your prosperity & success in any new literary enterprise to which you may devote your genius & your talents.

Did you receive the paper I sent you on your article in the *London Quarterly* on *Politian*? It was much talked of.

Did I mention to you in my last hurried note that the lady in whose album (as Mr. Didier claims) the *Scribner* facsimile poem was written was Mrs. Judge Balderston?

I knew nothing of the Poe letter or letters to me of which you wrote having been published in the *Graphic*, and have not yet seen them.

Gill has had no new facts from *me* since the winter of 1873–74, when you first wrote to me, but there are some interesting papers in his Laurel Leaf article. I wish I had a copy to send you.

And now, my dear friend, I subscribe myself for *time* & *eternity* (dastardly Northerner though I am), your sincere friend,

S. H. Whitman

P.S. I have not had a line from Rose since she went away from us. Her father told me last night that she was *well*.

137. *Sarah Helen Whitman to John H. Ingram.*   Item 283

My dear Mr. Ingram,   Feb. 13, 1876
In your letter of 19th Jan. you remind me "that some of your questions are still unanswered," "that I have never denied the authorship of that letter to Mrs. Oakes Smith."

I think I told you that I had no copy of Mrs. Smith's article on Poe. I vaguely remember that either in a private letter to me, or in a published article on Poe, perhaps in *both*, she said that Poe, with all his charm of manner, impressed her as being *insincere*!

I think that I earnestly controverted this charge, admitting that he had his faults, but that a want of sincerity was not one of them. If I ever said or wrote to her anything in relation to his faults, it was in this connection.

In truth, he was *not* a Sir Galahad, nor "One who ever / Moved among us in white armor." He could, doubtless, have said with Hamlet, "I am very proud, *revengeful*, ambitious."

His letters are eloquent with expressions of heartfelt contrition & remorse.

It is enough that his faults & his errors were not of a nature to alienate my heart's love & loyalty. There *are* faults of baseness & perfidy & dishonor which would inevitably change love & loyalty into sorrowful indignation & disdainful pity.

I will copy for you the letter of Mrs. Oakes Smith to me, after reading the little volume which brought to me the pleasure of your acquaintance, a friendship uninterrupted for two years, until an impalpable cloud from some wild weird clime out of space, out of time, seems to have overshadowed it. *Sic transit.*

In relation to your introduction to certain portions of Mrs. N[ichol]s' paper. You will remember that having urged me to criticise your "Memoir," saying, "There must be so much you could suggest for revision, omission, or addition," I pointed out the passages which seemed to me "too painful" for publication in Mrs. Nichols' interesting paper. In your reply, dated March 14, 1875, you say, "Mrs. N[ichols] was, as I have said, the author of the *Sixpenny Maga.* paper. Now, strictly between ourselves & the post, I cannot rely very much upon either the accuracy or the *friendliness* of either the Dr. or his wife. I trust I am not misjudging them."

Certainly, *I* had no idea of questioning Mrs. N[ichol]s' friendliness to you when I expressed my regret that these papers were retained in Widdleton's volume. The article was in many respects *admirable*, & in objecting to certain passages I certainly had no idea that I was wounding your feelings or transgressing the critical license which you had so generously asked me to exercise.

I frankly explained to you my relations with Mr. Gill when you first sought information from me. I have dealt frankly & openly & disinterestedly with both. I believe I told you in my last that Mr. Gill had had nothing from me since the winter of 1873–74.

I think he sincerely regrets the impulsive & aggressive letter which he wrote to Widdleton, but he is a Northerner & what can be expected of him? As for me, my Southern relatives, before the War, were "thick as the leaves in Vallombrossa." I was even named for the wife of a Governor of South Carolina & a Senator from that state to the Congress of the United States, that is to say, for my Aunt Sarah Power, wife of Gov. David R. Williams, so that I ought to have some claim to consideration.

But enough. I am too sad for jesting. And so, *bon soir*, your friend,
                                                                    S.H. Whitman

P.S. I have answered the questions *you* proposed to *me*. Will *you* tell *me* what friend & correspondent of *mine* it was who wrote to you that "even your grandchildren would curse the day that your name became associated with that rogue's"? He [Gill] is a bankrupt in business and doubtless in reputation, but so are all, or nearly all, the "solid men" of Boston & New York—even the Capital of the nation is suspected of having some people of problematical reputation under its marble domes. It's "a bad lot," as you Englishmen say, *n'est ce pas*?

There are so many arrows in your two last letters that I had almost forgotten one of the sharpest. In your letter of the 13th Jan. you say, "I have found my *Southern* correspondents strictly *honorable*, not answering questions where they were not certain." Is it, then, that your Northern correspondents have *willfully* misled you by answering questions where they were not certain?

                                                                    Semper Idem

138. *John H. Ingram to Sarah Helen Whitman*

My ever dear Friend,   14 Feby. 1876
    I am profoundly grieved that I have so wounded your feelings as the tone of yours dated the 1st shows that I have, but pray forgive me.

It was not the mere fact of Gill's impudence, nor the audacity of Widdleton giving my apparent sanction to the claim, but what wounded me to the quick, *was* your apparent indifference. Had your letter contained a single sentence of disgust at Gill's conduct, I should have felt satisfied, but seeing, so it seemed to me, that although you expressed your disbelief (*not positive knowledge*, which, however, *you had*) of his said "Romance of Edgar A. Poe" having been written, you took his claim as a matter of course, I felt utterly despairing of having done, or being able to do, anything towards proving *my* theory of Poe's life. I read, and reread your letter, but vainly sought for any expression of disapprobation of this Gill's behaviour. It seemed to me that I was being placed on a level with him, & so long as I worked for the same end it did not matter who or what I was, or how my character suffered. Had you but expressed disgust at the man's conduct I should have felt *you* were true to me, & with your sympathy I would have been encouraged to continue the fight.

Quickly following your information of the claim came letters from American correspondents expressing sympathy & assuring me, long before my "Disclaimer" could reach them, of their disbelief in Gill's claim, & asking me to write something for them to publish in contradiction. Since the "Disclaimer" appeared, strong expressions of confidence in my veracity have reached me from unknown readers in France & this country.

Having to publish the "Disclaimer" has been a very bitter pill to me, because it seemed to me as if I were striving to abrogate to myself the sole right to vindicate Poe—as if I were jealous of others attempting to rival me there. On my soul, I was never inspired by such feelings! Had any properly qualified person have undertaken the task of writing Poe's life I would willingly, & without hope or wish for any kind of reward, have assisted him or her, & have given every scrap I possessed about the poet. When Gill asked me for information, I willingly sent him such published papers as I had, & would have sent him more had I have been able to trust to him. However, enough of this subject. Gill is bankrupt, I see, &, I suppose, will take to some other method of living.

I have been *very* unwell since I wrote to you—am still so, & have had cares & worries numberless, but the more I have thought over it, the less I feel *able* to resign the completion of my work. *I must finish my "Memoir" of Poe.* My mind can never rest until it has disburdened itself of the accumulation of ideas it has made on this subject. But I am still willing to take a partner in the work if I could only find anyone in America willing to labour on it as I have laboured here. But I feel that health & *everything* urge the speedy completion of this work, so I have begun to gather together rapidly the scattered ends of my story. You will be astounded at the immense amount of reliable *data* I have garnered together.

By the way, the name of the person who supplied Stoddard's rigmarole of Poe's early life was a Mrs. Dixon of Richmond, but he altered & garbled it very much.[1]

I presume you know that Gill offered to write the Memorial biography & was refused by Mr. Widdleton. I have heard from Baltimore that he forced himself upon the Memorial Committee.

Miss Rice has written to ask me to permit them to use my "Memoir" for the Baltimore Memorial Book. I could not, of course, having allowed Widdleton to for his, although he did not use the revised copy, as requested. I have asked Miss Rice to try for permission of the

International Review to use their paper by me, and have made several revisions in it for her.

Don't say anything about the 1827 edition of the poems. I have found it! & written a paper about it![2] Mr. Harris shall have copy of the paper. I am negotiating for advance sheets for America.

"Siope" was the earliest name for "Silence"; it appeared in the *Baltimore Book* for 1838.

My chief blank in Poe's life now is between 1838–1844 (his stay in Philadelphia), although I have some interesting items even for that period. I have no correspondent in that city. Mrs. Hale nor Mr. Godey ever answered.

You will find that I was quite right about "The Bells" & the *Union Magazine, alias Sartain's Union Magazine.*

I do not think you need ignore Widdleton. *I* have not answered his letter offering to publish any further matter &c. and excusing his conduct, because he *knowingly* has treated *me* badly, but you have nothing to do with that.

Pray do not let my words about the North be misunderstood. *You* know that I have real & true friends there. Why, I have quite recently received two charming letters from your Providence Rose, who is growing quite French. I have not answered her last, although it contained—don't be jealous!—a charming little vignette of an Italian girl model. She seems enjoying herself now.

I did receive a *cutting re.* my *Politian* paper, from the Providence *Journal.* I *hear* the paper was more noticed than anything in the *London,* but I saw very few—only two, I think, of the notices.

Where did you get your extract from Mrs. Browning's letter *re.* Poe, which I quoted? Browning has been very annoyed, *entre nous,* about Poe. Buchanan-Read told him that *Poe told him* (Read) that "The Raven" was founded on a line in "Lady Geraldine's Courtship," but on a subsequent occasion said that was *"all a lie"* and that it was as described in "The Philosophy of Composition." He (Browning) says he could not have told Thompson (*vide* my extract from letter to Davidson) that he hoped to see Poe's memory cleared from aspersion, as he was not aware it had been aspersed! What do you say? I shall, of course, cut all *that* out.

Do you know anything more of the "Alone" verses? I believe them to be Poe's, but not in Poe's handwriting. It is as like Didier's as it possibly can be.

I will get *Laurel Leaves* and see if there be anything new to me in it.

"The Beautiful Physician" has not come to hand—only some half-remembered lines. I believe it will turn up, however. Look out for a bunch of new true authenticated poems!

And now, forgive me, and believe that my warmth of feeling has been invoked because I value your approbation in this matter more than anyone's, and to doubt it was intolerable.

May all "The winged seraphs" you believe in, and all the good I *hope* for, guard & protect you, is the faithful wish, oh, believe me, of yours,

John H. Ingram

P.S. Do you know anything of Wm. Ross Wallace, the poet? He, an acquaintance of Poe's (I have met several who say they knew Poe) tells me, was *very* intimate with Poe & knew more of him than anyone in New York. Wallace wrote *some* very fine poems. Is he alive?[3] He wrote a poem to Mary Star! We shall find her some day.

J.H.I.

1. This account by Mrs. Dixon, and, presumably, Mrs. Ellis, related stories of Poe's mischievous propensities as a youth, debts the Allans had to pay for champagne he had drunk, seventeen broadcloth coats he had bought, of his forcing his way into John Allan's sickroom, the probable illegitimacy of Poe's sister Rosalie, and had stated that Poe's mother had died in a poorhouse.

2. This was indeed a triumph for John Ingram. Poe had said in the prefaces to his 1829 and 1831 volumes of poetry that he had included poems that were copied verbatim from the volume he had published in 1827. Poe did not leave a copy of the volume among his other books, and no one could remember having seen such a volume.

Ingram had disbelieved Griswold and Stoddard on principle, and, as letters above show, he had long questioned Mrs. Whitman and her wealthy bibliophile friend and neighbor Caleb Fiske Harris about the existence of an 1827 volume. When Ingram later learned that Harris had seen or thought he had seen *Tamerlane* listed in Kettell's *Specimens of American Poetry* (1829) as a volume of unpublished poems "which the author has seen in print," he had all he needed: the title of the 1827 volume, the circumstances of its publication and suppression, and, most important, outside evidence that the volume had been actually sighted. Now to find the volume itself.

And find it he did. Searching through literally bales of books and pamphlets sent to the British Museum Library by American booksellers, he finally held in his hands a small volume, with front and back covers missing, that had been sent over probably in 1866 and priced at one shilling to the Library, and he knew immediately that he had located the first known copy of Poe's 1827 *Tamerlane*!

Very likely Ingram had made this remarkable find early in 1876, shortly before writing to Mrs. Whitman about it in this letter of Feb. 14. The paper he mentioned having written on *Tamerlane* appeared in the *Belgravia Magazine* for June 1876 and was partially reprinted in the New York *Daily Graphic* on June 8, 1876, as "Poe's Suppressed Poetry." Ingram reprinted the title poem and six of the nine fugitive pieces in the unknown volume; the other three had been reprinted almost verbatim in current collections of Poe's poetry. With this widely reprinted article Ingram was able to silence forever the debates about Poe's unknown edition; he could prove too that Poe had told the truth, about which the dead Griswold and the living Stoddard had lied. In addition, Ingram increased immeasurably his own reputation as a Poe scholar and researcher.

Ingram then proceeded to do what no other writer about Poe had been able to do: he wrote and published in the *Athenaeum* for July 29, 1876, "The Bibliography of Edgar

Poe," which traced Poe's development as a poet through all four of his published volumes.

3. William Ross Wallace (1819–1881) was first a lawyer, then an author and poet. He is best remembered for his lines "And the hand that rocks the cradle . . . Is the hand that rules the world."

139. *A Reply from William F. Gill to John H. Ingram,* American Bookseller, *1 (Feb. 15, 1876), 130–32*

A Reply from William F. Gill to John H. Ingram

To the Editor of The American Bookseller:

Dear Sir—In the London *Athenaeum* of January 15th, and in several American journals, appears a circular signed by J. H. Ingram, relating to some matters connected with his biography of Edgar A. Poe. The American publisher of the memorial edition of Poe's works prefaces Mr. Ingram's memoir with the following statement: "It should be stated that a considerable portion of Mr. Ingram's memoir is gathered from material previously used by Mr. William F. Gill in his lecture, *The Romance of Edgar A Poe*, written in September, 1873, which forms the first complete vindication of Poe from the calumnies of Rufus W. Griswold. Mr. Gill has kindly permitted the use of the material derived from this source, in order that Mr. Ingram's memoir might appear in its original form." Mr. Ingram chooses to deny that any portion of his memoir was gathered from material first utilized by me, and ventures to charge that I copied portions of his article on Poe in my paper printed in *Lotos Leaves*, which he states was not published until January, 1875.

It is quite true that *Lotos Leaves* did not appear in England until the time mentioned, but it was published in this country six or eight weeks in advance of its appearance in London, and was in type here some two months in advance of its issue in a bound volume. Mr. Ingram states that his sketch was issued in October, 1874, which was fully one year after the material in question was utilized in my lecture on Poe, and *three months* after the same material, in the form of an essay, had been submitted to Mr. Howells, editor of *The Atlantic Monthly*, and returned by him with certain suggestions, that were adopted almost immediately thereafter, in *Lotos Leaves*. In corroboration of this statement, I append a copy of a letter received today from Mr. Howells in answer to a note of inquiry from me regarding this matter:

Editorial Office of The Atlantic Monthly,
Cambridge, Mass., Feb. 4, 1876.

My Dear Mr. Gill:—I very well remember seeing your paper on Poe in MS., and suggesting some modifications, with a view to its use by us. So many MSS. have passed through my hands since that I can't recall just when I read yours, but I am pretty sure it was in the summer of 1874.

> Yours truly,
> (Signed) W. D. Howells.

As a matter of fact, the first announcements of my lecture were made in the Boston *Daily Advertiser* and other Boston papers as early as June, 1873. The full descriptive advertisement of the same will be found in the circular issued by the American Literary Bureau in August, 1873, and ample documentary evidence is at hand to substantiate Mr. Widdleton's statement that a considerable portion of Mr. Ingram's memoir is gathered from material previously used by me in this lecture. How it happens that Mr. Ingram gathered his facts from unpublished materials will appear. Early in the month of January, 1874, I received letters from the owner of original papers and MSS. pertaining to Edgar A. Poe, stating that applications had been made by an English gentleman for copies of the letters then in my hands, and incorporated in my lecture, and the return of these, with other material that had been placed in my hands, was requested. The following extract from one of these letters will explain the nature of the request:

Will you lend me for a few days the extract which I gave you from the literary recollections of Mr. Gowans, the New York bookseller. I have recently received a letter from an English gentleman, who has written an article on Griswold's memoir, which he tells me will shortly appear in an English monthly. He asks my aid as to certain points in his history, and it is in furtherance of his request that I wish to send him the favorable testimony of the "truthful and uncompromising Scotch bookseller." I will return the copy in a few days. I have seen many pleasant and complimentary articles about you in the Boston papers this winter, and am always glad to hear of your success. If you have at hand ———'s letter to me regarding Poe, written in the autumn of 1849, I should like to have send them [*sic*]. I think you said you had left them with other papers at your summer residence when you wrote last. Very truly your friend,

——— ———

In another letter the same writer especially mentions Mr. Ingram, as follows:

I should like to see your lecture or such parts of it as may refer to matters connected with my communications to you. If you do not object, perhaps you will allow me to copy the letter of Mr. ———. Poe's friend. *I have promised Mr. Ingram to ask you for a copy.* With grateful acknowledgments, your friend,

——— ———

The Gowans paper and all others asked of me on Mr. Ingram's account were, with a single exception, which by an oversight was not copied, duly forwarded and must have reached Mr. Ingram, as the major part of the papers were private, and could have come from no other source. This correspondence appears in his memoir, and as I was subjected to very considerable trouble in having it copied in order to return the originals or the copies which the owner transmitted to him, it would seem evident that Mr. Ingram is somewhat indebted to me for the privilege of using them. The coincidence that he mentions of an erroneous date appearing in my paper, in *Lotos Leaves*, which was also made by him in his magazine article, is due to the fact that our information came from the one source mentioned, and must be coincident. The error in question was pointed out to me by the owner of the original papers from whom the information was elicited, and duly corrected by me. As regards Mr. Ingram's quotations from my private correspondence to him, they are substantially correct. The gentleman had expressed especial solicitude in obtaining the life of Poe, written by T. C. Clarke, Esq., of Philadelphia. This memoir I had, with more zeal than discretion, purchased from Mr. Clarke, early in September, 1873, at a considerable price, in the hope of getting some new points for my lecture, then nearly completed. I found that Mr. Clarke's memoir could not be made available without completely rewriting the lecture, and I set it aside for the time being. When, therefore, Mr. Ingram's letter was received, making especial inquiries for Mr. Clarke and his memoir, I was open to a possible negotiation. I felt convinced, from Mr. Ingram's next letter, that he would not be willing to reimburse me for my outlay, and replied in the words quoted in his circular. It is true, again, that I had not at that time completed a life of Poe. Indeed I felt convinced that there was not sufficient material then attainable to justify a new life of the poet. Since then my researches have developed new mines, and my views have been modified accordingly. In a letter dated July 6, 1874, Mr. Ingram writes me as follows: *"I do not wish, moreover, to interfere with your projected memoir; there is plenty of scope for a new American life, towards which my work would assist."* Notwithstanding this and other similar assurances, Mr. Ingram has taken every available means of putting his memoir before the American public, knowing that much of his material was identical with that in my hands. When warned by Mr. Widdleton that I had raised objections to the reprinting of his memoir in America, the professional etiquette which should govern all authors, and does govern most authors, should have induced him to desist from any further overtures to the American publishers. Mr. Widdleton answered his unwarrantable charge as to my copying from him, according to his light at the time. Later, when a personal interview with me enabled me to present all the facts, accompanied by full documentary evidence, he offered that deference to my prior claims that justice and courtesy demanded. Knowing that Mr. Ingram's biography was, with the exception of the material previously assigned to me, scarcely more than a compilation of familiar facts from familiar magazines, I had not thought it incumbent upon me to offer more than a personal protest against the issue of his innocuous sketch here. My only regret is that I did not absolutely insist upon the rights which the copyright law of this country gives to an author to his manuscript, rights which I could have incontestably proved. In conclusion, I wish to state distinctly, that not a line or a word printed over my name has ever been copied from any of Mr. Ingram's writings; that I do not charge that he has copied from any printed article of mine. I claim simply that a considerable portion of the material which he used in 1874 in his memoir had previously been used in a manuscript lecture written by me in 1873, a year previous, and that he had been made aware that the material had been so used by me before he had printed a line of the portion in question. My claim will not, I venture to think, be regarded as unprecedented or unreasonable. Thanks to the courtesy that usually prevails among authors, it is of a kind that would seldom be called in question. Asking your indulgence for this trespass upon your patience and that of your readers, and trusting that the nature of the explanation demanded will excuse this incursion upon your valuable space, I am,

Yours very truly,
William F. Gill.

140. *Sarah Helen Whitman to John H. Ingram.* Item 285

My dear Mr. Ingram, Feb. 29, [18]76
    Since reading the "Reply" to your "Disclaimer," a copy of which was sent me yesterday by the author, I am not so much surprised at the aggressive tone of your last letters. It may be that his letter to Widdleton contained an insinuation that I approved his course. The "Reply" shows that he is utterly reckless in his statements.
    I wrote him a letter yesterday, a verbatim copy of which I send you. While I deeply feel the wrong & the pain inflicted by the tone of your last letters—your resentment of my disposition to make some allowance for the irritation Gill felt in finding that you had forestalled him in his desire to write the life of Poe seems to me *somewhat* more intelligible.
    I told him in my letter that I felt it due to you & to myself to make to

you the same explanation of the quoted paragraphs from my letters, paragraphs which he had printed without consulting me on the subject, that I had made to *him*.

I received this morning from Wm. D. O'Connor a press copy of a letter to Miss Rice, written at her request for the Memorial volume which she is preparing. It is an eloquent & superb defence & characterization of Poe. The pressure of O'Connor's official duties had delayed it beyond the time when she had hoped to receive it, but it will doubtless soon be printed, if not in that volume, in some magazine or literary journal.

You say you have "wiped your hands of the Poe matters," but you may not object to read an allusion made to your own work on one of its closing pages, or rather its closing paragraph:

> For I know that his vindication draws nigh. He has been long coffined ⟨ I cannot distinctly make out all the words in the press copy ⟩ in slander, but the miserable tangle of the lies & forgeries of Griswold & his allies will soon be cleared away forever. Thanks for this to the movement begun by Mrs. Whitman in her beautiful little book, *Edgar Poe & His Critics*, & soon to be completed by the patient research & clear insight of Ingram. Thanks also to you & your coadjutors for fresh glory upon his memory and the flower of marble upon his grave. I am, dear Miss Rice

Yours faithfully,
W. D. O'Connor

Dec. 9, 1876[1875]

[Enclosure: Sarah Helen Whitman to William F. Gill.   Copy]

Feb. 27, [18]76

I have read with regret & amazement your "Reply" to Mr. Ingram's "Disclaimer." It were far better to have abandoned a claim which you must see to be untenable and which in your recent interview with me I thought you frankly admitted to be so. The only evidence you adduce of Mr. Ingram's having been permitted to use "material previously assigned" to you, is assumed to be presented in extracts from two of my letters to you, containing three requests. The first request cited is:

> Will you lend me for a few days the extract which I gave you from the literary recollections of Mr. Gowans, the New York bookseller? I have recently received a letter from an English gentleman who has written an article on Griswold's "Memoir" of Poe, which he tells me will shortly appear in an English monthly. He asks my aid as to certain points of Mr. Poe's history, & as it is in furtherance of his request that I wish to send him the favorable testimony of "the truthful & uncompromising Scotch bookseller." I will return the copy in a few days.

The paper in question was a *printed* slip from the New York *Evening Mail*. I had no idea that in asking the privilege of copying it for an English correspondent I was violating the International

Copyright Law, as a paragraph in your "Reply" seems to charge me with doing. On the contrary, I thought you would be glad to give further publicity to testimony so valid & so favorable to one whose cause you were generously proposing to advocate. Your prompt compliance with my request, which I gratefully acknowledged, was unaccompanied by any intimation that my request was a presumptuous one.

Your second citation from the same letter is an incorrectly quoted request for the return of a letter addressed to me in the autumn of 1849 by Dr. Rufus W. Griswold, a letter which I had *lent* to you for your private perusal, under the strictest injunctions of secrecy—a letter which you had apologised for *not sooner returning*, under date of October 13, 1873, *three months before I had any correspondence with Mr. Ingram*, who has never *used* the letter, never even *seen* it. Yet you have quoted my request for its return in evidence that you had kindly *permitted* Mr. Ingram to *use* material which had exclusively been assigned to you!—which had been asked & *obtained* of you "on his account."

Your third & last extract from my letters was a request to be allowed to copy an autograph letter from Mr. John Willis of Orange County, Virginia—one of Poe's classmates at the University. I *had* promised Mr. Ingram to ask you for a copy of this letter, but you will remember that you never *answered* this request. You had an undoubted right to withhold the letter, since I had given it to you unconditionally, nor did I *blame* you for withholding it, knowing how valuable all such "material" had become. But was it right, in quoting my letter, to leave it to be inferred that you had complied with it?

————————

There were other corrections of unfair statements, but this covers the principal misinterpretations.

I am anxious to know how he will meet this sifting of evidence.

141. *Sarah Helen Whitman to John H. Ingram.   Item 286*

Dear Mr. Ingram,   March 7, [18]76
Your letter of Feb. 14th was received the day after mine was mailed.
To the letter of which I sent you a copy Mr. Gill returned an evasive answer, affecting to sustain his plea by the most futile representations. But what he says now about anything can avail him little. I was informed yesterday that his creditors, who had consented to receive 13 cents on a dollar, had just learned that he had withheld from the account rendered to them of his assets $60,000. They are filled with

indignation against him and intend to hold him to a strict account.

The popular feeling is entirely against him. The publisher's pamphlet in which he inserted his "Reply" has "no circulation," so I was informed by a bookseller of this city. Nothing that he could say could injure you. If he does not clear himself from his present business "*complications*" (to speak mildly), he will not have the temerity to return to the charge against me. For I have shown him that it is with *me* that he will have to measure swords in this contest, and though I shrink from "broil & battle," I can meet him in the cause of truth & justice in a fair fight.

I cannot understand you when you say in your letter of Feb. 14th that I took Gill's claim "as a matter of course." Was there not an exclamation point to indicate my surprise at the assertion? It was to me so palpably absurd a pretension that I *may* not have thought it necessary even to indicate my surprise in any way. I had told you frankly from the beginning of my correspondence with you *all that I knew or thought* about the proceedings of the author of "The Romance of Edgar Poe" and about the inception & progress of the work. I did not suspect that you were in any doubt about what I might feel or say on the subject.

I do not remember where the quotation of Mrs. Browning's letter was first seen by me. I *have* seen it in many publishers' articles, but cannot at this moment recall where.

I am very weary & heavyhearted and can only say *goodnight*, with sincerest wishes for your happiness & success. Ever your friend,

Sarah Helen Whitman

I am too tired tonight to say much that I wished to say. Perhaps another time will come for all.

142. *John H. Ingram to Sarah Helen Whitman*

My dear Friend,   14 March 1876

Yours of the 29th Ultimo, just received, shows that you have not yet received mine of the 14th Ultimo. I trust it has now reached you safely and that you have *forgiven if you cannot ever forget.*

You will see by the enclosed rough proof what my "Rejoinder" to Gill is.[1] I do not think, unless you had the whole correspondence which has passed under my eyes, that you can fully comprehend how utterly despicable this Gill is. Apart from other sources, the communications Mr. Widdleton has forwarded me show his true nature—a *portion* of the correspondence which I must return (although not asked for) to Mr. Widdleton, I forward to you, as I do not think I break any confidence in so doing. The papers were sent me by Widdleton without any stipulation. Kindly forward them to their proper address (*i.e.*, Widdleton's).

You are mistaken in deeming that Gill was irritated at my forestalling him with your information—in his last letter to me *he expressed the hope* that I should be able to make use of the Gowans &c. testimony! I should never have heard anything *publicly* of his claims had Mr. Widdleton not declined his offer to write a "Memoir" of Poe for his edition of Poe's works. Mr. W[iddleton] is now thoroughly disgusted with Gill & although still doubting what my attitude might be, wrote to the New York *Evening Post* a letter apologizing for having given, *as if with my sanction*, publicity to Gill's claim. He is now reprinting the "Memoir" for the 4–vol. edition of the works, & has sent me the first proof for revision—if he follows out my corrections he will greatly enhance the value of the life.[2]

I have already told you that the 1827 volume has reached my hands, but this I wish kept quiet *pro tem*. It was printed but *not published*, & to *me* is, from a biographical point of view, the most interesting of his vols. You will hear fully of it ere long.

Pray let us dismiss this Gill affair for all eternity & be as we were of yore. I have been very unwell—the thought of being regarded by you merely as an instrument to be used for a purpose & then cast aside broke me down utterly. You must bear somewhat with me. I have suffered such mental torments in my short life as few mortals undergo & remain sane. I clung to your friendship as a sheet anchor and then, the utterly heartless way in which *you seemed* to regard me wrung my heart. But enough! Forgive & forget.

As regards Gill, he sees that he cannot expect you to shield his falsehoods & misrepresentations. Pray do not be drawn into a correspondence with him. To you, I need scarcely repeat that I never gave him *the slightest reason to believe* that I would not publish in America.

I sent copy of my "Rejoinder" to the *American Bookseller*, where, I believe, Gill's "Reply" was first sent, but a copy sent to a printer for a few proofs got lost, & has only just turned up. I enclose you one. I cannot help feeling that this touching "pitch" does not improve my own feelings, or other people's—it is unworthy of my aims—& unless Gill does something very outrageous I shall drop the subject now. Just note the amusing way in which he alludes, however, to Ingram being only a "clerk in a public office"—are Americans generally so ignorant of our social institutions, or is Gill only presuming on Widdleton's ignorance? It is a well-known fact that our leading scientific & literary men are in the Civil Service, for instance, Sir R. Airey, Herschell, Professor Owen, Sir Arthur Helps, W. Rossetti, are or were in Civil

Service. Anthony Trollope & E. Yates were in the same Dept. as myself. A clerkship in our Civil Service is permanent, & is indicative of a certain amount of influence & *education*.[3]

You know Horne's works of course? "Orion," &c.? He is a noble old fellow & has just published a revised edition of *Cosmo*. I will send you a copy next mail day. If you care to publish any remarks in the P[rovidence] *Journal*, Horne will be glad to see them. He has one weakness—he does not like to be deemed *too* old! It is nearly 50 years ago since first edition of *Cosmo*.

Reverting to our *own* subject: can you give any suggestions as to the origin of "The Raven" other than those contained in "The Philosophy of Composition"? Do you know when or where "El Dorado" was published, prior to Poe's death?[4] "For Annie," I believe, you have answered. I wish someone would give me a list of Poe's contributions to *Graham's Magazine*, Vols. 18, 21, up to 1850, & of those to *The Gift*, 1831–1850. Are they in your Athenaeum? I think *you* have looked?

I shall tell Widdleton that I have sent his Gill correspondence per you, as "I wished you to see it." It follows on Thursday.

Ever yours,

John H. Ingram

1. Ingram's "Rejoinder" follows these notes.
2. See page 378, n. 4.
3. Ingram had received his commission in the British Civil Service in 1868. The birth certificate he had to furnish at that time led to my discovery that the date he gave to *Who's Who*, 1849, had to be false, for he could not have been commissioned at the age of nineteen. See my article "The Birthdate of John Henry Ingram," *Poe Studies*, 7 (June 1974), 24.
4. In the *Flag of Our Union*, Apr. 21, 1849.

143. *Ingram's Rejoinder to Gill's Reply,* American Bookseller, 1 (Apr. 1, 1876), 233–34

Ingram's Rejoinder to Gill's Reply

Editor of The American Bookseller:

Sir—As Mr. W. F. Gill, of Boston, in his so-called "Reply" to my repudiation of his claim of having furnished me information for my "Memoirs of Poe," really admits the accuracy of my statements, and, what is more important, as Mr. Widdleton, the publisher, has publicly stated that his seeming recognition of Mr. Gill's pretensions was made without my knowledge, any further discussion on my part may be deemed supererogatory. Mr. Gill, however, has contrived to involve his confession in so much irrelevant matter that the real points at issue are in danger of being lost sight of; permit me, therefore, to reiterate them:

1. That I have never received a single item of information about Edgar Poe from Mr. Gill.

2. That I have never made use of anything written by him on the same subject.

3. That his sketch in *Lotos Leaves* contained information previously incorporated in my publications, copies of which I had sent Mr. Gill.

Nos. 1 and 2 are corroborated by his public acknowledgment that the extracts I have published from his letters are "substantially correct." These extracts prove that up to August 27, 1874, Mr. Gill had neither sent me any information about Poe, nor, *unless he wrote what was not correct*, had he then written anything about the poet. But Mr. Gill, taking advantage of the unwonted luxury of getting into print, avers that, as early as September, 1873, *he had written* a "lecture" about Poe, and had advertised this embryo lecture earlier still. No amount of sophistry can extricate him from the horns of the dilemma upon which he thus so recklessly fixes himself. About "the summer" of 1874, this lecture, Mr. Gill states, was metamorphosed into an essay and submitted to the editor of the *Atlantic Monthly*. Unfortunately, the manuscript had to be returned unpublished, and unless Mr. Gill can prove that Mr. Howells allowed me to peruse it, or in any way gather information from it, the mere fact of its existence is of no value. From what American friends tell me, I should fancy every editor of position in the States rejects manuscript[s] every week about Edgar Poe. Am I to be deemed conversant with the contents of all this unpublished rubbish?

Unable to soften editorial hearts into printing his paper, Mr. Gill finally hit upon the plan of publishing it himself. Accordingly, the long delayed "lecture-essay" appeared in *Lotos Leaves*, heralded by its author's remark that it had been prepared at "a somewhat brief notice." Gibbon took twenty-three years for his History, so we must not begrudge Gill a less number of months for *his*, nor, merely regarding the quantity of matter he has compiled, exclaim *"Parturiunt montes, nascitur ridiculus mus!"*

As regards the date of the *Lotos Leaves* publication, I may mention, for Mr. Gill's information, that my copy bears this imprint: "Boston: William F. Gill & Co., 1875." If this date be false the fault is not mine.

Mr. Gill's declaration that I promised not to publish my "Memoir of Poe" in America is not only an insult to me but to common-sense, and is unsupported by a tittle of fact. He, forsooth, might publish his diluted copies of my papers in England, whilst I, even if I could have prevented it, was not to allow the publication of my works in America! I never did, and never would give Mr. Gill, or anyone else, such a promise.

Having said so much for Mr. Gill, allow me to say a few words about myself, and my third point. In response to Mr. Gill's request I sent him the following papers, which I had written, about Edgar Poe: "New Facts about Edgar Poe," and "More New Facts," *published* in the London *Mirror* January 24 and February 21, 1874, respectively; a life of Edgar Poe, published in *Temple Bar* Magazine, June, 1874, and an account of Poe's poetry and Life at West Point, published in the *Gentlemen's* Magazine for May, 1874. When these papers were *written* is of little consequence as evidence, but I may remark that the *Temple Bar* manuscript was sent to Messrs. Bentley & Son on December 1, 1873, long before I knew of Mr. Gill's existence, whilst the last proof of my "Memoir of Poe" was sent to Messrs. A. & C. Black on the 18th of July, 1874. Some of the above-named papers *did* reach Mr. Gill; all of them, I believe, have been reprinted in America; and every fact of interest in Mr. Gill's sketch had already appeared in them; indeed, I think he will find it as difficult to prove the originality of his letterpress as of the engraving which accompanies it—both had done duty previously in England. It is hard for Mr. Gill to find that "the ancients have stolen his ideas," but, as it is to be presumed that he is still very young, he may have another opportunity of appearing in print, in which case let me advise him to steer clear of all chances of that which, in the words of Byron, is likely to prove

> "A 'strange coincidence,' to use a phrase
> By which such things are settled now-a-days."

London, March 6, 1876.   John H. Ingram

144. *Sarah Helen Whitman to John H. Ingram.*   Item 288

My dear Mr. Ingram,   March 24, [18]76
  On the last day of Feb. I mailed a letter to you. I was very tired & ill & in my haste (as I afterwards remembered) put a three-cent stamp only on the envelope. I had been preparing a number of letters for the mail, all of which required a three-cent stamp only, & unconsciously placed the same on yours. I hope this did not prevent it from going into the foreign mail bag at New York.
  The next day, March 1st, I received a letter from you in a more friendly & cordial tone than the two immediately preceding it. Since that time I have been very unwell & have been waiting to hear from you in relation to Gill's proceeding in publishing garbled extracts from my letters. I sent you copies of my letter to him, of which I took copies also for such of my friends as knew of his "Reply" to your "Disclaimer."
  Widdleton, I see, has issued a volume of the poems recently to

which Gill's *Lotus Leaves* article is used as introductory! It is brought out in small quarto form & sold for a dollar.[1] Mrs. Oakes Smith has republished a portion of *her* essay on Poe in the *Home Journal* of Wednesday, March 15th.[2] A copy was sent me from the office of the Providence *Journal* this morning. It has the passage which, as I imagine, called forth the *protest* of which I spoke in defending myself against the charge which you brought against me, *viz.*, that I had said he was "unscrupulous & revengeful." I promised to copy for you her letter about my book. I will do it tonight.

In the *Home Journal* article, Mrs. Oakes Smith repeats the charge of insincerity. She says, "Mr. Poe was not one to inspire a true confidence, as a rule of life." Much that she says in this connection does not have the ring of true friendship, & it was doubtless in reply to something of this kind which called forth my protest & comments, such as they were, on *his faults*. All allusion to my letter, which you quote, is omitted in this article. There is a passage which I do not remember to have seen before & which puzzles me. She speaks of the myriad little loves ". . . not one in a million of which is of sufficient magnitude to be at all noteworthy," etc., etc.

I will cut out the passages in this connection & enclose them. Were they in the previous editions of her article? It has been often published before. If in the earlier copies, I should think, by the trumpeter of the "little loves" made up of vanity, jealousy, spleen, & selfishness, she meant Griswold, but I know of no later which have been open to the charge, nor indeed was *his*, unless his allusion to Mrs. Osgood could be so interpreted.

Mrs. Smith was no friend to Mrs. Osgood, I well know. She could not have meant me as one of "the little loves," because she introduces in the present revised (?) copy the astonishing paragraph about his "installing" Helena & herself & a few others as queens, etc., etc.!!!

Can you enlighten me about "the myriad little loves"—can you tell me if it was in the earlier copies, such as *Beadle's*, which I think you said you had, and can you copy for me the exact phrase used by her in the words you say are quoted from one of my letters?

Send me back the cutting from the *Home Journal* article, which I enclose.

You ask if I know anything of Mr. Ross Wallace. I know that he wrote for the magazines in 1848 & that Poe greatly admired some of his poetry. There was an article, a poem by Wallace in the same no. of *Graham's*, that contained Poe's "Lines to Helen" (they were headed "Lines to ———"). He read them to me to show how much he felt they had lost by the omission of the line of which I told you in a former letter. He then read me a poem by Wallace from the same magazine,

Oct., I think, and pointed out two or three phrases as of surpassing excellence. The idea contained in them that pleased him so much was "To live is Victory." I have forgotten the words and remember only the idea. I did not know that he was intimate with Wallace. Mr. Wallace afterwards wrote regularly for the New York *Ledger*. I believe his *habits* were very *ir*regular, but he was a writer of undoubted genius. I think you might hear of him by addressing a letter to Mr. Bonner, if he still edits the *Ledger*, but *that* I do not know. I had an impression that Wallace was not living, but it may be without foundation. Perhaps he is one of the "contemporaries" who helped forward the Raven in Sandy Welsh's cellar.

I had a letter from Mr. O'Connor lately in which he says, "Ingram's review of Stoddard in the *Civil Service Review* is *splendid*! I *do* hope that fraud will get his due some day."

My Rose does not write a single word. I told her just before we parted in the street, when I saw her for the last time, that if I did not answer her letters always, she must not think it was because I did not love her. She has gathered up all her sweetness & hidden it away from me forever. When my heart is once wounded by cruel thorns it will not heal readily. I am sorry, but I can only say "a dio." Don't tell her this.

I am sorry that you are not well & that you have had "worries & annoyances." I have never for a single moment wavered in my loyalty to you as a trusted friend. I have never uttered a word of disparagement or of criticism about you or your work to *any*body—on the contrary, I have always spoken of both as you would like to have heard me speak. I have been perfectly sincere with you about Gill from the beginning, and I thought you ought to have known me better than to have written to me as you did, but I will not say another word, *nevermore*. Forgive the grammar & all my sins small & great & take my heart's blessing,

S.H.W.

St. Mark's Place, New York
Friday Evening, Feb. 9, [18]60

My dear Helena,

I have just finished your book of *Edgar Poe & His Critics*.

You have strangely fallen into the sphere of this weird child of genius & the impression left by your book is precisely that left by his character. We are thrown into a sad musing melancholy mood in which we yield to the spell of the enchanter without question or comment. It is enough for you & him to write—others will be the commentators. Your book is a marvel as much as was Poe. The angels will bring their harps nearer to your casement for the penning of this tribute.

[Elizabeth Oakes Smith]

After all it is not much—it furnishes no evidence that she had faith

in him—it did not spring so much from genuine friendliness & regard
as from other motives which are betrayed in some of the—but I will
not carp or criticise.

Have you forgiven me for being troubled about Mrs. Nichols'
anecdotes?

I am glad that you have found "Siope," etc.

1. *The Poetical Works of Edgar Allan Poe, with Memoir and Vindication* (New York:
W. J. Widdleton, 1876).

2. This article of four and one-half columns is Item 680 in the Ingram Poe Collection.

145. *John H. Ingram to Sarah Helen Whitman*

My dear Friend,   5 April 1876

Your long-looked-for letter has arrived, I mean yours of the 24th
Ultimo. Your last—the one you call the 3 cent—was so short & so stiff
that I have been half crazy with myself for having written as I have
done to you. How can mind speak to mind by these cursed crooked
pothooks & hangers! How can I learn to express my thoughts by these
up & down crooked strokes? *I* cannot exercise the "Power of Words."

Do not deem that it is *your* criticism of my deeds—my writings—
that I fear. You could not speak more severely of my weak attempts
than I can and have done myself. No one could scarify my writings as I
could, & when anyone flatters, or speaks well of my writings, I never
feel as if I could thoroughly believe them. From my friends—from
you, I should never feel annoyed at dispraise for my literary efforts, nor
for pointing out my shortcomings. I speak truthfully, my friend. But
what "riles" me—what turns all my hot blood to steam is to find myself
made a tool of—played with to suit someone's purpose. And the fact
that I loved you so truly—admired & reverenced you so faithfully—
made my thought that you were wearied with me—regarded me only
as a puppet to be played with—red hot agony.

In some things I am as proud as Lucifer. I must speak of myself
now—and in *my mind* deem myself as great as any being that ever
breathed this world's air. I would not change my entity for
Shakespeare's nor Shelley's—and often I feel half mad to think that I
have ever published a line, knowing that I have written nothing
worthy of living, & yet knowing that my thoughts are so grand—so
daring. *I* can but judge myself by what I feel, & it is gall & wormwood
to know that the few—how few!—whom I love & reverence can
misjudge me—not by what I have attempted, but by what they deem
me fit.

What am I talking about? I can't begin again, so must let this wild farrago go to you. And now to real facts & be "Mr. Worldly Wiseman" again.

I am surprised at what you say about Widdleton publishing *Lotos Leaves*—so different to what I have imagined from his letters to me. I have returned him the correspondence with Gill he sent me *direct*, as it struck me that asking you to forward it from Providence seemed to draw you into the controversy. I might, certainly, have sent it to you, & then had it back. There! it was of no value! but it would have shown you what pressure Gill put upon Widdleton, threatening even legal proceedings, & accusing me of perjury. Declaring that I knew certain matter was contained first in *Lotos Leaves*, & then in a *written* lecture, & that *I had solemnly pledged my word not to publish in America!* In one paragraph of one of his letters he asked Mr. W[iddleton] why he was aiding Ingram "in *stealing* from me (*i.e.*, Gill) the right which properly belongs to me, as the *first* to undertake to effectually vindicate E. A. Poe." And, alluding to an intention of pressing the matter as to the question of legal rights, remarks, "If it comes to that the law is explicit & all in my favour upon this point." Then calls attention to the fact that he, Mr. Gill, is "nearly affiliated with literature (sic)" & that Ingram "is only a clerk in some office."

That you had *assigned* any material to him I knew at once was false—as false as that I had made *any* promise to him. That he had taken portions of my "New Facts" &c. without acknowledgment, did not matter a pin. I don't think I called any attention to it—until this claim of his—*Mais, c'est assez—ne c'est pas?*

I have had a copy of the *Home Journal* with Mrs. E. O. Smith's paper—'tis the same she sent me. Her fiction is better than her fact. When I read the paper in print I was half inclined, for the moment, to answer it, but *reason* instantly showed me the folly of thus wasting my time & energies. These newspaper & magazine articles are forgotten in a week.

Did you see Mr. Lathrop's half-hearted attempt to say a word for Fairfield's *idea* of Poe in *Scribner's* for this month? In the paper "Irving, Poe & Hawthorne."[1] These things "won't wash" & do no real ultimate harm. Fifty years hence when we are dead and—most of us—forgotten, Poe will be a classic, & his personal character no more discussed than Homer's.

Returning to Mrs. Smith—whose extract I return. In her paper on Poe in *Beadle's Monthly* for Feby. 1867, she says: Mrs. Whitman writes Poe "was, it is true, vindictive, revengeful, unscrupulous in the use of expedients to attain his ends"—I shall be glad to know that "Helena" did *not* write it. Mrs. S[mith], although so imaginative, might have the good sense to correct where she has been shown correction is necessary. What a hobby she has for misspelling names: her letters are full of it: Helen*a*, Fann*ie*, [*illegible*], H*u*rst, &c.

Poe gave her more than she deserved: she might have remained content without inventing for him things that he *could* not have said. I have not *Beadle's*, but can "look it up" in the British Museum again, but 'tis no consequence, is it? We can now drop *her*: *she* is played out. I cannot understand her "little loves" & fancy it is only a random shot to hit all round. This paper is not a republication, so far as I know, but it is partly made up from her former articles. She "pitches into" Mrs. Lewis vigorously in writing—not in print. The extract from your letter, here sent, is only a small portion of the tirade quoted from you.

Strange is that Memorial letter of S. D. Lewis. I always thought Mrs. Lewis a widow. Would we could meet & *talk* of these matters.

I cannot find that W. Ross Wallace is dead, & yet cannot hear of his being alive; he wrote *some* fine poems, *some* of the finest American lines, I deem, in some respects.

Poe's lines to Helen (headed "Lines to ———") appeared in *Sartain's Union Magazine* for November. How then about *Graham's*? I would be so glad to get a simple record of all Poe wrote in *Graham's Maga.* for Vols. 18, 21 & then to 1850. Where can this be done? I'll try Davidson again—he cards me that after 1st his address will be once more P. O. Box 567, New York. Wallace was, so I am told, very dissipated. By the way, "The Raven" when first published was slightly different from the present version. I believe I have discovered what suggested the poem, so far as the refrain &c. is concerned, but I don't think I need take the public into my confidence. "Sandy Welsh's Cellar" is good enough for them.

Your Rose is doubtless loyal but working hard. I have never answered her pretty last letter so, perhaps, she thinks to punish you for my faults.

Never mind *my* unwellness. I am never well & always worried & anxious—all my nerves are living ones. I am a perpetual anxiety. And yet life *is* a luxury to me. To live & feel that I live *is* something worth "a cycle of Cathay."

A grand Memorial volume is preparing at Baltimore to include the letters &c. & "my Life" from the *International*, slightly revised. By the way, I fancy this last item is not to be told. I mean that the life is to be therein, so "mum's the word."

Mrs. Nichols has written her "Recollections," but I have suggested its appearing in some magazine, as I am not sure how much, or what portion of it, I can use. I have not seen the paper. I still believe the Nichols too ready "to point a moral & adorn a tale" to stick to the strict letter of literary law—that is, friendly to Poe, but desirous of filling up blanks. Can you comprehend?

My dear friend, Mrs. Houghton, writes but scraps just now—she has domestic trouble, I fear.

And now, forget the "thorns," & ever believe me, as of yore, & for evermore, yours devotedly,

John H. Ingram

P.S. Hutcheson Poë (son of the head of the Irish Poës) and an officer in the Royal Marines, called upon me & seemed very desirous of gathering information about the Poe family in America. He had been to Baltimore & called upon the Poes, on Neilson Poe, *Junior,* and from him did not get a very favorable reception. N[eilson] P[oe], Junior, said he did not know & *did not want to know* who his grandfather was, or something to that effect.

Hutcheson Poë is apparently really an innate gentleman & a handsome-looking fellow. He gave me an extract from the *Annual Register* for July 14, 1817, page 60, containing an account of some Scotch emigrants taken over to his Polish estates by *Count Poë* of Doospouda, Poland.[2]

J.H.I.

1. George Parsons Lathrop's article in defense of Fairfield's allegation that Poe was a madman of letters was printed in *Scribner's Monthly,* 11 (Apr. 1876), 799–808.

2. This eighteen-line extract is Item 1 in the Ingram Poe Collection.

146. *Sarah Helen Whitman to John H. Ingram.   Item 289*

My dear friend,   April 7, 1876

I duly received yours of the 14th Ulto., & on Saturday last a copy of Mr. Horne's *Cosmo,* of which I will speak hereafter. Many thanks. I have always been an admirer of his "Orion," & his "New Spirit of the Age," was, to my thinking, better than Hazlitt's. His correspondence with Mrs. Browning, as published in the *Contemporary Review,* I read with great interest.

Your "Rejoinder" I handed to two gentlemen who happened to be present when I received it, & who had read with high approval your *Civil Service* "showing *up*" of Stoddard's *Poetic* enterprise. They read, also, with apparent zest your "Rejoinder." Doubtless it is very pungent & exasperating, damaging not only to Poe's too ambitious champion, but to the testimony, such as it is, presented in his behalf. Doubtless, too, Gill deserved all this, not only for having published documents which I had expressly *forbidden* him to publish, & for neglecting to submit to me his Lotus Leaf MS., as he had *promised* to do, but more especially for having put forth his audacious claim to have "kindly permitted you to use material" etc., etc. which had been previously used by himself! That was a felicitous allusion of yours to the *embryo* lecture, & tells the whole story.

I assumed that your injunction to secrecy about the 1827 edition of the poems would not exclude Mr. Harris from the knowledge of a matter in which he has taken so great an interest. I had an interview with him last evening & he wishes me to ask you if the owner of the copy to which you allude was willing to dispose of it (provided you did not wish to purchase it yourself), to ask you if you would use your influence to obtain it for him. Being a collector of rare books & the owner of the largest collection of American poetry in the country, he will give all & more that the book would be likely to command from any other purchaser. He will be gratified to receive your article on the little vol. He has been aware of the existence of such a copy through a gentleman who has been in correspondence with him on the subject, a Mr. Lee, I think he said, of Baltimore or Richmond, a bookseller.

Was it the *Philobiblion* in which Stoddard first published his insinuations that no such volume had been printed? Whatever it was, Mr. Harris says that if you wish to see the article he will mail to you the number of the periodical containing it, the numbers still being unbound.

I wonder if you have heard about a scandalous paragraph which is going the rounds of the press? This is the paragraph: "Elizabeth Oakes Smith writes in the *Home Journal* that the immediate cause of Edgar A. Poe's death was a severe beating which he received from the friend of a woman whom he had deceived & betrayed."

I have received several letters bitterly denouncing Mrs. Smith for this scandalous story. Now, I do not believe that Mrs. S[mith] ever wrote such a paragraph or would *authorise* its insertion in any paper.[1]

Some of the tribe of secret slanderers who are forever lying in wait for an occasion to sully his memory & obscure his fame have doubtless seized upon an idle & absurd story told by Mrs. S[mith] in that article which she wrote long ago for one of her own magazines, & which (as I think I told you in my last letter) she has lately republished in the *Home Journal*.

If you have a copy of that article, you will see that her account of the cause of Poe's death has been misrepresented & misquoted, & doubtless with malign intent, by some of Poe's enemies. If I knew her present address, I would write to her at once to confirm or deny this story, which is being so widely circulated under her name. Cannot you do it? I think that Mrs. S[mith], in getting up an article on Poe, had introduced a garbled & inaccurate account of Griswold's story about the lady who had lent him money and whom, refusing to pay, he had threatened to expose by showing letters that would make her "infamous." We know on what basis this perfidious & wicked story was constructed. Mrs. S[mith], who, as I told you, is constitutionally inaccurate, probably did not trouble herself to correct or verify the story so long as it was found sensational & acceptable to the lovers of light literature.

She assumes to like & admire Poe, in the somewhat contradictory article lately republished in the *Home Journal*, & I think must be indignant at this malign perversion of her words. Do ask her about it.

I long to see your article on the suppressed poems.

It is an hour past midnight, and so, goodnight. Forget anything & everything that I may have said to give you pain & believe that I have never faltered in my wish to be to you what you have so often called me, your beneficent "Providence,"

S.H.W.

1. In the article "Recollections of Poe," by Mrs. Elizabeth Oakes Smith, New York *Home Journal*, Mar. 15, 1876, these lines do appear: "He was not a diseased man from his cups at the time of his death, nor did he die from *delirium tremens*, as has been asserted. The whole sad story will probably never be known, but he had corresponded with a woman whose name I withhold, and they having subsequently quarrelled, he refused to return her letters, nor did she receive them till Dr. Griswold gave them back after Poe's death. This retention not only alarmed but exasperated the woman, and she sent an emissary of her own to force the delivery, and who, failing of success, beat the unhappy man in a most ruffianly manner. A brain fever supervened, and a few friends went with him to Baltimore, his native city, which he barely reached when he died."

147. *Sarah Helen Whitman to John H. Ingram.* Item 290

My dear friend, April 18, [18]76

Yours of the 6th [5th] just arrived. I will only say one word tonight in reply to one of your questions, and write at *once* so as to avail myself of tomorrow's steamer.

You say, "Poe's Lines to Helen (headed 'Lines to —— ——') appeared in *Sartain's Union Magazine* for Novr. 1848 How then about *Graham's Magazine*?" They could not of course have appeared in *both*, nor did they appear as "To —— ——," but "To —— —— ——."

The first article in the number in which they appeared was a poem by Ross Wallace. All this I told you in one of my recent letters.

Now will you tell me on what authority you ask me, "How then about *Graham*?"

I had the very number long in the house which Poe brought to me &

from which he read to me both his poem to me and the poem of
Wallace. I have a very particular reason for wishing you to write on the
enclosed card the reason for your statement the *authority* on which
you question mine, and ask it from you as you value my friendship to
reply *at once*. I will explain to you my *reason* as soon as I hear from
you.

Why did you cross out the date 1848? That was the true date of the
first publication of the poem.

Sincerely and affectionately your friend,

P.S. I send you a little poem which I wrote on a spray of trailing
arbutus which was presented to me in the street last Thursday,
because the *reply*, entitled "Epigea," another name for the arbutus,
was written by a young poet & botanist, the one who read with such
keen enjoyment your "Rejoinder" to the "Reply" of W[m] F. G[ill],
W.W.B. W.W.B. is Professor W. W. Bailey.

I long to hear about the [18]27 edition of the poems.

Faithfully your friend,

S. H. Whitman

Mr. Bailey thinks of Stoddard just what we think of him. He saw
much of him when S. was editor of the *Aldine*.

George Parsons Lathrop is, I *think*, the assistant editor of the
Atlantic. The mention of Fairfield as an "ingenious writer who has
carried his theory too far" and the whole tone of the article show that
he is in league with the enemies of Poe who have taken opportunity to
assail him behind the flimsy mantle of Fairfield.

148. *John H. Ingram to Sarah Helen Whitman*

My dear Providence,   22 April 1876

I duly received yours dated 4th [7th] and will briefly reply. I cannot
say much, as I am feeling unwell again. I might almost say "light" or
rather *misty*-headed & ready every now & then to lapse into
insensibility. I am working hard at *something*—when 'tis done I must
vegetate again for a while, at least as regards literature.

Re. Horne—have you seen his paper on *Psyche Apocalypté*, from *St.
James's*? It is a drama he & Mrs. Browning were to have written
together. He reprinted a few copies (only 25, I think) of the article, &
gave me a copy, &, I fancy, (at my suggestion) sent Hand Browne one.[1]
If there be a spare copy I'll get him to send it to you. You'll value it.

The *American Bookseller* has sent me some copies with my

"Rejoinder." From same number I learn that at "The Book Fair" books sold very badly—far below all expectation—the only works realizing good prices being *Widdleton's editions of Poe*. The "unhappy master" does not seem decreasing in popularity, although the Stoddards, Fairfields, &c. "o'er his cold ashes upbraid him."

Mallarmé is publishing translations of Poe's "Marginalia" in *La République des Lettres*. Did I send you a copy? I fear not, but will, 'Tis the best periodical of the day.

Re. the 1827 edition. Of course I cannot object to Mr. Harris knowing, but I am anxious that the matter goes no further until my paper has appeared. Even in that I have suppressed the fact that the poems are "by a Bostonian," instead of bearing Poe's name on imprint. This fact has hitherto baffled inquirers, and I trust you & Mr. Harris will oblige me by still keeping it *sub rosa* for a while. I enclose such particulars as may interest Mr. Harris. Although I am, probably, the only person in England knowing that this little book is by Poe, it is not in my possession, but in the national collections, & I do [not] suppose could be bought for any money. I would give *something* to obtain a copy, as you may imagine. I would not have republished these poems, at least until my life was ready, but feared they might come to light elsewhere. Oh! have I told you there are several *un*published pieces in the collection?

How did you know that "Alone" appeared in Mrs. Balderston's album? I have her address, but have not had time to write yet. Swinburne says he thinks it "worthy of its alleged parentage."

Did you see the death of Revd. Dr. Houghton, Mrs. Houghton's husband?[2] Suddenly. She sent me the news. I wish she'd come to Europe for a change. She could tell me more facts than anyone.

Mrs. Nichols has sent me her "Recollections," they are short & contain little beyond a reproduction of the *Sixpenny Magazine* paper. Nothing of any value whatever.

In my next edition of Poe's *Works* I hope to give the whole of his poems—will you tell Mr. Harris? I cannot find time to write him, or might send him some useful notes. Does he want to know anything in the British Museum? I had better send him copy of Mrs. Lewis's (i.e., "Stella's") drama *Sappho*.[3]

Philobiblion, I fancy, was the *first* place (as far as I know) where Stoddard "published his insinuation." In *Round Table*, &c. he repeated it. I have not thought it worth while to refute Mrs. Smith's stupid scandal: all her "facts" as I told her when she sent her paper (the MS.) to me were fictions. I like her mental deductions, in part, but her imagination is very diseased. Her article is only the repetition of an old, effete, & utterly exploded pack of scandal. By this post, I send you a number of *New York Review* containing a reply to her *Beadle* paper (the basis of the *Home Journal* [article]). Kindly return it to me when perused—also, the enclosed scraps published at time of the poet's death. Be assured Mrs. Smith wrote the *Home Journal* paper. I don't think you could do any good by writing to her. I forget her address but will look it up & send it to you. A personal letter, I feel assured, however, will not obtain any satisfaction.

The account of Poe's death I gave in the *International Review* was the true one, be assured. It was the "cooping" which murdered him.

I cannot say anymore now, so, for a while, goodbye.

John H. Ingram

1. *Psyche Apocalypté: A lyrical drama.* Projected by E. B. Browning and R. H. Horne. Reprinted from the *St. James Magazine & United Empire Review*, Feb. 1876.

2. Dr. Roland Stebbins Houghton had died in Hartford, Conn., Thursday, Mar. 23, 1876. See Item 681 in the Ingram Poe Collection for an obituary.

3. Stella Lewis, *Sappho: A Tragedy in Five Acts* (London: Trübner & Co., 1875).

149.   *John H. Ingram to Sarah Helen Whitman*

My dear Providence,   2 May 1876

Yours dated the 18th Ultimo to hand and, in compliance with your request, I reply at once. You say reply on enclosed *card*, but no card was enclosed—only a most fragrant bunch of Arbutus—not the European Arbutus evidently, but a sweeter & an earlier flowering bloom.

Your lines *are most beautiful*—truly redolent of spring sweetness &, *for once*, I must confess the reply is not unworthy of the lines replied to. Why are you so chary of your poems? Why not republish during your earthly life?

As nothing in the shape of a card was enclosed, I give my "authority" for the *Graham* testimony on the next scrap. You will see that "S.H.W."—whose authority I always accept—gave me the information. But all is put right now. 'Twas evidently only a slip of the pen.

The Didier herein referred to is, I am told, *meditating* a new life of Poe. He has been so doing for some years, he says, but, if his facts are not more reliable than those prefixed to the "Alone" lines, I am afraid we shall not get much useful information therefrom. I suppose he'll be on the right side.

Looking over the *Literary World* (New York) for *1850*, I see that in reviewing Vol. iii of Poe's works, Griswold was severely handled &, *even then*, accused of inserting into Poe's critiques things Poe had not put there. The notice, however, cannot be styled friendly to Poe.

I'll send a *Sappho* to you for Mr. Harris in course of a few posts. "Stella" is, of course, Mrs. Lewis. Did I ever tell you *she* gave me the MS. of *Politian*? Keep this *sub rosa*—I have reasons. I have done much for her. "What a lot" we shall have for our *viva voce* exchanges!

Ever yours,

John H. Ingram

In yours dated 27 May 1875 you say, after telling how the MS. of "To Helen" passed into the hands of Dr. Buchanan: "The lines to Helen were first published in *Graham's Magazine* in Oct. 1848. Poe brought me the number & pointed out to me that they had left out the words, 'Oh God, oh heaven! how my heart beats in coupling those two words.'" I need not send the leaf, need I? I fear to lose a line of yours (save two pistol & dagger epistles, & those I keep in lieu of sackcloth & ashes). I at once entered the above date in a book I keep of Poe's first publications. I mean a list of when his various productions appeared. I have only two vols. of *Graham's* & some odd parts. There are none in the British Museum & I still await a full list of Poe's contributions to the magazine, but his *acknowledged* pieces is nearly full. Recently I was investigating *Sartain's Union Maga.* & found the "Lines to ——."* I noted the discrepancy at once & wrote to you. This is the whole story.[1]

Mallarmé is translating & publishing Poe's "Marginalia" in *La République des Lettres*. I have given you information *re.* the 1827 vol.—in my last—as soon as I can get the paper published you shall have copies.

Do you see *Notes & Queries*? No. 121 for 22 April, page 336, headed "Philadelphia Authors," contained a charge against Poe of plagiarism.[2] I have responded & have let a certain plagiaristic "cat out of the bag," where I have long kept it, that will startle *one* Philadelphia author, I fancy. My reply should appear next Saturday the 6th.[3]

At last Scribner's have responded politely with respect to my communication on "Alone." They state:

> After receiving your letter we sent to Baltimore & got from Mr. Didier the original copy of the Poe verses. We had already submitted the photo of it to a "Poe expert" who pronounced the poem & the handwriting as probably genuine. Upon examination of MS. we found that the date and, also, the title had been added by another hand—but we think there is no doubt as to the authenticity of the poem itself.

I had no idea you possessed "Poe experts"! The "probably" is very

*[*Mrs. Whitman's note:*] It was not *Sartains's*, neither *Graham's*, but the *Union*.

convincing, *n'est ce pas*? The poem is doubtless genuine, but it will need a goodly array of Poe experts to convince me that the handwriting is that of "The Raven's" author.

Mrs. E. O. Smith's address is Hollywood, Carteret County, North Carolina—but I send her last letter. Pray let *it be private* & return it, because it is so full of misapprehensions, to speak mildly, that I have not cared to answer it. I returned her MS. at once.

1. Mrs. Whitman's letter of May 27, 1875, contains neither an account of the "To Helen" manuscript nor the sentences Ingram here quotes. But Ingram's date is surely correct (he seldom erred in this respect), for the quoted passage cannot be found in the surviving correspondence (the Buchanan affair is discussed several times). In its present state the six-page holograph is clearly incomplete (see p. 296), lacking one leaf. When Mrs. Whitman persisted in pursuing this question (see her next letter, No. 150), Ingram apparently returned this leaf in his letter of May 31, 1876 (No. 151), with the request that she return it (see p. 422). It has not survived.

2. *Notes and Queries*, 5th ser., 5 (Apr. 22, 1876), 336: "Mr. Francis Harold is living, and is a member of the Philadelphia board of stockbrokers. He is a gentleman of decided literary taste[. . . .] Some years ago, Mr. Duffee proved that Poe (a most unprincipled man) was a plagiary of his most celebrated story, The Gold Bug[. . . .] UNEDA, Philadelphia."

3. Ingram's reply appeared on schedule, May 6, 1876, 377: "UNEDA, in speaking of a Philadelphian, a certain Mr. Duffee, alleges, 'Some years ago Mr. Duffee proved that Poe (a most unprincipled man) was a plagiarist of his most celebrated story, *The Gold Bug*.' If your correspondent means, and the construction of his sentence is somewhat curious, that Edgar Poe stole the story from some one else, will he or she be good enough to state how, when, and where the charge was proved? As your readers are aware, similar charges have been frequently trumped up against the author of *The Raven*; but hitherto, upon examination, they have been proved utterly false. Speaking with a full knowledge of Poe's life and character, I emphatically deny that he was 'a most unprincipled man.'"

150. *Sarah Helen Whitman to John H. Ingram.   Item 292*

My dear friend,   May 19, 1876

I have waited *so* impatiently the receipt of an answer to my question as to the paragraph in your letter of April 6 [5] in which you say, "Poe's lines to Helen (headed 'Lines to —— ——') appeared in *Sartain's Union Magazine* for *Novr*. How then about *Graham's*?" I have underlined the words just as you wrote them.

You say in your letter of May 2 that you, your*self*, found the lines in *Sartain's Union Magazine*, noted the discrepancy, & at once wrote to me. This, you say, "is the whole story."

If you found the lines in *Sartain's Union Magazine*, all that I told you about them was a fiction, not to say a *falsehood*, since *Sartain's*

Union Magazine was not published until January 1849, after Edgar Poe
& I had parted never again to meet.

I was so *sure* of this that on the very day when I last wrote to *you*, I
addressed a letter to Mrs. Sarah Josepha Hale, requesting her to
ascertain for me, if possible, the date of Sartain's first number. On the
first of May I received the enclosed card verifying my impression.

Either you have been *mistaken* about seeing the lines in *Sartain's
Magazine* or all that I told you is to use the mildest term—well I will
not characterize it.

You cannot wonder that I feel acutely the imputation which your
words, "How then about *Graham's*?" has charged me with.

This is *not a trivial matter*, as your strongly emphasized words show
that *it was not*, in your own mind. This was not a mere "slip of the
pen."

You have not, I fear, dealt frankly with me. You have had reasons for
thus calling me to question about the matter which you are unwilling
to confide to me.

You need not fear to do so. I will not betray you. I will keep your
secret, if you will only tell me frankly *why* you asked the question. If
you will not do this, you certainly will not refuse to reexamine the
Sartain magazines in which you say that you found the "Lines to ——
——" and tell me the *month* & *year* in which they appeared there.

I have told you before that they appeared in *Graham's* in the
autumn of 1848. I was not quite sure of the *month*, as I think I told
you. I have, however, satisfied myself that it was in *November*. Though
I have long ago lost every copy of the magazine & have never seen a
copy since, save those contained in the two bound volumes of the
magazine from which I copied for you Graham's letter two years ago,
volumes which I obtained after long enquiry & of which you yourself
afterward obtained a copy.

I read with interest Mrs. Smith's letter. I will venture to keep it a few
days longer because I wish to copy a portion of it. I will return it soon.
I had many things to say to you, but must wait for the next steamer,
having been interrupted till I have only time to send a parting word. I
have had a beautiful letter from Mallarmé telling me that he had
ordered a copy of his *Raven* sent me which I might receive possibly a
few days after the receipt of his letter, or, perhaps a few days before.
His letter was dated April 4, and the book has not yet come. I wrote
him yesterday. The postmaster here has sent orders to have the matter
looked up in New York, but I am afraid it has been intercepted. I told
him that I was glad to learn from you that he was translating some of
the critical papers.

I think with you about the handwriting of the "Alone," that it bears no resemblance to Poe's. On the other [hand?],there are unmistakable indications that the "March 17, 1829" *are* Mr. Didier's. But I think he may have been *told* that the lines were in Poe's handwriting & have believed it. It was Miss Rice who told me the name of Mrs. Balderston, the lady in whose album the poem was assumed to have been written.

I received from Miss Rice some time ago an intimation that Mr. Didier would be most happy to be of use to me in any way that I might point out. I had asked her if she knew Mr. Didier, the gentleman who had sent a poem purporting to have been a facsimile copy of the original to *Scribner's*. She told me that he was an intimate friend of hers & would be most happy to serve me in any way in his power, &c. I made no reply to this statement, but asked her if she knew the name of the lady, & she replied that it was Mrs. Judge Balderston. Recently I have had two letters from Mr. Didier, who, it seems, is proposing to bring out a life of Poe!! He says he has obtained much valuable information about his early life, etc. He, of course, wanted something from me. But I was reticent in my reply, tho' cordial & glad of any new light on the subject, etc., etc. I hear absolutely nothing of Gill. I fancy he has dematerialized, as our spiritualistic friends say.

Mr. Harris sent a long message to you a few evenings ago. He advises that you print the [18]27 poems without letting it be known *where* the copy is or that the title was etc., etc., *By a Bostonian*. He knows, or thinks he knows, how this copy came to find its way to England. He has left the city for a few weeks. He apparently envies you the sight of this little book. There is nothing in the world like the exultation of a book collector over a new & rare pamphlet. He wishes to know if you can find in the National Collection the pamphlet of which I spoke to you summer before last, called *The Musiad or Ninead*, by Diabolus, which was published in Baltimore in 1830, & which was a poem with *notes* about the authors of that day, in which Poe was spoken of.[1] I wrote to John Neal about it. The notes were torn off. Mr. H[arris] thinks we might find something of great interest in them. I think I wrote to you about it.

You will remember my friend Lyman Dwight who died a little more than a year ago in New Providence (Nassau), & who took such an interest in your proposed life of Poe, but did not live to see it in print. I wrote something about his newly erected monument a few days ago under the title of "An Old Graveyard," which I enclose & which may bring you near to me in my Rhode Island home.

Goodbye, & may heaven bless you & keep you. I hope we shall not lose faith in each other, for it is hard to get back again when lost. *Vale, vale.*

                                                                S.H.W.

1. The late Professor T. O. Mabbott firmly rejected this 101-line pamphlet as Poe's work.

151. *John H. Ingram to Sarah Helen Whitman*

My dear Friend,   31 May 1876
  On the 2nd Instant I answered yours dated 18th April, and, therefore, you should have received it before the 19th May, which is the date of yours just to hand. If my delayed letter has now reached you, you will therein find a full statement why I asked about the "Lines to ——" being accredited to *Graham's*. You were my authority, but I presume it was only a slip of your pen which we have now rectified. To satisfy your mind, however, I return you your MS. (that is, the portion of your letter containing the statement). When read, pray return this piece, as I keep all *your letters—a sacred trust—most carefully.*
  I see, after all, you have my letter of the 2nd & it still does not explain. Pray forgive my stupidity. I am worked & worried with neuralgic pain, beyond endurance.
  You say that I could not have found the lines in *Sartain's Union Magazine* (I always underline *titles* of books, &c. so there's nothing in that) because said magazine did not begin until January 1849, but this is wrong. "Lines to ——" appeared in it in *Oct. 1848,* & the "Enigma" to Mrs. Lewis in *March 1848.* Or, perhaps, I am wrong somewhere. I'll go to the British Museum on Saturday 3rd & look again & send you precise *data.* But the whole matter is not, cannot, be of the importance you put upon it. I cannot imagine what you are fearing. A few moments' conversation would clear up the whole affair.
  You gave me—*vide* the enclosed—*Graham's,* Oct. 1848. Well & good. I put it in my *data* book. Looking over *Sartain's Union,* I there found the "Lines" (one omitted) just as you had described them. I wrote you, thinking *Sartain's* might have copied from *Graham's* & wanting to discover the original publication.
  Your reply of the 18th April made me deem that *Sartain's* was right. Now this seems wrong.
  I could not understand you wishing me to write on an "enclosed card"—which card never came. In your present letter you again say you have enclosed card from Mrs. Hale, but you have omitted again to enclose anything of the kind. But all this is needless worry. The point is easily got at without you being agitated.
  I have no secret reasons for so natural a question as asking about a

date!! I am, certainly, anxious to have all the dates correct, but fear I shall never succeed. I shall be afraid to ask you any questions if you worry yourself so much about nothing. As for my underscoring, I do that too much—'tis a bad habit.

Perhaps *Sartain's* had a duplicate copy of the lines? I fancy this did sometimes happen with Poe's poems. But I'll get the exact date on Saturday.

I am glad Mallarmé has written & hope you have received *Le Corbeau*. After I asked him to send it, he was unable, for some time, to find means of sending it.

I do not think Mallarmé but Mendès was (is) the translator of the "Marginalia."[1]

Didier has written several papers on Poe matters but they are worthless for want of accuracy. He is said to be at work on a Life, but I don't fancy will publish. Gill, I believe, has collapsed. A very polite letter from Mr. Widdleton just to hand. Mrs. Judge Balderston's address I have, but cannot get time to write to her.

Pray do not ever be reticent of giving information about Poe to Didier, or anyone, on my account. The only favour in that way I ask is—if you allow Poe's letters to you to be published, let me publish them. I know my life, when it is published, will not suffer from any others having preceded it.

I ask you, however, not to let anyone, save Mr. Harris, know anything about the 1827 edition more than I have told in *Belgravia* for June, copy of which I sent you by yesterday's mail.[2] The copy over here, Mr. Harris may like to know, seems to have been acquired in 1866. It was as much as I could do to keep from stealing it!

I will try & find the pamphlet you mention. I don't *think* you mentioned it before, but I *must be careful with you* or you will make more fuss than my foes would.

The "Old Grave Yard" I keep for a quiet moment. I have never replied to Miss Peckham, so I expect she will not notice me anymore.

If you really like me, find fault with me, but don't go making hobgoblins out of slips of the pen—slips which only go before our four eyes.

Yours ever & always,

John H. Ingram

1. Catulle Mendès did publish an introduction to excerpts from Poe's "Marginalia" in *La République des Lettres*, Mar. 20, 1876, pp. 131–32.

2. Ingram's article in the *Belgravia Magazine*, "The Unknown Poetry of Edgar Poe," was partially reprinted in the New York *Daily Graphic*, June 8, 1876, as "Poe's Suppressed Poetry." The article is here reproduced in its entirety immediately following.

152. "The Unknown Poetry of Edgar Poe," by John H. Ingram,
Belgravia Magazine, 29 *(June 1876)*, 502–13

The Unknown Poetry of Edgar Poe
John H. Ingram

THE MENTAL STRUGGLES which frequently beset the editor of a deceased writer's unknown works in the present instance, fortunately, could not arise. The desire of making public the literary remains of one whose name and fame have become the world's property does not, in this case, conflict with that duty to the dead which should restrain from publication posthumous writings calculated to detract from their author's reputation. Apart from the belief that a portion at least of the unknown poetry of Poe, now first brought to light, is as meritorious as some of the known pieces, there is the fact to rely on that it was printed for publication by its author, and only suppressed through circumstances of a private nature—through private circumstances which can no longer affect anyone. The 1845 edition of Poe's poems was the last collection published during their author's lifetime, and, although many of his early pieces were omitted from it, there does not appear to be any reason for supposing that he would have objected to the republication of the remainder, as long as they were circulated *as they were written*, and devoid of the "improvements" which some of his compositions were subjected to whilst going "the rounds of the press." The appearance, moreover, of the following verse will have the advantage of confuting one of those reckless charges made by a follower of Griswold, that it was "mendacious" of Poe to assert that he had printed the volume whence it is now extracted.

This—Edgar Poe's first book—was printed, although not published, in Boston in 1827. It is entitled "Tamerlane and Other Poems," and contains only forty pages. The title-page is graced by a couplet from Cowper:

> Young heads are giddy and young hearts are warm,
> And make mistakes for manhood to reform.

From the preface to the little volume thus modestly heralded is learned that its contents were chiefly written in the years 1821–2, when the author had not completed his fourteenth year. "They were not, of course," he remarks, "intended for publication, and why they are now published concerns no one but himself." He deems that "the smaller pieces, perhaps, savor too much of egotism; but they were written," he adds, "by one too young to have any knowledge of the world but from his own breast." "In 'Tamerlane,'" the boy-poet tells us, "he has endeavoured to expose the folly of even *risking* the best feelings of the heart at the shrine of Ambition. He is conscious that in this there are many faults, (besides that of the general character of the poem), which he flatters himself he could, with little trouble, have corrected, but, unlike many of his predecessors, has been too fond of his early productions to amend them in his *old age*." In conclusion, "he will not say that he is indifferent as to the success of these poems—it might stimulate him to other attempts—but he can safely assert that failure will not at all influence him in a resolution already adopted. This is challenging criticism," he confesses; but adds, "let it be so. *Nos haec novimus esse nihil.*" An assertion, it may be remarked, he lived to prove the falsity of.

Besides "Tamerlane," which occupies seventeen pages of this booklet, there are nine "Fugitive Pieces": three of these are reprinted, nearly *verbatim*, in the current collections, and another, in a somewhat altered style, reappeared in the rare edition of 1829. As even the revised copy of this poem is almost unknown to general readers, the original version of it is given here, together with the remaining five pieces, which will be quite new to the world, the little volume containing them having hitherto escaped the most diligent search of bibliographists and admirers of Poe. At that period of his life in which these poems were written, their youthful author was strongly influenced by Byronism, and "Tamerlane," as, indeed, Hannay pointed out, shows traces of it. This influence is even more marked in the little book before us than in the 1829 volume, of which all the later editions, save that of 1831, are reprints. This unknown original is, indeed, very different in many respects from the later "Tamerlane," into which several new passages have been interpolated, and from which many other passages have been omitted. The variations between the two copies are so numerous and so lengthy that little less than the entire republication of the first draft would suffice to show them all, and as that is, of course, out of the question here, we purpose to cite only the most interesting of the omissions. Different in structure, and explaining some things which, in later copies, are left to the imagination, the "Tamerlane" of 1827, is, however, in many parts quite equal to the present poem. Eleven explanatory notes, suppressed in all subsequent editions, are given to the chief poem, but only the first and fifth of them call for notice. In the first note, Poe says that very little is really known of Tamerlane's history, "and with that little I have taken the full liberty of a poet. . . . How shall I account for giving him 'a friar' as a death-bed confessor, I cannot exactly determine. He wanted someone to listen to his tale—and why not a friar? It does not pass the bounds of possibility—quite sufficient for my purpose—and I have, at least, good authority on my side for such innovation."

Details of the slight plot of this poem are almost needless. Tamerlane, lord of half the known world, is on his death-bed. Before his troubled spirit can pass away he longs to disburden his mind of its weight of woe, and, accordingly, sends for a friar, and confesses to him the story of his life. *Now,* when the world is at his feet, he forgets all his projects of empire and visions of glory, and has but for

> "Memory's eye
> One object—and but one"—

the ideal of his bygone boyhood:

> " 'Tis not to thee that I should name—
> Thou can'st not, would'st not dare to think
> The magic empire of a flame
> Which even upon this perilous brink
> Hath fixed my soul, though unforgiven
> By what it lost for passion—Heaven!
> I loved.
>
>   . . . . .
>
> I loved her as an angel might
> With ray of the all-living light
> Which blazes upon Edis' shrine.
> It is not surely sin to name,
> With such as mine—that mystic flame—
> I had no being but in thee!
> The world with all its train of bright
> And happy beauty (for to me
> All was an undefined delight),
> The world—its joys—its share of pain,
> Which I felt not, its bodied forms
> Of varied being, which contain
> The bodiless spirits of the storms,
> The sunshine and the calm—the ideal
> And fleeting vanities of dreams,
> Fearfully beautiful! The real
> Nothings of mid-day waking life—
> Of an enchanted life, which seems,
> Now as I look back, the strife
> Of some ill demon, with a power
> Which left me in an evil hour,
> All that I felt, or saw, or thought,
> Crowding, confused became
> (With thine unearthly beauty fraught)
> Thou—and the nothing of a name . . .
> The passionate spirit which hath known,
> And deeply felt the silent tone
> Of its own self-supremacy—
> (I speak thus openly to thee,

'Twere folly now to veil a thought
With which this aching breast is fraught)
The soul which feels its innate right—
The mystic empire and high power
Given by the energetic might
Of Genius at its natal hour;
Which knows (believe me at this time,
When falsehood were a tenfold crime,
There is a power in the high spirit
To *know* the fate it will inherit),
The soul, which knows such power, will still
Find *Pride* the ruler of its will.
Yes! I was proud—and ye who know
The magic of that meaning word,
So oft perverted, will bestow
Your scorn, perhaps, when ye have heard
That the proud spirit had been broken,
The proud heart burst in agony
At one upbraiding word or token
Of her, that heart's idolatry.
I was ambitious.
    . . . . .
          In her eyes
I read (perhaps too carelessly)
A mingled feeling with my own;
The flush on her bright cheek, to me,
Seemed to become a queenly throne. . . .

Then—in that hour—a thought came o'er
My mind it had not known before:
To leave her while we both were young—
To follow my high fate among
The strife of nations, and redeem
The idle words which, as a dream,
Now sounded to her heedless ear—
I held no doubt—I knew no fear
Of peril in my wild career;
To gain an empire and throw down—
As nuptial dowry—a queen's crown.
The only feeling which possest,
With her own image my fond breast—
Who, that had known the secret thought
Of a young peasant's bosom then,
Had deemed him, in compassion, aught
But one whom fantasy had led
Astray from reason. Among men
Ambition is chained down—nor fed
(As in the desert, where the grand,

The wild, the beautiful conspire
With their own breath to fan its fire)
With thoughts such feeling can command;
Unchecked by sarcasm and scorn
Of those, who hardly will conceive
That any should become 'great,' born
In their own sphere—will not believe
That they shall stoop in life to one
Whom daily they are wont to see
Familiarly—whom Fortune's sun
Hath ne'er shone dazzlingly upon,
Lowly—and of their own degree."

The idea which Poe here enuciates in verse, of those

"who hardly will conceive
That any should become 'great,' born
In *their* own sphere,"

he explains still further in a very characteristic note; it is too idiosyn-
cratic of its author to be ignored. He remarks that "it is a matter of the
greatest difficulty to make the generality of mankind believe that one
with whom they are upon terms of intimacy should be called in the
world a 'great man.' The reason is evident. There are few great men.
Their actions are constantly viewed by the mass of people through the
medium of distance. The prominent parts of their character are alone
noted, and those properties which are minute and common to every
one, not being observed, seem to have no connection with a great character. Who ever read the private memorials, correspondence, &c., which
have become so common in our time," demands the astute lad, "without
wondering that 'great men' should act and think 'so abominably?'"
Returning to "Tamerlane," the suppressed edition continues:

"I pictured to my fancy's eye
Her silent, deep astonishment,
When, a few fleeting years gone by
(For short the time my high hope lent
To its most desperate intent),
She might recall in him whom fame
Had gilded with a conqueror's name
(With glory—such as might inspire,
Perforce, a passing thought of one
Whom she had deemed in his own fire
Withered and blasted; who had gone
A traitor, violate of the truth
So plighted in his early youth),
Her own Alexis, who should plight
The love he plighted *then*—again,

And raise his infancy's delight
The bride and queen of Tamerlane.

"One noon of a bright summer's day
I passed from out the matted bower
Where in a deep still slumber lay
My Ada. In that peaceful hour,
A silent gaze was my farewell,
I had no other solace—then
T'awake her, and a falsehood tell
Of a feigned journey, were again
To trust the weakness of my heart
To her soft thrilling voice. To part
Thus, haply, while in sleep she dreamed
Of long delight, nor yet had deemed,
Awake, that I held a thought
Of parting, were with madness fraught;
I knew not woman's heart, alas!
Though loved and loving—let it pass

I went from out the matted bower
And hurried madly on my way,
And felt with every flying hour
That bore me from my home more gay;
There is of earth an agony
Which, ideal, still may be
The worst ill of mortality.
'Tis bliss, in its own reality.
Too real, to *his* breast, who lives
Not within himself, but gives
A portion of his willing soul
To God, and to the great whole—
To him, whose loving spirit will dwell
With Nature, in her wild paths; tell
Of her wondrous ways and telling, bless
Her overpowering loveliness!
A more than agony to him
Whose failing sight will grow dim
With its own living gaze upon
That loveliness around: the sun—
The blue sky—the misty light
Of the pale cloud therein, whose hue
Is grace to its heavenly bed of blue;
Dim! though looking on all bright!
O God! when thoughts that may not pass
Will burst upon him, and, alas!
For the flight on earth to fancy given
There are no words—unless of Heaven.
. . . . .

When Fortune marked me for her own,
And my proud heart had reached a throne
(It boots me not, good friar, to tell
A tale the world but knows too well,
How by what hidden deeds of might
I clambered to the tottering height),
I still was young; and well I ween
My spirit what it e'er had been.
My eyes still were on pomp and power,
My wildered heart was far away,
In valleys of the wild Taglay,
In mine own Ada's matted bower.
I dwelt not long in Samarcand
Ere, in a peasant's lowly guise,
I sought my long abandoned land:
In sunset did its mountains rise
In dusky grandeur to my eyes.
I reached my home—my home no more—
For all was flown that made it so—
I passed from out its mossy door
In vacant idleness of woe.
There met me on its threshold stone
A mountain hunter I had known,
In childhood, but he knew me not.
Something he spoke of the old cot:
It had seen better days, he said;
There rose a fountain once, and *there*
Full many a fair flower raised its head:
But she who reared them was long dead,
And in such follies had no part.
What was there left me *now*? despair—
A kingdom for a broken heart."

The "Fugitive Pieces" which follow "Tamerlane" call for little comment. They are all more or less strongly tinged with the same cast of
thought which from first to last distinguished their author. The verses
entitled "Evening Star," and the lines beginning "The happiest day,"
are perhaps too indicative of the influence of the boy's contemporaries,
and too crude to be of any remarkable value; but the attention of Poe's
admirers may be confidently claimed for the other four as not only illustrative of his mental history, but as poems of real worth. These are they:

Dreams

Oh! that my young life were a lasting dream!
My spirit not awakened till the beam
Of an eternity should bring the morrow.

Yes! though that long dream were of hopeless
    sorrow,
'Twere better than the cold reality
Of waking life to him whose heart must be
And hath been still upon the lovely earth,
A chaos of deep passion from his birth.
But should it be—that dream eternally
Continuing—as dreams have been to me
In my young boyhood—should it thus be given,
'Twere folly still to hope for higher heaven.
For I have revelled, when the sun was bright
I' the summer sky, in dreams of living light
And loveliness—have left my very heart
In climes of mine imagining apart
From mine own home, with beings that have been
Of mine own thought—what more could I have seen?
'Twas once—and only once—and the wild hour
From my remembrance shall not pass—some power
Or spell had bound me—'twas the chilly wind
Came o'er me in the night, and left behind
Its image on my spirit; or the moon
Shone on my slumbers in her lofty noon
Too coldly, or the stars; however it was,
That dream was at that night wind—let it pass.
I have been happy, though in a dream.
I have been happy, and I love the theme:
Dreams! in their vivid coloring of life
As in that fleeting, shadowy, misty strife
Of semblance with reality, which brings
To the delirious eye more lovely things
Of Paradise and Love—and all our own!—
Than young Hope in his sunniest days hath known.

Visit of the Dead

Thy soul shall find itself alone—
Alone of all on earth—unknown
The cause; but none are near to pry
Into thine hour of secrecy.
Be silent in that solitude,
Which is not loneliness—for then
The spirits of the dead who stood
In life before thee are again
In death around thee, and their will
Shall then o'ershadow thee—be still:
For the night, though clear, shall frown,
And the stars shall not look down

From their thrones in the dark heaven
With light like hope to mortals given;
But their red orbs without beam
To thy withering heart shall seem
As a burning, and a fever
Which would cling to thee forever.
But 'twill leave thee, as each star
In the morning light afar
Will fly thee—and vanish:
But its thought thou canst not banish,
The breath of God will be still;
And the mist upon the hill
By that summer breeze unbroken
Shall charm thee—as a token
And a symbol which shall be
Secrecy in thee.

Evening Star

'Twas noontide of summer,
     And midtime of night;
And stars, in their orbits,
     Shone pale through the light
Of the brighter pale moon.
     'Mid planets her slaves,
Herself in the heavens,
     Her beam on the waves.
     I gazed awhile
     On her cold smile;
Too cold—too cold for me
     There passed, as a shroud,
     A fleecy cloud,
And I turned away to thee,
     Proud Evening Star,
     In thy glory afar,
And dearer thy beam shall be;
     For joy to my heart
     Is the proud part
Thou bearest in heaven at night,
     And more I admire
     Thy distant fire,
Than the colder, lowly light.

Imitation

A dark unfathomed tide
Of interminable pride—
A mystery and a dream
Should my early life seem;

I should say that dream was fraught
With a wild and waking thought
Of beings that have been
Which my spirit hath not seen,
Had I let them pass me by,
With a dreaming eye!
Let none of earth inherit
That vision on my spirit;
Those thoughts I would control
As a spell upon his soul;
For that bright hope at last
And that light time have past.
And my worldly rest hath gone
With a sigh as it passed on:
I care not though it perish
With a thought I then did cherish.

[Stanzas]

How often we forget all time, when lone
Admiring Nature's universal throne;
Her woods—her wiles—her mountains—the intense
Reply of HERS to OUR intelligence!

1.

In youth I have known one with whom the earth
In secret communing held—as he with it,
In daylight, and in beauty, from his birth:
Whose fervid flickering torch of life was lit
From the sun and stars, whence he had drawn forth
A passionate light such for his spirit was fit;
And yet that spirit knew—not in the hour
Of its own fervor—what had o'er it power.

2.

Perhaps it may be that my mind is wrought
To a fever by the moonbeam that hangs o'er,
But I will half believe that wild light fraught
With more of Sov'reignty than ancient lore
Hath ever told—or is it of a thought
The unembodied essence, and no more,
That with a quickening spell doth o'er us pass
As dew of the night time o'er the summer grass?

3.

Doth o'er us pass, when, as th' expanding eve
To the loved object—so the tear to the lid

Will start, which lately slept in apathy?
And yet it need not be—(that object) hid
From us in life—but common—which doth lie
Each hour before us—but *then* only bid
With a strange sound, as a harp-string broken
T' awake us—'tis a symbol and a token

4.

Of what in other worlds shall be—and given
In beauty by our God, to those alone
Who otherwise would fall from life and heaven
Drawn by their heart's passion, and that tone,
That high tone of the spirit which hath striven
Though not with Faith—with godliness—whose
    throne
With desperate energy 't hath beaten down;
Wearing its own deep feeling as a crown.

———————

The happiest day—the happiest hour
    My seared and blighted heart hath known.
The highest hope of pride and power,
    I feel hath flown.

Of power! said I? yes! such I ween;
    But they have vanished long, alas!
The visions of my youth have been—
    But let them pass.

And, pride, what have I now with thee?
    Another brow may ev'n inherit
The venom thou hast poured on me—
    Be still, my spirit.

The happiest day—the happiest hour
    Mine eyes shall see—have even seen,
The brightest glance of pride and power
    I feel—have been:

But were that hope of pride and power
    Now offered, with the pain
Ev'n *then* I felt—that brightest hour
    I would not live again:

For on its wing was dark alloy,
    And as it fluttered fell
An essence powerful to destroy
    A soul that knew it well.

153. *John H. Ingram to Sarah Helen Whitman.   Postcard*

                                                                                     3 June 1876
Yours containing Mrs. H[oughton?]'s card, Mrs. S[mith?]'s letter, &c.
to hand. Do you see our *Notes & Queries*? I have taken up cudgels
there once or twice of late for E.A.P. *v.* your countrymen. I am writing
at the British Museum. The *Union Magazine* (not called *Sartain's
Magazine* until Jany 1849) is before me: in the number for *November*
1848, page 200, is the poem "To ——" by E.A.P. *Graham's* for that
date, or any date, is not here. Up to Jany 1849 the magazine was called
the *Union*, thence to Jany 1850 *Sartain's*, & after Jany 1850 *Sartain's
Union Magazine*. I was, therefore, really correct.

                                                                                           J.H.I.

If the lines appeared in Graham's for Oct. 1848, as you fancy, then
they were probably sent to both magazines, but it is strange that both
should have omitted the same line. The work by "Diabolus" I cannot
discover here.

                                                                                           J.H.I.

154. *Sarah Helen Whitman to John H. Ingram.   Item 214*

My dear friend,   June 16, 1876
Your letter of May 1 [31] with the copy of your article in the
Belgravia duly reached me on the 12th, & yesterday came your card of
June 3. Thanks for your prompt compliance with my request about the
magazine. I am *quite* satisfied now that you had no covert meaning in
proposing the question about *Graham's*. Had you said the poem
appeared in the *Union Magazine*, I should at once have recalled the
fact, but your assertion that it was first published in *Sartain's Union
Magazine*, which *I felt well assured* was not then in existence, made
me think that somebody had *told you* this in order to discredit my
assertion.
We were *both* mistaken as to the name of the magazine, it seems. I
had only my memory to depend upon & I thought it was *Graham's*, &
that it was published in the Oct. number. I have, since receiving your
card, corrected this impression by obtaining with some difficulty a
bound vol. of the *Union* for 1848, and there found the poem which I
told you Poe read to me & also the poem by Wallace, which I
remembered was in the same number & of which I could recall but
one line or couplet. It was not (as I supposed) the first poem in the

number, nor was the line precisely as I quoted it, though the *thought* was identical. Did you notice it?

> No matter what our future fate may be
> To *live* is in itself a majesty!

These were the lines which Poe commented upon.[1]

I do not think that there was any connection whatever between the *New York Magazine* edited by Mrs. Kirkland & *Sartain's Magazine* afterwards published in Philadelphia.[2] But at all events my doubts are satisfied. I am sorry that you were troubled by my making "such a fuss" about it. Do not be afraid to ask me any questions that suggest themselves to you. I will answer them as well as I can, & at all events with sincerity.

I was greatly interested in your extracts from the suppressed "booklet." I have as yet only had time to read them hurriedly. I will be careful not to say where you found them. Mr. Harris said that he wished you *had* appropriated the jewel, so that his conscience was unburthened.

Did I send you an extract or article from the Brooklyn *Times* referring to a letter from Mrs. Weiss? The letter was published in the *Herald*, but I did not see it.

I have lately heard that a paragraph had been going the rounds of the papers stating that the house in which Poe was born is still standing. I doubt not that innumerable tales & anecdotes, true & false, will continue to flood the press about our mysterious poet.

I have just received another letter from Didier. He says Widdleton has written that his MS. must be forwarded by the 2nd week in July. This looks like business. I hope he may add something of value if he enters the arena, but the facts must be better borne out than the *Scribner* facsimile would seem to promise.

I have not yet heard from M. Mallarmé in reply to the letter I mailed to him on the 19th of May, I think, nor have I yet received the book. I begin to fear that it will not come, but I shall cherish his beautiful letter not the less. I have heard nothing of the literary merit of the translation, save what was intimated in Swinburne's letter. The *London Quarterly* is quite savage on Swinburne, I see.

I have been looking at *Notes & Queries*, which is taken at the Athenaeum Library, for the replies to certain attacks on Poe. I did not find them in the last issue. I wish you would name the monthly number in which I can find them.

I have not had a single line from Rose, not even a message through her sister! What can be the matter? They have had some family jars at home which have caused a great scandal here, *i.e.*, her stepmother's father sued his daughters for the care of the property which their uncle left to them, & (being incensed at his having taken a wife) they refused to pay the debt, leaving him utterly destitute. He went to law about it & was so overcome in stating the case that he dropt down dead in the courthouse. Mrs. Peckham was in possession of a hundred & fifty thousand dollars at the time. It is talked of openly as a King Lear tragedy. But Rose, happily, is in no way responsible for her stepdame's delinquencies.

I am grieved to the heart by what you tell me of your ill health & other annoyances; above all, I am sorry that my causeless suspicions should have added to your troubles or given you a moment's unnecessary pain. I should not have been so stirred by having my testimony doubted if the letters received from you last winter had not so deeply wounded me. But it is over & I will not distrust you anymore. Your friendship & sympathy were very dear to me in the strange isolation of my life & I should be sorry indeed to lose them.

You know something of the anxieties of my life. These have increased alarmingly with the last year. It is true that I have hosts of friends and correspondents who look to me for sympathy & cheer, for counsel & inspiration. But they are not near enough to react on my own spirit, which would often be desolate indeed but for the few who understand & love me. And these few are often excluded by the morbid moods & baseless antipathies of the one whose peace of mind it is the object of my life to preserve at any sacrifice.

You will understand & will keep sacred the confidence I repose in you. But my whole life seems sometimes a sacrifice to this object. It may lead you to understand much that may otherwise seem incomprehensible. Yet I doubt not the whole will seem in that life which awaits us not only just & right but supremely beautiful & good.

I will try to write again soon. In the meantime think of me as faithfully and sincerely your friend,

S. H. Whitman

Ask me *any* questions you like. I will not make "a fuss," nevermore.

1. William Ross Wallace's poem "Chant of a Soul" appeared in the *Union Magazine of Literature and Art*, Oct. 1848, p. 215.
2. For Mrs. Caroline Kirkland, see p. 114, n. 3.

155. *John H. Ingram to Sarah Helen Whitman*

My dear Friend, 28 June 1876

That is a title I cannot improve. Let us now be as we were of yore before the clouds swept across the horizon of our hope.

I am glad you got the *Belgravia* paper safely. Were you not deeply interested in the lines? You cannot believe how I valued them—knowing how those shorter pieces were poured forth from the poet's heart of hearts.

I sent the advance sheets to Browne to copyright; he did so, but the New York *Daily Graphic* of the 8th Instant has published nearly the whole paper, & it is, doubtless, by this time, all over the States—it is too bad.

I am glad you are satisfied about the *bona fides* of my question of the "Lines." It was rude & wrong of me to use such a word as "fuss," but all is now forgiven, *n'est ce pas*? Let me, however, say that nothing told me by *any*one could ever have shaken my faith in you—only *my own* feelings & fancies could ever have dimmed my trust (not in your fidelity—but) in your feelings.

I have nearly completed the chronological list of the first publications of poems & tales. A *complete* list of *The Gift* might add one or two to the latter. Burton's last & Graham's first vols., under Poe, are now *en route* to me.

I do not think it matters now about the author being given as "a Bostonian," but we'll "wait a wee."

At editorial request I have written a paper for the *Athenaeum* on "The Bibliography of Poe"—poems only. When this appears I will send an extra copy for Mr. Harris, & if he will kindly send any notes or comments his knowledge may suggest, I shall be thankful.

The true date as to the publication of the tales &c. resolves into thin air many of the idle lies told of Poe.

Do you not see *Notes & Queries*? 'Tis much read in America. I'll send you the numbers containing my present correspondence & if you see your way to speak a word it will be valuable. Did you ever hear of Miss Georgiana Sherburne, or her story of "Imogene; or the Miser's Treasure" from which Poe's "The Gold-Bug" shall be plagiarized? I shall utterly break up the accusation, I feel assured, if they will only continue the correspondence. Did you know this Duffee?

I am very poorly & worn & 'tis late—so wait till tomorrow for the rest of this scrawl.

29 June 1876

I have found the address of Wallace & written to him. I hope something from him—if he has not been silenced by the Philistines—for he *was* a true poet in days of yore,—one from whom I should have predicted great things.

I think you sent me copy of Mrs. Weiss' letter—at all events four or five copies are to hand. I need scarcely remark that it is not quite correct as to *data*.[1]

How I long for a verbal—*viva voce*—communication. I have so many things to tell & be inquired about.

I doubt about the existence of the birthplace, but have not seen the paragraph—let me, if you get copy. I hope we may get some gleams of light from Didier, but his evidence will need sifting.

Mallarmé is a bad correspondent. He said he had sent *Le Corbeau* a long time ago. I sent him your slip & begged him to send copy. He could not find means of transport for some time. Pray do not be disappointed with it when you get it. 'Tis *outre*. He has recently produced an edition *de* luxe of a poem of his own, *L'Apres-Midi d'un Faune*, & a reprint of Beckford's *Vathek* from 1st edition.[2] So he has had plenty to do.

The "Marginalia" I fancy is translated by Camille Mendès. It includes a note I hate & would have liked to suppress, but that I know Poe wrote it.

I *must* send you *La République des Lettres* when I can get another copy. I have so much to think of.

Notes & Queries nos. for 22 April, 6 May, 24 June contain my Poe correspondence with "Uneda."[3] Attack was begun under heading "Philadelphia Authors." I give these particulars, as I see you say you have *N&Q* in your Athenaeum. If it turn out well I may republish the correspondence, with a few notes of my own.

I have never answered Miss Peckham. What atrocity!

We should sympathize. *My* life has been so far a sacrifice—perhaps is sacrificed—for others. So you must not think me bad natured that I cannot bear *all* with lamblike resignation, or sometimes grow cross.

I trust your pains in reading this scrawl will not equal mine in writing it, and ever am, pray believe, *tout á vous*.

John H. Ingram

1. Mrs. Susan Archer Talley Weiss addressed a letter on Apr. 10, 1876, to the editor of the New York *Herald* in which she denied Elizabeth Oakes Smith's story of Poe's having been beaten to death (New York *Home Journal*, Mar. 15, 1876) and offered her account of Poe's last visit to Richmond in the summer of 1849. See Item 683 in the Ingram Poe Collection.

2. Mallarmé, *L'Après-Midi d'un Faune* (Paris: Alphonse Derenne, 1876); William Beckford, *Vathek* (Paris: Labitte, 1876).

3. Uneda's answer to Ingram, *Notes and Queries*, 5th ser., 5 (June 24, 1876), 526: "Mr. J.H. INGRAM has taken exception to an opinion of mine that Poe was a most unprincipled man, and also to my assertion that he borrowed his story of *The Gold Bug* without acknowledging his indebtedness. The columns of 'N.&Q.' are not the proper place for argument upon the first point. Mr. INGRAM says that he knew Poe—I also knew him. I have written, privately, to Mr. INGRAM my reasons for the very decided opinion that I entertain upon Poe's moral character. It is one thing to admit the excellence of a writer's imagination, and another thing to believe him a valuable member of society. I will only

add that I never heard any one in this country express any other opinion than that which I entertain respecting the character of Poe. Mr. Duffee has furnished me with the following remarks upon the subject of Poe's borrowing the story of *The Gold Bug*:— 'I did accuse Edgar A Poe of plagiarism, a charge which was never disproved. He borrowed not only the plot but the language of Miss Georgiana Sherburne's tale of *Imogene; or, the Pirate's Treasure*. In fact, Miss Sherburne (daughter of Col. Sherburne, U.S.A.) informed me, in the first place, of the plagiarism, and I exposed Poe in an article in one of our daily papers, for which he commenced a libel suit, and employed Mr. David Paul Brown, who, after receiving a letter from me, soon dismissed the matter, for very good reasons.'

"I may add to the above that the authoress of Imogene is now residing in New York, the wife of a son of one of the most distinguished commodores in the American navy."

156.   *Sarah Helen Whitman to John H. Ingram.   Item 295*

My dear Friend,   July 11, [18]76

I have just received yours of the 28th. Thanks for sending me the numbers of *Notes & Queries* containing your correspondence with "Uneda." I shall try to look at it this P.M. if the intense heat does not prevent, but not in time I fear to revert to it in this letter.

I shall look with interest for the *Athenaeum* paper.

I am curious to know what note you would like to have suppressed in the "Marginalia," as published by Mendès. Is it suppressed in your edition of the works?[1] I am heartily in favor of suppressing (at least in all matters not affecting important truths) whatever may seem to an editor irrelevant or likely to injure the reputation of his author. I rely on your usual prompt kindness to enlighten me. I have been looking over Griswold's edition & yours, but cannot find any note in either which seems to call for so strong a word as that you have applied to it.

You speak of having received many copies of Mrs. Weiss's letter, one of which you think was sent by me. On the contrary, I have not even *seen* it. Can you spare me one of the copies in your possession? I wish very much to see it.

Mrs. Von Weiss, it seems, is the Susan Archer Talley whose poems have been spoken of so favorably by Griswold. The specimens given by him being chiefly haunting echoes or variations from Tennyson's "Lady of Shalott."

I was profoundly interested in the specimens of Poe's first published collection of poems. Mr. Harris was surprised not to find the three classic stanzas "To Helen." Were not you?

All that you say about your discoveries as to the order of his prose articles, stories, & poems is intensely interesting to me.

In answer to certain questions put to me by Mr. Didier as to the discrepancy between Mr. Willis's statements & my own concerning the time of Poe's removal to Fordham, I had an opportunity to refute some recent scandals pretty effectively. The letter which I commenced with the intention of writing only a brief note grew to an unexpected length, & he thinks if published *just as it stands* will have great weight in disproving them. I know my treatment of the subject will interest you & will meet with your cordial sympathy. Some benignant Fate gave me the opportunity to refute them almost without an effort on my part. There is nothing personal in the communication, not a word in allusion to myself.

I have not yet answered my letter from Rose. The domestic atmosphere is not serener than when I last wrote, and a thunderstorm, most grateful after the long continued heat & drought of the last three weeks, is rolling & crashing overhead.

Will write next week. Ever faithfully your friend,

S.H.W.

My dear friend,   July 18, 1876
A week of intolerable heat has passed since I wrote the enclosed hurried note. Prevented from mailing it by the storm of Tuesday evening last, I have been hoping day after day to write you more fully, but disappointed in the hope, will send off a delayed note.

I have been twice to the Athenaeum to examine the *Notes & Queries*. Have seen the April & May numbers with the astonishing claim put forth in them! The June number has not yet arrived. I never heard of Miss Georgiana Sherburne or her story of Imogene! I think her bug, if examined by an entomologist, will turn out a humbug. As soon as I can get the June number, I will take note of it.

I have been pondering over that note to which you refer in "Marginalia." If I am not mistaken, it was intended as a mere play upon words, or an *extravaganza*, like the recipe to cure a boy from squinting. *N'est ce pas*? It is absurd, but I should hardly say "hateful." Tell me about it.

I have not seen Mr. Harris since I received your last. He called last week, but I was too unwell to see him.

Ever sincerely your friend, who would fain be your "Providence,"
S.H.W.

I have not yet found time to answer my letter from Rose. Her sister Grace called on me yesterday & told me Rose would stay another year. The family have given up their house in town.

I did not know that the early poems had been republished in the *Graphic*. I have been completely *insulated* during the devitalizing weather of the last four or five weeks.

---

1. The note in Poe's "Marginalia" Ingram wanted to suppress reads, "That man is not truly brave who is afraid either to seem or to be, when it suits him, a coward."

157. "The Bibliography of Edgar Poe," by John H. Ingram, London Athenaeum, *July 29, 1876, pp. 145–46*

The Bibliography of Edgar Poe

HALF A CENTURY has not elapsed since the author of "The Raven" printed his first little volume of verse, and yet, not only it, but also two later editions or collections, have become so extremely rare that the most diligent bibliographers seek for them in vain. Even the fourth and latest collection of the poems of Edgar Poe issued during their author's lifetime, is becoming scarce. These early editions being so rare, and a large portion of their contents quite unknown, some account of them cannot fail to prove interesting. Like some other modern poets, Edgar Poe, in the later part of his short career, discarded a very large portion of his juvenile verse, and refined and abridged much of that which he retained. Doubtless, what has been lost in quantity has been regained in quality, nevertheless, it will not be an inglorious occupation for the student to gather up the few chips still left in the master's workshop.

Edgar Poe's first tiny tome, consisting of only forty pages, was printed in the author's natal city of Boston in 1827, but suppressed previous to publication. It bears upon its title-page:—

TAMERLANE

AND

OTHER POEMS .

BY A BOSTONIAN.

"Young heads are giddy, and young hearts are warm,
And make mistakes for manhood to reform."—*Cowper.*

BOSTON: CALVIN F. S. THOMAS.

1827.

Having so recently given a full description of, and lengthy extracts from, this unknown volume (*Belgravia Magazine*, for June, 1876), many further particulars are no longer necessary; the coincidence may, however, be pointed out that the excerpt from Martial—*"Nos haec novimus esse nihil,"*—with which Poe's Preface concludes, was also that selected as a motto for the title-page of "Poems by Two Brothers," published in the same year, and generally considered to be Tennyson's first publication. There are several palpable *errata* in Edgar Poe's first book, which was anything but an *édition de luxe*, so that, apart from private reasons, its author was justified in its suppression. The Preface is followed by "Tamerlane," which occupies 17 pp., and is an almost entirely different poem to that now known by the same title; nothing less than the entire republication of the former could show all the variations between the two. The later draft being indented and better punctuated, is more pleasing to the eye, but the older version contains many passages fully equal in beauty to the best of its successor. A more connected story is afforded by the 1827 version of "Tamerlane" than by the later editions; in it the heroine is named as Ada, and the hero is styled Alexis, Tamerlane being deemed only a *nom de guerre*: eleven notes, suppressed in the later editions, accompany the poem. Following "Tamerlane" are nine "Fugitive Pieces"; five of these have never been reprinted until now; one other, somewhat revised, reappeared in the 1829 collection, whilst the remaining three are reprinted, nearly *verbatim*, in the present editions. Dreams are the chief theme of Poe's first volume, and in it first appeared, but with the following stanza (now omitted) prefixed, the little lyric entitled "A Dream":—

> A wildered being from my birth,
>   My spirit spurned control,
> But now, abroad on the wide earth,
>   Where wanderest thou my soul?

Poe's first acknowledged collection, that of 1829, bears the following title-page:—

AL AARAAF,

TAMERLANE

AND

MINOR POEMS.

BY EDGAR A. POE.

BALTIMORE: HATCH AND DUNNING.

1829.

This volume was printed for private circulation. It contains only 66 pp. and many of those are merely extra leaves and bastard titles. The real contents include "Al Aaraaf," substantially as now printed, and prefixed to it, but then unnamed, the sonnet now styled "To Science." Dedicated to John Neal, follows the present version of "Tamerlane," and, thereafter, several Miscellaneous Poems: these smaller pieces include the lines now known as "Romance," but then called "Preface";

the song, "I saw thee on thy bridal day"; "The Lake," from the suppressed volume of 1827; and six other pieces. Five of these latter are, save some trifling corrections, as still published, but in the following lines "To M———" appear three stanzas not yet reprinted; the whole poem, as it stands in the 1829 edition, reads thus:—

> O! I care not that my earthly lot
>   Hath—little of earth in it—
> That years of love have been forgot
>   In the fever of a minute—
>
> I heed not that the desolate
>   Are happier, sweet than I—
> But that *you* meddle with *my* fate
>   Who am a passer-by.
>
> It *is* not that my founts of bliss
>   Are gushing—strange! with tears—
> Or that the thrill of a single kiss
>   Hath palsied many years—
>
> 'Tis not that the flowers of twenty springs
>   Which have withered as they rose
> Lie dead on my heart-strings
>   With the weight of an age of snows.
>
> Nor that the grass—O! may it thrive!
>   On my grave is growing or grown—
> But that, while I am dead yet alive,
>   I cannot be, lady, alone.

The title-page of the 1831 collection is:—

POEMS

By

EDGAR A. POE

"Tout le monde a raison." Rochefoucauld.

SECOND EDITION.

New York: Elam Bliss.

1831.

This volume contains 124 pp.; it is dedicated to the United States Corps of Cadets, and is prefaced by a letter to a "Mr. B———," doubtless a mythical person. This letter, dated from West Point, Poe afterwards republished, with some slight alterations, as a magazine paper. The shorter poems lead the van, beginning with a poetical "Introduction" of sixty-six lines, an expansion of the twenty-one lines known as "Preface" in 1829. These additional lines were subsequently suppressed; but the following exerpt will show that they are worthy of preservation, not only as a fair sample of the idiosyncracies, but also of the poetic powers, of their author. After verse 10, the suppressed lines run:—

> Succeeding years too wild for song,
> Then rolled like tropic storms along,
> Where, tho' the garish lights that fly
> Dying along the troubled sky,
> Lay bare, thro' vistas thunder-riven,
> The blackness of the general Heaven,
> That very blackness yet doth fling
> Light on the lightning's silver wing.
>
> For, being an idle boy lang syne,
> Who read Anacreon and drank wine,
> I early found Anacreon rhymes
> Were almost passionate sometimes—
> And by strange alchemy of brain
> His pleasures always turn'd to pain—
> His naiveté to wild desire—
> His wit to love—his wine to fire—
> And so, being young and dipt in folly
> I fell in love with melancholy,
> And used to throw my earthly rest
> And quiet all away in jest—
> I could not love except where Death
> Was mingling his with Beauty's breath—
> Or Hymen, Time, and Destiny
> Were stalking between her and me. . . . .
>
> But *now* my soul hath too much room—
> Gone are the glory and the gloom—
> The black hath mellowed into grey,
> And all the fires are fading away.
>
> My draught of passion hath been deep—
> I revell'd and I now would sleep—
> And after drunkenness of soul
> Succeed the glories of the bowl—
> And idle longing night and day
> To dream my very life away.
>
> But dreams—of those who dream as I,
> Aspiringly, are damned and die:
> Yet should I swear I mean alone,

By notes so very shrilly blown,
To break upon Time's monotone,
And yet my vapid joy and grief
Are tintless of the yellow leaf—
Why not an imp the greybeard hath,
Will shake his shadow in my path—
And even the greybeard will o'erlook
Connivingly my dreaming-book.

These lines are followed by the exquisite lyric, "To Helen"; by the earliest known version of "Israfel"; by "The Doomed City," afterwards improved and rechristened "The City in the Sea"; by a much expanded and weakened version of "Fairyland"; by "Irene," subsequently much altered and abridged, and published as "The Sleeper"; by "A Paean," chiefly remarkable as being the germ of that melodious and exultant defiance of Death, the poem of "Lenore"; and, finally, as far as the "Miscellaneous Poems" are concerned, by some lines entitled "The Valley Nis," which lines ultimately, much curtailed and revised, were renamed "The Valley of Unrest." This 1831 collection consists chiefly, however, of enlarged but scarcely improved versions of "Al Aaraaf" and "Tamerlane"; the variations, indeed, in this edition are inferior in poetic value to those in the earlier volumes, and the punctuation is neither so good nor so characteristic, and leads one to the conclusion that the little book was very hastily prepared for the press. Both the longer poems, upon republication, were again reduced to their original dimensions of 1829; from the suppressed portions the following lines, from the Prelude to "Al Aaraaf," will be interesting:—

Thy world has not the dross of ours
Yet all the beauty—all the flowers
That list our love or deck our bowers
In dreamy gardens where do lie
Dreamy maidens all the day;
While the silver winds of Circassy
On violet couches faint away.

Little—oh! little dwells in thee
Like unto what on earth we see:
Beauty's eye is here the bluest
In the falsest and untruest—
On the sweetest air doth float
The most sad and solemn note—
If with thee be broken hearts,
Joy so peacefully departs,
That its echo still doth dwell,
Like the murmur in the shell.
Thou! thy truest type of grief

> Is the gently falling leaf—
> Thou! thy framing is so holy,
> Sorrow is not melancholy.

From 1831 to 1844, Poe scarcely wrote any poetry, although he occasionally revised and republished in periodicals much that had appeared in his juvenile volumes. Midway, however, in this poetically barren period, he published two of his finest, if not the finest of all his poems, "The Haunted Palace" and "The Conqueror Worm." This long interregnum of poetic silence was succeeded by a period of great brilliancy inaugurated in February, 1845, by the universally admired "Raven," and only ending (at the poet's death) in October, 1849, with the posthumous publication of "Annabel Lee." The *furore* created by "The Raven," undoubtedly encouraged its author to return to poesy, and to publish, in November, 1845, his final but incomplete collection of poems, as,—

THE RAVEN,

AND

OTHER POEMS.

BY

EDGAR A. POE.

NEW YORK:
WILEY AND PUTNAM, 161, BROADWAY.
1845.

The little book, although it only contains 90 pp., holds much more matter than its still punier predecessors. It is most enthusiastically dedicated "to the noblest of her sex," to Mrs. Browning (then Miss Barrett), and is heralded by the same Preface which introduces all the posthumous editions. "The Raven," which takes the lead in the volume, is as now reprinted; in earlier publications there had been many variations and gradual changes, of which the most noteworthy is the alteration, at the end of the 11th stanza, from the original reading of,—

> So, when Hope he would adjure,
> Stern Despair returned, instead of the sweet
> Hope he dared adjure,
> That sad answer, Nevermore.

to its present masterly roll of melancholy music. Besides the poems confessedly "Written in Youth," the work contains several others which are but revisions of his juvenile labours; an amended draft of the "Coliseum," for which a prize had been awarded him in 1833; scenes from his unpublished tragedy of "Politian," written somewhat about the same period; the few pieces which had had written during his married life, and the definitive republications of his two longer poems, "Al Aaraaf" and "Tamerlane."

Of the incomplete collection of Edgar Poe's poems published upon his death, and of the innumerable native and foreign editions and translations published since, there is no need for me to now speak.

John H. Ingram

158. *John H. Ingram to Sarah Helen Whitman*

My dear Providence,   3 Aug. 1876
   I was *so* thankful to get yours dated 11th & 28th Ultimo, as it seemed ages since I had heard from you.
   With respect to the Marginal note I alluded to, perhaps I overestimated its value, but I feared it might be used as a handle to countenance cruel slanders, besides that it is quite contrary to my ideas. You will find it on page 368, Vol. iii, of my edition—called "Cowardice," & numbered xxxviii. Had I not *known* it was by Poe I would have omitted it, but he published it and I could not safely cancel it, without chance of it reappearing some day.
   When the "Uneda" v. J. H. Ingram correspondence is concluded I will send you full copies. I mean the *Notes & Queries* affair. "Uneda" has written to me accusing Poe of all kinds of *filthy* crimes, but my letter (of which you shall have eventually have copy) will be a "shutter up" I fancy.[1]
   You will have got my paper on "The Bibliography of Poe" in *Athenaeum*, I trust, before this. I'll send another copy as soon as I can get one. They sold out, the newsvender tells me.
   I return Miss Peckham's note with many thanks. I wrote to her at once, & asked her where she is to be found. I expect to leave for France on Saturday. I am quite knocked up, but must not get beyond two days' post of London just now.
   I will look out & send you a copy of Mrs. Weiss's letter. I thought you sent me one copy. I send it in my next.
   My earliest dates of the tales (as to the publication) are nearly complete—only a few (most of which appeared or reappeared) in the *Broadway J[ournal]* are not yet certain.
   I am not surprised that the lyric "To Helen" did not appear in the

1827 volume. It is my firm opinion that Poe did not know Mrs. S[tanard] so early in life as we thought—more of this some day.

I have been waiting for a letter from Mrs. Richmond, who promised a mutual friend to write, but no news *yet*.

W. Ross Wallace has not answered yet.

Pray do not be reluctant to give Mr. Didier any information on my account. I should be glad to help him myself, if I were *sure* he were on our side. Pray publish your letter.

I should be glad if you could find time to write a *short* note to Editor (Dr. Doran) of *Notes & Queries* (asking for information, say, as to when & where "Imogene" was published) & alluding to the allegation that no American spoke well of Poe.

I am quite exhausted. I shall try & [write] a more connected letter from Normandy.

Meanwhile & ever, I am, pray believe me, yours most faithfully,

John H. Ingram

1. Although Uneda's personal letter to Ingram has not survived, the "shutter up" letter to Uneda was printed in *Notes and Queries*, 5th ser., 6 (July 22, 1876), 78: "I agree with UNEDA that the columns of 'N. & Q.' are not the proper place for discussing a man's character, even though that man be celebrated, and regret that the discussion has been forced upon me by the imputation cast upon POE. UNEDA will scarcely expect me to recount the long list of Americans who have not only expressed verbally, but even in print, an opinion respecting Poe's character different from that he entertains, and I content myself with referring to John P. Kennedy, John Neal, Frances S. Osgood, Mrs. Whitman, N. P. Willis, Mrs. Gove Nichols, W. J. Pabodie, Thomas C. Clarke, L. A. Godey, and George R. Graham, all American authors, and four of them from Philadelphia. Of Miss Georgiana Sherburne or of *Imogene; or, the Pirate's Treasure*, I cannot find any trace in Duyckinck's *Cyclopaedia of American Literature*, in Allibone's *Dictionary*, or in Trubner's *Guide*. This last omission is almost conclusive that Miss Sherburne's tale was not published in book form; I am, therefore, again compelled to ask UNEDA, in justice to the dead, and for the satisfaction of the living, to state how, when, and where this charge of literary theft was proved against Edgar A. Poe. Mr. Duffee's letter gives no particulars as to the necessary *data*."

More than a year passed before Uneda replied, and by that time relations between Ingram and Mrs. Whitman were so strained there is no way of knowing whether she ever saw Uneda's abject surrender. *Notes and Queries*, 5th ser., 8 (Aug. 11, 1877), 115–16:

"Since the appearance of the demand made by MR. INGRAM in the communication last above referred to, I have been of opinion that it should have been addressed to Mr. Duffee, and ought to have been answered by him. As he has remained silent, I feel it to be my duty to state that, after much trouble and a considerable expenditure of time, I have come across a copy of *Imogene*. It is a very extraordinary work for a girl of thirteen to produce, but it does not bear the slightest resemblance to Poe's story of the Gold Bug, either in its incidents or its style. I cannot imagine why my friend Mr. Duffee was made the victim of so silly a hoax.

"Miss Sherburne has been married to a Mr. Hull; but I am informed that he is not of the family of our distinguished commodores. She resides in Brooklyn, N.Y., and is one of the writers for the New York *Tribune*."

159. Sarah Helen Whitman to John H. Ingram.   Item 299

My dear Mr. Ingram,   Aug. 25, [18]76
    I duly received your welcome letter of ten days ago [Aug. 3?], &
have since received two copies of the London *Athenaeum* containing
your valuable paper on the poems. Learning that Mr. Harris was in
town yesterday (I have not *seen* him for weeks, having been too ill to
see anyone), I sent him the copy intended for him. I have been utterly
prostrated by the weather and write even this brief note with difficulty.
I have *tried* to write by every Wednesday & Saturday steamer since I
received your last, but without being able to accomplish my purpose.
    Have not yet answered the letter of our friend Rose. (Our friend and
mine), Mrs. Paulina Wright Davis, died last night. She knew your
friends, Mrs. Nichols & Mrs. Houghton. I shall have much to say to
Rose if I live to write her as I wish. Tell her this, if you see her.
    I told you that I had not hesitated to deny that paragraph in the
Home Journal attributed to Mrs. Oakes Smith about a personal assault
on Poe by the friends of one whom he had ruined & betrayed. I wrote
to her for the first time in ten or twelve years to tell her that I had done
so, that is, to express my conviction that it did not emanate from her,
was not written by her, not authorized by her. I send you her card in
reply. Since then I have had two most kind letters from her. In the last,
dated August 18, she says, "Mr. Ingram is doing a just & true work in
regard to Mr. Poe. He tells me he dedicated it to you. Is it not strange
how malice follows up this dead-living genius?"
    I enclose to you a copy of an article which I wrote for the Providence
Journal some five weeks ago. Perhaps the work treating of the
challenge sent by Pinckney, and challenge which he dared to refuse,
may have some bearing on the question involved in the *note* which
you would have expunged from "Marginalia."
    I am getting very tired. Will write by Wednesday's steamer, if
possible.
    I long to see the whole of the Uneda correspondence & Mrs. Weiss's
article in the *Herald*. I long to know all you have learned about Mrs.
Stanard.
    Everything here is in a state of collapse. Is the world coming to an
end, think you?
    I hope your visit to Paris will make you quite well. Gill has been
achieving notoriety by sliding down a ravine of the White mountains!
To me he is as the "missing link" or the "Lost Pleiad."
    Benedicte,

                                                    S. H. Whitman
    I want you to tear off the outside leaf of this sheet & send it back to

me. What if it should go before the world with all its blots, in some coming era when your residuary legatees come into possession!

160. *John H. Ingram to Sarah Helen Whitman*

My dear Providence,   12 Sept. 1876
   Still my Providence—although I am *now* Mr. "Ingram".
   I am just returned to town after an absence (from office) of five weeks, and meet your ever welcome epistle (Aug. 25). I have had to give up America this year as my engagements would not well permit me to go beyond two or three days' post from London.
   I went through Normandy, came back to town, & then went to Weymouth, a pleasant English seaside place, where a party of my relatives were staying. Among young people—children—I grew quite a boy once more, & can scarcely, as yet, buckle to the stern matter-of-factness of work.
   My health, I am thankful to relate, is marvellously improved, and I feel in that state when open air life—even an agricultural labourer's—would be preferable to this prison-like existence here. However, I must be grateful for even a temporary lease of health—it won't last long!
   I wish you had better news of yourself to give, but the terribly hot weather has been most trying. Now *we* are are complaining in London of the cold.
   I have heard twice lately from Miss Peckham & owe her a letter. Had the first letter arrived two days sooner I should have sought her out in Holland, but it was too late. I had already made my plans & left for France. But this is not very interesting for you.
   Many thanks for the memo. about John Neal. I had received a letter & papers announcing his decease from his daughter, but had no time to notice his death here. I must do so, though.
   Did you see the letters in *Athenaeum* by Forman & Theodore Watts, which my paper "Bibliography of Poe" invoked?[1] As soon as settled down, I shall answer latter.
   I have several letters needing reply from Browne, Davidson, & others in America.
   Mrs. Houghton has just written & *so has Mrs. Richmond.* Latter writes a long letter declaring the purity & beauty of Poe's character. Shall I not be able to produce an unassailable & exhaustive protraiture of our hero? I feel that I must live to do it.
   The *République des Lettres* is now giving translations of the poems,

452   *Poe's Helen Remembers*

&c. The last (by Mallarmé) was the "Lines to Helen"—to you. I must get you a copy. I have thoroughly stirred up Young France, through some of its leaders, about Poe.

Entre nous, I regret to say that I do not believe a single word of your imaginative friend "Eva"'s denial of the paragraph in the *Home Journal. I had the MS. in my own hands, in her writing, containing it!* Pray be careful about accepting her denial in print. I will return her card in my next, but do not ask for the outside leaf of your letter back. I do not wish to part with a scrap of your letters to me, & there is nothing in the leaf for you to be ashamed of, my dear Providence.

I fancy "Uneda" has collapsed. My private letter was too much for her, or him.

I will look up a copy of the letter from Mrs. Weiss to send in my next.

My heap of unanswered communications is so terrible that I must forego all further news for the present, save that relating to a portrait of Poe.

Do you know Bruckmann's *Gallery of Celebrated Men*—poets, musicians, &c.?[2] Well known in Europe & America. From my portraits (especially the one used for my "Memoir") he has had a portrait painted, & photographed in various sizes, & as soon as it is copyrighted in Washington you shall have one of the largest size. Then let me know your opinion. Though, necessarily, an ideal portrait, I deem it, in most respects, doubtless a good one. It will be published & known all over the globe. Even my poor efforts, you see, spread the fame of our hero & I shall never cease, whilst life & brain remain, to continue these efforts, & to be, yours most devotedly,

J. H. Ingram

1. Harry Buxton Forman (1842–1917) had asked in the London *Athenaeum*, Aug. 5, 1876, p. 177, for clarification of Ingram's statement in his recent paper on the bibliography of Poe that there had been "earlier publications" of the title poem before it appeared in the 1845 *The Raven and Earlier Poems*. Foreman added that while both Tennyson and Poe had Southey's example of the familiar epigraph from Martial before them, Tennyson had reversed the opening words to *Haec nos*, while both Poe and Southey had used *Nos Haec novimus esse nihil.*

Ingram answered Forman in the *Athenaeum*, Aug. 19, 1876, p. 241, that "The Raven" had been published earlier in various periodicals and under Poe's supervision before it appeared in book form.

Theodore Watts-Dunton (1832–1914) on Sept. 2, 1876, brought up in the *Athenaeum*, p. 306, the old question about Poe's having adapted "The Raven" from the Persian, and suggested that Poe had read Mr. Mudford's story in *Blackwood's* before he composed "The Pit and the Pendulum," as well as suggesting that Poe's "Arthur Gordon Pym" owed something to Coleridge's "Mariner," a Scottish story, "Allan Gordon," and another remarkable story, "The Lonely Man of the Ocean," which had appeared in the *Monthly Magazine*, four years before "Pym" came out in the *Southern Literary Messenger*.

Ingram did not answer Watts-Dunton.

2. Friedrich Bruckmann (1814–1898) was a well-known photographer, certainly, although a search through both the Library of Congress and the British Museum Library catalogues failed to reveal a book with this title.

161.   *Sarah Helen Whitman to John H. Ingram.*   Item 302

My dear friend,   Oct. 19, [18]76

It gave me heartfelt joy to hear of your health & happiness in your letter of September the 12th. I wish that you could pass more of your time in that open air, congenial life you describe so felicitously.

I found on the Athenaeum table the allusion to your admirable paper on the poetry of Poe by Forman, but have not yet seen that by Theodore Watts which you say you shall answer soon. Our copies of the London periodicals are always behindtime.

If you would give me the *date* of any article on subjects referred to in your letters, I could obtain them from Mr. Bartlett. He informed me that he had seen several allusions to your paper in that & other journals which he is in the habit of sending to friends in Cambridge, soon after he receives them.

I saw in a Southern paper among the names of the writers who were to contribute to the Memorial volume to be published in Baltimore, that you were to furnish a "Memoir" of Poe.

At the request of Miss Rice, W. D. O'Connor wrote an article which the advisers of Miss Rice wished him to modify in one or two particulars which it was apprehended would have a tendency to affect its local popularity. The volume being assumed to rely specially for its immediate success on the favor of the Baltimoreans. This *entre nous*. Whether O'Connor will consent to the modification is still a question.

If you can tell me where I can obtain a copy of the *République des Lettres*, the number containing the translation of the poem *a moi meme*, I should like to obtain one.

Mr. Bartlett told me last week that he saw some time ago at a bookstore in New York a copy of the illustrated *Corbeau*. He did not like the work of the artist, Manet. I have since seen an artist from Boston, Henri Bacon, who has just returned from Paris, knows & likes Manet, but does not like his work. Did you see Mallarmé when you were in Paris?

I shall be delighted to receive the portrait you promise me, the Bruckmann Gallery portrait.

I should like to know the true date & history of the daguerreotype given you by Mrs. Lewis & copied by Fredericks into Gill's *Laurel Leaves*.

I am glad that you have had in the letter of Mrs. Richmond such a gracious tribute to Poe's genuine goodness of heart & character. The letters which Mrs. Clemm sent me from that lady, letters received after her return from a long visit to Lowell—a whole winter spent at her house, convinced me of her fidelity to his memory.

Mr. Didier's "Memoir" is to preface the Household Edition of Poe's poems. I can hardly doubt that it will be favorable to him. We shall soon see.

As to E[lizabeth] O[akes] S[mith], your assertion that you had in your possession the MS. of the offensive *paragraph* published in the *Home Journal*—surely you do not mean that the paragraph stating that Poe came to his death through a brutal personal assault "from the brothers of a woman whom he had *betrayed & ruined*"—you do not mean that the MS. of *this* (a brief paragraph) was, or had been in your hands? If so, all human testimony would seem questionable. She admits the story of an assault from the brothers of a woman whose letters he had declined to return, as you know, but this is *altogether a different charge*.

I saw last evening in looking over a bound volume of *Scribner's* for the last half of the year 1875 a paragraph in the Bric-a-Brac department of the magazine for Nov. referring to the publication of a facsimile poem by Poe, as presented in the Sept. number. It purported to come from R. L. P. Allen, "late superintendent of the Kentucky Military Institue," who says Poe was a classmate of his, etc., etc. that he entered West Point Academy with him in 1830 & finding the routine uncongenial to him, *withdrew* in less than a year, that he, Mr. Allen, on leaving the Military School in 1834, went to Baltimore where he was informed that Poe was at that time engaged in a Baltimore brickyard wheeling bricks, like "rare Ben Jonson." This sounds somewhat Brick-a-Brackish. Did you see the item? You will find the story in the November *Scribner* for 1875.[1]

Gill has just turned up again after a year's silence, and in a very characteristic way, I have received within a week two letters from him. I will tell you about them next time.

I must close now, with a Benedicite. Yours faithfully,

S. H. Whitman

1. *Scribner's Magazine*, 11 (1875), 142–143:

Farmdale, Kentucky
September 10, 1875

I notice in your September number fac-simile of a poem by Poe, dated March, 1829, and said to have been written after he left West Point. E. L. D. is in error. Poe was a member of my class at the Military Academy—which entered the Academy in June, 1830, and he left the Institution sometime in 1831. I remember him well. While at the Academy he published a small volume of poems which were not thought to have much merit. He was too much occupied with his poetry to attend to the severe studies of the course at the Academy, and hence resigned, in order to devote his whole time to poetry.

The writer, having graduated, left the Academy in 1834, and, while visiting a friend in Baltimore in the fall of that year, was asked by a casual acquaintance if he knew Edgar Allan Poe, who had informed the gentleman alluded to that he was acquainted with me. On responding in the affirmative, I was told that *Poe was then working in a brickyard in Baltimore, being engaged in wheeling clay in a wheelbarrow.* This may throw light on that part of his history immediately after his leaving the Academy.　　　R.T.P.A.

(R.T.P. Allen, of the Class of 1834, late Superintendent of Kentucky Military Institute.)

162.　*John H. Ingram to Sarah Helen Whitman*

My dear Providence,　　　　　　　　　　　　　　　　　　　2 Nov. 1876
Yours dated 19 Ultimo just to hand, & at risk of only sending you a short scribble, I answer right away. I was becoming very anxious at your long silence, but continually deferred my reply in hopes—from day to day—of hearing from you. I feared you were unwell (—you do not speak now of your health—) & not having yet replied to Miss Peckham, of course I have not heard through her. I have so much to say, too!

In the first place, let me tell you about "Landor's Cottage": it must have been written about the time of your engagement; was sent to the *Metropolitan* (magazine?) in Dec. 1848 or Jany. [18]49; and was returned to Poe in March, unpublished, upon the stoppage of said publication.

Did you know & remember anything of the *Flag of the Nation?* Of Boston. I can also tell you that when Poe obtained no reply to his last letter of appeal to you, begging that you would contradict the scandals about his conduct at your last interview, he believed that his letter had been intercepted & kept from you.

Did you, or do you, know a Mrs. Osborne? Mr. O. Dodge has died suddenly, & I fear neither his portrait of Poe, or the promised copy, will now be obtainable, but I'll try for it.

I take tea with Mrs. Lewis today, & will again ask about the portrait she has—copies are everywhere.

Bruckmann has lost two different photos I had of Poe, which you sent me but, happily, not the one my engraved portrait is from. His portrait is, I think, very good & I don't know why he is delaying publication. I will call on him at earliest moment.

The Baltimore Memorial is to have a *very fine unknown* portrait, I am informed. We shall see. There are about 20 different portraits in existence that I know of.

This winter, Mallarmé assures me, his translation of the poems, with biographic sketch & portrait of Poe will appear—portrait from mine. The book will be inscribed to Mrs. S. H. Whitman—so you will not need the *République des Lettres*, with the translation, though you may get that.

I seem to have made Poe quite the hero in French literary society just now, although Mallarmé has long worshipped him. He says he sent you the *Corbeau*, but, as you have not received it, has sent another. I have not yet met him in the flesh, not having time to go to the watering place he was at this year. We shall, doubtless, soon meet.

Letters in *Athenaeum* & *N&Q*: "Uneda" in latter seems to have "shut up." In former, I have not had time to answer Theodore Watts. It was so poor, & self-answered, that I don't think I shall bother about it now.

Anent H. B. Forman (my friend): he is now bringing out the *complete & best* edition of Shelley in 4 vols—Vol. i ready.[1] I am reading all the proofs with him. 'Tis an interesting labour.

My "Memoir" of Poe for the Baltimore Memorial is the *International Review* life revised. I wonder what was "objectionable" in O'Connor's article! I received the *Two Rivulets* vol. from Walt Whitman a week or two ago, with fine portrait & autograph.[2]

Mrs. Richmond speaks in the highest terms of Poe. She, I fancy, saw nothing but his brightest side. I think she was very glad at the prospect of his marriage with you, but I cannot help deeming the result was the best that could have happened—at least for you. Oh, how I wish I could see you & *talk* all over with you. I shall never be able to publish my final biography until I have *seen* you. But there is no hurry.

I have never been able to get Gill's Laurel Leaf. Should you have any objection to lend it to me? I would return it quickly. If you have *any* disinclination do not hesitate for one moment to say so.

Didier will, doubtless, be very favourable to Poe, but as to his reliability? Well, you may remember the note heading the "Alone" poem in *Scribner's*. However, we have turned the tide in the right direction & now all will be easy sailing.

As to E[lizabeth] O[akes] S[mith], I had the MS. in my possession certainly, & certainly all, or nearly all, had been previously published by her: as to the *exact* words, I would not dare to assert anything, & my remarks to you referred to the *whole paper* & not to any sentence. I read your meaning that she denied authorship of the whole article. I did not notice (but will reread) "a woman whom he had *betrayed & ruined." I thought I had read it* "a woman whose letters he had declined" &c. I will look to *Scribner* for the brickyard story:—it looks "very like a whale."

I suppose Gill won't sell out—if he has anything to sell? I wonder if Stoddard would?

Did you hear of Mr. Cleaveland's death? I wrote a short notice of John Neal for the *Athenaeum*—unfortunately it, through a mistake, got put into the *Miscellanea* at the end.³ Miss Neal sent me a fine photo of the brave old man.

Happily, my health & spirits are very good. I mean to live & labour, & be famous yet, my dear friend. Like poor Chenier, "I have so much here" (in my brain) which must someday be wrought out.

Meanwhile, & *forever*, believe me to be your *amicus fidelissimus*,

John H. Ingram

1. H. Buxton Forman's four-volume edition of Shelley was published in 1880 (London: Reeves and Turner).

2. *Two Rivulets*, including "Democratic Vistas," "Centennial Songs," and "Passage to India," was published as a companion volume to the 1876 (sixth) edition of *Leaves of Grass* in Camden, N.J., 1876.

3. John Neal's obituary, signed "I," appeared in the London *Athenaeum*, Oct. 14, 1876.

163. *Sarah Helen Whitman to John H. Ingram.* Item 303

My dear friend,   Nov. 14, [18]76

The contents of your letter [Nov. 2] interested me more than I can tell you, what you say about "Landor's Cottage," more especially. I had so often asked the question of persons likely to know, & now, when I had given up all hope of its being answered, it is answered in accordance with my dearest wishes. I have told you under what circumstances Poe told me of his intention to write *a pendant* to his "Domain of Arnheim." Assuredly you were destined to the work which you are so effectually performing.

A beautiful letter from Mallarmé speaks of your "noble work as having avenged his memory."

How did you find out that the "pendant" had been offered to *Post*?

Mallarmé wrote to explain about the *Corbeau* & to tell me if nothing further was heard from it before November—his letter was dated October 19—he would send me one of his own copies, with every precaution that it should not fail to reach its destination. He also told me of his wish to dedicate to me the volume of translations from Poe's poems, which he hoped to bring out during the ensuing winter, or spring, or later.

I wonder if he has yet attempted "Ulalume"? I think any translator would find it difficult to translate a poem which English readers still find so difficult to interpret.

I have explained to him carefully all that Poe said to me on the subject, & in doing so a light broke on me as to the meaning of that last verse, and I began to feel that it is *necessary* to the comprehension of the poem. Above all, it explains that the planet, whose "duplicate horns" were seen on the eastern horizon, was a mirage of the fancy; for, of course, he could not normally, with the natural eye, have distinguished the crescent phase of the star; and in the last verse he *tells* us that it was the "*Spectre* of a planet" which the pitiful wood-demons had miraculously evoked to lure him from sorrowful thoughts & beguile him with visionary hopes of love & happiness that might yet be his, until he discovered that the planet was rising directly over the sepulchre wherein his Virginia lay entombed. Then, overwhelmed with that remorseful sorrow that seems always to have visited him when his thoughts reverted from some dream of present happiness to the memory of a lost love, he explains, "Oh what demon has tempted me here?" In this view of the theme of the poem, is not the last verse, however obscure, necessary to its elucidation?

You ask what were the passages in O'Connor's paper which Miss Rice wished him to qualify. It was, I think, something indicative of Walt Whitman's supremacy as a poet, & some expressions of indignation at the want of sympathy shown by some of the American *literati* as to the erection of a monument to the memory of Edgar Poe—only this & nothing more.

About Gill's *Laurel Leaves*, which you tell me you have not seen. He is now, as he informs me, about to publish the two articles on Poe in a volume, with some quotations from my book! & requests permission to engrave for his work "the oval portrait," the same which you have of me from an oil painting. On this proposition I put a decided veto. Miss Rice proposed the same thing to me last spring, in relation to the Memorial volume, but I told her that without having the terms of the engraver & the privilege, in case I acceded to them, of purchasing & withholding the engraved portrait, if not satisfied with the result, I could not consent to the use of the photograph, which cannot legally be used without the consent of the artist who painted & has a copyright of the picture. I moreover demanded to see the proofs of what he, Gill, had taken from my book & the revision of anything which he had published in relation to me. The book will probably be of the compact size of the Bric-a-Brac volumes. As soon as it is issued (it is now going through the press as he writes), I will send you the volume.

The *Laurel Leaves* form a large & very heavy volume. Perhaps it will be better to wait for this. If you think so, I will send the book as soon as it is out.

This is the matter which he wanted Widdleton to buy & publish *with* Didier's, making one volume. Didier would not consent to this, &

now Widdleton having finally rejected the proposal, Gill intends, I believe, to publish it himself.

Much delay has ensued as to Widdleton's publication of Didier's "Memoir", & now the intense excitement attending the presidential election will probably prolong the delay.

I want my letter to go by tomorrow's mail & must try to bring it to a close.

My dear MacRaven,

It is now the *20th of November* & the letter which began on the 14th is still unfinished. Engagements which could not be avoided interrupted the completion of my letter. The week has been a week of political anxiety & elemental storm. Everything is at a deadlock until we know under what king we are to serve. Many think that we are on the brink of another Civil War!

You ask if I knew anything of a Mrs. Osborne. Probably not the one of whom you speak. The one of whom I knew something did not, I think, know Poe. Again, you ask if I know anything of the *Flag of the Nation*. Was it not the paper in which the lines "For Annie" first appeared?[1] You speak of the loss of two photographs I sent you. They were the two taken by Coleman from copies (one from a photograph & the other from a lithograph) of the "Ultima Thule" portrait. Well, a *daguerreotype* taken years ago from the original daguerreotype has recently been recovered by Mr. Lewin, now of Boston, an artist of fine genius, after having been lent & lost or withheld for twelve years!

Knowing that I had been making enquiries for this portrait, Mrs. Lewin brought the daguerreotype to me on a recent visit to Providence & at my request took it to Manchester and allowed him to take a negative from it. Mr. Lewin would not consent to have a daguerreotype taken from it. But I purchased from Manchester half a dozen copies, of which the enclosed is one. Does this resemble the daguerreotype which Ossian Dodge told you Poe gave *him*?

In your last you told me you were going to take tea with Mrs. Lewis & would try to find out about the date of *hers*. *Did* she inform you?

I have heard nothing about the Baltimore Memorial for some three weeks. I fancy the unsettled state of business in consequence of uncertainty as to the presidential election has delayed all publishing enterprises in Baltimore.

A young friend of mine, an artist, leaves tomorrow, intending to pass the winter in Paris; he will sail on Wednesday. I have given him an introductory note to our friend Rose & one to M. Mallarmé. I have also at Mallarmé's request, *given him* a note to Rose. He writes that I told him I had a friend residing in Paris & hopes it is not too late to make her acquaintance. But I think it must have been from *you* that he learned it. I do not remember having told him, but perhaps I did.

The *Corbeau* has not yet alighted on my bust of Apollo! I am sorry that he has had so much trouble about it. I shall look eagerly for your friend's life of Shelley. I see that Mrs. Browning's correspondence with Horne is to be published. You did not tell me in what *number* of the *Athenaeum* was your notice of Neal.

And now once more, ave atque vale, and believe me ever & ever your "Providence,"

S. H. Whitman

P.S. Did you tell me that you had found a copy of Lowell's article on Poe in *Graham's* for February 1845? If not, I could send you one. It is an odd number that was found by me among a pile of old newspapers in the garret. The covers are torn off & the portrait that must originally have accompanied it is gone. I have just found it & have not yet had time to see how it compares with the one in Griswold's compilation.

There is *one word* in the extract you give from Mrs. Gove Nichols' account of her visit to the Fordham cottage that I *do* earnestly wish you would change, if you publish the extract in future editions. It is to be found at the foot of the 62nd page of your "Memoir" in the sentence, "There he stood with his arms crossed before the tormented bird." etc. Can you not in any future edition say the "imprisoned bird" instead of the "tormented"? It may seem a slight thing, but I never recur to it without pain.

Has Mrs. Nichols ever published her "Reminiscences of Poe," as you told me she proposed to do? And do you ever see her now? Don't forget to tell me how you found out about "Landor's Cottage."

And now, once more, bon soir & benedicite.

S. H. W.

Nothing recently from Didier about Widdleton's intentions.

1. The *Flag of Our Union* was founded by Frederick Gleason in 1846 and quickly became a leading American weekly in circulation, with Park Benjamin, Horatio Alger, Frances Osgood, and Edgar Poe among its contributors. Poe said that it was not very respectable but that it paid well ($5 a "Graham" page, $5 for a sonnet). Gleason sold out to his editor, Martin M. Ballou, in 1854, and the magazine continued to publish until 1870.

164. *John H. Ingram to Sarah Helen Whitman*

My dear Providence,   12 Dec. 1876
    At the risk of only sending a few lines I will try & scribble off an

acknowledgment of yours of 14th Nov. answering, to the best of my abilities, your questions therein.

As regards "Landor's Cottage": I derived my information from two of Poe's own letters relative to his then literary adventures—in the first he speaks of the forthcoming appearance of "Landor's Cottage" in the magazine, & in the second of the magazine's failure & the return of his MS.

As regards Mallarmé—I believe him to be a noble fellow. I have repeatedly urged him to send you *Le Corbeau*: he says one copy was sent, but as that has not reached you another is going, *or gone*—I think he said gone—but his letter is "to hum." He promised to look after a copy of the translation of "To Helen," but said if that did not reach you it would not matter, as you would get it in the vol. of his translations. I have not seen his translation of "Ulalume," but feel certain that he has made one, & will ask for it, so that I may see whether he has quite comprehended the various points you have drawn my attention to, although I dare say your explanation to him will have sufficed. The last stanza, however valuable to us, the students, is not a happy ending for those who read poetry only for its sound & should, therefore, be kept separate.

Thanks *re.* the O'Connor's deleted remarks. From your words I should say Miss Rice's—or her advisers'?—"qualifications" were right.

I should like, of course, to see the Gill book—or, indeed, *anything* about Poe—from any quarter & will—where needed—return same.

I must get Didier's sketch from New York, but fear it will be more to confuse than elucidate matters.

The *Flag of the Nation* was, I fancy, the one in which lines "For Annie" appeared. She (Mrs. Richmond) is now in correspondence with me.

Have you heard from Miss Neal? I have not since I sent her the *Athenaeum*. I will look up the number with my notice of Neal in— 'twas a *short* paper, & published at the end under *Miscellanea* through a mistake of mine, as it appeared.

Many thinks for the photo. It does much resemble the two lost ones. I hope they'll be found. I cannot hear of the publication of the Bruckmann portrait, although I had the proofs months ago. Yes! poor Dodge's—I told you, did I not, that he was dead?—photo did resemble the lost two, even more than the one you now send. Mrs. L[ewis]'s information about hers is—like all her information—very vague.

The Baltimore Memorial, I hear, is in the press & proceeding.

It was I who told Malarmé of Miss Peckham & I wondered he never spoke of her in his letters.

You speak of Horne & Mrs. Browning's correspondence. I *fancy* Browning is very annoyed at this publication.[1]

Two vols. of Forman's Shelley are published, & two to appear. They are the poems & not the life of Shelley, & will be the only complete edition. Reviews will appear when last vol. is published.

Many thanks, but I have Lowell's paper on Poe in *Graham's Mag*.

Mrs. Nichols has *not* yet published her "Recollections." She is much engaged just now at Malvern with illness. I hope to meet her in London this winter. My *suggestions may* have delayed her publishing.

Have you heard of Moncure Conway?[2] I was at his wife's weekly reception yesterday.

Haste for mail. Always & ever yours,

John H. Ingram

P.S. You do not say how your health is now.

1. *Letters of Elizabeth Barrett Browning Addressed to Richard Hengist Horne*, ed. S. R. Townshend Mayer, 2 vols. (London: Richard Bentley and Son, 1877).

2. Moncure Daniel Conway (1832–1907), was a minister and an author. He was a cousin of Moncure Daniel, the editor of the Richmond *Examiner*, who had written the so-called "Eulogium" of Poe which was published in the *Southern Literary Messenger*, 16 (Mar. 1850), 172–87.

165. *Sarah Helen Whitman to John H. Ingram.*   Item 305

My dear friend,   Dec. 15, [18]76

Gill's proofs, which I have been impatiently awaiting (having by the exercise of some diplomacy prevailed upon him to submit them to me), came yesterday.

They are a curious *melange* of *everything* comprised in Mr. Widdleton's Memorial volume of last year with some business papers in relation to the *Stylus*, claimed to be derived from Thomas C. Clarke, & some recollections of the domestic life of the family while residing in Philadelphia, also ascribed to Mr. Clarke, but not written in his accustomed style certainly, & of no special interest.

There is a story, however, about the house where Poe wrote "The Raven," "important if true"—that is to say, interesting—& by no means improbable, which does not conflict with any known facts as to the matter, so far as I am aware. (I will copy it for you presently). These, with some elaborate speculations of his own concerning the true meaning lying perdu in "The Raven," the Griswold and Pabodie letters, & certain portions of Poe's letters to me (published without my consent or knowledge in the Lotos & Laurel Leaf papers) comprise about the whole of the "Memoir." G[ill] has the grace to make honorable mention of you from time to time in the "Memoir"—as a sop to Cerberus, peut-être (moi meme).

The collection may perhaps be called, to use the word of Mr. G. P. Lathrop as applied to Poe's style, promiscuous. (See the enclosed article on Lathrop's "Study of Hawthorne.")

But there is one thing in it to me entirely new & profoundly interesting. Through your correspondence with Mrs. Richmond & Poe's friends in Lowell, you may perhaps have seen it. Indeed I am half inclined to think it may have been written by the Mrs. Osborne of whom you spoke in your last letter, was it not? I refer to a beautiful, & beautifully written, record of Poe as seen by a young lady, then in her teens, who heard his Lowell lecture on poetry in the early summer of 1848 (soon after he had sent me the "Lines to Helen"), and of other interviews with him "when he visited Lowell [in the autumn] some months afterwards."[1] This was the time undoubtedly when he visited Lowell at the invitation of friends who hoped to make arrangements for his giving another lecture there, a hope which was defeated by the excitement attending the presidential election before the inauguration of Zachary Taylor.

As you may already have seen this record, or if not, will soon read it in the book, which I shall send you as soon as it is issued, I will not copy her recollections here. I think I know "the lady who differed from Mr. Poe, & expressed her opinions somehwat strongly," as mentioned in the narrative.

To return to "the house where 'The Raven'" was written—Just as I wrote the last word I received a card from Gill asking for return of his proofs by the 3 P.M. train.

The book will be out at least in a day or two. Will write again by Tuesday's mail.

In haste, sincerely your *guardant "Providence,"*

S.H.W.

1. These recollections of Poe were written by Sarah Heywood Trumbull, Mrs. Richmond's younger sister, who spent much time in the Richmonds' home in Lowell, especially during the time Poe visited that city.

166. *Sarah Helen Whitman to John H. Ingram.*   Item 307

My dear friend,   Dec. 31, 1876
Yours of December 12 received. Thanks for the information about "Landor's Cottage," so long sought for in vain! How many, *many* things

of interest to me & to all the friends of our poet your researches have brought to light.

Gill's book is not yet out; as soon as it appears you shall receive a copy. The Household Edition of the poems, accompanied by Didier's "Memoir," anticipates him & adds a very interesting chapter to the story of Poe's early life, for the rest of the story is briefly outlined as we already know it.[1] I fancy Gill is waiting to incorporate whatever new matter he can find in it in his own *omnium gatherum*. Widdleton has send me a copy of the Household Edition of the poems for the New Year. I will send it with Gill's, as soon as that is issued, which will probably be within a few days.

The portraits you send—copies of your Coleman & Remington photo—though superficially well executed, seem to me utterly divested of all *characteristic* expression. The eyes are vacant & wandering, the mouth nerveless, & the whole bearing & attitude of the figure stiff & conventional. How different from the engraving in your volume! I do not think anyone who had ever seen Poe would recognize this copy as even a "counterfeit presentment." I would not pain the artist by having this opinion made public. So, let it be strictly *entre nous.*

Have you seen the photo in the Baltimore Memorial volume? *That* would be *recognized* at once, but *so* changed in expression that I would much prefer the likeness had been omitted with all that gave to it its characteristic impress of pride & nobility. A profane collegian, a great admirer of Poe's genius, wittily says, "It looks like a cross between a stage villain & a retired clergyman whose sands of life had nearly run out," as the quack doctors say. What do *you* think?

The engraving from the new Household Edition is from the portrait by Osgood (Fanny's husband) in the rooms of the Historical Society of New York. It is the best from that portrait, but has something of the rigid & formal character of the painting.

Two facts which I had heard before but which I had assumed to be apocryphal are in Didier's "Memoir," told as authentic: one, the impressive and tragic deaths of Poe's parents in the doomed theatre at Richmond; and the other the fact that Mrs. Poe, Edgar's mother, was a wife before the young law student saw and loved her![2] Stoddard, in his letters to me, made a great point of the fact that Poe's mother was *not* (as Mrs. Clemm said in one of the letters I entrusted to you & quoted by me in *Poe & His Critics*) "herself but a child," but was at least 6 or 7 years older than her husband. He accented the fact, apparently to show Mrs. Clemm's unreliability as an authority.

By the way, *be very careful of those letters of Mrs. Clemm's, with my marginal comments appended.* Do not let them pass into other hands, & someday when you are *quite at leisure,* copy for me the phrase, *the lines* in which she says, "You will never know how he loved you nor his agony at parting with you." Only this & nothing more—with the date of the letter & signature.

I find that in the new "Memoir" a very prominent place is given to my letter. To my surprise, it was printed as an "Introductory Letter." When I wrote it I did not know that Poe's parents perished in the doomed theatre at Richmond! If I had known it I could have made my allusion to Maudsley's article still more impressive.[3]

I will send you a copy of the volume if you have not already received one. Of course I gave Didier no personal details. Such as he has published were gathered from your "Memoir" & Gill's papers. Gill's book is not yet out. I fancy he is waiting to make use of such new material as he can find in Didier's narrative. But I have told you this already.

The Baltimoreans seem greatly pleased with your "Memoir," as prepared for their Memorial volume.

But my dear MacRaven you have not yet toned down that "fierce flame" against which I so long ago remonstrated.[4]

Why not say, "unconscious of the interest she had aroused," or "the profound impression she had left," or, if you will permit *me* to arrange the story of the incident, I think I could relate it more accurately than Griswold has done, & in a manner not less interesting, & you could introduce it, if you think proper, in your completed Life! What say you? You see, Poe's wife was still *living* at the time, & it is not permitted under the circumstances to cherish "a fierce flame" for another lady, in "sober prose," you know, though it may be when the memory has crystallized into poetry in after years. But there is nothing of earthly passion in the poem he sent me—*is* there?

I like & heartily approve the other alterations in relation to the introduction of my name, but this is one which I have looked for in vain. I know you will not overlook it now that I have reminded you of your promise.

Mallarmé has sent copies of *La République des Lettres*. He will send the *Corbeau* by Mrs. Moulton or my friend Walter Brown. He is indeed, as you say, "a noble fellow." He says beautiful things of you, & has, I *know*, a most sweet & generous nature. I have just sent him some unbound sheets of my defense of Poe. He says Rose & her sister gave him a most cordial reception. She has not written to me since she saw him.

I should have sent my letter by the last mail, but I have been "under the weather," which has been terrific!

Ever & ever your friend,

S. H. Whitman

Did I send you a copy of my article on Lathrop's "Study of Hawthorne"?

1. *The Life and Poems of Edgar Allan Poe and Additional Poems, a New Memoir by E. L. Didier.* (New York: W. J. Widdleton, 1877).

2. Elizabeth Arnold had been married in 1802 to Charles Hopkins, also an actor. Hopkins died on Oct. 26, 1805, and his widow's marriage to David Poe, Jr., took place sometime between Mar. 14 and Apr. 9, 1806. See Quinn, pp. 23–24.

3. Henry Maudsley asserted in his article "Edgar Allan Poe," *American Journal of Insanity*, Oct., 1860, pp. 152–98, that Edgar had inherited infirmities of mind from his father, David Poe, and was "destitute of that faculty of reasonable insight, by which a man sees in human life something more than what is weak, sinful, and contemptible."

4. Ingram had written in his first "Memoir" of Poe that prefaced his 1874–75 edition of Poe's *Works*:

"In the early summer of 1848 we find Poe delivering a lecture at Lowell, on the 'Female Poets of America.' 'In an analysis of the comparative merits of the New England poetesses,' says the Hon. James Atkinson, who attended the lecture, 'the lecturer awarded to Mrs. Osgood the palm of facility, ingenuity, and grace;—to Mrs. Whitman, a pre-eminence in refinement of art, enthusiasm, imagination, and genius, properly so called;—to Miss Lynch he ascribed an unequalled success in the concentrated and forcible enunciation of the sentiment of heroism and duty.' Mrs. Whitman, undoubtedly the finest female poet New England has produced, had been first seen by Poe, says Griswold, 'on his way from Boston, when he visited that city to deliver a poem before the Lyceum there. Restless, near midnight, he wandered from his hotel near where she lived, until he saw her walking in a garden. He related the incident afterwards in one of his most exquisite poems, worthy of himself, of her, and of the most exalted passion.'

"Meanwhile the beautiful young widow lived on perfectly unconscious of the fierce flame she had aroused in the poet's heart" (I, lxxiii–lxxiv).

This passage was repeated in the long sketch of Poe's life, "Edgar Allan Poe," that Ingram contributed to the *International Review*, 2 (Mar. 1875), 169, published in New York, and in the memorial volume, published in Baltimore, after the unveiling of the monument to Poe's memory on Nov. 17, 1875.

167. *Sarah Helen Whitman to John H. Ingram.*   Item 309

My dear friend,   Jan. 9, 1877

I have just received the life-size copy of the photograph. It is superb! *So* good that I am sorry I criticized so searchingly the smaller copies received before. The nerveless look of the under lip seems entirely absent from this beautiful copy, and the air of the head & figure seem much finer. I am delighted to have so beautiful a copy of the little photograph I sent you.

Mr. Coleman tells me that he has had several requests to allow the daguerreotype I gave him to be copied. Gill among others has asked him to allow him the use of it, but he has invariably refused. He says that he regrets having given away one of the copies taken at the time I sent you the copy from which your engraving was taken. He tells me thousands of copies have been sold from it, and all *wretched*. I want him to see this. I think he will be greatly pleased.

Gill has been burnt out, I believe, & the publication of his Life is still delayed. I will endeavor to get a copy of Didier's to send by tomorrow's steamer. I cannot say more now than to give once more a word of fervent thanks & Benediction for all.

I am suffering intensely from a severe bronchial affection which is an epidemic here & has proved fatal to many in my immediate neighborhood. Among others the President of Brown University, whose sudden death was announced this morning.[1] The weather has been frightful.

Ever devotedly your friend,

S. H. Whitman

I have not heard from Rose since she saw Mallarmé. I wish I could fitly translate his sonnet. There are some things in it which baffle me. I wish they had given a facsimile of it. There are apparently one or two misprints in it. Some of our Brunonians to whom I have shown it think so.

S.H.W.

I have been comparing the smaller photo with the copy received today & think it may be improved by a few slight changes. The shadow between the under lip & the chin should be *shorter*, as it *is* in the life-size copy—the lip itself not carried out so far as it is toward the corner of the mouth on the left side of the picture, & the lights on the cheek & forehead toned down on the right side—and above all the corner of the lip should be shadowed.

1. Alexis Caswell (1799–1877), president of Brown University, 1868–1872, died suddenly on Jan. 8, 1877.

168. *John H. Ingram to Sarah Helen Whitman*

My dear Friend, 18 January 1877

Great stress of correspondence prevented my immediate response to yours of 15th Ultimo. I, therefore, have now to respond to two communications.

You begin with Gill's book. I shall be glad to see it *when* it does appear but do not anticipate much profit from it—if there be aught in it of value I shall use, referring to my authority, of course.

Didier's book, I shall, also, be glad to see. Hearing from Baltimore that it was out, I have written Davidson to get me a copy from Widdleton—might I trouble you to ask Davidson (P. O. Box 567, as of yore) whether he has got me a copy? It would save you sending.

It is my hope to make something, however, very different from all these sketches. I wish to paint a living, breathing man—to feel with his feelings—suffer with his sufferings—succeed with his successes. *Data*, of course, I need, but I now feel that I know the *man* and, if I do not reproduce Poe as he lived and felt, then it will not be from want of knowledge but from want of power. To you & to you only do I say this thing—for if I fail to add more than a few paving stones to the fabled inferno, I do not want to proclaim the fact upon the housetops. A biography—fit meat for the multitude at least, I can produce.

Returning from this high-flown ramble to our muttons. House where Poe wrote "The Raven"—"important if true," as you say. I shall put it under the glass of truth & inspect it.

En passant, you once spoke of Swinburne's *Under the Microscope*. I have read it twice since. It chiefly consists of crushing with a vindictive heel some critic-vipers, but, *in a note*, refers to Poe as the one poetic voice &c. of America. Have you seen Swinburne's last pamphlet on Carlyle, alias "the Muscovite Crusade &c."[1] If ever anyone was flayed by words, the egotistic old Chelsea Mightmonger must be raw.

Have you heard aught of Forman's *Shelley*? Only 2 vols. out yet. I read every proof & enjoy it. But our muttons are out of sight again!

Gill from Clarke. I have some items about Poe & Clarke that G[ill] is likely not to wot of.

Thanks for you on Lathrop's Hawthorne. It was scarcely worth your manipulation & deserved (*i.e.*, Lathrop) scarification.

As regards the young Lowell lady's reminiscences—this is, probably, Mrs. Richmond's sister? If so, I have her record. Mrs. Richmond, besides much information, letters &c. has sent me the 2-vol. edition of *Tales* of 1839.[2]

Yours of the 31st Ultimo. *Re*. Didier's sketch & its new & interesting chapter. This probably refers to 1831–33 epoch &, if so, & *reliable*, will be interesting.

I am sorry you do not like the "Memorial" portrait I sent you because it is—although really an ideal—likely to be wider known & more lastingly known, both in Europe & America, than any other yet published. Personally, I must say that I liked it, but the *Academy's*—probably W. M. Rossetti—speaker, seems of your opinion. The artist is some German.

Portrait in Baltimore Mem[orial] Vol[ume] I believe to be very like, but like the last remnants of life—worn, haggard, shadowed already by "coming events" of the latter days.

The two events—"*facts*"—in Didier's vol. are as unveracious, as, I fear, the whole sketch is. Mrs. Poe died in her bed two or three weeks before the Richmond theatre was burned. Mr. Poe's fate seems hidden in mystery. The tale of Mrs. P[oe] having been twice married would seem to be about as true as the very common story that their son had been married two or three times. Stoddard's "point" of her not being young I think I shall be able to "put out of court."

Mrs. Clemm's letters (indeed, every scrap you have sent me) are safe & ready to return to you at a moment's notice. Mrs. Clemm's unreliability as to dates has been made too much of. I find her *very exact*—even to the dates of the Stanard incident—having followed other accounts I had got wrong. His friendship with Mrs. S[tanard] ("Helen") was later—I *believe*—than you deem. Mrs. C[lemm] was wrong, however, I *should think* about the Poes having ever done anything for Edgar's mother.

I shall be glad to see your letter to Didier. I had not heard of it before.

What do you think of the Baltimore Mem[orial] Vol[ume]? Very pretty, *n'est ce pas*? But I think there is too much of "Ingram" & other unknowns, & too little of Poe.

As regards "the fierce flame" &c., I only had a few hours to scribble off *by post* a few omissions & corrections & never saw any proofs, so must not be held responsible for *anything*. I did not note that Virginia was *then* alive—but send me your narrative. I shall be glad to see it, if you will send it but don't "cast me off" for saying that I am not sure of using it. I can only fly as my own wings will carry me in this matter, though all *must* please you.

So you have not yet received the *Corbeau*? Mallarmé is, I do believe, a capital fellow.

I am just tearing through Mrs. E. B. Browning's correspondence— the small portion of it published by Horne.[3] I nearly always agree with E. B. B[rowning] against *Orion*, but I think it a great mistake that it has been published. It, the book, does neither credit to Horne nor E. B. B[rowning]—certainly not to the former. Whilst the remarks of latter on Mrs. Norton should not have been published during Mrs. N[orton]'s life.

Would that we could meet! How much I should have to tell & explain.

In haste. *Semper idem*—

John H. Ingram

P.S. I may run over to Paris *Salon* in May, & then hope to hunt out your Rhode Island Rose.

1. Algernon Charles Swinburne, *Note on the Muscovite Crusade* (London: Chatto & Windus, 1876).

2. These volumes of *Tales of the Grotesque and Arabesque* had been found in Poe's trunk, forwarded from Baltimore by Neilson Poe to Mrs. Clemm in Lowell, after Poe's death in 1849.

3. *Two Letters from Elizabeth Barrett Browning to Richard Hengist Horne*, Printed for private circulation only (London: R. Clay, n.d.).

169. *Sarah Helen Whitman to John H. Ingram.* Item 313

My dear MacRaven,   Feb. 2, [18]77
   Your of the 18th Ulto. just received. I sent you a copy of Didier's "Memoir" etc., on the 12th January. I hope it arrived safely. I will write at once to Davidson to countermand your order for a copy from Widdleton.
   I believe he, Didier, intends writing a separate work on the subject. When all the evidence is in & fairly sifted we can judge better of its value. I was greatly surprised, in truth, at the two statements to which you refer. He seems to have been in correspondence with Neilson Poe, & surely *he* must know. Yet I believe the story as told by Didier has not been publicly contradicted. It throws a weird glamour over the romance of Poe's life, which seems never fully to emerge from "The Demon of the Shadow" which so dominated his imagination.
   When I said I did not like the Bruckmann copies of your photograph, I referred to the small ones *only*. The other is superb. Do you not find that the large portrait has a quite different expression from the other? Mr. Coleman, who remembers Poe & who owns the daguerreotype from which the copy I sent you was taken, thinks the large one the best ever published of him. But in the *smaller* pictures the resemblance is somehow strangely altered or left out; the corners of the mouth, on which so much depends, are specially wanting in vraisemblance. Compare them with the engraving in your book & tell me which is the more characteristic of the man.
   I hear nothing of late in relation to Gill's book. I fancy he is waiting till we know under what king we are to serve, & until business returns to its accustomed channels.
   Lathrop is assistant editor of the *Atlantic*. He married Rose Hawthorne. Her brother, Julian Hawthorne, is very much incensed at his publication of a private journal which the great novelist or tale writer would have suppressed.[1]
   Yes, I have read Swinburne's noble rebuke of Carlyle's barbarous & brutal policy. It is not less admirable in tone & temper than in the relentless truth of its brave utterances. There is nothing like it in the language. How will Carlyle endure his life after it? Will he not wear sackcloth & ashes for the rest of his dishonored days?

I wish you had told me in what number of the *Academy* was to be found the notice of the photograph. Can you think that a portrait or face so serene & noble as that from which the life-size Bruckmann portrait was taken could in less than a year have become, as you say, worn & haggard like the face in the Baltimore Memorial? *I* think it more likely that the fault was in the printing of the photo.

The Raven [*Le Corbeau*] has at last arrived & wherever he puts in an appearance the page is nobly illustrated, but in one of the etchings we see only what passes for his *shadow on the floor*. This is something out of the range of my appreciation.

But two of the illustrations grow upon me every time I look at them—the one where he is seen swooping toward the window of the poet, & the other where he sits enthroned in shadows on the bust of Pallas. These two flank the portrait you sent me and add a new interest & lend a new character to my "Hall of Dreams."

When you come to Providence you will see them there if I, myself, am there to welcome you.

I have many questions to ask, but must wait till next time.

Semper Idem. Your Providence of Providence,

Helen Whitman

1. George Parsons Lathrop edited and published *A Study of Hawthorne* (Boston: J. R. Osgood and Co., 1876) in which he quotes from Hawthorne's *English Notebooks*.

170. *John H. Ingram to Sarah Helen Whitman*

My dear Friend, 3 Feb. 1877

A severe bronchial attack, which has kept me confined to the house for some days and rendered me unfit for anything, prevented my writing sooner to acknowledge yours of the 9th and Didier's *Life*, the first copy of this latter yet to hand. I shall be anxious to get your next, as in this (of 9th) you speak of suffering from an attack of bronchitis yourself.

We are having the most singular winter that I ever recollect—no cold or snow since early in November, but "the rain it raineth every day." England will soon be swamped.

I am glad you like the large copy of the portrait. It has not been much liked here. The *Athenaeum* was cruel on it, & the *Academy* was not very enthusiastic—of the smaller copies folks are very severe. I shall try & get your suggestions about it carried into effect.

The Balt[imore] Mem[orial] Vol[ume] portrait is, doubtless, very good for Poe *in those latter days*. Didier's is a vulgar copy of the

Osgood one; in fact, Didier seems to vulgarize all he touches. I prefer Griswold's ghastly, gaunt, & even fiendish portraiture, to Didier's man-milliner sort of puppet. As for his *data*, as you, of course, have detected, they are more mischievous & *misleading* than those of any work on Poe yet published—scarcely a page but is full of errors. He has copied my vindication extensively, as you see, but even then, he has either copied me when I have been in error, or he has made a "muddle" of my facts. As I have told you, Mrs. Poe died before the fire. Stoddard was quite right there—& that alone would have invalidated the statements of old Mr. Clarke. *Entre nous*, I do not believe the old man the sole author of all that fictitious tale—*vide* Colonel Preston's "Reminiscences," which are, undoubtedly correct.[1] Poe *was* in England 1816–21–22. From birth to death the book is unreliable, untrue, & some statements are, evidently, purposely mistold—such as the date of Poe's marriage, so as to make his letter to Mr. Kennedy (really *written many months before wedding*) (that is from the extract of the letter I give) seem written in dejection because of his separation from his wife. The account of Virginia's death, purposely, or otherwise, given out of Mrs. Nichols' recollections (in my "Memoir"), of her illness, as her death-bed—is all fictitious. *I have letters of Poe & Mrs. Clemm* which prove how *everything needed* for their darling was provided—by Mrs. Houghton & others. *Mais, c'est assez—n'est ce pas?*

What I object to most is not the errors of fact—and *you* must not accept aught in the book without corroboration—but the tone. I would rather see Poe enveloped in clouds of horror & mystery than made a dandyfied Minerva-press hero. My Baltimore friends are, apparently, of my way of thinking. By the way, how comes it that Didier boasts of the acquaintanceship of Neilson Poe, & many others who knew Poe—classmates, &c. (*who have given me correct statements*) & yet makes such stupid mistakes? This looks queer. Besides, Mrs. Clemm *could not* have told him some of the things here.

I have, you see, between 40 & 50 of Poe's & Mrs. Clemm's (mostly unpublished) letters to go by, besides other *data* numberless.

I have lent Didier to two *literati*, who are well-versed in Poeana, & they may review it. *Entre nous*, one is the author of the *British Q[uarterly] Review* article.

I wrote some time ago to Miss Peckham but have not had reply—this I must expect after my long silence to her.

Mallarmé's sonnet, as pointed out to Browne, was full of *errata*. He says an exact copy was made but copy Mallarmé has sent me is very different. Pity *facsimile* was not made.

I want to *facsimile* many of Poe's poems—*of which I possess the originals*—beginning with "The Coliseum" & ending with "The Bells." By the way, do you know anything of "El Dorado"? When &

where it was first published?[2] It is about the only one of which I have
not the history—was it, think you, *posthumous & unfinished?*

How tiresome about Gill's book being put off! But then! Doubtless
there was nothing much new in it. It would not be worth buying (his
material, I mean) through a third party, think you? I could never get a
copy of *Laurel Leaves.*

Balt[imore] Mem[orial] Vol[ume] is much liked here. It is very
pleasantly "got up," but I should have liked my name left out of the
different letters included in it.

Your "Introductory Letter" was the best part of Didier's book. I see
he has a line or two more of Poe's letters to you than hitherto
published. Which are the "Additional Poems"?

Do you know any possessors of large collections of autographs in
America who may have letters of Poe's they would permit copies of?

Did I tell you I had obtained the *Tales of the Grotesque &
Arabesque?* 1840 edition.

I have been reading Mrs. Browning's letters, published by Horne.
She speaks of Poe's "The Raven."

Was that a *correct* translation of Mallarmé's letter in Didier's *Life?*
Au revoir,

John H. Ingram

1. Col. J. T. L. Preston and Edgar Poe had been schoolmates at a classical school in
Richmond. The speech he delivered during the ceremonies at the unveiling of the monument to Poe in Baltimore on Nov. 17, 1875, was printed in the memorial volume, pp.
37–42, as "Some Reminiscences of Edgar A. Poe as a Schoolboy."

2. "El Dorado" was first published in the *Flag of our Union,* Apr. 21, 1849.

171. *John H. Ingram to Sarah Helen Whitman*

My dear Providence,   14 Feb. 1877

Yours dated 2nd is just to hand. I seem to have a large budget to
unfold if I can but remember all.

As you will have already learned, from mine of 3rd Instant, I have
received Didier's book. I have already spoken of its contents so need
not go over ground again, but I beg you will not accept a single
unproved statement of his. I do not credit the story of widowhood, &
feel assured that I shall be able to disprove it, as easily as the death in
the theatre is disprovable. Mrs. Poe died several days before the
Richmond theatre was burned, as, indeed, Stoddard pointed out—
reprinting the obituary record from Richmond *Enquirer.*[1] I cannot think
Didier can have had any personal communication with the Poes, as his
book directly contradicts their written statements—statements which

contemporary evidence confirms. Only last Saturday an English poet lent me some letters (*un*published) of Poe's, & in one of them, dated June 1836, he informs Kennedy of his marriage having just taken place—this is correct, but Didier's date is given incorrectly on purpose to make the letter he got from my "Memoir" agree with his theory.[2] Old Clarke's testimony is all humbug & the book is one mass of mistakes, some, indeed, caused by blindly following my "Memoir", & knowing so little of the subject.

I have lent the book to several of Poe's admirers here & expect some reviews which I will get copies of for you. The book had a rather severe "skull dragging" in *Athenaeum* for last Saturday 10th.[3] This you will see.

I have just turned up Didier's letter to me & send it to you for comparison with the *facsimile* poem in *Scribner's*—Ed[itor] of which wrote me that *Didier acknowledged having* written the date & signature!! After that, I fear "Alone" is shaky—not, indeed, that I, for one moment, believe *Didier* to have *composed* the lines. Please return Didier's letter.[4] You will see what he says about Poe's mother in his *Life*; he has only gone by an anonymous newspaper slip.

I think it not improbable that Miss Arnold (a woman of no small talent, apparently) was born at sea—but all will be revealed.

By the way, did I tell you that the *Allen* who gave the story of Poe working in the brickyard "late in the fall of 1834" was a witness *against* Poe in the West Point courtmartial, & that the *Gibson* who wrote the account of *Harper's* "Poe at West Point" was *tried* at the same time as Poe was?

Oh, for a few hours chat! I could tell *you* so much—much that I can never print. More than half Poe's letters, unfortunately, are so personal—affect so many living people—that I can not print them.

I have heard several times lately from Mrs. Richmond. She is very kind, and has placed a large number of letters, &c. at my service. Gill's description of Poe by the young schoolgirl was from her—by her sister—& the MS. of "The Bells," which he announced himself owner of, was only borrowed from Mrs. R[ichmond].

Do you ever see Mr. Harris? I should be glad to hear, if, at any time, he knew of Poe's early vols. for sale, *for an English poet*. Do you think he would permit a copy of Diabolus' *Musiad* to be taken in MS. for me? If so, could you press anyone into your service to do it for me? It is, I believe, only 8 pps. Title page, &c. Doubtless, I could find out *something* by it.

Having recently discovered Miss Anna Blackwell's address, I wrote to her, and this morning received her reply—and very strange it is! Some mistake somewhere. I will quote some portions:

Your letter greatly surprised me. . . I never saw him ⊰ Poe ⊱ but twice, & really know nothing about him, except from hearsay. Some lady (whose very name I have forgotten) once invited me to go with her to take a basket of delicacies, suitable for an invalid, to Mr. Poe, who was then recovering from illness, & in very straitened circumstances. I . . . went with her to a little place in the country (I have not the slightest remembrance *where*) in which he & his wife were living. The visit was a short one & I remember nothing of the incidents . . . short time afterwards Mr. Poe returned my visit. Those, to the best of my remembrance were the only times I saw him. I left New York shortly afterwards, & returned to England, the following year ⊰ 1848 ⊱.

Do you not think there must be some mistake about Miss Blackwell having ever stayed at Fordham, as you have described? Who could have given you the information? Nothing one gets about Poe seems to be reliable. Sometimes I fancy that he never lived & sometimes, I think *there must* have been two Poes!

Without giving name of my informant to Miss Blackwell, I alluded to a letter I had seen copy of to her from Poe, & asked if she had any other letters of his. She says, "I do not think I ever received a line from him . . . there must be some mistake . . . the extreme slightness of my acquaintance with him precluding all probability of his having ever written to me," & so forth. And you have seen the letter![5]

I hope Davidson will send you another copy of Didier's [book], as I may never get my copy back.

I am thankful you have got the *Corbeau* at last. Did I tell you that I had obtained the Latin translation of "The Raven"? I will enclose the *Academy* notice of Bruckmann's portrait.[6] Your always & ever,

John H. Ingram

P.S. I have found Mr. Wellford's address & will try him—but I want letters! letters! Do you know any American autograph collectors?

1. Edward V. Valentine had copied the notice of Elizabeth Arnold's death from the Richmond *Daily Enquirer*, Dec. 10, 1811, and had sent it to Ingram on July 2, 1875. See Item 236 in the Ingram Poe Collection.

2. Ingram printed portions of this letter from Poe to John P. Kennedy in his 1880 *Life*, I, 140–41. For a complete text see Ostrom, I, 95–96.

3. The "severe skull dragging" accorded Didier's book is reproduced following these notes. It is unsigned, but John Ingram wrote it.

4. Oct. 1, 1874. Item 174 in the Ingram Poe Collection.

5. Miss Blackwell lies throughout her letter to Ingram, which is Item 315 in the Ingram Poe Collection. See Ostrom, II, 369–71, for complete text of the letter Poe addressed to her from Fordham, June 14, 1848, the letter which Miss Blackwell *gave* to Mrs. Whitman, who copied it verbatim for Ingram.

6. On Jan. 13, 1877, p. 40, under "Notes on Art and Archaeology," an *Academy* writer said of Poe's portrait: "Mr. F. Bruckmann of 17 Southampton Street, has published a 'Memorial Portrait' of Edgar Poe. It is a well-taken sightly photograph, head and shoul-

ders, of about two-thirds the size of life; ... it clearly represents the poet in the later period of his life, and does not give a very agreeable idea of his face, ... here he looks somewhat jaded, shifty, and supercilious."

The adjectives used disqualify Ingram as the author of this paragraph.

172. *Review of Eugene L. Didier's* Life and Poems of Edgar Allan Poe, *by John H. Ingram, London* Athenaeum, *Feb. 10, 1877, pp. 188–89*

The Life and Poems of Edgar Allan Poe; and Additional Poems. Edited by E. L. Didier. (New York, Widdleton.)
[John H. Ingram]

FOR A QUARTER of a century his countrymen allowed Poe's memory to moulder under the obloquy heaped upon it by Griswold: some of the poet's friends, it is true, uttered faint protests and then relapsed into silence. In Europe it was otherwise; Baudelaire, Hannay, and Mr. Moy Thomas—notably the last—chose to disregard the biographer's deductions, and drew from Poe's life a very different moral from that accepted, or at least acquiesced in, by his countrymen. The view which these writers arrived at by instinct was amply confirmed by Mr. Ingram's "Memoir of Poe," published in Edinburgh in 1874, and thrice republished in the United States. Finally, the Americans seem to have come to the conclusion that a little hero-worship on their own behalf may prove acceptable, and during the last two years have not only erected a "Memorial" to, but have also published six or seven biographies of Poe, and, if the essay before us may be regarded as expressive of their opinion, have adopted the belief that he was one of the noblest, best, and most virtuous of mortals. Whether Mr. Didier, the writer of the present "Life" will convert many persons on this side of the Atlantic to this creed may be a matter of opinion, but as to his manner of setting about it there cannot be two opinions.

In his preface, Mr. Didier proclaims that the true story of Poe's life has not yet been told, and that he, in now telling it for the first time, has corrected "many false statements heretofore accepted without question"; he also avers that "much fresh and interesting information has been obtained," that "every person accessible to the writer, who possessed any information upon the subject, has been approached, and seldom in vain," and that the dedicatee of the volume has permitted him to have "extracts from Poe's letters." After this preliminary flourish of trumpets, those who sympathize with Dr. Johnson's avowal, "I am a famished man for literary anecdote," will not be gratified to learn that this essay contains scarcely anything true which has not been already published and republished *ad nauseam*; scarcely anything new which is not palpably incorrect; not a single line, apparently, from any letters of Poe, which has not been previously printed,—not anything, indeed, addressed to the gentleman named in the dedication,—and that nearly every page abounds with blunders, which even a slight knowledge of the subject might have prevented. An "Introductory Letter" by Mrs. Whitman, whose "Edgar Poe and his Critics" is laid under heavy contribution, follows the Preface: it is, of course, written in an authoritative tone, but, in following out some such subtle researches in the domain of "antenatal influences" as those which inclined Mr. Shandy to forbode misfortunes for Tristram, the lady has been somewhat out in her reckoning; it would scarcely be safe to carry such delicate investigations back further than nine months, even for such a phenomenal person as Poe, who was born on the 19th of January, 1809—just 276 days after his parents appeared as the leading characters in an English version of Schiller's "Robbers." A lucky coincidence, truly, for the admirers of "prenatal influence!"

Few will care to hear retold the old story of how Poe's father, when a law student, beheld and married a pretty English actress; but it is but right to warn those who may meet with Mr. Didier's sketch, that there is no truth in his ultra-romantic story of the young couple having been killed in the burning of Richmond Theatre, on the 26th of December, 1811: Mrs. Poe died in her bed on the 8th day of the said December, as reference to a file of any Richmond paper for the current month would have shown: when and where the poet's father died is still a mystery.

The school experiences of Poe, as given on the authority of a Mr. Clarke, formerly a tutor in Richmond, Virginia, are equally untrustworthy. This gentleman, who, it is stated, has attained the age of eighty-six, must be gifted with a wonderful memory, if the reminiscences he supplies are to be relied on. He states:—

"In September, 1818, Mr. John Allan, a wealthy Scotch merchant residing in Richmond, brought to my school a little boy between eight and nine years old. 'This is my adopted son, Edgar Poe,' Mr. Allan said. 'His parents were burned to death when the theatre was destroyed. The little fellow has recently returned from a residence of two years in Scotland, where he has been studying English and Latin. I want to place him under your instruction.' I asked Edgar about his Latin. He said he had studied the grammar as far as the regular verbs. He declined *penna, domus, fructus*, and *res*. I then asked him whether he could decline the

adjective *bonus*. I was struck by the way in which he did it: he said,
'*bonus*, a good man; *bona*, a good woman; *bonum*, a good thing.' Edgar
Poe was five years in my school. During that time he read Ovid, Caesar,
Virgil, Cicero, and Horace in Latin, and Xenophon and Homer in Greek."

Unfortunately for this circumstantial introduction to Mr. Clarke's recollections of Poe, there is abundant evidence extant, including that of
the poet himself and of his mother-in-law, to prove that during this epoch (1816–1821) of his life he was at school in England.

Other data proffered by Mr. Didier, in his anxiety to correct the "many
false statements" of previous biographers, are equally unfortunate. It is
not necessary that we should adduce all his errors; but, in perusing this
compilation, we noted, amongst other inaccuracies of detail, the following needing correction. Poe's first volume of poems was *not* published
in 1824; it was *not* styled "Al Aaraaf, Tamerlane, and Minor Poems"; it
was *not* stated to be "by a Virginian"; it did *not* contain the lines "To
Helen," nor were those lines written by their author when thirteen
years of age. At p. 42, Mr. Didier declares that Poe was "the least creditable cadet that ever entered the Military Academy" at West Point,
which proves how little he knows of the history of that institution, whilst
his account of the poet's few months' stay at it shows how little he knows
of *that*. At p. 53, speaking of the "Tales of the Folio Club," a collection
of six of the poet's earliest prose pieces, he contrives to give an incorrect
catalogue of them, although he must have had their proper titles before
him; and, moreover, declares that they were perfect when they left their
author's hands—an opinion from which Poe certainly differed, as he
subsequently greatly revised them. At p. 58, the date of Poe's marriage
is misstated, in order to explain certain expressions contained in a letter
of the poet, and which really was written eight months before, instead
of the nine days after, his wedding; whilst the statement that, to gratify
his wife's taste for music, Poe—then living on 100*l.* a year—"had her
taught by the best masters," is not only contrary to reason, but to what
Mrs. Clemm, in a well-known letter, tells of the matter. In January, 1837,
Poe who had not then as here declared already "made a brilliant reputation," was not offered the associate editorship of the New York *Quarterly Review*, with a salary larger than he was receiving on the *Literary
Messenger*, nor did he contribute to said Review critiques on current
literature: he left Richmond for other reasons; he was never offered any
position on the Review, and never wrote but one critique for it, and then
at his own request. The magazine which Mr. Didier speaks about at
p. 65, upon investigation, he will doubtless find was known as the *North
American Magazine*, and not the *Museum*, as he repeatedly styles it,
and even makes Poe so name it. The statement that Graham bought the

Gentleman's Magazine of Burton in the "autumn" of 1840 is also incorrect; it had changed hands some time before, as the title-page proves. There is no truth in the allegations that Poe was "the first to proclaim the genius of Mrs. Browning to the world," or that "he was the first to introduce to American readers the then unknown poet, Tennyson, . . . at a time when the English critics had failed to discover the genius of the future Poet Laureate." Long before Poe had published a sentence about either of these English poets, their works were well known in both hemispheres. Nor did Poe declare that Dickens—for whom he had intense admiration—owed his great success as a novelist to the delineation of characters that "were grossly exaggerated caricatures," whether the truth of such an assertion be, or be not, "now generally admitted," as Mr. Didier avers.

It was in April, and not November, 1840, that Poe retired from editing *Graham's Magazine*; and it was from the *Dollar Newspaper,* and not the *Dollar Magazine,* that he obtained a prize for "The Gold Bug." "The Raven" was not, by a great many, the only composition that its author published under a *nom de plume*; nor is it correct to state, as Mr. Didier does, that "not a stanza, not a line, not a word, was changed" after it was first printed. Poe frequently altered it, as has been recently pointed out in the *Athenaeum,* in a letter which has been widely circulated in the United States. The note which originally headed "The Raven" was undoubtedly the production of Poe himself—a fact that will probably astonish Mr. Didier, who deems the author of it "could not have been long out of his short-clothes," but that it was never written as published in this book is as certain as it is that Poe never said he intended to limit the projected poem to 108 lines precisely. Indeed, Mr. Didier would appear throughout to have read his hero's works as witches said the Lord's Prayer. The account of a visit paid to the Poes at Fordham, derived from Mr. Ingram's "Memoir of Edgar Poe," and, like many other lengthy extracts from the same source, taken without acknowledgment by the compiler, exhibits other blunders: the visit was not paid by "a gentleman," but by the well-known Mrs. Gove-Nichols, and the account given by Mr. Didier, at pp. 99–102, of Mrs. Poe's death, notwithstanding its circumstantiality, is fictitious: letters from Poe and Mrs. Clemm are in existence which prove that, thanks to the generosity of Mrs. Houghton and other noble-hearted women, the poet's wife, during the last days of her existence, wanted for nothing that money and kindness could procure.

Enough has, doubtless, been said to prove the incorrectness of this "Life of Poe," and to show that if, as its author avers, the world has remained, up to the time of this publication "in ignorance of the *true* story of the poet's life," it is certain to remain some time longer in the same unenlightened condition. This *soi-disant* memoir, indeed, has nothing new of value to offer us, and even ignores entirely some of the most interesting episodes of Poe's career, such as his school-days at Stoke Newington; his subsequent adventures in Europe; the story of his first love, and of the fidelity and generosity of the friends of his latter years; nor does it, notwithstanding its pretensions, furnish a scrap not already well known of Poe's correspondence. Had Mr. Didier possessed the industry and ability necessary for the work he has attempted, he might have succeeded better than any of his predecessors, of whose labours he has so largely made use, but to not one of whom he has proffered a single word of acknowledgment. He lives among many of the surviving friends and relatives of the poet, and near to the scenes and abodes in which a large portion of Poe's life was passed. He claims to have been intimate with Mrs. Clemm, and to have had placed at his disposal details and letters which were inaccessible to others, and the result of the advantages which he appears to have enjoyed is this incongrous compilation of hackneyed details and ludicrous blunders.

Mr. Didier's critical acumen and brilliancy of style a few specimens will suffice to prove, whilst his classical learning may be inferred from such remarks as that of schoolboys writing Latin odes "after the style of the '*O jam Satis* (sic) of Horace." Poe's tales, Mr. Didier tells us, fascinate and astonish the reader with "the verisimilitude of their improbability"; and his reviews, he deems, prove their author to have been "the most consummate critic that ever lived." "The Raven," this same authority asserts, placed its writer "in the front rank of the poets of the world"; and that to Poe America is indebted—"prenatal influences" notwithstanding—for conferring upon it the glory of having produced "the most original poet of the century," and a genius who "always dressed with extreme elegance and in perfect taste," and who "generally wore grey clothes, a loose black cravat, and turn-down collar." With the misascription of "Genius is patience," Mr. Didier informs us that "there never was a more patient genius than Edgar A. Poe"; that he was "never idle, never lounging; when not engaged upon a critique, he was writing a tale or a poem"; and that he knew English literature "from the very source—from Chaucer, the first Poet Laureate"; which latter information will, doubtless, prove acceptable to *Notes and Queries*.

Space will not admit of any of Mr. Didier's varied portraitures of his hero—with his brow "white as a girl's and as beautiful as a god's"—who "did not attempt to shake any man's religion," and "seduced no one from the path of virtue by the voluptuous enchantment of his writings. Byron did this," concludes Mr. Didier, "and more than this: to the evil influence of his writings he added the evil example of his life." After this parting kick at a Britisher, we must bid farewell to the whitewasher of the Raven. As for the "Additional Poems" of the title-page, there is not one discoverable in the book itself.

173. Sarah Helen Whitman to John H. Ingram. Item 316

Dear Mr. Ingram, March 2, [18]77
 Yours of Feb. 14 just received. Something in its tone pains me more than I can express. Are there then *two Ingrams* as well as "two Poes"?
 Since you are disposed to question and cross-examine my testimony so peremptorily with regard to Miss Blackwell, let me once more tell you, very briefly, that *all* that I have said to you with regard to her knowledge of Poe & of the Fordham cottage was derived from *herself.* She it was who told me of her visit to Fordham in company with a lady whose name she seems now to have "forgotten," Mrs. Gove Nichols.
 Her visit of a few weeks at the cottage for the benefit of country air and rest from protracted labors was also, as I understood her to say, induced by the kind advice of the same lady in the spring of 1847, while she was under her medical treatment.
 You quote from Miss Blackwell's letter to you the words "I do not think I ever received a line from him . . . . there must be some mistake . . . the extreme slightness of my acquaintance with him precluding all probability of his having ever written to me."
 Now it is possible that Miss Blackwell never did receive from Poe any letter save that of which I sent you a copy. The letter was written in reply to one which she had addressed to him as to the publication of a volume of poems which had already appeared in the magazines of the time.
 The passage in which he spoke of his interest in me, etc. etc., his seeing me *but once,* & his wish that she should write to him of me could have had little interest for *her,* since she did not speak of it to me until she had had it more than a fortnight, although we saw each other daily. I have told you how she happened to give me the letter. I have told you also that in Feb. 1861 I gave the letter to the Hon. John R. Bartlett of this city, at his earnest request for an autograph of Poe, which, though intimate with many of Poe's intimate friends, he had long sought for in vain. He had perhaps the finest collection of autographs in New England, superbly bound in heavy folios. He is brother-in-law to Senator Anthony, & like him, was an intimate friend of Mrs. Osgood, yet neither of these gentlemen had been able to procure a fragment of Poe's writing. Mr. Bartlett is also an intimate friend of our friend, Mr. C. Fiske Harris. They are both enthusiastic bibliophiles.
 But to the letter just received from you. You say, "Do you not think there must be some mistake about Miss Blackwell's ever having stayed at Fordham as you have described? Who could have given you the information? Nothing one gets about Poe seems reliable." Again, "If my memory serves me right, Mrs. Gove Nichols, who, *you* thought

introduced Miss A[nna] Blackwell to the Poes, did not *know* Miss Blackwell."[1]

Let me once more remind you, since you seem to have forgotten, that you wrote me you had spoken to Mrs. Nichols about Miss *Elizabeth* Blackwell, & she replied that she was not acquainted with her, and that I then wrote to you that it was not Dr. *Elizabeth* Blackwell but Miss *Anna* Blackwell of whom I had spoken to you.

Write once more to Mrs. Nichols & I doubt not she will confirm all that Miss Blackwell told me in relation to the Fordham visit.

As to the letter, you can find all that I have said *authenticated* by addressing a line to Hon. John R. Bartlett.

If Mrs. Nichols does not confirm my report, I shall think that there is either no Miss Anna Blackwell or that there are *two* Mrs. Nichols.

In the meantime, I enclose a letter from Miss Blackwell written from England in the spring of [18]49 to her Providence friend, lest you should think there is no

                                                                  Providence

"Tis bitter cold & I am sick at heart."

I should not have felt so deeply wounded by the acrimonious tone of your letter had you not *evaded* a request I made to you, for a copy of a paragraph in one of Mrs. Clemm's letters to me, by saying all my papers, etc. should be returned to me when *demanded*![2]

I will apprise Mr. Harris of your request.

Return Miss Blackwell's letter at your convenience. It contains nothing of importance save the verification of identity, but I should like to retain it.

Benedicite.

I am not aware that Mr. Didier has ever spoken an unkind or disparaging word of you. Why should you be enemies?

1. The first of these two quotations is in Ingram's letter of Feb. 14, 1877, p. 475; the second is on a stray page from one of Ingram's letters which Mrs. Whitman must have returned to him to prove her point, for it is filmed with his papers on Roll No. 2, following Item 174.

2. This exact wording is not discoverable in any of the surviving Ingram letters.

174.   *Sarah Helen Whitman to John H. Ingram.   Item 319*

To one who calls himself my "friend,"   April [March] 13, [18]77

In your letter of March 19 [Feb. 14], [18]77, you informed me that you had *lent* Didier's "Memoir" which I sent you to "a friend,"—that I should find his notice of it in the London *Athenaeum* for Feb. 10. On

Saturday, April [March] 3, the day after I mailed my reply to you, I went to our Providence Library to look at the notice.

As I entered the reading room, Mr. C. Fiske Harris, who was standing near one of the alcoves, came to meet me & asked if I had seen your attack on me in the London *Athenaeum*.[1]

I thought at first there was some mistake. The paper had been removed from the reading room for later issues, but Mr. Harris presently procured me a copy from the Librarian.

That you should have directed my attention to this singular performance surprises me. Mr. Bartlett has just procured me a copy from Cambridge, the periodical being furnished here only to subscribers, and I have re-read the virulent article with renewed astonishment.

Of course these gentlemen who are devotedly my friends feel that no friend of mine would have written or *authorized* such an unprovoked assault.

Let us not revert to it. The matter itself was of little moment, but the *animus* of it gave a rude shock to all my previous impressions of the young Englishman who in his generous advocacy of an American poet had invoked my aid, sought my confidence and my criticism, and hailed me as his "Providence"!

"It was not an enemy who had done this"—it was my trusted friend & correspondent, a gentleman of whom no one had previously written to me or spoken in my presence a single word which might not have been written or spoken to one known as your faithful & inviolable friend! It was a startling & strange revelation—a wound that time cannot heal.

Let me briefly revert to your letter. You say you did not know that I was acquainted with Miss Blackwell! It seems incredible that you should so soon have forgotten all that I have told you in relation to her. Not very long ago I sent you a brief note from her, dated Sept. 1848, in which she speaks of her regret at not having been well enough to see me when I called at her hotel in the morning with E.A.P., & makes playful allusion to the *rose-garden*, asking if the *roses were still blooming*. Apparently you must have returned her note to me without reading it.

And now you tell me you do not think Poe was in Richmond until June 1849, having "*pretty full knowledge of Poe's whole time for 1848.*" If you have still in your possession the copy made at your request of Poe's long letter to me, dated Sunday evening, October 1, 1848, you will see what Poe himself says about this matter.[2] If you have any doubts of the *genuineness* of the letter you can apply to our friend Davidson who had the *original* in his possession from March 1858 to June 21 of the same year.

I have had no correspondence with Mr. Didier for months & the only intelligence which I have communicated to him was contained in the letter which he introduced as an "Introductory" one, but the few brief letters which I have received from him have had a character of manliness, sincerity, & courtesy which impressed me very favorably, & his book has confirmed the impression, nor do I yet understand the ground of your displeasure against him. As to the *Scribner* poem, I have long known from friends in Baltimore that the facsimile was a genuine one. Mr. Didier himself has never *alluded* to the subject in his correspondence with me. But there are other papers in the same handwriting whose authenticity is *unquestionable* & which I understand will soon be published by another collector of autographs.

We seem to have been "like ships that speak each other on the sea, then pass to meet no more."

Vale atque vale.

S.H.W.

1. This is, of course, the "severe skull dragging" Ingram mentioned, p. 474.

2. See Ostrom, II, 387, for complete text. Poe says clearly that he was in Richmond in the summer of 1848.

175. *John H. Ingram to Sarah Helen Whitman*

My dear Friend,   19 March 1877
(For I cannot help deeming that your are *that* at heart, & so I shall, therefore, address you until you restrain me)—I must confess that I am somewhat at a loss how to answer yours of the 2nd. My letter of the 14th Feby. was—*certainly, as regards you*—written with all my usual affection and regard for you, & without any reserve, & yet you say "something in its tone pains" you, & that you felt "deeply wounded by its acrimonious tone," & by my evading a request "for a copy of a paragraph in one of Mrs. Clemm's letters" to you, & that I said all your papers should be returned when *demanded.*

Let me take up these remarks of yours categorically: as regards my tone I really know not what to say—I have, & have had for some years, several American correspondents (I will not say "friends," for *all my friends*, save mother & sisters, are gone to seek that bourne whence no traveller returns)—and have been in constant correspondence with them a long while, but not to one of them have I opened my heart & mind as I have to you, nor treated any of them with the confidence & unwavering reliance which I have you, & yet I have not had a single ripple to disturb the surface of our acquaintanceship—that has been reserved for *our* correspondence—but why? Is it that you have some *nearer* "friend"—who instills suspicion & mistrust into your mind? Cast a glance over all our past communion &, *unaided by anyone,* think whether I have ever behaved towards you & your wishes, *knowingly,* other than you could have desired. I have deferred to your wishes in the matter of my writings about Poe more than I would to any other living person—and shall continue to do so.

As regards "evading" the request. Your letter is at home which asked me to copy the paragraph, but I feel certain that you said "some day when at leisure," or words to that effect, & *never gave me any reason to think you wanted the copy at once.*

As regards the interpretation you put upon "demanded." I am certain that if you read the context, so far from there being anything "acrimonious," you will find it jocular—or an attempt to be.

I return that letter of Mrs. Clemm's, & will return the others in my next.

You will find that Mrs. C[lemm] was more reliable than you seem to think. I do not think that Poe was in Richmond until June 1849, for his second visit. I was misled myself by those reminiscences of J[ohn] Thompson's. I have pretty full knowledge of Poe's whole time for 1848, & do not see that he could have visited Richmond. He certainly did not renew his acquaintance with Mrs. Shelton until latter half of 1849.

I never was "disposed to question & cross examine *your* testimony" with regard to Miss Blackwell, whose letter to me as well as hers to you, I enclose—but it did seem to me at first flush that I had written to the wrong woman. And you must remember that I nearly always write to you in the midst of official worry & without any means at hand for reference, & that *I had quite forgotten for the time that you had any personal* knowledge of Miss Blackwell, and in my letter to her I was so careful of your feelings that I in no way hinted that you had communicated the contents of Poe's letter to her to me. *Your* testimony I do not for one instant question, & did not, only at the moment thought you might have been misinformed—forgetting, as said above, your personal knowledge of Miss B[lackwell]: had I mentioned *that* she could not so readily have repudiated the affair. Kindly let me have her letter to me, which I have not, & shall not answer.

I have just heard from Mrs. Gove Nichols—not about the Blackwells—to say she thinks of coming to reside in London permanently & hopes then to see me, so we shall be able to have some long chats, I hope. Mrs. Lewis either does not, or *will not,* know anything about Poe,—recountable. Mrs. Houghton, who is a dear creature, has had terrible domestic troubles, but is firm as a rock. Mrs. Richmond has been most kind. The *Tales of the Grotesque and A[rabesque]*, she sent me, were in Poe's portmanteau when he was found dying.

Pray ask Mr. Harris to let me have the copy of his copy of the *Diabolus* brochure at his *earliest convenience*. I hope to have another work, if not two! out soon, & before the life!

I want Davidson to undertake something that way also—all my knowledge & collection is at his service. He, & Browne, & Valentine, are ceaseless in their aid.

Could not Mr. Bartlett name some American collectors of autographs to whom I could apply for copies of Poe's letters? Mrs. H[arriet] B[eecher] Stowe probably has one or more of Poe's letters in her immense collection, but I never could bring myself to write & ask a favour of *her*!

You wind up your terrible letter with remark about Didier, & say that you are not aware that he has ever spoken "an unkind or disparaging word" about me. Nor am I—why should he? He has, indeed, been very careful not to make a single allusion to the Mr. Ingram whose researches he has not only availed himself of but whose writing he has copied—paragraph after paragraph—without the addition of even inverted commas. Facts are everybody's when published, & although want of courtesy or honesty may cause the acknowledgment of their authority to be omitted, the *ideas* of other people are only appropriated by rogues. Poe's cause can never be aided by making him out, either, to have been an industrious commonplace dandy.

As regards the letter I sent you of D[idier]'s, & the accompanying information, I did so in remembrance of what you had said in former days, that you were so afraid of things not by Poe, being imputed to him. Poe may have composed "Alone," but any court of law would decide that Mr. D[idier] wrote the MS. of which *facsimile* appeared in *Scribner's*. He has taken what he deems a popular side *now*, but his whole conduct is beneath contempt, whilst his *facts* are as fictitious, &, therefore, as hurtful as Griswold's. My *data* were not always right, but I never, knowingly, misstated.

Goodbye for a few days. Ere this reaches you I sincerely hope that you will be free from the misguiding influence, & once more be prepared to look upon, as your ever faithful friend,

John H. Ingram

P.S. I have written to Miss Peckham & had reply & written to her again.

176. John H. Ingram to Sarah Helen Whitman.

26 April 1877

I little thought that the day would come when I should receive such a letter [Mar. 13] as that you have just sent me, although the tone of your previous one should have prepared me for it.

It is only another illusion dispelled, another of the few joys I had left in this world gone—to find that I deceived myself in believing you my friend.

In parting from one from whom I have never swerved in sincere respect and affection, & to whom I shall ever display a loyal fidelity, it ill becomes me to refer to tokens—known or unknown—I have invariably given of the truth of my professions but, with regard to what you call "an attack upon you," but in which I fail to see anything but *a kindly allusion, I here declare that the words are not mine.* Not that it matters now. I see that you wish to be free from me & one way is as good as another.

I will take an early opportunity of looking out all that I have of yours & will return it. I trust that your next *protégé* will serve you as faithfully as I have ever done.

Do not think, however, that this time I relinquish the work I have so long meditated upon. I shall not be false to myself in that, and, as it will be impossible to omit your name, I trust you will still permit me to avail myself of such matter relating to you as has *already been published*?

That amid my many works, griefs, & occupations, I should have *pro tem* overlooked what you have said about Miss Blackwell, only those most prejudiced against me could have been surprised at, but that Miss B[lackwell] & Mrs. Nichols, who *says Miss B[lackwell] certainly never stayed at Fordham,* should have forgotten *events* in their own lives does seem strange. I am quite willing to accept your testimony—as you well know—that Poe was in Richmond in 1848, although it can only have been for a day or two &, probably, without Mrs. Clemm's knowledge—not, indeed, that I am likely to take her evidence without additional testimony.

You know in your heart of hearts that I never have doubted *your words,* but that I was mistaken in your ideas with regard to myself, I frankly confess is a fact. I was so foolish as to deem you actuated towards me with the same feelings of regard & friendship that I felt towards you.

That you deem Mr. Didier a representative of "manliness, sincerity, & courtesy" certainly proves how different are our gauges of such characteristics. A man who obtains money under false pretenses &

steals other persons' property would not, according to my standard, be *chevalier sans reproche.*

You do not say that you received the letter of Mrs. Clemm's which I enclosed, but I trust it reached you safely.

I cannot palter with words any longer, & only pray that if there be any protecting spirits to this most wretched and delplorable sphere they may ever guard you, & be as truly faithful to you as has ever been,

John H. Ingram

P.S. I have twice requested Mr. Davidson to obtain & forward you copy of Mr. Didier's *Life.* If he has not done so, I will obtain & return the one you sent.[1]

1. John Ingram could not have afforded to return Mrs. Whitman's copy of Didier's book, for he had annotated it heavily, as was his invariable custom when reading other persons' attempts at writing Poe biography, and some of the same remarks in the margins of the pages, in Ingram's script, were later used in the printed review of the book, as Mrs. Whitman would have clearly recognized, had she needed any further proof that Ingram had indeed written the review. Nine months were to pass before Ingram again wrote to Mrs. Whitman.

177.   Review of William F. Gill's Life of Edgar Allan Poe, *by John H. Ingram, London* Athenaeum, *Oct. 6, 1877, p. 539*

The Life of Edgar Allan Poe. By William F. Gill.
(New York, C. T. Dillingham.)
[John Ingram]

ILL-FATED IN his life, Edgar Poe has been still more ill-fated in his biographies, especially those of his native land. Beyond a short critique by Prof. Lowell, and Mrs. Whitman's eloquent little volume on "Poe and his Critics," we know of no American publication affording the slightest evidence of its author's capability to appreciate the poet's genius. And yet, under the title of "Original Memoir of Poe," *réchauffé* compilations, seasoned with a few additional scandals more or less pertinent to the poet's story, follow one another with the greatest regularity in the United States. A few months ago we noticed one of the most pretentious of these volumes; and now we have to allude to another, replete with most of its predecessor's faults, and only less vulgar because containing less of its editor's own phraseology. This "Life of Poe" is written, its author informs us, to correct Griswold's "numerous inconsistencies" and "glaring falsehoods"; but, after perusal of the book, we are forced to the conclusion that its compiler cannot have read his predecessor's work through, or he would not make the many erroneous statements about it that he does. Some of his misstatements, indeed, are so singular, that it seems strange that they can have been made unintentionally; whilst his blunders, whenever he attempts to give information derived from "original investigation," are most ludicrous.

"Another *raison d'etre* of this book is," says Mr. Gill, the complaint of an English author that "no trustworthy biography of Poe has yet appeared in his own country." If Mr. Gill intended this Life to remove the reproach, he has failed utterly. Unwilling or unable to thoroughly investigate personally the subject of his work, he has contented himself with taking Mr. Ingram's recent "Memoir of Poe" as the basis and main source of his compilation, added several pages from Mrs. Whitman's book, a few untrustworthy *data* from an old sketch by Mr. Stoddard, interlarded some irretrievably vulgar anecdotes, and, concluding with a republication of the threadbare "Memorial Ceremonies" of 1875, entitles the collection "the first complete life of Edgar Poe yet published." Could he have seen our recent review of Mr. Didier's volume, he would, doubtless, have deferred publication of this book until he had corrected some of the many preposterous errors with which it abounds. His most glaring fault is want of knowledge of the subject he is writing upon; in reprinting quotations from the writers whose works he makes so free with, he almost invariably betrays the fact that, instead of referring to the original source, he is citing at second-hand. He continually indulges in long *verbatim* or slightly altered excerpts from his predecessors, without affording the least acknowledgment of his indebtedness; and, whenever he does confessedly quote, he nearly always fathers the quotation upon the wrong person, as when he ascribes to Hannay the twaddle quoted at page 113, whilst Griswold and some mythical "London editor" are made responsible for much that outside Mr. Gill's Life it will be difficult to discover. Mr. Ingram's Memoir is followed with blind reverence, although, of course, without acknowledgment, and the consequences are often quite laughable. For instance, catching at an allusion to an article on Poe in the *Northern Monthly* for 1868, Mr. Gill misreads it, and states that Poe was engaged upon that periodical, although it was not started until nearly twenty years after his decease.

Mr. Gill's *errata* and blunders would require several pages of the *Athenaeum* to set forth, but we can only allot a few words to the bare mention of some of the most self-evident. Poe did not plead guilty to all of the specifications of the West Point court-martial, nor were they "innumerable," nor were some of them "thoroughly absurd." It was long before, instead of after, his career at West Point that the poet met Miss Royster; nor was it previous to, but after, his departure for Richmond that he married. He was not a regular contributor to the *New York Quarterly Review*. He did try to start a magazine of his own whilst with Mr.

Burton; and did do many other thing which Mr. Gill alleges that he did not, and did not do many things which he declares that he did do; whilst to assert that he had no "craving for stimulants" is to falsify his story, and is in direct contradiction to Poe's own written words (*vide* Mrs. Whitman, pp. 74, 75). Where Poe's "expressed dictum" that his earlier poems should not be published is to be found we should be glad to learn, as also Mr. Gill's authority for several other equally unsupported statements; and we only regret that, in return, we may not promise to say of this Life what he tells the newspaper correspondents said of his reading, viz. that it was "the finest rendition of 'The Raven'" to which they had ever listened, and that Mr. Gill's "resemblance to the recognized ideals of Mr. Poe himself made the personation of his horror and despair almost painful."

178. *Gill's Reply to Ingram's Review, New York* Herald, *Nov. 11, 1877*

Gill's Life of Poe.

How the "Athenaeum" Criticism Came to Be Written—The
Claims of Mr. Ingram Controverted—Mr. Gill's Reply.

To the Editor of the Herald: In the SUNDAY HERALD of Oct. 28 appeared a criticism of my "Life of Edgar A. Poe," copied from the London Athenaeum, the source of which explains its virulent animus.

As my veracity has been called in question it becomes necessary, in order to explain the significance of the Athenaeum article, to revert at some length, to a controversy, incited nearly ten years ago by Mr. J. H. Ingram of London, who is repeatedly referred to in a complimentary manner by the critic of the Athenaeum. This Mr. Ingram, it should be stated, is a clerk in the London Postoffice, and also an attache of the Athenaeum, a journal that has for some years past distinguished itself in the abuse of American authors. Mr. Ingram, like Mark Meddle in "London Assurance" courts notoriety, and, having failed to enlist any attention in his memoir of Poe has, since its publication, groped among the outskirts of the literary circles, and with his shoulders laden to his ears with chips, craving, like Meddle, a blow or a kick. Nearly two years ago (February, 1876) he got what he had for some time desired in this way, in a letter published by me in the London Athenaeum, and copied here in the New York Evening Post and other journals.

[. . . . .]

As regards the charge that I have not given credit to authors from whom I have quoted in my "Life," it is equally false [as was Ingram's charge that Gill had reverently followed and copied Ingram's Memoir of Poe], as any one who will examine its pages will at once perceive. I repeatedly credit Mrs. Whitman facts derived from her. On page 22 I specially mention Mr. Stoddard as authority for the only statement quoted from him, and devote three pages (265, 266, 267), to the mention of writers, including Mr. Ingram, who have written concerning Poe.

As to the "mythical London editor," mentioned in the article, the disingenuousness of the writer is clearly shown; for I expressly *quote* Mr. Thomas Cottrell Clarke as authority for the statement made, not claiming them as original.

When the writer stigmatizes as untrue my account of Poe's dismissal from West Point, he controverts the written testimony of the poet himself, from which my statement is made. If Poe did not himself know the facts connected with his dismissal from West Point, then the Athenaeum is right and I am wrong, but it would seem to be a matter in which the poet's own testimony was significant.

Again, the Athenaeum "critic" who, it needs no ghost come from the other world to tell us, is

MR. INGRAM HIMSELF

states that he was not married before leaving for Richmond. Now, as I have seen a copy of the marriage certificate in the hands of the sister of the poet's wife, I may also be permitted to put this testimony against this writer's erroneous statement of the fact in his book.

As regards any actual errors in my biography, I am well aware that such exist, but not those which the Athenaeum critic has enumerated. In the closing page of my "Life," I expressly abnegate any claim to adequacy or perfection for it.

Since its issue, I have gathered much new material, and, in a new and enlarged edition of the work, shall utilize it, to its improvement, I trust. Mr. Ingram, probably aware that my "Life" is to be republished in England, and sensible of the effect that its disclosure of the unreliability of his memoir will produce, took the only available means of modifying this unpleasant effect by animadverting upon the trustworthiness of my biography in the columns of the journal to which he is attached. A noteworthy fact, in connection with Mr. Ingram's criticism, is that no copy of my book has yet been sent by the publishers to the Athenaeum, or to any other English journal, for review.

The enterprising gentleman must have ordered a copy from America for the express purpose to which it was devoted.

In conclusion, permit me to state that Mr. Ingram's memoir, which the Athenaeum accuses me of "blindly following," is comprised in 99 12mo. pages, while my "Life," also a 12mo., contains 315 pages.

Dr. Johnson has said that he never knew that he had succeeded until "he felt the rebound." According to this test Mr. Ingram has paid my "Life" a compliment by his virulent attack which should compensate for the bad temper brought to it. Yours respectfully,
Boston, Nov, 7, 1877.   William F. Gill

179. *Sarah Helen Whitman to John H. Ingram.*   Item 329

Dear Mr. Ingram,   Jan. 16, [18]78
   Thanks for your interesting enclosures and for the significant quotation from George Sand.[1]
   I might transcribe it as my sole reply, in heartfelt sincerity & good-will.
   If your words in some of those letters of the past, to me, eventful year, caused me profound pain at the time, the *via dolorosa* which I have of late been called to tread has effaced all minor sorrows, and regrets.
   I remember only the happiness I felt in your earlier sympathy & friendship.
   I have had from my dear Rose a letter that cheered and blessed me. Tell her this when you write. I am for the present in the beautiful home of the Dailey's, which she knows well, doubtless, with all my household gods around me, saving such as fell under the auctioneer's hammer.[2] The walls of my room are hung with mirrors old & new, & with pictures of the same diverse epochs of history.
   I am sitting before a cheerful wood fire in an upper-room looking out on fields & meadows & pleasant gardens. Apollo—*my* Apollo stands on a pedestal at the door of entrance in the upper hall—my Venus of Milo adorns the lower hall, and my bronze censer from the palace of the Emperor of Peking breathes myrrh & sandalwood from its dragon's mouth, whenever the company in the parlor below wishes to be "drowsed in the Orient's dusky thought."
   I do not know that I ever sent you the lines written in my old home & dedicated to a friend who had just died at St. Helena, S.C. The picture of the old place is dearer to me *now*, since I shall never see it again as it was.
   I read with interest your paper & the article by J.H.I. which it contained.[3]
   I write in haste.
   With dearest love to Rose, to whom I will write soon.
   I am most sincerely your friend,
                                                    S. H. Whitman

Davidson has been very ill of malarial fever since his autumnal visit to Florida, but writes that he is recovering.

1. If Mrs. Whitman dated this letter accurately, there is a missing Ingram letter. Although Ingram writes in his next letter (No. 180, Feb. 2, 1878) as if it were his first communication with her since his embittered farewell of Apr. 26, 1877, the dates on both holographs (Nos. 179 and 180) are clear, and internal evidence suggests that the missing letter was written in early December 1877 (see p. 493 and page 494, n.1). If both writers are referring to the same enclosures (which have not survived), Ingram may have sent in December only enclosures and an apparently conciliatory quotation from George Sand in an effort to determine Mrs. Whitman's feelings toward him, and Number 180 may be his first real letter since their break, hence his phrasing and tone.

2. After her sister's death, Mrs. Whitman disposed of many of her personal possessions and moved, by gracious invitation, into the home of Mrs. Albert Dailey and her daughters in Providence.

3. Almost certainly an account of Ingram's discovery of Poe's "The Journal of Julius Rodman," which was printed in the London *Athenaeum*, Nov. 3, 1877.

180. *John H. Ingram to Sarah Helen Whitman*

My dear Friend,   2 Feb. [18]78
For such I again venture to address you now—as I hope our clouds have disappeared.

Your great sorrow I heard of through our dear "mutual friend" of Paris but not, of course until I had sent off my enclosures.[1]

Since last we exchanged penned thoughts across the ocean so much of sad & glad things have happened. You have parted for awhile with almost the other half of your life—I—I have had my trials. A dear little nephew, whom I looked to as the future representative of our ill-omened & hapless family, has been placed in the bosom of Mother Earth. "Other friends have flown *before*." But the world spins on & the winds, the tides, all nature performs her duties as of heretofore, & we *must* do the same.

The last few months have been a period of immense literary activity with me. I cannot mention a tithe of my published papers—too many for goodness, indeed. I wrote two papers on De Quincey, the longer & better for America (in the *International Review*) as a critique on a new life of the Opium Eater by Japp, the man who wrote the review of Poe for the B[ritish] Q[uarterly] R[eview].[2] Then recently I have had articles on "Fernán Caballero," the Spanish female novelist who died recently, in the *Dublin University Maga[zine]* & on (for the same publication) "J. C. Mangan"—but this latter—I fancy—was sent you.[3] Then papers in English & French (in U. States & France) on a young English poet, O'Shaughnessy—(Irish, rather). I met him yesterday at another poet's to hear Villon read. Then I have had papers weekly in the *Mirror*, which has revived. This week's I send you with a medley therein, about authors including Poe.[4]

I have just written a paper for *New York, London, Paris, & Leipzig!* on the "Unknown Correspondence of Edgar Poe." It will startle the literary world, I fancy. It only refers, as a rule, to the three last years of his life, but will give the chief portions of 15 or more unknown letters about new, unknown incidents in his life.[5]

This is only a sample of the immense amount of material I have accumulated about our hero. I hope to visit America this year for, without such a visit, I fancy, I cannot do this subject justice. What an amount I shall have to tell you.

I have written for next week or so a short hurried paper on Oliver Madox Brown's literary remains.[6] Have you heard of the poor boy? Not 20 when he died & yet already a genius! Son of F[ord] Madox Brown, the artist & brother-in-law to W. Rossetti & Dr. F. Hueffer.

Have you heard of *poor Mrs. Houghton's death?*[7] She was true to the last & thought of me & my objects with almost her last thoughts—or rather words. I quite loved her.

Your have not, of course, hear [*sic*] of how Mrs. Richmond's MSS. of "The Bells" & "A Dream within a Dream" were stolen—at the photographers?[8]

Last Oct. in Paris I had many chats with Mallarmé over Poe matters—but more of this hereafter.

You will—or have—heard of *your* dear Rose, and of how she so kindly consented to immortalize my weary face on canvas. I cannot express the joy it was to me to meet her & her graceful sister Kate in the dreary wastes of Paris life.

In a day or so, my friend H. B. Forman, the Shelley editor, of whom you wot, will publish the love letters of Keats from the original MSS.[9] Quite a treat. They will appear in New York at same time—and now, pray write again & forgive this hurried scrawl from he who has never really swerved in his allegiance to you—from

John H. Ingram

1. Mrs. Whitman's sister, Susan Anna Power, had died on Dec. 8, 1877.

2. H. A. Page [A. H. Japp], *Thomas DeQuincey; his life and writings, with unpublished correspondence* (London: J. Hogg & Co., 1877).

3. These articles were later printed in book form, as part of the Illustrated Library of Fairy Tales: *The Bird of Truth* (translated from the Spanish) of Fernán Caballero. By John H. Ingram. (London: Sonneschein & Allan, 1881). An announcement in the London *Athenaeum*, Nov. 17, 1877, stated that "a critical and biographical article by Mr. John H. Ingram, on James Clarence Mangan, the Irish poet, will appear in the December number of the *Dublin University Magazine*."

4. The most important of these papers in the newly revived London *Mirror of Liter-*

ature appeared Nov. 3, 1877, displaying another triumph of Ingram's: " 'The Journal of Julius Rodman,' a Newly-Discovered Work by the Late Edgar A. Poe."

A paper Ingram did *not* mention in this letter as having recently published was his long, blistering review in the London *Athenaeum* of Gill's *Life of Poe*, which was reprinted in the Boston *Herald*, Oct. 28, 1877, forwarded, without doubt, by Ingram. A copy of Gill's reply is pasted in one of Mrs. Whitman's scrapbooks, now in the Brown University Library.

5. Ingram's calling Mrs. Whitman's attention to this forthcoming publication was surely malicious in intent, as was his subsequent sending her copies of the article (Apr. 9, 1878). See page 497, n.1.

6. As he usually did, Ingram expanded this paper and others on the same subject into a book, *Oliver Madox-Brown: A Biographical Sketch* (London: Elliot Stock, 1883).

7. Mrs. Marie Louise Shew Houghton had died on Sept. 3, 1877.

8. While "stolen" is inaccurate, the story of the manuscripts being lost and found by the photographer is detailed in Mrs. Richmond's letters to Ingram, Jan. 8 and Feb. 5, 1878, in *Building Poe Biography*, pp. 182–84. Items 328 and 330 in the Ingram Poe Collection.

9. Harry Buxton Forman, *Letters of John Keats to Fanny Brawn written in the years MDCCCXIX and MDCCCXX and now given from the original manuscripts and notes*, Printed for private circulation (London: Reeves & Turner, 1878), 128 pp.

181. Sarah Helen Whitman to John H. Ingram. Item 333

Dear Mr. Ingram,   March 9, 1878
Do not think that I have failed to acknowledge your very interesting letter through indifference or neglect. I have much to say to you— much to ask of you.

I am preparing at intervals of leisure something to leave to those who love me after my "de-materialization," as the seance circles of our friend Mrs. Nichols might say.[1]

All through the month of February I have been suffering from pneumonial fever—my annual experience—I have not even written to dear Rose to thank her for the vivid & speaking photo which she sent me—nor to any foreign correspondent—so busy & so weary have I been with the cares & changes incident to leaving my home of the last ten years.

I ~~enclose to you~~ will write very soon if possible.
Your sorrow is a sorrow to me always. Benedicite.
                                                      S.H.W.

P.S. Mrs. Clemm's letters came safely.

1. Mrs. Whitman spent her last days sorting her papers and preparing her poems for publication after her death. They were published in 1879 by Houghton, Osgood & Co., of Boston.

182.   John H. Ingram to Sarah Helen Whitman

My dear Friend,   9 April 1878
    For such I must still style you, & such, when we are dematerialized,
I trust you shall be found to be.
    Your little note [Mar. 9] came, & I have long longed to reply but,
apart from the ever pressing duties of life, & *the voluminous
correspondence in several languages* far beyond my control, I have
been suffering from, for some time, a most depressing melancholia &
am quite unable to cast it off. So pray forgive my not acknowledging
yours at once.
    I was working very hard on the *Mirror* & other publications—so
hard that I had not time to think—when suddenly that erratic journal
was stopped & I was flung into a semi-state of idleness—no, not
idleness, for I have always plenty of irons in the furnace, but the
urgency was gone, & I have suffered from the collapse.
    During the interregnum in our correspondence so much has
happened that our letters cannot gather up again, that I look forward to
an interview for the clearing ups, detailments of all intervening
matters.
    The "boulders" of fact & fiction, anent the *Library Table*–Ellet affair,
duly passed through my hand, & I was sorely driven to "put in my oar"
but wisely abstained. The Briggs venom, however, is still working &
only a few days ago I received a Boston paper, a religious publication,
declaring all kinds of *mysterious* crimes & *unnamed* misdeeds had
been done by the Raven. But anonymous ephemeral paragraphs are
not worth notice, save in a general way, such as in my "Unknown
Correspondence by E. Poe"—two copies of which I have desired
Appleton's to send you.
    You will find therein a copy of *his* letter to Miss Blackwell. I thought
it right that that should appear & that you could not have any objection
to its publication. But it does not appear in the English version, which
is confined to Poe's relations with Mrs. Shew, Mrs. Richmond, & Mrs.
Royster [Shelton].
    I shall be anxious to hear your views on this paper.[1] You will see how
widely spread its circulation will be, by the little slip from the
Athenaeum I sent you. I am doing all I can, now-a-days, to spread
Poe's fame & vindication in *foreign lands*!!! In collecting all possible
editions of his works, I am astounded at their number. French
numberless—German 5—Italian & Spanish 2—that I know of. I shall
give a list of all editions some day.

                                                       10 April 1878
    I was stopped so often yesterday that I could not get finished by 4

P.M.., when a literary man called for me, & I had to forego the conclusion, & today my brain is so dull & vacant that I do not know what to ask, tell, or say.

Did I tell you that "Rose"—your New England Rose—had painted my portrait in oils? I cannot tell you how I value this painting, not merely on account of its likeness, & fine painting even as a picture, but also because of its artist's sake, & because I saw it grow into being— touch by touch. "Rose" is a real artist and, I am certain, will have few equals in America. She should be duly appreciated by your Providence.

Did you get my paper on J. C. Mangan? Either the English or American issues? Have you followed English literature of late? Seen Rossetti's new edition of works & "Memoir" of Shelley? That Gilfillan will publish a new life of Burns? &c.[2]

Did you ever hear of C. Kent's edition of Charles Lamb's works, with a short *vindicatory* "Memoir?"[3] Some unscrupulous scandal-mongers had put upon record that Lamb was a drunkard &, latterly, a maniac, & C. Kent has thoroughly "shut them up." He writes me that he was the first to introduce Poe's name & works (in 1852) to Bulwer, & that he was writing a vindication of E.A.P. some years back—from *intuition*, & without documentary evidence, when he was stopped by Lord Lytton (the present not the late Lord L.), informing him that I was just completing such a work.

All Europe that knew & appreciated Poe's poetry seemed eager & ready to prepare his vindication. How strange that my poor efforts should have been the first to effect anything—& stranger still, that his own countrymen should be the last to gloat over the virus spewed over his grave.

Happily, time puts all these things right as, I hope & trust, it will our mutual intercommunications.

I wish you would publish a new edition of *E[dgar] P[oe] & His Critics*—'tis always being asked for, & would be even more appreciated here than with you.

Always, believe me, here & *hereafter*, yours,

John H. Ingram

1. Ingram's "Unpublished Correspondence by Edgar Poe" was published in *Appleton's Journal* for May. This issue must have been out in mid-April, for Ingram had time to send Mrs. Whitman two copies of the article, and she had time to read it carefully and annotate it heavily. From these notes she prepared her first and only public attack on Ingram, an attack that focused on his ethical and scholarly deficiencies. It is reprinted here immediately following. A copy of Ingram's article, annotated in Mrs. Whitman's script, and a manuscript copy of her article, unsigned but probably written by Charlotte Dailey, are in Mrs. Whitman's papers in the John Hay Special Collections Library, Brown University.

In this article Ingram gave portions of a number of unpublished letters from Poe. (The article is not reprinted here; for complete texts of the letters therein, see Ostrom, II, 340, 350–51, 372–74, 400–404, 405–6, 414–15, 417–20, 425–26, 429–32, 434–36, 437–39, 446–48.) Ingram concludes with an account of Poe's "first and last love," Mrs. Shelton. When Mrs. Whitman read this article, she knew for the first time that at the same time Edgar Poe was engaged to marry her and was writing passionate literary love letters to her, he was also writing passionate personal love letters to another man's wife. Her attack is notable for its restraint and its wit: Ingram, she suggests, has done an unmistakable disservice to Poe's reputation, which he had spent so many years trying to redeem.

2. William Michael Rossetti, *The Poetical Works of Percy Bysshe Shelley, with a Critical Memoir* (London: Ward, Locke & Co., 1879). The Rev. George Gilfillan's first *Life of Robert Burns, with Memoir* had been published in 1856 (Edinburgh: J. Nichols).

3. *The Works of Charles Lamb*, ed. Charles Kent (London: Routledge & Sons, 1876).

183.   Review of John H. Ingram's "Unpublished Correspondence by Edgar A. Poe" (Appleton's Journal, 4 [May 1878], pp. 421–29), by Sarah Helen Whitman, Providence Journal, May 4, 1878

"The Unpublished Correspondence of Edgar Allan Poe"

Moore was blamed for burning the biographical memoranda confided to him for publication. Some of Poe's later memorialists may perhaps be blamed for *not* burning material confided to them for publication by Poe's nearest and dearest friends.

It will be remembered that in the March number of Scribner's Monthly for 1878, Mrs. Susan A. T. Weiss gave to the public her recollections of the "Last Days of Edgar Allan Poe," including the "true" story of his intentional rupture of an engagement with Mrs. Elmira Shelton, née Royster.

In the "Unpublished Correspondence" presented in the May number of Appleton's Journal, all this is reversed. The other side of the shield is now presented. Mrs. Shelton, after having been importuned on the subject for twenty-nine years, has at last spoken. We have the story, which Mr. Ingram assures us he was "graciously permitted to publish," in the lady's own words. It is direct and to the point. She was *not* engaged to Mr. Poe; but there was an *understanding* between them. Her version of the story is a very matter-of-fact, discreet, straightforward story, not *very* romantic, but very credible, and so realistic in some of its details, that Balzac himself might have written it.

Mr. Ingram enthusiastically calls it "the story of Poe's first and last love, as romantic and interesting as was ever penned by poet." This first and last love, however, does not seem to have precluded other romantic episodes whose epistolary records have also been confided to him, whether with a gracious permission for their publication does not appear.

The first letter in the series, Number one, purports to be a copy of "perhaps the only letter ever written by Poe to his wife," a somewhat startling assumption, intended "perhaps," to discourage future autograph hunters from wasting their time in fruitless research. Then follow the letters addressed to Mrs. Shew, a lady of generous impulses and great personal attraction, who at the period of Mrs. Poe's last illness is said to have been presiding over a private medical and water-cure establishment in upper Broadway. In November, 1850, she was married to Dr. Roland S. Houghton.

In the absence of all testimony as to the verbal authenticity of the letters presented under this heading, it is due to the literary reputation of the poet to whom they are ascribed to make certain statements omitted by their compiler.

In the spring of 1875, copies of some of these letters were submitted to me by Mr. Ingram. The first note, dated January 28, 1847, was claimed to be from a note in Poe's handwriting; the others were avowedly from *copies* of Poe's letters sent him by the same lady. Admitting their value as a record of facts, I frankly told him that from certain peculiarities of style and phraseology, so unlike the nervous rhythmical and emphatic style of Poe, I could not readily accept them as literal transcripts from the originals, and that however interesting in their details, they ought not to be presented to the public as verbatim copies of autograph letters.

In his reply, Mr. Ingram repeatedly and earnestly assured me that he entirely concurred with my opinion, and that I might rest assured that he would publish nothing until it had been carefully revised and "recast."

Whether the letters "To Annie" were subjected to this process does not appear, but one can hardly imagine Poe to have said, "You are the only being in the whole world whom I have loved at the same time with truth and with purity."

It is true that in Lowell as elsewhere the disturbing elements which had always developed themselves among the friends who could best appreciate his genius and the charm of his society, soon began to manifest themselves. Mutual misrepresentations and recriminations, attended by rash and compromising statements, seem to have followed, until driven to desperation he may have permitted himself to say unmanly things of those whom he believed to have injured him.

As an offset to the confused and contradictory impression which these letters must inevitably leave on the mind of the reader, we would refer those interested in the subject to the "Recollections" of a lady known as the "sister," so often spoken of in the letters "To Annie."

They will be found in the seventh chapter of Gill's Life of Poe, under the head of "*Suggestive Recollections.*" The delineation of Poe as seen by this lady in his earlier visits to Lowell, is so delicately, truthfully and tenderly treated, that, all who knew him will recognize the exquisite fidelity of the portrait.

Whether, as Mr. Ingram claims, the "unpublished correspondence" as a whole, will throw new lights on some of the dark and troubled phases of Poe's strange and sorrowful history, may be doubted. Observant and critical readers cannot fail to perceive that some of the new lights are cross-lights, tending to obliterate the outlines, obscure the colors and destroy what artists call the "values" of his illuminated record. To those who can read between the lines the letters undoubtedly supply some missing links, fix some suggestive and very significant dates, and furnish a clue to some important facts yet unrevealed.

If we must concede—since so many of the wayward poet's friends and "vindicators" will have it so—that Poe was like Hamlet, "very proud, revengeful, ambitious," we are not yet prepared to believe he was deliberately treacherous and perfidious.

One thing is certain, if Boileau's celebrated axiom is to be received as valid, *Le style c'est l'homme meme*, a man's style is the man himself, we do not always in these letters find the man in the style.

A specimen of the avidity with which the most preposterous charges against Poe are received and circulated, appeared recently in the N.Y. *Evening Post.* A contributor affirming that one of Poe's intimate friends assured him that Poe insisted that he saw no reason why a man should not kill an objectionable person for his own convenience, while he was convinced that the maker of a false rhyme ought to be hanged for the offence. And this was put forth in a prominent journal as an evidence of Poe's moral obliquity. As well might Dr. Johnson have been denounced as a hardened reprobate, devoid of all moral sense, when, on being told that Boswell was preparing a life of him for posthumous publication, he exclaimed: "Sir, if I thought that Bozzy was preparing to write my life, I should be tempted to anticipate him by taking his."

S.H.W.

184. Rose Peckham to John H. Ingram.   Item 337

59 Snow St.
Providence, R.I., U.S.A.
My dear Mr. Ingram,   July 3, 1878
I have neither time nor heart to send you this morning the answer your kind letter merits. Still I feel that I ought not to postpone any

longer telling you the sad news that will probably have reached you before this does of the death of our dear friend, Mrs. Whitman.

She called to see me the day after we reached home. It was the last time she went out. I saw her twice afterward, spending two most delightful afternoons with her, when she threw off her illness entirely—talked, chatted, laughed, gossiped, and brought her various treasures from hidden nooks for my inspection. When I first went in she was troubled for breath, almost suffocated, but that passed off and she became more herself than I ever remember her.

Of course she talked much about you, and I am sure you occupied a great place in the thoughts of her latter days. When I last saw her, I was to return to her *as soon* as I should receive a letter from you, as she had something to say to you which she wished me to write in reply.

Your letter came Tuesday. Father was so ill, I did not go that day. Next day a gentleman called to tell me she was failing fast, but she spoke so earnestly of wishing to see me that he came to tell me to go at once. I went home from my studio to carry out his injunction when I found sister Grace just returned from Mrs. Whitman who was then dying and could see no one. Next day she was gone.

I cannot express to you my regret at not seeing her again. It will always be a grief to me. Father gained nicely for five weeks after our return, but we have had excessively warm weather of late which has been very trying for him. He became well enough to enjoy talking with us over varied experiences and took such a quiet satisfaction in seeing us about him that it will always be a blessing to me to remember it. I cannot write even to you my dear friend of the anguish of hope and fear we live in from day to day, with the dread certainty always in the background that there *is no* hope. It is heartbreaking. It seems an era of suffering and affliction for everyone we know, and we seem to live in an atmosphere of death and desolation.

Thank you for your kindest of letters. Is there no hope that you will come to America this summer? I am sorry to think that you have any cause for bitterness toward American critics, but I am glad you do not include *me* in your resentment. If you go to Paris, I hope you will call on Mrs. Rein, my friend of whom you have heard me speak. I enclose a card—also clipping from the *Journal* in regard to Mrs. Whitman.

I am sorry to trouble you about the pictures. I pray you not to do anything at present, just keep the "Little Bess" for me until I have a clearer mind to decide what to do to relieve you of it.

I know this letter does not deserve an answer, but I hope you will find time to write me a line. Kate joins in kindest regards.

Believe me as always, yours truly,

Rose Peckham

The first I knew of Mrs. Whitman's funeral was from Mr. Thomas Davis who called to see us and told us about it after it was all over. I could not help feeling hurt that no word was sent me, as I am sure Mrs. W[hitman] had very few friends nearer or dearer to her than I was. I thought I should see some notice in the *Journal*, but it seems she requested it should not be printed till after her burial. It seems as if I was fated to be deprived of all pertaining to a last look or word.

Mr. Davis wanted to marry Mrs. W[hitman] about 35 years ago. He said she looked like a woman in the prime of life, after her death. She did not long survive her sister. She told me that her greatest fear was that she might die first.

[Enclosures: Newspaper clippings from the Providence *Journal*.   Item 739]

Mrs. Sarah Helen Whitman died last night at half-past nine o'clock at the home of Mrs. Albert Dailey, 97 Bowen Street, of affection of the heart, complicated by other ailments. Although for some weeks it has been evident that her tenure of life was feeble and uncertain, her friends were beguiled by her cheerful, uncomplaining manner into the hope that not quite yet was she to be called to the great change which she contemplated with entire complacency and satisfaction. We will not this morning speak of the lovely life just closed, nor of the rare intellectual gifts now lost to earth. At some fitting time, the memory of Mrs. Whitman will receive the tribute of appreciative affection that her elevated character and gentle manners have inspired in the hearts of all who enjoyed her acquaintance. [June 28, 1878]

By Mrs. Whitman's special request, the formal announcement of her death was not sent to the papers until after her funeral, and no invitations to the funeral were sent out. But the affection of friends supplied the place of the usual means of communication, as was shown by the spontaneous gathering of so large a number. An account of the touching exercises appears in another column.

The Funeral of Mrs. Whitman

The remains of Mrs. Sarah Helen Whitman were laid to rest Saturday afternoon towards the closing of the day, at the North Burial Ground. The funeral exercises were held at the residence of Mrs. Albert Dailey, and were strikingly impressive and beautiful. There was a strict avoidance of all ostentation, and the obsequies were in a certain sense private. Only those who knew Mrs. Whitman best, or who admired her rare gifts and kindly character most, were present. The remains lay in a casket, covered with a cloth of white. The features were placid and natural. The hands pressed to the breast a bunch of beautiful roses. On the casket lid lay a wreath of green leaves, from which sprang a few heads of ripened wheat. Beautiful flowers were arranged in beds upon stands, one at the head and one at the foot of the coffin.

The exercises were conducted by Miss Anna C. Garlin. After reading a selection from the Scriptures, Miss Garlin, in graceful language, spoke of the personal qualities of the deceased [. . . .]

At the close of her remarks, Miss Garlin offered up thanksgiving for the beautiful life passed away. She then read from the works of Mrs. Whitman her ode to the Angel of Death [. . . .]

It was then announced that the casket was about to be closed, and that an opportunity would be given to all who wished to take a parting look at the features of the deceased. And while the people were gathering about the casket, Hon. Thomas Davis, standing near-by, paid a tribute to the memory of her whose mortal remains lay within it[. . . .]

Mr. Davis spoke very feelingly, but his remarks could not be heard distinctly, save by those who were in the room with him[. . . .]

At the Cemetery

The grave was completely lined with branches of laurel and evergreen so that the naked earth was nowhere seen. It was appropriate that the grave of Sarah Helen Whitman should be the first one in Providence thus simply and beautifully embowered with emblems of immortality. After the casket was lowered, friends tossed upon it sprays of laurel and evergreen, and then each one scattered flowers. [July 1, 1878]

185. Rose Peckham to John H. Ingram. Item 338

My dear Mr. Ingram,   Aug. 14, 1878

Your last letter and the copy of the number of the *Athenaeum* containing the obituary notice of Mrs. Whitman reached me in our country home in Connecticut. I sent you a *Journal* with a notice of Father's accomplishment of his one great longing, to get to his beloved Heights once more. He bore the journey wonderfully, and instead of suffering any reaction has seemed to be gaining slowly but steadily ever since. He takes a little promenade about the house daily, sits on the porch, and insists that the daily paper shall be read to him. Accordingly, I felt quite resigned to quit the breezy Heights for a few days in order to complete some work left unfinished in the haste and anxiety of our hegira. It is very warm in the city, and I shall not be sorry to return to the bosom of the family.

Before replying to your letter, I wished to be able to give you definite information concerning your correspondence with Mrs. Whitman. Yesterday I met Dr. Channing, who is one of her literary executors; Caleb Harris is the other. I made known your wishes to him, and he informed me that all Mrs. Whitman's correspondence in reference to Poe would be carefully guarded for future use, and as yours came under that head, it would probably be useful in the memoir of the Poe affair, the mystery of which I believe it is a part of the executors' duty to clear up from notes left by Mrs. Whitman and from the letters that passed between her and Poe. The letters of which you have copies—I learned from both Dr. Channing and the gentleman who transcribed them for your use—form a part of the manuscript from which the executors will get their facts. They have never been given in their entirety to any person yet, the *copies* you have being only *extracts*. Mrs. Whitman was very cautious and prudent, with all her amiability and generosity, and as this memoir has long been one of her cherished plans, I dare to say any information she gave other writers was duly noted, and will probably be supplemented by unsuspected reserves.

I saw a copy of Mrs. Whitman's will. She gave about $2500 in legacies to charitable institutions, $2000 for the publishing of her work and literary remains in a suitable form, the balance of her money to be equally divided between Lottie and Maud Dailey, daughters of the friend with whom she died—about $2500 apiece. They did everything to make her last days comfortable.

There has been much complaint of the manner in which her funeral was ordered. Even her kinsman received no word. I am not entirely surprised, when I reflect how apart my friendship was for her, from any sect or society, that word did not reach me as it passed around among the spiritualists and radicals. I saw her alone almost always, and no one but ourselves knew how intimate we were.

You ask for my *aims* and *plans*. I hardly know myself. We have no plans. When Father is better we draw a long breath once more. Now we feel, after passing through such a long period of suspense and anxiety—most harrowing—that we may take a little courage, and hope that he may continue indefinitely in this state of gentle invalidism. We never know, however, what a day may bring forth, and this uncertainty is always the sombre background of all our hopes. When I can, I shall continue to paint at whatever comes first—it seems to be mostly portraits now. I have finished one order, commenced another, and have two others ahead, and this without making any pretense of working very assiduously. In the autumn when I get back to my studio I daresay there will be no lack of work.

I wish I knew someone who would bring me over my "little Bess." I received an invitation to contribute to the next Dudley Gallery, but it is too far away and implies too much exertion. Could I but try my hand at remodelling little Bess' countenance, I should not fear to send it. As it is, I must beg you to keep it a while longer.

I heard from Mr. Warner some time ago. He had been travelling on the Continent—had missed seeing our friend the late Miss Alcott in Paris.

I trust I have made plain the executors' intentions in regard to Mrs. Whitman's correspondence. Should there remain, or arise, any point on which you wish to satisfy yourself, I am sure a note addressed to Dr. Wm. F. Channing, Providence, R.I., would receive attention.

You say nothing in reference to your health. I hope you are quite well, better by far than when I saw you last, for then I was impressed with the evidence of your indisposition. So you gave up the trip to Paris. I learn that our friends there, the Reins, are to spend the winter in Norway. Everybody wants them to come home.

If "kind sister Kate" were here, I know she would enjoin me to express to you her pleasantest remembrances.

Hoping to hear from you when you have leisure, I remain as ever, very truly your friend,

Rose F. Peckham

The grave of Sarah Helen Whitman, North Burial Grounds, Providence, R.I.

*186. "Mrs. Sarah Helen Whitman," Obituary Notice by John H.
Ingram, London Athenaeum, July 20, 1878, p. 88*

Mrs. Sarah Helen Whitman

Information of the death of Mrs. Sarah Helen Whitman, the American
author and the heroine of Edgar Poe's lines "To Helen," has just reached
me. She died on the 27th ultimo, at her native city of Providence,
wherein the greater portion of her seventy-five years of life had been
spent, and where her ancestors, the Powers, had resided for two centuries or more. To the world at large she is merely known as an author of
considerable talent and rich and varied reading, but, to those acquainted with the secret of her inner life, she will always be remembered as a brave-hearted woman, who for many years endured
unrepiningly a condition of continuous self-sacrifice and anxiety, only
paralled by the intermittent martyrdom of Charles Lamb. It could not
have failed to comfort her in her last hours to know that the near and
dear one for whom she had suffered so much had preceded her by some
months in her journey to the grave.

A large portion of Mrs. Whitman's literary labour, consisting chiefly of
critical articles and fugitive verse, is unedited, and she steadfastly refused to have republished during her lifetime the two volumes by which
she is best known in the world of letters. In 1853 she collected and
published at Providence a thick volume of verse, entitled *Hours of Life
and Other Poems*, which not only attracted much attention on account
of its melancholy beauty, but because many of the pieces were devoted
to the memory of Edgar Poe. In 1860 Mrs. Whitman drew much more
marked attention to her admiration for the author of "The Raven" by the
publication of *Edgar Poe and His Critics*. This impassioned defence of
her celebrated countryman created a profound impression in American
coteries. The reputation which her little book so materially helped to
clear from slander and misrepresentation was consistently and devotedly cherished by her to the last, and this is no improper moment for me
to acknowledge that to Mrs. Whitman's unwearying kindness and cooperation is due a considerable portion of the data upon which my vindicatory *Memoir* of Poe is based. Towards affording a clearer impression
of her great countryman's character she furnished me with the whole of
the romantic history of her engagement with Edgar Poe, the cause of
the rupture of that engagement, and the poet's correspondence with her,
only stipulating that the latter should not be published during her
lifetime[. . . .]

The spontaneous and affecting scene at Mrs. Whitman's funeral
[. . .]proved the strong affection she had inspired the hearts of many
with.

                                                      John H. Ingram

Sarah Helen Whitman

John H. Ingram

Index

Index

The abbreviation "id." is used for "identification."